THE NEW LAW OF PEACEFUL PROTEST

The right to demonstrate is considered fundamental to any democratic system of government, yet in recent years it has received little academic attention. However, events following the recent G20 protests in April 2009 make this a particularly timely work.

Setting out and explaining in detail the domestic legal framework that surrounds the right of peaceful protest, the book provides the first extensive analysis of the Strasbourg jurisprudence under Articles 10 and 11 of the European Convention on Human Rights, offering a critical look at cases such as *Öllinger, Vajnai, Bukta, Oya Ataman, Patyi* and *Ziliberberg*, as well as the older cases that form its bedrock. The principles drawn from this case law are then synthesised into the remainder of the book to see how the right of protest enshrined in the Human Rights Act 1998 now operates. The five central chapters show how the right is defined: the restrictions on the choice of location of a protest; the constraints imposed on peaceful, persuasive protest; the near total intolerance of any form of obstructive or disruptive protest; the scope of preventive action by the police; and the extent to which commercial targets can avail themselves of private law remedies. This contemporary landscape is highlighted by critical analysis of the principles and case law—including the leading decisions in *Laporte, Austin, Jones and Lloyd* and *Kay*. The book also highlights and develops themes that are currently under-theorised or ignored, including the interplay of the public and the private in regulating protest; the pivotal role played by land ownership rules; and the disjuncture between the law in the books and the law in action.

While the book will appeal primarily to scholars, students and practitioners of law—as well as to campaigners and interest groups—it also offers political and socio-legal insights, which will be of interest equally to non-specialists.

The New Law of Peaceful Protest

Rights and Regulation in the Human Rights Act Era

David Mead

·HART·
PUBLISHING

OXFORD AND PORTLAND, OREGON
2010

Published in the United Kingdom by Hart Publishing Ltd
16C Worcester Place, Oxford, OX1 2JW
Telephone: +44 (0)1865 517530
Fax: +44 (0)1865 510710
E-mail: mail@hartpub.co.uk
Website: http://www.hartpub.co.uk

Published in North America (US and Canada) by
Hart Publishing
c/o International Specialized Book Services
920 NE 58th Avenue, Suite 300
Portland, OR 97213-3786
USA
Tel: +1 503 287 3093 or toll-free: (1) 800 944 6190
Fax: +1 503 280 8832
E-mail: orders@isbs.com
Website: http://www.isbs.com

© David Mead 2010

David Mead has asserted his right under the Copyright, Designs and Patents Act 1988,
to be identified as the author of this work.

All rights reserved. No part of this publication may be reproduced, stored in a retrieval system,
or transmitted, in any form or by any means, without the prior permission of Hart Publishing, or as expressly
permitted by law or under the terms agreed with the appropriate reprographic rights organisation.
Enquiries concerning reproduction which may not be covered by the above should be addressed to
Hart Publishing Ltd at the address above.

British Library Cataloguing in Publication Data
Data Available

ISBN: 978-1-84113-621-9

Typeset by Hope Services, Abingdon
Printed and bound in Great Britain by
TJ International Ltd, Padstow

PREFACE

The final chapters of this book were completed towards the end of 2009, a year that marked several significant anniversaries in the history of political dissent and peaceful protest. It was 25 years since the miners' strike started and 30 years since Blair Peach was killed by the Special Patrol Group at an anti-racist rally in Southall. *Liberty* had begun life 75 years before, in 1934, as the National Council for Civil Liberties, founded by journalist Ronald Kidd in response to the brutal treatment of Hunger Marchers two years previously. It was a whole 360 years since Gerard Winstanley's Diggers claimed St George's Hill in Surrey during the age of civil unrest in the 1640s. It was also the year, of course, when the media and political discourse turned to the subject, at least from the time of the London G20 summit in April onwards.

Though much of this book was written before the images from the G20 monopolised our screens over the Easter period, I completed and reflected on it in the light of what unfurled. This book, though it is far from being a study of *mass* protests and dissent, cannot now be read without at the very least an awareness of the police tactic of 'kettling' and be read by people who may well have been shocked and distressed witnessing what seemed like gratuitous and wanton violence, even if it was sporadic and out of the mainstream.

In one way this has been incredibly beneficial. The G20 summit, alongside the various inquiries, reports and media attention during the year, has provided a tremendous fillip for this oft-neglected and—certainly in comparison with free speech—underplayed area of public life and public interaction. In this I have been unintentionally assisted by my own tardiness. This book in fact should have been growing dusty on booksellers' shelves long before, sadly, we became aware of Ian Tomlinson and Nicola Fisher. It has had a rather longer than usual, or longer than planned, gestation period for many reasons. This has meant that this is an ideal time to be immersed in the academic legal study of protests and dissent. This book provides the first detailed treatment of the right to protest under the Human Rights Act at a time, like no other in recent political memory, when the need to debate and discuss issues relating to political engagement would struggle to feel more contemporary, more relevant and more pressing.

The G20 though has focussed public attention—and disquiet?—on what are not run-of-the-mill peaceful protest events. One of the points I try to stress in this book is how the legal framework that deals with the seeming social harm of disruptive or disturbing protest is not rational, planned or coherent. It has overlaps or has small gaps that are filled with a massive plug or creates new offences where there is no need, laws that are then used in an unforeseen or unpredictable manner. There is a political tendency to knee-jerkism, reacting to events—the 'need to do something and be seen to do something' attitude; the sort of political attitude that gave us the Dangerous Dogs Act of 1991. Legal responses are skewed by a host of non-legal factors. The problem that the G20 has thrown up and the various inquiries, reports and media attention during the year is that it overlooks the mundane and the everyday: angry parents gathering signatures in the High Street trying to prevent yet another fast food outlet opening or the placard-bearing teenager as the maverick politician visits their school. *These* are the sorts of events that shape the reality of protest just as much as, and probably more than, half a million members of the Countryside Alliance marching through London for 'Liberty and Livelihood' . . . yet it is these that do not make the front pages or the law reports. That last point is important. After all, if the Metropolitan Police gently move a protesting group on, to the far side of a street away from public gaze as *The Guardian* (26 January 2010) alleged was the case in the run up to Tony Blair's appearance before the Chilcott Inquiry into the Iraq war, and no one brings a case, the right to protest has probably been denied but with impunity.

The New Law of Peaceful Protest has been written for a variety of readers. I hope that interested lay readers will find as much in its pages to stimulate thought and to prompt reflection as the dedicated academic or activist adviser. It has been written with one single aim: to set out a detailed—though not complete or comprehensive—critical account of the state of the law. In doing so I also intended—but it would in any event have been unavoidable had that not been so—to provide that analysis and explanation in context: to note underlying themes or historical development; to see cross-currents and cross-overs; and to consider the impact of the law as it pans and plays out. Those who prefer their law not to be so entirely black-letter will also I hope find reward dotted within its pages. The cover photo was deliberately chosen with that approach in mind. How was Mark Wallinger's installation *State Britain* able to win the Turner Prize for art in 2007 when Brian Haw's Westminster peace-camp, of which it is a direct replica, was seen as a 'demonstration'—so, it was argued, requiring authorisation under the provisions of the Serious Organised Crime and Police Act 2005?

Five years ago, when I set out on this project, I wanted to write a book that would prompt us to think about why it is so important that we should be able to protest; about how the law should respond and how it should balance the competing rights and interests at stake; about whether there are some types of protest or protester or topics that the law should treat differently and if so, more harshly or more sympathetically; and about the growing interdependence of public and private regulation of the right. Now it is complete, I hope it will plot a route by which we might seek to resolve those issues.

This book sets out the law as of 1st August 2009 though Hart have been good enough to allow me to incorporate at the proof stage a little detail on some recent developments surrounding the policing of protest. These can be found at the tail end of chapter seven. They mostly concern the Strasbourg decision in the stop and search case, *Gillan v UK* decided by the European Court in January 2010. A few more unfortunately missed the cut. First, since the book was completed, after long years in the political wilderness, the common law offence of sedition (p 233) was finally abolished in early January 2010. This was the result of section 73 and section 182 of the Coroners and Justice Act 2009. Second, the Government appears to have started a process of review and reflection, perhaps a re-siting and reconfiguring. The Home Office's latest policing White Paper *Protecting the Public: Supporting the Police to Succeed* (published in early December 2009) featured an immediate commitment from the Home Secretary to 'set out clear principles for the policing of protest' and an aim to implement a Code of Practice on Protest by June 2010. We shall just have to wait to see how much this echoes the agenda for change set out in the conclusion to this book.

The indulgence afforded me in allowing late entries some six weeks before publication would be reason enough to thank all those at Hart who have contributed to the eventual publication of this book. In particular, Jo, Rachel and Mel have all been wonderfully supportive from my first tentative proposal in 2005 to its reaching the shelves some five years later as, in its later stages, were the copy editors and indexers. Especially though, I would like to thank Richard Hart himself. He has shown enormous tolerance, tact and understanding, far more perhaps than a first-time academic author could expect, and I hope that this book goes some way towards repaying that faith.

It is 25 years since I started as an undergraduate. Since that time, I have met, worked with and been taught by some very knowledgeable lawyers, far too many to name and thank here. I hope that being exposed to how they think, how they write and how they approach matters has rubbed off in some way and influenced my own thoughts, writing and approach. This book is the better for all that ... though of course its conclusions and its interpretations, its views on where the law has gone wrong and all infelicities in language are attributable only to me.

I should like to single out four. In my first week studying law, just after the Miners' Strike and the decision in the *GCHQ* case, I met Conor Gearty. His description of public law as being about the power the state wields—'it's all the trendy lefty cases, David'—inspired me then and has continued to do so. In my first post, fresh from commercial legal practice with only an LLM behind me, Ian MacLeod was—and has remained—wonderfully supportive. That this book features far fewer six-line sentences with sub-sub clauses is down to the help (and dogged resilience) shown by Mark Stallworthy in my early days at UEA. In more recent times, Brigid Hadfield has shown me similar patience and has offered very wise counsel on several occasions. More generally, I have been fortunate to have spent the past 10 years among friends in the intellectually supportive and welcoming atmosphere of the Law School at UEA. Amongst those no one deserves more special mention than Claudina Richards, a true chum when things get tough.

For all the help of those colleagues in law, this book is really a product of my involvement with my family and friends. Without them to provide welcome relief from academic turmoil this book would never have been started—let alone finished—and so it is to them that I dedicate it. My dad has been silently supportive and publicly proud of the first Mead to go to university. I hope this book goes some way towards redressing my self-acknowledged failures at DIY and car mechanics. My sister has been a shining example of fortitude and optimism for many years. I would gladly have swapped this book for a measure of improvement in her health any day. My late mother did not even know this book had been started, let alone that it has come to fruition but a mix of her steadfast belief and her high expectations kept me going whenever a mental block took hold. In the past few years, university work—especially paperwork rather than writing-work—has eaten into 'spare' time far more than I would have liked. Inevitably, my children have lost out by having grumpy dad around for far too long. I'm very sorry for that. Ned and Posy— I think he's gone.

The fact that I was still able to spend weekends at football training or watching dance shows meant that evenings became tied up. One person more than anyone suffered from this selfishness. More than just making me sit down and finish—when I felt I just couldn't let go—and proof reading, Jude has proved to be a rock in the storm of life—not just when writing this book but throughout the past two decades. She lightens my mood, chivvies me along, tempers my excesses, holds us all together ... and even laughs at my jokes. Thanks for everything; this book is for you.

CONTENTS

Preface   v
Table of Cases   xi
Table of UK Legislation   xxv

1: Introduction   1

    I.   Overview   1
    II. Historical Development of The Right   4
    III. The Function of Free Speech and Protest   6
    IV. Protest and Democracy   9
    V. A Simple Dichotomy: Protest v Direct Action   11
    VI. Deciding to Engage in Collective Action   12
    VII. The Socio-Legal Aspect   14
    VIII. The Role and Behaviour of the Police   18
    IX. Protest and Protesters at the Start of the New Millenium   20

2: Protecting Human Rights in the Human Rights Act Era   25

    I.   The Right to Protest at Common Law   26
    II. The European Convention on Human Rights   29
    III. A Home-Grown Bill of Rights? The Human Rights Act 1998   38
    IV. Conclusion: The Likely Influence of the Human Rights Act on Peaceful Protest   55

3: Strasbourg Case Law on the Right to Peaceful Protest   57

    I.   Introduction   57
    II. A Content Study of Protest Cases   59
    III. The Scope of the Right to Peaceful Protest   63
    IV. The Extent of Lawful Interferences with the Right   76
    V. Conclusions   114

4: The Locus of Protest   118

    I.   Introduction and Overview   118
    II. Rights of Access Over Land for the Purpose of Protest   121
    III. Place-Specific Restrictions on Protest   138
    IV. Police Powers in Relation to Protests on Land   162
    V. Conclusion   167

x Contents

5: Peaceful Persuasion and Communicating Dissent   168
    I.   Overview   168
    II. Marching, Meeting and Holding Demonstrations: The Statutory Scheme
         in the Public Order Act 1986   169
    III. Showing Support for Causes and Campaigns   213
    IV. Conclusion   233

6: Taking Direct Action   237
    I.   Introduction and Overview   237
    II. Direct Action Protesters as Terrorists   239
    III. Crimes of Violence and Damage   241
    IV. Aggravated Trespass   252
    V.   Harassment and Intimidation   264
    VI. Other Criminal Measures to Control Direct Action   292
    VII. Conclusion   306

7: Preventive Action by the Police   311
    I.   The General Duties of the Police   311
    II. Stop and Search Powers   313
    III. Preventing Breaches of the Peace   319
    IV. Anti-Social Behaviour Orders   362
    V.   Dispersal Orders   364
    VI. Strasbourg Case Law   373
    VII. Conclusions   375

8: Private Law Remedies and Proceedings   381
    I.   Introduction   382
    II. Possible Claims by Private Parties   384
    III. Conclusions   398

9: Conclusion   399
    I.   A Strasbourg Snapshot: The Right of Peaceful Protest under the ECHR in 2010 400
    II. A Domestic Snapshot: The Right of Peaceful Protest in England and Wales
         in 2010   401
    III. The Wider Picture: A Recap of Some Key Themes   408
    IV. An Agenda for Change   412

Appendix I: European Convention for the Protection of Human Rights and
        Fundamental Freedoms 1950   426
Appendix II: Bringing an Individual Case to Strasbourg: An Overview   431
Appendix III: A Summary of Strasbourg Case Law on the Right to Peaceful Protest 433
Appendix IV: Human Rights Act 1998, Chapter 42   467

Bibliography   477
Index   485

TABLE OF CASES

UNITED KINGDOM CASES

A and Others v Secretary of State for the Home Dept. [2004] UKHL 56 ......54, 101, 154, 394
A-G's Reference (No 2 of 1983) [1984] QB 456 251
Albert v Lavin [1982] AC 546 ....321, 334–5, 337, 338
American Cyanamid Co v Ethicon Ltd [1975] AC 396 395
Arrowsmith v Jenkins [1963] 2 QB 561 139
Ashbury Rly Carriage and Iron Co v Riche (1875) LR 7 HL 653 124
Ashworth Hospital Authority v MGN Ltd [2002] UKHKL 29 288
Atkin v DPP (1989) 89 Cr App R 199 221
Attorney-General v Fulham Corporation [1921] 1 Ch 440 124
Attorney-General v Great Eastern Rly Co (1880) 5 App Cas 473 124
Austin v Commissioner of Police for the Metropolis [2005] EWHC 480; [2007]
   EWCA 989; [2009] UKHL 5 ....51, 182, 189, 349–356, 370–2, 379, 399
Ayliffe v DPP; Swain v DPP; Percy v DPP [2005] EWHC Admin 684 258
Baillie v DPP [1995] Crim LR 426 ....174, 190
Banks v Ablex Ltd [2005] EWCA Civ 173 266
Barnard v DPP CO/ 4814/98 unreported Divisional Court 15th October 1999
   [2000] Crim LR 371 ....144, 253–4
Bayer v DPP [2003] EWHC 2567 Admin 251, 259, 412
Bayer v Shook [2004] EWHC 332 266
Beatty v Gillbanks (1882) 9 QBD 308 ....185, 220, 328, 330, 333–4
Bellinger v Bellinger [2003] UKHL 21 43
Bibby v Chief Constable of Essex (2000) 164 JP 297 326
Birch v DPP [2000] Crim LR 301 ....140–1, 407
Blake v DPP [1993] Crim LR 586 ....141, 247–9, 412
Blathwayte v Cawley [1976] AC 397 51
*Bloomsbury Publishing Group v News Group Newspapers Ltd (Continuation of
   Injunction)* [2003] EWHC 1205 390
Boddington v British Transport Police [1999] 2 AC 143 170
Bonnard v Perryman [1891] 2 Ch 269 ....4, 395
Brickley & Kitson v Police unreported *Legal Action* July 1988 184
British Oxygen Co Ltd v Minister of Technology [1971] AC 610 126
Broadwith v DPP CO/4073/99 [2000] Crim LR 924 DC 187, 190–2
Bromley LBC v Susannah (1999) JPL 361 (1998) 7 Env LM 11 390
Broome v DPP [1974] AC 587 394
Brown v Stott [2001] 2 WLR 817 54
Brutus v Cozens [1973] AC 854 222
Bucknell v DPP [2006] EWHC 1888 Admin 365–6

xii   Table of Cases

Bugg v DPP (1993) QB 473 332
Burris v Adzani [1995] 4 All ER 802 ....279, 283–4
Butler v Derby City Council [2005] EWHC 2835 Admin 120
Cameron v Network Rail [2006] EWHC 1133...48
Campbell v MGN (No 2) (Costs) [2005] UKHL 61 387
Campbell v MGN [2004] UKHL 22 ....47, 298
Capon v DPP CO/3496/97 unreported Divisional Court decision
    4th March 1998...262–4, 309
Carson v Secretary of State for Work and Pensions [2005] UKHL 37 128
Cawley v Frost [1976] 1 WLR 1207 171
Chambers and Edwards v DPP (1995) COD 321 223
Chancellor of the University of Oxford v Broughton [2004] EWHC 2543 Admin 275, 283
Chancellor of the University of Oxford v Broughton [2006] EWHC 1233 Admin......275, 280
Chancellor of the University of Oxford v Broughton [2008] EWHC 75
    QB 268, 279, 282, 404
Chandler v DPP [1964] AC 763..142, 246
Charman v Orion Publishing [2007] EWCA Civ 927 386
Chiron Industries v Avery [2004] EWHC 493 QB 300
Church of Jesus Christ of the Latter Day Saints and Others v Price [2004]
    EWHC 3245 QB 267–8, 279, 284, 397
Cole v Turner (1704) 6 Mod Rep 149 245
Conn v Council of the City of Sunderland [2007]EWCA Civ 1492 268
Connolly v DPP [2007] EWHC 237 Admin......................................55,137, 224, 229,
                                                                                                236, 296–8, 382, 403, 406
Cream Holdings v Banerjee [2004] UKHL 44 ....275, 397
Culla Park v Richards [2007] EWHC 1850...385
Daiichi Pharmaceuticals v Stop Huntingdon Animal Cruelty (SHAC) [2003]
    EWHC 2337 274
Davis v Lisle [1936] 2 KB 434...256
De Freitas v Permanent Minister of Agriculture, Fisheries Lands and Housing
    [1999] 1 AC 69...53
Dehal v CPS [2005] EWHC Admin 2154 225
Department of Transport v Williams unreported Court of Appeal *The
    Times* 7th December 1993 388
Derbyshire County Council v Times Newspapers [1992] 3 WLR 28 CA;
    [1993] AC 534...28, 387
Dino Services v Prudential Assurance Co Ltd [1989]1 All ER 422 244
DPP v Avery [2001] EWHC Admin 748 216
DPP v Clarke (1991) 94 Cr App Rep 359; [1992] Crim LR 60 ....220, 222, 364
DPP v Collins [2006] UKHL 40 295
DPP v Dunn [2001] 1 Cr App R 352 276
DPP v Dziurzynski [2002] EWHC 1380 ....273, 275–6
DPP v Fidler [1992] 1 WLR 91 222
DPP v Haw [2005] EWHC 2061 Admin; [2006] EWCA Civ 532 ....154–7, 402
DPP v Haw [2007] EWHC 1931 Admin 150, 155
DPP v Hutchinson [1990] 2 All ER 836 188
DPP v Jones [2002] EWHC 110 188–9

Table of Cases xiii

DPP v Jones and Lloyd [1999] 2 AC 240 ....5, 130, 139, 163, 190, 192, 194–203, 231, 236, 257, 383, 395, 407–8
DPP v Little (1992) 1 All ER 299..245
DPP v Moseley, Selvanayagam and Woodling unreported High Court decision 9th June 1999 *The Times* 23rd June 1999 ....272–3, 278, 309, 363, 391
DPP v Orum [1989] 1 WLR 88 220–1
DPP v Parmenter [1992] 1 AC 699...245
DPP v Smith [1961] AC 290..246
DPP v Tilly [2001] EWHC Admin 821 ....144, 254–5, 309, 403
Dr Bonham's case (1610) 8 Co Rep 113b 26
Drake v DPP [1994] Crim LR 855, DC..247
Duncan v Jones [1936]1 KB 218 ....4, 327–9, 331, 333, 335, 340, 346, 403
EDO Technology Ltd (EDO) v Campaign to Smash EDO (Preliminary Issues) [2005] EWHC 2490 ....270–2, 407, 412
EDO Technology Ltd v Campaign to Smash EDO [2005] EWHC 837 QB 261, 265–6, 277, 279, 282, 404
Emerson Developments Ltd v Avery [2004] EWHC 194 274
Epsom BC v Nicholls (1999) 78 P & CR 348 QBD. 390
Ettridge v Morrell (1986) 85 LGR 100..123
Evans and Blum v DPP [2006] EWHC 3209 Admin.............................18, 160–141, 402, 406
Fidler v DPP [1992] 1 WLR 91..291–2
Fitzpatrick v Sterling HA [1999] 3 WLR 1113 41
Flockhart v Robinson [1950] 2 KB 498..171, 173–4, 181
Foulkes v Chief Constable of Merseyside [1988] 3 All ER 705 326
Foy v Chief Constable of Kent unreported 20th March 1984 342
Galloway v Telegraph Group [2006] EWCA Civ 17 386
Gayford v Chouler [1898] 1 QB 316. ....164, 247
Getty v Antrim County Council [1950] NI 114..247
Gough v CC Derbyshire [2002] EWCA Civ 351 ....53, 204, 354
Hall v Save Newchurch Guinea Pigs Campaign [2005] EWHC 372 ....275, 277, 280, 305
Hammond v DPP [2004] EWHC Admin 69..224, 226–7, 404
Hampshire Waste Services Ltd v Intending Trespassers in Chineham Incinerating Site [2004] EWHC 1738 Ch 390
Hardman v Chief Constable of Avon and Somerset [1986] Crim LR 330. 247
Harrison v Duke of Rutland [1893] 1 QB 142 196–8
Heathrow Airport Ltd v Garman [2007] EWHC 1957 QB 241, 265, 269, 276–7, 282, 419
Henderson v Battley Unreported Court of Appeal decision 29th November 1984...........247
Hibberd v DPP unreported 27th November 1996 (Staughton LJ and Tucker J) noted [1997] CLY 1251 ....255, 259
Hickman v Maisey [1900] 1 QB 752 ....196, 198
High Tech International AG v Deripaska [2006] EWHC 3276 QB.................................164
Hipgrave v Jones [2001] EWHC 2901 QB..265, 267
Hirst and Agu v Chief Constable of West Yorkshire (1987) 85 Cr App R 143 ....5, 140, 197, 200, 407, 417
Holgate–Mohammed v Duke [1984] AC 437 189
Homer v Cadman (1886) 16 Cox CC 51 DC..138
Hubbard v Pitt [1976] QB 142..4, 27, 197, 385, 394–7

xiv *Table of Cases*

Hughes v Holley (1988) 86 Cr App R 130 356
Humphries v Connor 17 Ir CLR 1...323, 335
Hunter v Canary Wharf [1997] AC 655..47, 394
Huntingdon Life Sciences v Curtin Unreported Court of Appeal 15th October 1997
    (Thorpe LJ and Schiemann LJ) 273
Huntingdon Life Sciences v Curtin and Others Unreported High Court
    The Times 11th December 1997...272, 309, 391, 403
Huntingdon Life Sciences Group Plc v SHAC [2003] EWHC 1967...........................277
Huntingdon Life Sciences Group plc v SHAC [2007] EWHC 522 276–7
Hutchinson v DPP unreported *The Independent* 20th November 2000....................249
*International Transport Roth Gmbh v Secretary of State for the Home
    Department* [2002] EWCA Civ 158 54
Iveson v Harris 7 Ves Jun 251 276
J Lyons & Sons v Wilkins [1899] 1 Ch 255 ....290, 294, 395–6
Jameel v Wall Street Journal [2006] UKHL 44..386
Jordan v Burgoyne [1963] 2 QB 744..220
Kay v Commissioner of Police for the Metropolis [2006] EWHC 1536 Admin;
    [2007] EWCA Civ 477; [2008] UKHL 69..172, 175–182, 403
Kay v Lambeth LBC; Price v Leeds CC [2006] UKHL 10 (conjoined appeals) 41
Kaye v Robertson [1991] FSR 62..26
KD v Chief Constable Hampshire [2005] EWHC 2550 270
Kearns v General Council of the Bar [2003] 1 WLR 1357 386
Kebilene v DPP [2000] 2 AC 326 ....145, 273
Kelly v Chief Constable of Hampshire unreported *The Independent*
    25th March 1993..326
Kelly v DPP [2002] EWHC 1428..267
Kent v Commissioner of Police for the Metropolis unreported *The Times*
    15th May 1981 ....170–1, 181, 204–5
Khan v Commissioner of Police for the Metropolis [2008] EWCA Civ 723 286
Knuller v DPP [1973] AC 435 246
Lamb v DPP [1990] Crim LR 58...323
Lau v DPP [2000] 1 FLR 799 267
Lewis v Chief Constable of Manchester Unreported Court of Appeal
    The Independent 23rd October 1991 320
Lewis v DPP, unreported Divisional Court decision 1995 221
Lippiatt v South Gloucestershire CC [2000] QB 51..394
Litster v Forth Dry Dock Engineering [1990] 1 AC 546 43
London Borough of Lewisham v Commissioner of Police for the Metropolis
    unreported *The Times* 12th August 1977..170
London County Council v Attorney-General [1902] AC 165 124
Lucy v DPP unreported 22nd November 1996 (Staughton LJ and Tucker J)
    noted (1997) 73 P & CR D25...253, 258
M Michaels (Furriers) v Askew unreported Court of Appeal 23rd June 1983
    (Dunn and Purchas LJJ) *The Times* 25th June 1983..276, 391
MacLaine Watson v DTI [1990] 2 AC 418 27
Maguire v Chief Constable of Cumbria unreported Court of Appeal 26th April 2001 326
Mainstream Properties v Young; OBG v Allan; Douglas v Hello! [2007] UKHL 21............302

Majrowski v Guy's and St Thomas's NHS Trust [2006] UKHL 34 268
Manchester Airport v Dutton [2000] QB 133 CA 390
Marsh v Arscott (1982) 75 Cr App R 211 ....171, 221
McAdam v Urquhart 2004 SLT 790 ....257, 259
McConnell v Chief Constable of Greater Manchester [1990] 1 All ER 423.....................322
McDonalds v Steel and Morris unreported Court of Appeal decision
   31st March 1999 (Pill and May LJJ; Keane J)..386
McKennit v Ash [2006] EWCA Civ 1714 382
McLeod v Commissioner of Police for the Metropolis [1999] 4 All ER 553....................323
Mendoza v Ghaidan [2002] EWCA Civ 1533; [2004] UKHL 30 ......41, 43, 55, 127, 137, 206
Middlebrook Mushrooms v TGWU [1993] ICR 612 28
Monsanto v Tilly unreported Court of Appeal decision 25th November
   1999 [2000] Env LR 313 ....277, 281, 390–3, 398
Morris v Knight [1999] CLY 3682 268
Morrow and others v DPP [1994] Crim LR 58..222
Mosley v News Group Newspapers [2008] EWHC 1777 QB 46
Moss v McLachlan [1985] IRLR 76 ....335, 337–8, 341–3
Murray v MoD [1988] 2 All ER 521 HL 318
Nagy v Weston [1965] 1 WLR 280...139
Nelder v DPP Unreported Divisional Court 3rd June 1998, *The Times*
   11th June 1998 ....252, 259
News Group v SOGAT '82 [1986] IRLR 337 ....391, 397
Nicol v DPP unreported Divisional Court decision 10th November 1995
   The Times 22nd November1995, [1996] Crim LR 318 ....10, 223, 326,330–3, 357, 403
NIREX v Barton unreported High Court decision *The Times*
   14th December 1986. 391
Norwood v DPP [2003] EWHC Admin 1564 ....219, 221, 223–4, 227–30
O'Hara v Chief Constable of the RUC [1997] AC 286 187
O'Kelly v Harvey (1882) 10 LR Ir 285 ....323, 335, 344–5, 348
O'Moran v DPP [1975] QB 864 DC 214–6
Osman (Mustapha) v Southwark Crown Court [1999] COD 446 217
Palmer v R [1971] AC 814 250
Papworth v Coventry [1967] 1 WLR 663 DC 145, 147–8
*Parochial Church Council of the Parish of Aston Cantlow, Wilmcote with Billesley,
   Warwickshire v Wallbank* [2003] UKHL 37 46
Pay v Lancashire Probation Service [2004] ICR 187 48
Percy v DPP [1995] 1 WLR 1382 DC 320, 332, 360
Percy v DPP [2001] EWHC Admin 1125...51, 224–9, 272, 407, 411
Peterkin v Chief Constable of Cheshire unreported *The Times* 16th
   November 1999 342
Phytopharm Plc v Avery [2004] EWHC 503 277
Piddington v Bates [1961] 1WLR 162 ....337, 340, 342
Police v Lorna Reid [1987] Crim LR 702 186
Poplar Housing v Donoghue [2001] EWCA.Civ 595 ....46, 254
Porter v Magill [2001] UKHL 67...126
Pratt v DPP [2001] EWHC Admin 483 267
Pursell v Horn (1838) 8 Ad and El 602 245

xvi Table of Cases

R (Anderson) v Secretary of State for the Home Department [2002] UKHL 46 43
R (Animal Defenders International) v Secretary of State for Culture, Media
    and Sport [2008] UKHL 15 234
R (Begum) v Governors of Denbigh High School [2006] UKHL 15 ....53, 103
R (Bono) v Harlow DC [2002] EWHC 423 Admin..52
R (Brehony) v Chief Constable of Greater Manchester[2005] EWHC
    640 Admin 50, 165, 184, 189, 205, 211, 213, 406
R (Countryside Alliance) v Attorney-General [2007] UKHL 52..384
R (Daly) v Secretary of State for the Home Department [2001] UKHL 26 ....53, 197, 331
R (EE) v Secretary of State for the Home Department [2007] UKHL 47 353
R (Fuller) v Chief Constable of Dorset [2001] EWHC 1057 Admin 162, 165–7
R (Gentle) v Prime Minister [2008] UKHL 20..393
R (Gillan) v Commissioner of Police for the Metropolis [2006]
    UKHL 12 ....216, 316–9, 353, 379, 411
R (Heather) v Leonard Cheshire Foundation [2002] EWCA Civ 366 46
R (Huang) v Secretary of State for the Home Department [2007] UKHL 11 204
R (JJ) v Secretary of State for the Home Department [2007] UKHL 45............................353
R (Laporte) v Chief Constable of Gloucestershire [2004] 2 All ER 874; [2005]
    QB 678; [2006] UKHL 55 ....51, 55, 170, 319, 328,
                                             334–348, 360, 372, 398, 403, 409, 423
R (MB) v Secretary of State for the Home Department [2007] UKHL 46 353
R (McCann) v Crown Court at Manchester [2002] UKHL 39 363
R (Morgan Grenfell) v Inland Revenue Commissioners [2002] UKHL 21 ....28, 187, 367
R (O'Brien) v Basildon DC [2006] EWHC 1346 Admin 165
R (Prolife Alliance) v BBC [2003] UKHL 23..54, 221, 297
R (Q) v Secretary of State for the Home Department [2003] EWHC 195 27
R (Singh) v Chief Constable of West Midlands [2005] EWHC 2840 Admin;
    [2006] EWCA Civ 1118 ....366–73, 403
R (Ullah) v Special Adjudicator [2004] UKHL 26 41
R (W) v Commissioner of Police for the Metropolis [2006] EWCA Civ 458 367
R (Weaver) v London and Quadrant Housing Trust [2009] EWCA Civ 587 ....46, 131
R v A [2002] 1 AC 45..42
R v Bow Street Metropolitan Stipendiary Magistrates' Court ex p USA (No 2)
    sub nom Re Allison [2000] AC 216..298
R v BSC ex p BBC [2000] 3 All ER 989 ....135, 137
R v Burns (1886) 16 Cox CC 355..233
R v Central Independent Television plc [1994] Fam 192..28
R v Chief Constable of Devon and Cornwall ex p Central Electricity Generating
    Board [1982] QB 458...5, 312, 320
R v Chief Constable of Sussex v International Trader's Ferry [1999] 2 AC 418.................235
R v Chief Metropolitan Stipendiary Magistrate ex p Choudhury [1991] 1 QB 429...........233
R v Clarke (No. 2) [1964] 2 QB 315 293
R v Colohan (Sean Peter) [2001] EWCA Crim 1251 ....268, 270
R v Commissioner of Police of the Metropolis ex p Blackburn [1968] 2 QB 118 312
R v Constanza (Gaetano)(1997) 2 Cr App 492...245
R v County Quarter Sessions Appeals Committee, ex p Metropolitan Police
    Commissioner [1948] 1 KB 260 321

R v Cousins [1982] QB 526...249
R v Coventry City Council ex p Phoenix Aviation [1995] 3 All ER 37................................312
R v Davis [2008] UKHL 36 28
R v Debnath [2005] EWCA Crim 3472..279
R v Donovan [1934] 2 KB 498..245
R v Ealing LBC ex p Times Newspapers [1978] IRLR 129..124–5
R v Fiak [2005] EWCA Crim 2381 247
R v Fisher (1865) LR 1 CCR 7 247
R v Gibson [1990] 2 QB 619..221, 246
R v Hill (1988) 89 Cr App R 74 247
R v Hobbs [2002] 2 Cr App R 324 CA..249
R v Horseferry Road Metropolitan Stipendiary Magistrate ex p Sidiatan
  [1991] 1 QB 260 218
R v Howell [1982] QB 416 [1981] 3 All ER 383 ....320, 325, 342–3, 348, 360–1
R v Hunt (1989) Cr App R 74 248
R v Ireland; R v Burstow [1998] AC 147...245–6
R v Jones (1974) 59 Cr App R 120..291
R v Jones [2006] UKHL 16 ....11–12, 249–50, 259–60, 270, 307, 393, 412
R v Keogh [2007] EWCA Crim 528 ....165, 173, 188
R v Kirk [2006] EWCA Crim 725..294, 296
R v Lambert [2001] UKHL 37 ....165–6, 173, 184, 188, 263
R v Lewisham LBC ex p Shell UK Ltd [1988] 1 All ER 938 387
R v London Quarter Sessions Ex parte Metropolitan Police Commissioner
  [1940] 1 KB 670..357
R v Lord Chancellor ex p Witham [1997] 2 All ER 27..28
R v Lord Saville of Newdigate ex p B [2000] 1 WLR 1855 29
R v Madden [1975] 3 All ER 155 CA 293
R v MAFF ex p Callaghan (2000) 32 HLR 8...165
R v Mansfield JJ ex p Sharkey [1985] 1 All ER 193 DC..358, 423
R v Ministry of Defence ex p Smith and Lustig–Prean [1996] QB 517.......................28, 124
R v Morpeth Ward Justices ex p Ward [1992] 95 Cr App R 215...................329–32, 357, 403
R v Panel on Takeovers & Mergers ex p Datafin [1987] 1 QB 815 46
R v Rimmington [2005] UKHL 63 ....284, 293, 319, 394
R v Rogers [2007] UKHL 8 228
R v Savage [1992] 1 AC 699...245
R v Secretary of State for Employment ex p EOC [1995] 1 AC 1 42
R v Secretary of State for Foreign & Commonwealth Affairs ex p World
  Development Movement [2001] 1 All ER 908 50
R v Secretary of State for Social Security ex p JCWI [1996] 4 All ER 385 ....27, 50
R v Secretary of State for the Home Department ex p Brind [1991] 1 AC 696...........27, 44
R v Secretary of State for the Home Department ex p McQuillan [1995]
  4 All ER 400..27–8
R v Secretary of State for the Home Department ex p Norney (1995)
  7 Admin LR 861...28
R v Secretary of State for the Home Department ex p Pierson [1998] AC 539 366
R v Secretary of State for the Home Department ex p Simms and O'Brien
  [2000] 2 AC 115..4, 366

xviii Table of Cases

R v Secretary of State for Transport ex p Factortame (No. 2) [1991] 1 AC 603.....................42
R v Sefton MBC ex p BASC [2001] Env LR 10 124
R v Shayler [2002] UKHL 11 252
R v Shivpuri [1987] AC 1..249
R v Shorrock [1994] QB 279...293
R v Somerset CC ex p Fewings [1995] 1 WLR 1037 124–6
R v Whiteley (1991) 93 Cr App Rep 25..247
R v Williams (Gladstone) [1987] 3 All ER 411 250
R v Williams (Michael) Unreported Divisional Court 28th July 1998..............................266
Raissi v Commissioner of Police for the Metropolis [2008] EWCA Civ 1237......................187
Rankin v Murray (2004) SLT 1164, High Court of Justiciary 217
Raymond v Honey [1983] 1 AC 1..28
Re A (Conjoined Twins) [2001] 2 WLR 480..252
Re de Keyser's Royal Hotel (1920) AC 508...319
Re E (A Child) [2008] UKHL 66...3
Re S (Child Care Plan) [2002] UKHL 10..43, 206
Re Waste Management plc [2003] EWHC 2065 Ch..389
*Re Wykeham Terrace, Brighton, Sussex, ex p Territorial Auxiliary &Volunteer Reserve
  Association for the South East* [1971] Ch 204 276
Redfearn v Serco (t/a West Yorkshire Transport Service) [2006] EWCA Civ 659 126
Redmond–Bate v DPP [2000] HRLR 249 ....6, 111, 223, 227, 320,
                                                                        326, 329, 332–4, 345–6, 403
Reynolds v Times Newspapers [2001] 2 AC 127 386
Robson v Hallett [1967] 2 QB 939..256–7
Roe v Kingerlee [1986] Crim LR 735, DC. 247
Rogers v DPP unreported Divisional Court decision 22nd July 1999..............................218
RWE npower Plc v Carroll [2007] EWHC 947 277
Seaga v Harper [2008] UKPC 9...386
Secretary of State for Education v Tameside MBC [1977] AC 1014 187
Secretary of State for Transport v Fillingham unreported High Court decision
  26th March 1996 noted [1997] Env LR 73...390
Secretary of State for Transport v Haughian [1997] 2 CMLR 497 CA 390, 398
Showboat Entertainment v Owens [1984] 1 WLR 384 126
*Shrewsbury & Atcham BC v Secretary of State for Communities and Local
  Government* [2008] EWCA Civ 148...124
Sierny v DPP [2006] EWHC 716 Admin 364
Silverton v Gravett unreported High Court decision 19th October 2001....................279, 391
Sim v Stretch (1936) 62 TLR 669..385
Smith v Thomasson (1891) 16 Cox CC 740 DC..291
SmithKline Beecham plc v Avery [2007] EWHC 948...277
Snook v Mannion [1982] Crim LR 601..256
Stephens v Myers (1830) 4 C and P 349 245
Tabernacle v Secretary of State for Defence [2009] EWCA
  Civ 23 ....41, 51, 100, 122, 142, 399
Tate & Lyle Industries Ltd v GLC [1983] 2 AC 509 394
Thomas v News Group Newspapers [2001] EWCA Civ 1233 ....233, 268
Thomas v NUM (South Wales Area) [1986] Ch 20...284, 290, 302, 394, 396

Thomas v Sawkins [1935] 2 KB 249 ....322–5, 404
Todd v DPP [1996] COD 111, DC 291
Total Network SL v Revenue and Customs Commissioners [2008] UKHL 19 388
Turberville v Savage (1669) 1 Mod Rep 3 245
United Kingdom Nirex Ltd v Barton Unreported *The Times*, 13th October 1986. 277
Venables & Thompson v News Group Newspapers [2001] 1 All ER 908 47
Verrall v Great Yarmouth BC [1981] QB 202..5, 123, 125
Waddington v Miah [1974] 2 All ER 377 28
Wainwright v Home Office [2003] UKHL 53...301
Waite v Taylor (1985) 149 JP 551 140
Ward, Lock and Co v The Operative Printers' Society (1906) 22 TLR 327...............290, 395–6
Webster v Southwark LBC [1983] QB 698 ....123, 125
Westminster City Council v Haw [2002] EWHC 2073 Admin 120
Wheeler v Leicester City Council [1985] AC 1054..124–5
Whelan v DPP [1975] QB 864 DC..214–6
Williams (Richard) v DPP (1992) 95 Cr App R 415..171
Winder v DPP (1996) 160 JP 713 DC 254, 260, 302, 309, 402
Wise v Dunning (1902) 1 KB 162...330, 333, 334, 346
Wood v Commissioner of Police for the Metropolis [2008] EWHC 1105
   Admin; [2009] EWCA Civ 414...117, 376–8, 399, 422
X v Y [2004] EWCA Civ 662 48
YL v Birmingham City Council [2007] UKHL 27 ....46–9, 127, 131, 135

STRASBOURG HUMAN RIGHTS CASES

A v UK (1999) 27 EHRR 611 33
Abdulaziz, Cabales and Balkandali v UK (1985) 7 EHRR 471 127
Adali v Turkey App 38187/97 ECtHR judgment 31st March 2003 ....62, 71, 85
Airey v Ireland (1979) 2 EHRR 305..32, 67, 74, 128, 317, 325, 420
Aldemir v Turkey App 32124/02 ECtHR 18th December 2007 ....62, 78, 107, 111, 116,
                                                                    127, 139, 158–9, 207, 212, 308, 400
Amuur v France (1993) 22 EHRR 533 352
Anderson v UK App 33689/96 ECnHR inadmissibility decision 27th
   October 1997 74
Andersson v Sweden App 12781/87 ECnHR inadmissibility decision
   13th December 1987...207
Appleby v UK (2003) 37 EHRR 38 ....64, 74, 129, 132–6, 163, 200, 324, 383, 408
Arrowsmith v UK App 7050/75 (1978) 19 DR 5...230, 232
Ashughyan v Armenia App 33268/03 ECtHR judgment 17th July 2008.............................62
Baczkowski v Poland App 1543/06 ECtHR judgment 3rd
   May 2007..62, 67, 71, 78, 80, 89, 95, 375
Balçik v Turkey App 25/02 ECtHR judgment 29th
   November 2007..........................61, 71, 92, 95, 106, 116, 127, 139, 193, 207, 308, 375, 422
Barankevich v Russia App10519/03 ECtHR judgment 26th July 2007 58
Bozano v France (1987) 9 EHRR 297..353
Bramelid v Sweden App 8588-9/79 (1982) 29 DR 64 383

xx *Table of Cases*

Bukta v Hungary App 25691/04 ECtHR 17th July 2007 ....62, 73, 81–3, 108, 111,
 115, 157, 159, 173, 207, 212–3, 232, 308, 371, 406
Castells v Spain (1992) 14 EHRR 445 230
Cetinkaya v Turkey App 75569/01 ECtHR judgment 27th June 2006 65
Cetinkaya v Turkey App 3921/02 ECtHR judgment 23rd January 2007........58, 210–11, 230
Chappell v UK App 12587/86 ECnHR inadmissibility decision 14th July 1987 206
Chassagnou v France (2000) 29 EHRR 615...36, 297
Chorherr v Austria (1994) 17 EHRR 358 ....75, 92, 96, 110–11,
 114, 116, 211, 231, 346–7, 400
Christian Democratic People's Party v Moldova App 28793/02 ECtHR
 judgment 14th February 2006 ....58, 86, 90, 94–5, 98, 207
Christians Against Racism and Fascism (CARAF) v UK App 8440/78
 (1980) 21 DR 138..64–5, 68, 77, 92, 111, 170, 206–11, 242, 344
Çiloglu v Turkey App 73333/01 ECtHR judgment 6th March 2007............62, 116, 207, 400
Cissé v France App 51346/99 ECtHR judgment 9th April 2002 ....61, 65, 70, 81, 85, 93, 97
CS v Germany App 13858/88 ECnHR inadmissibility decision
 6th March 1989 ....65–6, 68, 86, 91–2, 106, 141
Csánics v Hungary App 12188/06 ECtHR judgment 20th January 2009 ....59, 105
Custers and Others v Denmark App 11843/03 ECtHR judgment 3rd May 2007 58
Denmark, Norway, Sweden and the Netherlands v Greece (The Greek case)
 Apps 3321-4/67 and 3344/67 Commission report 5 November 1969.............................84
Direkçi v Turkey App 47826/99 ECtHR inadmissibility decision
 3rd October 2006...207
Djavit An v Turkey App 20652/92 ECtHR judgment 20th February
 2003 ....66. 70, 79, 85, 94, 375
Donnan v UK App 3811/04 ECtHR inadmissibility decision 8th November 2005 374
Drieman v Norway App 33678/96 ECtHR inadmissibility decision
 4th May 2000 ....85, 89, 97, 100, 249, 308, 374
Dudgeon v UK (1981) 4 EHRR 149..30, 38, 50, 78, 96
Duzgoren v Turkey App 56827/00 ECtHR 9th November 2006 230
Engel v Netherlands (1976) 1 EHRR 647 ....30, 351
Ezelin v France (1992) 14 EHRR 362................63, 68, 77, 85, 93, 105, 115, 164, 193, 206–7,
 238, 242, 315, 344, 371, 374, 388, 400, 416
Fairfield, Tredea and Cox v UK App 00024790/04 ECtHR inadmissibility
 decision 8th March 2005 227
Friedl v Austria App 15225/89 ECnHR inadmissibility decision 30th November
 1992 ....65, 79
G and E v Norway Apps 9278/81 and 9415/81, ECnHR inadmissibility
 decision 3rd October 1983 ....75, 91, 106, 139, 165, 213, 400
G v Germany App 13079/87 ECnHR inadmissibility decision
 6th March 1989 ....65, 86, 92, 94, 106, 141, 308
Galstyan v Armenia App 26986/03 ECtHR 15th November 2007...........62, 66, 69, 105, 108,
 111, 116, 127, 139, 207, 212, 308, 371, 374, 416
Gillan and Quinton v UK App 4158/05 ECtHR judgment 12th January 2010 380
Golder v UK (1975) 1 EHRR 524 31
Goodwin v UK (1996) 22 EHRR 123 32
Goodwin v UK (2002) 35 EHRR 447 38

Gorzelik v Poland (2005) 40 EHRR 4 ....32, 34, 36, 58
GS v Austria App 14923/89 ECnHR inadmissibility decision
    30th November 1992...65, 76, 90, 92, 106, 139, 213, 374, 400, 407
Guenat v Switzerland App 24722/94 ECnHR admissibility decision 10th April 1995......353
Gül v Turkey App 4870/02 62–3
Guliyev and Ramazanov v Azerbaijan App 34553/02 ECtHR judgment
    19th June 2008 207
Güneri v Turkey Apps 42853/98, 43609/98 and 44291/98 ECtHR judgment
    12th July 2005 ....207, 210–11, 230
Guzzardi v Italy (1980) 3 EHRR 333 ....316, 351–2
Gypsy Council v UK App 66336/01 ECtHR inadmissibility decision
    14th May 2002...78, 90–2, 95, 100, 103, 206
Handyside v UK (1976) 1 EHRR 737 ....32, 36–8, 67, 88
Hashman and Harrup v UK (2000) 30 EHRR 241..................................34, 61, 75–6, 86–7,
                                                                            219–220, 238, 282, 308, 361
Heikkila v Finland App 25472/94 ECnHR inadmissibility decision
    15th May 1996..101, 207, 209
HL v UK (2005) 40 EHRR 32..352
HM v Switzerland 353
Hyde Park v Moldova App 18491/07 ECtHR judgment 7th April 2009...............................62
Incal v Turkey App 22678/93 ECtHR judgment 9th June 1998..230
Informationsverein Lentia and Others v Austria Series A no. 276 p. 16................................98
Ivanov v Bulgaria App 46336/99 ECtHR judgment 24th November 2005..........90, 189, 207
Jersild v Denmark (1994) 19 EHRR 1 ....38, 96
JK v Netherlands App15928/89 ECnHR inadmissibility decision
    13th May 1992..64, 101, 115, 232
Kandzhov v Bulgaria App 68294/01 ECtHR judgment
    6th November 2008 ....62, 71, 108, 230, 400
Kara v UK App No 36528/97 ECnHR inadmissibility decision 22nd October 1998. 215
Karakaya and Piroglou v Turkey Apps 37581/02 & 36370/02 ECtHR
    18th March 2008 ....62, 84, 86, 230
Klass v FRG (1978) 2 EHRR 214 ....38, 50, 78
Kutznetsov v Russia App 10877/04 ECtHR judgment
    23rd October 2008 ....62, 76, 81, 83, 104–5, 107–8, 116, 159, 230, 400, 406, 417
LCB v UK (1998) 27 EHRR 212 32
Leander v Sweden (1987) 9 EHRR 433 38
Lindon v France (2008) 46 EHRR 35 98
Lopez Ostra v Spain (1994) 20 EHRR 277 32
Loukanov v Bulgaria (1997) 24 EHRR 12 353
Lucas v UK App 39013/02 ECtHR inadmissibility decision
    18th March 2003 ....92, 104–5, 374
Makhmaduv v Russia App 35082/04 ECtHR 26th July 2007 ....58, 62, 76, 210, 212, 374
McBride v UK App 27786/95 ECtHR inadmissibility decision
    5th July 2001...66, 89, 190, 207, 348, 374
McCann v UK (1996) 21 EHRR 97 ....32, 50
McKay v UK (2006) 44 EHRR 827 354
McLeod v UK (1999) 27 EHRR 493 ....321, 323, 325

xxii *Table of Cases*

Mkrtchyan v Armenia App 6562/03 ECtHR 11th January 2007 .... 62, 65, 202
Molnar v Hungary App 10346/05 ECtHR judgment
　7th October 2008 .... 62–3, 73, 80–1, 82, 90, 95, 103, 173, 212, 400
Moosman v Austria App 14093/88 friendly settlement 9th July 1992 .... 64, 169, 232
Moseley, Selvanayagam and Woodling v UK App 57981/00 ECtHR
　inadmissibility decision 12th December 2002 .... 75, 273, 364
MS v Sweden (1999) 28 EHRR 313 31
Murphy v Ireland (2004) 38 EHRR 13 234
Murray v UK (1996) 22 EHRR 29 50
N v UK (2008) 47 EHRR 885 351–2
Nicol and Selvanayagam v UK App 32213/96 ECtHR admissibility
　decision 11th January 2001 .... 89, 332, 361
Nielsen v Denmark (1988) 11 EHRR 175 352–3
Niemitz v Germany (1993) 16 EHRR 97 .... 297, 384
Norwood v UK App 23131/03 ECtHR inadmissibility decision 16th November 2004 229
O'Halloran and Francis v UK (2007) 46 EHRR 397 351–2
Öllinger v Austria (2008) 48 EHRR 38 .... 67. 73, 89, 99, 104, 111–14, 116, 127,
　　　　　　　　　　　　　　　　　　　　　　　205, 207, 210, 231, 308, 344, 347, 375, 400
Oner v Turkey App 64684/01 ECtHR inadmissibility decision
　1st June 2004 .... 65, 83, 92, 95
Osmani v FYR Macedonia App 50841/99 ECtHR inadmissibility
　decision 11th October 2001 .... 63, 69, 95–6, 230–1
Ouranio Toxo v Greece App 74989/01 ECtHR judgment 20th October 2005 73
Oya Ataman v Turkey App 74552/01 ECtHR judgment
　5th December 2006 .... 71, 73, 80, 92, 103, 107, 116, 127,
　　　　　　　　　　　　　　　139, 159, 193, 207, 230, 232, 238, 308, 325, 374, 400
Patyi v Hungary App 5529/05 ECtHR judgment
　7th October 2008 .... 62, 67, 78, 80, 91, 103, 139, 204, 207, 210, 212, 400
Pendragon v UK App 31416/96 ECnHR inadmissibility decision
　19th October 1998 .... 58, 78, 85, 100, 102, 190, 206
Petropavlovskis v Latvia App 44230/06 .... 62–3, 77
Piermont v France App 15773-4/89 ECtHR judgment 3rd December 1992 .... 207, 230
Plattform "Arzte fur das Leben" v Austria (1991)
　13 EHRR 204 .... 32, 67, 71, 73, 97–8, 113, 128, 207–8, 375
Pretty v UK (2002) 35 EHRR 1 .... 31, 38, 96, 297, 384
Protopapa v Turkey App 16084/90 ECtHR judgment 24th February 2009 .... 62, 70
Rai, Allmond and Negotiate Now! v UK App 25522/94 ECnHR inadmissibility
　decision 6th April 1995 .... 87, 93–4, 101, 109, 111, 127, 147, 203, 206–11, 400
Rassemblement Jurassien et Unité Jurassienne v Switzerland App
　8191/78 (1980) 17 DR 93 .... 64–6, 79–80, 92, 94, 97,
　　　　　　　　　　　　　　　　　　　　　　　　　　　　　100, 109, 111, 157, 207, 209–11
Refah Partisi v Turkey (2003) 37 EHRR 1 58
S v Austria App 13812/88 ECnHR inadmissibility decision
　3rd November 1990 .... 75, 90, 103, 106, 139, 207, 211, 374
Saadi v UK (2008) 48 EHRR 17 Grand Chamber 353
Sahin v Turkey App 68253/01 ECtHR judgment 21st December 2006 58
Sahin v Turkey (2007) 44 EHRR 5 (Grand Chamber) 215

Salabiaku v France (1991) 13 EHRR 379 357
Salduz v Turkey App 36391/02 ECtHR inadmissibility decision
    28th March 2006 ....83, 92, 95, 207
Saya v Turkey App 4327/02 ECtHR judgment 7th October 2008.......................................62
Schiefer v Germany App 13389/89 ECnHR inadmissibility decision
    6th March 1989 ....86, 92, 106, 114, 141
Segerstedt-Wiberg v Sweden App 62332/00, ECtHR judgment 6th June 2006 79
Soering v UK (1989) 11 EHRR 439..31, 33, 351–2
Solomou v Turkey App 36832/97 ECtHR judgment 24th June 2008 61–2
Sporrong and Lonnroth v Sweden (1983) 5 EHRR 35 ....33, 383
Stankov and Ilinden v Bulgaria App 29221/95 and 29225/95 ECtHR
    judgment 2nd October 2001 ......64, 66–7, 79, 85, 96, 99, 102, 107, 109, 189, 207, 210–11
Steel and Morris v UK (2005) 45 EHRR 22. ....33, 51, 75, 386–7
Steel and Others v UK (1998) 28 EHRR 603.....................61, 75, 77, 85, 88, 105–6, 114, 200,
                               207, 231, 238, 320–1, 324, 334, 348, 356, 357–61, 388
Stefanec v Czech Republic App 75615/01 ECtHR judgment 18th July 2006 ....62, 86, 203
Stjerna v Finland (1994) 24 EHRR 194 ....70, 133
Sunday Times v UK (1979) 2 EHRR 245 ....34, 85
Tre Traktörer AB v Sweden (1989) 13 EHRR 309 383
Tsavachidis v Greece App 28802/95 ECnHR report 28th October 1997 79
TV Vest v Norway App 21132/05 ECtHR judgment 11th December 2008
    (2009) 48 EHRR 51 ....62, 234
Tyrer v UK (1978) 2 EHRR 1 31
UMO Ilinden v Bulgaria App 44079/98 ECtHR judgment 20th October
    2005 ....109, 189, 207
United Turkish Communist Party v Turkey (1998) 26 EHRR 121 ....32, 58
Vajnai v Hungary App 33629/06 ECtHR judgment
    8th July 2008...62, 99, 102, 105, 109, 215, 236
van Marle v Belgium (1986) 8 EHRR 483 383
Verein gegen Tierfabriken (VgT) v Switzerland (2002) 32 EHRR 4 ....231, 234
Verein gegen Tierfabriken (VgT) v Switzerland (No 2) App 32772/02
    ECtHR (GC) judgment 30th June 2009...234
Von Hannover v Germany (2006) 43 EHRR 7 31
WG v Austria App 15509/89 ECnHR inadmissibility decision
    30th November 1992 ....76, 81, 90, 115, 158, 213, 238
Wingrove v UK (1997) 24 EHRR 1 222
Witold Litwa v Poland (2001) 33 EHRR 1267 353
WM and HO v Germany App 13235/87 ECnHR inadmissibility decision
    6th March 1989 ....86, 92, 106, 141
X v Sweden App 6094/73 (1977) 9 DR 5 65
X & Y v Netherlands (1986) 8 EHRR 235 33
X v Federal Republic of Germany (1981) 24 DR 158...352–3
XYZ v UK (1997) 24 EHRR 143 38
Ziliberberg v Moldova App 61821/00 ECtHR inadmissibility decision
    4th May 2004..69, 79–81, 82, 87, 91, 94, 104–5,
                                   115, 157–61, 174, 181, 207, 242, 344, 406

INTERNATIONAL CASES

Brooker v Police [2007] NZSC 30 .... 219, 228
Cohen v California 403 US 15 (1971) 217
Collin v Smith 447 F Supp 676 (1978) 117, 170
Commission v France C-265/95 [1997] ECR I-6959 235
Committee for the Commonwealth of Canada v Canada (1991) 77 DLR (4th) 385 118
Eugen Schmidberger Internationale Transporte Planzuge v Austria (C-112/00)
    [2003] ECR I-5659 235
Forsyth Co v Nationalist Movement 505 US 123 (1992) 23, 117
Hudgens v NLRB 424 US 507 (1976) 134
Minto v Police [1987] 1 NZLR 374 337
New York Times v Sullivan 376 US 254 (1964) 385
RAV v City of St Paul Minnesota 505 US 377 (1992) 129
RJR-McDonald v Canada (AG) [1993] 3 SCR 199 54
Robins v Pruneyard Shopping 447 US 74 (1980) 133
SA Societé Esso v Association Greenpeace France judgment of the Parisian
    Court of Appeal 14th chamber 26th February 2003 233
SA Societé Esso v Association Greenpeace France judgment of the Parisian
    Court of Appeal 4th chamber 16th November 2005 233
Terminiello v City of Chicago 337 US 1 (1949) 7
Texas v Johnson 491 US 397 (1989) 225
Ward v Rock Against Racism 491 US 781 (1989) 100

TABLE OF UK LEGISLATION

Anti-Social Behaviour Act 2003 3
   s 30–32 .... 364–373, 404
   s 36 365
   Sched 3, para 1 252
Broadcasting Act 1981
   s 29 27
City of London Police Act 1839
   s 22 147
Communications Act 2003
   s 127 295–6
   s 237 293
   s 321 .... 234, 405
Companies Act 1985
   s 723B–F 298
Companies Act 2006
   s 119 299
   ss 163–165 299
   ss 240–246 299
   s 1088 299
Computer Misuse Act 1990 298
Conspiracy and Protection of Property Act 1875
   s 7 290
Contempt of Court 1981
   s 10 288
Counter Terrorism Act 2008
   s 76 376
Countryside and Rights of Way Act 2000
   s 2 136–138
   s 42 137
   Part II 257
   Sched 2 136–138
Crime and Disorder Act 1998 .... 3, 121
   s 1 .... 314, 362–4
   ss 28–33 .... 218, 228
Criminal Attempts Act 1981
   s 1 249
Criminal Damage Act 1971
   s 1 .... 11, 247
   s 5 .... 141, 247, 251

Criminal Justice Act 1988
  s 39 245
Criminal Justice and Immigration Act 2008 ....
  s 76 249
Criminal Law Act 1967
  s 3 ....141, 249–252, 259–260, 263
Criminal Law Act 1977
  s 1 248
  s 51 ....246, 294
Criminal Justice and Police Act 2001 ....
  s 42 ....15, 284–9, 290, 311, 401–2, 405
  s 42A 288–9, 290, 402
  s 43 294
  s 44 277
  s 45 298
Criminal Justice and Public Order Act 1994 ....
  ss 33–38 27
  s 60 ....216, 315
  s 61 ....162–7, 247, 252, 257, 378
  s 68 ....11, 16, 19, 56, 120, 144, 249, 252–261,
                                     263, 288, 302, 309, 381, 402, 405, 416
  s 69 ....19, 24, 261–4, 288, 309, 311, 318, 378
Cycle Tracks Act 1984 257
Education Act 1986
  s 43 123
Employment Rights Act 1996
  s 98 51
European Communities Act 1972 40
Equality Act 2006 39
Geneva Conventions Act 1957 270
Highways Act 1980
  s 137 ....24, 138–141, 196, 199–200, 292–3
  s 303 388
Human Rights Act 1998 ....38–54, 126–129, 203–206, 405–6
  s 2 ....40, 63, 234, 360
  s 3 ....1, 40–44, 51, 55, 137,139, 145, 152, 156, 160, 164,
                                     193, 205–206, 223, 235, 248, 255–6, 260, 263, 270,
                                     281, 285, 287, 288, 291, 296, 304, 382, 402, 406
  s 4 ....40, 42–44, 51
  s 6 ....1, 40, 44–48, 52–53, 126, 131, 150, 200,
                                     311, 334, 382–3, 388, 397, 406, 415, 420
  s 7 ....1, 40, 44, 50–56, 145, 148, 203–5, 215, 242, 248, 340, 341, 347, 385, 406
  s 10 42
  s 12 ....275, 397
  s 19 40
  Sched 1 39
International Criminal Court Act 2001 250

Justice of the Peace Act 1361 356–7
Local Government Act 1972 ....
   s 120 124–6
Magistrates' Courts Act 1980
   s 115 356–7
Malicious Communications Act 1988
   s 1 .... 224, 293–8, 403
Metropolitan Police Act 1839
   s 52 147
   s 54 .... 147, 246
   s 60 246
National Parks and Access to Countryside Act 1949
   s 5 137
Obscene Publications Act 1959
   s 2 295
Offences against the Person Act 1861
   s 18 246
   s 20 246
   s 47 245–6
Official Secrets Act 1911
   s 1 .... 141–2, 246
   s 2 141–2
Open Spaces Act 1906 124
Police Act 1996
   s 89 .... 147, 251, 321
Police and Criminal Evidence Act 1984
   s 1–3 .... 313–5, 380, 411–2
   s 17(6) 322
   s 24–24A 251, 338
   s 28 251
   Code of Practice A 314
Police Reform Act 2002
   s 50 .... 314, 362, 411, 423
Political Parties, Elections and Referendums Act 2000 ....
   s 22 13
   s 37 13
Postal Services Act 2000
   s 85 .... 294, 296
Prevention of Crime Act 1953
   s 1 246
Private Security Industry Act 2001 24
Protection from Harassment Act 1997 .... 16, 21–22, 24, 56, 233, 264–284,
                                                    286, 295, 299, 302, 363, 391, 397–8, 403–5, 409–10
   s 1 .... 265, 267, 270–3, 286, 407
   s 1A 265–6, 305
   s 2 .... 264, 272, 276, 284, 286, 304–5, 382, 410
   s 3 .... 261, 264–6, 284, 286, 420

xxviii Table of UK Legislation

   s 4 ....244–5, 265, 273
   s 5 ....265, 273
   s 7 ....266–9, 274, 277–8
Public Libraries and Museums Act 1964
   s 7 125
Public Meetings Act 1908
   s 1 123
Public Order Act 1936
   s 1 213–6
   s 2 14
Public Order Act 1986 169–171
   s 1–3 ....242–4, 320
   s 4 ....218–9, 228, 291
   s 4A 218–220, 223–4, 228, 330
   s 5 ....24, 146, 218–230, 233, 235, 272, 286, 289, 291,
                       321, 347, 357, 364, 370, 398, 404–5, 409–10, 417, 419
   s 6 ....219, 225, 242–3
   s 8 ....243, 285
   s 12–14A 2, 146, 182–213, 234–6, 313, 319, 336, 338, 347–8, 350, 373, 408
   s 11 ....171–182, 279, 365, 403
   s 12 ....52, 180–,1, 182–3, 206, 212, 279, 417, 346,
   s 13 ....52, 170, 179–180, 182–3, 208, 212, 346–7
   s 14 ....24, 138,148–150, 153–4, 156,
                      183–5, 206, 212, 368, 370, 372–3, 405, 419
   s 14A–C 24, 120, 153, 183–5, 192–203, 212, 252, 261, 419
   s 16 184
   s 38
   s 39 162
Prevention of Terrorism Act 2005 240
Race Relations Act 1976 126
   s 71 125
Representation of the People Act 1983 ....
   ss 95–97 ....123, 126
Seditious Meetings Act 1817 146
Serious Crime Act 2007
   s 44–46 248
   s 59 248
Serious Organised Crime and Police Act 2005
   s 125 ....265, 274
   s 126 288
   s 127 286
   ss 128–131 ....142–5, 146
   ss 132–138 ....16, 59, 148–161, 179, 402, 405, 419
   s 145 ....15, 23–24, 300–306, 381, 388, 405, 419
   s 146 ....24, 291, 304–6, 381, 388, 405
   s 148 300
   s 149 303

Table of UK Legislation xxix

Supreme Court Act 1981
  s 37 275
Terrorism Act 2000
  s 1 ....14, 216–7, 239, 241, 294, 405
  s 3 14
  s 11–15 14
  s 13 217
  ss 44–47 ....216, 241, 309, 314, 315–9, 379–80, 411
  Sched 2 14
Terrorism Act 2006
  s 12 143
Theft Act 1968
  s 1 246
  s 9 246
  s 15 294
  s 21 246
Theft Act 1978 294
Town Clauses Act 1847
  s 28 246
Town and Country Planning Act 1990 120
Trade Union and Labour Relations (Consolidation) Act 1992
  s 219 388
  s 220 ....285, 365
  s 241 ....19, 290, 305, 416
Tumultuous Petitioning Act 1661 146
Vagrancy Act 1824
  s 4 246
War Crimes Act 2001 270
Wildlife and Countryside Act 1981
  Part III 257
The European Convention on Human Rights 1950 29–38,
  Art 1 ....39, 128
  Art 2 ....32, 34
  Art 3 ....33, 256, 272
  Art 4 33
  Art 5 ....30, 33–4, 51, 89, 200, 232, 304, 316–8,
                                321, 334, 336, 349–356, 357–361, 380
  Art 6 ....30, 32, 165–6, 173, 184, 188, 219, 229, 321, 357–8, 363–4, 409
  Art 7 ....156, 293
  Art 8 ....30, 38, 135, 166, 215, 228, 256, 272, 311, 316–8, 323, 376–8, 380, 383
  Art 9 ....31, 34, 89, 104, 111–4, 210, 227, 229, 231, 296–8
  Art 10 ....1, 31, 33, 63–64, 75–6, 81, 132–6, 143, 150, 164,
              200–203, 206–213, 215, 220, 225–9, 230–6, 238, 248, 254,
              260, 267, 272, 279, 287, 291, 296–8, 303–4, 311–3,
              316, 324–5, 357–361, 363, 368, 371, 376, 383, 388
  Art 11 ....1, 31–6, 55–56, 57–116, 127–9, 143, 150, 153–5,
              157–161, 164–5, 181, 197, 200–203, 206–213, 214, 231, 235, 238,

242, 244, 248, 254, 260, 267, 271, 282, 287, 291–2, 303–4, 311–3,
316, 324–5, 343–4, 347, 357–361, 363, 368, 371, 383, 388, 415, 418, 420
Art 13 ....39, 71–2
Art 14 ....31, 127–8, 214, 227, 229, 303
Art 15 33
Art 17 ....8, 229
Art 34 ....50, 227
Art 41 40
The First Protocol ....
Art 1 ....31, 133, 135, 166, 198–9, 272, 311, 383
The Fourth Protocol ....
Art 2 ....73, 201
The Serious Organised Crime and Police Act 2005 (Designated Sites)
    Order 2005 SI 2005/3447..143
The Serious Organised Crime and Police Act 2005 (Designated Sites
    under Section 128) Order 2007 SI 2007/930..143
The Serious Organised Crime and Police Act 2005 (Designated Sites
    under Section 128) (Amendment) Order 2007 SI2007/1387 143
The Serious Organised Crime and Police Act 2005 (Designated Area)
    Order 2005 SI 2005/1537..149
The Serious Organised Crime and Police Act 2005 (Commencement
    No.1 & Transitory Provisions) Order 2005 SI 2005/1521 155
The Companies (Disclosure of Address) Regulations 2009 SI 2009/214 299
Rules of the Supreme Court (RSC) ....
Part 54..50
Civil Procedure Rules (CPR)..
Rule 19.6 ....274, 276, 278, 421
Rule 50 (formerly RSC Ord 113) 390

1
Introduction

'If voting changed anything, they'd abolish it' (attributed to Emma Goldman).

The effectiveness of elections in a democracy is not the subject of this book. Our focus will be on what fills the gap and provides the safety-valve in the five-year period in between, as well as providing the fuel and the framework for political discussion, debate and development. This is the ability we all have to participate in different forms of political protest. This book, though primarily doctrinal in outlook and tone, is not exclusively so. It will consider protest and public order law, especially the policing and control of it as a social construct, as something operating in practice, on the ground on streets and in meeting halls across the country. Though its concerns are primarily on how the law permits and limits when, where and in what way people can protest, we must accept that the law is played out in real life by real people.

I. Overview

The book has nine chapters. The first, this introduction, provides a general overview of some key themes and ideas. It will also plot the development over time of the 'right' to protest or to assemble in domestic law and will set out some well-known material on the value and function of free speech and protest, as well as identifying the links between protest and democracy. It also touches on some socio-legal perspectives: the role of the police, the construction of deviance and the gap between the law in the books and the law in action. The second chapter is a short one. It provides a general grounding in the general principles of the Human Rights Act 1998 (HRA) and the European Convention on Human Rights (ECHR) that we can draw on throughout the remainder of the book. Its scope is therefore limited to key aspects: the scope of the interpretative duty under section 3 of the HRA; the bodies that are bound by the new duty on public authorities in section 6; how Convention rights can be used as either a sword or shield. It will also highlight some aspects of ECHR jurisprudence that underpin the cases: proportionality, positive obligations and the 'prescribed by law' test. The next chapter, chapter three, contains a detailed analysis of what we shall call the right of peaceful protest (an amalgam of elements of the rights to freedom of speech under Article 10 and of peaceful assembly under Article 11) and its case law at Strasbourg level. We will consider what it means to categorise a protest or an assembly as 'peaceful', whether there are positive duties imposed on states alongside negative duties of restraint, and how the balancing or proportionality test in Articles 10(2) and 11(2)—which

2 *Introduction*

permits states lawfully to restrict the right—plays out before the Strasbourg Court. This is the first time that Strasbourg jurisprudence on the right of peaceful protest has been analysed on this scale and to this degree. These two chapters comprise the first, scene-setting part of the book. Together they show the scope of the right and the modalities of its protection, in the abstract, in England and Wales.

The second, lengthier part is broken into five chapters. Together these depict how protest is regulated in law today, in light of the HRA. By 'regulation' (in this book) we mean how the socio-political activity of protest is controlled by means of coercive legal rules and restrictions. It resembles therefore the type of regulation beloved by certain types of lawyers, political scientists and economists dealing with markets and competition but with these provisos. We will not distinguish between general laws (created by legislatures and by judges) and tailored regulations by administrative agency 'rule-makers'. Secondly, we will not engage in any analysis of the efficiency or the appropriateness of the laws, rules and regulations at achieving their desired outcome. That is, do they and can they achieve what they set out to achieve or are there better measures to do so? Thirdly we will not engage in any debate about transparency, due process, or legitimacy surrounding the creation of the regulatory framework.[1]

Chapter four is entitled 'The Locus of Protest'. This contains a detailed look at the laws surrounding where protests can take place, in both general and place-specific terms, such as around Westminster. As we shall see, a crucial element determining not just the success of any proposed protest but whether the protest can take place at all will be whether there is somewhere to hold it. If there is no right to hold a protest anywhere—except on land owned by the protesting group—this will diminish, perhaps even emasculate, the right in practice. We shall encounter here one of the main themes in this book, the increasing interplay of the public and private spheres in the regulation of protest. We shall develop this a little more at the end of this introduction. The remaining four chapters each represent contrasting pairs of topics. In chapter five, 'Peaceful Persuasion and Communicating Dissent', we consider how and the extent to which the law is able to constrain protesters who want merely to convey a view, to drum up public support or to demonstrate opposition to a plan or policy. We will in the main look at two aspects: regulating marches and assemblies under sections 11–14A of the Public Order Act (POA) 1986 and using the criminal law to restrict the speech of protesters. This might be by uttering actual words that are insulting or abusive—'You baby killer, we know where you live'—or symbolic speech: eg trade union leaders wearing pig masks to illustrate the lucrative bonuses paid to company directors with their snouts in the trough. Where protesters move from seeking to engage with the polity and the wider public to staging protests that obstruct or disrupt the target enterprise or activity itself, protesters have moved into the realm of direct action. How the law responds to protest of that nature is the subject-matter of chapter six, 'Direct Action'. The law here, as we shall see, adopts an even less favourable position. There will be little that a direct action protester can do that will be lawful under domestic law; whether a jury will convict is, of course, another matter. Chapters seven and eight are fairly self-explanatory: 'Preventive Action by the Police' and 'Private Law Remedies'. In the first, we will assess the extent of the powers the police possess (together with any duties imposed on them) to

---

[1] We will not specifically consider any of the various laws and rules in terms of the Government's five Principles of Good Regulation (proportionality, accountability, consistency, transparency and targeting), save that we will often do so as part of our more general legal analysis: www.berr.gov.uk/whatwedo/bre/index.html, accessed 8 May 2009.

prevent protests either occurring at all or becoming disorderly or violent. This will be at both micro-level—the officer in the street—and macro-level—the Bronze Commander in the station. We shall focus on an area that has been the subject of two recent House of Lords decisions, the power to take action so as to prevent a breach of the peace. This power lays behind the controversial tactic of 'kettling', whereby large numbers of people—both violent and peaceful protesters as well as those on their way home from work—are herded and then contained en masse. We shall also consider powers to seek Anti-Social Behaviour Orders against protesters and to order the dispersal of anti-social groups, as well conducting surveillance by photographing protesters as they attend meetings. Chapter eight allows a little more insight into a theme we identified earlier: the increasing interdependence of the private and the public, the civil and the criminal. Our conclusion, chapter nine, sums up and reviews what has preceded it but also offers an agenda for change. The concluding chapter calls for a Royal Commission on protest and suggests what might be its terms of reference and the areas it would need to investigate.

I should offer two caveats. The law we shall explore is the law of England and Wales. I profess no knowledge of Scottish or Northern Irish law so far as it differs either in general terms or as it relates to protest.[2] Even more offensively, this book will largely use the shorthand 'English law'—because it is just that, shorter—when what is really meant is 'English and Welsh law'. More neutrally, 'domestic law' is used interchangeably to mean 'English and Welsh' but to exclude Scottish or Northern Irish. A second justifiable criticism of this book is that it offers little comparative insight into domestic regulation. It draws on only limited, isolated instances of the experience and jurisprudence of other states, whether European (save as an incident of the ECHR) or Anglo-Commonwealth, let alone from other less familiar legal systems.[3] This must be even less forgivable in an era marked by formal human rights protection for the first time in the United Kingdom where so much could be learned from, say, the Canadian Charter or the German Grundgesetz.[4] It is an omission of considerable weight, one of which I am acutely aware. Should this book extend to a second edition, one that I would gladly remedy. I can only offer the fact that a book that is already some 150 pages longer than originally planned but which sets its stall as a critical consideration must have as its focus the position in England and Wales.

---

[2] We shall not look in any detail at the crucial role, given the historical backdrop, played by the Parades Commission, constituted under the Public Processions (Northern Ireland) Act 1998. See generally D MacAusland, 'Policing parades and protest in Northern Ireland' [2007] *European Human Rights Law Review* 211. For the issue of protest in transitional/conflict areas as it applies in Northern Ireland, see M Hamilton, 'Freedom of assembly, consequential harms and the rule of law: liberty-limiting principles in the context of transition' (2007) 27 *Oxford Journal of Legal Studies* 75 and *Re E (A Child)* [2008] UKHL 66.

[3] At international level, the book only takes account of the ECHR and not the right under the ICCPR. There is one rather dated comparative account: T Murphy, 'Freedom of assembly' in D Harris and S Joseph (eds), *The International Covenant on Civil and Political Rights and UK Law* (Oxford, Clarendon Press, 1995). An overview can be found in S Joseph, J Schultz, and M Castan, *The International Covenant on Civil and Political Rights Cases, Materials, and Commentary*, 2nd edn (Oxford, Oxford University Press, 2003) ch 19.

[4] Taking that last example, there is a good, short overview of three cases from 2007 in which the *Bundesverfassungsgericht* (German federal constitutional court) had to balance the right of assembly against public order and national security: R Youngs, 'G8 protests: controlling the right to demonstrate' (2008) 14 *European Public Law* 69. Taking another jurisdiction, TA El-Haj, 'The neglected right of assembly' 56 *UCLA Law Review* 543 (2009) contains a look at the development and current state of the right of assembly in the USA.

4 Introduction

II. Historical Development of The Right

There is no time at which one can easily plot the entry of a right of assembly and protest into legal and judicial discourse in England. As we shall see in chapter two—and this is perhaps the most well-known aspect of the British constitution—before 1998 and the passing of the HRA there were no such things as 'rights' in either the Hohfeldian sense (with concomitant duties) or in the sense of enforceable, higher forms of law. Judges were—and not solely in the context of free speech and protest—wont to talk of liberties, a negative residual concept: what is left after all legal restrictions have been imposed and taken account of is that I have the freedom to do X. Since of course everyone else has the freedom to do anti-X or even prevent me doing X, I might not be able to do X after all. All of this, as is well-known, is the function of the UK's historic attachment to an unwritten or at least uncodified constitution.

In the late nineteenth century, Dicey wrote, of the right of public meeting, that 'it can hardly be said that our constitution knows of such a thing as any specific right of public meeting'.[5] Yet only a few years later, in *Bonnard v Perryman* in the late Victorian era we have probably the earliest mention of a right of free speech—though not assembly or protest. The court there considered that the 'right of free speech is one which it is for the public interest that individuals should possess, and, indeed, that they should exercise without impediment, so long as no wrongful act is done'.[6] That though was a libel case where the issue was whether or not to grant interim relief before trial. From then on, we can see a clear line of cases establishing what was in fact a clearly and deliberately elucidated right to freedom of expression at common law culminating in the House of Lords in *Simms*. There a prisoner was claiming the right to speak to and be interviewed by a journalist after the Home Secretary in effect banned him from doing so. Although decided in 1999, it was not decided by reference to the HRA but at common law. For Lord Steyn, the starting point for analysis of the lawfulness of the Home Secretary's policy was 'the right of freedom of expression. In a democracy it is the primary right: without it an effective rule of law is not possible'.[7]

The lineage of a distinct right to demonstrate, to protest or to assemble is more mixed and more difficult to trace. In 1936, Lord Hewart CJ asserted that 'English law does not recognize any special right of public meeting for political or other purposes'.[8] It is probable that we first come across it in the judgment of Lord Denning MR in *Hubbard v Pitt*, a case from the 1970s.[9] A group of local residents in Islington, North London had organised a picket outside the offices of an estate agency they alleged were behind land development practices that sailed distinctly close to the wind. In the course of his dissenting judgment (which we shall explore in detail in chapter eight) the Master of the Rolls asserted that now 'the right of protest is one aspect of the right of free speech'.[10] Stamp LJ also talked similarly but in terms of a liberty, not a right: 'liberty to speak, the liberty to assemble and the liberty

---

[5] AV Dicey, *An Introduction to the Study of the Law of the Constitution*, 10th edn (London, MacMillan 1959) 271.
[6] *Bonnard v Perryman* [1891] 2 Ch 269 (CA) 284. The court comprised Lord Coleridge CJ, Lord Esher MR, Lindley LJ, Bowen LJ and Lopes LJ. Contrast Dicey's view: 'At no time has there in England been any proclamation of the right to liberty of thought or to freedom of speech' (*An Introduction to the Study of the Law of the Constitution*, above 239–40).
[7] *R v Secretary of State for the Home Department ex parte Simms* [2000] 2 AC 115 (HL) 125.
[8] *Duncan v Jones* [1936] 1 KB 218, 222.
[9] *Hubbard v Pitt* [1976] QB 142 (CA).
[10] ibid, 178–9.

to protest or communicate information'.[11] Lord Denning was at pains to stress the value of the right to a pathologically healthy democracy:[12]

> The right to demonstrate and the right to protest on matters of public concern ... are rights which it is in the public interest that individuals should possess; and, indeed, that they should exercise without impediment so long as no wrongful act is done. It is often the only means by which grievances can be brought to the knowledge of those in authority—at any rate with such impact as to gain a remedy. Our history is full of warnings against suppression of these rights. Most notable was the demonstration at St. Peter's Fields, Manchester, in 1819 in support of universal suffrage. The magistrates sought to stop it. At least 12 were killed and hundreds injured. Afterwards the Court of Common Council of London affirmed 'the undoubted right of Englishmen to assemble together for the purpose of deliberating upon public grievances'. Such is the right of assembly. So also is the right to meet together, to go in procession, to demonstrate and to protest on matters of public concern. As long as all is done peaceably and in good order, without threats or incitement to violence or obstruction to traffic, it is not prohibited.

A few years later, in the *CEGB* case, he seemed clear that his own speech was the view of the Court: 'English law upholds to the full the right of people to demonstrate and to make their views known so long as all is done peaceably and in good order: see Hubbard v. Pitt'.[13] Shortly after that, in *Hirst and Agu v Chief Constable of West Yorkshire*, Otton J began by stating that the 'courts have long recognised the right to free speech to protest on matters of public concern'.[14] Almost the entirety of the rest of his speech took the form of repeating the words of Lord Denning in *Hubbard* above. The confusion between a 'right' and a 'liberty' or 'freedom' is evident in his concluding words: that 'freedom of protest on issues of public concern' should be given the recognition it deserves. Similarly, in *Verrall v Great Yarmouth BC*, Lord Denning (again) asserted that 'freedom of assembly is another of our precious freedoms. Everyone is entitled to meet and assemble with his fellows to discuss their affairs and to promote their views: so long as it is not done to propagate violence or do anything unlawful'.[15] There the issue was whether the National Front was entitled to an order of specific performance after the council, following local elections and new political control, rescinded the licence to use a council venue for the party's annual conference.

Again, as with the right of free speech, in 1999—at common law still not under the HRA—the majority of the House of Lords in *DPP v Jones and Lloyd* held that there was a right of peaceful public assembly in the highway (at least).[16] The case, as we shall see when we consider it in depth in chapter five, is not a clear-cut ringing endorsement of a general right of protest and assembly against all-comers—though not necessarily absolute—in all places and at all times. The decision, arising out of a banned protest near Stonehenge, is largely one—despite the language of rights used by Lord Irvine, Lord Clyde and Lord Hutton—based primarily on a different, more long-standing right: the right of access to and use of land. In fact it is only Lord Hutton that departs from the specifics of rights over/on the public highway. He in fact begins his analysis with the general proposition that

---

[11] *ibid*, 187.
[12] *ibid*, 174.
[13] *R v Chief Constable of Devon and Cornwall ex parte Central Electricity Generating Board* [1982] QB 458, 470.
[14] *Hirst and Agu v Chief Constable of West Yorkshire* (1987) 85 Cr App R 143.
[15] *Verrall v Great Yarmouth Borough Council* [1981] QB 202 (CA) 217, Lord Denning MR. See also Cumming-Bruce LJ: 'If there is a case for silencing a group which wishes to organise as a political party, it is for the Crown in Parliament by statute to restrict the right of free speech or free association' (at 222–3).
[16] *Director of Public Prosecutions v Jones and Lloyd* [1999] 2 AC 240 (HL): Lord Irvine at 255, Lord Clyde at 280, and Lord Hutton at 286.

the common law recognises that there is a right for members of the public to assemble together to express views on matters of public concern, 'one of the fundamental rights of citizens in a democracy'. This is based on both *Hubbard* and *Hirst*, and he reasons deductively that the right will be unduly restricted unless it can be exercised in some circumstances on the public highway.[17]

Whether there is a right at common law to protest, to assemble and to demonstrate, where we can find it and when it arose is, of course of purely academic interest. It is hard to conceive of the necessity to rely on a 'right' at common law over and above, or in the alternative to, the HRA. What the preceding discussion does illustrate is the perhaps more fragile, perhaps less generally accepted nature of that right, and *DPP v Jones* is no better example. It is hard to count the number of books in the Anglo-Commonwealth world dedicated to the topic of free speech. Those on the topic of protest and assembly would probably not utilise the fingers of both hands. There is a near homogeneity about the value and necessity of freedom to speak, even to speak offensively or baselessly; the same cannot be said about the right to protest and demonstrate despite the allied, symbiotic nature of the two rights. Too often, and we have seen this in recent times during the G20 protests, it is argued that the right to protest should quite properly be countervailed by the convenience of others, business disruption and the 'unreasonable' nature of the protest.[18] It is, quite simply, inconceivable that sensible people would argue that free speech should be curtailed because others might be 'inconvenienced' or 'because I disagree with you'. There is, however—and we shall see this in both domestic and Strasbourg cases—a near equivalence between the right to protest and the right to drive unhindered on the road or the right to shop without disturbance on a Saturday afternoon, even though 'a demonstration without some form of disruption is both counter-intuitive and inevitably sterile'[19]. Taking such a perspective does not bode well for the protection of the right and seems markedly to underplay the functional value of protest, as an element of and aside from, free speech. It is that we shall turn to now.

III. The Function of Free Speech and Protest

In the well-known words of Sedley LJ, free speech includes 'not only the inoffensive but the irritating, the contentious, the eccentric, the heretical, the unwelcome and the provocative provided it does not tend to provoke violence. Freedom only to speak inoffensively is not worth having'.[20]

The literature on the value and role of free speech is considerable but for our purposes we can distill its essence into a few short propositions.[21] This is not the place to dispute the

---

[17] *ibid*, 287–8.
[18] JCHR 7th report of session 2008–09 'Demonstrating respect for rights? A human rights approach to policing protest', 23 March 2009 at para 64: www.publications.parliament.uk/pa/jt200809/jtselect/jtrights/47/4702.htm, accessed 15 June 2009. This was not, so as to be clear, the JCHR's view but a summary of evidence submitted by witnesses.
[19] B Fitzpatrick and N Taylor, 'A Case of Highway Robbery' (1997) 147 *New Law Journal* 338, 339.
[20] *Redmond-Bate v DPP* (1999) 7 BHRC 375 (DC) at [20].
[21] See generally E Barendt, *Freedom of Speech*, 2nd edn (Oxford, Oxford University Press, 2007) ch 1, together with K Greenwalt, 'Free speech justifications' (1989) 89 *Columbia Law Review* 119, A Meikeljohn, 'The First Amendment is an absolute' (1961) *Supreme Court Review* 245, F Schauer, *Free speech: a philosophical enquiry* (Cambridge, Cambridge University Press, 1982) and W Waluchow (ed), *Free expression: essays in law and philosophy* (Oxford, Clarendon Press, 1994).

various claims made on behalf of free speech and protest but rather to set them out so we can draw on them and refer to them in the rest of this book. Free speech and, by extension, the right of peaceful protest might be justified or asserted as being valuable, either deontologically or teleologically—or both. Knowing the basis on which it is being asserted that free speech or a particular protest are good things is important, as it means that any restrictions imposed must confront and deal with those assertions. Different assertions or justifications might possess different strengths depending on what is actually taking place: justifying a march as contributing to enhancing democracy may well not stand up where the protest itself is avowedly anti-democratic.

Being able to speak my own mind without restriction, to read what I want and to hear whatever views of others I wish is intrinsically valuable, since it respects my autonomy, dignity and self-worth. Restricting free speech and protest rights is censorship by any other name—what Sedley LJ referred to as 'State control of unofficial ideas'[22]—and so allows someone else to judge what I can see or hear or view or say. To do so not only deprives me of my choices but places someone else, no better qualified and in fact, since they are not me, worse qualified to assess what is best for me. That deprives me of my own moral authority. We might—most obviously, say, in the context of expressive choice in the types of clothing worn or haircuts paraded—see it linked to aspects of personal identity and self-development and self-fulfilment, though in that latter case free speech is as much valued for its consequences, as it is about being intrinsically good. To the extent that free speech informs and supports what we choose to do and how we choose to live our lives, it is both instrumental and also integral to concerns about privacy in both its informational and autonomy senses. There is a close symbiosis between the two rights. Without a guarantee of privacy/confidentiality, will people feel able to speak freely? Without free speech and the right to receive information, on what can I base my life-choices? How will I know whether to go on holiday to Pembrokeshire or to Peru? Reading, hearing or viewing certain types of words or speech can also serve an important confirmatory role or reinforce negative (self-)images: the absence (say) of certain types of characters in soap operas (or their stereotypical portrayal) illustrates this well. To that extent again, what seems to be an intrinsically valuable role can be seen equally as performing an instrumental role: longer term social cohesion by the validating of different demographic groups.

One function of free speech

> is to invite dispute. It may indeed best serve its high purpose when it induces a condition of unrest, creates dissatisfaction with conditions as they are, or even stirs people to anger. Speech is often provocative and challenging. It may strike at prejudices and preconceptions and have profound unsettling effects as it presses for acceptance of an idea.

So said Douglas J in *Terminiello* in the American Supreme Court in 1949.[23] We can view free speech and the right to hold demonstrations and marches as serving more functional or consequentialist imperatives. These are usually viewed as one of two. Free speech creates a so-called market place of ideas. It also contributes to the development of and sustaining of democracy. By allowing people to say whatever they want, the 'truth' will out or, if we are considering more value-laden content, better ideas, thoughts and views will survive and flourish. Truthful speech ultimately defeats falsity by showing it to be . . . false! Poor ideas and thoughts are defeated by rational discourse. Thus, goes the argument, we should defend

---

[22] *Redmond-Bate*, above n 20.
[23] *Terminiello v City of Chicago* 337 US 1, 4 (1949).

even racist or hate speech: groups like the British National Party should be taken on and defeated on their own terms, their ideas and values shown to be baseless and debased, not silenced and driven underground. Linked to this is the value of free speech in promoting general human wellbeing and advance. Without being able to refute or even just test accepted (scientific) views, there would be moribund stagnation: we would still believe the world was flat. Even 'untruths' have a valuable role to play. Most pertinent for us is the role that free speech and protest play in political discourse. Without a free press—and our own ability to read and decipher texts and messages—we would be exercising our right to vote in a vacuum. It thus sustains an informed participatory electorate that can read about alternatives when they come to choose new governments and parliaments. It plays a role too outside that more formal five-year period. Journalists and protesters alike probe and criticise politicians and public officials; they engage in debate about—to choose three examples—a cleaner more sustainable environment, the availability of abortion and the supposed urban skew of policy-making. They publicise minority viewpoints and thus contribute to a more rounded, comprehensive public policy debate. Free speech thus provides a safety-valve, a corrective to formal (Westminster) politics. Over time, a sustained campaign of protest might alert others that something is amiss, might attract publicity that might signify that a decision or policy is significantly out of line with public expectation or preferences. This, of course, does not mean it is 'wrong' but does mean it needs at least a better more persuasive case to be made in its defence, which might in time lead to a complete rethink. Thus deliberative democracy comes about in the market place of political ideas and ideology.

The normative justification proffered for protecting and guaranteeing the right of protest should—though often in hard cases does not—dictate how and why it might be restricted and how likely it is that a counter-claim or counter-justification would succeed. At its simplest, for example, a claim founded on the democratic rationale will—or should—most likely founder if the protest being proposed is one by advocates of an overthrow of democracy or those who reject democratic means as the solution to problems. This is often the case for extremists at either end of the political spectrum, more usually right-wing racists, and can be found in legal form in Article 17 of the ECHR. A claim by a right-wing *party* to hold a march could not be sustained by autonomy and self-worth—though of course its members, rather than the party, may consider a ban would defeat those two values. Alternatively, claims based on dignity and choice can be made not where a march or meeting is banned but where conditions as to time and place (among other matters) are imposed. If, after all, an organiser wanted to hold a march for five minutes, two miles from where the object of his group's ire lives at 9:00 on a Sunday evening, when no one else would be around, surely she would have chosen to do so? Anyone seeking to impose those conditions could—but again oftentimes will not—be asked to explain why conditions which sought to respect autonomy were not sufficient to, say, prevent disorder or disruption.[24]

---

[24] See further on this H Fenwick and G Phillipson, 'Direct Action, Convention Values and the Human Rights Act' (2001) 21 *Legal Studies* 535, 543–5.

IV. Protest and Democracy

Whether new social movements[25] and collective action, especially on single-issue campaigns, subvert or supplement what we traditionally envisage as the democratic process is a question that goes to the heart of the debate about legitimacy of protest. Whatever is the answer we need not resolve here, but we do need to touch upon it so as to provide context for much of what follows.[26]

What is true is the rise in the western world of what Amitai Etzioni has referred to as 'demonstration democracy'.[27] In fact, whether political protest is an adjunct or an alternative to voting and campaigning by organised, established political parties is not the right question to ask.[28] At its heart it fails to recognise that different types of protest, in differing ways and to different extents, both support and sideline Westminster politics and democracy. Put simply, communicative protest—that is, standing on street corners shouting slogans, marching through London to denounce the War on Iraq or rallying support for a petition to ban fox-hunting—is seen as essential to support an informed, participatory and active electorate, playing its role at persuading and cajoling MPs, officials and private commercial targets. On the other hand, direct action protest—obstructing the runway at Stansted, dismantling bombers destined for Israel or Iraq or pulling up GM crops in a field—cannot be seen in the same light. It cannot be an exercise of democratic power for me and my like-minded friends to attempt to impose my will on others who are reluctant to change. Of course it could quite properly be argued that our version of democracy—in the United Kingdom—is flawed: it is unrepresentative in so far as the government of the day may be formed with the support of only a minority of the popular vote, usually between 33 and 40 per cent. In other words, far more of those who voted (let alone the nation as a whole) did not want Tony Blair or Margaret Thatcher as Prime Minister or his/her party in government. That is a very big question and a whole different ball-game. Does it therefore render direct action protest less justifiable in countries that use, say, a form of Proportional Representation for general elections? It is true that in the UK, at least, it is not just the voting system that is at the heart of protesters' complaints. What happens when there is a clear, demonstrable public view on a given topic but which is ignored? The example of course is the decision to wage war on Iraq, taken in March 2003 against a backdrop of a

---

[25] There is a wealth of literature on New Social Movements, particularly by Donatella della Porta: see H Kriesi et al, *New Social Movements in Western Europe: A Comparative Analysis* (Minneapolis MN, University of Minnesota Press, 1995); H Kriesi, D Della Porta and D Rucht (eds), *Social Movements in a Globalizing World* (London, Macmillan, 1998) and D Della Porta and M Diani, *Social Movements* (Oxford, Blackwell Publishers, 1999).

[26] Other interesting (sub-) questions would appear to include why people protest—can we predict which sort of people do or do not and whether there are indicators, of people or circumstances, which predict protest as more likely, what Alan Marsh has called 'protest potential': see A Marsh, 'Explorations in Unorthodox Political Behaviour: A Scale to Measure Protest Potential' (1974) 2 *European Journal of Political Research* 107 and A Marsh, *Protest and Political Consciousness* (Beverley Hills CA, Sage, 1977) and see generally S Barnes and M Kaase (eds), *Political Action: Mass Participation in Five Western Democracies* (Beverley Hills CA, Sage, 1979).

[27] A Etzioni, *Demonstration Democracy* (New York, Gordon and Breach, 1977).

[28] Whether or not there are in fact significant differences in terms of citizen participation between large scale protests groups—such as Friends of the Earth, Greenpeace, Amnesty International—and formal party political structures is a matter of some debate: see G Jordan and W Moloney, 'Protest businesses and democratic activity' in G Jordan and W Moloney, *The Protest Business—Mobilizing Campaign Groups* (Manchester, Manchester University Press, 1997).

march in central London of a million or so in the February.[29] Does that make it morally right to take the law into our own hands? Are there criteria—should there be criteria—by which we can evaluate the legitimacy of large-scale collective dissent so as to defeat or temper the 'decisional autonomy' of Burkean representatives at Westminster?[30] What if there is evidence of serious democratic malaise—for example civil servants and BAA officials colluding to produce (to doctor?) data on pollution targets and environmental impact that eventually led to the conclusion that expansion at Heathrow could occur without breaching EU targets and rules?[31] Would that justify direct action—even if only climbing on the roof or Parliament and draping banners indicating Westminster was BAA's HQ?[32]

There is a real danger that we cede neutrality to sympathy for outcomes and causes, letting our views on the subject-matter flavour our response to the question of the legality or even the morality of the protest. What *is* it about climate change that disposes many to agree not only with the objectives but with the interventionist methods employed by Plane Stupid and Greenpeace, whereas few—and probably not the same people and that is the point—would concede the same privilege to groups campaigning against the perceived liberalisation of abortion laws, or to neighbourhoods that take protection against paedophiles in their midst into their own hands? Can we be sure that one is 'wrong' and if so, by what measure? Can it be the weight of scientific evidence—if so that rules out much other direct action on most other topics? At what point is it illegitimate for me to protest, to dissent, to object, to seek to alter things that happen to me, that concern me or simply that I do not like? Might it in this context be important to consider whether the protesting group is 'mainstream': could we normally and properly expect it to participate in the (flawed) democratic process and to abide by the results or is the group on the margins, perhaps espousing an unpopular cause? What is its impact on this particular target: is the target a company with resources enough to swallow and deflect (most forms of) direct action or is it private fishermen, whose activities are objected to by animal welfare campaigners who throw stones into a pond?[33]

This book does not set out to provide detailed answers to those questions or a revised theory of participative protest but it will show the differentiated way that the law deals with certain types or forms of protest. It is to reflect a little more on that that we now turn. After that we might be better placed to consider the relationship of protest to democratic values.

---

[29] The police estimate was 750 000. Participants put the figure at nearer two million: news.bbc.co.uk/1/hi/uk/2765041.stm, accessed 12 May 2009.
[30] See D Beetham, 'Political Participation Mass Protest and Representative Democracy' (2003) 56 *Parliamentary Affairs* 597.
[31] 'Evidence fix led to third runway being approved', *The Sunday Times*, 9 March 2008, at: www.timesonline.co.uk/tol/news/politics/article3512042.ece, accessed 12 May 2009.
[32] Five 'Plane Stupid' environment protesters were fined in November 2008 for what seems to have been (media reports being unclear) criminal trespass, though whether this was aggravated trespass, trespass on a designated site or holding an unauthorised demonstration within 1 km of Westminster is unclear. It must be doubted given the nature of the protest that it was direct action properly called. The aim of the protest was not to disrupt or intimidate or obstruct the building of the runway or the airport generally—though this has been done and will be continued when building starts. To that extent, Gordon Brown's words that 'Decisions should be made in this house and not on the roof of this house' seems in fact misplaced: this was at best a tangentially disruptive protest designed to heighten awareness and to enlist public sympathy.
[33] The case in which this occurred is *Nicol v DPP* [1996] *Criminal Law Review* 318 and the general discussion of the normative issues or framework is found in Fenwick and Phillipson, above n 24, 546–7.

V. A Simple Dichotomy: Protest v Direct Action?

In short, domestic law and Strasbourg decisions—certainly historically—have not been especially responsive to nuances between different types and forms of, and motivations for, protest. Largely, the law has taken a very black and white approach: peaceful communication—marching, pamphletting, rallies, meetings, slogans and banners—if not fully protected, have been looked on relatively favourably in comparison with any form of disruptive or obstructive protest. Broadly speaking protests of that type have been banned or restricted largely at will, with states being asked to show very little need or justification: the disruption or obstruction is presumed to be enough. Such demarcation raises two concerns: first, that the black and white line is drawn in the wrong place and secondly, that it does not allow for shades of grey. There is considerable difference between what Fenwick and Phillipson call 'symbolically disruptive' direct action protest—perhaps because of its short duration or the fact that it is easily remedied or because its relative impact is minimal—and direct action that causes significant obstruction such that there is a risk that the group will actually succeed in their aims, outwith the democratic process.[34]

We might also typify protests either as incidentally and inevitably disruptive—where those affected are other citizens in their daily lives whose support is needed for any successful campaign to change the law democratically—or as intentionally obstructive and disruptive protests, aimed at closing down the activity itself. Similarly, direct action that causes or threatens harm to people must be qualitatively different to that which 'merely' threatens harm to property, or even which does cause such harm. To call both groups 'violent' protesters—or to equate non-violent with peaceful—seems (at best) to be an infelicity of language and at worst a deliberate misuse, though as a label, one that has important sociological consequences for perceptions of protesters. We might further look at protests—direct action as well as peaceful communication—and consider whether the law should (and does) respond differently to actual than to potential harms. There is considerable debate, as we shall see in many chapters, surrounding the pre-emptive use of coercive—usually state—power, especially where the innocent (either those later shown to be or those who even at the time can obviously be said to be) are caught up. This is one of the major concerns arising from the G20 protest but is not reserved for that. In April 2009, over 100 environmental protesters were arrested on suspicion of conspiracy to commit aggravated trespass and criminal damage, in anticipation of a planned protest at an Eon power station. All were quickly released without charge but subject to quite onerous bail conditions.[35]

This book will take as its premise the following. First, what I am calling peaceful communication and both symbolic obstructive/disruptive protest together with incidentally and

---

[34] The use of legal proceedings brought after perhaps a short-lived staged direct action event, with no risk of preventing the activity, as a part of the protest has been heavily criticised: see Lord Hoffman in *R v Jones* [2006] UKHL 16 [90]–[94]. He talks of 'the emergence of a new phenomenon, namely litigation as the continuation of protest by other means . . . [by which] protesters claim that their honestly held opinion of the legality or dangerous character of the activities in question justifies trespass, causing damage to property or the use of force. By this means they invite the court to adjudicate upon the merits of their opinions and provide themselves with a platform from which to address the media on the subject. They seek to cause expense and, if possible, embarrassment to the prosecution by exorbitant demands for disclosure, such as happened in this case'. Protesters had damaged fighters that were due to be used in the bombing of Iraq contrary to international law, it was alleged by the protesters.

[35] 'Nottingham power station suspects "treated like terrorists"', *The Guardian*, 18 April 2009. www.guardian.co.uk/environment/2009/apr/18/climate-protestors-arrest-nottingham, accessed 16 June 2009.

inevitably obstructive/disruptive protest should be considered legitimate civic responses to perceived democratic deficits and should, unless a pressing case is made out, on evidence, be presumed to be lawful. To that extent this position is in line with, but also a development of, that adopted by Fenwick and Phillipson.[36] It is, in other words, a more generous realignment of the historic position, one that broadly equates to the difference between direct action and civil disobedience:[37] one side seeks to effect change directly, by obstruction, intimidation, even violence and causing significant damage. The other, the symbolic protester, seeks to highlight a concern, but is willing to incur a penalty and acts in a measured, balanced way, all things considered. As Lord Hoffman stated,

> civil disobedience on conscientious grounds has a long and honourable history in this country. People who break the law to affirm their belief in the injustice of a law or government action are sometimes vindicated by history. The suffragettes are an example which comes immediately to mind. It is the mark of a civilised community that it can accommodate protests and demonstrations of this kind. But there are conventions which are generally accepted by the law-breakers on one side and the law-enforcers on the other. The protesters behave with a sense of proportion and do not cause excessive damage or inconvenience. And they vouch the sincerity of their beliefs by accepting the penalties imposed by the law. The police and prosecutors, on the other hand, behave with restraint and the magistrates impose sentences which take the conscientious motives of the protesters into account. The conditional discharges ordered by the magistrates in the cases which came before them exemplifies their sensitivity to these conventions.[38]

Where protest is not a form of civil disobedience—where the disruption is minimal in time or effect and so largely symbolic—but does genuinely and actually cause disruption to the activity itself such that there is a serious risk the activity will cease purely as a result of the direct action protest itself, this should be presumed to be unlawful.[39] Thus it would be unprotected absent a pressing case, made out on evidence, that there were absolutely no alternative means and there was a clear democratic imperative to act in that fashion. That would rule out 99 per cent of intimidatory or disruptive or obstructive targeted direct action but would leave open the opportunity to argue that in a particular circumstance the democratic system of representative government has been shown to be so unresponsive as to demand that we take action into our own hands.

VI. Deciding to Engage In Collective Action

Protest tends not to be a solitary activity; those who feel strongly about an issue will want to come together to form a protest group. That needs one person to be aware of the existence of other like-minded, concerned individuals. With the dissemination of information made easier by the explosion in communications technology and capability from the 1990s onwards this must be less of a problem—though it was probably never a problem in the past

---

[36] Above n 24.
[37] See too R Dworkin, *Taking Rights Seriously* (Cambridge MA, Harvard University Press, 1977) 186–7.
[38] *Jones*, above n 34, at [89].
[39] We might extend the ambit of presumptive lawfulness by positing that in addition to being 'serious', the risk should also be clear. Alternatively, we might restrict it by positing that if the activity ceases largely, but not purely, as a result of the direct action, then it would be an unlawful protest.

if there was an emotive local issue generating a highly-focused collective campaign.[40] Examples are easy to think of: a decision to close a local school or post office or to grant planning permission to allow a quarry to be built in unspoilt countryside or to build a bypass.[41] That said, issues that because of their nature garner immediate publicity either due to their divisive and emotive nature, their wider impact or because they strike a (temporary) chord of public disquiet may well cause a rallying round. We might think of *Make Poverty History* or the anti-war campaign *Not In My Name*. The proliferation, cost, speed and ease of communication not only aids isolated individuals seeking protest 'soulmates' but of course assists in drumming up support, keeping members and potential members informed of planned activities and acting as a rallying point.

Once aware of other like-minded souls, an individual's decision to engage collectively with and to protest about an issue will be dictated by weighing up the strengths and weaknesses of taking collective action.[42] Obviously there is power in numbers: being able to persuade others that you are right and they are wrong can only be enhanced by showing collective strength. It also means a sharing of skills, strengths and expertise according to ability and a pooling of resources. The larger the group, too, the more and further reaching the network of contacts and people who may be called upon to help and to promote the cause. The greater the collective, the greater will be the group dynamic. This might well improve the quality of internal debate on means and ends and ultimately its decision-making but clearly will lead to an increase in tensions within the group. The gains will also need to be balanced and offset against the near-certain loss of individual autonomy over tactics and goals, as the individual is subsumed within the imperatives of a group, and the likely greater organisational costs.

In domestic law, there is little restriction on organising and establishing political or protest groups.[43] There is no need for prior permission and the only public regulation is that a protest group must register if it wishes to stand for election as a political party. Under section 22 of the Political Parties, Elections and Referendums Act 2000, nominations in UK elections can only be made for candidates standing for a qualifying registered party or standing as 'an independent', that is to say someone who does not purport to represent any party, or someone where there is no description given on the ballot paper.[44] The only two

---

[40] To refer to some issues as 'local' misses the point, of course, that many are symptomatic of macro-policy on education and the environment and may in turn be the focus of an on-going national campaign or one that develops subsequently from that initial single example.

[41] That last raises a point of considerable interest. Many inhabitants of villages or towns may desire to see an over-subscribed trunk road diverted some distance away for a variety of reasons. They may well (rightly or wrongly) consider that bypassing their town would make the town safer, their lives healthier and less disrupted and the value of property prices to rise. Equally some in the town—and certainly wider afield—may be members of environmental or green groups who object to what they see as further desecration of the countryside in the interests of road developers or the temporary selfish interests of others in the town over and above the greater and longer term good of access to the country.

[42] See for example M Hornsey et al, 'Why Do People Engage in Collective Action? Revisiting the Role of Perceived Effectiveness' (2006) 36 *Journal of Applied Social Psychology* 1701 in which the authors argue that 'perceived effectiveness' as a determinant of initial engagement is not related solely to influencing decision makers. Other criteria might also be relevant: does it influence the public, does it build an oppositional movement, does it express values? What follows in the text is based largely on the writings of someone else whose words of wisdom I have kept on a scrap of paper. I do not know whose but would be happy to make a proper attribution in future editions.

[43] Under the ECHR the only real restriction on forming political associations is their un- or anti-democratic nature and objectives: see as a summary S Sottiaux, 'Anti-democratic associations: content and consequences in Article 11 adjudication' (2004) 22 *Netherlands Quarterly of Human Rights* 585.

[44] It is only registered parties that are entitled to party political broadcasts: s 37 forbids broadcasters from including in its broadcasting services any party political broadcast made on behalf of a party which is not a registered party. We touch upon the contentious area of political broadcasting and political advertising later towards the end of chapter five.

real obstacles in the path of groups that seek to achieve a political objective by collective strength are the prohibition on quasi-military organisations under section 2 of the POA 1936 and the fact that certain terrorist groups can be subject to proscription under the Terrorism Act 2000.[45] 'Terrorism' is defined very widely in section 1 of the 2000 Act and could conceivably capture certain forms of direct action protest. We consider this in a little more detail in chapter six. Both are more theoretical than real obstacles.

Section 2 of the 1936 Act makes it unlawful to organise, control, manage or train an association for the purpose of enabling it either

(a) to be employed in usurping the functions of the police or armed forces, or
(b) to be organised and trained or organised and equipped either (i) for the purpose of enabling it to be to be employed for the use of or display of physical force in the promotion of any political object or (ii) in such a manner as to arouse reasonable apprehension that they are organised and trained or organised and equipped for that purpose.

It seems highly unlikely that any protest group *simpliciter* would fall foul of (a) but newspaper reports setting out the change in tactics of some extreme animal rights protest groups indicate that the width of (b) could remain a potential weapon in the armoury against them.[46] Secondly, groups may be proscribed either by being named in Schedule 2 to the 2000 Act or by Ministerial order under section 3(3)–(4) if the Home Secretary believes the organisation is 'concerned in terrorism' by committing or participating in acts of terrorism; by preparing for terrorism; by promoting or encouraging terrorism; or otherwise by being concerned in terrorism. Once a group is proscribed, certain proscription offences follow under sections 11–15. These relate to membership of (or professed membership of) a proscribed organisation; arranging, managing or assisting at meetings that support a proscribed organisation, that further its activities or that are to be addressed by a member of a proscribed organisation; wearing clothing or carrying an article in public in such a way or in such circumstances as to arouse reasonable suspicion that the person is a member or supporter of a proscribed organisation; and fundraising and inviting support.

VII. The Socio-Legal Aspect

This book is largely a consideration of the law that regulates protests and protesters, or alternatively empowers them, distinguishing various types by motivation, impact or the methods utilised. What though of the operation of those laws? How do these restrictions play out on the ground? What is the effect of the law on the socio-political phenomenon of protest and its interplay with it? Although such perspectives will not dominate our book, it is important for a fuller and better understanding of how the law regulates any human activity that we appreciate the political and social dimension in which it operates. This is particularly so when, as here in general, we are looking at the exercise of state power through its police.

[45] See generally H Fenwick, *Civil liberties and human rights*, 4th edn (Abingdon, Routledge-Cavendish, 2007) 1381–1406.
[46] 'Revealed: animal rights extremists set up combat skills training camp in Britain', *The Independent*, 25 July 2004, at: www.independent.co.uk/environment/revealed-animal-rights-extremists-set-up-combat-skills-training-camp-in-britain-554343.html, accessed 16 June 2009.

The history of the law in this area is reactive. Aside from the HRA, it is all one-way traffic: incremental restriction, regulation and encroachment. There is no over-arching 'big picture', no theoretical underpinning, no normative framework within which proposed changes in the law are plotted and evaluated. None of this is novel and none of it is confined to the law of protest and public order. The law seems forever to be playing 'catch-up' with protesters. As each new devious, mendacious strategy or tactic comes into play, so does the 'we must (be seen to) do something now' knee-jerkism (with apologies to Bittner[47])—but there is no, or only limited, grappling with whether that 'something' is needed, is appropriate and whether it properly balances the competing rights, interests and tensions. The development of the law is largely informed by problems and filling the gaps and the need to forge what are proposed as tailored solutions, capturing those perceived to fall outside the ambit of the existing law. No thought seems ever to be given to whether the 'problem' of intimidation towards suppliers of credit to animal research labs, or the 'problem' of people camping outside homes belonging to directors of arms manufacturers—to choose two examples—is not one of insufficient law on the books to prevent it but is rather that whatever law exists is hard to enforce. If *that* were the problem, how will creating further and more specific, better-targeted laws solve it? If the problem is really more one of identifying culprits or obtaining enough evidence, it is moot whether fashioning a bespoke law (The Banning Sending Razor Blades Through The Post To Abortionists Act 2009, perhaps?) will be the answer. Yet the political response has been exactly that in our two examples: section 145 of SOCPA 2005 and section 142 of the CJPA 2001.

We consider those two measures in detail presently in chapter six but for now, our concerns are different. There are three of them. The first is the increase in discretion caused by the problem of overbreadth. The second is the distortion of existing powers to fill a gap. The third is the questionable necessity of the changes at all. If overly broad laws are being passed—or developed and expanded at common law by the courts—and existing laws are being adapted to meet new types of protest, is there really a pressing social need (to use Strasbourg terminology) to enact yet more? Is it really the case that there was no other way to deal with protesters who stand at the gates of abortionists' houses berating them in fairly rudimentary language and warning them of the dire consequences for their families if they continue, than creating the specific offence of harassing someone in the vicinity of their home? It is not contradictory to maintain, as we shall in this book, that there are too many vague, broad laws regulating protest while also asserting that they should be used rather than more being created solely to cater for whatever is this year's chosen protest tactic.

Let us take the first two in turn. It might not be hard to draft a precise enough law so as to capture only those who 'post animal excrement to people working in an animal experimentation laboratory' so as to convince them not to work there any more. Worded that way, the law would leave workers exposed to human excrement or (if it were worded as 'excrement') to entrails, to mutilated body parts as well as razor blades and syringes being delivered by hand. The gaps would soon be exposed by wily determined protesters. Any law has to be wide enough to capture the intended current practice and provide limited 'wiggle room' for the future. A broader law that criminalised 'sending or delivering material that causes anyone connected with [list of activities or targets] to fear for their safety with the intention of persuading or intimidating the recipient' would bring an inevitable,

---

[47] Bittner uses the phrase 'something that ought not to be happening and about which someone had better do something now': M Bittner, 'Florence Nightingale in search of Willie Sutton: a theory of the police' in H Jacob (ed), *The potential for reform of criminal justice* (Beverley Hills CA, Sage, 1974) 30.

consequential increase in discretion to those operating the law. It sets up the police on the ground (and the Criminal Prosecution Service in deciding to bring charges) as what Doreen McBarnet has called the 'fall guys'.[48] Let us take one concrete example. In 2005 those organising a 'demonstration' in an area around Westminster became required for the first time to obtain prior authorisation from the police. Previously, constraints had been imposed on assemblies and processions only so it was clear the drafters wanted to capture something wider, something more ethereal, something less organised and less institutionalised... but what? Is reading out the names of those who died in the Iraq war a 'demonstration'—or a publicity stunt? What about political activists dressing up in Father Christmas costumes to plague the Prime Minister? The first was considered by the Metropolitan Police to be a demonstration, the second a publicity stunt.[49] Many would view it as the other way around. Wide discretion reposed in the hands of decision-makers such as the police, with rules that do not limit or structure it, has the potential to undermine the legitimacy of any decisions and thus undermine the legitimacy of any 'powers to compel tolerance on the part of rationally self-interested citizens in a pluralist democracy'.[50]

The second concern is the reverse of that first: laws that are passed to deal with a recognised social problem, totally unrelated to protest, but which are worded as possibly to encompass restrictions on protest—or at least not to exclude it. The legal framework that surrounds harassment is a case in point. The PFHA 1997 was originally drafted, as a private member's bill, to deal with the problem of women (in the main) being stalked. As we shall see in chapter six, it has featured regularly and increasingly as a tool to deal with peaceful (that is, not violent) albeit unwelcome protest. Changes to the law of aggravated trespass (also discussed in chapter six) provide another example of how laws can be misdirected as a result of a perceived gap. In short, aggravated trespass is committed where X trespasses on land and disrupts or obstructs the lawful activity of Y nearby. It was introduced largely to deal with fox-hunt saboteurs. Until 2004, it could only be committed outdoors. Since then it has embraced those who trespass inside buildings, changed on the government's own case to 'close loopholes in the law which were being exploited by animal rights protesters' trespassing inside research labs to release the caged animals.[51] Yet it has been used since then to arrest students protesting in their own university senate building.[52]

Our last concern is the necessity for new laws. It is a harder case to sustain and one that should largely be derived empirically—rather than driven anecdotally from the police. To some extent it is a function of the first two. I hope in this book to show that the range, number and extent of criminal offences and administrative regulation (where certain demonstrations need authorisation and certain marches need notification) make it difficult to conceive quite where the gaps are. A joint Home Office/DTI consultation paper in 2004 on animal research and animal rights protests illustrates well the self-defeating nature of the government's case and more generally. In the foreword the then Prime Minister and Home

---

[48] D McBarnet, *Conviction* (London, MacMillan, 1981) 156 and see too 'The Police and the State' in G Littlejohn et al, *Power and the State* (London, Croom-Helm, 1978).

[49] See further the discussion in chapter four pp 152 below.

[50] D Feldman, 'Protest and tolerance: legal values and the control of public-order policing' in R Cohen-Almagor (ed), *Liberal democracy and the limits of tolerance—essays in honor and memory of Yitzhak Rabin* (Ann Arbor MI, University of Michigan Press, 2000) 48. Feldman posits four conditions for this legitimacy of which this is part of the second. There is a good discussion of discretion and rule-making as it applies to the police (at 50–53).

[51] *Animal Welfare—Human Rights: protecting people from animal rights extremists*, at: police.homeoffice.gov.uk/news-and-publications/publication/operational-policing/humanrights.pdf, p 12, accessed 30 July 2007.

[52] 'Lancaster Six Lose Appeal', *The Guardian*, 17 March 2006, at: education.guardian.co.uk/higher/news/story/0,,1733511,00.html, accessed 30 July 2007.

Secretary told us that animal research, together with its scientific advances and economic success story, is under threat from a

> tiny minority of animal rights extremists who are behind an illegal campaign of intimidation and violence against individuals and firms involved in this vital work... The Government, police and courts are stepping up efforts to stamp out this illegal and sometimes violent conduct.[53]

The tension at the heart of our discussion is thrown into sharp relief by this catch-22. If their conduct and campaigns are 'illegal', why are newer and greater powers needed to deal with them? Their activities are already against the law. If their activities are not already against the law, how can they be 'illegal'? We are back to our starting point: it is not because the crimes do not exist they cannot be arrested but because of enforcement problems—identification of the wrongdoers, insufficient resources for the police, lack of witnesses. Logically, none of these problems will be rectified by creating another crime or series of crimes. The problem is not insufficient law but how it is applied.

That extract also tells us how legal responses play a major role in constructing deviance and in moulding perceptions about protesters. None of what follows is to condone the extreme behaviour of some animal rights protesters, those who commit very serious crimes of violence or hatred. Surely no one would excuse behaviour such as the well-documented theft of the remains of an 82 year-old woman from her grave, a woman whose only crime was to be the mother-in-law of the owner of a controversial farm that bred guinea pigs for animal research.[54] Neither would more than a handful of dedicated activists excuse campaigns of violent intimidation, firebombing, sending hoax letter bombs or packages containing razor blades, publishing false claims that someone is a paedophile, throwing bricks through windows, spraying graffiti on cars and physical assault.[55] However, as we shall see, many forms of protest activity are still not permitted even if they are not violent, do not even threaten it but are at worst disruptive and difficult for their targets to tolerate. Inevitably, this leads us to reflect on what is being categorised as unlawful behaviour, why and by whom? Again, these are questions the detailed investigation of which is largely beyond the confines of a book like this. We might in this regard though usefully consider this example. Until recently, hunting with dogs was classified as a lawful activity and any activities that interfered with it as unlawful, a very simple dichotomy between socially permitted (even socially encouraged) activity and activities that are proscribed for interfering with that which is permitted. Clearly, as was the case with hunting, as one side of the equation shifts—hitherto lawful activity is at some time banned—so does the other. The protest activity that is outlawed is not being outlawed because it is unlawful per se (if any is?) but functionally because its prohibition allows the achievement of that which society deems beneficial or tolerable at least. Categorising certain forms of behaviour as undesirable (and thus unlawful) creates folk devils whom we might more easily marginalise.[56] The ensuing moral panic, described by Stan Cohen as a 'threat to societal

---

[53] *Animal Welfare—Human Rights: protecting people from animal rights extremists*, above n 51.

[54] A group of three was found guilty of inter alia conspiracy to blackmail and jailed for 12 years each in May 2006. The family run business ceased operations in January 2006 after a six-year campaign including hate mail, malicious phone calls, hoax bombs and arson attacks: see various news agencies such as: news.bbc.co.uk/1/hi/england/staffordshire/4762481.stm (11 May 2006) and www.guardian.co.uk/animalrights/story/0,,1773153,00.html (12 May 2006) accessed both 30 July 2007.

[55] *Animal Welfare—Human Rights: protecting people from animal rights extremists*, above n 51, pp 9–11.

[56] S Cohen, *Folk Devils and Moral Panics* (St Albans, Paladin, 1973). See also S Hall et al, *Policing the Crisis: Mugging, the State and Law and Order* (London, MacMillan, 1978) and more recently C Critcher, *Critical readings: Moral Panics in the Media* (Berkshire, Open University Press, 2006). The media portrayal of (certain types) of protesters makes an interesting study in its own right: see as one example of misreporting and hyperbole G Monbiot, 'Attack of the baby eaters', *The Guardian*, 18 August 2007.

values and interests',[57] has two outcomes. It sows the seeds for and legitimises further crack downs on what was hitherto lawful activity and, by collectively casting out those who continue to engage in socially disapproved of activities or 'otherising', effects social reinforcement.[58]

VIII. The Role and Behaviour of the Police

Clearly pivotal in any account of protest and protesters is the involvement of the police.[59] It will be officers on the ground who respond on an individual level by making arrests, by issuing warnings and where there are large scale protests, by keeping rival groups at bay and by controlling marches and assemblies. The extent (and source) of the legal controls on this discretion is one of the themes in this book. There is a wealth of literature on this type of policing, most notably in the UK the various empirical studies carried out during the 1980s and 1990s by Jim 'Tank' Waddington,[60] David Waddington and Chas Critcher.[61] These though are not confined solely to policing protests and demonstrations but cover public order—and disorder—more generally: public carnivals, industrial disputes, sporting events and riots. Several interesting questions—outside the more doctrinal remit of this book—deserve greater exploration as factors that do and should shape and structure the policing response.[62] First, an analysis of what accounts for different national approaches; we have yet to see water cannon deployed on mainland Britain, yet such scenes are commonplace across continental Europe.[63] Equally important would be to contemplate whether and how the sorts of events and incidents that require police intervention and control have changed over the past 20 years or so,[64] as would a similar understanding of those doing the challenging and confronting: why does the 'crowd'—as opposed to its members—act as it does?[65]

---

[57] Cohen, *ibid*, p 9.

[58] There are of course internal/individual consequences of labelling—such as self-fulfilling expectations of deviance—as well as external and social: see generally H Becker, *Outsiders* (New York, Free Press, 1963) and discussions/developments of his work.

[59] Still a very good overview of policing as a subject of study and specifically the various influences and constraints on police discretion is R Reiner, 'Policing and the police' in M Maguire, R Morgan and R Reiner, *The Oxford Handbook of Criminology*, 4th edn (Oxford, Oxford University Press, 2007).

[60] See PAJ Waddington, *The strong arm of the law: armed and public order policing*, esp chs 5–7 (Oxford, Oxford University Press, 1991); 'Dying in a ditch: the use of police powers in public order' (1993) 21 *International Journal of the Sociology of Law* 335; *Liberty and order: public order policing in a capital city* (London, UCL Press, 1994); and 'Policing public order and political contention' in T Newburn (ed), *Handbook of Policing* (Cullumpton, Willan, 2003).

[61] D Waddington, K Jones and C Critcher, *Flashpoints—studies in public disorder* (London, Routledge, 1989); D Waddington, *Contemporary issues in public disorder: a comparative and historical approach* (London, Routledge, 1992); D Waddington and C Critcher (eds), *Policing public order: theoretical and practical issues* esp chs 6–8 (Aldershot, Ashgate, 1996); and D Waddington, 'Seattle and its aftershock: some implications for theory and practice' (2007) 1 *Policing* 380.

[62] For a challenge to the traditional theory of the crowd, that they are largely and inherently irrational, which—in the authors' opinion—misinforms the policing intervention, see S Reicher et al, 'Knowledge-based public order policing: principles and practice' (2007) 1 *Policing* 403.

[63] See for example D Della Porta, *The Policing of Protest in Contemporary Democracies* (San Domenico Italy, European University Institute, Robert Schuman Centre, 1997) and D Della Porta and H Reiter (eds), *Policing Protest: The Control of Mass Demonstrations in Western Democracies* (Minneapolis MN, University of Minnesota Press 1998).

[64] A good historical overview of public order during the twentieth century can be found in C Townshend, *Making the peace: public order and public security in modern Britain* (Oxford, Oxford University, Press, 1993) or more specifically R Geary, *Policing industrial disputes 1893–1985* (Cambridge, Cambridge University Press, 1985).

[65] See G LeBon, *The crowd—a study of the popular mind* (New Brunswick NJ, Viking Press, 1895) *cf* C McPhail, *The Myth of the Madding Crowd* (New York, Aldine de Gruyter, 1991) via R Turner and L Killian, *Collective Behavior* 4th edn (Englewood Cliffs NJ, Prentice-Hall, 1957, 1993).

The research studies indicate a clear divide between those who see the police as having adopted a far more aggressive stance, akin to para-militarism when confronted with and dealing with large scale disorder and those who still see public order policing as, largely, by consent and 'negotiated management'[66] wherever possible—with violence and force a long, long way down the list of possible solutions. The former view, probably subscribed to by a majority, is certainly the more mainstream and characterised by Jim Waddington as orthodoxy. The latter is typified by his own work, in 'splendid isolation' as he himself refers to it.[67] Whether or not the orthodox view will gain yet greater currency after the G20 disturbances in April 2009 is obviously something that will pan out over time. But it is, as Waddington says, a false dichotomy. The real question is why do some protests flare up and some pass off peacefully and so why do some necessitate or prompt an 'upping of the ante' by the police? These studies all focus on the macro-level, the operational, the large-scale rather than the interaction between individual protester and individual officer: How and why do officers decided to arrest for breach of the peace, rather than for aggravated trespass or obstruction? How and why do officers decide to arrest at all rather than give directions to desist (under, say, section 69 of the Criminal Justice and Public Order Act (CJPOA) 1994, which we will look at in chapter six) or even deal with it more informally? What accounts for the vastly differing uses and reliance on different crimes in order to make arrests across England and Wales? My own research—admittedly only using data about defendants proceeded against at magistrates courts[68]—shows that of the 63 defendants proceeded against for watching and besetting under section 241 of the Trade Unions and Labour Relations Consolidation Act 1992 (TULRCA) in 2003 (though of course not all these may have been protesters) 49 occurred in one county, Surrey, with 11 in Hertfordshire. Suffolk seems to prefer using aggravated trespass under section 68 of CJPOA 1994 (19 out of 54 across England and Wales in 2002, 12 out of 74 in 2003). It is impossible to imagine that incidents of aggravated trespass occur in only a few counties. This data raises the usual concerns about discretion that we considered above. The existence and control of discretion at both macro- and micro-levels on the street will be one of the themes of this book.[69]

There are two clear differences between public order/protest policing and ordinary 'bobby on the beat' policing. These both might determine the police response but also our perceptions of the policing of protest. The first is that policing protest is necessarily political whereas patrolling on the street, making arrests and conducting searches is not—or is so only in so far as any exercise of state power is political.[70] Rather than 'necessarily', perhaps

[66] C McPhail et al, 'Policing Protest in the United States: 1960–1995' in Della Porta and Reiter, above n 63. See too D Baker, 'From Batons to Negotiated Management: The Transformation of Policing Industrial Disputes in Australia' (2007) 1 *Policing* 390.

[67] PAJ Waddington, 'Both arms of the law: institutionalised protest and the policing of public order' British Society of Criminology conference 1995 available at: www.britsoccrim.org/volume1/008.pdf, accessed 11 June 2009. This contains an excellent summary of the conflicting positions and seeks to reconcile the two by positing that the key determinant was the institutionalised, or amenability to being institutionalised, nature of the activity: 'Conspicuous occasions of disorder to which the police respond with heavy-handed suppression are almost entirely uninstitutionalised' (unpaginated in original).

[68] Source: RDS within Office for Criminal Justice Reform, supplied in 2005 under the Freedom of Information Act 2000.

[69] It is the relative rather than the absolute use of various powers that prompts interest. The absolute use overall might show that a new power was not actually needed—the gap is not there—or might show that police tactics are to seek consensus in the shadow of the law: see T Bucke and Z James, *Trespass and Protest: Policing under the Criminal Justice and Public Order Act 1994* HORS 190 (London, Home Office, 1998) 40–41.

[70] That is aside from the observation that any system of law, and thus its enforcement, in a capitalist social democracy gives pre-eminence to private property, what Steven Lukes calls the third dimension of power: see S Lukes, *Power—a radical view* (London, MacMillan, 1974).

20 *Introduction*

we might conclude that policing protest is *overtly* political.[71] When this is allied to the discretion inherent in any policing, but especially policing protest, we can see why there is such a fine line for officers to tread—and are being seen to tread: maintaining the status quo during, or even the holding the ring between, competing protests outside an arms factory or animal exporters essentially engages the police in politicised decision-making. This brings us to the second difference: policing protest is almost always, certainly far more so than 'ordinary' policing, carried out in the public eye.[72] It is here perhaps we might notice the greatest change—perhaps in the eyes of the police the greatest threat: citizen journalism, the democratisation of the media and 24-hour rolling news. We no longer need to rely on official news sources and we no longer have to wait for the next edition of the daily paper; instead we are able to engage in a continuous process of updating our understanding of the world from constantly changing user-generated content. Protesters and bystanders alike are all able to photograph what the police are doing, upload them onto websites like YouTube[73] and 'blog or twitter about them as they catch the tube or bus home.[74] It is something of an irony that during the build up to the G20 summit in April 2009 the worry had been about undercover and underhand police surveillance, whereas it was a camera-phone belonging to a US holidaymaker that captured the last moments in the life of newsagent Ian Tomlinson, who died after being pushed over by officers in the City of London. Similarly it is only because of the new participatory media that we know that a police search for 'evidence of a political nature' would include removing copies of *The New Statesman* but not letters from an MP. After environmental protester Bertie Russell was arrested after taking over a coal train bound for Drax power station in June 2008, his bedroom was searched. His father filmed the whole police operation and this was loaded onto the site of *The Guardian* newspaper.[75]

IX. Protest and Protesters at the Start of the New Millennium

Bertie Russell is a good example of the emergence of a new phenomenon, the professional protester and activist, concerned with environmental issues or animal rights or anti-abortion or anti-arms trade.[76] Dating from the protests against the motorway extension at

---

[71] By contrast, not all public order policing is political—Trooping the Colour or the Notting Hill Carnival would be good examples whereas, by definition, policing protest must be.

[72] PAJ Waddington (editorial) 'Policing of public order' (2007) 1 *Policing* 375.

[73] As just one example, 'Riot police knock down protester on Gaza demo', at: www.youtube.com/watch?v=NPB5q8gvCWo, accessed 11 June 2009.

[74] The impact on policy making and public attitudes of increasingly media-savvy protesters is worthy of a study itself: media pictures of members of Plane Stupid occupying Westminster protesting at alleged collusion show them on phones to selected sympathetic journalists (confirmed in personal conversation between the author and one of those arrested): see 'Anti-airport protesters scale Parliament's roof' *The Independent*, 27 February 2008, at: www.independent.co.uk/news/uk/home-news/antiairport-protesters-scale-parliaments-roof-788107.html (accessed 11 June 2009).

[75] 'Police confiscate property of a "political nature" from a suspected environmental activist', *The Guardian*, 19 April 2009, at: www.guardian.co.uk/environment/video/2009/apr/19/police-activism, accessed 11 June 2009. His father was reported as saying 'We are a completely clean, middle-class family from west London and I was the sort of person who would ask a policeman for the time, but now I would steer clear. I no longer have any trust in the police and especially after seeing the vast violence by police against the G20 protesters I worry about the safety of anyone near them'.

[76] M Button, T John and N Brearley, 'New challenges in public order policing: the professionalisation of environmental protest and the emergence of the militant environmental activist' (2002) 30 Int J Soc Law 17. They

Twyford Down in 1994 and the Newbury bypass in 1996, the 1990s saw an 'intensification of protests using direct action . . . [with] strategies . . . that have differed significantly from traditional protests'. The innovative, sophisticated and extensive range of tactics employed by these protesters has posed new challenges to policing organisations.[77] Their geographical spread, with protest sites springing up across the country, meant each force had to try to deal anew and single-handedly with veterans of previous campaigns.[78] This fragmentation created an obvious imbalance between police and protesters. One response was the creation of cross-force co-ordination by bodies such as the National Extremist Tactical Co-ordination Unit. NETCU was set up under the auspices of ACPO, the Association of Chief Police Officers to respond to the threat of domestic extremism. It is not an operational unit in that it does not actively investigate criminal activity. According to its own website, its role is to support others to prevent, reduce and disrupt criminal activity associated with domestic extremism and single issue campaigning. It works, its websites states, with police forces across the country to provide tactical advice and guidance in order to promote a coordinated and consistent approach to tackling domestic extremism. It supports industry, academia and other organisations that have been targeted or could be targeted by extremists, providing security advice, risk assessments and information that can help minimise disruption and keep their employees safe. It also provides the Government, police, CPS and industry with information about trends and types of domestic extremist incidents and crimes.[79]

The extent to which it spies on and undertakes general surveillance of legitimate protesters is a matter of some considerable concern and tension. NETCU is publicly committed—as one would imagine—to supporting the right to demonstrate lawfully and recognises that most protest campaigns are conducted peacefully and legally. Its work, it states, is focused on the small minority in any campaign with extreme views and who are prepared to break the law in order to further their cause, and not the majority of lawful campaigners. There have been credible media reports that indicate this is not always the case. The *Guardian* journalist and environmental campaigner George Monbiot highlighted the fact that NETCU refused to remove from its list of High Court injunctions granted against 'domestic extremists' the name of a 70-year-old former university physicist. His 'crime' had been to campaign against the use of a beauty spot in Oxfordshire, Radley Lakes, as a dumping ground by RWE Npower after which the company sought and obtained an injunction under the PFHA 1997 to prevent further harassment.[80] This is despite the fact that NETCU's view is that environmental protesters do not pose a threat of violence to any individual.[81]

The changing types of protest, the changes in methods and motivations of protesters and the changes in police responses is a key theme that provides the backdrop to our discussion

---

highlight not only the change in tactics and methods but the preparedness to break the law for example and to run the risk of imprisonment, the emergence of full-time protesters, a growing and identifiable counter-culture (with websites, publications and gatherings) and moves towards a more highly trained and expert protester, well-versed in different forms of protest and resistance, organised along non-bureaucratic, non-hierarchical lines: *ibid*, 18–21.

[77] *ibid*, 18.
[78] *ibid*, 20.
[79] www.netcu.org.uk/about/about.jsp, accessed on 11 June 2009.
[80] G Monbiot, 'Otter-spotting and birdwatching; the dark heart of the eco-terrorist peril', *The Guardian* 'Comment Is Free', 23 December 2008, at: www.guardian.co.uk/commentisfree/2008/dec/23/activists-conservation-police, accessed 16 June 2009.
[81] ACC A Setchell (National Co-ordinator for Domestic Extremism (sic), the head of NETCU) speaking on the 8 May 2009 on Radio 4's 'The Report' but he refused to indicate how many had their details stored on its database. The programme is available via: www.bbc.co.uk/programmes/b00k4g57 (access 16 June 2009).

in the rest of this book.[82] Before we embark on that, let us lastly flag up—or emphasise where we have already done so—some other threads that run through this whole area of law.

A major theme will be the interdependence of the public and the private spheres. We shall see this in many ways. Perhaps the most immediate are those private law rules relating to land ownership which remain pivotal to the location and success of any protest, whether peacefully communicating a view or direct action. Whether a group is holding a march or trying to handcuff themselves to a JCB, the same question about rights of access to land hold true: protests need to occur somewhere. That 'somewhere' will belong to someone and if that 'someone' is not a protester or sympathetic to the cause, there is a very strong chance that the protest will not be able to go ahead. In due course (mainly in chapter four) we shall see how the reality of protest is a function of the interplay of a variety of factors: the socio-economic demography of land ownership; political decisions regarding public space; how the extent and development of private common law remedies relating to land shape public law remedies and constraints. This is our second point. Much of the public regulation of protest, either through administrative powers (such as banning assemblies) or through criminal enforcement is dependent on private law concepts. This is mainly, but not exclusively, the law of trespass. Many powers 'kick in' only once a protester has—or perhaps is reasonably believed to have—exceeded whatever permission—if any—she has to be at the protest site in the first place.[83] Our third point is the reverse of this. Recent years have witnessed a shift from the public regulation of protest to its privatisation: mechanisms of control are no longer purely criminal or administrative in origin. Decisions about whether a protest takes place at all and what is and is not tolerated have been placed in the hands of private bodies, the corporate and individual targets of the protests, rather than being the remit solely of the police or local councils. A good example would be where the civil jurisdiction to grant injunctive relief to prevent actual or threatened harassment has been opened up under the Protection From Harassment Act (PFHA) 1997. Thus, those who own armaments factories or run private abortion clinics might be able to claim a buffer or exclusion zone around their properties to prevent harassing protests taking place. Equally, a coal mining company might try to change its Articles of Association to restrict environmental protesters being able to buy up single shares so that they might propose motions at the AGM. Alternatively, protesters might face libel actions for publishing false material—or material they cannot show is true. Indeed, the threat of libel might hang over them and create a 'chilling effect' on their protesting activities. Thus, and this is our last point, the same protest might be governed by overlapping regimes, civil and criminal, which creates room

---

[82] One matter that appears to be under-researched in the literature is the effect of modern technology, especially communications technology, on protest and protesters. Several areas spring to mind. The first is changes in ways of protesting by using viral campaigning and social networking sites: see for example 'Swivelchair activism', *The Guardian*, 11 December 2007. The second is that it has made mobilising tens or even hundreds in a short space of time is no longer or far less of a problem for protesters—but is correspondingly more of one for the police—than it was 10 or 15 years ago. The third (see p 20 above) is not only the impact on surveillance *by* the police but, as part of what John Keane calls a monitory democracy, how it facilitates surveillance *on* the police: see J Keane, *The Life and Death of Democracy* (London, Simon and Schuster, 2009).

[83] Some commentary on the Theft Bill and eventual Theft Act 1968 hint at the issues surrounding the application of civil law concepts in the criminal sphere, such as trespass in the context of burglary and property in the definition of theft, but without really developing the conceptual difficulties of this cross-over: see T Hadden, 'The draft Theft Bill' [1967] *Crim LR* 669, 657–7; JC Smith, 'Burglary under the Theft Bill' [1968] *Crim LR* 295, 298–302; and J Collins, 'The Theft Act and it commentators' [1968] *Crim LR* 638, 642–4. I am grateful to Ian McLeod for pointing me in that direction.

for choice but also confusion. Harassing someone is both a civil wrong, entitling the victim to injunctive relief, and a crime under the PFHA. Making the situation more entwined is the fact that breach of a civil PFHA injunction is without more a criminal offence. Similarly, protesters who induce breaches of contract between suppliers and target companies are no longer only potentially liable for one of the economic torts. If they are animal rights protesters, they now run the risk of committing the offence of interfering with contractual relations so as to harm an animal research organisation under section 145 of the Serious Organised Crime and Police Act (SOCPA) 2005.

This more fragmented yet duplicatory framework brings a further important consequence—intended or not. It allows the costs and the burdens (and of course the risks) of preventing protests to be shifted or spread onto those who have been directly affected by it. This could be advantageous if we consider the impact on the public purse of maintaining the status quo and maintaining order. Policing the G20 protests in London in April 2009 was estimated by the Metropolitan Police Commissioner to have cost £7.2m and policing the Tamil protest outside Westminster in the Spring of 2009 (after 43 days of continuous protest) to have cost about £8m.[84] The disproportionate impact for the Met of the costs of policing London, given the site of 'obvious' political protest targets should not be underestimated. While it is clear in the US (but has yet to be litigated in the UK or at Strasbourg) that charging a speaker or marcher or protester the cost of policing, so as to offset it, is an unconstitutional abridgement of the 1st Amendment, what if the private targets of protest take action to prevent or restrict it—and bear the costs themselves?[85] Is this something to be welcomed? The legitimate public interest in protest is one that generally should require public funding lest its continued existence and extent is left to the private market to regulate. Decisions about whether or not protests go ahead might be taken on a cost/benefit analysis, weighing up the legal costs of an injunction against the loss in business. That said, of course the public purse could benefit from some of the costs being defrayed: in the late 1990s, Hill Grove Farm in Oxfordshire that bred cats solely to be sold on for animal experimentation was targeted by protesters hoping to 'persuade' the owner to close. Their campaign of violence and intimidation, including death threats and firebombs, led him to do so in 1999 but the costs of policing the property for two and a half years from March 1997 were estimated to be £2.8m to August 1999.[86] The costs of protest include both the real and opportunity costs of (usually) intimidatory direct action. The matrix of balancing rights and interests has been complicated recently by their addition to the equation. A considerable amount of the government's recent legislative tightening can be put down to justifiable fear about the fiscal consequences of failing to act.[87] How long will companies,

---

[84] Uncorrected evidence on 19 May 2009 from Sir Paul Stephenson to the Home Affairs Select Committee investigation into the policing of protests QQ 306–7 and 368, at: www.publications.parliament.uk/pa/cm200809/cmselect/cmhaff/uc418-iv/uc41802.htm (accessed 12 June 2009).

[85] *Forsyth County v Nationalist Movement* 505 US 123, 136 (1992) 'a tax based on the content of speech does not become more constitutional because it is a small tax' (Blackmun J).

[86] 'Embattled breeding farm closes', *The Guardian*, 14 August 1999, at: www.guardian.co.uk/uk/1999/aug/14/davidpallister, accessed 12 June 2009. In that light, the estimated £142,000 cost of policing the six-mile M77 extension in Scotland in the mid 1990s seems good value! See D Donnelly, 'Anti-roads protests, the community and the police' (July 1996) *Police Journal* 207, 213.

[87] *Animal Welfare—Human Rights: protecting people from animal rights extremists*, above n 51, paras 30–35 'Economic contribution to the bioscience sector'. It was estimated that in 2004 the sector employed 80 000 people directly and annual investment in research and development was worth £3.5bn to the UK. The UK trade in pharmaceuticals was worth £12bn in 2003 creating a trade surplus of £3.4bn (HMG, *Protecting People from Animal Rights Extremists: A Progress Report*, July 2006, at: www.netcu.org.uk/downloads/hmg_are_progress_report_july_2006.pdf, accessed 17 September 2007).

whose directors have their cars daubed with graffiti or about whom false allegations of paedophilia are made, remain in the UK or decide not to invest here at all? In May 2005, as the government was announcing plans to tighten the law so as to criminalise economic sabotage[88] Aegis Defence Services predicted that 'up to £16bn of investment per annum could be lost in the pharmaceutical and biotech industries unless the government took action to protect companies'.[89] The appropriate response to these dilemma is one of the challenges facing law- and policy-makers in the near future.

Our last point—and one which leads into the various chapters that follow—is this. Any protest is likely to fall foul or interact with not just criminal and civil law but with totally different parts of the criminal and civil 'codes'. The regulation of protest therefore is multi-agency.[90] Let us take just one example which will allow us incidentally to see the point made earlier: with so much 'law' do we really need yet more? A group stands on the pavement outside an arms factory, chanting and seeking to persuade workers not to go in. The individuals (there being no such thing as an unlawful assembly or group in English law) would need to be wary of a host of infractions. They might be unlawfully obstructing the highway contrary to section 137 of the Highways Act 1980. They might constitute a public assembly and therefore subject to administrative regulation by the police or council under the POA 1986. They might run into trouble with section 5 of the POA 1986 by using threatening, abusive or insulting language whereby someone might be caused harassment, alarm or distress. If they stray one foot off the public highway they will be trespassing and thus open to civil claims for injunctions at the suit of the company but, more immediately, to charges of aggravated trespass under section 69 of the CJPOA 1994. If it continues for more than one day, equally the terms of the PFHA come into play; harassment is defined as 'a course of conduct' hence the need for a second day of protest. There is always the risk of breaches of the peace—if not from the protesters themselves, then from the workers or other third parties. Again, depending on what is shouted or written on placards or leaflets, there is the risk that any of the protesters might defame the company or its directors.

With that entwining firmly in mind, let us now turn to see how the right of peaceful protest is regulated and guaranteed in the UK under the Human Rights Act. First we shall consider the HRA itself and the ECHR in general terms before our detailed assessment of the right at Strasbourg level itself. This will be followed by five chapters each outlining different protest scenarios or issues: the locus of protest; peacefully communicating dissent; direct action; preventive action by the police; and private law remedies.

---

[88] These were contained in s 145 and s 146 of SOCPA 2005, which we shall cover in chapter six.
[89] 'New law against animal activists', *The Guardian*, 21 January 2005. The same article made reference to an ABPI (Association of British Pharmaceutical Industry) report that, inter alia, 113 suppliers had pulled out of deals with animal research companies because of intimidation. See also 'Animal rights activists force drug firm to rethink UK role', *The Guardian*, 15 November 2004, about Novartis, the Swiss pharmaceutical company. In December 2002, the estimated cost of providing cover to the directors of Huntingdon life Science was estimated to be costing its insurers Marsh and McLennan millions of pounds so much so that the Government was forced to provide emergency insurance cover: 'Auditors under fire over animal rights', *The Guardian*, 20 February 2003.
[90] This could extend at, say, a motorway construction site to private security guards (now regulated under the Private Security Industry Act 2001) and bailiffs serving eviction papers on trespassers and perhaps, the Health and Safety Executive overseeing the physical removal of protesters from tree houses or underground tunnels. A different take on the multi-agency approach is revealed by reports that civil servants passed police intelligence about protesters to power company executives: 'Secret police intelligence was given to E.On before planned demo', *The Guardian*, 20 April 2009, at: www.guardian.co.uk/uk/2009/apr/20/police-intelligence-e-on-berr, accessed 16 June 2009.

2

Protecting Human Rights in the Human Rights Act Era

This chapter offers an explanation, in very broad terms, of how human rights have been and are protected in domestic law. Our review will commence with a reflection on the United Kingdom's common law heritage in which the concept of positive 'rights' was alien. In this, until the dying days of the last millennium, we were out of kilter with mainland Europe (as well as large numbers of other states), where citizens largely had constitutional rights, judicially enforceable in their own courts. For many of those states, this meant doing no more than enshrining in domestic law the protection given by the ECHR. The provisions of the ECHR and some of its underpinning and overarching jurisprudence are the focus of the second part of the chapter. We shall analyse in detail the case law of the European Court of Human Rights at Strasbourg on the right to peaceful protest (under Articles 10 and 11) in chapter three. The final part of this chapter outlines the scheme of the Human Rights Act 1998 (HRA) to see how that right, in the words of the accompanying White Paper, has been 'brought home'. Having looked at its key terms, to gauge at a general level how the HRA operates, the chapter will conclude with a scene-setter for chapters four to eight. By looking at a few examples, we shall see the means by which English law is now able to protect the right to peaceful protest. The scope and extent of that protection forms the remainder of the book.

What will be clear in this chapter, and this cannot be stressed strongly enough, is that there is now a fully-fledged right to protest. It encompasses aspects of the rights of free speech under Article 10 and peaceful assembly contained within Article 11. We shall explore its limitations at Strasbourg level in the next chapter. This marks, as we shall soon see and as was alluded to in our introduction, a sea-change in legal thought in the UK. What should be borne in mind for what follows in chapters four to eight, therefore, should be the overarching and underpinning nature of that right. This may not always be clear from the nature of those chapters, which seem to be arranged into scenarios—location, peaceful protest, direct action, preventive policing and private law remedies—where the focus of each is not always the positive right. Although each of the remaining five substantive chapters seems to comprise a study of current domestic restrictions on that primary right, analysed in terms of their lawfulness—proportionality—under the ECHR, this book, if read as a whole, provides a comprehensive insight into both the right and its regulation in the Human Rights Act era.

I. The Right to Protest at Common Law

Before the HRA came into force in England in October 2000, the UK's common law constitution was based on the idea of residual liberty. This reflected an historic attachment to Dicey, rather than one that adopted and enshrined positive rights: people were free to do whatever they liked provided they did not at the same time break the law. If I was largely free to act so were others—so they were free to do to me what I was free to do to them; unless specifically restrained by law, I had no 'right' to prevent them.[1]

From this, three observations flow. First, whatever 'rights' I had protecting me against the activities of others were simply the culmination of discrete legal rules governing (quite possibly) some other legally constructed activity. Thus, private, common law rules relating to land ownership would give some degree of protection against invasions of privacy—absent a formal *right* of privacy—in the form of an action in trespass.[2] Secondly, without a system of positive rights, those who sought protection for their 'right' to act—or to be protected against the actions of others—had to find a pre-existing remedy to ground their claim. Thus, though there was no right to liberty, the ancient remedy of habeas corpus allowed those who had been detained unlawfully a measure of protection of their liberty.

The third observation is this. If I wanted to engage in what we might now call rights-protected activity—such as going on a peaceful march—I would only be able to do so, and certainly not as a *right*, if there was no rule, at common law or in statute, forbidding me. As we shall see, there was (and still is) a catalogue of laws making it broadly unlawful to engage in most forms of protest activity, certainly so if the protest was even vaguely disruptive or obstructive. This throws into sharp relief the near irresoluble conflict between two of Dicey's constitutional fundamentals: the rule of law and the sovereignty of the Westminster Parliament.[3] In Dicey's view British subjects were fully protected—in terms of fairness of trials, free speech, rights to liberty and property—because British judges had decreed it so: there was no need for intolerable European decrees of rights. The unforeseen problem was this: what would occur if the Parliament decreed it not so? The days of Coke CJ in *Dr Bonham's case* had long since gone:[4]

> In many cases the common law will control Acts of Parliament, and sometimes adjudge them to be utterly void: for when an Act of Parliament is against common right and reason, or repugnant, or impossible to be performed, the common law will control it and adjudge such an Act to be void.[5]

---

[1] AV Dicey, *An Introduction to the Study of the Law of the Constitution*, 10th edn (London, MacMillan, 1959).

[2] In one leading pre-HRA case *Kaye v Robertson* [1991] FSR 62, the actor Gordon Kaye was left dependent on his claim for malicious falsehood—falsely implying that he consented to an interview while critically ill in hospital—rather than being able to claim an invasion of privacy after a journalist published a story based on the interview having obtained entry by deception.

[3] It is the third limb of Dicey's propositions concerning the rule of law that has an impact here: freedoms are best protected by the judges and courts of the common law, imbued as they are with an historical and sympathetic heritage, rather than being imposed from above by a constitution that may be out of line with public wishes and support. The contrast in his mind was between the pan-European turmoil of the Age of Revolutions in the nineteenth century and the slower, more evolutionary approach in Britain with its singular constant—the common law.

[4] *Dr Bonham's case* (1610) 8 Co Rep 113b 118a.

[5] That said, academics and judges writing extra-judicially have hinted that parliamentary sovereignty as a common law construct must itself be limited by certain underpinning higher constitutional principles. If Parliament sought to legislate in breach of, for example, the constitutional 'right' of access to courts or to abolish elections, would the judges sit idly by? See Lord Woolf, 'Droit Public—English style' [1995] *Public Law* 57, 69; TRS Allen, 'Parliamentary Sovereignty: Law Politics and Revolution' (1997) 113 *Law Quarterly Review* 443, 449; and *Jackson v Attorney-General* [2005] UKHL 56 at [102] (Lord Steyn, obiter).

Since the 1689 Revolution it had been accepted—by parliamentarians, by judges and by academics—that the final word must rest with the democratically elected chamber. Thus in 1994 Parliament was free to legislate to remove the 'right of silence' (technically, a privilege against self-incrimination) in sections 33–38 of the Criminal Justice and Public Order Act. More relevant to us was Parliament's decision in 2005 for the first time to impose a requirement of prior authorisation on those who wished to exercise the long-held 'right' to assemble outside the House of Commons.[6]

It was not true that the common law did not know of human rights. As the century wore on, the courts 'discovered' certain rights that were inherent in the common law or at least informed its development,[7] so much so that Sedley J suggested 'the standards of the ECHR march with those of the common law'.[8] We saw in our introductory chapter the recognition of a 'right to a protest' (and its sibling the right of free speech) in the judgment of Lord Denning MR in *Hubbard v Pitt*, albeit of doubtful parentage.[9] What was still true was the very limited infusion into domestic law of *European* rights. On one level, the ECHR was technically irrelevant. Under English law's dualist system, the ECHR—as any other international treaty—bound the government only to the other states parties. It did not confer benefits or impose burdens on citizens.[10]

Before 1998, the ECHR was not even a measure against which executive discretion could be gauged or by which it could be reined in. The ECHR did not bind the government in its day-to-day dealings with citizens, despite the government of the day agreeing to guarantee the rights contained in the ECHR, when it signed the Treaty in 1950, to all those within the jurisdiction. An argument along those lines was put in *R v Secretary of State for the Home Department ex parte Brind* but such an analysis of the public law duties on Ministers was rejected by the House of Lords.[11] As Lord Bridge indicated, that approach would amount

---

[6] Sections 132–138 of the Serious Organised Crime and Police Act 2005, analysed more fully below in chapter four.

[7] See Sir John Laws, 'Is the High Court the guardian of fundamental constitutional rights?' [1993] *PL* 59.

[8] *R v Secretary of State for the Home Department ex parte McQuillan* [1995] 4 All ER 400, 421 but compare K Ewing and C Gearty, *The Struggle for Civil Liberties* (Oxford, Oxford University Press, 2000) 403. It is true these tended to be what human rights theorists would call 1st generation or civil and political rights; the common law largely did not recognise socio-economic rights relating to (say) shelter or medical care—though see *R v Secretary of State for Social Security ex parte JCWI* [1996] 4 All ER 385 and *R (Q) v Secretary of State for the Home Department* [2003] EWHC 195. Even Ewing and Gearty do not assert that judges failed to protect the catalogue of what we now call '(human) rights'; in that period, and throughout the century, they were very keen to protect certain sorts of rights—the property rights of employers, in the form of business, capital and profit, as against unionists or more traditional rights of liberty and the person such as fair trials, arbitrary arrest and torture. As such, judges were broadly sympathetic towards a liberal, individualistic political settlement rather than more social forms of engagement with 'the public'. These latter Ewing and Geary categorise as 'civil liberties' or *droits du citoyen*—rights relating to civic and democratic participation—after which 'human rights' can be contested and their scope and content decided. Civil liberties, so construed, would include voting rights, rights of expression, rights of collectivity and association as well, of course, as the right to protest.

[9] *Hubbard v Pitt* [1976] QB 142 (CA) 174 and above 4.

[10] In order for any Treaty to take effect in domestic law—and thus to 'bite' on citizens (either empowering or constraining them)—there needs to be incorporation by Parliament. This gives a democratic imprimatur to the exercise of the sovereign prerogative treaty-making power: *MacLaine Watson v Department of Trade and Industry* [1990] 2 AC 418 (HL).

[11] *R v Secretary of State for the Home Department ex parte Brind* [1991] 1 AC 696 (HL). Four journalists challenged the Home Secretary's decision, taken under the wide statutory power in s 29 of the Broadcasting Act 1981, to ban the media from using the direct speech of members of Sinn Fein. The judicial review was based, inter alia, on this being a violation of the journalists' rights under Art 10. Rather than seeking to rely on this directly, Lord Lester QC argued that the Home Secretary was bound to bear in mind that right and only act in a manner consistent with it when exercising the statutory power.

to 'judicial usurpation of the legislative function'.[12] It was for Parliament to incorporate the ECHR, not for judges to do so by the back door of judicial invention. Despite that, the ECHR did have a level of practical significance in the UK before 1998. Where the common law was uncertain or incomplete the ECHR was used to inform its development;[13] where a statute was ambiguous, it could be called on as an aid to interpretation (since Parliament could be presumed not to legislate in breach of the UK's international obligations);[14] and any exercise of judicial discretion during the course of or at the outcome of a case should bear in mind and take account of the ECHR.[15]

Before the HRA, alongside this nascent Europeanisation, judges—having exposed long-hidden, dormant common law rights such as free speech,[16] unimpeded access to the courts and to legal advice[17] and the right to life[18]—felt able to provide a measure of protection for 'rights' in two main ways.[19] First, alongside the ambiguity principle, judges also presume Parliament does not intend to legislate contrary to these common law rights. If courts are to give effect to Parliament's words in such cases, Parliament must explicitly indicate a clear intention to remove or to limit these rights.[20] If not, primary legislation will be interpreted as not sanctioning a removal or restriction. Secondary or subordinate legislation will be struck down as ultra vires if it restricts or removes a common law right unless that restriction or removal was permitted by express words in the parent Act or it is an obvious and necessary implication of those words that such a restriction or removal was foreseen.[21]

Secondly, the courts developed traditional judicial review so as to require more rigorous scrutiny when assessing the rationality of government decisions affecting common law rights. We can see this so-called super-*Wednesbury* test in cases such as *Lustig Prean*.[22] There the courts were asked to review the legality of the Ministry of Defence decision to dismiss service personnel who were discovered to be, or admitted to being, gay or lesbian. The challenge was based partly on the ground that this was an unlawful discrimination and interference with the right of private (sexual) life. The applicants lost the case but in the course of judgment, Sir Thomas Bingham MR iterated a new 'anxious scrutiny' test: 'the more substantial the interference with human rights, the more the court will require by way

---

[12] *ibid*, 748.

[13] *Derbyshire County Council v Times Newspapers* [1992] 3 WLR 28 (CA), decided on different grounds in the House of Lords: [1993] AC 534.

[14] *Waddington v Miah* [1974] 2 All ER 377, the more so when Parliament legislated specifically to give effect to an earlier ECHR decision: *R v Secretary of State for the Home Department ex parte Norney* (1995) 7 Admin LR 861.

[15] *Middlebrook Mushrooms v Transport & General Workers' Union* [1993] ICR 612 (decisions concerning the grant of injunctive relief in favour of an employer during an industrial dispute must bear in mind the Art 11 rights of the union and its members).

[16] As two examples see *Derbyshire County Council v Times Newspapers Ltd* [1993] AC 534 and *R v Central Independent Television plc* [1994] Fam 192 (CA) 203, Hoffman LJ.

[17] *Raymond v Honey* [1983] 1 AC 1.

[18] *McQuillan*, above n 8.

[19] Common law human rights are not extinguished by the HRA so the two systems of protection may overlap: see *R v Davis* [2008] UKHL 36 on fair trials at common law and under Art 6. To the extent that common law rights might be wider or in situations where the ECHR is silent on a matter, then analysis of this nature might come to the fore.

[20] In *R (Morgan Grenfell) v Inland Revenue Commissioners* [2002] UKHL 21 the House of Lords concluded that absent specific wording, the statutory regime for enforcing income tax did not embrace a power for the Commissioners to seek possession of legally privileged correspondence: Lord Hobhouse at [44]–[45].

[21] Thus, in *R v Lord Chancellor ex parte Witham* [1997] 2 All ER 27, regulations that increased court fees, pursuant to a general statutory power but in the absence of specific statutory authorisation, were ultra vires where the effect was to deprive impecunious litigants of the opportunity to bring proceedings in breach of the common law right of unimpeded access to the courts.

[22] *R v Ministry of Defence ex parte Smith and Lustig-Prean* [1996] QB 517.

of justification before it is satisfied that the decision is reasonable in the sense [that it is beyond the range of reasonable responses]'.[23] In *R v Lord Saville of Newdigate ex parte B* Lord Woolf explained the reasoning for the adoption of this heightened test as follows:

> [W]hen a fundamental right ... is engaged, the options available to the reasonable decision maker are curtailed. They are curtailed because it is unreasonable to reach a decision which contravenes or could contravene human rights unless there are sufficiently significant countervailing considerations. In other words it is not open to the decision maker to risk interfering with fundamental rights in the absence of compelling justification. Even the broadest discretion is constrained by the need for there to be countervailing circumstances justifying interference with human rights. The courts will anxiously scrutinise the strength of the countervailing circumstances and the degree of the interference with the human right involved.[24]

As we shall see, this heightened test goes some way towards effecting better protection for the right of peaceful protest by restricting the scope of permissible executive action more than would be possible under a 'mere' irrationality challenge, but is still someway short of what Strasbourg expects by means of rights-review.

II. The European Convention on Human Rights

The ECHR is the longest-standing binding international human rights instrument.[25] It was drawn up in 1950—with the UK ratifying it in 1951—and entered into force in 1953. It therefore predates both UN Covenants by some 15 years. It was drawn up under the auspices of the Council of Europe for whose operation it remains responsible today. The Council's remit is primarily in the field of human rights, along with development and cooperation, with the ECHR probably its most well-known contribution.[26] The ECHR was very clearly a response to the atrocities of the inter-war years and of World War II itself. The aim of its framers was to avoid European-wide conflict by providing an irreducible core of basic standards of humanity. It was hoped that creating a minimum guarantee of judicially-enforceable rights, such as liberty, fair trial, freedom of expression and of conscience, would reduce the likelihood of political extremism, seen to flourish in times when political leaders were able to dispense with the rule of law with impunity.[27] Membership of the Council of Europe (in June 2009) stands at 47. There has been a significant increase in membership from the 1990s with the break up of the former Soviet bloc and in the Balkans. This in turn has caused significant difficulties as the European Court of Human Rights (ECtHR) in

---

[23] *ibid*, 554. The formulation proposed by counsel for the applicants, and accepted by the Court, was in turn largely adopted from the test proposed by Sir John Laws, above n 7.

[24] *R v Lord Saville of Newdigate ex parte B* [2000] 1 WLR 1855 at [37].

[25] The main English language reference books dedicated to the ECHR are C Ovey and R White, *Jacobs and White: The European Convention on Human Rights*, 4th edn (Oxford, Oxford University Press, 2006); P van Dijk et al, *The Theory and Practice of the European Convention on Human Rights*, 4th edn (Antwerp, Intersentia, 2006) and D Harris, M O'Boyle, E Bates and C Buckley, *The Law of the European Convention on Human Rights*, 2nd edn (Oxford, Oxford University Press, 2009).

[26] The homepage of the Council is www.coe.int/ (accessed 16 June 2008). It has taken responsibility for human rights in discrete areas such as torture and minority languages.

[27] In contrast the founders of what became the EEC several years later saw the way forward as being primarily a free market and ever closer socio-economic ties where increasing trading interdependence would make war less likely.

Strasbourg seeks to administer the same rules about torture, freedom of religion and fairness of trials for both fully developed and fledgling democracies throughout the region.[28]

A. The Scope of the ECHR and Jurisprudence of the Court

The ECHR is very clearly a product of its time and of the political heritage of its drafters and proponents: its substantive focus is almost entirely on first generation civil and political rights rather than on second generation socio-economic rights, such as the rights to housing, welfare, education or healthcare.[29] Appendix I sets out the rights in the ECHR in full. For our study, it is likely that the only ones we will need to consider are those below, in summary. Chapter three considers Strasbourg case law on the right of peaceful protest under Articles 10 and 11 in depth. Other rights will be looked at in greater detail as we come across them in chapters four to eight.

- Article 5 guarantees the right to liberty and to security. It allows for deprivations of liberty in one of only six limited situations set out in Article 5(1). These include conviction by a competent court; non-compliance with the lawful order of a court, or in order to secure fulfilment of any obligation imposed by law; or where it is effected for the purpose of bringing someone before a competent legal authority on reasonable suspicion of having committed an offence; or when it is reasonably considered necessary to prevent his committing an offence or fleeing after having done so. In all cases, arrests or detention must be made 'in accordance with a procedure prescribed by law' and must be 'lawful', words with autonomous Convention meanings.[30] In addition, the rights in Article 5(2), 5(3), 5(4) and 5(5) provide a measure of further procedural protection for all those arrested or detained: the right to be informed promptly of the reason for arrest and of any charge; the right to trial within a reasonable time or to release; the right to take proceedings by which the lawfulness of detention shall be decided speedily (with release ordered if detention is not lawful); and the right to compensation for anyone arrested or detained in violation of Article 5.
- Article 6 guarantees the right to a fair and public hearing where civil rights and obligations are being determined or where someone has been subjected to a criminal charge, both (again) autonomous Convention concepts. The right to a fair trial in Article 6(1) encompasses an independent and impartial tribunal as well as the concept of 'equality of arms' for both sides. Those who have been charged with a crime also have additional rights (in Article 6(2)–(3)), including the presumption of innocence and procedural protection such as legal aid and the right to cross-examine witnesses.
- Article 8 guarantees the right to respect for private life, family life, home and correspondence. The concept of private life means more than just physical privacy (a spatially-based concept) but extends to rights in relation to sex life and partners[31] as well as rights of

---

[28] For ease, Appendix II provides an overview of some of the procedural aspects of the ECHR.
[29] The Council of Europe was not alone in this. It was decided at a political level to adopt a separate charter dealing with such matters and to have them enforced not by judicial means but by a reporting procedure. The Council of Europe Charter of Social Rights came into being in 1961 and was revised in 1996, entering into force in 1999.
[30] In short, this means that the Court will construct its own criteria for determining a concept, irrespective of any categorisation or determination by domestic law. For example, the notion of 'criminal charge' under Art 6 (see below) is one that the Strasbourg Court may attach to proceedings that a domestic court has already construed as administrative or regulatory or even civil but not criminal: see *Engel v Netherlands* (1976) 1 EHRR 647 and the cases that follow it.
[31] *Dudgeon v UK* (1981) 4 EHRR 149.

informational privacy.[32] Underlying these wider notions we can see the nascence of an approach founded on protecting choice and individual autonomy.[33]
- Article 9 grants the right to freedom of thought, conscience and religion and includes the right to change religions or beliefs and the freedom to manifest that religion or belief.
- Article 10 guarantees the right to freedom of expression; a right which includes freedom to hold opinions and to receive and impart information and ideas without interference.
- Article 11 guarantees the rights to associate with others (including the right to form and join trade unions for the protection of their interests) and to peaceful assembly.
- Article 14 establishes a right not to be discriminated against. Crucially, this is not a free-standing right but one that is parasitic: it is the right to have other rights in the ECHR secured and enjoyed on a non-discriminatory basis. The list providing the actionable grounds of discrimination—the 'suspect categories'—is much wider than under even UK discrimination law, including as it does 'political or other opinion' 'national or social origin' 'property' 'language' 'birth' 'association with a national minority' (as well as sex, race, colour and religion) but its inclusion of 'or other status' has meant an even wider category of permitted challenges.
- Article 1 to the First Protocol (effectively an addendum) guarantees to individuals the right of peaceful enjoyment of their possessions, though individuals can be deprived of their possessions in the public interest.

The ECHR was the first human rights instrument to be enforced exclusively by judicial means rather than by regular reporting or by ad hoc inspection.[34] Since the first cases starting coming through in any numbers in the 1970s, the ECtHR in Strasbourg has built up a lengthy and detailed corpus of decisions. We shall now look at some of the general, overarching principles that underpin the Court's reasoning and analysis of cases before it.

The ECtHR has on many occasions expressed the view that there needs to be a purposive interpretation. It aims to give effect to the central purpose: protecting individual human rights (rather than laying down mutual obligations as between states) within a framework of democratic ideals and values.[35] The Court sees the ECHR as a 'living instrument' requiring a 'teleological approach in light of present day conditions'.[36] Interpretation evolves over time rather than being set in the stone of the 1950s and overly reliant or fixed on the intention of the parties at the time of contracting to the Treaty. This tends to reduce the precedential value of the case law over time.

That approach also means that a mere reading of the words of the various articles will give only a partial picture of the scope of the protection afforded by the ECHR and it may on occasion be positively misleading. Although the text of the ECHR is always the first place to look, it will not always clearly or completely show its extent or limitations. Giving effect to the ECHR as a living instrument protecting pan-European democratic ideals has meant that the ECtHR on times too numerous to mention has read rights into the text or has refined its approach so as to offer much wider protection than would appear on its face. In *Lopez Ostra v Spain*, the ECtHR decided that an individual's right to respect for the home included a duty on states to take certain measures to protect homes against environmental

---

[32] *Von Hannover v Germany* (2006) 43 EHRR 7; *MS v Sweden* (1999) 28 EHRR 313.
[33] *Pretty v United Kingdom* (2002) 35 EHRR 1.
[34] Since 1998, the Council of Europe's revised Social Charter has been enforced partly by a system of collective complaints.
[35] See eg *Golder v United Kingdom* (1975) 1 EHRR 524 and *Soering v United Kingdom* (1989) 11 EHRR 439 at [87].
[36] *Tyrer v United Kingdom* (1978) 2 EHRR 1 at [31].

pollution by private companies.[37] In *Goodwin v UK*, so as to avoid the 'chilling effect' on the right of free speech—since it played such a pivotal role in sustaining a freely functioning democracy—a necessary adjunct was that a journalist should rarely, if ever, be obliged to disclose a source.[38]

We can identify certain underlying principles within the case law. One would be the common European heritage and its democratic political tradition, with its hallmark values of 'pluralism, tolerance and broadmindedness', individual freedom and the rule of law.[39] In *Gorzelik v Poland* the Grand Chamber asserted that

> democracy does not simply mean that the views of a majority must always prevail: [although individual interests must on occasion be subordinated to those of a group] a balance must be achieved which ensures the fair and proper treatment of minorities and avoids any abuse of a dominant position.[40]

Another, less aspirational principle is that rights in the ECHR must be practical and effective, not theoretical and illusory. In *Airey v Ireland* the ECtHR considered that the failure to provide legal aid for those seeking judicial separation or divorce in Ireland violated Article 6(1), one aspect of which was a right of access to a court.[41] Without access to legal aid, Mrs. Airey could never ask a court to determine her civil rights and obligations; she would never have a trial, let alone one that was fair.

That echoes the third principle, a more important and more recent development in the jurisprudence of the ECtHR: the preparedness on the part of the Court to countenance the imposition of positive obligations upon states. Primarily the ECHR is framed so as to require mere forbearance by signatory states. All a state needs to do to ensure compliance with, say, the right of freedom of expression is not to impose some form of state censorship on the media. However, a host of cases now indicate an acceptance of a more limited positive duty on states to guarantee the effective enjoyment of rights. Under Article 2 states must now not merely refrain from killing anyone but must investigate suspicious deaths, whether caused by the state or not, and must provide information about dangers that may threaten life.[42] Under Article 11 the Court has accepted there is a limited duty to facilitate peaceful protest by requiring states to provide an adequate police presence, especially in the face of violent opposition determined to be disruptive.[43] If the Court construes the reach of an Article to include a limited positive duty, a state can no longer just argue that it did not interfere with the right—that is the point. That said, there is understandable reluctance to extend the scope of patent negative duties to abstain into a system of large-scale judicially created positive duties.[44] The area is under development on a piecemeal basis.[45]

If the ECtHR is not entirely comfortable with requiring states themselves to act on pain of violating the ECHR, it is all the more reluctant to impose obligations on states requiring

---

[37] *Lopez Ostra v Spain* (1994) 20 EHRR 277.
[38] *Goodwin v United Kingdom* (1996) 22 EHRR 123.
[39] See *United Turkish Communist Party v Turkey* (1998) 26 EHRR 121 and *Handyside v United Kingdom* (1976) 1 EHRR 737.
[40] *Gorzelik v Poland* (2005) 40 EHRR at [90], order of original wording altered slightly.
[41] *Airey v Ireland* (1979–80) EHRR 305 at [24] and see too *Golder*, above n 35, at [35].
[42] See *McCann v United Kingdom* (1996) 21 EHRR 97 and *LCB v United Kingdom* (1998) 27 EHRR 212 respectively.
[43] *Plattform Ärzte für das Leben v Austria* (1988) 13 EHRR 204, discussed in greater detail in chapter three.
[44] This has largely been on practical grounds—because imposing such obligations generally requires expenditure—and the linked philosophical objections about the nature of rights and duties.
[45] See generally A Mowbray, *The Development of Positive Obligations under the European Convention on Human Rights* (Oxford, Hart Publishing, 2004).

them to regulate the purely private sphere. That said, it has done so again in order to ensure a proper and full realisation of rights. This is a concept known as *drittwirkung*. Under this, state liability is imposed where a third party's actions, which the state has failed to regulate or to prevent, violate someone's human rights. Thus in *A v UK* the violation of Article 3 was founded on the failure of domestic law to protect a child against a physical punishment beating: the threshold set by the (then) 'reasonable chastisement' defence to a charge of assault did not deter or allow the step-father to be punished after the event and so did not confer adequate safeguards.[46] More recently, in the 'McLibel Two' case, Article 10 was interpreted to hold that a failure by the UK to provide legal aid in a defamation case brought by a private company against a private individual might constitute a breach of Article 10, especially when there is a considerable disparity in the resources of the litigating parties.[47]

The last and probably the most important concept that we need be aware of is proportionality.[48] In one of many similar judgments, *Sporrong and Lonnroth v Sweden*, the ECtHR concluded that its role was to

> determine whether a fair balance was struck between the demands of the general interest of the community and the requirements of the protection of the individual's fundamental rights. The search for this balance is inherent in the whole of the Convention and is also reflected in the structure of Article 1.[49]

The ECtHR utilises the proportionality test, and the notion of balance that underpins it, in several ways. It plays a role when the court is deciding whether or not to impose a positive obligation on a state in any given situation. It is also one of the key factors in the analysis of what are termed qualified rights—such as the right to peaceful protest—by providing a framework for arbitrating between the competing individual and wider social claims. It is to those we now turn.

B. Absolute and Relative Rights

Very few rights in the ECHR are absolute. That is to say very few are incapable of being defeated by a more pressing public interest. The only two that are—Article 3, the prohibition on torture and on inhuman or degrading punishment or treatment and Article 4(1), which outlaws slavery and servitude—are unlikely to arise in any public order scenario.[50] There are in essence three ways in which seemingly far-reaching rights can be reined in (restricted, qualified or limited) on ostensibly public interest grounds: derogation or temporary opt-out in time of war or other public emergency threatening the life of the nation

---

[46] *A v United Kingdom* (1999) 27 EHRR 611 and also *X and Y v Netherlands* (1986) 8 EHRR 235.
[47] *Steel and Morris v United Kingdom* (2005) 41 EHRR 22 and see below chapter eight p 386.
[48] R Clayton and H Tomlinson, *The Law of Human Rights* (Oxford, Oxford University Press, 2001) 279 identify six areas where it is used. These include determining: whether or not dissimilar treatment of analogous groups constitutes unlawful discrimination under Art 14; the lawfulness of the so-called 'claw-backs' under Arts 8–11; the limit of or the extent of any rights that are to be implied into an Article (ie they are not self-evident on its face); and to determine whether or not to impose a positive obligation on a state.
[49] *Sporrong and Lonnroth v Sweden* (1983) 5 EHRR 35 at [69] though this was for the puporse of assessing the reasonableness of expropriations of property or of restrictions on using property, both in the public interest. See also *Soering*, above n 35, at [89] in the context of deportations to face torture or death.
[50] It could certainly be argued that herding or 'kettling' protesters, as occurred at the G20 protests in April 2009, into a cordon for hours on end without toilet facilities is inhuman treatment.

under Article 15;[51] self-evident restrictions on the face of an article (such as under Article 5(1) which allows for lawful deprivations in six limited and finite categories);[52] and the claw-backs contained in Articles 8–11. Each of these claw-backs is in a similar but not entirely identical form.[53] It is here that many of the major battles over rights have been fought and which will continue to be at the forefront in human rights arguments under the HRA when it comes to the regulation of peaceful protest. It is for this reason we need to dwell a little more on the interplay under these four articles.

Let us construct an archetype around Article 11. Individual protester (P) wants to undertake some form of protest activity X—forming a protest group, organising a march, taking part in a rally, burning flags during a sit-in—and the state responds by doing Y or making decision Y—outlawing the group, banning the march, photographing all those at the rally, arresting all those at the sit-in. To ascertain whether or not P's rights under Article 11 have been violated any court seised of the matter will work through the five stages below:

1. P must show that doing X (in Strasbourg-speak) 'engages' Article 11.
2. P must show that the state doing Y constitutes a restriction on her Article 11 rights.

In most peaceful protest situations, P will usually have little difficulty demonstrating these two. We shall consider the Court's case law on the ambit of Article 11 in detail in chapter three. For now we need merely to note that it will be rare for any type of protest activity, even obstructive direct action, not to fall within the scope of the Article provided it is peaceful, that is provided P herself is not violent. It also seems unlikely that A will not be able to show that in doing Y, the state has not restricted her rights under Article 11 in that she is less able to assemble peacefully or to associate than would have been the case absent the state deciding Y or performing activity Y.

3. The state must show that the restriction on A's right was 'prescribed by law'.

Here, the state must do more than just show a basis for the restriction that is lawful domestically—though if it cannot do that, the restriction will be unlawful per se. The phrase has an autonomous Convention meaning. It is designed to maintain and to promote the rule of law and to remove elements of arbitrariness. For a restriction to be 'prescribed by law' it must also be shown to have the twin qualities of accessibility and certainty. In *Sunday Times v UK* the Strasbourg Court set out a two-limbed test.[54] In general, it indicated that

---

[51] Some rights are non-derogable but in respect of the rights most likely to crop up in a public order context (Art 5, the right to liberty, and Arts 10 and 11, free speech and peaceful assembly respectively), it would be permissible, in an emergency or war, for states to derogate. A state may only do so proportionately so as to deal with the emergency. The existence of the threat and the measure(s) needed to deal with it are primarily an assessment for the member state within its margin of appreciation (see below) with the Strasbourg Court taking a more supervisory role.

[52] Similarly, Art 2(2) which removes any state liability where someone is intentionally deprived of their life if it is the result of no more force than is absolutely necessary and is used to defend another from unlawful violence; to effect a lawful arrest or to prevent the escape of someone lawfully detained; or for the purpose of quelling a riot or insurrection. The last may be of direct albeit (it is hoped) of rare application in the context of public order. The death of teacher Blair Peach in 1979 after he clashed with paramilitary officers (the Special Patrol Group) during an Anti-Nazi League rally in London springs to mind, as does the more recent death of Ian Tomlinson at the G20 protest in the City of London in April 2009—though he was not actually protesting but walking home.

[53] Under Art 9, only the right to manifest one's religion either alone or in community with others and either publicly or privately can be qualified. The right to freedom of thought, conscience and religion (and the right to change religion or beliefs) is absolute.

[54] *Sunday Times v United Kingdom* (1979) 2 EHRR 245.

Firstly, the law must be adequately accessible: the citizen must be able to have an indication that is adequate in the circumstances of the legal rule applicable to a given case. Secondly, a norm cannot be regarded as 'law' unless it is formulated with sufficient precision to enable the citizen to regulate his conduct: he must be able—if need be with appropriate advice—to foresee, to a degree that is reasonable in the circumstances, the consequences which a given action may entail.[55]

The test means that vague rules or rules that are incapable of objective measurement may fall foul of Article 11. Unless it can be said with sufficiently certainty, clarity and precision in advance—which seems to be the key—that participating in a march or staging a demonstration will render participants liable to arrest or some other such penalty, then any domestic law which does impose penalties runs the risk of being held unlawful. It is designed, as the judgment makes clear, so as to allow potential protesters to know their likely liability and thus to assess whether or not to protest at all.[56] In *Hashman and Harrup v UK*, fox-hunt protesters were bound over to keep the peace and to be of good behaviour or, rather, not to engage in behaviour contra bonos mores.[57] That requirement—where such behaviour was defined as 'wrong rather than right in the judgement of contemporary fellow citizens'[58]—was too vague, being too subjective, to be predictable. The restrictions imposed therefore violated Article 11.

The Grand Chamber has recently set out some of its thinking on the vexed issue of vague laws. *Gorzelik v Poland*, although it is a case on the right of association in Article 11, provides a good general example of the Court's approach.[59] The Polish electoral authorities refused to recognise The Union of People of Silesian Nationality because they considered there was no Silesian national minority in Poland. 'National minority' was the term used in the relevant legislation but without any criteria for assessing what it meant. The association challenged the refusal—and the legal framework on which it was based—as not being prescribed by law. The Grand Chamber, finding for the Polish authorities, stated that it was:

a logical consequence of the principle that laws must be of general application that the wording of statutes is not always precise. The need to avoid excessive rigidity and to keep pace with changing circumstances means that many laws are inevitably couched in terms which, to a greater or lesser extent, are vague. The interpretation and application of such enactments depend on practice ... The scope of the notion of foreseeability depends to a considerable degree on the content of the instrument in question, the field it is designed to cover and the number and status of those to whom it is addressed ... It must also be borne in mind that, however clearly drafted a legal provision may be, its application involves an inevitable element of judicial interpretation, since there will always be a need for clarification of doubtful points and for adaptation to particular circumstances. A margin of doubt in relation to borderline facts does not by itself make a legal provision unforeseeable in its application. Nor does the mere fact that such a provision is capable of more than one construction mean that it fails to meet the requirement of 'foreseeability' for the purposes of the Convention. The role of adjudication vested in the courts is precisely to dissipate such interpretational doubts as remain, taking into account the changes in everyday practice.[60]

---

[55] ibid, at [49].
[56] It would appear that best advice for legislators would be to frame laws broadly or overly generally so as more easily to avoid being held in violation—though as we shall see, such blanket laws, unless discretion is exercised under them narrowly and specifically, will likely lead to violations on grounds of disproportionality.
[57] *Hashman and Harrup v UK* (2000) 30 EHRR 241. Domestic law on binding over is dealt with in chapter seven.
[58] ibid, at [38].
[59] *Gorzelik v Poland*, above n 40.
[60] ibid, at [64]–[65].

4. The state must show that the restriction seeks to achieve one or more of the social interests or public policy goals listed in Article 11(2), viz national security or public safety, preventing disorder or crime, protecting health or morals or protecting the rights and freedoms of others.

Again, we shall analyse this in depth in the next chapter. Nonetheless, as Clare Ovey and Robin White put it looking at Articles 8–11 generally, '[the prevention of disorder or crime] justification for interferences is the most frequently raised before the court and the most frequently accepted by it'.[61] However, the same authors continue,

> it is relatively easy for a Contracting State to bring its action within one of the stated exceptions, and the Court seldom has to spend much time analysing the nature of the limitation to satisfy itself that it falls within one of them.[62]

The Strasbourg Court has also made it clear on repeated occasions, if the claw-backs themselves were not wide enough, the reference to 'rights of others' need not even be a right recognised as worthy of protection as a free-standing Convention right.[63]

5. The state must show that the restriction is 'necessary in a democratic society'.

This tends to be the focus of attention and contention between applicants and respondent states. That a state can show there is a legitimate reason for restricting protest—that is (4) above—is not the end of the story. Not only must there be a recognisably legitimate aim, found in the exhaustive list in Article 11(2), but any restriction or interference imposed on protest must also be proportionate: it must meet a 'pressing social need'.[64] Here, the state is required properly to balance the rights of individuals comprised in Article 11(1) against the general (perhaps more nebulous?) community interest comprised in Article 11(2).

The role of the Court in scrutinising a state's actions or decisions is not confined to ascertaining whether the state exercised its discretion reasonably, carefully and in good faith. States seeking to justify an interference must demonstrate reasons that are 'relevant and sufficient' and that the decision was based on an 'acceptable assessment of relevant facts':[65] if they fail to do so, a violation is very likely to be the outcome. The Court will ask whether or not there is an objectively rational connection between the measure taken and the end sought. If the measure cannot achieve its aim or if the measure could achieve its aim but in a manner that is more intrusive of an individual's right than an alternative, then the measure is likely to be seen as disproportionate. The Court's role here is not appellate but one of review: its task is not to substitute its own view for that of the national authorities on

---

[61] Ovey and White, above n 25, at 206.
[62] ibid, at 204.
[63] In *Chassagnou v France* (2000) 29 EHRR 615, the issue was whether it was an unlawful restriction on the negative right of association for French law to require certain small landholders to transfer the hunting rights over their land to approved municipal hunters' associations in order to create municipal hunting grounds. The Court was prepared to accept that given the duty to ensure, on behalf of the community, the safety of people and property, it was a legitimate state aim to organise and to regulate a leisure activity the main purpose of which 'was to provide pleasure and relaxation to those who took part in it while respecting its traditions'. Thus the legislation secured the legitimate aim of protecting the rights and freedoms of others: at [106]–[108].
[64] *Handyside v UK* (1979–80) 1 EHRR 737 at [48]. The Court added that the word 'necessary' was not synonymous with 'indispensable', neither had it the flexibility of such expressions as 'admissible', 'ordinary', 'useful', 'reasonable' or 'desirable'.
[65] *Gorzelik*, above n 40, at [96].

legislative policy and measures of implementation but to review the decisions they reached in the exercise of their discretion.[66]

Within this, however, states will be accorded some room to manoeuvre. This discretion, what Strasbourg refers to as a margin of appreciation, is flexible and its width varies, depending on circumstances. The court calls on the margin of appreciation when it assesses two matters: whether a state needs to restrict the right to protest and what measures are necessary to do so. The Court in *Handyside* explained:

> By reason of their direct and continuous contact with the vital forces of their countries, State authorities are in principle in a better position than the international judge to give an opinion on the exact content of these requirements as well as on the 'necessity' of a 'restriction' or 'penalty' intended to meet them ... [I]t is for the national authorities to make the initial assessment of the reality of the pressing social need implied by the notion of 'necessity' in this context. Consequently, Article 10 (2) leaves to the Contracting States a margin of appreciation. This margin is given both to the domestic legislator ('prescribed by law') and to the bodies, judicial amongst others, that are called upon to interpret and apply the laws in force ... Nevertheless, Article 10 (2) does not give the Contracting States an unlimited power of appreciation. The Court, which, with the Commission, is responsible for ensuring the observance of those States' engagements, is empowered to give the final ruling on whether a 'restriction' or 'penalty' is reconcilable with freedom of expression as protected by Article 10. The domestic margin of appreciation thus goes hand in hand with a European supervision.[67]

The margin of appreciation thus depicted is an entirely judge-made solution—it does not appear anywhere in the text—to the diplomatic conundrum of how, in a single pan-European treaty binding all equally, to cater for individual country responses to any given socio-political problem. In affording member states 'wiggle room', the margin of appreciation assumes Europe is not homogenous, whether culturally, morally, religiously, historically or politically. It also serves the political purpose, identified in the passage above, of placing the primary responsibility for ensuring and guaranteeing human rights onto states parties, with the Strasbourg Court playing only a back-stop supervisory role. Nonetheless, the concept is far from immune to criticism. The detail of this need not detain us much further but some familiarity is necessary so as to understand a little better the complexities, nuances and limits relating to the law of protest at Strasbourg level.

Let us briefly consider two: the lack of articulation of its scope and its varying width. When confronted with the broadly formulaic nature of a Strasbourg judgment, the first-time reader may well think of the margin of appreciation as resembling the US Cavalry on the hill of old. Just when it seems that the government being challenged is arguing a hopeless case, with the weight of the judicial reasoning seemingly against it, like a magical rabbit from a hat, the margin of appreciation is summoned up from nowhere to vindicate the government's position and to save the day. Given the degree of discretion it allows, it is surprising that the ECtHR rarely engages in any real analysis of its reasoning: hardly ever do we discover why what state A did was within its margin or, if a violation is found, what else it could have done to bring itself within it. In several cases, it appears as little more than a fait accompli or an ex post facto justification.

The second concern, which compounds the first, for scholars and adviser alike[68] is that the width of the margin of appreciation varies—so allowing greater or lesser discretion—

---

[66] ibid.
[67] *Handyside*, above n 64, at [48]–[49].
[68] Ironically, its uncertainty and unpredictability might well put Strasbourg decisions in breach of its own 'prescribed by law' test as set out in the *Sunday Times* case above.

depending on factors such as the right in issue or the competing social interest 'claw-back'. Freedom of expression has historically been valued very highly, given its functional role in enhancing and maintaining an informed democracy.[69] As such it attracts a narrow margin of appreciation. The result is that Strasbourg permits limited deviation from a pan-European norm.[70] Certain aspects of private life, especially in the area of autonomy and sexual choice, have also been construed as having narrow margins,[71] whereas when the issue in question relates to a moral viewpoint, cultural difference or where there is no uniform European view (for any other reason), then the practice has been to allow a wide margin of appreciation.[72] Similarly, where the limiting factor or claw-back is national security, Strasbourg has historically permitted states a good deal of discretion, under the guise of the margin of appreciation, in cases such as *Leander v Sweden*[73] and *Klass v Federal Republic of Gemany*.[74] What the Strasbourg court is not adept at explaining is what happens when free speech is restricted on grounds, say, of national security: how does it balance out the overlapping contemporaneous need for both a narrow margin and a wide margin?

III. A Home-Grown Bill of Rights? The Human Rights Act 1998

Since the 1950s, both major political parties in Britain had been united in opposing any form of domestic bill of rights. However, in the early 1990s official Labour Party policy changed in favour of a home grown Bill of Rights. In 1996, with a General Election looming, the shadow Home Office team issued its consultation paper 'Bringing Rights Home',[75] followed, after Labour's 1997 election victory, with the White Paper 'Rights Brought Home'.[76] What became the Human Rights Act was to be a cornerstone of Labour's first term package of constitutional reform, described at the time by the late Lord Williams of Mostyn (then a Home Officer Minister) as 'comparable to the introduction of the NHS in 1948'.[77] The Act was passed in 1998 and entered into force in England and Wales in October 2000.[78] The White Paper gave four main aims behind the legislation:

- Ensuring UK citizens can have their rights under the ECHR protected in UK courts by UK judges;
- Making the process of protecting rights under the ECHR less costly and quicker than proceeding to Strasbourg;

[69] *Handyside* above n 64 at [48].
[70] See such cases as *Handyside* above n 64 and *Jersild v Denmark* (1994) 19 EHRR 1.
[71] See as an example *Dudgeon v UK* (1982) 4 EHRR 149.
[72] Examples would include issues such as rights for transsexuals and euthanasia: see respectively cases such as *XYZ v UK* (1997) 24 EHRR 143 (though *cf* now *Goodwin v UK* (2002) 35 EHRR 447) and *Pretty v UK* (2002) 35 EHRR 1.
[73] *Leander v Sweden* (1987) 9 EHRR 433.
[74] *Klass v FRG* (1979–80) 2 EHRR 214.
[75] See J Straw and P Boateng [1997] *European Human Rights Law Review* 71.
[76] Cmnd 3782 available at: www.archive.official-documents.co.uk/document/hoffice/rights/rights.htm (accessed 2 July 2009).
[77] Public lecture at LSE, 4 February 1998.
[78] Books on the HRA abound. Good places to start for further detail would be H Fenwick, *Civil Liberties and Human Rights*, 4th edn (Abingdon, Routledge, 2007) or Clayton and Tomlinson, *The Law of Human Rights*, above n 48. Appendix IV sets out the key sections of the HRA.

- Allowing UK judges to make a distinctively UK contribution to the development of human rights in Europe by ruling on cases in the UK on the basis of familiarity and sensitivity; and
- Leading to closer scrutiny of the human rights implications of new legislation and policies.

As the Bill passed through Parliament, debates crystallised around a few key themes.[79] The Conservative opposition took the politically pragmatic decision not to oppose the Bill in principle but to oppose aspects of its mechanics and proposed structure. The key issues for resolution were: the strength the HRA should have and its relationship with other Acts; the effect on Parliamentary Sovereignty of bringing rights home and the extent to which decision-making under the HRA would lead to a politicised judiciary; and the need for a fully-fledged Human Rights Commission. Despite considerable parliamentary support, nothing was established; the Equality and Human Rights Commission (which came into being in October 2007 as a result of the Equality Act 2006),[80] however, has the role of promoting and fostering human rights by campaigning, by advising and by taking legal action. At an institutional level, a large amount of the publicising and scrutinising work that a Human Rights Commission might have undertaken has been performed by the Joint Select Committee on Human Rights (JCHR), established in February 2001 by Parliament itself.[81] The JCHR is a highly regarded and august body, comprising 12 members drawn from both Houses.[82] It conducts several thematic inquiries every year and scrutinises all public bills, producing large numbers of reports annually.[83] We shall make regular reference to these throughout the remainder of this book.

The HRA has been referred to as 'our Bill of Rights'.[84] Crucial to our understanding is to grasp its limitations as well as its potential to promote and guarantee effective protection of human rights domestically. As the Long Title makes clear, the HRA is designed 'to give further effect' to the ECHR; it does not incorporate 'Convention rights'. Instead it 'brings them home' or domesticates them.[85] As Lord Irvine made clear at Report stage in the House of Lords,

---

[79] See JUSTICE, *Legislating for Human Rights—the parliamentary debates on the Human Rights Bill* (Oxford, Hart Publishing, 2000).

[80] Its homepage is at: www.equalityhumanrights.com/en/Pages/default.aspx, accessed 17 June 2008.

[81] Its homepage is at: www.publications.parliament.uk/pa/jt/jtrights.htm, accessed 17 June 2008.

[82] Its terms of reference are to consider (a) matters relating to human rights in the UK (but excluding consideration of individual cases); (b) proposals for remedial orders, draft remedial orders and remedial orders made under s 10 of and laid under Sch 2 to the HRA; and (c) in respect of draft remedial orders and remedial orders, whether the special attention of the House should be drawn to them on any of the grounds specified in Standing Order 73 (Joint Committee on Statutory Instruments), at: www.parliament.uk/parliamentary_committees/joint_committee_on_human_rights/jchrabout.cfm, accessed 17 June 2008.

[83] For example, in March 2009 it produced a report into the policing of protest: JCHR 7th Report of session 2008–09 *Demonstrating respect for protest: a human rights approach to policing protest* available at: www.publications.parliament.uk/pa/jt200809/jtselect/jtrights/47/4702.htm (accessed 2 July 2009).

[84] *Brown v Stott* [2001] 2 WLR 817 (HL) 839 (Lord Steyn).

[85] The HRA does not 'bring home' all the rights in the Convention. Schedule 1 to the HRA creates the concept of 'Convention rights', which excludes Art 1 and Art 13. The HRA itself after all is the mechanism by which the UK (in the words of Art 1) 'secures to everyone within the jurisdiction the rights and freedoms' within the remainder of the ECHR so to include that Article as a Convention right would veer towards surplusage. There was much greater dispute about the absence of Art 13, guaranteeing the right to an effective national remedy for violations of the ECHR. The Labour Government defended its decision by pointing out that, as with Art 1, the HRA itself was to be the effective domestic remedy. Opponents pointed out that the limitations of the HRA would mean this could not be guaranteed and highlighted what they assumed was the government's fear: its inclusion in Sch 1 would empower the judiciary to fashion effective domestic remedies outwith their powers in the remainder of the HRA.

40 *Protecting Human Rights in the Human Rights Act Era*

> The ECHR under this Bill is not made part of our law . . . it does not make [it] directly justiciable as it would be if it were expressly made part of our law. I want there to be no ambiguity about that.[86]

The difference between the ECHR and EC law, brought into the UK by the European Communities Act 1972 could not be starker. Section 2 of the 1972 Act makes EC rights directly enforceable before British courts and as directly and immediately a part of English law as if enacted by Westminster; the ECHR is not part of the substantive law of the UK. The thinking behind the HRA was different. Lord Irvine again made this clear. Reflecting two years on he stated that the HRA had

> a clear starting point—a pragmatic view of our constitutional arrangements. That view is of an accommodation between the State and the individual; and of a new and dynamic co-operative endeavour that is developing between the Executive, the Judiciary and Parliament; one in which each works within its respective constitutional sphere to give ever developing practical effect to the values embodied in the Act.[87]

The 'pragmatic view of our constitutional arrangements'—the triptych of parliamentary sovereignty, the rule of law and the separation of powers—explains the HRA's twin-track approach to guaranteeing the rights enshrined in the ECHR.[88] First, section 3 heralds a new dawn for statutory interpretation; all legislation whenever enacted should 'so far as possible' be read and given effect to in a manner that is compatible with Convention rights. Where that is not possible section 4 permits judges to grant a 'declaration of incompatibility' as a remedy. This we shall call the new canon of legislative compatibility. Secondly, section 6 imposes on public authorities a new public law duty, a duty not to act incompatibly with Convention rights. We shall refer to this as the duty of Convention compliance. Under section 7(1), victims may enforce this duty by using Convention rights either as a sword (to found a claim) or collaterally as a shield in proceedings.

In the remainder of this chapter we shall consider the mechanism of that twin track approach in more detail.[89]

A. The New Canon of Legislative Compatibility

What is the status of Strasbourg case law in this new interpretative landscape? Section 2 of the HRA requires judges, when determining a question which has arisen in connection with a Convention right, to take account of ECHR case law when in its opinion it is relevant. Judges are not bound by the ECHR: they are not enjoined to 'decide in accordance with'.[90]

---

[86] Hansard HL Report 29 January 1998, vol 585 col 421.

[87] Lord Irvine, 'The Human Rights Act Two Years On: An Analysis' a talk given at Durham University in November 2002 reprinted at [2003] *PL* 308.

[88] At an institutional level, the HRA also seeks to ensure the better protection of Convention rights by requiring Government ministers to make a compatibility statement before Second Reading: see s 19. It is important to note that a s 19 Ministerial statement of compatibility is a very different legal animal to a judicial declaration of incompatibility under s 4.

[89] The only other aspect of the HRA to be aware is s 8. This confers on a court the discretion to grant a remedy or relief that is 'just and appropriate' where public authorities act unlawfully. Courts may only do so within their existing powers and jurisdiction so a tribunal that has no power to grant injunctions is not suddenly empowered by virtue of s 8. Damages can be awarded but have tended to be low, reflecting Strasbourg practice that in most cases, nominal damages or even the finding of a violation provide 'just satisfaction' under Article 41.

[90] Given Strasbourg's purposive 'living instrument' approach, when domestic courts are taking account of Strasbourg case-law, reflexively this ought to empower them to take organic and dynamic approaches to interpretation so as to protect human rights and the values of a democratic society. Taking account of ECHR case-law

That said, the presumption is that 'clear and constant Strasbourg jurisprudence' should only be departed from in special circumstances with good reason.[91] One good reason would be the need for certainty that comes with a hierarchical system of domestic precedent: only in the very rarest of cases should the decision of a higher court be rejected in favour of a Strasbourg decision,[92] though a clear and obvious incompatibility between Strasbourg and pre-1998 precedent might be sufficient to create, effectively, a 'Year Zero'.[93] The nature of the section 2 duty has meant that since 2000 we have witnessed the development of legal argument and decisions in the same structured manner as Strasbourg and an increased 'borrowing' from and reliance on protections contained in Bills of Rights in similar—usually Commonwealth or Anglo-American—jurisdictions.

Let us turn to section 3 itself. It was drafted deliberately to maintain the supremacy of the Wesminster Parliament, and so clearly rejects both US-style strong constitutional review and even the weaker Canadian form. Either were thought still to have the potential overly to empower the judiciary and to upset the delicate constitutional balance between lawmakers and interpreters.[94] Instead our HRA is most closely modelled on the New Zealand Bill of Rights Act 1990.

(i) The Terms of Section 3

Whenever a court is called upon to interpret statutory words and phrases, section 3(1) requires them to to do so in a way that is Convention-compatible but only 'so far as [that is] possible'. That statutory formula appears to preserve parliamentary sovereignty: judges may only (re-) interpret statutory meanings where the new proposed Convention-compatible meaning is a possible meaning. Nothing in the HRA permits judges to set aside primary legislation or to refuse to apply incompatible primary legislation: under section 3(2)(b) 'the validity, continuing operation or enforcement' of primary legislation remains unaffected by the fact that it can only be read in an incompatible manner.[95] Incompatible primary legislation must continue to be upheld as valid whenever it was enacted:[96] in human rights cases, no longer can courts call upon the doctrine of implied repeal to uphold

---

might also engender more precedential fluidity, given the nature of stare decisis at Strasbourg. There is still a question over the extent to which account should be taken where the outcome was based on the margin of appreciation, especially where the case did not involve the UK.

[91] The leading case is *R (Ullah) v Special Adjudicator* [2004] UKHL 26 and see R Masterman, 'Section 2(1) of the Human Rights Act 1998: Binding Domestic Courts to Strasbourg?' [2004] *PL* 725. This leaves, at best, only limited room for judges to generate and to develop an autonomous municipal corpus of human rights law.

[92] *Kay v Lambeth London Borough Council; Price v Leeds City Council* [2006] UKHL 10.

[93] The Court of Appeal in *Mendoza v Ghaidan* [2002] EWCA Civ 1533 adopted a statutory meaning that had been specifically rejected by the House of Lords only three years before in *Fitzpatrick v Sterling Health Authority* [1999] 3 WLR 1113 (HL).

[94] Canadian judges are empowered to strike down legislation that violates any of the rights guaranteed under the 1982 Charter of Rights and Freedoms unless the legislation contains what is usually referred to as a 'notwithstanding' clause. The effect of this is that the primacy of the allegedly conflicting legislation is asserted over any other possible judicial meaning, even where that judicial meaning would otherwise lead to a holding that there was a violation.

[95] Under s 3(2)(c) furthermore, the validity, continuing operation or enforcement of any incompatible *subordinate* legislation remains unaffected by its own incompatibility if primary legislation prevents the removal of the incompatibility. Where subordinate legislation violates a Convention right, it can be declared as such even to the extent of being struck down unless, effectively, the parent Act required the subordinate legislation to be passed and to be passed in that form. In other words, secondary legislation passed under under the vires of general, all-encompassing primary legislation that imposes a dispropotoinate restriction on peaceful protest is precarious: see as one example, *Tabernacle v Secretary of State for Defence* [2009] EWCA Civ 23.

[96] Section 3(2)(a).

later Acts—here the HRA—over earlier inconsistent Acts or provisions. Thus at a domestic level even the new Convention right of peaceful protest would have to bow to contradictory statutory imperatives, perhaps centuries-old, if it was not possible to 'read' that earlier legislation compatibly with Parliament's later pro-protest pronouncement on the matter in 1998, in the HRA. In cases where it is not possible to read legislation compatibly, section 4 permits (but does not require) judges in the High Court and above to grant a declaration of incompatibility. This will not 'affect the validity, continuing operation or enforcement' of the legislation declared incompatible and neither is it binding on the parties—though it may kick-start the section 10 'fast-track' procedure.[97] In short, section 4 is a 'booby prize':[98] criminal provisions that breach the right of peaceful protest will still apply and those whose detentions were unlawful deprivations of liberty will not be freed.[99] Though section 4 was much heralded, it is in fact less of a remedy than the power that obtains under the European Communities Act 1972 either to declare legislation incompatible with EC law or to suspend its operation on grounds of incompatibility.[100]

(ii) The Extent of Section 3

What then (in Lord Lester's words) is 'the art of the possible' under section 3?[101] What does case-law predict about how judges might wield their new power in peaceful protest cases coming before them? Clearly the new duty in section 3 goes further than previous reliance on the ECHR in interpreting legislation, limited as that was to cases where legislation was ambiguous or had been introduced so as to give effect to a Strasbourg judgment.[102] Section 3 establishes what has been called a 'rebuttable presumption in favour of Convention rights'.[103] Judges are no longer asked to search for the literal or true meaning of Parliament's intention in using word X. Instead, they are asked to engage in more generous, broader and purposive interpretations. In one of the first cases under section 3, *R v A*,[104] Lord Steyn expressed it thus:

> [T]he interpretative obligation under section 3 of the 1998 Act is a strong one. It applies even if there is no ambiguity in the language in the sense of the language being capable of two different

---

[97] Section 10 permits the taking of action to remedy either a domestic finding that there has been a violation of a Convention right (under s 4) or the Strasbourg Court finding there has been a violation of the ECHR. In either case—but only if there are compelling reasons—the violation can be remedied without the need to pass amending primary legislation. Instead, a Minister may by order make such amendments to legislation, even primary legislation, as she considers necessary to remove the incompatibility, an archetype 'Henry VIII' clause.

[98] G Marshall, 'Two kinds of compatibility: more about section 3 of the Human Rights Act 1998' [1999] PL 377, 382.

[99] The interplay between the two sections highlights an important constitutional tension that inheres in any system purporting to protect, to value and to prioritise fundamental rights. Section 3 allows judges to do justice as between the parties at the possible expense of parliament's explicit wishes (contained in the incompatible legislation). Section 4 allows them to maintain the delicate constitutional balance but only by depriving one of the litigant of realistic success and immediate protection—but does, it is said, open up 'democratic dialogue' between judges, parliament and people.

[100] See respectively *R v Secretary of State for Employment ex parte Equal Opportunities Commission* [1995] 1 AC 1 and *R v Secretary of State for Transport ex parte Factortame (No 2)* [1991] 1 AC 603.

[101] Lord Lester, 'The art of the possible—interpreting statutes under the Human Rights Act' [1998] EHRLR 665.

[102] Above text to n 14.

[103] Lord Cooke of Thorndon, Hansard, HL Deb 3 November 1997, col 1272.

[104] *R v A* [2002] 1 AC 45 (HL). The House of Lords was asked to interpret the so-called 'rape-shield' provisions in the Youth Justice and Criminal Evidence Act 1999 which imposed a considerable restriction on the rights of defendants to cross-examine complainant witnesses. It was argued such restrictions violated Art 6, the right to a fair trial.

meanings. It is an emphatic adjuration by the legislature . . . Under ordinary methods of interpretation a court may depart from the language of the statute to avoid absurd consequences: section 3 goes much further. Undoubtedly, a court must always look for a contextual and purposive interpretation: section 3 is more radical in its effect . . . In accordance with the will of Parliament as reflected in section 3 it will sometimes be necessary to adopt an interpretation which linguistically may appear strained. The techniques to be used will not only involve the reading down of express language in a statute but also the implication of provisions. A declaration of incompatibility is a measure of last resort. It must be avoided unless it is plainly impossible to do so. If a *clear* limitation on Convention rights is stated *in terms*, such an impossibility will arise.[105]

The 'implication of provisions', that is 'reading in' or adding words or phrases, so as to render an otherwise ostensibly incompatible statutory phrase was not novel: it had been used previously in the EC context.[106] 'Reading down' is a less contentious technique. Rather than adding words, this involves narrowing overly broad or general words (or perhaps widening the express terms of a defence to a criminal charge) so as to confine their ambit to Convention-compatible circumstances. In truth, the difference between reading in and reading down is one that is blurred and academic; it need concern us no longer.

A measure of qualification to the radical re-writing favoured in *A* (where provisions relating to cross-examination of rape victims were re-written broadly to resemble the *status quo ante* Parliamentary intervention in 1999) was added in the next major case, *Re S*.[107] Along with *Anderson*[108] and *Bellinger*[109] the House provided clearer guidance on the boundary between permissible creative interpretation and impermissible re-drafting or judicial legislating. Lord Nicholls identified two factors as indicating the line had been transgressed: first, where a meaning departs substantially from a fundamental feature of the Act, and secondly that would be especially so where the departure has important practical repercussions which the court is not equipped to evaluate.[110]

Two years later, in *Mendoza v Ghaidan*, the House was clear about the relative merits of section 3 and section 4.[111] Section 3 requires a Convention-compatible meaning to be adopted wherever possible unless to do so would be inconsistent with a fundamental feature of the Act. Lord Steyn (and to some extent Lord Rodger) was clear that the law had taken a wrong turn: 'the linch-pin [of remedying the mischief by "bringing rights home"] was section 3(1). Rights could only be effectively brought home if section 3(1) was the prime remedial measure and section 4 a measure of last resort'.[112] All their Lordships agreed that Parliament did not intend, when passing section 3, that judges should be overly concerned with the linguistic niceties of allegedly incompatible legislation. It was permissible to read words in, read words down, to modify their meaning and even to put 'the

[105] *ibid*, at [44]–[45].
[106] *Litster v Forth Dry Dock Engineering* [1990] 1 AC 546, interpreting UK employment law in the light of an EC Directive.
[107] *Re S (Care Plan)* [2002] UKHL 10.
[108] *R (Anderson) v Secretary of State for the Home Department* [2002] UKHL 46.
[109] *Bellinger v Bellinger* [2003] UKHL 21.
[110] *Re S*, above n 107, at [40] The House had been asked to decide the legitimacy of the 'starring' system read into the Children Act 1989 by the Court of Appeal when interpreting a court's powers in care proceedings. That system essentially empowered a court both to identify essential milestones in a care plan and to require local authorities to take action if they were not achieved within a certain time. The House decided such an approach could not be justified as a legitimate interpretation of the 1989 Act: it was a cardinal principle of the 1989 Act that the courts were not empowered to intervene in the discharge of a local authority's parental responsibilities under a final care order.
[111] *Mendoza v Ghaidan* [2004] UKHL 30.
[112] *ibid*, at [46] and Lord Rodger at [122].

offending part of the provision into different words',[113] provided courts did not adopt meanings inconsistent with a fundamental feature of the legislation or which had wide-reaching or practical/economic ramifications. As Lord Rodger indicated 'What matters is not so much the particular phraseology chosen by the draftsman as the substance of the measure which Parliament enacted in those words'.[114] Lord Millett, in the minority as to the outcome, even went so far as to say that in certain contexts, it was possible for black to mean 'black or white' (but never 'not black') and for 'cat' to encompass 'cat or dog'.[115]

It is clear that judges now have considerable scope, given by Parliament itself, to recast statutes in a more Convention-compatible hue, should that be seen as needed. Whether or not they choose to do so, and the extent to which they have done so, will be one of the matters that we shall cover in the remainder of the book.

B. The Duty of Convention Compliance

The other technique by which Convention rights are domesticated and given protection without full-blown incorporation is by imposing on public authorities the duty of Convention compliance contained in section 6(1): it is unlawful for them to act in a way that is incompatible with a Convention right. This new public law duty is enforceable by victims under section 7. Section 7(1) states:

> a person who claims that a public authority has acted (or proposes to act) in a way which is made unlawful by section 6(1) may—
>
> (a) bring proceedings against the authority under this Act in the appropriate court or tribunal, or
> (b) rely on the Convention right or rights concerned in any legal proceedings, but only if he is (or would be) a victim of the unlawful act.

In short, the 'sword' of section 7(1)(a) expands the traditional three heads of judicial review to permit challenges based on an actual or potential breach of the section 6 duty. In effect this permits *Brind*-like challenges, arguing that decisions taken by governmental and quasi-governmental bodies have violated or will violate the ECHR. As many rights can be qualified, this ushers into domestic law judicial review challenges based around the European notion of proportionality. The 'shield' of section 7(1)(b) allows, for example, those charged with criminal offences to set up a Convention right collaterally as (part of) their defence.

Whether or not the HRA has promoted an *internalising* of rights-protection by public bodies rather than facilitating external, ex post facto court challenges has been moot in the early years of the HRA. A full assessment of the extent to which the right to peaceful protest has been brought home would consider not only the extent to which judicial decisions now favour protesters when previously they did not (and the extent to which legislation does not unnecessarily encroach) but also the extent to which 'rights-consciousness' pervades the minds of police officers on the beat as they weigh up whether or not to arrest or to impose conditions on a march. That said, however, the major focus of this book will be on judicial and legal means to promote and protect the right to protest rather than considering the

---

[113] ibid, at [124] Lord Rodger.
[114] ibid, at [123].
[115] ibid, at [70]–[72].

socio-legal realities of everyday policing decisions taken in the shadow of the law using what Robert Reiner has called the 'Ways and Means Act'[116]—or indeed decisions taken without any lawful basis but which are just accepted.[117]

An analysis of the operation of sections 6–7 requires us to address three questions. We shall look at each briefly below.

1. What is a public authority upon whom the duty rests?
2. How are Convention rights enforced by victims?
3. How is Convention compliance assessed?

(i) What is a Public Authority?

Much has been written by public lawyers on the boundaries of the state—where does and should the HRA cast the public law/private law divide? As we are interested only in providing a backdrop for public order, our task is much simpler.

There is no list in the HRA of 'public authorities' unlike the Freedom of Information Act 2000. Instead section 6 defines a public authority partly functionally:

> (3) In this section, 'public authority' includes –
>
>   (a) any court or tribunal, and
>   (b) any person, certain of whose functions are functions of a public nature,
>
> but does not include either House of Parliament or a person exercising functions in connection with proceedings in Parliament.
> (4) In subsection (3), 'Parliament' does not include the House of Lords in its judicial capacity.
> (5) In relation to a particular act, a person is not a public authority by virtue only of subsection (3)(b) if the nature of the act is private.
> (6) 'An act' includes a failure to act but does not include a failure to—
>
>   (a) introduce in, or lay before, Parliament a proposal for legislation; or
>   (b) make primary legislation or remedial order.

A combined reading of section 6(3)(b) and 6(5) leads to a three-fold division—a distinction supported by Hansard, the Government's intention and case law since 2000—between:[118]

1. 'standard' 'pure' or 'core' public authorities;
2. quasi or hybrid or functional public authorities; and
3. purely private bodies.

Courts and tribunals will always be bound by the duty of Convention compliance by virtue of section 6(3)(a), whereas Parliament, other than the Appellate Committee of the House of Lords, will not be liable under section 6(1) for failing to legislate to remedy a convention violation, either actual or putative.

---

[116] R Reiner, 'Policing the police' in M Maguire, R Morgan and R Reiner, *The Oxford Handbook of Criminology*, 2nd edn (Oxford, Oxford University Press, 1997) 1002. The phrase has not appeared in subsequent editions.

[117] This might be for a variety of reasons—a misunderstanding of the law, or more likely now a failure to realise the Convention implications—but whatever the officer's reasoning, citizens tend not to challenge directions given by uniformed officers at demonstrations, seemingly with the weight of the law behind them. An example might be a requirement to remove an inoffensive banner from a protest site where there is no power to do so.

[118] See also Clayton and Tomlinson, *The Law of Human Rights*, above n 48, para 5.08 et seq.

In turn, section 6(3) and (5) in effect require answers to these three questions: first, does body X undertake or perform any public functions?[119] Secondly, assuming it has some public functions—and if not, it would be in category (c)—are all or only some of its functions public? Last, if only some, is the nature of the act it is performing and on which it is being challenged one that is 'public' or 'private' in nature?[120] The issue of real importance and no small measure of difficulty is what distinguishes 'pure' from 'functional' public authorities.[121] All the functions of the former are functions of a public nature. It has been accepted that they are bound always to act in a Convention-compliant fashion even when acting 'privately'. Functional authorities by contrast, although some (but not all) of their functions are of a public nature, are liable under section 6(1) only for acts that are not private in nature—whatever these may be! Purely private bodies, that is bodies with no public functions at all, have no duties under section 6(1) imposed on them *directly*.

What for us, in our study of peaceful protest, is going to be the problem or the issue? It would be fair to say that it is likely to be peripheral but potentially pivotal: the potential liability under section 6 of functional bodies for decisions that affect the right to protest. It is likely to be peripheral, as most of the protagonists involved in any protest are likely to polarise into obviously pure public authorities and clearly private companies, increasingly the targets of protest, on the one hand and groups of private individuals protesting on the other. It is beyond argument that both central and local government, together with the police, will be pure public authorities.[122] If so, all decisions—arrests, bans, conditions, directions—taken by ministers, councils, Chief Constables and officers that both engage and then restrict the right of peaceful protest would be subject to scrutiny under section 6 and section 7. At the other end of the spectrum, let us imagine some decisions affecting someone's ability to protest, taken by purely private bodies. Maybe an arms manufacturer dismisses all employees who attend the 'No War in Iraq' march. Alternatively, a powerful GM crop company terminates the contract of its farm equipment supplier without notice after the supplier founds the 'Say Yes to Natural Foods: Say Yes to a Cleaner World' campaign. A condition in the supply contract specifically forbids suppliers doing anything that

---

[119] Although domestic cases on amenability to judicial review (such as *R v Panel on Takeovers & Mergers ex parte Datafin* [1987] 1 QB 815) will be relevant they will not be determinative: see eg *Parochial Church Council of the Parish of Aston Cantlow, Wilmcote with Billesley, Warwickshire v Wallbank* [2003] UKHL 37 at [42] (Lord Hope).

[120] To that extent, the analysis adopted by Lord Scott in *YL v Birmingham City Council* [2007] UKHL 27 is preferable to that of Lord Bingham. *R (Weaver) v London and Quadrant Housing Trust* [2009] EWCA Civ 587 appears to confirm that the correct approach and the focus of the judicial inquiry should be on the nature of the specific act complained about—is it private or public in nature?—once it has been established the body has (some) public functions.

[121] The categorisation of bodies appears now, in light of the House of Lords decision in *YL*, above n 120, to be one that is functional in origin, and thus truer to the wording of s 6 than what Landau called the previous 'institutional-relational' approach of the earlier Court of Appeal decisions *Poplar Housing v Donoghue* [2001] EWCA.Civ 595 and *R (Heather) v Leonard Cheshire Foundation* [2002] EWCA Civ 366: see J Landau, 'Functional Public Authorities after YL' [2007] *PL* 630, 632.

[122] In *Aston Cantlow*, above n 119, at [7] and [12]—the only case of any note on pure public authorities—Lord Nicholls referred to pure authorities as being 'essentially a reference to a body whose nature is governmental in a broad sense of that expression [and] in respect of which the government is answerable [at Strasbourg]'. Factors which he outlined and which might assist in the 'instinctive classification' of a body as a core public authority included: possessing special powers or exercising statutory powers, democratic accountability, taking the place of central or local authorities, public funding in whole or in part, an obligation to act only in the public interest or providing a public service and a statutory constitution. The police were considered to be pure authorities by Lord Irvine (Hansard HL Deb 16 November 1997 col 1231) and in none of the various cases since October 2000 has a point been taken. In *Aston Cantlow*, Lord Nicholls specifically lists them (at [7]): contrast private security guards at a construction site.

might indicate the environmental harm attributed to GM food manufacture. In neither case can a protester rely on section 7(1)(a) to mount a claim directly against the company alleging a violation of their Convention rights as there is no duty of convention compliance imposed *directly* on purely private bodies.

(ii) The Position of Private Bodies

That is not to say that individual citizens, private firms—whether sole traders, partnerships or multi-national conglomerates—and unincorporated associations such as charities or NGOs cannot be liable for restricting the Convention rights of protesters if they are subjected to a peaceful protest and try to stop it. It is merely that section 6 gives victims no rights to challenge those bodies directly in court; this reflects the historic idea that states pose the greatest threat to liberty. On its face, the HRA says nothing about protecting individuals against breaches by other individuals. However, as we have seen, courts and tribunals are specifically defined as public authorities and so are bound by the section 6 duty when, for example, hearing cases between competing private litigants. This is the indirect horizontal effect of the HRA on the private sphere. Judges must decide cases or exercise their discretion in a way that accords with and gives effect to Convention rights; they would be in breach of their own duties under section 6 if they were to act in a manner that is not Convention compliant. Convention rights are therefore capable of 'biting' on private individuals not because they themselves are bound by section 6(1) but because judges are.[123] Not only does such a view have the imprimatur of government,[124] but case law has followed this approach. It is now firmly established that the HRA creates or confers on individuals no new cause of action—such as the tort of violating Convention rights—where none previously existed.[125] It is also equally clear that judges, where cases are brought to court on the basis of existing, established private law causes of action and remedies—in say tort or contract—will need to mould and develop those common law principles so as to ensure that neither party to the litigation is deprived of their Convention rights (or is restricted in the exercise of them) by the outcome.[126] Where this has been seen most is in the area of privacy. There, courts have felt obliged to develop the principles of confidentiality to protect against media intrusion while, it is true, not disproportionately restricting a newspaper's freedom of expression.[127]

How might this affect peaceful protest? It might mean demonstrators arguing that the rules relating to trespass should be developed to allow for some measure of peaceful protest on a third party's land or that nuisance should not automatically entitle someone to an injunction requiring a protest to end.[128] We shall consider these in chapter eight. We can

---

[123] See further Clayton and Tomlinson, *The Law of Human Rights*, above n 48, at paras 5.80–5.99.

[124] During debate, Lord Irvine indicated his view that although the government had 'not provided for the Convention rights to be directly justiciable between private individuals' (Hansard HL Deb 3rd December 1998 col 1231) he believed it was right 'as a matter of principle for the courts to have the duty of acting compatibly with the Convention not only in cases involving public authorities but also in developing the common law in deciding cases between individuals' (Hansard HL Deb 24 November 1997 col 783).

[125] *Campbell v MGN* [2004] UKHL 22 where it was expressly held that the HRA created no direct cause of action between private parties individuals, such as the press and an individual.

[126] *Venables and Thompson v News Group Newspapers* [2001] 1 All ER 908 (HC) Butler-Sloss P at [108]–[109] and [126].

[127] *Campbell*, above n 125, *McKennit v Ash* [2006] EWCA Civ 1714 and [2008] EWHC 1777 QB.

[128] In *Hunter v Canary Wharf* [1997] AC 655, Lord Cooke in his dissent thought that—in line with international human rights instruments—the common law of nuisance should be developed to allow residents, not solely those with a proprietary interest as has held the majority, to maintain an action.

see this in one of two examples above where the farm supplier would be asking the court as a section 6 public authority to re-write basic principles of English contract law so as to protect his independent right—conferred by a sovereign Parliament—to protest. In the other, the anti-war employee would be using the HRA to argue that it would not normally be fair for a private sector employer to dismiss an employee for a reason which amounted to an unjustified interference with that employee's right to protest.[129] This is not the development in the private sphere of common law *simpliciter* but instead the protesters would be arguing for a Convention-compatible meaning to be adopted in an 'essentially private law dispute arising from a relationship that is underpinned or informed by statute'.[130] This is not to say that either or both might succeed—it is unlikely either would[131]—but to illustrate how such claims might be brought.

(iii) (Possibly) Functional Bodies

Having dealt with the two extremes, we have accounted for most parties affected by a peaceful protest. Let us look at the position of those bodies that straddle the thornier middle ground; those that are neither purely public nor purely private. It is almost impossible to conceive—in the arena of protest—a *YL*-type decision—a decision restricting someone's ability to protest is taken by a private company carrying out the state's own statutory or public functions on behalf of the state under some form of contracting-out mechanism.[132] If one were—eg the police enlisting the paid help of a private security firm to undertake the policing of a protest[133]—then on the view of the majority of the House of Lords in *YL*, the decision taken by the private security firm would be outside the confines of the controlling influence of the HRA, though the police themselves would remain liable as a pure authority for any decisions they took.

Three more bodies deserve attention. It seems almost certain that state schools would meet most or all of Lord Nicholls's criteria in *Aston Cantlow* and would have no private functions: they would be pure authorities.[134] If they tried to restrict protesters worried about the employment of a convicted paedophile at the school, they could only do so proportionately. Universities and hospitals might not be in the same category; they might be thought of as performing a mixture of roles or functions.[135] A university educating 18–21 year olds might well be seen as performing a public function, but when academics

---

[129] See *X v Y* [2004] EWCA Civ 662, *cf Pay v Lancashire Probation Service* [2004] ICR 187.

[130] D Mead, 'Rights, relationships and retrospectivity: the impact of Convention rights on pre-existing private law relationships following *Wilson* and *Ghaidan*' [2005] PL 459, 460.

[131] In the latter, the farm supplier, the chances of success, given freedom of (and not to) contract would seem to be very low. That said, many proponents would argue that putting rights at the forefront of legal discourse—perhaps even leading to the overturning of centuries of orthodoxy—is exactly what the HRA is about.

[132] *YL*, above n 120. The decision has been subjected to almost wholesale academic criticism: see as examples Landau, above n 121, S Palmer, 'Public private and the Human Rights Act 1998—an ideological divide' (2007) 66 *Cambridge Law Journal* 559 and A Williams, '*YL v Birmingham City Council*: contracting out and "functions of a public nature"' [2007] *EHRLR* 524.

[133] A more complicated issue would be if a pure authority such as a university paid for private security to control a student sit-in rather than use the police or its own security team.

[134] It seems to be accepted by all that private schools would be outwith the reach of s 6. This must be because the act of educating children *pursuant to a contract* is one that is private—educating children *per se* must be engaging in a public function.

[135] It is thought that regulatory and privatised bodies will be functional bodies: in the case of the former body Railtrack, its public function would be in respect of rail safety but it would engage in private functions if buying and selling land: see Lord Irvine at Committee stage Hansard, HL Deb 24 November 1997, col 796 and *Cameron v Network Rail* [2006] EWHC 1133.

undertake research, especially if that is privately-funded, that would no more be a public function than if a pharmaceutical company undertook it in-house. A university must then be a functional authority with a mix of public and private functions. Similarly, hospitals may perform NHS operations and private operations under the same roof, meaning they cannot be pure authorities.[136] Both the university and hospital then would only be liable under section 6 for acts which are public in nature.[137] What is the position for a group demonstrating to publicise their opposition to abortions carried out in NHS hospitals or protesting about animal experimentation at a university laboratory? The problem is this. Under section 6(5) the university or the hospital would only be liable for a breach of section 6(1) if the *act* they perform (decision they take?) when restricting peaceful protest were not private. How—and on what basis—should we categorise decisions such as banning from premises, refusing entry, applying for an injunction alleging harassment of its employees or suing for damages for the economic tort of inducing breach of contract?[138]

Discussion of the qualities that make an act private—or public—is beyond the confines of a book on peaceful protest and on which limited HRA ink has so far been spilled. It is quite clear that just because an act is performed by a state or quasi-state entity that will not render it 'public' in nature—otherwise what would be the point of section 6(5)? Quite possibly, the benchmark of 'publicness' is the ability to do something that ordinary citizens cannot perform. On that reading, the examples above are no more than the exercise of private law rights: we can all decide we do not want someone on our land[139] and we can all sue for damages—there is nothing quintessentially public about a hospital doing so. What *is* it about those acts that might make them public in nature if done by (using Lord Nicholls's words) an 'instinctively' governmental body? It cannot be that an act is public in nature if it has a (detrimental) effect on Convention rights: that would be circular and would again deprive the qualification in section 6(5) of any meaning. Functional bodies would be liable for all acts, even private ones, where that act defeated a Convention right. Since no one would be bringing a case unless their rights were affected, this would bring all acts within the ambit of section 6, not what Parliament intended.

Let us dwell here no longer; for our purposes the issue is largely academic. Even if a university or hospital is deemed to be performing private acts when it evicts those who protest on its property or refuses entry to them or sues for an injunction or damages, that does not deprive the protesters of a right of challenge. As we saw above, they may call on the court to mould private, common law remedies using the notion of indirect horizontal effect. What it does do is to deprive them of the right to challenge that decision directly using the sword of section 7(1)(a), since judicial review can lie only against public authorities. It is the mechanism under section 7 that we now turn to.

[136] See Lord Irvine, *ibid*, col 811. On the same basis, is this because the act of private treatment is a private one or because treating the ill is a public function? It is submitted that the reason a task is performed cannot alter its public or private flavour (*cf* Lord Scott and Lord Mance in *YL*, above n 120, who, as Landau points out, could be read as introducing a third distinguishing criteria, motivation: Landau, above n 636) and so it must be that where a surgeon operates because they have been paid to rather than because of any statutory duty, we alter our perception of the nature of the act. Fully private hospitals would be outwith the HRA on either score: any possibly public functions they perform involve acts of a private nature.

[137] It must be mentioned that in none of the many cases since 2000 involving any of these three bodies has it ever been doubted that they are amenable to review for their decisions as public authorities but in none has the basis of liability been established.

[138] These latter two private law remedies are discussed in detail in chap. 7.

[139] We shall leave aside for now the issues surrounding use of land belonging to others for holding a protest, whether or not one group is able to use land belonging to a third party for a protest raises significant and different issues that we shall consider below in chap. 4.

(iv) How are Convention Rights Enforced by Victims?

Victims may lay claim to their Convention rights, including obviously the rights in Articles 10 and 11, by using section 7(1) of the HRA as either a sword or a shield.

(a) Who is a Victim?

Only those who are victims—defined in section 7(7)—may challenge public authority decisions as being potentially in breach of section 6. The test is explicitly the same test as applied at Strasbourg under Article 34. Under Article 34, individual applications may only be brought by persons, groups of persons or NGOs 'claiming to be a victim of the violation'. Broadly, this means only those actually and directly affected by violations (or where the victim is deceased, their relatives[140]), removing from NGOs the right to bring cases on behalf of others. They may only do so where they themselves have suffered a direct violation—their own march banned, their group disbanded or their advertisements censored.[141] The only dilution of the strict rule is that Strasbourg has also permitted claims by members of a class all of whom could have been affected by the restriction or upon all of whom it can be said there was a chilling effect on their potential activities.[142] The test in section 7(7) is narrower than the test applied at common law for judicial review: it leaves no room for public interest challenges by pressure groups who, provided they fulfill certain criteria, are taken as demonstrating a 'sufficient interest' within Part 54 of the Rules of the Supreme Court.[143] The effect of section 7(7) is that pressure groups such as Liberty would be unable to bring a representative public interest challenge for breaches of the right to protest unless the group itself were directly affected by a restriction.[144]

(b) Using Section 7(1) as a Sword and a Shield

Having established how potential challengers assert their standing, let us consider how claims might be brought and the sort of claims they might be. Section 7(1)(a) allows victims to 'bring proceedings under this Act in the appropriate court or tribunal'—the sword—and section 7(1)(b) allows victims to 'rely on the Convention right . . . concerned in any legal proceedings', the shield.

In practice, this means the possibility of protesters using section 7(1)(a):

1. To apply for judicial review against a public authority arguing a breach of the duty contained in section 6(1). There are many examples in just the area of peaceful protest. One would be a challenge to the imposition of conditions on a public assembly as being a disproportionate restriction on protest as occurred in *R (Brehony) v Chief Constable of Greater Manchester*.[145] Equally, victims could seek judicial review not just of Ministers' decisions which they allege are violations of the right of peaceful protest for being

---

[140] *McCann v UK*, above n 42.

[141] They may be heard as *amicus curiae* at Strasbourg as was the UK human rights campaigning group Liberty in *Murray v United Kingdom* (1996) 22 EHRR 29.

[142] *Klass v Federal Republic of Germany* (1978) 2 EHRR 214 at [33]. In *Dudgeon v United Kingdom* (1981) 4 EHRR 149 the applicant had not been prosecuted but he was permitted to challenge the Northern Irish criminalisation of homosexual conduct even between consenting adults in private.

[143] Most notably *R v Secretary of State for Social Security ex parte JCWI* [1996] 4 All ER 385 and *R v Secretary of State for Foreign and Commonwealth Affairs ex parte World Development Movement* [2001] 1 All ER 908.

[144] In practical terms, such groups would very likely either be able to put up one 'victim' for a case and then act for or advise them or seek leave to intervene as a third party.

[145] *R (Brehony) v Chief Constable of Greater Manchester* [2005] EWHC 640 (Admin).

disproportionate decisions, but of secondary legislation put forward by them. A Minister's duty under section 6 to act compatibly with the right of peaceful protest—that is not to act disproportionately in respect of it—extends to all decisions they take, including the decision to promulgate it. Such a challenge would be to the vires of the secondary legislation. The argument would not be that the byelaw, statutory instrument or regulation is ultra vires the parent Act but that it is ultra vires the Minister's powers for being a breach of Article 11, on the basis that it is a disproportionate restriction on the right. A good example is the successful challenge by the Aldermaston Women's Peace Camp to MoD byelaws restricting its fortnightly weekend camp on controlled areas at Aldermaston, the atomic weapons establishment.[146] Alternatively, though it could never result in a quashing order given the terms of section 3(2) of the HRA (unlike for secondary legislation), protesters could still apply for judicial review of primary legislation seeking the political remedy of a section 4 declaration of incompatibility.
2. To sue a public authority in tort for damages for breach of section 6 statutory duty.

Alternatively, protesters could use section 7(1)(b):

3. To institute proceedings, against either public or private bodies, using an existing, recognised head of liability—founded on statute or common law—and then utilising the HRA to argue that the case should be decided in a way that preserves the victim's Convention rights. This would be our farm equipment supplier suing the GM company for breach of contract—indirect horizontal effect—arguing (perhaps) that the condition should be void as a matter of public policy as being a restraint on Convention rights enshrined by Parliament[147] or that condition be read as only forbidding protesting activities that can be seen as directly harmful to the company.[148] This would also cover the unfair dismissal of the arms manufacturer employees, a 'publicly infused private law'[149] action based on section 98 of the Employment Rights Act 1996.[150]
4. To call on the Convention collaterally as a defence to claims brought against them (at common law or under statutory provisions) by a third party, whether private individual or government body. This would encompass protesters defending both private law claims and criminal charges. Both may provide fruitful opportunities in the field of public order and peaceful protest. For example, in the domestic proceedings that became *Steel and Morris v UK* (the so-called 'McLibel Two') at Strasbourg, the Court of Appeal was asked (but refused) to re-shape the tort of defamation so as to preclude multinational corporations from being able to sue in libel.[151] In *Percy v DPP*, a peace protester

---

[146] *Tabernacle v Secretary of State for Defence* [2009] EWCA Civ 23 (Laws, Wall and Stanley Burnton LJJ).

[147] See, for a similar argument about a testamentary disposition, *Blathwayte v Cawley* [1976] AC 397 (HL).

[148] In reality, the only case that has come close is *Austin v Commissioner of Police for the Metropolis* [2009] UKHL 5, the case arising out of what is now known as 'kettling' at the May Day disturbances in 2001. At first instance and to some extent in the Court of Appeal, the claim was for damages for false imprisonment at common law. The action brought by the detained protesters, and the case in part revolved around the defence of necessity—and the extent to which it should be adapted and developed in light of the right of peaceful protest a and liberty under Art 5. We discuss *Austin* in detail in chapter seven.

[149] Mead, above n 130.

[150] By contrast, claims—by the police or other authorities—that judges should extend the reach of the common law so as better or more easily to control protests would be met by Lord Bingham's adjuration in *Laporte*: 'assessment of whether a new restriction meets the exacting Convention test of necessity calls in the first instance for the wide consultation and inquiry and democratic consideration which should characterise the legislative process, not the more narrowly focused process of judicial decision. This is not a field in which judicial development of the law is at all appropriate': *R (Laporte) v Chief Constable of Gloucestershire* [2006] UKHL 55 at [52].

[151] Court of Appeal summary taken from the ECtHR decision (2005) 41 EHRR 22 at [30]–[32].

successfully challenged her conviction for using threatening, abusive or insulting words likely to cause harassment, alarm or distress (contrary to section 5 of the Public Order Act 1986) after she daubed 'Stop Star Wars' on the US flag and placed it on the road outside a US Air Force airbase. It was held that the magistrates who originally convicted her had given insufficient weight to her rights under Article 10.

The same scenario can give rise to opportunities to use Convention rights as both a sword and shield. As we shall see, under sections 12 and 13 of the POA 1986 the police are able to impose conditions on public processions so as to be able to control them on public order grounds. If a protester feels that a condition has been imposed that is disproportionate, they may challenge it in advance by judicial review, using the sword of section 7(1)(a) to argue the condition violates Article 11 (and so the police in imposing it are in breach of section 6 of the HRA). Alternatively, they may wait until they are arrested for taking part in a march knowingly in breach of a condition, and set up its disproportionality/illegality as a shield to any charges brought.

(v) How is Convention Compliance Assessed?

It is axiomatic but public authorities will only be acting unlawfully under section 6(1) if they 'act in a way that is incompatible with a Convention right'.[152] What does it mean to say that a public authority has acted in a way that is incompatible with the right of peaceful protest?

Primarily—for the court on a challenge at least—this involves assessing the proportionality of any measure that purports to, or does, restrict or limit the right to protest. Most rights in the ECHR, as we have seen, are not absolute. If a council intervenes in an assembly by banning a march, or the police interfere with the right of free speech by making arrests for offensive placards at demonstrations, these will not per se breach either Article 10 or 11. It will only do so if the measure fails to satisfy the three-pronged 'claw-back' test that we looked at earlier in this chapter:

- Is it prescribed by law?
- Does it seek to achieve a listed social aim?
- Is it necessary in a democratic society?

The public authority imposing the restriction must satisfy the court—whether on a judicial review challenge under section 7(1)(a) or (if Article 11 is used collaterally) under section 7(1)(b) as a defence—that each part is made out in turn. Defeat on any one will mean the measure is unlawful. That said, success or failure tends to turn on the last, with argument focusing on the proportionality of the proposed measure in terms of an external and retro-

---

[152] Although see s 6(2) which provides a measure of exculpation from s 6(1): section 6(1) is inapplicable 'to an act if (a) as the result of one or more provisions of primary legislation, the authority could not have acted differently; or (b) in the case of one or more provisions of, or made under, primary legislation which cannot be read or given effect in a way which is compatible with the Convention rights, the authority was acting so as to give effect to or enforce those provisions'. The effect is that the duty of Convention compliance only applies where public authorities have discretion, or a choice, first as to whether or not to act and second, as to what act(s) to perform or decisions to take. If instead of discretion a public authority is required to act or to decide and then to act in only one particular way or to take only one particular decision, the public authority will not be acting unlawfully even if its action or decision means the restriction of someone's Convention rights: see eg *R (Bono) v Harlow District Council* [2002] EWHC 423 (Admin).

spective judicial assessment.[153] Is it one that is shown to be suitable, necessary and balanced?[154] We can see that the courts have constructed a new standard for review. The ability to utilise Convention rights as a sword has brought with it a change

> from enforcing public duties, the traditional judicial review approach, to protecting the public rights of the individual, the new HRA approach, [which] has meant that the focus of the courts has moved 180 degrees from the public body to the individual.[155]

We have moved from *Wednesbury* irrationality-based review, through and past super-*Wednesbury* review, and ended up with a much more fleshed-out proportionality review, one that is much closer to a review on the merits. The new approach can be seen most clearly in *R (Daly) v Secretary of State for the Home Department*,[156] as interpreted in *Gough v CC Derbyshire*.[157] *Daly* involved an assessment of the lawfulness of a blanket policy relating to searches of prison cells and examination of correspondence with a lawyer. The outcome depended on the legitimacy and hence proportionality of the restriction on a prisoner's Article 8 rights. Lord Steyn adopted the formula put forward in the Privy Council case of *de Freitas*.[158] He concluded that the court should ask whether

> (i) the legislative objective is sufficiently important to justify limiting a fundamental right; (ii) the measures designed to meet the legislative objective are rationally connected to it; and (iii) the means used to impair the right or freedom are no more than is necessary to accomplish the objective.

The contrast between proportionality or HRA-review and traditional review is that the latter is more intense.

> First, the doctrine of proportionality may require the reviewing court to assess the balance which the decision maker has struck, not merely whether it is within the range of rational or reasonable decisions. Secondly, the proportionality test may go further than the traditional grounds of review inasmuch as it may require attention to be directed to the relative weight accorded to interests and considerations. Thirdly, even the heightened scrutiny test developed in [*ex parte Smith*] is not necessarily appropriate to the protection of human rights . . . In other words, the intensity of the review, in similar cases, is guaranteed by the twin requirements that the limitation of the right was

---

[153] Public law duties, such as those under s 6, can equally have internal, prospective value: before taking any decision public bodies should ask themselves—'is this compatible with Convention'. Public law decision makers should—for *each* decision that affects the right to protest—assess internally as follows by asking: What am I trying to achieve? Will X achieve what I want it to do? What other means are available? What is the effect on individual Y of choosing option A over option B? Is there sufficient reason to justify option A over option B? If so, what is it and can I demonstrate it? The move from negative residual liberties to positive rights means that rights can only be limited or removed if a public authority makes a case that it is proportionate and legitimate to do so; if it cannot, the action should be declared unlawful. It might also have been thought to mean that unless in advance the body addresses the need for careful tailoring—using the least drastic means, with carefully tailored restrictions, not overly broad and based on individual circumstances—a measure would fall foul. This was not the view taken by the House of Lords and its 'outcomes is all approach' in *R (Begum) v Governors of Denbigh High School* [2006] UKHL 15: see See D Mead, 'Judicial mis-behavin': a defence of process-based review of public authority decisions under the Human Rights Act' (Norwich Law School Working Papers 08/02), at: lawwp.webapp2.uea.ac.uk/wp/index.php/workingpapers/issue/view/14 (accessed 2 July 2009).
[154] M Supperstone and J Coppel, 'Judicial review after the Human Rights Act' [1999] *EHRLR* 301, 313.
[155] Lord Woolf, British Academy Lecture October 2002: 'Human Rights: Have the Public Benefitted?' available at: www.proc.britac.ac.uk/cgi-bin/somsid.cgi?page=121p301&type=header (accessed 2 July 2009). In turn this does not seem to have provoked great changes in judicial investigation despite it seeming to presuppose an increased likelihood of judges analysing and evaluating the means used and alternatives open to a public law decision makers.
[156] *R (Daly) v Secretary of State for the Home Department* [2001] 2 WLR 1622 (HL) at [26]–[28] (Lord Steyn).
[157] *Gough v Chief Constable of Derbyshire* [2002] EWCA Civ 351 at [68].
[158] *De Freitas v Permanent Minister of Agriculture, Fisheries Lands and Housing* [1999] 1 AC 69 (PC) 80.

necessary in a democratic society, in the sense of meeting a pressing social need, and the question whether the interference was really proportionate to the legitimate aim being pursued.

The qualification added by *Gough* is that restrictions on rights (here, Football Banning Orders) could only lawfully be imposed after giving individual consideration to each individual involved: only then would they be a proportionate restriction on freedom of movement. The effect of *Daly* and *Gough* is that blanket approaches to the policing of public order are likely to be susceptible to challenge on human rights grounds as being disproportionate interferences with Articles 10 or 11.[159] Thus banning all marches in an area or arresting all in one group for public order offences may be met with the claim (if challenged under section 7(1)(a)) or the defence (under section 7(1)(b) if charged with an offence) that the measure was not rationally connected (*Daly*) or imposed without individual consideration (*Gough*) to each prospective protester. In a similar fashion, decisions taken in relation to protests where alternative, less restrictive or less intrusive measures could have achieved the same result will also be disproportionate.[160]

We considered the key Strasbourg concept of the margin of appreciation earlier, a judicial construction influenced by matters such as European heterogeneity and state sovereignty, and reflecting a desire to ensure continued adherence to the ECHR where members states may only do so if they know they will not be held in breach for every minor deviation from a pan-European 'norm'. Depicted thus, it is easy to see how the concept can and must have limited use in a national setting. Domestic courts *do*, though, permit public authorities room to manoeuvre, but under the autonomous concept of judicial deference—what was referred to in 1998 as the 'discretionary area of judgement in relation to policy decisions [that reflects the fact that other bodies] are better placed than the judiciary to decide'.[161] Deference may work at the level of legislative choice, such as framing or wording an Act. Examples would be *Brown v Stott*[162] or *International Transport Roth Gmbh v Secretary of State for the Home Department*.[163] Alternatively, it may work at the level of executive decision-making or administrative rule-making as in *R (A) v Secretary of State for the Home Department*[164] or *R (Prolife Alliance) v BBC*.[165] At a wider constitutional level, the concept of deference raises concerns and tensions that need not concern us overly in this book.[166] Whatever can be said on that, those studying peaceful protest need to be aware of the possibility that judges may defer to the choices of Parliament, the police and government—though this tends to be done more explicitly than the Strasbourg Court on the margin of appreciation.

---

[159] See under the Canadian Charter *RJR-McDonald v Canada (AG)* [1993] 3 SCR 199.

[160] In fact, a decision might be disproportionate in one of three ways. Though it is far from accurate, we might better see this mathematically. If a restriction cannot ever achieve the social goal—say preventing crime—because a restriction is imposed too late it will be disproportionate. If that measure could achieve, say, a 75% prevention of crime but a measure that was only 50% as restrictive could also do so, the first measure will be disproportionate. If that second measure could still achieve a 66% prevention of crime but was still only 50% as restrictive, then there is a strong argument that the first measure is still disproportionate as the losses still outweigh the gains in comparison.

[161] D Pannick, 'Principles of interpretation of Convention rights under the Human Rights Act and the discretionary area of judgment' [1999] PL 545.

[162] *Brown v Stott* [2001] 2 WLR 817 (HL).

[163] *International Transport Roth Gmbh v Secretary of State for the Home Department* [2002] EWCA Civ 158.

[164] *R (A) v Secretary of State for the Home Department* [2004] UKHL 56.

[165] *R (Prolife Alliance) v British Broadcasting Corp* [2003] UKHL 23.

[166] It will suffice that this partially articulated concept currently provides yet another battleground for discussion: does judicial 'interference' diminish the concepts of the rule of law and separation of powers (thus justifying the need for deference) or is a failure to regulate government (and perhaps legislature) by employing deference an abdication of judicial duty and constitutional responsiblity?

IV. Conclusion: The Likely Influence of the Human Rights Act on Peaceful Protest

The foregoing should have provided us with the tools with which we can start to assess the changes to the 'traditional' regulation of public order and policing of peaceful protest in later chapters. Before turning to look at that in depth, we might reflect briefly on how the HRA might play a role in 'bringing home' the right of peaceful protest. We might here usefully reflect on the framework provided by Lord Bingham in *Laporte*.[167] Much of what he says draws on what we might call ECHR basics, but as a succinct distillation of the position, it provides a good starting point.

> Article 10 confers a right to freedom of expression and article 11 to freedom of peaceful assembly. Neither right is absolute. The exercise of these rights may be restricted if the restriction is prescribed by law, necessary in a democratic society and directed to any one of a number of specified ends. The Strasbourg court has recognised that exercise of the right to freedom of assembly and exercise of the right to free expression are often, in practice, closely associated. The fundamental importance of these rights has been stressed. [His Lordship here referred to cases such as *Steel v UK* (1998) 28 EHRR 603, *Ezelin v France* (1991) 14 EHRR 362 and *Ziliberberg v Moldova* (App 61821/00) ECtHR inadmissibility decision 4 May 2004]. It is the duty of member states to take reasonable and appropriate measures to enable lawful demonstrations to proceed peacefully ... Thus the protection of the articles may be denied if the demonstration is unauthorised and unlawful ... or if conduct is such as actually to disturb public order ... But (*Ziliberberg*) 'an individual does not cease to enjoy the right to peaceful assembly as a result of sporadic violence or other punishable acts committed by others in the course of the demonstration, if the individual in question remains peaceful in his or her own intentions or behaviour' ... Any prior restraint on freedom of expression calls for the most careful scrutiny ... The Strasbourg court will wish to be satisfied not merely that a state exercised its discretion reasonably, carefully and in good faith, but also that it applied standards in conformity with Convention standards and based its decisions on an acceptable assessment of the relevant facts.

The imaginary Mass Meetings Act 2009 regulates indoor meetings of more than five people. Under section 1 anyone who 'without reasonable excuse' organises or participates in a meeting 'not in open space' at which five or more people are present commits an offence unless the organiser has first obtained a meetings licence from their local council. Clearly, those hosting a party would claim they had a 'reasonable excuse'. What about those arranging or merely attending a public meeting in a village hall to rally opposition to a road-building scheme? Anyone charged after attending would be entitled to rely in those criminal proceedings on their Convention right—collaterally under section 7(1)(b)—to protest. In effect, they would be constructing a defence along these lines: 'My reasonable excuse is Article 11'.[168] The phrase 'without reasonable excuse' must under section 3 of the HRA be 'read and given effect' so as to include as a reasonable excuse the right of peaceful protest. There is little complication in that and it may not have been so greatly different before 1998.

What, though, if there was no 'reasonable excuse' defence: is all lost? Unless it would defeat the overall scheme of the 2009 Act or it has wider ramifications—such as cost, social implications or practical consequences—it seems from *Mendoza* that courts should strive

---

[167] *Laporte*, above n 150, at [35]–[37], ECHR citations omitted.
[168] See, as an example of this in practice, *Connolly v DPP* [2007] EWHC 237 (Admin).

(unless it is impossible?) to construe the Act compatibly (assuming on its face it is not[169]). At its simplest, 'a reasonable excuse' defence could be read in or words along the lines of 'unless to convict someone merely attending would constitute a disproportionate restriction on the right of peaceful assembly under Article 11'. If the organisers sought a licence and were refused or onerous conditions were imposed, they could challenge the council's decision under section 7(1)(a)—using Article 11 as a sword to have either the refusal or the onerous conditions struck down and, for the refusal, an order that a new decision be reached that properly took account of everyone's rights under Article 11. We shall consider in the next chapter whether the group could force the hand of a reluctant landowner so as to be allowed to protest on his or her land. If, after the meeting, the group decided to target the private road-building company who in turn might respond with attempts to obtain injunctions—based on harassment under the Protection From Harassment Act (PFHA) 1997—or to prevent repeat nuisances outside their HQ, this is where the courts would be prevailed upon to develop or mould (respectively) the statutory remedy contained in the 1997 Act or tort at common law so as properly to balance the rights of the protesting group and the company. Similarly, if the group decided, instead of picketing and leafletting, to adopt more obstructive or disruptive direct action techniques, they could still call on their right of peaceful protest if charged, say, with aggravated trespass under section 68 CJPOA 1994 . . . but would stand little chance of success. That is because of the very limited protection given by the ECtHR to that sort of protest activity. It is to that that we shall now turn.

---

[169] We shall address whether or not it is in fact a breach of Article 11 to require prior authorisation for meetings and marches in chapter three. If it is not, the Act on its face is compatible and no further issue arises.

3

Strasbourg Case Law on the Right to Peaceful Protest

Article 11 of the European Convention guarantees freedom of peaceful assembly and of association. It states that

> 11(1) Everyone has the right to freedom of peaceful assembly and to freedom of association with others, including the right to form and to join trade unions for the protection of his interests.
>
> 11(2) No restrictions shall be placed on the exercise of these rights other than such as are prescribed by law and are necessary in a democratic society in the interests of national security or public safety, for the prevention of disorder or crime, for the protection of health or morals or for the protection of the rights and freedoms of others. This article shall not prevent the imposition of lawful restrictions on the exercise of these rights by members of the armed forces, of the police or of the administration of the State.

I. Introduction

This chapter considers those Strasbourg judgments and admissibility decisions—of both the Court and the former European Commission for Human Rights (EComHR)—which feature a restriction on a protest of some form or other. The aim is to establish the scope and extent of the right of peaceful protest at Strasbourg level which we can draw on for our domestic analysis in chapters four to eight. This chapter is in two main parts. The first part draws heavily on my own 2007 content study, which provided some basic quantitative, statistical data on the right.[1] The second comprises the bulk and analyses the constituent parts of Article 11(1) and the claw-backs of Article 11(2). It is not intended to be a detailed study of cases, case by case, but rather of general principles, issues and themes extracted from them. Summaries of facts, outcomes and reasoning are contained in Appendix III.

The Court has long recognised that the right of peaceful assembly enshrined in Article 11 is a fundamental right in a democratic society and, like the right to freedom of expression, one of its foundations. Not only is democracy a fundamental feature of the European public order but the Convention was designed to promote and maintain the ideals and values of a democratic society. Democracy, the Court has stressed, is the only political model contemplated by the ECHR and the only one compatible with it. By virtue of the wording of

---

[1] D Mead, 'The right to peaceful protest under the European Convention on Human Rights—a content study of Strasbourg case law' [2007] *European Human Rights Law Review* 345.

Article 11(2), the only necessity capable of justifying an interference with the rights enshrined in that Article is one that may claim to spring from 'democratic society'.[2]

Some qualifications and caveats are needed at the outset. First, there is no right of peaceful protest in the ECHR. It is used in this book as shorthand for the amalgam of the right of peaceful assembly under Article 11 and those aspects of freedom of political expression under Article 10 that can truly be said to be forms of protest. This chapter will in fact address a few Article 10 cases that relate to protest but in which there is no overlap with Article 11, either in terms of the factual scenario or the way the application is framed. Secondly, this is not a study of peaceful assembly case law: cases in which applicants have claimed a breach of Article 11 when an assembly was banned or conditions imposed have been excluded from our survey where that assembly was not going to engage in any form of protest.[3] Last and conversely, neither is this a study of Article 11 case law: we will not look at the right to associate under Article 11 save where it is incidental to an actual protest.[4] This is a study of peaceful protest. In order to elicit some principles, all those cases in which one issue was people 'protesting' needed to be found.[5] That led, in my original content study, to some definitional problems. Given that researching all Article 11 cases would have been simple to conduct but would have produced results of limited value to the project, the first task was conceptualising all 'protest' cases so as to identify them.[6] In short, that study—and this chapter's more detailed qualitative survey—adopted four criteria as the hallmarks of protest to identify not just the 'archetypal core' but those cases on the penumbra. These four related to motive, forum, content and actor.

> First, the activity must be politically participative. Protesting connotes a deliberate choice to contribute directly to influencing policy choices and outcomes by becoming constructively engaged with an issue ... [Thus] protest, as we think about it, is located properly in the public, rather than private, domain. This means, secondly, that the protest is directed towards the body that is capable of making—or preventing—the change (government, parliament, multi-national company) or at the public seeking to persuade against or cajole for change ... thirdly, the subject-matter of the protest has to be of wider concern rather than being primarily peculiar or more important to a single individual, what Bedau calls 'personal hand-washing'. Fourthly and last, protest runs alongside and outside (perhaps even counters?) formal party structures, whether supplanting or supplementing the formal democratic system ... [recognising] that at its heart protest is generally about airing grievances because 'traditional' politics is incapable of responding.[7]

---

[2] Examples abound: see *Christian Democratic People's Party v Moldova* (App 28793/02) ECtHR judgment 14 February 2006, at [62]–[63] and *Makhmaduv v Russia* (App 35082/04) ECtHR 26 July 2007, at [63].

[3] This would include cases such as *Pendragon v UK* (App 31416/96) EComHR inadmissibility decision 19 October 1998 (the use of Stonehenge by druids for the summer solstice) and others where religious observance meetings were disrupted such as *Barankevich v Russia* (App10519/03) ECtHR, judgment 26 July 2007, violation of Arts 9 and 11.

[4] There were, in late 2006, about 30 or so cases where individuals were prevented from forming political or campaigning / protest groups. The key principles can be discerned from Grand Chamber decisions in cases such as *Gorzelik v Poland* (2005) 40 EHRR 4 at [88]–[96] and *Refah Partisi v Turkey* (2003) 37 EHRR 1 at [86]–[105] and the Court judgment in *United Turkish Communist Party v Turkey* (1998) 26 EHRR 121 at [42]–[47].

[5] There are a few cases in which protesters have been punished by their own domestic courts or action taken against them yet their Strasbourg challenge was not founded on an alleged violation of the right to peaceful protest. These cases do not feature either. They would include, for example, *Custers and Others v Denmark* (App 11843/03) ECtHR, judgment 3 May 2007 (unsuccessful application by members of Greenpeace complaining that their convictions for trespassing on a USAF airbase breached Art 7), *Sahin v Turkey* (App 68253/01) ECtHR, judgment 21 December 2006 (excessive use of force at a demonstration as a breach of Art 3) and *Cetinkaya v Turkey* (App 3921/02) ECtHR, judgment 23 January 2007 (possible violations of Art 5 for six-day police detention following arrest at an unauthorised demonstration). The case reports give no indication why no application under Art 11 was made.

[6] Mead, above n 1, 347.

[7] ibid, 349–50.

This definition is by no means complete or even workable: why did the study exclude cases where those campaigning for the return of an MP were subjected to sanction, unless it was either a minority MP fighting vested state interests or party officials canvassing for the election of an avowedly anti-government MP?[8] Why should a protest against human rights abuses in the form of self-immolation be a protest but emailing one's MP not be seen in the same light? That said, it might provide a useful starting point for thinking more conceptually and philosophically about the nature of protest, about political participation and about how protest and protesters are labelled. We shall return to some of these matters as we conclude this book. At a more mundane level, although domestic law has largely managed without needing a definition of protest, given its historical focus on (public) order maintenance and the absence of positive rights at common law, in 2005 Parliament legislated for the first time to regulate not marches or assemblies, more easily captured, but 'demonstrations'. If the police are able lawfully to take action against unauthorised demonstrators in the vicinity of Parliament, under sections 132–136 of the Serious Organised Crime and Police Act 2005, then they surely need to be able to determine what constitutes a 'demonstration'? Why is Brian Haw, with his long-running solo campaign against the Iraq War in Westminster Square, a 'demonstrator', whereas Mark Wallinger, whose nearby Tate Modern installation exactly replicated Haw's peace camp, is an 'artist'?[9] Such definitional value judgements are clearly problematic for all concerned—from those who enforce the law, who need to know the extent of their powers, to those against whom it is enforced, who need to know the extent of the power available against them. As well as being value-laden, it is easy to see too how protest is context specific. My sitting on a seat on a bus might be thought of as a million miles from the sorts of matters we will be engaged with ... But if I am black and I sit on a seat reserved for whites, at a time of segregation and racial inequality, this becomes very much a political act of protest and dissent.

Cases reaching Strasbourg under Article 11 are not confined to assemblies in the narrow sense of 'public meeting' but have encompassed, more widely, marches and a host of other forms of protest activity. Within that latter category, there is some overlap with the wider more general right of freedom of expression, both being forms of communicative political activity. Which of those articles should govern any given scenario is one matter we shall consider below along with assessing the scope of the right contained in Article 11; the extent of any positive duties under Article 11; the issue of counter-demonstrations and the hecklers' charter; and the role and duties of the police. We shall also consider what Strasbourg has had to say about qualifications to the right under Article 11(2).

II. A Content Study of Protest Cases

This part largely summarises my own content study of 72 cases, updated to take account of 25 more decided up to May 2009. Appendix III produces this data in tabulated form.[10] It

---

[8] Thus *Csánics v Hungary* (App 12188/06) ECtHR judgment 20 January 2009 was excluded from consideration. During a labour dispute, a union leader made 'colourful' comments in the media and at a demonstration about the managing director of the company taking over his own, comments which were offensive and damaged managing director's reputation. The sanction imposed €300 was held to be disproportionate as the comments, though heated, did not overstep the mark. Though it is arguable, this is not protest on our definition but a private denunciation.

[9] Mead above n 1, 348 fn 17.

[10] *ibid*, 352–8. I am grateful to Sweet and Maxwell, the publishers of the European Human Rights Law Review, for allowing me to reproduce the tabulated data.

sets out all the peaceful protest cases to have entered the Strasbourg system, including those declared inadmissible, struck out or which resulted in a friendly settlement, as well as all cases to have reached the Court for judgment. These were obtained after searching the Council of Europe's HUDOC database using various search terms (such as 'assembly' and 'protest') against both Article 10 and Article 11.[11] The cases that were discovered were then categorised A–D, to represent, in turn: demonstrations, assemblies and rallies (A); marches and processions (B); persuasive or symbolic protest (C); and obstructive, disruptive or intimidatory protest (D). This was largely a judgement-call, not especially refined and with some obvious overlaps.[12]

The first matter is to note the spread of states against which applications have been brought. Turkey by far outnumbers any other but there are several notable exceptions. States against which no applications have been brought include Sweden, Denmark, Spain, Italy and Belgium while France, Switzerland, Norway, the Netherlands and the Czech Republic have two or fewer. The tendency has been for newer signatories—from the former Slavic states and former soviet bloc—to dominate alongside Turkey, which with the United Kingdom comprises about half the Court's caseload. For demonstration protests, recent years have seen the appearance of Moldova, Armenia, Azerbaijan, Hungary and Bulgaria as well as the continued presence of Austria, France, Finland and the UK. This is probably representative of the ECHR as a whole: newer members are being taken to task on matters long since reformed in longer-standing members.

This pattern raises questions beyond a book of this nature and length. First, it clearly cannot be the case—we might properly assume—that protesters are better protected in Italy than in the UK or that Italians and the French have less to protest about. What might account for the disparity? My own study offered four possibilities for further exploration: cultural differences as to what might be an acceptable level of protest; different levels of deference to political institutions; differences in the political mainstreaming of protest; and institutional responsiveness to dissent.[13] For some—such as Turkey—the data represents the attempt to cope with underlying geo-political dimensions, tensions and even fragility. But of course Turkey is not alone in this yet features very heavily. Similarly and this is our second point, the data does not allow us to measure the reality of pan-European protest. The study cannot capture the fact that in many countries a good deal of low-level protest might well not be against the law or might be unlawful but tolerated (because the authorities choose not to proceed against the protesters) and it omits any cases where protesters are penalised but do not wish to incur the risk and cost of proceeding through the domestic courts and onto Strasbourg, choosing instead to pay a token administrative fine or to spend an hour in the cells.

What can we glean from all this about the nature of protest—and its protection—at Strasbourg level? First, we might well have expected 'traditional' forms of protest to feature far less heavily than they do. Instead, in terms of applications—perhaps the best 'gut feeling' of what citizens perceive has gone awry in any country—assemblies prevail. Well

---

[11] A fuller account of the methodology is set out *ibid*, 351–2.

[12] Parenthetic categorisation indicates a 'flavour' of another category. There are a few categorised as (E)—direct political engagement and on our definition of protest above, broadly something that was not seen as a protest but they were listed as they involved clear minority political parties or figures.

[13] Mead above n 1, 353, fn 34. One further factor might be differences in policing style: some will aim for more 'negotiated management', which we discussed in our introduction. See further D della Porta, M Andretta, L Mosea and H Reiter, *Globalization from below: transnational activists and protest networks* (Minneapolis MN, University of Minnesota Press, 2006) ch 6.

over half the cases brought to Strasbourg stemmed from restrictions or bans on assemblies, rallies or demonstrations: out of 97 applications, 56 could be so categorised.[14] This indicates that what we might consider to be the core of the right is not (or at least not thought to be) adequately protected by states parties, police and militia. Indeed, a clear majority of violation findings involve interferences with rallies and demonstrations: 20 out of 37. These figures must be a worry: they show that a right that is so 'quintessentially part of the right to peaceful protest, has become neither culturally accepted nor legally embedded unquestioningly within pan-European domestic law'.[15] Why do cases involving demonstrations feature so heavily when more modern forms of protest do not? Intuitively, we might think that states would struggle more to negotiate an appropriate balance when protesters decide to engage in pickets, vigils, symbolic speech and obstruction that when catering for assemblies.

Secondly, it is important for much of our analysis of domestic law to appreciate the limited protection given at Strasbourg to direct action or any form of protest that causes more than merely incidental obstruction. Only five such cases have passed though to a full hearing on the merits and succeeded; of these, two are very much on the edge. In *Cissé*, the protest took the form of an occupation of a church with the consent of the church authorities.[16] In *Balçik* the protest against F-type prisons manifested as a gathering and blocking of a tram line. It would be fair to say that the Court side-lined that issue in its judgment; only a close reading of the facts brings it out.[17] The only three that are clearly direct action cases are *Solomou*, *Steel and Others v UK* and *Hashman and Harrup*.[18] In none was a violation found—though in each the Court did hold there was a violation of the ECHR—on a substantive, proportionate basis. In *Solomou*, there was no separate finding once Turkey had been found in breach of both limbs of Article 2 (including the right to an effective investigation).[19] Although *Hashman* might appear to support the idea that Strasbourg is receptive to protest which is (minimally) obstructive and disruptive but which is more than incidental, the finding was clearly based not on whether the restriction on the right to protest imposed by the binding over order was necessary, or proportionate, but on the fact that it was not prescribed by law. It is very clearly predicated upon the vagueness of the English law of binding over to be of good behaviour. There is little doubt that had the law been clearer and more readily predictable and apparent on what the couple was and was not permitted to do, the decision would have gone against them, as it did for the first two direct action applicants in *Steel and Others v UK*. In that case, the only findings of a violation were in respect of the three peaceful protesters communicating a view, using placards and banners, outside an arms conference.

Our third point is merely to note what any ECHR scholar would instinctively guess: that by and large the Strasbourg Court when it does reach a decision that there has been a

---

[14] Very few (eight), from reading the judgments, could truly be said to involve marches. About 40% (39) were classified as involving some form of peaceful communication or persuasion or engagement in public debate as a means of protest. Just over a fifth (17) were cases where the protest took the form of direct action, that is deliberately obstructive or disruptive (rather than that being an incident of any group gathering together) behaviour—or worse.
[15] Mead, above n 1, 553.
[16] *Cissé v France* (App 51346/99) ECtHR judgment 9 April 2002.
[17] *Balçik v Turkey* (App 25/02 EctHR) judgment 29 November 2007.
[18] Respectively, *Solomou v Turkey* (App 36832/97) ECtHR judgment 24 June 2008, and *Steel and Others v UK* (1998) 28 EHRR 603 and *Hashman and Harrup v UK* (2000) 30 EHRR 241.
[19] In fact, technically although the Art 10 application had been declared admissible, it is not included in the 'no separate finding' list in the Court's judgment.

violation of the right to protest does so because the restriction is not necessary.[20] Cases that arise from the quality of law are very much in the minority. As well as *Hashman*, findings based on the 'prescribed by law test' are: *Stefanec, Mkrtchyan, Karakaya and Piroglou, Baczkowski, Hyde Park, Kandzhov* and *Adali*.[21] Largely, the Court is asked to decide whether the interference was a proportionate one or whether the reasons given were relevant and sufficient to meet a pressing social need; effectively the same thing. In the vast majority of those cases, states rely on the need to prevent disorder (in tandem in many cases with the need to prevent crime) as the legitimate aim prayed in aid. While this is not at all surprising, given the historic link between protest and public order maintenance, both here and abroad, nearer the end of this chapter we shall 'unpick' the nature and quality of these claims of disorder that stand behind a state's justifications. We shall see it is not all it might seem.

The overall picture we have of the right to peaceful protest in Strasbourg case law could be summarised as follows. Cases tend to involve situations where protesters en masse have been denied the right to take part in a demonstration or a march. Those who engage in direct action—certainly in recent times—tend not even bothering to apply[22] and those that do have, statistically speaking, a mountain to climb, first to convince the Court to declare the case admissible and then to win on the merits. While the reason for the relative paucity of case law overall might reflect the fact that generally in Europe the right is protected adequately before domestic constitutional courts or by the domestic legal order, this seems unlikely first for fledgling states and secondly for direct protest. Given the larger numbers of cases involving restrictions on more traditional forms, it seems fair to conclude that direct action would be protected less at domestic level. In fact, the workload of the Court is on the increase when it comes to protest. In the two and a half years since the work for the original content study was completed in the Autumn of 2006, the Court has given judgment in 18 cases[23] (finding violations in all bar three), struck five out of the list and declared two more admissible. Of the 97 peaceful protest applications to have come before the Strasbourg Court in its history, 37 have been disposed of—by being struck out, declared inadmissible or resulting in a finding of a violation—in the period from January 2006 until

---

[20] There have now been 36 separate holdings of a violation of the right to peaceful protest by the Court, well over two-thirds of those declared admissible, and a substantial proportion of the 43 to have reached the Court for a full hearing on the merits of the peaceful protest claim.

[21] This makes eight from 36. Respectively, *Stefanec v Czech Republic* (App 75615/01) ECtHR judgment 18 July 2006; *Mkrtchyan v Armenia* (App 6562/03) ECtHR 11 January 2007; *Karakaya and Piroglou v Turkey* (Apps 37581/02 and 36370/02) ECtHR 18 March 2008; *Makhmaduv v Russia* above n 2; *Baczkowski v Poland* (App 1543/06) ECtHR judgment 3 May 2007; *Hyde Park v Moldova* (App 18491/07) ECtHR judgment 7 April 2009; *Kandzhov v Bulgaria* (App 68294/01) ECtHR judgment 6 November 2008; and *Adali v Turkey* (App 38187/97) ECtHR judgment 31 March 2003.

[22] In fact overall, broadly the chances of an application clearing the first hurdle and being declared admissible were 60:40. This success rate has increased in the period 2006–09 from 50:50. Of the 97 cases lodged, 37 were declared inadmissible and 49 admissible. Ten were struck out of the list and two—*Gül v Turkey* (App 4870/02) and *Petropavlovskis v Latvia* (App 44230/06)—have been adjourned on the issue of Arts 10 and 11.

[23] These were: *Karakaya, Baczkowski* (both above n 21) *Solomou* (above n 18) *Balçik* (above n 17) *Aldemir and Others v Turkey* (App 32124/02) ECtHR 18 December 2007; *Bukta v Hungary* (App 25691/04) ECtHR 17 July 2007; *Galstyan v Armenia* (App 26986/03) ECtHR 15 November 2007; *Makhmaduv* above n 2; *Hyde Park* above n 21; *Kandzhov* above n 21; *Kutznetsov v Russia* (App 10877/04) ECtHR judgment 23 October 2008; *Molnar v Hungary* (App 10346/05) ECtHR judgment 7 October 2008; *Ashughyan v Armenia* (App 33268/03) ECtHR judgment 17 July 2008; *Patyi v Hungary* (App 5529/05) ECtHR judgment 7 October 2008; *Saya v Turkey* (App 4327/02) ECtHR judgment 7 October 2008; *Vajnai v Hungary* (App 33629/06) ECtHR judgment 8 July 2008; *Çiloglu v Turkey* (App 73333/01) ECtHR judgment 6 March 2007; *TV Vest v Norway* (App 21132/05) ECtHR judgment 29 November 2007; and *Protopapa v Turkey* (App 16084/90) ECtHR judgment 24 February 2009.

May 2009. Hearings are awaited in two: *Gül* and *Petropavloskis*. That is, over one-third of its output has come in the last three and a half years. Over time, although the respondent states have changed, the subject-matter of applications—as between the four categories outlined in the study—has remained fairly static. It is to the detail of these that we will now turn.

III. The Scope of the Right to Peaceful Protest

The bulk of this chapter provides a detailed analysis of the Court's case law, which will inform our understanding of the right to peaceful protest in the HRA era, given the duty on courts under section 2 of the Human Rights Act 1998 to take account of Strasbourg jurisprudence. The analysis will be in two parts—first, the scope of the primary right and second, the extent of permitted restrictions.

The Court's workload fits into a reasonably narrow archetype. Even the less traditional, less communicative/expressive protests tend to be sit-ins or obstructive direct action. The Strasbourg Court—even at admissibility level—has not been asked to consider other protest activities that are increasingly the norm in the UK. To give but three examples: harassment outside the homes of those who finance arms manufacturers; the organised mass-emailing by environmental protesters worried about deforestation in South America, designed to cause an overload and breakdown of a fast food chain's IT system; and sending photos of aborted foetuses through the post to those who work at abortion clinics. As we shall see in chapters four to eight, we can only hypothesise about the approach Strasbourg would take in the absence of any hard cases.

A. Article 10 or Article 11?

Many applications alleging an interference with the ability to mount a protest rely upon both Article 11 and Article 10, which guarantees the right to freedom of expression. This includes the 'free expression of opinions by word, gesture or even silence by persons assembled on the streets or in other public places'.[24] Thus we can see the close link and overlap between Article 10 and Article 11. The Court has noted in several cases the functional synergy between the two:

> [N]otwithstanding its autonomous role and particular sphere of application, Article 11 must also be considered in the light of Article 10. The protection of opinions and the freedom to express them is one of the objectives of the freedoms of assembly and association as enshrined in Article 11.[25]

In other words, people come together in groups to assemble and to associate so as to be able to express a view more effectively and in fact to 'secure a forum for public debate and open expression'.[26] The two articles inter-depend in this way too: restrictions on assemblies and

---

[24] *Osmani v FYR Macedonia* (App 50841/99) ECtHR inadmissibility decision 11 October 2001.
[25] *Ezelin v France* (1992) 14 EHRR 362 at [37].
[26] *Molnar*, above n 23, at [42]. Of course people assemble and associate for non-expressive purposes and, conversely, people engage in expressive protest or politically communicative activity without forming assemblies no matter how widely construed that concept might be.

rallies may well be attributable to the exercise of the free speech rights of certain participants. In *Stankov*, the Court said that the close link between the two articles was 'particularly relevant where—as here—the authorities' intervention against an assembly or an association was, at least in part, in reaction to views held or statements made by participants or members'.[27]

In several cases the Strasbourg Court has confronted the interplay between the two and tried to establish which should be *lex specialis*. In most cases the decision is that of the applicants and their advisers rather than the Court; unless the facts speak clearly to one or other, applicants tend to rely on leaving the Court either to dispense with one or, in a few cases, effectively to merge them together. There is no case in which the Court has considered both Article 10 and Article 11 separately, and no application has been rejected or a violation not been found under one where it would have been under the other. That said, the Court and Commission has tended to adopt a common-sense, gut feeling approach to deciding which one 'leads' without iterating any specific principles for the categorisation. In *Rassemblement Jurassien* a challenge was made to a general ban on all political meetings, through applications under both Articles 10 and 11.[28] The Commission decided that

> the allegation concerning Article 10 may be considered as subsidiary in relation to that concerning the right of peaceful assembly. The problem of freedom of expression cannot in this case be separated from that of freedom of assembly, as guaranteed by Article 11, and it is the latter freedom which is primarily involved in this issue. In the circumstances of the present case, it is accordingly not necessary to consider Article 10.[29]

As a rule of thumb, traditional protests by groups—whether by way of a march, a rally, a meeting or a demonstration—not unsurprisingly tend to be viewed as the exercise of the right of peaceful assembly. Where someone has a more explicit aim of persuading—other than by force of numbers or mere collective presence—or communicating a viewpoint (or that is what they are punished for),[30] or where protest takes a more symbolic form[31] or is more obstructive and disruptive direct action, Article 10 is likely to come to the fore. Thus in *Appleby* a group had been banned from assembling in a shopping centre, as the aim had been to enlist signatures for a petition and to distribute leaflets from a stall; the case was decided under Article 10.[32] In truth, little probably turns on this. The only difference is that Article 10(2) comprises a wider selection of legitimate aims—territorial integrity, protecting the reputation of others, or preventing disclosure of material obtained in confidence of for maintaining the authority or impartiality of the judiciary—but these bear so little on situations where people are protesting as to be paper differences only. As we shall see, the vast majority of state defences are based on preventing disorder or crime and protecting the rights of others; legitimate aims common to both Article 10 and Article 11.

---

[27] *Stankov v Bulgaria* (App 29221/95 and 29225/95) ECtHR judgment 2 October 2001.

[28] *Rassemblement Jurassien et Unité Jurassienne v Switzerland* (App 8191/78) (1980) 17 DR 93, 119

[29] See also *Christians Against Racism and Fascism (CARAF) v UK* (App 8440/78) (1980) 21 DR 138, 147–8

[30] *JK v Netherlands* (App 15928/89) EComHR inadmissibility decision 13 May 1992: arrested after unfurling a 'No Olympics' banner at Amsterdam railway station (as the official delegation left for Lausanne) in protest at Amsterdam's candidature.

[31] The best example of symbolic speech constituting a protest is probably *Moosman v Austria* (App 14093/88)—the removal of crosses on M's land (symbolising the death of nature)—by those involved in a road building project on the instructions of a government official: declared admissible on 15 October 1991 but which ended in a friendly settlement on 9 July 1992. There are very few such cases.

[32] *Appleby v UK* (2003) 37 EHRR 38. In *WG v Austria* (App 15509/89) EComHR inadmissibility decision 30 November 1992, a similar protest—a pair of environmental campaigners set up an information stands and handed out pamphlets—the Commission decided it did not need to decide the issue and approached the case under Article 10.

B. An Assembly

The term 'assembly' covers formal meetings—whether in the form of a demonstration (trying to convert or to communicate) or a rally to show strength—but also more ad hoc, informal gatherings where people have come together to protest:[33] 'a demonstration by means of repeated sit-ins blocking a public road fell within the ambit of Article 11(1)'.[34] It seems unlikely that a one-off sit-in would be viewed as being outside the scope of Article 11: in *CS v Germany*, the applicant had undertaken only two sit-ins outside US air bases.[35] By contrast, in *Cissé*, it was argued by the French government that an occupation of several months' duration could not per se constitute an 'assembly'. Since the Court found a violation, we can assume that it attaches no temporal limit to the term 'assembly'. The Greenham Common camps would presumably still be seen as assemblies on that basis. 'Assembly' also covers mere presence at a press conference during which various statements and communications were read out, rendering such presence in Turkish law an illegal assembly.[36] Article 11 sensibly makes no distinction between static groups and those that are marching or in procession—both are covered—so as to avoid a gap in protection and to avoid having to assess when one becomes the other.[37] Article 11 protects meetings in private and meetings that take place on public thoroughfares.[38] It is a right belonging to both those who organise and those who take part in meetings or processions.[39]

Strasbourg has yet to consider what level of formality or structure is implicit in an assembly or a procession: does the meeting have to be deliberate and organised or can an assembly happen spontaneously, by chance? Must it have some common purpose,[40] some sense of communality—and if so must it exist at the outset? Is it an 'assembly' in Strasbourg terms to congregate outside a police station protesting about someone just brought in for questioning? Sensibly it would be. The Court after all has stressed the functional connection between Article 10 and Article 11, as we saw above. If that were the case, there seems no reason why it should not protect a loose grouping which happens to meet, becomes vexed and decides to march to the local council offices to complain. Domestic courts have wrestled with such a conundrum: in *GS v Austria*, we learn that in the eyes of the Austrian Constitutional Court a group of people meeting was only an assembly

> if it was organised with the intention of inducing the participants to a common action (debate, discussion, demonstration), and if it resulted in a particular association of the participants. Thus

---

[33] *Cissé* above n 16. *Oner v Turkey* (App 16091/90) ECtHR admissibility decision 6 June 2004 seems to extend Article 11 to a group protesting by way of a hunger strike. The application under Article 11 was rejected but because the applicants were considered to have been taken into custody not as a result of their hunger strike but because of suspicions about their criminal activity.

[34] *Friedl v Austria* (App 15225/89) EComHR inadmissibility decision 30 November 1992, referring to *G v Germany* (App 13079/87) EComHR inadmissibility decision 6 March 1989.

[35] *CS v Germany* (App 13858/88) EComHR decision 6 March 1989: Article 11 application declared inadmissible on grounds that the measure it was not disproportionate to the aim of preventing disorder.

[36] *Cetinkaya v Turkey* (App 75569/01) ECtHR judgment 27 June 2006.

[37] *CARAF*, above n 29, at [4] and *Mkrtychan v Armenia* above n 21. As we shall see, English law applies a different regulatory regime to assemblies as to processions. The end of one and the start of the other has not yet been the subject of judicial decision in England.

[38] *Rassemblement Jurassien* n 28, 119. The case does not tell us about other publicly-owned land that is not a thoroughfare.

[39] *CARAF*, above n 29, 148.

[40] It is certainly the Commission's view that the right of *association*, under Article 11, is a right for individuals to associate 'in order to attain various ends': *X v Sweden* (App 6094/73) (1977) 9 DR 5, 7

an assembly [is] a meeting of persons for the common purpose of discussing opinions or of impart-
ing opinions to others. A meeting of persons by coincidence [does] not amount to an assembly.[41]

As the case was not declared inadmissible on the basis that the facts didn't engage Article 11—but rather because the convictions were necessary—we can assume the Austrian position was rejected.

What about minimum numbers? Does an 'assembly' imply a gathering, so two people at least, or even a critical mass or can a solitary protester constitute an assembly? In the various German sit-in cases—such as *CS v Germany*[42]—no question was ever raised about these not constituting assemblies but in each case those arrested were not demonstrating by themselves. So far as can be seen, the short case reports indicate no case in which a solitary protester has utilised Article 11—though clearly Article 10 could apply. However in two cases—*McBride v UK*[43] and *Galstyan v Armenia*[44]—individuals were allowed to rely on Article 11 or, in McBride's case, not debarred from doing so purely because they were not at the time acting in common. In both, demonstrations were taking place. In *McBride*, action was taken that interfered with M's ability to join it and in *Galstyan* action was taken that was premised on G's distant connection with it. McBride was arrested for breach of the peace and detained for 90 minutes as she walked from the site of an anti arms trade demonstration in the direction of an arms fair some 10 minutes away. McBride challenged this at Strasbourg under, inter alia, Articles 10 and 11 'because she was wholly prevented from pursuing a completely peaceful demonstration'. The application was ruled inadmissible on proportionality grounds not as incompatible *rationae materiae*; achieving the legitimate aim of preventing disorder and protecting the rights of others. The Court did not consider it relevant that at the point of arrest—though there was an assembly—she herself was neither assembling nor demonstrating but walking towards it.[45] The decision is open to the interpretation that it has widened the reach of Article 11 by eliding the word 'assembly' with the word 'protest'—such that it no longer means a coming together of persons—or by eliding 'assembly' with procession thence with ambulation. In *Galstyan*, the applicant (an authorised official for an opposition candidate) was successful in arguing a violation of Article 11 following his arrest, according to the police, for obstructing traffic and anti-social behaviour, after observing an anti-government demonstration some 100–150 metres away. It was clear though that he was in fact arrested for participating in the demonstration and for violating public order during it.

The right in Article 11 is to hold an assembly of one's own choosing in terms of content and activities that are undertaken. Therefore, it will be an interference, albeit it one capable of justification on proportionality grounds, with the right if a march or meeting is allowed but held on terms dictated by the state. It thus endorses the element of autonomy inherent in the right. In *Stankov v Bulgaria*, a commemorative meeting at an historical site was

---

[41] *GS v Austria* (App 14923/89) EComHR inadmissibility decision 30 November 1992.
[42] *CS v Germany* (App 13858/88) EComHR inadmissibility decision 6 March 1989.
[43] *McBride v United Kingdom* (App 27786/95) ECtHR inadmissibility decision 5 July 2001.
[44] *Galstyan* above n 23.
[45] *Djavit An v Turkey* (App 20652/92) ECtHR judgment 20 February 2003 (though not a protest case and so not in Appendix III) does provide support for a reading of Article 11 that encompasses travel or getting to a meeting or an assembly that is already taking place—perhaps rather than moving to start one. There, a violation of Article 11 was found when the applicant was denied permission to cross to Southern Cyprus for a bi-communal meeting. We learn little more about the substantive legality of such a ban—the interference was founded on the absence of a legal regime surrounding the granting of permits, thus making the interference one that was not prescribed by law.

banned every year save one year, in which the applicant group was allowed to attend but no one was permitted to have placards, to make speeches or to hold a separate demonstration.[46] It is also a right to hold meetings at a time (and place?) of one's choosing. It is clear in *Öllinger* that the authority's decision to ban the meeting was informed as much by the proposed date—All Saints' Day—as by its content, target and likely impact.[47]

Quite what level of inchoate protection is offered by Article 11 remains to be seen. Intuitively if the authorities prevented someone from beginning a demonstration and without that person, it was clear the protest would not—and indeed did not—come to fruition, that would as much be an interference with the right to assemble (of either those who did not then meet, or the arrested leader) as would those cases where the police wade into a meeting and disperse it. The Court's general view—expressed in *Airey*—is that rights must be more than theoretical and illusory but must also be practical and effective.[48] It would not be much of a right if an assembly were protected only once it was in operation but not those that were inchoate. The Court established in *Patyi* that freedom of peaceful assembly protects the abstract possibility of holding an assembly undisturbed.[49] Thus a refusal to authorise a demonstration undoubtedly concerns, in a personal and direct manner, the right to peaceful protest, but whose? It is clear that those organising a cancelled demonstration would have a sufficient interest in bringing a claim but what about possible participants? At first sight, *Patyi* would appear not to extend protection to those who do not actually ever assemble. In fact the decision is not quite so clear-cut and dead-end. We should be wary of extrapolating too much from it. The 47 other named applicants, whose cases were declared inadmissible, were outwith the protection of Article 11 as they were not victims. Their only connection to the protest outside the Prime Minister's house was that, along with thousands of others, they had lost money when a company went insolvent and had been unable to recoup their losses—hence the planned protest. There was no evidence that any of them intended to protest.[50] We cannot conclude from the case that anyone who intends or wishes to join a protest but is debarred would be so unlucky. Article 11 is perfectly capable of holding the authorities to account where they interfere with the preparations for a protest by way of a 'chilling effect', as in *Baczkowski*.[51]

C. Peaceful Assembly

The close link to and support for the guarantee of free speech in Article 10 means that 'freedom of assembly as enshrined in Article 11 of the Convention protects a demonstration that may annoy or give offence to persons opposed to the ideas or claims that it is seeking to promote'.[52] Any assembly—whether static meeting or procession—will clearly lose the protection of Article 11 if it is not peaceful. There has been considerable case law on this. It does not simply mean that if a demonstration turns violent all those present forfeit any

---

[46] *Stankov v Bulgaria*, above n 27, at [79]–[80].
[47] *Öllinger v Austria* (2008) 48 EHRR 38 and see also *Stankov* (above n 27, at [109]) 'the time and the place ... were crucial' and so restricted the state's margin of appreciation to deal with possible disturbances.
[48] *Airey v Ireland* (1979) 2 EHRR 305.
[49] *Patyi*, above n 23, at [25]–[27].
[50] ibid, [26].
[51] *Baczkowski v Poland*, above n 21, and see text to nn 97–98 below.
[52] *Stankov v Bulgaria*, above n 27, at [86], relying on *Plattform 'Ärzte fur das Leben'* (1991) 13 EHRR 204 at [32]: 'a demonstration may annoy or give offence to persons opposed to the ideas or claims it is seeking to promote' in turn derived from the famous passage in *Handyside v UK* (1976) 1 EHRR 737 at [49].

Convention protection. What if it only becomes violent as a result of hijacking by a subgroup intent on violence and havoc, or in response to threats from third parties, perhaps counter-demonstrators? Case law is clear: what matters is the intention of its organisers and participants. In *CS v Germany*, the Commission stated that the right to freedom of peaceful assembly 'is secured to everyone who organises or participates in a peaceful demonstration. The notion of "peaceful assembly" does not, however, cover a demonstration where the organisers and participants have violent intentions which result in public disorder'.[53] The Commission appeared then to qualify this by referring to the fact that none of the demonstrators had been 'actively violent in the course of the sit-ins', which is, of course, a different matter. In its earlier *CARAF* decision, the Commission set out that the right is secured to

> everyone who has the intention of organising a peaceful demonstration. In the Commission's opinion the possibility of violent counter-demonstrations, or the possibility of extremists with violent intentions, not members of the organising association, joining the demonstration cannot as such take away that right. Even if there is a real risk of a public procession resulting in disorder by developments outside the control of those organising it, such procession does not for this reason alone fall outside the scope of Article 11(1) of the Convention.[54]

Careful reading of those dicta in *CS v Germany* tells us that not only must violence be intended, it must also be the result. A demonstration that its organisers hope and want to become violent will not lose protection for its participants if it remains (for whatever reason) peaceful. Strasbourg does not yet appear to have confronted the situation where conditions are imposed on an assembly—thereby constituting a restriction—so that it remained peaceful and someone afterwards (rather ironically) tries to claim their right to peaceful protest was restricted where without those conditions violence would have broken out. The conjunctive 'and' linking organisers and participants to intended violence is important: if an organiser intends, and uses violence, without the knowledge or support of others, innocent participants ought not to be penalised by having imputed to them the intentions of the organisers, let alone any violent turns that a march or meeting actually takes.

Many states take the view that once some participants become violent, the march or assembly itself becomes 'illegal' or 'unlawful' and can properly be stopped in its entirety. Turkey is one such state under its Law No 2911.[55] The ECHR takes the view that it is not assemblies that are violent or unlawful but people. Arresting someone arbitrarily purely because they are wrapped up in what has become (perhaps what was intended to be) a violent demonstration, as a way perhaps of managing it, is clearly a restriction and cannot be justified solely on the basis that that person has lost the protection of Article 11. On this, *Ezelin v France* is instructive. A barrister took part in a demonstration that had not been prohibited but which did, over its course, change its nature. He was later disciplined by his professional body for failing to dissociate himself (either by leaving the procession or by himself verbally condemning the chanting and placards) from those demonstrators who had become offensive and insulting. The ECtHR held that the imposition of even the minor penalty here was a violation of the applicant's rights under Article 11: 'freedom to take part

[53] *CS v Germany* (App 13858/88) EComHR inadmissibility decision 6 March 1989, at [2].
[54] *CARAF*, above n 29, at [4].
[55] In 2007, according to Saadettin Iskan (Deputy Head Security Dept, Turkish National Police), a liberalising reform of this law was planned but research has not discovered the status of this: talk given at EU TAIEX seminar on freedom of assembly, June 2007 in Ankara.

in a peaceful assembly . . . is of such importance that it cannot be restricted in any way . . . so long as the person concerned does not himself commit any reprehensible act on such an occasion'.[56] Similarly, in *Galstyan*, the Court considered that

> the very essence of the right to freedom of peaceful assembly would be impaired, if the State was not to prohibit a demonstration but was then to impose sanctions, especially such severe ones, on its participants for the mere fact of [being present and proactive at the demonstration in question] . . . without committing anything reprehensible [illegal, violent or obscene in the course of it], as happened in the applicant's case.[57]

But what about an organiser who fully intends the march should remain peaceful but it turns violent as a result not of a counter-demonstration but hotheads among the ranks who intended all along to become violent? Is there a duty to crack down on those within the group, failing which Convention protection is lost? In *Ziliberberg v Moldova*, the Court stated that protesters do not cease to enjoy the right 'as a result of *sporadic* violence or other punishable acts committed by others in the course of the demonstration, if the individual in question remains peaceful in his or her own intentions or behaviour'.[58]

We might take the reference to 'sporadic violence' as implying that if it continued, the right would be lost. But if the organiser could not stop it, what is she to do? It is clear from *Ezelin* that there is no duty to dissociate oneself from the violence of others, though of course Ezelin was a participant, not an organiser. The better view must continue to be that a protester will only liable for her own intended violence—extending perhaps to those whom it would be reasonable to expect her to control, though that is rather unquantifiable. Such a protester would 'remain peaceful in his or her intentions or behaviour'.

In *Osmani v FYR Macedonia*, the applicant mayor was convicted of stirring up national and racial hatred after he organised and then spoke at a public meeting at which he vociferously and ferociously defended the Albanian flag and language.[59] His application to Strasbourg under Articles 10 and 11 was ruled inadmissible as manifestly ill-founded: his sentence was not disproportionate in view of his encouragement for armed resistance and riot. The Court did note first that his 'speech, his actions and the meeting organised by him . . . undoubtedly played a substantial part in the occurrence of the violent events that followed', and secondly that he

> directly called the citizens of Albanian ethnic origin to resist the implementation of a final judicial decision, thereby causing hatred, intolerance and tensions in a very sensitive inter-ethnic situation, as well as a feeling of insecurity among the rest of the population and had revived the painful memories of the Second World War.

The first limb of the Court's words seems to equate cause and effect with intention. Without engaging in the semantic vagaries of 'intent' can it be said that Osmani intended the violence that subsequently occurred? In the second limb—and generally in this area—the danger of what we might call the Mandela problem arises: why is it per se lawful to restrict the free speech and rights of peaceful assembly of someone who urges mass civil disobedience even in fiery tones or, more problematically, who themselves actually engage in it? This is a normative question, which requires better justification than is usually possible in admissibility decisions where the issue is whether a claim is manifestly ill-founded. We should be

---

[56] *Ezelin*, above n 25, at [53].
[57] *Galstyan*, above n 23, at [117].
[58] *Ziliberberg v Moldova* (App 61821/00) ECtHR inadmissibility decision 4 May 2004.
[59] *Osmani v FYR Macedonia*, above n 24.

clear too that *Osmani* does not indicate—even in extreme situations—that the protection of Article 11 might be lost not for being violent but for stirring violence up. *Osmani* did not say that such behaviour was outwith the definition of peaceful assembly but rather that restrictions would likely be proportionate. It is implicit in the judgment that even such incitement does not turn a peaceful assembly into a violent one. In *Protopapa v Turkey*, the application was not declared inadmissible but instead was rejected on its merits even though there, in the Court's view, it was clear that the demonstration against the TRNC had engaged in widespread violence.[60]

'Peaceful' has an autonomous Convention meaning. It does not equate solely to an assembly that is not unlawful in domestic law, such as one that is unauthorised or even unconstitutional: so to hold would denude the right of any international protection. In *Cissé v France* a large group occupied a church—albeit with permission and support from the priest and parish council—for several months to highlight their own immigration status and to protest about French immigration rules.[61] The French government argued that the eventual forcible evacuation of the group did not engage Article 11, as an unlawful occupation could not constitute a peaceful assembly. It argued that Article 11 'did not extend to events intended by the organisers and participants to disturb public order or which, irrespective of the purpose for which they had been organised, unreasonably curtailed the right of others to assemble freely'. In its view, there was a particularly flagrant unlawful flavour to the assembly. First, its very purpose entailed a breach of public order. The aim of the assembly and the occupation was to defend and to legitimise a deliberate breach of French immigration rules. Secondly, occupying a church for several months could not be classed as peaceful:[62] it indisputably hindered the local congregation in their worship, a form of freedom of assembly that enjoyed the protection of French law. The Court did not agree— it stated curtly, without explanation, that the evacuation of the church amounted to an interference in the exercise of the applicant's right to freedom of peaceful assembly. As the applicant put it, an assembly does not cease to be peaceful simply because its purpose does not meet with the approval of the government of the day: the legality or otherwise of the assembly under domestic law was under no circumstances to be used as a criterion for determining whether it was peaceful. This is a welcome confirmation of an obvious point, one to which the Court should continue to adhere.

D. Positive Duties Under Article 11

We saw in chapter two how even articles framed in negative terms may imply a positive duty on states to act so as to facilitate or guarantee the protection of a right. The proportionality test set out in *Stjerna v Finland*—balancing the interests of an individual against the wider social interest—is used to determine whether or not an article comprises the positive right argued for and whether or not on the facts it is engaged.[63] The right of peaceful assembly under Article 11 is no different. *Djavit An v Turkey* concerned the imposition of travel restrictions on someone hoping to cross the buffer zone in Cyprus to attend a bi-communal meeting in the south. It is not a protest case within our definition, although it does involve

---

[60] *Protopapa v Turkey* (App 16084/90) ECtHR judgment 24 February 2009.
[61] *Cissé v France*, above n 16.
[62] *ibid.*
[63] *Stjerna v Finland* (1994) 24 EHRR 194.

people peacefully assembling, so it is not included in Appendix III.[64] There, the Court did consider the scope of the duty comprised in Article 11. It noted that states

> must not only safeguard the right to assemble peacefully but also refrain from applying unreasonable indirect restrictions upon that right ... [A]lthough the essential object of Article 11 is to protect the individual against arbitrary interference by public authorities with the exercise of the rights protected, there may in addition be positive obligations to secure the effective enjoyment of these rights.[65]

The Court in pure protest cases has iterated this as its general approach.[66] We can draw from this various conclusions. At its simplest, states must refrain from acting in ways that may directly interfere with the right even to the extent, as we shall see, of imposing effective restrictions by penalties after the event. Secondly, states must not interfere indirectly where such a restriction or interference would be unreasonable. Thus, where a council requires protesters to pay a relatively high charge for use of public land to hold a demonstration, or charges the group for a licence for an activity taking place on a march, this may be viewed as unlawful interference.[67] Thirdly, states may be under a positive duty to act so as to safeguard the right; an obligation, as the Court noted in *Baczkowski*, of 'particular importance for persons holding unpopular views or belonging to minorities because they are more vulnerable to victimisation'.[68]

Positive obligations to secure the right peacefully to assemble might take one of two forms. There might be a positive duty on states themselves to facilitate a protest taking place, perhaps by providing an adequate level of policing at a march or by providing access to public protest space. Alternatively, states may have a positive duty to ensure third parties themselves do not act so as to deprive protesters of their rights (or, indeed, do act so as not to), perhaps by imposing requirements or measures upon them. If private shop-holders, companies or landowners can too easily prevent groups protesting about the business or activities they carry out on their own land—by obtaining injunctions to prevent harassment or by using the right of absolute enjoyment over their land to ban all-comers—then the right to protest might not be 'effectively enjoyed'. Let us look at each of those in turn.

The first naturally leads us to discuss what, if anything, states should do to guarantee the right to protest in the face of counter-demonstrators' objections. To some extent this also follows from our discussion about the qualities of a 'peaceful' protest and the point at which protests cease to be peaceful. The *locus classicus* is *Plattform 'Ärzte für das Leben' v Austria* in 1988.[69] The applicants' Article 11 claim had earlier been declared inadmissible by the Commission as being manifestly ill-founded, so by the time it reached the Court it was nominally only concerned with Article 13. Despite that, the Court had to decide the question of a possible breach of Article 11 on the facts in order to assess the issue of a violation

---

[64] Compare *Adali v Turkey*, above n 21, which is included because of its slightly different facts.
[65] *Djavit An v Turkey*, above n 45, at [57].
[66] *Balçik*, above n 17, at [46]–[47] and *Oya Ataman v Turkey* (App 74552/01) ECtHR judgment 5 December 2006, at [36].
[67] Salford Council was proposing to charge four schoolgirls more than £2000 to march through the city protesting at the council's plans to close their own school. The sum was said to cover the expenses of closing roads. Similar attempts to charge indirectly for protest might include demanding a fee for consent to distributing non-political leaflets and requiring payment for a live entertainment license for groups utilising, say, music or 'street theatre' as part of a protest: [Summer 2008] *Liberty* magazine p 8–9.
[68] *Baczkowski*, above n 21, at [64]. This contrasts with the extra restraint required of government and the authorities—especially where alternative means exist to reply to attacks—given their dominant position: *Kandzhov*, above n 21, at [73].
[69] *Plattform 'Ärzte für das Leben' v Austria* (1991) 13 EHRR 204.

of Article 13, as that right—to an effective national remedy—only applies where there is an arguable breach of another right in the ECHR. The Court's judgment therefore offered its view on the nature of Article 11, in particular the nature of any positive duty to guarantee, to safeguard, even to promote peaceful assembly.[70] The applicants were a group of doctors united in their opposition to Austria's abortion laws and who wished to campaign for change. Their Strasbourg challenge was to what they saw as inadequate police protection that led to two of their planned demonstrations being disrupted, both of which were authorised under Austrian law. At both, large numbers of opponents caused trouble: eggs and clods of grass were thrown, chanting over loudspeakers was used to drown out the words of the anti-abortionists, and each protest verged on violence. At the second, the situation was made more tense by the unlawful presence of a right-wing group determined to support the doctors. The police had in fact refused permission to opponents of the doctors' group who had planned to hold counter-demonstrations, as it had to the Austrian Socialist Party for the date and time of the second demonstration. There was a last-minute change of plan and a new route for the first demonstration and the police had warned that it was not likely to be as amenable to crowd control.

In respect of that demonstration, the group brought disciplinary and constitutional proceedings in the Austrian courts alleging failure to provide sufficient protection. None succeeded. It was these that became the basis of the Article 13 challenge at Strasbourg. This ultimately failed too but not before the ECtHR had determined the scope of Article 11. Contrary to the Austrian Government's argument, the ECtHR decided that in order properly to dispose of the Article 13 claim it had to determine the extent of Article 11. The Court considered that

> [g]enuine, effective freedom of peaceful assembly cannot, therefore, be reduced to a mere duty on the part of the State not to interfere: a purely negative conception would not be compatible with the object and purpose of Article 11. Like Article 8, Article 11 sometimes requires positive measures to be taken, even in the sphere of relations between individuals, if need be ... While it is the duty of Contracting States to take reasonable and appropriate measures to enable lawful demonstrations to proceed peacefully, they cannot guarantee this absolutely and they have a wide discretion in the choice of the means to be used. In this area the obligation they enter into under Article 11 of the Convention is an obligation as to measures to be taken and not as to results to be achieved.[71]

Protest groups must

> be able to hold the demonstration without having to fear that they will be subjected to physical violence by their opponents; such a fear would be liable to deter associations or other groups supporting common ideas or interests from openly expressing their opinions on highly controversial issues affecting the community. In a democracy the right to counter-demonstrate cannot extend to inhibiting the exercise of the right to demonstrate.[72]

On the facts, the ECtHR decided the Austrian authorities had not failed to take reasonable and appropriate measures. The police did not remain passive at either time—one hundred were deployed at one venue and were used to separate the protagonists and to clear the area. A large number were deployed for the first demo even though the route was changed.

---

[70] In light of the time dedicated to it by the Court, it must be asked whether the claim that there had been a breach of the positive duty under Article was *manifestly* ill-founded.
[71] Above n 69 at [32] and [34] (citations omitted).
[72] *ibid*, at [32].

For both demonstrations, other protests were prohibited including the annual Labour Day parade.[73]

The fact that 'authorities have a duty to take appropriate measures with regard to lawful demonstrations in order to ensure their peaceful conduct and the safety of all citizens'[74] can very easily justify the necessity of some form of advance notification procedure perhaps even to the extent of sanctioning the need for prior authorisation. This was the Hungarian government's argument in *Bukta v Hungary*, a case we shall look at more fully below.

> On certain occasions, positive measures had to be taken in order to ensure [the peacefulness of an assembly]. The three-day time-limit was therefore necessary to enable the police, *inter alia*, to co-ordinate with other authorities, to redeploy police forces, to secure fire brigades, and to clear vehicles. They drew attention to the fact that if more than one organisation notified the authorities of their intention to hold a demonstration at the same place and time, additional negotiations might be necessary.[75]

Thus authorisation/notification can assist states in responding to other rights, and not just Article 11 rights of other groups, such as the right of free movement rights of citizens in their everyday lives, contained in the Fourth Protocol.[76]

Another positive measure that might be used to preserve and to guarantee the rights of protesters would be to ban any counter-demonstration. Implementing such a measure though will necessarily affect the rights of the counter-demonstrators themselves. In essence what we have—and *Plattform 'Ärzte für das Leben'* is a good example—is an unrecognised clash of competing Article 11 rights. It is not reasoned as such: not only the group of doctors but also the counter-demonstrators had a right to hold protest meetings and marches.[77] So far the only Article 11 case reasoned on that basis is *Öllinger v Austria*.[78] There, a majority of the ECtHR held that banning a meeting in Salzburg cemetery commemorating those Jews killed by the SS, deliberately timed to coincide with an SS memorial service, violated Ö's rights under Article 11. The meeting was banned in order to safeguard the religious rights of cemetery visitors (under Article 9) on All Saints' Day as well as to prevent an endangering to public order and security. We shall consider the case in detail when we consider the proportionality of restrictions under Article 11.

The second aspect of the positive duties within Article 11 raises questions about state regulation of the private sphere so as to accord proper and effective protection of the right to protest. So far there has been only limited discussion of this element at Strasbourg; the focus

---

[73] Similarly, in the context of the right of association in Art 11, in *Ouranio Toxo v Greece* (App 74989/01) ECtHR judgment 20 October 2005, the Court stated (at [37])—in light of the police failing to protect a political party's HQ from violent attacks and threats to its officials (with allegations of complicity on the part of local clergy and municipal officials)—that 'it is incumbent upon public authorities to guarantee the proper functioning of an association or political party, even when they annoy or give offence to persons opposed to the lawful ideas or claims that they are seeking to promote. Their members must be able to hold meetings without having to fear that they will be subjected to physical violence by their opponents. Such a fear would be liable to deter other associations or political parties from openly expressing their opinions on highly controversial issues affecting the community. In a democracy the right to counter-demonstrate cannot extend to inhibiting the exercise of the right of association'.
[74] *Oya Ataman* above n 66, at [35].
[75] *Bukta v Hungary*, above n 23, at [29].
[76] See *Molnar*, above n 23, at [37].
[77] Such clashes of rights cases are not rare: the archetype is probably the conflict between the right to privacy and the right to free speech that arises whenever the media wishes to print gossip about a public figure.
[78] *Öllinger v Austria*, above n 47. The Court divided 6:1 with Judge Loucaides dissenting. I discuss the case more fully in 'Strasbourg discovers the right to counter-demonstrate: a case-note on *Öllinger v Austria* [2007] EHRLR 133.

of the Court's workload has been almost exclusively on criminal enforcement or administrative regulations, that is arrests or bans and conditions, but each within the public sphere. We shall see in chapters four to seven that a concern in this area domestically has been the increasing ease—and willingness—with which those private parties directly affected by a protest are able to take action against protesters outside that more traditional public law paradigm, a paradigm that is more capable of responding more appropriately to the various public concerns and tensions. Our last substantive chapter, chapter eight, is dedicated to this developing area—private law enforcement and remedies.

The only two situations that have arisen have involved consideration of the extent to which states are required to secure access to privately-owned land in order to facilitate the holding of protests and of the seeming inequality between litigants in the operation of defamation laws. We shall look in more detail at the first in the next chapter. In brief, the state in Western Europe underwent significant ideological change in the late twentieth century, withdrawing from many elements of socio-economic life including direct ownership or management of land. Certainly in the UK swathes of land that was previously publicly held passed—under the guise of privatisation or public/private finance initiatives—into private hands. Clearly, the right to protest—if it is to be practical and effective rather than theoretical and illusory[79]—should not be dependent on the vagaries of land ownership: if almost all land is privately owned, where would demonstrators go?

Two cases, both against the UK, demonstrate that private law rights relating to land—and an owner's ability to exclude all-comers—will trump the public right of peaceful protest. A state cannot be required—as an aspect of the positive obligation under Article 11—to re-order its private law so as to establish a right of access to land to disseminate ideas, to publicise a cause or even just to hold a meeting so long as other means are open and available to protesters who want to bring an issue to public attention. The first case—the admissibility decision in *Anderson v UK*—was not a protest case. A group of 10 youths was barred from a shopping centre on grounds of alleged misconduct and disorderly behaviour.[80] The group's complaint under Article 11 was dismissed as incompatible *rationae materiae*: there was no indication in the Commission's case law that freedom of assembly was intended to guarantee a right to pass and re-pass in public places or to assemble for purely social purposes anywhere one wishes. The second case was clearly a protest case; the ECtHR decision in *Appleby v UK*.[81] Again the land involved was quasi-public land: land once owned by a public body but now owned, or controlled at least, by a private company. The group in *Appleby* wanted to protest and to impart information about proposed local development plans. The company which owned the local shopping centre refused them permission to set up a stall distributing leaflets and to collect signatures for a petition. The application to the Court under Articles 10 and 11 was unsuccessful. The Court agreed with the contention that Article 10 in situations such as the present could comprise a positive obligation, but on the facts—a majority decided[82]—there was no failure by the UK to protect the applicants' freedom of expression. That is, there was no duty to guarantee a positive right of access to land for the purposes of protest or freedom of expression enforceable against the land owner. The key determinant was the availability of alternative means of

---

[79] *Airey v Ireland*, above n 48.
[80] *Anderson v United Kingdom* (App 33689/96) EComHR inadmissibility decision 27 October 1997.
[81] *Appleby v United Kingdom* (2003) 37 EHRR 38.
[82] Judge Maruste dissented from the majority on this point. In his view, the majority's decision gave the owners' property rights unnecessary priority over the applicants' rights of freedom of expression and of assembly.

communicating their ideas. The case has been subject to considerable criticism and comment. We shall look at this in detail in chapter four.

The other situation arose in *Steel and Morris v UK*.[83] The so-called McLibel Two were successfully sued for defamation in the UK for their part in distributing a pamphlet that was heavily critical of and hostile to MacDonalds. The pair made an application to Strasbourg arguing a breach of Article 10. The Court found for them largely on the basis that procedurally British defamation law did not strike the right balance between the two opposing parties—one element was the lack of legal aid and another was the size of the award relative to the pair's income and resources. We shall look at this in detail in chapter eight.

E. Direct Action Protests

The Court has been asked on many occasions to consider restrictions not on peaceful communication—marching, demonstrating or campaigning—but on obstructive or disruptive protest, protest aimed not at changing minds but at stopping an activity in the first place. Probably the most important case was *Steel and Others v UK*, in which the Court accepted that direct action could constitute a form of symbolic speech within Article 10.[84] Five protesters at three separate events were arrested for breaching the peace and were detained at least temporarily: one was actively disrupting a grouse shoot, one actively attempted to disrupt building works on a motorway extension and a group of three waged a campaign against the arms trade which involved them distributing leaflets outside an arms sales conference. At Strasbourg Article 11 was considered to raise no new issues and so the case proceeded under Article 10: even the protests by the first two activists, who had physically impeded activities of which they disapproved, constituted expressions of opinion.[85] Reliance on Article 10, with direct action protests seen as forms of expression (and the consequent relegation of Article 11), has been followed in several cases since such as, to name but four, *Selvanayagam v UK, Hashman and Harrup v UK, G and E v Norway* and *Chorherr v Austria*.[86] Strasbourg, though, is by no means consistent. In *S v Austria* no reference was made to Article 10 in an application concerning the prohibition of a demonstration protesting about

---

[83] *Steel and Morris v United Kingdom* (2005) 45 EHRR 22.

[84] *Steel and Others v UK*, above n 18.

[85] The Court seemed to distinguish, as it does for Art 11, between protected peaceful and unprotected non-peaceful speech but unlike in Art 11 it did not in the *Steel* case clearly set out what it considered to be peaceful: can we equate it with violent intentions as under Article 11 or is there a subtle difference?

[86] In *Selvanayagam v UK* (App 57981/00) ECtHR inadmissibility decision 12 December 2002, it was argued that it was disproportionate for English law to adopt the position that the very act of breaching a *civil* anti-harassment injunction (even if granted ex parte) was 'unreasonable' conduct and so debarring those charged with *criminal* harassment from arguing a reasonableness defence, as permitted in statute. That aspect of the application under Art 10 was declared inadmissible on the ground that such a position was not disproportionate to the legitimate aim of preventing disorder or crime or to protecting the rights of the owners of the mink farm, the object of the protest. In *Hashman and Harrup*, above n 18, binding over powers—this time used against fox hunt saboteurs to be of good behaviour, rather than to keep the peace (as in *Steel*)—were challenged. In *G and E v Norway* (App 9278/81 and 9415/81) EComHR inadmissibility decision 3 October 1983, a group of six Laplanders camped outside the Norwegian parliament to protest about the environment and the treatment of the Lapp minority. They were granted authority to assemble for four hours on one day. They were ordered to move on after four days and those who refused were arrested and convicted, first, of setting up camp for an unauthorised time and second for failing to leave when ordered. The Commission decided that no separate issues were raised under Art 11; the demonstration, by setting up the tent in front of the Parliament, was certainly an expression of opinion. The protester in *Chorherr v Austria* (1994) 17 EHRR 358 was arrested for distributing anti-arms trade leaflets at a public ceremony marking 40 years of peace. Despite that fact that he was asked by the police 'to cease what could only be regarded as a demonstration' at no stage did Art 11 feature in the court's reasoning.

'repression in Austria', which took the form of shouting slogans and making excessive noise.[87] Contrariwise, in both *WG v Austria* and *GS v Austria* the Commission decided to assess under Article 10 the arrests for unlawful unauthorised use of the road of two groups that had set up information tables in a pedestrian area and had distributed pamphlets setting out the group's position on matters of political concern. Applications were made under Article 10 and under Article 11 but both of those cases were decided by reference solely to the 'more general guarantee' of Article 10.[88]

As we saw at the start of this chapter, if a protest is one that is construed as obstructive or disruptive—or worse—there is a very high chance the application will be declared inadmissible, given the width of the margin of appreciation afforded to member states in this area. This is so whether the protest is incidentally and inevitably disruptive or obstructive or is intentionally and directly disruptive or obstructive. Only the latter is aimed at preventing the activity complained about from continuing or taking place. In only one such case— *Hashman and Harrup*—has the Court found a violation and that was on the basis that the restriction was not 'prescribed by law'.[89]

IV. The Extent of Lawful Interferences with the Right

Having established the scope of the right we need now to consider how it might lawfully be qualified. In chapter two, we saw how ostensibly extensive rights may have restrictions imposed upon them. Restrictions—or interferences—must be prescribed by law, must serve a legitimate aim and may interfere with the exercise of the right no more than is necessary in a democratic society. The 'only restriction capable of justifying an interference is one that may claim to spring from democratic society'.[90] Largely, as we saw at the start of this chapter, the focus of the Court's decision-making process is around that last issue, the issue of proportionality. We will consider here the nature of that 'claw-back', looking at each of the three limbs in turn: what does it mean to say that an interference has been 'prescribed by law?; what can we learn from the Court's jurisprudence about the prescribed aims?; and in what situations have interferences been declared disproportionate? The Court elucidated its role in *Makhmaduv v Russia*.

> In view of the essential nature of freedom of assembly and its close relationship with democracy there must be convincing and compelling reasons to justify an interference with this right ... In carrying out its scrutiny of the impugned interference, the Court has to ascertain whether the respondent State exercised its discretion reasonably, carefully and in good faith. It must also look at the interference complained of in the light of the case as a whole and determine whether it was 'proportionate to the legitimate aim pursued' and whether the reasons adduced by the national authorities to justify it are 'relevant and sufficient'. In so doing, the Court has to satisfy itself that the national authorities applied standards which were in conformity with the principles embodied in Article 11 and, moreover, that they based their decisions on an acceptable assessment of the relevant facts.[91]

---

[87] *S v Austria* (App 13812/88) EComHR inadmissibility decision 3 November 1990.
[88] Above p 63–64.
[89] *Hashman and Harrup*, above n 18.
[90] *Kuznetsov v Russia*, above n 23, at [39] and *Djavit An*, above n 45, at [56].
[91] *Makhmaduv v Russia*, above n 2. The Court held for the applicant on the basis that Russia had been unable to provide any credible evidence substantiating its claim that a terrorist threat was the reason for withdrawing authorisation for a meeting protesting about local government policies in Moscow itself.

That analysis is dependent on the applicant establishing that an interference has occurred. It is to that we turn first.

A. The Nature of the Interference

It is clear from *Ezelin* that taking a measure afterwards, such as punishing someone for protesting for participating in an assembly, interferes as much with the right as doing something beforehand—such as banning a march—or during its course, such as arresting someone peacefully holding aloft a placard.[92] Examples of each type abound.

(i) Punishment

Ezelin is a good an example of punishment after the event. As we saw, a disciplinary reprimand was imposed on a barrister for actively participating in a protest meeting (by holding a placard) and for not dissociating himself from violence that ensued. Strasbourg considered that this was an 'interference' even though the measure—a reprimand—was neither especially serious nor criminal in nature. In Ezelin's case, it affected his professional status and only attached to him because of his additional professional responsibilities. Criminal convictions will clearly constitute an interference after the event but so might something short of being found guilty: three of the five applicants in *Steel and Others v UK* were never convicted yet the very act of removing them from the scene of a protest about arms sales— they were arrested and charged but magistrates ordered their release some seven hours later—was enough to require the UK to justify (ultimately unsuccessfully) the necessity of the interference with their rights to freedom of expression.[93] It is possible that the Court will take an even more expansive view of what constitutes an interference when the *Petrovpavlovskis v Latvia* case comes before it for full hearing.[94] The claim there is that a refusal to grant naturalisation, because the applicant had led a campaign against the removal of rights for Russian-speaking minorities in the Latvian education system, was an interference with his right of peaceful protest. The case was declared admissible despite Latvia arguing that this was an attempt to claim a right not protected in the ECHR, relating to citizenship.

(ii) Bans in advance

Even temporary bans for short periods can constitute an interference. In *(CARAF) v UK* a two-month ban on all marches, aimed at preventing the National Front (an extreme right-wing group) from marching but which coincidentally affected the applicant group, meant that they had suffered an interference with their right under Article 11.[95] Bans on meetings

---

[92] *Ezelin*, above n 25, at [39] although it was on this point that Judge Pettiti dissented: 'it is not clear that the minimal sanction imposed after the event, a purely moral sanction, had an effect such as to place an obstacle in the way of freedom to demonstrate ... [and] the majority has not, in my view, explained its conclusion that a subsequent sanction could be sufficient to deter the person concerned from participating in another demonstration at a later stage'.
[93] *Steel*, above n 18. The three were arrested at 8:25 am, charged and were taken to be detained at the magistrates' court at 10:40 am They were brought before the magistrates at 3:45 pm at which time they were released, a little over seven hours after first arrested.
[94] *Petrovpavlovskis v Latvia* (App 44230/06), declared admissible on 3 June 2008.
[95] *CARAF* above n 29.

of four days and three and a half days' duration were enough to constitute interferences.[96] In two cases, governments have argued that if a march has actually gone ahead—perhaps a ban has been overturned or simply ignored—or that if a march was ended by security forces without anyone being charged or convicted, that meant there had been no interference. In both cases, the Court held for the applicants. In *Baczkowski v Poland*, the regional mayor banned a march and several static assemblies.[97] Both went ahead—in the case of the march with police protection. In each case the decision to impose a ban was overturned on appeal *after* the event had taken place. The government argued there had been no interference. On this, the Court said:

> However, the applicants took a risk in holding [the march and the assemblies] given the official ban in force at that time. The assemblies were held without a presumption of legality, such a presumption constituting a vital aspect of effective and unhindered exercise of the freedom of assembly and freedom of expression. The Court observes that the refusals to give authorisation could have had a chilling effect on the applicants and other participants in the assemblies. It could also have discouraged other persons from participating in the assemblies on the ground that they did not have official authorisation and that, therefore, no official protection against possible hostile counter-demonstrators would be ensured by the authorities . . . Hence, the Court is of the view that, when the assemblies were held, the applicants were negatively affected by the refusals to authorise them.[98]

We should note that the applicant was an organiser of the march. In *Aldemir and Others v Turkey*, the Court held that the forcible disruption of a demonstration (on the ground that the location was not permitted) and subsequent prosecutions, even though the only two charged were acquitted, both interfered with the right on the basis of a chilling effect: ie it may have discouraged others from taking part in similar meetings.[99] What about a challenge to a general ban, brought by an applicant 'A' who did not even try to hold a march—though, had she tried, she would have fallen foul of the ban? Would A be able to show any adverse effect?—How could she be a victim? Of what has she been deprived? It is a markedly different scenario to cases such as *Klass v Federal Republic of Germany* or *Dudgeon v UK*, where the court has permitted general provisions to be attacked by those who can show that those provisions were capable of being applied to them but had not yet been applied.[100] In each of those, there was a very strong case that each had been affected: each may well have changed their position by altering or modifying their behaviour in knowledge of the existence, respectively, of phone-tapping and laws prohibiting certain homosexual activity. As we saw in *Patyi*, which drew specifically upon *Baczkowski*, the Court permitted a challenge to be brought by the organiser who had planned a protest by 20 or so people outside the Prime Minister's house but which was banned.[101] It declared inadmissible claims by all the other named applicants as they were merely some of thousands who had lost money but, on the facts, this was because there was no evidence of their intention to protest. It is not clear what would have been the outcome had any of the other 47 indicated a desire to hold their peaceful vigil.

---

[96] *Pendragon*, above n 3, and *Gypsy Council v UK* (App 66336/01) ECtHR inadmissibility decision 14 May 2002.
[97] *Baczkowski*, above n 21.
[98] ibid, at [67]–[68].
[99] *Aldemir*, above n 23, at [34].
[100] *Klass v FRG* (1978) 2 EHRR 214; and *Dudgeon v UK* (1981) 4 EHRR 149.
[101] *Patyi*, above n 23.

The claim would be stronger if the reality were as follows: 'I wanted to hold a protest meeting on Monday but was caught by a general ban aimed at others. The first opportunity I had was the day the ban ended but by then it was too late to make known our concerns about XYZ . . . so we didn't try'. In such a situation, given the importance of being able to choose the time and venue of the protest (see *Stankov v Bulgaria*[102]) A could argue she was a victim of an interference under Article 11.

(iii) Permission and Authorisation

Another question that exercises judicial minds at Strasbourg is whether or not requiring permission or authorisation constitutes an interference.[103] It is clear that refusing to grant permission will constitute an interference, as it is akin to a ban. In *Djavit An v Turkey*, the ECtHR construed a refusal to grant a permit to travel into Southern Cyprus from the Turkish North as an interference on the right to assemble under Article 11, as it

> in effect barred his participation in bi-communal meetings there, preventing him consequently from engaging in peaceful assembly with people from both communities. In this connection the Court observes that hindrance can amount to a violation of the Convention just like a legal impediment.[104]

There is a clear difference, however, between subjecting a march or an assembly to the need for prior authorisation or permission—with the possibility of refusal or of conditions being imposed—and merely requiring prior notification—with the possibility of penalties for failing to do so—where the police have no power to refuse or any greater powers to regulate. If the former is not an interference, the latter less onerous restriction certainly cannot be. The orthodox Strasbourg position is that subjecting public assemblies to prior authorisation does not normally encroach on the right under Article 11 and so is not an interference.[105] With that power inevitably comes a power to impose sanctions for assembling without authorisation.[106] The Court's thinking here is by no means clear and simple.

(a) *Ziliberberg* and analysis

In *Ziliberberg*, the Court grappled with the question of the arrest and conviction of protester for 'active participation' in an unauthorised demonstration, as was required under

---

[102] *Stankov*, above n 27.
[103] A further issue has been whether or not state surveillance and police intelligence gathering at rallies are forms of interference with the right of peaceful protest. These have generally been viewed as restrictions on the right to respect for privacy under Article 8 rather than as restrictions on the right to protest. In *Friedl v Germany*, above n 34, the applicant did not even allege that surveillance was a breach of his rights under Art 11. Instead, he argued that taking, recording and keeping photographs (even anonymously without noting the names of the subjects of each photo) when protesters refused to move on from a sit-in on the road constituted a disproportionate interference with his private life. It was disposed of by friendly settlement. In *Tsavachidis v Greece* (App 28802/95) EComHR report 28 October 1997. Regular—and at times constant surveillance—by the Greek National Intelligence Service on account of his leading involvement with the Jehovah's Witnesses was held by the Commission as a violation of Art 8 (by 13 votes to four) with no separate issue under Art 11 (by 14 votes to three) and no violation of Art 9 (by nine votes to eight). Again the case was eventually resolved by friendly settlement (21 January 1999). In *Segerstedt-Wiberg v Sweden* (App 62332/00) ECtHR judgment 6 June 2006 (at [107]) the Court held that collating and storing personal data relating to political opinion, affiliations and activities that is deemed unjustified for the purposes of Art 8(2) ipso facto constituted an unjustified interference with the rights protected by Arts 10 and 11.
[104] *Djavit An*, above n 45.
[105] *Rassemblement Jurassien*, above n 28, at 119.
[106] *Ziliberberg v Moldova* above n 58.

Moldovan law. On one hand, the Court decided that the conviction undoubtedly constituted an interference but on the other, in approaching the three-limbed test under Article 11(2), the Court continued:

> [subjecting meetings on public thoroughfares] to an authorisation procedure does not normally encroach upon the essence of the right. Such a procedure is in keeping with the requirements of Article 11(1), if only in order that the authorities may be in a position to ensure the peaceful nature of a meeting, and accordingly does not as such constitute interference with the exercise of the right.[107]

It cannot of course be the case that an action can simultaneously be both an interference and not an interference with a right. The Court is distinguishing the need for an authorisation—generally not an interference—from penalising someone for failing to obtain one: this latter measure must be proportionate. Such an approach is not without its problems. It prevents the ECtHR from assessing the proportionality of the authorisation process because the three-stage process only kicks in once an interference has been found—so if draconian conditions were imposed under an authorisation system but were reluctantly complied with, since no one would have been arrested, there would have been no interference and so no one could challenge the conditions as being excessive.

Construing the need to obtain an authorisation as an interference would be a more favourable approach under a system of supra-national adjudication. It chimes well too with the 'chilling effect' concept at the heart of *Backzowski* and *Patyi*.[108] If draconian authorisation conditions are imposed and the march is then called off, under the orthodox *Ziliberberg* position, there will be nothing for the court to assess. In that regard, the Court has recently observed the importance of domestic procedural safeguards—in the context of bans in response to authorisation requests (and there is no reason why it should not apply to the imposition of conditions)—in preventing unreasonable restrictions on freedom of assembly.[109] It would allow courts to assess the proportionality of requiring permission rather than, if the reverse were true, possibly rendering the right to peaceful protest illusory or subverted by states imposing permission rules for any type of march, meeting, rally or assembly. It is to a large extent implicit in the recent *Ataman* case.[110] The demonstration there too was unlawful under Turkish law, for the organisers had not given prior notification 72 hours in advance, but the result was different. That failure meant, under Turkish law, that the demonstration could be dispersed by the police, once a request to do so had been made and refused. The Court did not consider prior notification unreasonable, but on the facts the manner of its dispersal—the speedy and heavy-handed response, allied to the fact that the demonstrators posed no threat to public order and were not themselves violent—meant there was a violation of Article 11.

> In the absence of violent acts on the part of the demonstrators, it is important that the public powers demonstrate a certain tolerance of peaceful gatherings so that the freedom of assembly as guaranteed by Article 11 is not deprived of all its meaning.[111]

---

[107] The Commission here adopted the wording mutatis mutandis in *Rassemblement Jurassien*, above n 28, at 119.
[108] Discussed above, text to nn 97–98.
[109] *Molnar*, above n 23, at [40].
[110] *Oya Ataman*, above n 66.
[111] *Ataman*, above n 66, at [42].

In so holding, the Court relied on its earlier decision in *Cissé v France* to underline its view that an irregular (domestically unlawful) situation does not justify a breach of the right of peaceful assembly.[112] It would also be consonant with the approach adopted by the EComHR in the case of *WG v Austria*, no mention of which is made by the Court in its *Ziliberberg* admissibility decision.[113] The applicant was convicted of unlawfully using a public road without authorisation. He and about 10 others were all staunchly opposed to nuclear power and wanted to inform the public about Austria's energy policy. On a single day (from 10 am to 6 pm) over four consecutive weeks, a table was set up in a pedestrian area so as to impart information and to distribute pamphlets. The applicant notified the police, but as he did not seek or obtain authorisation as required under Austrian law, he was arrested, convicted and fined.[114] Before the EComHR, both parties agreed that punishing someone for not having obtained an authorisation constituted an interference with their right to freedom of expression under the more general guarantee contained in Article 10(1). On the question of proportionality, the Commission concluded that

> balancing the interests of the prevention of disorder, in particular of an unhindered and safe traffic on public streets, and the interest of the applicant in the exercise of his right to freedom of expression ... in the present circumstances, the *requirement of prior authorisation of his activities could be regarded as justified*. The application of the Regulations by the Austrian authorities and the fine ... do not appear disproportionate to the legitimate aim pursued (emphasis added).[115]

It is important, though, that any administrative process or requirements—to be lawful under the ECHR—do not 'represent a hidden obstruction to'[116] peaceful protest and that their purpose is to 'allow the authorities to take reasonable and appropriate measures in order to guarantee the smooth conduct'[117] of the protest. If so, authorisation and notification does not normally encroach unnecessarily on the right.

(b) *Bukta* and analysis

To a great extent all of that must now take account of the ECtHR decision in *Bukta v Hungary*.[118] There the Court did not simply assume that the ability to apply sanctions was a necessary corollary of the power to require an authorisation.

A group of some 150 or so people met to demonstrate about the attendance of the Hungarian Prime Minister at an official reception hosted by the Rumanian Prime Minister, during the latter's official visit, on Rumania's National Day, a date commemorating the transfer of Hungarian Transylvania to Rumania. The group was dispersed by the police at the sound of a sharp noise. The group sought judicial review of the police decision in an attempt to have it declared unlawful. The action failed at first instance and on appeal: the

---

[112] ibid, [39], referring to *Cissé v France*, above n 16.
[113] *WG v Austria*, above n 32.
[114] Austrian law states that the use of public roads for purposes other than road traffic, in particular for commercial purposes or for advertising, requires an authorisation. No authorisation was required for meetings that constitute an assembly within the Assembly Act. In the eyes of the Austrian courts, this was not such a meeting as it was not one organised for the common purpose of inducing the participants to common action.
[115] Although *WG* was decided under Art 10 and *Ziliberberg* under Art 11—with the need for an authorisation being defined out of the scope of the primary right—there can be no difference surely between interfering with free speech and interfering with peaceful assembly? Either the need for an authorisation is an interference or it is not, and either is or is not proportionate.
[116] *Molnar*, above n 23, at [37].
[117] *Kuznetsov*, above n 23, at [42].
[118] *Bukta*, above n 23.

appeal court decided that the three-day notification rule—which had not been complied with, as the Hungarian Prime Minister only announced his intention the day before—applied to all demonstrations including spontaneous ones; any shortcomings were matters for the legislature not judges. That court further found that such a system could serve the public interest and the rights of others, namely, by protecting the free flow of traffic and the right to freedom of movement. The Strasbourg Court considered that the real reason for the disbanding—as evidenced in domestic decisions—was the absence of notice and not, as was alleged, the detonation and presumed security risk. The domestic courts had given no thought to the peaceful nature of the demonstration and founded their decision solely on the lack of any prior warning. The ECtHR went on:

> [I]n the circumstances of the present case, the failure to inform the public sufficiently in advance of the Prime Minister's intention to attend the reception left the applicants with the option of either foregoing their right to peaceful assembly altogether, or of exercising it in defiance of the administrative requirements. In the Court's view, in special circumstances when an immediate response, in the form of a demonstration, to a political event might be justified, a decision to disband the ensuing, peaceful assembly solely because of the absence of the requisite prior notice, without any illegal conduct by the participants, amounts to a disproportionate restriction on freedom of peaceful assembly.[119]

On one level, *Bukta* tells us only about the Court's approach to spontaneous protests where domestic laws do not allow such immediate responses. The general thrust though of the passage—particularly where the Court emphasises the need for a 'certain degree of tolerance towards peaceful gatherings' where 'demonstrators do not engage in acts of violence'—is not one that can so easily be confined and sits very uncomfortably with what the Court outlined in *Ziliberberg*:

> [S]ince States have the right to require authorisation, they must be able to apply sanctions to those who participate in demonstrations that do not comply with the requirement. The impossibility to impose such sanctions would render illusory the power of the State to require authorisation.[120]

The extent to which *Bukta* could be said to sanction a whole new approach to notice requirements was at the heart of *Molnar*: it could not be extended to the point that the absence of prior notification could never be a legitimate basis for crowd dispersal.

> The right to hold spontaneous demonstrations may override the obligation to give prior notification to public assemblies only in special circumstances, namely if an immediate response to a current event is warranted in the form of a demonstration. In particular, such derogation from the general rule may be justified if a delay would have rendered that response obsolete.[121]

On the facts, this was not the case. The election result, about which the applicants were so vexed, had been announced two months before. Nothing therefore justified holding a disruptive protest, on a main thoroughfare bridge, without notice. How the Strasbourg Court and English courts under the HRA will resolve this seeming conflict has yet to be worked out. The Court seems to have departed yet further from Ziliberberg in *Kuznetsov*: 'in the

---

[119] ibid, at [35]–[37].
[120] Unlike *Bukta*, in *Ziliberberg* the domestic rules did not solely prescribe that notice be given but empowered the local council inter alia to impose conditions on the conduct of the assembly: see Art 12 of the Moldovan Law of 21 June 1995 on the organisation and conduct of assemblies, set out in the ECtHR judgment. Intuitively one would imagine that a condition-imposing authorisation would be subject to greater scrutiny on proportionality grounds than a requirement merely to give notice.
[121] *Molnar*, above n 23, at [37]–[38].

circumstances ... merely formal breaches of the notification time-limit [were] neither relevant nor a sufficient reason for imposing administrative liability'.[122] The applicant had given only eight days' notice, not the required 10. The Court appears to be condoning a position that non-substantial deficiencies in complying with notification and authorisation rules; deficiencies that are minor in relation to both the rules and the event—certainly if they cause no additional burden on the authorities and still allow the police to maintain control—should not (cannot?) justify the imposition of penalties. We will return to all of this in the next chapter.

(iv) 'Non'-interferences

When considering the notion of 'interference' the Court can take a wrong turn by, on occasion, misconceptualising the nature of the measure. Two examples will make the point. In *Oner v Turkey*, an application under Article 11 was dismissed as being manifestly ill-founded in eight short lines.[123] Relatives of some PKK prisoners (on hunger strike at the arrest of Abdullah Oçalan) gathered at the regional offices of a sympathetic political party and went on hunger strike too. These offices were searched and all those present were taken into custody. It was alleged that PKK and other separatist literature was found there. Many were later convicted of aiding a terrorist organisation. Amongst the applications made to Strasbourg was one that alleged the arrest and taking into custody of all those at the offices was an unlawful interference with the right to peaceful assembly under Article 11. Having noted that Turkish law made it a crime to assist an illegal organisation, the Court continued:

> The applicants were taken into police custody not because of the fact they had gone on hunger strike, but because of the suspicion that their acts fell within the scope of [that offence]. They were later convicted since it was determined by the court that their acts fell within this provision. It follows that this complaint is manifestly ill-founded.

Similarly in *Salduz v Turkey*, S was convicted of aiding and abetting the PKK after participating in an illegal demonstration in support of Oçalan and hanging an illegal placard from a bridge.[124] The Court held that the applications under Articles 10 and 11 were manifestly ill-founded. S had not been convicted for expressing an opinion or for membership of a party but for aiding and abetting an illegal organisation.

While at first sight this seems an understandable and not particularly contentious position to adopt, treating and conceptualising the application in that way has the potential for significant concern. There is a strong line of cases—*Steel* being one—that flies in the face of these two decisions in which the Court appears to have been overly swayed by the domestic classification and construction of the wrongdoing. Arresting someone for an offence that is domestically defined and perceived as having nothing to do with restricting protest does not for that reason alone obviate the need for states to justify what is, on any definition, an interference with the right to assemble and to protest, more so in *Salduz* than in *Oner*. If such arguments were regularly allowed to succeed—that is, if the Court declared them inadmissible or found that there had not been a violation—it would open the door for states to 'define out' otherwise obvious interferences with the right to protest by framing their domestic laws to outlaw protest activity by the backdoor. It therefore limits what is inherent

---

[122] *Kuznetsov*, above n 23, at [43].
[123] *Oner v Turkey* (App 68684/01) ECtHR inadmissibility decision 1 June 2004.
[124] *Salduz v Turkey* (App 36391/02) ECtHR inadmissibility decision 28 March 2006.

in the ECHR, supra-national and pan-European protection for human rights. We could see laws making it not unlawful to protest but unlawful instead to stand outside an animal experimentation laboratory with a placard saying 'we don't like what you do' or to subject the Prime Minister to public ridicule. By analogy with *Salduz*, any conviction would not be for protesting but for that other discrete crime. An interference is an interference: being arrested must make it harder to continue with whatever form of protest has been chosen. The fact that they were later convicted by a court—and of what—is a 'red herring' in terms of assessing whether or not Article 11 is engaged, that is to say answering the question 'was there an interference?' Similarly irrelevant ought to have been—but was not—the fact that the applicants were accused of offering support to terrorists.

That is not to say that either application should have succeeded; it is to say that the proper resolution would have been to approach each case through the prism of necessity and proportionality. That seems to have been what occurred in *Karakaya and Piroglou v Turkey*, which expressly distinguished other freedom of expression cases against Turkey but not, it must be said, especially convincingly.[125] What really is the difference between *Salduz* and *Oner* on one hand and this one? Here the ECtHR decided that convicting someone for being involved in the 'Platform of Conscientious Objectors to War' (an organisation without any lawful status and thus contrary to the Turkish Associations Act) was in reality an interference with the right of free speech because their 'involvement' amounted only to the making of a collective press declaration in protest against the military operations of the USA in Afghanistan.

B. Prescribed by Law

The 'prescribed by law' test is designed to promote the rule of law and to eliminate arbitrary decision-making. The value and function of the test is ably demonstrated in one of the first cases to come before the Commission, *The Greek Case* in the late 1960s.[126] Applications were brought by Denmark, Norway, Sweden and The Netherlands alleging wholesale breaches of the ECHR during the rule of the Generals in Greece from 1967 to 1974. These included claims that freedom of assembly and association had been prohibited or restricted: 279 associations and organisations had been dissolved and had their property seized on the ground, the Government claimed, that they were Communist or Communist-inspired. Various laws and military proclamations prohibited, inter alia, all open-air gatherings of more than five people unless they were social or religious in nature or it was a lecture and the competent military authority had permitted it. All indoor gatherings were prohibited unless a competent public authority gave permission or the purpose was public entertainment, amusement or the gathering was of a social nature: a former Foreign Minister was sentenced to five years' imprisonment for holding a non-political dinner party attended by more than five people. In the Commission's opinion, none of the measures was lawful: the Commission considered that subjecting

> indoor meetings to the discretion of the police and lectures to that of the military authorities without any clear prescription in law as to how that discretion is to be exercised, and without further control, is to create a police state which is the antithesis of a 'democratic society'.

---

[125] *Karakaya and Piroglou v Turkey*, above n 21, at [48]–[49].
[126] *Denmark, Norway, Sweden and the Netherlands v Greece* (Apps 3321-4/67 and 3344/67) Commission report 5 November 1969.

The phrase bears the meaning of the two-limbed test set out in the *Sunday Times* case:[127] not only must there be a lawful domestic law basis for the interference,[128] but that domestic law must also be adequately accessible and certain. On the first limb, it does not matter that the law only entered into force a few days before the event in question, provided that in the national court's view, the (new) legal position was 'known to those who participated [in a protest] and all the applicants were aware of them when they committed the acts'.[129] A law is certain if it is 'formulated with sufficient precision to enable the citizen to regulate his conduct: he must be able ... to foresee, to a degree that is reasonable in the circumstances, the consequences which a given action may entail'. As we saw in chapter two, rules that are vague or have an uncertain scope or extent, or rules that are incapable of objective measurement may all lead to a finding of a violation of Article 11.[130] The test is designed to promote and to ensure the predictability of consequence X resulting from action Y: it should be clear to protesters in advance whether or not they will be subject to a penalty if they march or attend a rally or obstruct the road, so they can assess whether or not to protest at all.

Few cases turn on the domestic legal structure being insufficiently certain or accessible as to render the consequences of one's actions unforeseeable. Aside from the handful of Court decisions where the test has been determinative—which we considered at the start of this chapter—there are only a few more where it has even been an issue.[131] In the vast majority of cases, the issue of the quality of the law authorising the interference merits only a confirmatory paragraph or two in any one decision. We shall consider in turn the ways in which applicants have sought to use the requirement that an interference must be prescribed by law. The first is where there is no legal regime that governs the interference in question. The second, where the interference takes the form of a conviction for a discrete offence, is where it is argued that it was unforeseeable that that offence would be applied so as to criminalise the activity in question. The third is where vague or broad laws have been challenged as not providing adequate clarity and certainty. The fourth is where the Strasbourg Court holds that in fact domestic law has not been properly applied. Here it appears to be acting as a formal court of appeal rather than a review body but the danger of usurpation is minimised: in the one case where it has occurred—*Steel v UK*—no decision of a national court had ever been handed down.

(i) No Legal Regime at All

Adali v Turkey is probably the only example of the first category of cases that do not in fact depend on the operation of the *Sunday Times* test at all.[132] The Turkish government lost because there was no legal framework governing the interference in question, a requirement of permission to cross into Southern Cyprus from the Turkish controlled North. The decision to refuse permission to attend a public meeting (into deaths in custody and disappearances) organised by a radio station and attended by journalists was arbitrary and unlawful.

---

[127] *Sunday Times* case (1979) 2 EHRR 245 at [49].
[128] The Court and Commission have tended, sensibly and unsurprisingly, to defer to national courts and national institutions whenever they are asked to assess whether or not an interference had a legally valid domestic basis: see, as just one example, *Drieman v Norway* (App 33678/96) ECtHR inadmissibility decision 4 May 2000.
[129] *Drieman, ibid.*
[130] Broad, blanket laws might minimise the chances of a restriction not being 'prescribed by law'—but are also more likely to lead to a holding that a restriction is disproportionate.
[131] In addition to the cases discussed below in the text, this would include *Cissé*, above n 16; *Ezelin*, above n 25; *Pendragon* above n 3; and *Stankov v Bulgaria* above n 27.
[132] *Adali v Turkey*, above n 21, and see too *Djavit An* (above n 45), decided on the same basis a month before.

(ii) Unforeseeable Application

There have been a few cases of the second type, the focus of which was that the application of the law to a given event or activity was unforeseeable. In *Stefanec*, it was not a foreseeable interpretation of domestic law for the organiser of an illegal march to be fined for announcing publicly during its course that the march had been arbitrarily banned. Others were the four sit-in cases against Germany.[133] In each the Commission was asked to assess the legality, in Convention terms, of extending the offence of 'blameworthy coercion of another by force' (contrary to section 240 of the German Criminal Code) so as to criminalise those taking part in sit-ins on the road outside US Air Force airbases.[134] The applicants argued that the extension of the concept of force by the German courts was unlawful in terms of both Article 7 and under Article 11(2). No longer was physical force required; all that was now needed was expenditure of minimum energy by which the victim's freedom to decide what to do was inevitably influenced. Case law had not changed the essential elements of the offence to render criminal previously non-criminal situations. Instead, the Commission concluded that

> the progressively broader interpretation of the term 'force' ... has adapted the offence of 'unlawful coercion by force' to new circumstances and developments in society which can still reasonably be brought under the original concept of the offence.[135]

By contrast, in *Karakaya and Piroglou*, the Court held that the Turkish courts had extended the scope of a domestic rule on associations—that they may not form organisations—beyond that which could have been reasonably foreseen in the circumstances of the case. In the Court's view, this wording was not sufficiently clear to enable members of the association to have realised that rallying to a movement or 'platform' would lead to criminal sanctions being imposed on them: how could supporting such a movement be deemed to amount to the formation of an organisation within the meaning of the Act?[136]

(iii) Vague or Unclear Rules

The third type of case is where laws or rules are said to be too vague or unclear. One example is *Hashman and Harrup v UK*, which we considered earlier.[137] Fox-hunt protesters were bound over to keep the peace and not to engage in behaviour *contra bonos mores*, the latter

---

[133] *CS v Germany* (App 13858/88); *G v Germany* (App 13079/87); *Schiefer v Germany* (App 13389/89); and *WM and HO v Germany* (App 13235/87), all EComHR inadmissibility decisions 6 March 1989.

[134] Section 240(1) reads: 'Wer einen anderen rechtswidrig mit Gewalt oder durch Drohung mit einem empfindlichen Übel zu einer Handlung, Duldung oder Unterlassung nötigt, wird mit Freiheitsstrafe bis zu drei Jahren oder mit Geldstrafe, in besonders schweren Fällen mit Freiheitsstrafe von sechs Monaten bis zu fünf Jahren bestraft'. Section 240(2) reads: 'Rechtswidrig ist die Tat, wenn die Anwendung der Gewalt oder die Androhung des Übels zu dem angestrebten Zweck als verwerflich anzusehen ist'.

[135] *CS v Germany* above n 133.

[136] *Karakaya and Piroglou*, above n 125, at [54]. In *Christian Democratic People's Party v Moldova* above n 2, the Court may have found a violation based on the prescribed by law test but preferred instead to deal with the case on the surer footing of proportionality. A one-month ban was imposed on the applicant party's activities after it had organised an allegedly unauthorised demonstration it had been warned was illegal and unconstitutional. It was given three days to respond thereafter, the warning continued, the ban would be imposed. On the fourth day it was informed of the ban and three new—and more specific—grounds were invoked for justifying the ban. This led the Court to comment that the 'applicant party was not, therefore, informed in the warning letter of all the acts imputed to it, which reduced its ability to foresee all the consequences which the continued holding of meetings could entail. This in itself might be a sufficient basis for the conclusion that the impugned measures were not 'prescribed by law'. The Court did not consider it necessary finally to decide that issue.

[137] *Hashman and Harrup v UK* above p 61.

being defined as 'wrong rather than right in the judgement of contemporary fellow citizens'.[138] In the Court's view, such a requirement was too vague, that is to say too subjectively worded, to be predictable and was not prescribed by law.[139] *Ziliberberg v Moldova* revolved around the notion of 'active participation' in an unauthorised demonstration. The applicant argued that the term was insufficiently defined as to leave potential participants insufficiently certain whether or not their actual participation would be against the law. The Commission concluded that imposing a penalty on an 'active participant' was sufficiently clear as to be prescribed by law:

> [W]hilst certainty in the law is highly desirable, it may bring in its train excessive rigidity and the law must be able to keep pace with changing circumstances. Accordingly, many laws are inevitably couched in terms which, to a greater or lesser extent, are vague and whose interpretation and application are questions of practice . . . In the instant case the Court does not consider that the provision in question is so vague as to render the consequences of the applicant's actions unforeseeable. The 'active participation' in a demonstration might take so many forms that it might prove impossible to make an exhaustive list within a legal provision. It is therefore the duty of the courts to decide in every particular case what is 'active participation' and what is not.[140]

There have also been challenges to the scope of discretion conferred by widely framed domestic laws: broad, undefined discretion does not enable people to regulate their conduct or to foresee the consequences of any decision they take. *Rai, Allmond and Negotiate Now! v UK* featured a challenge to a decision not to permit any meetings or demonstrations in Trafalgar Square that related to Northern Ireland.[141] Regulations made in 1952 provided that permission was required, inter alia, to organise, conduct or take part in any assembly, parade or procession or to make or give a public speech or address in Trafalgar Square.[142] The refusal of permission to the applicants was in accordance with government policy on the exercise and structuring of permission under the 1952 Regulations, a policy announced to the House of Commons in a Ministerial statement in 1972. The Commission affirmed a position it had previously adopted that

> a law which confers a discretion is not in itself inconsistent with the requirement of foreseeability inherent in this concept, provided that the scope of the discretion and the manner of its exercise are indicated with sufficient clarity to give the individual protection against arbitrary interference.

---

[138] *ibid*, at [38].

[139] Judge Baka dissented on that point. In his opinion 'in the concrete circumstances of the case, the applicants should have known what kind of behaviour was *contra bonos mores* . . . [T]he "keep the peace or be of good behaviour" obligation has to be interpreted in the light of the specific anti-social behaviour committed by the applicants'. The case of *Chorherr* (above n 86) raised a similar question to that in *Hashman*. There, section IX(1) sub-para 1 of the Austrian Introductory Law of the Administrative Procedure Law makes it an offence for 'anyone who creates a breach of the peace by conduct likely to cause annoyance'. The applicant argued that its generality—and, we must imagine, the vagueness created by use of such imprecise and immeasurable terms—meant it fell foul of the *Sunday Times* formula. The Court decided 'that the level of precision required of the domestic legislation—which cannot in any case provide for every eventuality—depends to a considerable degree on the content of the instrument considered, the field it is designed to cover and the number and status of those to whom it is addressed . . . Furthermore it is primarily for the national authorities to interpret and apply domestic law . . . In the present case there is nothing in the Constitutional Court's judgment to lend weight to the proposition that the wording of the contested provision creates a situation incompatible with legal certainty . . . Mr Chorherr was therefore in a position to foresee to a reasonable extent the risks inherent in his conduct' (para [25]).

[140] *Ziliberberg v Moldova*, above n 58, at p 8 of the HUDOC transcript.

[141] *Rai, Allmond and Negotiate Now! v UK* (App 25522/94) (1995) EHRR CD 93, EComHR inadmissibility decision 6 April 1995.

[142] These were made pursuant to primary legislation in 1926, which empowered the making of such regulations as was considered 'necessary for securing the proper management of [any] park and the preservation of order and prevention of abuses therein'.

On the facts, the Commission concluded that although the power to regulate the Square was not subject to defined restrictions, the policy was formally and publicly announced and there had been numerous refusals subsequently. Thus, it was compatible with the requirements of foreseeability

> that terms which are on their face general and unlimited are explained by executive or administrative statements, since it is the provision of sufficiently precise guidance to individuals to regulate their conduct rather than the source of that guidance which is of relevance.

The Commission found the refusal was prescribed by law. The difficulty ignored by the Commission was the effect on foreseeability, and thus on the quality of law, of four cases (from 1976 to 1993) where permission to hold a rally or a demonstration was granted. The government view in the 1990s was that those cases were regarded as 'uncontroversial and non-partisan', and hence were exceptions. This is problematic in two ways. First, instituting a policy whereby only uncontroversial outpourings on the subject of Northern Ireland can be heard publicly in Trafalgar Square at a rally seems to fly in the face of what Article 10 is all about:[143] freedom of speech applies to information and ideas that 'offend, shock or disturb'.[144] Secondly, how can anyone know in advance if a rally is going to be uncontroversial? One person's controversy is another's certain truth. Such a term is so value-laden that using the term as a gauge virtually assures that it will be operated arbitrarily, without objective parameters, by government. Isn't this exactly the sort of thing that the 'prescribed by law' test was designed to minimise or remove? It was argued on behalf of the applicants that such a qualitative assessment of any one march or rally—the policy indicated that the only exceptions were for 'entirely uncontroversial peace demonstrations'—rendered it sufficiently vague or arbitrary as not to be prescribed by law. The Commission iterated that in its view the 'scope and manner of the exercise of the power to regulate assemblies in Trafalgar Square [were] indicated with the requisite degree of certainty to satisfy the minimum requirements of the criterion of "prescribed by law"'. That must be a conclusion open to some doubt: how can any one group predict that its rally will or will not be controversial given that (almost by definition) its controversiality is in the hands of the audience?

(iv) Improper Domestic Application

The last area of challenge is where it is accepted that the legal rules are clear, certain and foreseeable but it is argued they have not been properly applied by national authorities. This was the case in another of the breach of the peace cases—against the UK—to come before the Court. In *Steel and Others v UK* the issue was binding over to keep the peace.[145] Three separate groups of protesters challenged their arrest, temporary detention and, in the case of the first two applicants, subsequent detention after they refused to be bound over to keep the peace. The Court decided that the concept of breach of the peace and the relevant rules in national law were formulated with sufficient precision to allow citizens reasonably to foresee the consequences of their actions. However, in the case of the third, fourth and fifth

---

[143] In fact, it was argued by the applicants that permitting only uncontroversial marches and rallies—as explicitly set out in the policy—meant the policy was unlawful, in Convention terms. It was seeking to achieve a policy outcome—that all controversial marches be prohibited—that was not one of the listed legitimate social aims within Art 11(2).
[144] *Handyside v UK*, above n 52, at [49].
[145] *Steel* above n 18. The common law offence of breach of the peace, behind both the power to arrest and to bind over, was held to be sufficiently clear and precise.

applicants—whose protest was entirely peaceful, consisting of distributing leaflets outside an arms fair—the Court was not satisfied that the police were justified in fearing a breach of the peace. Unlike the first and second applicants, whose cases had been before the national courts, the third, fourth and fifth applicants were released without charge after their initial arrest and detention.[146] In the absence of a national decision, the Court was able to review the facts anew. It concluded that the arrests and detention of third, fourth and fifth applicants failed to comply with English law: the Court was not satisfied that any of the three had caused or was likely to cause a breach of the peace. That being so, the Court found a violation of Article 5(1)(c) in respect of the third to fifth applicants—as the deprivation of their liberty was not lawful, that is to say was not prescribed by law—and a violation of Article 10 on the same basis.[147]

C. Legitimate Aim

Article 11(2) provides seven permissible bases for states to found a claim that it was necessary to interfere with the primary right under Article 11. These are: the interests of national security or public safety; preventing disorder or crime; protecting health or morals; or protecting the rights and freedoms of others. There is considerable overlap with Article 10 but also bespoke measures arising specifically in the context of free speech. The latter permits restrictions that are necessary in the interests of 'territorial integrity' whereas Article 11 does not; it must be assumed that Article 11 was deliberately worded so as to exclude such state aims. Article 10 also permits—provided they are necessary—laws preventing disclosures received in confidence and for maintaining the authority and impartiality of the judiciary. Article 10 permits interferences that protect the 'reputation and rights' of others whereas Article 11 more widely allows for interferences that protect the 'rights and freedoms' of others.[148] This has been taken to include a host of claims that are not, and do not amount to, rights under the ECHR—or even rights at all—as well as those that do. An example of the latter type of claim is *Öllinger*.[149] Both sides agreed that the restriction on the proposed demonstration (objecting to an SS memorial ceremony in the same cemetery) would affect the rights under Article 9 of all visitors to the cemetery.

In terms of the former type of claim, let us consider *Nicol and Selvanayagam v UK*.[150] In the context of low-level, direct action protest against a fishing competition the Court

---

[146] The Court is reluctant to overturn the reasoned judgment of national courts on the issue even where the domestic case that is brought is a civil one for damages for wrongful arrest rather than a criminal one that assesses the liability for breach of the peace: see *McBride v UK* above n 43.

[147] The only similar case—but where the national courts were deemed to have misapplied a clear law—was *Baczkowski v Poland*, above n 21. There decisions by a local mayor to ban a march and several assemblies were overturned—after the dates for the march and assemblies had passed—on appeal. Despite the fact that the lower decisions lost their binding force once overturned, the ECtHR concluded the bans were not prescribed by law. It is not clear what the applicant hoped to achieve from their case given that the Constitutional Court confirmed the appellate decisions.

[148] In no case is there any discussion of what distinguishes a 'right' from a 'freedom'—they are elided: see as an example *Drieman v Norway*, above n 128. The Commission concluded that action taken against Greenpeace members who were obstructing a whaling ship could reasonably be viewed inter alia as for the protection of the rights and freedoms of others. The measure was 'aimed at securing the effective enforcement of the rules protecting whaling in the Norwegian exclusive economic zone'.

[149] *Öllinger*, above n 47.

[150] *Nicol and Selvanayagam v UK* (App 32213/96) ECtHR admissibility decision 11 January 2001, p 11 of the HUDOC transcript.

appears to have recognised a right—and not merely a freedom—to fish. To say that fishing is lawful under UK law does not mean that anyone has a right to fish. Absent any specific positive right—and none is apparent in the text of the decision—all that can be said is that the competitors were free—in the sense of not debarred or not prevented from being able—to catch fish. A does not have a 'right' but a Hohfeldian privilege—there is no duty on the state to permit fishing but no right to stop it. It is also clear that the Court accepts that the 'rights of others' extends to 'maintaining the orderly circulation of traffic'.[151] As with all other 'claw-backs', a fairly flexible approach has been taken at Strasbourg to what is an exhaustive list such that no protest application has been declared inadmissible or adjudged to be a violation for want of a legitimate aim.[152] In *The Gypsy Council v UK* the traditional annual Horsmonden Horse Fair (a 'significant cultural and social event in the life of the Romany gypsy community') was banned and the Court concluded that the ban struck a fair balance between the rights of the applicants and those of the community even though at no stage were any of their 'rights' actually identified.[153]

(i) The Range of 'Disorder'

As we saw earlier, the legitimate aim that has been claimed by far and away most often is preventing disorder, either alone or in combination with preventing crime. A consideration of some of these will give us a flavour of the types and range of cases that reach Strasbourg.

In *GS v Austria*, the Commission accepted that the desire for unhindered and safe traffic in public streets was a legitimate aspect of preventing disorder and so could be balanced against the applicant's right to freedom of expression (when he set up information stands and distributed leaflets in a pedestrian area). The application was declared inadmissible.[154] In *S v Austria*, the Commission held that banning a demonstration that was avowedly going to use music and rhythmical instruments was capable of being justified on the grounds of preventing disorder and protecting the rights of others given the likely excessive noise disturbance.[155] In contrast with its usually detailed analysis of the necessity of any given measure, the explanation of how and why the Commission considers the measure will achieve the aim is usually sparse: more often than not the explanation is little more than an assertion of a fait accompli.[156]

Historically, 'disorder' has been used by the Court less in the sense of the absence of order, turmoil, civil disturbance or chaos and more as a substitute for inconvenience,

---

[151] *Molnar*, above n 23, at [34].
[152] This is not peculiar to Article 11. Even in *Christian Democratic People's Party v Moldova*, above n 2, the pivotal issue was the necessity of a ban on the party's activities for organising an unauthorised demonstration, rather than the fact that the 'government did not make any particular submissions in respect' of there being a legitimate aim. It ought to have been the case that a finding of a violation (as did occur) was on that basis solely or at least as well as there being no relevant and sufficient reasons shown by the government for imposing the ban.
[153] *Gypsy Council v UK*, above n 96.
[154] *GS v Austria*, above n 41, and with similar facts and issues see *WG v Austria*, above n 32, which refers to ' the security and free flow of traffic'. Both were declared inadmissible.
[155] *S v Austria* (App 13812/88) EComHR inadmissibility decision 3 December 1990.
[156] We might with a measure of irony contrast this with the outcome and reasoning in one of the Court's own Article 11 decisions, *Ivanov v Bulgaria* (App 46336/99) ECtHR judgment 24 November 2005. There mayoral bans on rallies and demonstrations due to be held by UMO Ilinden were held to be unlawful violations of Article 11: the 'mayoral bans only made brief references to an alleged threat to public order, without stating the basis for such a conclusion or going into further detail . . . Thus, even assuming that the legitimate aims pursued were public safety and the prevention of disorder, it can hardly be concluded that the authorities gave relevant and sufficient reasons justifying the prohibitions'.

annoyance or disruption. Let us consider some further examples. Perhaps the best abdication of any need for an independent investigation of governmental claims that a measure is designed to achieve an aim comes in *Ziliberberg v Moldova*.[157] There the applicant was given an administrative fine for being an active participant in an unauthorised demonstration. In deciding that the application under Article 11 was inadmissible, the Commission had this to say about the legitimate aim:

> It is apparent that Mr Ziliberberg incurred a punishment provided for by the Code of Administrative Offences. Article 1 provides that the Code aims inter alia at the protection of public order. The interference was therefore in pursuit of a legitimate aim, the 'prevention of disorder'.

The Court does not question the motive of the government in punishing Ziliberberg or even the general purpose of the Code. On that basis, what is to prevent governments drafting laws that include bland, bald statements referring to at least one of the prescribed aims as part and parcel of any repressive, rights-restricting measure, so as to ensure it passes the first hurdle of the three-stage test in Article 11(2)? It is assumed that because the Code indicates its role is to protect public order—that is, preventing disorder—any penalty incurred for a breach must necessarily serve that legitimate aim.[158]

A similar presumption lies behind the finding of inadmissibility in *G and E v Norway*.[159] Here, a group of (at most) six Lapps erected a tent outside the Norwegian Parliament in order to make known their views about issues affecting them as an ethnic group. They were protesting specifically about the proposal to build a hydro-electric power station in their valley. The group had been authorised to demonstrate for five hours on a single day but they ended up staying for four days. They challenged their subsequent arrests at Strasbourg. The Commission declared the application inadmissible on every issue. As to Article 10, it said this: 'A demonstration by setting up a tent for several days in an area open to public traffic must necessarily cause disorder'. The Commission saw no need to explain how that would be the case. Without knowing the location and volume of pedestrian traffic, it is by no means obvious that any disruption would be caused. It is perfectly possible and reasonable to assume that no one would actually be disrupted by the presence of a single tent. There was surely a greater need to justify that assertion, given that a limited protest had been permitted: why was it thought, and we must assume, accepted that a five-hour protest in the middle of the day would not have caused disruption but a four-day one would have done?

By contrast, in the more recent case of *Patyi*, a five-metre-wide pavement was held to be an unlikely venue for disruption by a group of 20 (at most) protesting opposite the Prime Minister's house.[160] Passers-by could still use the pavement. Is there now a need for authorities to prove actual disruption or obstruction? In the German anti-nuclear sit-in cases the applicants challenged their convictions for unlawful coercion by force. They had blocked the road in front of US military barracks for several minutes, preventing military cars from using the road.[161] Their applications under Article 11 were declared inadmissible. The Commission found that the convictions could

---

[157] *Ziliberberg v Moldova*, above n 58.
[158] See, as one example, the holding and analysis in *Gypsy Council v UK*, discussed above n 153.
[159] *G and E v Norway*, above n 86.
[160] *Patyi v Hungary*, above n 23.
[161] *CS v Germany* above n 133. The Article 7 application was based around the fact that in convicting (and upholding that conviction) the German courts unforeseeably extended the remit of the existing offence and so punished her for a crime not known to law when the act was committed. This application too was rejected as manifestly ill-founded.

reasonably be considered as necessary in a democratic society for the prevention of disorder and crime ... [since] the applicant had not been punished for her participation in any demonstration as such, but for particular behaviour in the course of the demonstration, namely the blocking of a public road, thereby causing more obstruction than would normally arise from the exercise of the right of peaceful assembly.[162]

Aside from the issue of conceptualisation that we met in the cases of *Oner* and *Salduz*,[163] the Commission elides preventing crime with preventing disorder without feeling the need to grapple with what are clear distinctions between the two notions. Not only that, but at no stage does it seek to understand, or require any evidence so as to establish, why—and how—the sit-in created, caused or contributed to 'disorder'. Is blocking a road for a few minutes really something can be said to upset public order rather than to create a 'mere' inconvenience?[164]

The Gypsy Council case saw the Court treating as synonyms 'disorder' and 'disruption', effecting a subtle and worrying extension to an already vague and broad term, the more so if we consider the actual examples relied upon: historically disruption had been caused by the 'sheer volume' of visitors, indiscriminate parking, littering, a background level of increased crime and road closures. Obviously, combatting one of those side-effects— increased crime—is a legitimate and free-standing aim which, assuming the measure to be necessary, would mean the interference would be lawful, yet the Commission does not rely upon it for its holding. Why? Having said that, the elision of 'disorder' with annoyance and disruption has now largely been superseded by a more recent line of cases—such as *Balçik v Turkey* and *Oya Ataman v Turkey*—which show the Court taking a more favourable line on short-term, temporary blockages of roads and thoroughfares in the context of 'preventing disorder' claims.[165] We shall consider these below.

Positing cases such as *CS v Germany* and *GS v Austria* against a case such as *CARAF* shows the spectrum of disorder the prevention of which the Court is prepared to countenance as a legitimate aim. We can more easily see the risk of disorder in *CARAF*, where a clear and identifiable threat of violence either stemming from or aimed towards the participants in a National Front march was sufficient (alongside protecting public safety and the rights and freedoms of others) to justify a ban on all marches in London over a set period.[166] Similarly, the reasonable expectation of clashes between groups, based on past experience or with some other objective grounding, can be seen in *Rassemblement Jurassien et Unité Jurassienne v Switzerland*. There all demonstrations in public thoroughfares in the Jura were banned at a time of separatist tension between German- and French-speaking groups.[167] The Commission accepted that the tense situation meant a serious danger of disorder existed

---

[162] See mutatis mutandis on basically the same facts *G v Germany, Schiefer v Germany* and *WM and HO v Germany* all above n 133. In *Lucas v UK* (App 39013/02) ECtHR inadmissibility decision 18 March 2003 where arrests and convictions of those who staged a sit-in in the road leading to Faslane naval base were declared applications under Arts 10 and 11 following inadmissible: it considered the arrests and convictions could be regarded as pursuing the interests of public safety as well as preventing disorder.
[163] Above nn 123 and 124.
[164] See also *Chorherr*, above n 86, where the Court concluded that the arrest of a peaceful protester distributing anti-arms leaflets and holding a medium sized placard during a rally to celebrate the end of World War II 'pursued at least one of the legitimate aims referred to in Article 10(2) namely the prevention of disorder'. Even on the government's own contention Chorherr's behaviour was beginning to engender a commotion at most such that he himself had been threatened.
[165] Below p 106.
[166] *CARAF* above n 29.
[167] *Rassemblement Jurassien*, above n 28

and so it accepted the justifications of public safety and preventing disorder. At the other end of the spectrum is *Cissé v France*, the forcible evacuation of those participating in a two-month sit-in occupation of a church as part of a protest about France's immigration laws.[168] In the Court's view, 'the evacuation was ordered to put an end to the continuing occupation of a place of worship by persons, including the applicant, who had broken French law. The interference therefore pursued a legitimate aim, namely the prevention of disorder'. How can the occupation of a church—with the consent of the religious authorities and parishioners—be a cause of possible disorder? What does the element of breaking French law add—if not to make the aim one of 'preventing crime'? 'Preventing disorder' here smacks of being equated with 'they're doing something we don't like and if we don't act, they'll be seen to get away with it'. Accepting that argument edges the Court nearer to quite a slippery slope and the decision would have benefited from greater honesty, transparency and explanation.

The approach of the Court in *Ezelin v France* again appears to give short shrift to the question of legitimate aim: the Court appears to be hurrying to get to the interesting nub of any case, the proportionality of any measure. In *Ezelin*, punishment (very low-level professional discipline) was imposed on a lawyer who participated in a demonstration on Guadeloupe because he

> had not dissociated himself from the unruly incidents which occurred during the demonstration ... [and] such an attitude was a reflection of the fact that the applicant, as an avocat, endorsed and actively supported such excesses. The interference was therefore in pursuit of a legitimate aim, the 'prevention of disorder'.[169]

How does—or can—the continued peaceful participation of a lawyer in what began as a lawful, peaceful protest but which took a 'wrong turn' lead to an increased risk of disorder? How can—or does—his ex post facto disciplining prevent it, either from occurring or from becoming greater? Let us assume it is possible—what is the basis for such a conclusion? Where is the evidence, the data, the argument? Asking for such material might be seen as tantamount to importing the necessity test (though not necessarily the proportionality test) much earlier into the court's reasoning. Nonetheless, without some sort of case being made out—rather than merely accepting government assertion—the legitimate aim test is denuded of any value whatsoever.

The final case we will consider will demonstrate further the flexible nature and skew in favour of states. In *Rai, Allmond and Negotiate Now! v UK*, Negotiate Now! a non-partisan NGO, wished to hold a 'stationary' peaceful rally of up to 1000 people in Trafalgar Square in London in order to promote their views on how to achieve peace in Northern Ireland.[170] Permission was sought from the government but was refused on the basis that

> the policy of successive Governments since 1972 was to refuse permission for any public demonstrations or meetings on the issue of Northern Ireland in Trafalgar Square. This policy has been applied in an entirely impartial way. The only, very rare, exceptions have been approval for entirely uncontroversial peace demonstrations.

The NGO and two members challenged this decision at Strasbourg under Article 11. In the course of domestic judicial review proceedings the government had maintained that the

---

[168] *Cissé*, above n 16.
[169] *Ezelin*, above n 25.
[170] *Rai, Allmond and Negotiate Now! v UK*, above n 141

basis for its refusal was its public order concerns. The UK government defended the application by continuing that stance in Strasbourg. The problem was that the Metropolitan Police had been informed of the proposed rally and the Commissioner's view was that it would create no danger to public order. Nonetheless, the EComHR ruled that the UK's general policy of banning all demonstrations concerning Northern Ireland pursued the twin aims of preventing disorder and protecting the rights and freedoms of others, without giving any explanation of how this was so or even how it could be so other than an acknowledgement of the government's intention to avoid Trafalgar Square being used by those supporting violence. There was no *evidence* that this would be the case and in any event the firm view of the police was that there was no danger of disorder. The Commission noted that the circumstances of Northern Ireland led to sensitive and complex issues arising as to the causes of the conflict and any possible solutions. Nobody would dispute that but isn't that what free speech exercised through the medium of a peaceful assembly is about, contributing to public discussion on difficult topics that affect the polity? Is it defensible for the Commission of its own volition to have latched onto the legitimate aim of preventing disorder when that did not appear to be in the minds of the state's authorities at the time (or any time afterwards) and was not even predicted as a danger?[171]

D. Necessary in a Democratic Society

The last stage of the three-limbed test in Article 11(2) is the determination of where the balance should lie between the individual right peacefully to protest and the wider public interest in (say) preventing disorder. Only if it is a necessary—that is, measured and balanced—response will an interference be viewed as lawful in the eyes of the Strasbourg Court, because only then can it be said to meet a 'pressing social need'. We shall here refer to this test by its usual shorthand—proportionality. We saw earlier that the data bears out the view that proportionality plays a decisive role in determining the outcome of peaceful assembly cases at both the admissibility and substantive merits stages. We shall end this chapter by considering the detail of some of those cases so as to understand how this limb of the test plays out in practice.

On one side of the equation we can see that the Court has repeatedly stressed the functional importance of the right to peaceful protest and its valuable contribution to a pathologically healthy, informed participatory democracy. The right to freedom of assembly 'is a fundamental right in a democratic society and, like the right to freedom of expression, is one of the foundations of such a society. Thus, it should not be interpreted restrictively'.[172] There is a close symbiotic link between Articles 10 and 11: the 'protection of opinions and the freedom to express them is one of the objectives of the freedoms of assembly and association as enshrined in Article 11'.[173]

Against that important right and the political role it plays—as well of course as its value to individual autonomy—must be set the legitimate aims. These must be 'narrowly inter-

---

[171] If the Commission had one eye on delayed disorder elsewhere—perhaps making the 'troubles' in Northern Ireland harder to police—as a reaction to the rally taking place, was that really in the minds of the framers of the Convention? Is it a legitimate extension of the concept behind the restriction? If so, it has the potential to act as quite a considerable break on the rights of protesters.
[172] See *Rassemblement Jurassien*, above n 28, 119, *G v Germany* above n 133 p.256, *Djavit An*, above n 45, at [56] and *Ziliberberg* above n 58.
[173] *Christian Democratic People's Party v Moldova*, above n 2, at [62].

preted and the necessity for any restrictions must be convincingly established'.[174] Each can only serve as a limiter if it too serves the greater democratic interest: 'the only necessity capable of justifying an interference with any of the rights enshrined in those Articles is one that must claim to spring from a 'democratic society'.[175] The tension at the heart of any attempt by the Court to resolve protest cases satisfactorily, fairly or proportionately is immediately apparent. Interferences on peaceful protest must take account of the

> hallmarks of a 'democratic society' [giving] particular importance to pluralism, tolerance and broadmindedness. In that context, [the Court] has held that although individual interests must on occasion be subordinated to those of a group, democracy does not simply mean that the views of the majority must always prevail: a balance must be achieved which ensures the fair and proper treatment of minorities and avoids any abuse of a dominant position.[176]

That said, where the authorities imposed a ban on an historic, traditionally held Romany fair—out of fear of the disorder that would occur were it to be held—the Commission declared that the right is not absolute: 'where large gatherings are concerned the impact of the event on the community as a whole may legitimately be taken into consideration'.[177] That rather risks overplaying the social at the cost of the individual, even if the underpinning sentiment is sound: the nature of Article 11 requires a balance between, on one hand, rights and, on the other, what are usually community *interests*.[178] Conceptually, it is important always to bear in mind that the right to peaceful protest is competing against what might well be lesser interests, themselves not deemed worthy of protection by the Council of Europe as a full-blown right. Nonetheless, as we shall see, on numerous occasions the wider public interest has defeated individual rights—as occurs regularly throughout Articles 8–11.

The democratic underpinnings are interesting because they can cut both ways. The Court has stressed on several occasions that organisers and participants in demonstrations 'as actors in the democratic process should respect the rules governing that process by complying with the regulations in force'.[179] This has tended to arise in the context of administrative regulations in force—notification and authorisation—in which case the problem is a lesser one and one, in fact, that we have already addressed. If however 'regulations in force' is given a wider meaning such as the rules or framework governing the conduct of protests this raises a serious issue. If one of the regulations in force were 'No one may criticise the Prime Minister during a march', should protesters abide by that regulation in force? This is similar to the misconceptualisation point we came across in relation to *Oner* and *Salduz*.[180] The Court cannot surely have meant that they should, but if not, why not? Several solutions present themselves but each would benefit from clarification. First, the Court's comments

---

[174] *Osmani* above n 24, at p 13 of the HUDOC transcript.
[175] *Christian Democratic People's Party*, above n 2, at [63].
[176] ibid, para 64; see too *Baczkowski*, above n 21, at [63].
[177] *Gypsy Council v UK*, above n 96.
[178] Though of course community interests may well be relevant, they will only be so—and then only determinative if it is also 'necessary' to interfere—when 'the impact ... on the community as a whole' coincides with one or more of the legitimate aims in Art 11(2). Size alone—which would of course be a considerable impact—cannot sway the decision (on similar facts to these) to ban or to restrict a march or rally unless it can also be said that the rights and interests of others are concerned. It would have to be conceded, as we have already seen above, that the trigger for that is not set too high; it is hard not to imagine a case where the impact on the community would not also be said to raise the interests of others as a legitimate aim. That though is not ignore the important conceptual point that the impact on the community only plays a role when it can also be said to fall within Article 11(2).
[179] See *Balçik*, above n 17, at [49] and *Molnar*, above n 23, at [41].
[180] See text to nn 123 and 124 above.

relate only to matters of procedure not substance. It is only procedural rules that must be obeyed by respectful democratic actors. Secondly, the duty to obey regulations, even if of substance not form, does not extend to rules and regulations that denude the right of peaceful protest, Article 10 in particular, of any meaningful content and which undermine the participatory democracy underpinnings to the right itself.

(i) The Margin of Appreciation[181]

When assessing whether or not an interference is necessary, the Court has set out its approach in a large number of cases. We can draw on just one, *Stankov v Bulgaria*.

> Contracting States have a *certain* margin of appreciation in assessing whether [a pressing social need] exists, but it goes hand in hand with European supervision, embracing both the legislation and the decisions applying it, even those given by an independent court ... When the Court carries out its scrutiny, its task is not to substitute its own view for that of the relevant national authorities but rather to review under Article 11 the decisions they took. This does not mean that it has to confine itself to ascertaining whether the respondent State exercised its discretion reasonably, carefully and in good faith; it must look at the interference complained of in the light of the case as a whole and determine, after having established that it pursued a 'legitimate aim', whether it was proportionate to that aim and whether the reasons adduced by the national authorities to justify it are 'relevant and sufficient'. In so doing, the Court has to satisfy itself that the national authorities applied standards which were in conformity with the principles embodied in Article 11 and, moreover, that they based their decisions on an acceptable assessment of the relevant facts (emphasis added).[182]

Stating that states have a 'certain' margin of appreciation—or, as in *Osmani*, 'a certain but not unlimited margin of appreciation'[183]—tells us nothing about its extent and scope. In many other areas, the Court has expounded at least a basic scheme. We saw in chapter two that the margin of appreciation is likely to be narrow where restrictions are imposed on political journalism[184] or where the interference concerns a 'most intimate aspect' of private life[185] and wide where there is no European consensus on the scope of the right in question or where the right touches upon moral or ethical matters.[186] In very few of the peaceful protest cases has the Court undertaken any explicit analysis of the concept. In *Chorherr*, the Court stated that when assessing the margin of appreciation—the tolerance permitted to states in assessing both whether and to what extent it needs to interfere—'due regard must be had to the importance of freedom of expression in a democratic society'.[187] It added that the margin of appreciation 'extends in particular to the choice of the—reasonable and appropriate—means to be used by the authorities to ensure that lawful manifestations can take place peacefully'.[188]

---

[181] See generally H Yourow, *The Margin of Appreciation Doctrine in the Dynamics of European Human Rights Jurisprudence* (The Hague/Boston/London, Kluwer Law International, 1996); M Hutchinson, 'The margin of appreciation doctrine in the European Court of Human Rights' (1999) *International Comparative Law Quarterly* 638, S Greer, *The margin of appreciation: interpretation and discretion under the European convention on Human Rights: Human Rights files No 17* (Strasbourg, Council of Europe Publishing 2000).
[182] *Stankov*, above n 27, at [87].
[183] *Osmani*, above n 24, p 13 of the HUDOC transcript.
[184] *Jersild v Denmark* (1994) 19 EHRR 1.
[185] *Dudgeon v UK*, above n 100.
[186] *Pretty v UK* (2002) 35 EHRR 1.
[187] *Chorherr v Austria*, above n 86, at [31].
[188] ibid.

In only a few cases has the Court even ventured forth an opinion on the extent of the margin of appreciation. In each it has concluded that states should be allowed a deal of width. Greater clarification and exposition on this most important topic would indeed be most welcome. Given its close link—in many situations at least—to free political speech and, as we have seen, the functional role it plays in a healthy democracy, it would not be unreasonable to assume that the 'certain' margin granted to states should be reasonably narrowly constructed at least where the protest takes the form of peaceful communicative action—banner waving, marching, demonstrating—rather than being or becoming obstructive or disruptive. That would be consonant with *Drieman v Norway*, where Greenpeace members who obstructed a Norwegian whaling vessel were arrested. The Court considered that

> the disputed interference related to conduct which could not enjoy the same privileged protection under the Convention as political speech or debate on questions of public interests or the peaceful demonstration of opinions on such matters. On the contrary, the Court considers that the Contracting States must be allowed a wide margin of appreciation in their assessment of the necessity in taking measures to restrict such conduct.[189]

Clearly, greater width is needed where national authorities are grappling with and responding to an emergent crisis with a demonstrable effect on order. In one of its earliest pronouncements, *Rassemblement Jurassien*, the Commission was asked to assess a ban on all political meetings in one Swiss canton at a time of heightened separatist tension with consequent worries about public safety and preventing disorder. The report makes reference to the fact that given 'the number of sympathisers expected, serious clashes and disorder could be foreseen, as is proved by the subsequent discovery of explosive devices'. The Commission decided the applicants' challenge was inadmissible: a ban was necessary and was one that was within the state's margin of appreciation. The Commission declared that the margin of appreciation was 'fairly broad once the authority, as in this case, is confronted with a foreseeable danger affecting public safety and order and must decide, often at short notice, what means to employ to prevent it'.[190] This reflects the fact that national authorities are most obviously better placed to assess the risk and solutions than an international body some several years later. Notably, the Commission did not take account or even allude to the role and value of peaceful protest as part of the democratic process, as it did later in *Drieman*.

The acknowledgement in *Rassemblement Jurassien* of a 'fairly broad' margin in the circumstances is not the same as declaring as a rule that Article 11 attracts a wide margin of appreciation. That seems to be what the Court in *Cissé* considered to be the correct position: it said it would have 'regard to the wide margin of appreciation left to the States in this sphere'.[191] If this purports to be a general statement of the law it is doubtful if it is correct. The case on which it drew was the earlier Commission decision in *Plattform 'Ärzte'*. The comparison does not stand up. *Cissé* involved direct intervention and interference with a peaceful protest—the forcible eviction of squatters staging a sit-in in a church so as to protest about France's immigration rules. As we saw above, *Plattform 'Ärzte'* was a case in which the extent of the state's positive duty to facilitate and to safeguard the right to assemble was under the judicial microscope: it was in the context of that, more limited duty that the Commission stated:

---

[189] *Drieman*, above n 128, at p 10.
[190] *Rassemblement Jurassien*, above n 28, at 121.
[191] *Cisse v France*, above n 16, at [53].

While it is the duty of Contracting States to take reasonable and appropriate measures to enable lawful demonstrations to proceed peacefully, they cannot guarantee this absolutely and they have a wide discretion in the choice of the means to be used.[192]

There is no reason why as a rule the margin of appreciation should be wide under Article 11.

There are in fact clear, sound reasons for allowing states narrower room to manoeuvre when they interfere with protests traditionally seen as complementing the political process directly, such as rallies, meetings and marches. Though there is no case law directly on the point, it follows by implication from some of the holdings the Court has made in other free speech cases and on Article 11 cases concerning restrictions imposed on political parties. Taking just one example from the former category, in *Lindon v France*—arising out of the applicant's conviction before the domestic courts for defaming Jean-Marie Le Pen in a novel—the Court asserted that there is

> little scope under Article 10(2) ... for restrictions on freedom of expression in the area of political speech or debate—where freedom of expression is of the utmost importance ... Furthermore, the limits of acceptable criticism are wider as regards a politician as such than as regards a private individual. Unlike the latter, the former inevitably and knowingly lays himself open to close scrutiny of his every word and deed by both journalists and the public at large, and he must consequently display a greater degree of tolerance.[193]

Looking at our second category, one association case in particular is pertinent: it involved a temporary ban on the activities of a parliamentary party for having organised an unauthorised demonstration. In *The Christian Democratic People's Party (CDDP) v Moldova*, the Court held there was a violation of Article 11 because the reasons provided in support of the ban were neither relevant nor sufficient to justify it. The Court stressed, as it has in many other cases, the democratic underpinnings of the ECHR and of Articles 10 and 11, particularly in the case of formal party politics. It recalled earlier cases where the state was described as 'the ultimate guarantor of the principle of pluralism'[194] and noted how the guarantee of regular and free elections was a means to ensure the free expression of the people in their choice of legislature. It continued:

> Such expression is inconceivable without the participation of a plurality of political parties representing the different shades of opinion to be found within a country's population. By relaying this range of opinion, not only within political institutions but also—with the help of the media—at all levels of social life, political parties make an irreplaceable contribution to political debate, which is at the very core of the concept of a democratic society ... In view of the essential role played by political parties in the proper functioning of democracy, the exceptions set out in Article 11 are, where political parties are concerned, to be construed strictly; only convincing and compelling reasons can justify restrictions on such parties' freedom of association. In determining whether a necessity within the meaning of Article 11(2) exists, the Contracting States have only a limited margin of appreciation, which goes hand in hand with rigorous European supervision.[195]

That case is clearly about restrictions on formal political parties. While it could be used to support a narrow margin of appreciation in protest cases, it could also be said that protest—certainly as defined at the outset of this chapter—is the antithesis of organised political debate and discourse. In *Stankov v Bulgaria*, a case in which the Court considered whether

---

[192] *Plattform 'Ärzte'*, above n 52, at [34].
[193] *Lindon v France* (2008) 46 EHRR 35 at [46].
[194] *Informationsverein Lentia and Others v Austria*, Series A no 276 p 16, at [38].
[195] *Christian Democratic People's Party v Moldova*, above n 2, at [66]–[68].

or not banning meetings (and other activities) that an association planned to hold was compatible with Article 11, the Court stated:

> One of the principal characteristics of democracy is the possibility it offers of resolving a country's problems through dialogue, without recourse to violence, even when those problems are irksome. Democracy thrives on freedom of expression. From that point of view, there can be no justification for hindering a *group* solely because it seeks to debate in public the situation of part of the State's population and to find, according to democratic rules, solutions capable of satisfying everyone concerned (emphasis added).[196]

At its heart, the reasoning in *CDDP* and *Stankov* is concerned with ensuring an informed electorate able to weigh up and to choose between competing policy alternatives. If that is the basis of the rights guaranteed in Articles 10 and 11, why should rigorous supervision and scrutiny be reserved for formally constituted parties? Why should it not extend to those—such as pressure groups, NGOs and individuals outside the formal party structures—who want to meet, to march and to demonstrate in favour of or against one of those policy alternatives, a form of political engagement a small step removed from formal party politics? This must be all the more so given the close functional link between Article 10 and Article 11, whereby protecting 'opinions and the freedom to express them is one of the objectives of freedom of assembly and association enshrined in Article 11'.[197] If it is accepted that 'there is little scope under Article 10(2) for restrictions on political speech or on debate on questions of public interest',[198] then presumably the same applies for restrictions on the right to peaceful assembly under Article 11 in cases where a march or rally is being used as the means to communicate a political message or to engage with an issue of public interest. A prime example would be those marches organised to demonstrate opposition to the war in Iraq. Clearly, such reasoning would allow the Court—should it choose—to distinguish more obstructive or intimidatory protest and then to construe the margin more widely since those forms of direct action do not have as their aim engagement with the polity but intervention with the activity itself.

(ii) Factors Underpinning the Court's Approach

We saw in chapter two how the proportionality principle plays out at a general level. There needs to be an objective, rational connection between means and ends: a restriction must actually be capable of achieving the stated aim and if lesser means could achieve the same aim but at lesser 'cost' to rights, they should be utilised. We can glimpse the Court's approach in the following short extract from *Vajnai v Hungary*.[199] In deciding that a blanket restriction (by criminalising) on wearing the red star—as a totalitarian symbol—in public was a disproportionate restriction on free speech, the Court observed that 'apart from the ban in question, there are a number of offences sanctioned by Hungarian law which aim to suppress public disturbances even if they were to be provoked by the use of the red star'.[200] We shall conclude this chapter by analysing the Court's approach in selected cases to the question of the necessity of an interference, so as to elicit some of the factors considered relevant to the assessment.

---
[196] *Stankov*, above n 27, at [88].
[197] *Öllinger v Austria*, above n 47, at [38].
[198] ibid, and see also *Stankov*, above n 27, at [88].
[199] *Vajnai*, above n 23.
[200] ibid, [55].

(a) Time Manner and Place (TMP) Restrictions

In *Ward v Rock Against Racism* the US Supreme Court stated that government under the First Amendment

> may impose reasonable restrictions on time, place, or manner of protected speech, provided the restrictions are justified without reference to the content of the regulated speech, that they are narrowly tailored to serve a governmental interest, and that they leave open ample alternative channels for communication.[201]

Here the task a court is engaged in is assessing the extent to which restrictions deprive protesters of the essence or the substance of the right, either in its entirety or something approximating it, or whether the restrictions in reality only limit how the protest can take place, or where or when. This is by no means a simple task capable of clear-cut resolution: is a long-term camp the means by which the protesters choose to make their point known or is it the protest itself, something that has 'acquired a symbolic force inseparable from the protester's message'?[202]

One obvious way of looking at the issue is to consider the existence of alternative means for protesters to make their point. Strasbourg has stressed that this will reduce the likelihood of a restriction or interference being viewed as unnecessary. Clearly the provision or availability of reasonable alternatives has greater resonance as groups get nearer to obstructive direct action and is one factor in those applications that are almost uniformly being declared inadmissible. In *Drieman*, the Commission was greatly influenced by the fact that the Greenpeace protesters had alternative means open to them to demonstrate and to express their disapproval without restraint rather than coercing the whaling boats to stop a lawful activity.[203] In the *Gypsy Council* case the facts that an alternative site was being providing only 20 miles away and that a limited procession at the venue had been permitted by the police on the day in question were enough for the Commission to consider the ban on the traditional Romany horse-fair was necessary. If an interference has not fully impaired the ability to meet, demonstrate or march altogether this might sway the Court. In *Pendragon* although there was no alternative site to Stonehenge, the Commission emphasised the fact that this was not an absolute ban on the religious rights of the Druids, since they could meet in a smaller group of 19 or fewer.[204] In *Rassemblement Jurassien*, where all meetings in one area of one Swiss Canton were banned for a specified period, the Commission noted that

> the ban concerned only the territory of the Municipality of Moutier and its duration, indicated in advance, was limited in time. Proof of this is that a demonstration did take place, without any opposition from the authorities, less than one month after the planned date of the second demonstration.[205]

---

[201] *Ward v Rock Against Racism* 491 US 781, 791 (1989).

[202] *Tabernacle v Secretary of State for Defence* [2009] EWCA Civ 23 at [37] (Laws LJ). The issue was the legality, in ECHR terms, of a bye-law (promulgated by the Minister) which prohibited camping around the atomic weapons facility at Aldermaston, ostensibly on grounds of national security, public safety, preventing crime/disorder and right of others. It thus barred the women's peace camp, which twice a month for a weekend for 23 years had gathered there.

[203] *Drieman*, above n 128

[204] *Pendragon*, above n 3. As we shall see in chapter five, this was on the basis that at the time an 'assembly' constituted 20 or more in open air. It was only groups of that number that were regulated under the legislation in question. This is now less of get out of jail free card in the hands of the state as meetings of two or more have constituted an assembly for the purposes of imposing conditions since 2003.

[205] *Rassemblement Jurassien*, above n 28, at 121.

Taking such a stand requires a degree of circumspection for three reasons. First, holding that a ban was necessary where protesters were not deprived entirely of their ability to protest denies them any autonomy over the choice of time, manner or place of protest; as we have seen, the right to protest serves not only wide, public imperatives but can also support and sustain important private interests, such as choice and respect. Here, the Court is being overly swayed by the more obvious public utility of protest. Thus as the official delegation was departing Amsterdam railway station to put the city forward at Lausanne as a candidate to host the 1992 Games the removal of someone who unfurled a 'No Olympics' banner might seem justified as she was not prevented from protesting elsewhere. However, the removal did deprive her of the choice of the location where (presumably) she considered the protest would be most effective.[206] Secondly, it would still be the case that any meeting planned to take place during the prohibition period would not be allowed and the timing of this may in fact be crucial: there is after all no point in holding a public meeting to denounce the Prime Minister as a thief the day after a General Election.

(b) Blanket Bans

The third reason for taking a critical stance to TMP restrictions is that it will inevitably require a qualitative assessment of the point when a large-scale restriction—but with alternatives—becomes in effect an outright blanket ban. These, because by definition they are not tailored towards any threat but are applied in uniform fashion, without discrimination, have real risks of not meeting a pressing social need.

In *Rai, Allmond and Negotiate Now!*, the general policy of banning all rallies in Trafalgar Square where the subject-matter was the 'troubles' in Northern Ireland was proportionate because it was not a blanket ban.[207] The decision not to permit the applicants' rally only prevented them from being able to use that high-profile location; other locations were available. This factor was used by the government in argument and was relied on by the Court to hold that the applicants' rights were not truly or properly—or disproportionately—infringed. They seemed unaware that such a proposition cuts both ways—and indeed comes very close to being circular. At no stage did the Government explain why it was necessary—as a general policy—to prohibit rallies dealing with Northern Ireland in only one part of London while not adopting such a general policy for other high-profile locations, such as the many parks and open spaces.[208] Even if all 'high-profile' locations were subject either to a general policy or to individual bans, this leads to the second unexplained point: what is it about high-profile locations that justifies banning all rallies on the subject of Northern Ireland? If the rally had been banned in all areas in London—because of its subject-matter—then this *would* amount to a blanket ban and one based on subject-matter, lacking content neutrality, in the language of First Amendment jurisprudence. This the government would have struggled to justify. High-profile does not—we can assume—

---

[206] *JK v Netherlands* above n 30. See too *Heikkila v Finland* (App 25472/94) EComHR inadmissibility decision 15 May 1996: an group was ordered away from its chosen venue, outside the town hall, and refused. The measure was necessary to prevent disorder and in the interests of public safety—they had not been prevented from participating in an earlier demonstration.

[207] *Rai, Allmond and Negotiate Now!*, above n 141.

[208] It may seem convoluted but this argument is not dissimilar to the reasoning in *A and Others v Secretary of State for the Home Dept* [2004] UKHL 56. There the House of Lords struck down legislation that permitted detention without trial of foreign terrorist suspects. The legislation did not empower the detention of UK terrorist suspects, despite their being an admitted threat, and it was this partiality that indicated the legislative scheme was an arbitrary and unjustified restriction on liberty.

necessarily equate to 'large likely audience' so what is it about one high-profile location that makes it possible to ban *all* rallies on one subject there whereas if all rallies on the same topic were banned all over, this would undoubtedly amount to a disproportionate interferences? We shall never know. What is reasonably clear is that a general policy—which admits of few or no exceptions—tends to be disproportionate; as a matter of logic it can rarely be proportionate to impose blanket restrictions which are not tailored to individual circumstance and take no account of specific factors such as the threat posed, past history, the intention of the protesters, and impact and effect of the protest. A 'one size fits all' way of dealing with disorder, one that is not tempered by detail or situation, is one that is likely to struggle when it comes to the question of necessity. This is borne out by *Stankov*: 'an automatic reliance on the very fact that an organisation has been considered anti-constitutional—and refused registration—cannot suffice to justify under Article 11(2) of the Convention a practice of systematic bans on the holding of peaceful assemblies'.[209]

It is not just the policing or administrative response that needs to be tailored so as to avoid charges of being blanket—legislation must do so too. In *Vajnai*, the issue was the outright criminalisation of the wearing of the red star in public, as being symbolic of totalitarianism and thus eliciting memories of Hungary's past that many would prefer to have forgotten. The ban was unlawful as a disproportionate restriction on freedom of expression. The symbol had multiple meanings and therefore might be restricted in unjustified circumstances:

> [U]tmost care must be observed in applying any restrictions, especially when the case involves symbols which have multiple meanings. In such situations, the Court perceives a risk that a blanket ban on such symbols may also restrict their use in contexts in which no restriction would be justified ... the ban in question is too broad in view of the multiple meanings of the red star. The ban can encompass activities and ideas which clearly belong to those protected by Article 10, and there is no satisfactory way to sever the different meanings of the incriminated symbol. Indeed, the relevant Hungarian law does not attempt to do so. Moreover, even if such distinctions had existed, uncertainties might have arisen entailing a chilling effect on freedom of expression and self-censorship ... A symbol which may have several meanings in the context of the present case, where it was displayed by a leader of a registered political party with no known totalitarian ambitions, cannot be equated with dangerous propaganda. However, section 269/B of the Hungarian Criminal Code does not require proof that the actual display amounted to totalitarian propaganda. Instead, the mere display is irrefutably considered to be so [save in very limited situations]. For the Court, this indiscriminate feature of the prohibition corroborates the finding that it is unacceptably broad.[210]

(c) Rigidity of the Police Approach

In a similar vein, the Court has engaged in an assessment of policing tactics, considering if they were appropriate as a means to prevent disorder or to protect the rights and freedoms of others.[211] Strangely, this has not been a more pervasive theme in the Court's jurisprudence given that the notions of a 'pressing social need' and 'proportionality' tend to (though it must be conceded do not inevitably) require consideration—by the court at

---

[209] *Stankov*, above n 27, at [92].
[210] *Vajnai v Hungary*, above n 23, at [51], [54] and [56].
[211] Whether doctrinally speaking the seeming shift—evidenced at least in the *Pendragon* case, above n 3—in the onus of proof, from state to the applicant, is correct is moot. There, the applicants suggested how the ban could have been avoided. This led the Court to respond that it was 'not persuaded that this would have necessarily prevented the disorder and disruption which was anticipated'. Once a prima facie interference with a right is shown, is it really for the applicants to persuade the Court that it was one that was disproportionate? Those that restrict or remove rights should suffer the burden of justification.

least[212]—of the efficacy of alternatives, for both those individuals whose rights are under threat and for society generally as it strives to prevent disorder.

In *Gypsy Council v UK* (not a protest case), the applicants argued that the police decision to ban the horse-fair was disproportionate, as there were alternative measures that could have both accommodated the fair and assuaged concerns about disorder and disruption. These included: imposing reasonable conditions on conduct by regulating car parking; limiting the number of stall holders; ensuring sufficient policing and sufficient stewards were provided by the organisers; and ensuring that the village was cleaned afterwards by liaising with the gypsy representatives. The Court, in holding the Article 11 application to be inadmissible, was not persuaded that this would have necessarily prevented the anticipated disorder and disruption and so concluded the policing decision was proportionate. In *S v Austria*—the excessive noise protest—the Commission rejected the argument that alternative, less restrictive measures should have been taken. The applicant argued that instead of imposing a ban in advance, the authorities should have implemented a 'wait and see' policy. Failing to adopt that less restrictive measure (ending or dispersing the demonstration during its course) rendered the measure that was imposed a disproportionate one. Accepting that states have 'a certain margin of appreciation', the Commission considered

> that it was not disproportionate in the present case to [prevent excessive noise] by the prohibition of the demonstration rather than by its subsequent dissolution. Having regard to the previous experience it was in no way unreasonable or arbitrary to assume that the proposed demonstration would also lead to excessive noise. This assumption was supported, in particular, by the text of the applicant's notification to the authority and his subsequent admission that the noise should be loud enough to be heard by an inmate of a prison.

In *Patyi*, it was clear that one factor in the Court holding that there was a violation was the fact that the police had routinely and mechanistically repeated a ban on a demonstration outside the Prime Minister's house based on traffic disruption. Yet, on the day in question (Christmas Eve) it was accepted by both sides that no buses had run after 4:00 pm The Court was not convinced that a 20-minute protest by no more than 20 people on a five-metre-wide pavement would have hindered traffic.[213] It concluded that

> the authorities, when issuing repetitive prohibitions on the demonstrations, mechanically relying on the same reasons and not taking into account Mr Patyi's factual clarifications, failed to strike a fair balance between the rights of those wishing to exercise their freedom of assembly and those others whose freedom of movement may have been frustrated temporarily, if at all.

Another factor will be the speed of the police response in cracking down on protesters. This is what distinguishes, partially at least, the finding of a violation in *Oya Ataman* and the finding that there was no breach in *Molnar*. In the latter, the Court decided that the protesters had a reasonable length of time to make their point about the disputed elections, despite the disturbance to traffic and the fact that no advance notice had been given. The police had shown the necessary tolerance towards the demonstration and had not acted in too peremptory a fashion.[214] In *Oya Ataman*, the demonstration had been put down forcefully (another point of departure)—with tear gas—and very speedily after it started.[215]

---

[212] Under the HRA at least, public bodies are not required to assess the proportionality of decisions they take: *R (Begum) v Governors of Denbigh High School* [2006] UKHL 15.
[213] *Patyi*, above n 23, at [42].
[214] *Molnar*, above n 23, at [42]–[43].
[215] *Oya Ataman*, above n 66.

The Court in *Öllinger* adopted a more critical approach to policing strategy. Öllinger wished to commemorate those Salzburg Jews killed by the SS during the Second World War by holding a meeting at the war memorial in the municipal cemetery. It was planned specifically to coincide in time and place with an All Saints' Day commemoration by former members of the SS. The ECtHR decided that the ban imposed by the Austrian authorities was disproportionate even if it was designed to protect the right of cemetery-goers to manifest their religion under Article 9. The applicant argued that the authorities had not made any efforts to ensure that both assemblies could take place. In deciding the case in Öllinger's favour, the Court indicated its view that in the circumstances[216] it was

> not convinced by the Government's argument that allowing both meetings while taking preventive measures, such as ensuring police presence in order to keep the two assemblies apart, was not a viable alternative which would have preserved the applicant's right to freedom of assembly while at the same time offering a sufficient degree of protection as regards the rights of the cemetery's visitors.[217]

In contrast to the rigidity of the police, the Court has considered—or at least noted—that one factor in finding that a state did not have sufficient and relevant reasons to intervene (thus violating the right) would be the flexibility and readiness of the applicant to co-operate.[218]

(d) The Sanction Imposed

Another factor historically that has influenced the Court in finding for the state has been the size and type of the punishment imposed by the domestic courts for the breach of the law. Financial penalties or administrative penalties have tended to be upheld especially if they are 'relatively minor'. In *Lucas* a fine of £150 imposed after conviction for breach of the peace after staging a sit-in on the road outside Faslane naval base was one factor in holding her application inadmissible. Similarly, in *Ziliberberg* the Court declared as inadmissible the challenge to a conviction for active participation in an unauthorised demonstration, partly on the basis that the penalty (about €3) was at the lower end of the scale despite also acknowledging that it appeared 'heavy, relative to the applicant's revenue'. While that itself is a valid criticism, there are two more prominent objections. First, the amount of any penalty imposed may in fact be less of an interference than a 'mere' finding of guilt, with all that a criminal conviction entails: possible loss of job, criminal record to be declared and social stigma. Secondly, the scale of the punishment *after* the event may well have less of an impact on someone's ability to protest than removing them from the scene of a demonstration so as to be charged—or not—with a minor infraction of the law. Once the momentum and dynamic behind a march or rally has been lost, with several key protesters strategically removed to be bailed or released without charge, it may well be that the protest fizzles out: when those arrested are later released a few hours later, the march they had led may comprise little more than placards in the gutter.

---

[216] Those circumstances were: first and foremost, that Ö's assembly was in no way directed against the beliefs of other cemetery-goers or the manifestation of them. Moreover, the applicant expected only a small number of participants. They envisaged peaceful and silent means of expressing their opinion, namely the carrying of commemorative messages, and had explicitly ruled out the use of chanting or banners. Thus, the intended assembly in itself could not have hurt the feelings of cemetery-goers. Moreover, while the authorities feared that, as in previous years, heated debates might arise, it was not alleged that any incidents of violence had occurred on previous occasions.
[217] *Öllinger*, above n 47, at [48].
[218] *Kuznetsov*, above n 23, at [44].

It is not always the case that penalties on even a small-scale favours states. Criminal liability (as opposed to European administrative wrongdoing) or where the penalty is some form of incarceration even for a short period will make it harder for states to avoid liability. This was so in *Vajnai*, where the penalty for wearing the banned red star was the Hungarian equivalent of a suspended sentence.[219] Again there has been some shifting by the Court in the course of the millenium. In *Ezelin*, the punishment was minor—a professional disciplinary reprimand—and in *Steel* the third, fourth and fifth applicants were arrested, charged and detained but released after about seven hours without prosecutions being brought. In each case violations of the Convention were found: in *Ezelin* a majority of 6:3 held there was a violation of Article 11 with a clear acknowledgement that though the penalty was 'minimal' (para 53) the majority felt that the sanction was not necessary. It was primarily on the quantum of the penalty imposed that the three dissenting judges (Judges Ryssdal, Pettiti and Matscher) concluded the interference was proportionate. In *Steel*, the Court found unanimously that there had been a violation of Article 10 for the three peaceful anti-arms campaigners—though in truth there was no discussion of the size of the penalty. Instead the finding was based on the fact that, given that the three were released, the domestic courts had not assessed the proportionality of the arrests and detentions so the Court could effectively visit it de novo: in its view, there was no evidence for the police reasonably to fear a breach of the peace.[220] The fact that the three were clearly peaceful, non-obstructive protesters provides no distinction—so was the applicant in *Ziliberberg*. *Lucas* and *Ziliberberg* were both decided after *Ezelin* and *Steel* but neither judgment makes any reference to them. In its later *Galstyan* decision, the Court did draw on *Ezelin* (contrasting it with the instant case where the applicant was subjected to a more severe penalty, three days' loss of liberty) to assert this more general proposition:

> [F]reedom to take part in a peaceful assembly is of such importance that a person cannot be subjected to a sanction—even one at the lower end of the scale of disciplinary penalties—for participation in a demonstration which has not been prohibited, so long as this person does not himself commit any reprehensible act on such an occasion.[221]

There are echoes of this more critical approach in several other cases. We learn from *Çsanics* that even a mild sanction 'does not render a restriction compatible with the Convention if it is not in itself necessary in a democratic society'.[222] There the penalty was that he had to rectify his statement and pay court costs. Similarly, the fact that the amount of the fine for picketing a local court, to highlight issues over access to justice, was relatively small (€35) did not detract from the fact that the interference was not 'necessary in a democratic society'.[223]

---

[219] *Vajnai*, above n 23, at [29].
[220] It is clear too that in respect of the other two applicants, a key factor was the level of punishment. By five votes to four the Court decided the measures imposed on the first applicant (who intentionally impeded a shoot by walking in front as the members aimed their shotguns) who refused to be bound over was a proportionate measure. The four who voted in favour of the applicant stressed not the fact of the detention but the length of both the initial and subsequent detention. In the words of Judges Valticos and Markarczyk 'to detain for forty-four hours and then sentence to twenty-eight days' imprisonment a person who, albeit in an extreme manner, jumped up and down in front of a member of the shoot to prevent him from killing a feathered friend is so manifestly extreme, particularly in a country known for its fondness for animals, that it amounted, in our view, to a violation of the Convention'.
[221] *Galstyan v Armenia*, above n 23, at [115].
[222] *Çsanics v Hungary*, above n 8, at [46].
[223] *Kuznetsov*, above n 23, at [48].

(e) The Type of Protest

A further factor in the Court's reasoning has been the nature of the protest itself. The Court has consistently ruled against direct action protests—the essence of which is obstruction of the very activity being opposed—whenever the issue has come before it on a question of substantive disproportionality. Recently though the Court has started to look more favourably on obstructive protest where the obstruction or disruption is the undesired side-effect of the primary intention to communicate a political message or to persuade, what we referred to above as incidental or inevitable disruption rather than intended and direct disruption.[224]

Direct action protests do not succeed at Strasbourg and largely are declared inadmissible. Those few that have passed that hurdle—and may even have succeeded—have all done so on other grounds such as the 'prescribed by law' test. Historically, the Court has tended not to differentiate between cases where obstruction or disruption was intended and those where obstruction or disruption is a consequence of matters such as the time or place of the protest. Thus earlier in the chapter we saw the Court melding 'disorder' with 'disruption' in cases such as *G and E v Norway*[225] (the Laplanders' four day tent protest outside Parliament), *GS v Austria*[226] (the unauthorised demonstration on a public road, in the form of two small tables from which information was handed out), *S v Austria*[227] (the 'excessive noise' ban) and the four German sit-in cases.[228] Looking at just one, *G and E*, the Commission found that the interference with their rights could reasonably be considered necessary to protect public order: 'a demonstration by setting up a tent for several days in an area open to public traffic must necessarily cause disorder'. As well as failing to explain why disorder would 'necessarily' be caused, the Commission also fails to explain why it was consequently necessary (that is, proportionate) to arrest the group. This analysis is not an aberration on the part of the Commission. Strasbourg reasoning largely tended to assume disruption flowed from a protest (given the need to make a point or to highlight a concern which meant attracting attention) and that disruption equated to disorder, making it necessary for states to step in. Latterly, the Court has been giving greater consideration to the conduct and impact of the protest in question.

In a series of judgments from 2005 onwards, the Court has been at pains to stress that where marches and demonstrations are peaceful and there are no calls to, or threats of, violence national authorities should exercise considerable caution before imposing restrictions or stepping in, even if the protest is, under domestic law, unlawful and even if it has the potential to disrupt. In *Balçik*, the Court was asked whether it was necessary for the Turkish police violently to break up a demonstration and march by a group numbering just under 50.[229] The police had argued their intervention was needed because the protesters had not given 72 hours' advance notification, as required under Turkish law, and because they feared disruption and disorder at a busy time of day in a busy area in Istanbul. In holding that the forceful intervention by the police was disproportionate, the Court said:

---

[224] We might add the caveat that the obstruction must be more than de minimis: clearly for the first three applicants in *Steel and Others v UK*, there was some obstruction of the pavement and disruption for the participants at the arms conference by being subjected to unwelcome banners as they made their way inside.
[225] *G and E v Norway* above n 86.
[226] *GS v Austria* above n 41.
[227] *S v Austria* above n 87.
[228] *CS v Germany; G v Germany; Schiefer v Germany*; and *WM and HO v Germany*, all above n 133.
[229] *Balçik*, above n 17.

> [T]here is no evidence to suggest that the group presented a danger to public order, apart from possibly blocking the tram line. The Court notes that the group in question consisted of forty-six persons, who wished to draw attention to a topical issue, namely the F-type prison conditions. It is observed that the rally began at about noon and ended with the group's arrest within half an hour at 12.30 p.m. The Court is therefore particularly struck by the authorities' impatience in seeking to end the demonstration. At this point, the Court also recalls that although no notification had been given, the authorities had prior knowledge ... that such a demonstration would take place on that date and could have therefore taken preventive measures. In the Court's view, where demonstrators do not engage in acts of violence, it is important for the public authorities to show a certain degree of tolerance towards peaceful gatherings if the freedom of assembly guaranteed by Article 11 of the Convention is not to be deprived of all substance.[230]

In *Stankov v Bulgaria*—where the United Macedonian Organisation (UMO)-Ilinden was banned from holding public meetings because the association had been declared unconstitutional—the Court reiterated:

> that the fact that a group of persons calls for autonomy or even requests secession of part of the country's territory—thus demanding fundamental constitutional and territorial changes—cannot automatically justify a prohibition of its assemblies. Demanding territorial changes in speeches and demonstrations does not automatically amount to a threat to the country's territorial integrity and national security. Freedom of assembly and the right to express one's views through it are among the paramount values of a democratic society. The essence of democracy is its capacity to resolve problems through open debate. Sweeping measures of a preventive nature to suppress freedom of assembly and expression other than in cases of incitement to violence or rejection of democratic principles—however shocking and unacceptable certain views or words used may appear to the authorities, and however illegitimate the demands made may be—do a disservice to democracy and often even endanger it. In a democratic society based on the rule of law, political ideas which challenge the existing order and whose realisation is advocated by peaceful means must be afforded a proper opportunity of expression through the exercise of the right of assembly as well as by other lawful means.[231]

The Court found that the probability that separatist declarations would be made at the group's meetings could not justify the ban. In contrast to several earlier cases in which the Court (or Commission) appeared to value more highly the public's rather nebulous interest in not being disturbed—either physically or by noise—while going about its daily business, there has been a marked shift in approach on the part of the Court.

Aldemir v Turkey again involved the violent dispersal of trade union public meetings on the streets of Ankara protesting about a Trade Union bill then before Parliament.[232] Again, the requisite three days' advance notice had not been given and the meetings were forcibly ended on the ground that it was necessary to prevent disorder and to protect public safety: the meetings were being held in an impermissible area, irrespective of notice being given. The police gave—as the law required—a dispersal request, which was not obeyed. The police then turned to truncheons and tear gas, which led to a violent response from the demonstrators and consequent turmoil. While it was clear that 'authorities have a duty to take appropriate measures with regard to lawful demonstrations in order to ensure their peaceful conduct and safety of all citizens',[233] it also went without saying that 'any demonstration in

---

[230] ibid, at [51]–[52] following *Oya Ataman*, above n 66, at [41]–[42].
[231] *Stankov v Bulgaria*, above n 27, at [97]–[98] and see too *Kuznetsov*, above n 23, at [43].
[232] *Aldemir v Turkey*, above n 23.
[233] ibid, at [40].

a public place may cause a certain level of disruption to ordinary life and may encounter hostility'.[234] That latter did mean that those organising demonstrations should, 'as actors in the democratic process, respect the rules governing that process by complying with the regulations in force'. However, on the facts, there was no evidence to suggest the group 'initially presented a serious danger to public order [though] it was likely that they would have caused some disruption' in the area. Here, this meant that the swift intervention by force was unnecessary, given the tolerance required towards peaceful gatherings where the demonstrators do not engage in violence.

This distinction between disruption—a necessary incident of any protest in any event—and (serious) danger to public order, and the consequent implication that it is only the latter that can justify interferences with the right to protest, is given further support in *Galstyan v Armenia*.[235] In the context of deciding whether, inter alia, a conviction for 'making a loud noise' at a demonstration (as well as for obstructing street traffic) was proportionate, the Court had this to say:

> As to the loud noise ... there is no suggestion that this involved any obscenity or incitement to violence. The Court however finds it hard to imagine a huge political demonstration at which people express their opinion not generating a certain amount of noise.[236]

In *Bukta*, the Court was clearly swayed by the fact that there was no evidence to suggest a danger to public order 'beyond the level of the minor disturbance which is inevitably caused by an assembly in a public place', thus bringing into play the need for tolerance towards peaceful non-violent demonstrations.[237] The disjunction of disruption from disorder is a very marked and welcome contrast with the rationale of those earlier holdings of inadmissibility.

The Court has stressed the subject-matter of the demonstration in this sense: as we saw above, the closer the connection to the exercise of free speech or where its content is a matter of political concern, the greater will be its protection. Where the purpose of a picket was to attract public attention to the alleged dysfunction of aspects of the Russian judicial system, a serious matter, that was undeniably part of a political debate on a matter of general and public concern. The Court's constant approach has been

> to require very strong reasons for justifying restrictions on political speech or serious matters of public interest such as corruption in the judiciary, as broad restrictions imposed in individual cases would undoubtedly affect respect for the freedom of expression in general in the State concerned.[238]

A similar point was made by the Court in *Kandzhov*.[239] The applicant set up trestles seeking support for his campaign to force the Minister of Justice to resign. He advertised this by referring to him as a 'top idiot'.

> In a democratic system the actions and omissions of the government and of its members must be subject to close scrutiny by the press and public opinion. Furthermore, the dominant position which the government and its members occupy makes it necessary for them—and for the authorities in general—to display restraint in resorting to criminal proceedings and the associated

---

[234] *ibid*, at [42].
[235] *Galstyan*, above n 23.
[236] *ibid*, at [116].
[237] *Bukta*, above n 23, at [37].
[238] *Kuznetsov*, above n 23, at [47].
[239] *Kandzhov v Bulgaria*, above n 21.

custodial measures particularly where other means are available for replying to unjustified attacks and criticisms.[240]

In *Vajnai*—the 'red star' case—the Court asserted that 'when freedom of expression is exercised as political speech limitations are justified only in so far as there exists a clear, pressing and specific social need. Consequently, utmost care must be observed in applying any restrictions'.[241] Of course, all of this is rather a 'how long is a piece of string?' question and approach, given our politically-driven definition of protest. Nonetheless, it is a welcome affirmation.

(f) The Effect and Relevance of Third Parties

The last factor at play in the outcome of many protest applications before the Court is linked to the previous one. The Court has often had to grapple with cases where third parties either threaten to disrupt a proposed protest or threaten violence against it. Case law is far from consistent on this.

Let us reconsider *Rai, Allmond and Negotiate Now! v UK* and contrast it with the later case of *Stankov v Bulgaria*.[242] In *Rai* the Commission decided that the general banning policy served the twin legitimate aims of preventing disorder and protecting the rights and freedoms of others. It took account of the tense security situation in Northern Ireland, with no single view as to causes or solutions. This was despite the police being of the view that there was no danger of disorder. In *Stankov*, the applicants were also victims of a ban, this time for five years, on United Macedonian Organisation-Ilinden meetings intended to celebrate and to commemorate events of historical importance to Macedonians living in Bulgaria. Instead of the application being declared inadmissible, there was a finding of a violation of Article 11 by the Court. It was—as in *Rassemblement Jurassien* where a challenge to a ban on all political meetings was declared inadmissible because it was proportionate—a time of considerable potential separatist tension, with calls for independence for the area of Bulgaria known as Pirin. The aim of the association was to 'unite all Macedonians in Bulgaria on a regional and cultural basis' and to achieve 'the recognition of the Macedonian minority in Bulgaria'. There had, according to police reports, been provocation, incidents and clashes—both physical and verbal—at earlier commemorative meetings: anti-Bulgarian slogans had been chanted and beer was thrown into the face of an MP. Even though the Court accepted that the bans met one or more of the interests cited by the Bulgarian government (protecting national security and territorial integrity; protecting the rights and freedoms of others; guaranteeing public order in the local community; and preventing disorder and crime), it very clearly frowned on the policy of automatic bans irrespective of need, bans that were not tailored to individual circumstance even where they were based on past findings: 'automatic reliance on the very fact that an organisation has been considered anti-constitutional—and refused registration—cannot suffice to justify under Article 11(2) of the Convention a practice of systematic bans on the holding of peaceful assemblies'.[243]

---

[240] ibid, at [73].
[241] *Vajnai*, above n 23 at [51].
[242] We can also contrast it with *UMO Ilinden v Bulgaria* (App 44079/98) ECtHR judgment 20 October 2005, which was the application several years later complaining about the same problem.
[243] *Stankov v Bulgaria*, above n 27, at [92].

It is worth considering two further cases in more detail as they provide a sharp contrast with each other. The two are *Chorherr v Austria* and *Öllinger v Austria*.[244]

1. *Chorherr* The threat of disorder was of a very low level and the actions that were alleged to have prompted it were in themselves fairly innocuous, yet the Court still decided that the restriction on the applicant's rights under Article 11 was justified and proportionate. At a military ceremony and march-past in Vienna—attended by about 50,000 people—marking the 30th anniversary of Austrian neutrality and the 40th anniversary of the end of the Second World War, the applicant and a friend distributed leaflets calling for a referendum on the purchase of fighter aircraft by the Austrian armed forces. They wore rucksacks to the backs of which were attached enlargements of the leaflet; these measured about 50cm by 70cm, projected approximately 50cm above the heads of the persons carrying them and bore the slogan 'Austria does not need any interceptor fighter planes'. The actions of the two men caused a commotion among the spectators, whose view had been blocked. Two policemen informed the applicant and his friend that they were disturbing public order and instructed them to cease what could only be regarded as a demonstration. However, they refused to comply, asserting their right to freedom of expression. When they persisted despite further warnings from police officers and increasingly loud protests from the crowd, they were arrested and administrative criminal proceedings were instituted against them.

The key aspect is the antipathy that the applicant's behaviour was beginning to engender among those who wished to attend the parade peaceably. The Court indicated that the nature, importance and scale of the parade could appear to the police to justify strengthening the forces deployed to ensure that it passed off peacefully. It added that when he chose this event for his demonstration against the Austrian armed forces, the applicant must have realised that it might lead to a disturbance requiring measures of restraint, which the Court found not to be excessive. The Court appeared to approve the approach of the Austrian Constitutional Court: it expressly found that in the circumstances of the case the measures adopted had been intended to prevent breaches of the peace and not to frustrate the expression of an opinion. This conceptualisation of the issue echoes the approach taken above in the four German sit-in cases and is the one that is of most concern.[245] It is not clear why a peaceful protester should be arrested purely because a third party is so offended, annoyed or disturbed that they threaten violence themselves as a consequence, let alone why this should be considered a proportionate response. Might Herr Chorrherr's refusal to stop have been because he had an entirely different perspective? It seems eminently plausible for him to have reasoned that, as he had a constitutionally guaranteed right to express himself freely, he could legitimately and properly expect to have this right protected against those who were prepared to resort to violence to silence him and his views. We do not even know—not that it is necessarily decisive—if (m)any of those who were getting agitated actually disagreed with his views on the aircraft; it seems the commotion was caused because of a spoilt view. Is that really what the protection of free speech and peaceful protest comes down to—it is guaranteed provided it does not affect the 'right' to an unencumbered view of the military parade?

---

[244] *Öllinger v Austria*, above n 47, and *Chorherr v Austria*, above n 86

[245] See above n 133. In each, the Commission made clear its view that each 'had not been punished for her participation in any demonstration as such, but for particular behaviour in the course of the demonstration, namely the blocking of a public road, thereby causing more obstruction than would normally arise from the exercise of the right of peaceful assembly. The applicant and the other demonstrators had thereby intended to attract broader public attention to their political opinions concerning nuclear armament'.

We will consider these issues in greater detail in chapter seven when we look at the case of *Redmond-Bate v DPP* and what is referred to as the hecklers' veto.[246] The Court in fact has made a telling reference to the hecklers' veto in an important case—for peaceful protest and generally—that perceived public sensitivities cannot, without more, be a sound and sufficient reason to restrict the rights of another. In *Vajnai*, it declared its view that

> a legal system which applies restrictions on human rights in order to satisfy the dictates of public feeling—real or imaginary—cannot be regarded as meeting the pressing social needs recognised in a democratic society, since that society must remain reasonable in its judgement. To hold otherwise would mean that freedom of speech and opinion is subjected to the heckler's veto.[247]

Such a sentiment to some extent takes its flavour from a case decided a few years earlier, *Öllinger v Austria*.[248] It is to that case that we now turn.

2. Öllinger *Öllinger* indicates a new approach where the issue is a potentially violent third-party response to a protest. It provides a fine contrast with earlier cases—*Chorherr* being just one—in which the 'rights' of third parties, especially those that threaten violence, have been put before the rights of protesters. It is worth dwelling on *Öllinger* a little longer. As I have written elsewhere, we can see it as a departure from previous case law in one of three ways.[249] It is a clear-cut demonstration that one group's right to protest should not be overridden when the only risk if it goes ahead is that it will cause or trigger a disturbance or disorder generally: it sits out of line with both *Rai* and *Rassemblement Jurassien* here.[250] Secondly, it bucks the trend of cases that sanction restrictions on protest when there is a fear it will result in a violent conflagration started by those opposed to it: it is therefore a break with not only *Rai* and *Rassemblement Jurassien* but also with *CARAF v UK*[251] and *Chorherr* as well. Thirdly, it is the first time that a protest case has been conceptualised as a clash of competing rights—here Article 9 in opposition rather than (more usually) the Article 11 rights of counter-demonstrators—and the first time that Article 11 has been allowed to defeat the claims of other rights-holders. Whether the Court's decision can be sidelined and seen as a blip premised on a justified and rational dislike of the SS and the Nazis is of course for time to tell. Certainly what seemed like splendid isolation in June 2006 has become a mass gathering of pro-protest cases in the intervening two years. As we saw *Aldemir*, *Galstyan* and *Bukta* each feature a heightened concern for the rights of protesters despite the disruption their protest might cause.

Öllinger's ceremony at the war memorial in the municipal cemetery to commemorate the Salzburg Jews killed by the SS was designed to disturb the gathering of Comradeship IV—commemorating, as they had done for 40 years, former SS colleagues who died in the war. Öllinger expected about six participants, who would carry commemorative messages in their hands and attached to their clothes. No other means of expression (such as chanting or banners) which might offend piety or undermine public order would be used. Öllinger's meeting was banned in order to protect the general public against potential

---

[246] *Redmond-Bate v Director of Public Prosecutions* (1999) 7 BHRC 735.
[247] *Vajnai*, above n 23 at [57].
[248] *Öllinger v Austria*, above n 47.
[249] I have written about the case (see above n 78) on which this next part draws.
[250] *Rai*, above n 141, and *Rassemblement Jurassien*, above n 28.
[251] Above n 29. A ban on a planned march by a far-right group—where it was thought likely that violence would result—which incidentally prohibited all marches was upheld as by the ECtHR as a proportionate measure designed to prevent disorder, to preserve public safety and in the interests of the rights and freedoms of others.

disturbances: the gathering of Comradeship IV had in recent years been the target of activities aimed at disturbing them. The vehement discussions with members of Comradeship IV and other visitors to the cemetery that their very presence had elicited had caused considerable nuisance to other visitors of the cemetery and had each time required police intervention. Both meetings were to take place on All Saints' Day, an important religious holiday on which the population traditionally visited cemeteries in order to commemorate the dead. In Öllinger's case, it was felt that the disturbance of the Comradeship IV and other commemoration ceremonies was likely to offend the religious feelings of members of the public visiting the cemetery and would indisputably be regarded as disrespectful towards the dead soldiers of both world wars and thus as an unbearable provocation. Accordingly, there was a risk of protests by visitors to the cemetery which could degenerate into open conflict between them and those participating in the assembly.

Before the Austrian courts, the ban was upheld primarily as being a necessary and justified means to protect and to guarantee the manifestation of religion by others in the cemetery that same day against deliberate disturbance by others. The ban was thus an exercise of the positive obligation inherent within Article 9. It had been argued at domestic level that the ban was needed so as to protect the SS ceremony but that had been rejected by the Constitutional Court and was not pursued at Strasbourg. In fact, the Austrian government 'conceded that an assembly could not be prohibited solely on the ground of a certain likelihood of tensions and confrontations between opposing groups'.[252] If this is a statement about the legal position under the Convention at European level in 2006, based on previous case law, as we have seen that does not seem to be a concession it needed to make.

Öllinger applied to the Strasbourg Court arguing that his rights under Article 11 had been violated: the Austrian ban was not necessary. Implementing the ban disregarded the fact that the purpose of his meeting was to express an opinion, namely to remind the public of the crimes committed by the SS and to commemorate the Jews killed by its members. That the meeting coincided with the Comradeship IV ceremony was an essential part of the message he wished to convey. The authorities had failed to give sufficient reasons for prohibiting his meeting, nor had they correctly weighed up the interests of the applicant and of Comradeship IV in holding their respective meetings, or made any efforts to ensure that both assemblies could take place. The contested decisions were tantamount to protecting the commemoration ceremony for SS soldiers against legitimate criticism. Given its concession, the Austrian government was forced to argue that the ban was no more than necessary to maintain public order and to protect the rights and freedoms of others, namely the undisturbed worship of all those visiting the cemetery on All Saints' Day, an activity itself protected by Article 9 of the ECHR. In that, the government prayed in aid the fact that in its view Öllinger's assembly had been aimed mainly at disturbing the Comradeship IV ceremony, given the coincidence of time and venue, and the failure to assure the authorities that the Comradeship IV ceremony would not be disturbed. In reaching its decision, it argued it was entitled to rely on previous experiences in which similar assemblies had annoyed visitors, had led to heated discussions and had required police intervention. In its view, given that disturbances could not be ruled out, the authorities had not been under a positive obligation to allow both meetings, all the more so as measures designed to prevent confrontations (such as a police cordon) would themselves have disturbed the peace required at a cemetery on All Saints' Day.

[252] *Öllinger*, above n 47, at [30].

The Court concluded that on balance the rights of Öllinger's group should have outweighed the more limited rights of those manifesting their religion in the cemetery.[253] It is true that emphasis was placed on Öllinger's status as a Green Party MP but other factors came into play as well which of course might not be repeated in future cases:[254]

> First and foremost, the assembly was in no way directed against the cemetery-goers' beliefs or the manifestation of them. Moreover, the applicant expected only a small number of participants. They envisaged peaceful and silent means of expressing their opinion, namely the carrying of commemorative messages, and had explicitly ruled out the use of chanting or banners. Thus, the intended assembly in itself could not have hurt the feelings of cemetery-goers. Moreover, while the authorities feared that, as in previous years, heated debates might arise, it was not alleged that any incidents of violence had occurred on previous occasions.

The Court was struck by the fact that the domestic authorities, when banning Öllinger's meeting, attached no weight to the fact that an unconditional prohibition of a counter-demonstration was a very far-reaching measure requiring particular justification, especially where it is one designed to express an opinion on an issue of public interest.[255] Conversely, the unconditional prohibition on Öllinger's meeting, given that an adequate police presence might have allowed both meetings to take place (the point we addressed earlier in this chapter) placed too much weight on the interest of cemetery goers' not to be disturbed and too little on Öllinger's interest in holding the assembly. In its judgment, the Court did set out its view that

> under Article 11 the State is compelled to abstain from interfering with that right, which also extends to a demonstration that may annoy or give offence to persons opposed to the ideas or claims that it is seeking to promote. If every probability of tension and heated exchange between opposing groups during a demonstration was to warrant its prohibition, society would be faced with being deprived of the opportunity of hearing differing views ... On the other hand, States may be required under Article 11 to take positive measures in order to protect a lawful demonstration against counter-demonstrations.

Öllinger is not breaking new ground by declaring that Article 11 extends to demonstrations that cause offence to others, whether by design or by accident. In *Plattform 'Ärzte für das Leben'* in the 1980s the Commission made it clear that protest groups must

> be able to hold the demonstration without having to fear that they will be subjected to physical violence by their opponents; such a fear would be liable to deter associations or other groups supporting common ideas or interests from openly expressing their opinions on highly controversial issues affecting the community. In a democracy the right to counter-demonstrate cannot extend to inhibiting the exercise of the right to demonstrate.[256]

---

[253] Judge Loucaides dissented largely on the basis that the majority had substituted its own assessment of the facts and circumstances for that of the better-placed Austrian courts and, having done so, denied them any margin of appreciation.

[254] By placing elected representatives on a pedestal, this not only raises the spectre of (reverse) discrimination but it crystallises conventional party politics by preserving the status quo rather than allowing challenges to it: Mead, above n 78, at 141. Those not formally represented—those marginalised from formal party politics or on its extremes—might well be argued as deserving *more* protection so as to convince others and to get their views across. How else does someone away from the mainstream achieve election if all the prime-time television, speakers' corners and meeting places are reserved for those already elected?

[255] *Öllinger*, above n 47, at [44].

[256] *ibid*, at [32].

That line was not, as we have seen, consistently adhered to but it is to be hoped that *Öllinger* is laying down a new marker for the twenty-first century.

(g) Demonstration and Counter-demonstration

What the Court has not yet had to grapple with is to consider the point at which two demonstrations become a demonstration and a counter-demonstration and which is one and which the other. Presumably this would be 'first come first served' in the absence of any other indicia but why *should* a counter demonstration have fewer rights? They are both forms of protest and both are exercises of the right under Article 11 yet the demonstration is likely to be given a presumptive claim to legitimacy and thus to go ahead unimpeded. While this, it is submitted, should be so where the counter demonstrators acknowledge their own violent (or at least disruptive) intentions, such a formula should not be predictive where either (a) the counter demonstration is avowedly non-disruptive and non-violent or (b) where the greater—if not the first—violence is likely to come from the original demonstrators when they feel under verbal and minor physical attack. The first example is clearly what occurred in *Öllinger*. Although the decision is clearly premised on the countervailing religious rights of visitors to the cemetery, Öllinger's assembly was itself, if not a *counter-demonstration*, then at least a demonstration countering the Comradeshaft IV remembrance meeting that had been taking place for forty years. The question then becomes, as the Court properly identified, a matter of proper and effective policing to ensure two peaceful demonstrations or meetings (one of which happens to be labelled a 'counter-demonstration') take place as their organisers planned and intended. The right to protest here is more akin to a decision about managerial policing. An example of (b) would be where group A marches through a town and the local population (group B) comes out to make a point about the abhorrent views of groups A and a few locals throw rotten tomatoes. Members of group A react by starting a full-scale fight. This—but on a much smaller scale—is what occurred in *Chorherr*. A peaceful group—not protesting and so not even exercising a Convention right—was in the City Square when group B (comprising two members) staged a protest. This was peaceful but obstructive—their small placard obscured the view of some members of group A. Group A threatened violence yet it was against group B that action was taken. So, the group which threatens greater violence—in fact is the only group to threaten violence at all; the other group is merely disruptive—stands guaranteed of its 'rights' while the other loses Convention protection. It is impossible to view *Chorherr* as being anything except for implicitly overridden and overruled by *Öllinger*.

V. Conclusions

This chapter has shown how the Strasbourg Court has interpreted and developed the various elements within the concept of peaceful assembly under Article 11 which, when added to Article 10, founds the right of peaceful protest.

Strasbourg has been willing to accept forms of protest outside the traditional paradigm of marching, banner-waving and groups standing around shouting slogans; we need only look to *Schiefer* or to *Steel* as evidence that sit-ins or disrupting activities of which we disapprove at least engage Article 11 or Article 10—even if they almost certainly will not succeed on the merits. Protesters do not lose the guarantee of protection purely because the demonstration on which they find themselves becomes violent as long as they themselves commit no 'reprehensible acts' (*Ezelin*) or provided they 'remain peaceful in his or her own intentions or behaviour' (*Ziliberberg*). This applies only to more formal or traditional protests, ones which do not have obstruction or disruption as their modus operandi. For those direct action protests—even if they are not violent—the protection offered by Article 11—and so under the HRA—is limited if not invisible. Article 11 brings with it a limited duty on the part of the state to facilitate and to secure an effective right to peaceful protest—and so not only must the state (say) not ban a march unless it is 'necessary' to do so, the state may also be required to put measures in place or to take action, even if this costs money, to ensure protesters can protest freely without interference, disruption or intervention. As well as ensuring the proper policing of a march or meeting—in which context a certain amount of advance notice might be required—this might extend to imposing bans or restrictions on those who oppose the march or meeting. It does not, unless there is nowhere else to go, mean states must force the hand of private landowners and require them to grant access to protesters. We saw, primarily by reference to *Ziliberberg*, that a system of prior notification or even authorisation is not generally something that has overly exercised judicial minds at Strasbourg, though *Bukta* in 2007 provides some counter ballast where prior notification rules admit of no exceptions for urgent protests. It has also tended not to have been too problematic in Convention terms for states to impose blanket bans on demonstrations or marches—or as part of the effective guarantee, on counter-demonstrations alone—especially if they are short-lived and confined to a reasonably small area. Though these are clearly interferences, states have been able to justify them as proportionate in order to prevent disorder and to protect the rights of others.

We did see towards the end of the chapter how the past few years have seen a marked change in judicial attitudes at Strasbourg when it come to assessing a state's claim that it was necessary to restrict a march, ban an assembly or arrest a protester so as to prevent disorder. Historically, the Court was an easy target for critics asserting that it placed great weight on the 'rights' of citizens to go about their daily lives and to engage in socio-economic business undisturbed or inconvenienced by those who wish to highlight issues of concern to them.

In *WG v Austria*, someone who set up a stall in a pedestrian area so as to impart information and to distribute environmental protest leaflets was prosecuted and convicted of using a public road without authorisation.[257] His application was inadmissible; the Commission concluded that in undertaking the balancing test between 'the interests of the prevention of disorder, in particular of an unhindered and safe traffic on public streets, and the interest of the applicant in the exercise of his right to freedom of expression', the requirement of prior authorisation under Austrian Road Traffic Regulations could be regarded as justified. The application of the Regulations by the Austrian authorities and the fine did not appear disproportionate to the legitimate aim pursued. *JK v Netherlands* (the Amsterdam Olympics case) was declared inadmissible. The applicant had no permission to demonstrate on the platform as was required under Dutch law, which had the aim of preventing a disturbance of the order, safety or good running of operations in railway stations. In the Commission's view, the applicant was not prosecuted for having demonstrated (and neither was she prevented from protesting elsewhere) and the requirement of prior permission was a restriction which could be regarded as necessary in a democratic society for the

---

[257] Above n 32.

prevention of disorder. In *Chorherr* action taken against a pair of protesters who undertook very small-scale peaceful protest, seeking only to persuade and to inform by distributing leaflets, was held proportionate to the aim of preventing disorder.

Chorherr sits very uncomfortably with cases such as *Öllinger, Aldemir, Galstyan* and *Oya Ataman*. All of these cases indicate a greater dispensation towards those who engage in peaceful protest but whose protest may cause others either to react violently or to disrupt the protest or whose protest causes more than a modicum of disturbance and inconvenience to bystanders going about their business. As the Court said in *Öllinger*, if 'every probability of tension and heated exchange between opposing groups during a demonstration was to warrant its prohibition, society would be faced with being deprived of the opportunity of hearing differing views'. In terms (perhaps only?) of what occurs at a protest—conduct or words—again we see greater urging of tolerance and flexibility on states. In *Kuznetsov*, the Court reiterated that

> any measures interfering with the freedom of assembly and expression other than in cases of incitement to violence or rejection of democratic principles—however shocking and unacceptable certain views or words used may appear to the authorities—do a disservice to democracy and often even endanger it. In a democratic society based on the rule of law, the ideas which challenge the existing order must be afforded a proper opportunity of expression through the exercise of the right of assembly as well as by other lawful means.[258]

In fact, this more liberalising wind is not all one-way. In *Çiloglu v Turkey*, the Court (by a majority of 5:2) held for Turkey as having acted proportionately within its margin of appreciation in dispersing a crowd of 60 or so with tear gas.[259] They had been protesting in a public place on Saturdays for three years. It was unlawful under Turkish law (that is it was unauthorised) and the participants were informed of this. A majority concluded that the group had had adequate time and opportunity to attain their objective, drawing public attention to a matter of public concern—prisons policy—and the measures chosen were necessary to protect order and preserve the rights of others. The dissenting judges, Judges Popovic and Cabral Barreto, could see no difference between this case and the facts of *Oya Ataman*, where the Court unanimously found a violation, and so nothing on which to alter the Court's position. If the matter had been so pressing, why had the authorities waited for 170 weeks to resolve it?[260] If, as the majority asserted, the group had ample time to engage public opinion, why had the demonstration continued for so long and not ceased when its work was done?[261] In their view, neither the duration of the protest nor the number of instances are matters properly to be taken into account in the adjudication under Article 11(2).

In that regard we might recall—and end on—the words of the Court in both *Oya Ataman* and *Balçik*, that where demonstrators

---

[258] *Kuznetsov*, above n 23, at [45].
[259] *Çiloglu v Turkey* (App 73333/01) ECtHR judgment 6 March 2007, judgment in French only at the time of writing.
[260] This has echoes (though to a lesser degree) of one factor behind the Court of Appeal's holding in *Tabernacle v Secretary of State for Defence* [2009] EWCA Civ 23 that introducing a restriction on camping at Aldermaston was a disproportionate restriction on the rights of the Aldermaston Women's Peace Camp to protest peacefully. In the words of Laws LJ (at [41]), 'the fact that no steps were taken to put a stop to the camp for over 23 years . . . to my mind speaks loud'.
[261] This is rather disingenuous: the right in Article 10/11 is not to convert but to protest—it does not guarantee an outcome, that your views will be accepted.

do not engage in acts of violence, it is important for the public authorities to show a certain degree of tolerance towards peaceful gatherings if the freedom of assembly guaranteed by Article 11 of the Convention is not to be deprived of all substance.[262]

This has swiftly become a leitmotif for the Court, though the extent to which this has general application to all interferences by state authorities in protests—such as arrests or bans—or whether it will be confined to its peculiar facts of large-scale forceful police reaction and intervention will be seen as the case law pans out over time.

The remainder of this book will look at the right to peaceful protest in domestic law from five linked, sometimes overlapping, perspectives. Each chapter will endeavour to set out the legal framework regulating the right. Those five are: the locus of protest; peaceful communication; direct action; preventive action by the police; and private law remedies and enforcement. We shall see that for each of those five, most of the scenarios or interactions have come before Strasbourg in some shape for adjudication—if not on applications from the UK then from around Europe. Obviously, cases involving the conduct of marches, or action taken by the police to prevent breaches of the peace, or arrests for the content of banners at a rally are meat and drink to the ECtHR. We shall see however, as we progress through this book, that in England and Wales at least the law that regulates peaceful protest encompasses much more than that. Some of this regulation and legal interaction has yet to feature in the case law of the Court. To take just three examples, this would include situations where

- the private targets of a protest take action to stop it rather than leaving it to the state to do so, perhaps where a company bars a known share-holder activist from attending its AGM;[263]
- the police do not stop protests but create a 'chilling effect' surrounding those who do participate, perhaps by photographing protesters at a rally;[264]
- a public body doesn't act against a protest per se but a decision it takes means the protest is much less likely to be able to take place, perhaps by charging the group for a live entertainment licence for its street theatre protest.[265]

---

[262] *Balçik*, above n 17, at [51]–[52], *Oya Ataman v Turkey*, above n 66, at [41]–[42] and *Bukta*, above n 23, at [37].
[263] 'Burberry bans fur protester', *Eastern Daily Press*, 18 July 2008. The vice-president of animal rights groups PETA was banned from entering Burberry's AGM despite having a proxy voucher and attendance card.
[264] *Wood v Commissioner of Police for the Metropolis* [2009] EWCA Civ 414.
[265] [Summer 2008] Liberty magazine pp 8–9. One of the issues in the famous US Skokie litigation was the decision of the village to pass an ordinance requiring large-scale insurance cover for rallies in the village parks, a measure aimed at deterring the National Socialist Party of America from marching in the area. In *Collin v Smith* 447 F Supp 676 (1978) the measure was struck down as unconstitutional, imposing as it did a 'virtually insuperable obstacle' to the exercise of the group's free speech rights. See also *Forsyth Co v Nationalist Movement* 505 US 123 (1992).

4

The Locus of Protest

I. Introduction and Overview

Freedom of expression cannot be exercised in a vacuum . . . it necessarily implies the use of physical space in order to meet its underlying objectives. No one could agree that the exercise of the freedom of expression can be limited solely to places owned by the person wishing to communicate: such an approach would certainly deny the very foundation of the freedom of expression.[1]

This chapter considers the rules that regulate a protester's choice of venue for their protest. This framework has consequences for the underpinning rationale of the right of peaceful protest, given that it is underpinned not only by a wider functional democratic utility but by a need to respond to individual autonomy (relating to the type of message and means of communication), as we saw in chapter one. This chapter is divided into two: the general position governing rights of access to and over land for the purposes of holding a protest; and place-specific restrictions on protest, such as those that govern the area around Westminster.

An obvious and significant factor determining the success of any protest that seeks to persuade or to engage with voters is having somewhere to hold it. As we shall see, the rules that govern the availability of land, generally of private law, have wider ramifications in the public sphere: it is those rules that may well determine whether—and where—a protest may be held and so may determine levels of public participation and political engagement. It is generally accepted that publicly-owned land in the UK is on the decline—and with that comes a decline in public accountability and access. Since the 1980s, driven at first ideologically and then as well by economic concerns, land, property and buildings that were once in the hands of the Crown, government departments, local councils or statutory corporations and bodies have been privatised into the hands of (usually) the highest bidder to be run (mostly) for profit.[2]

---

[1] *Committee for the Commonwealth of Canada v Canada* (1991) 77 DLR (4th) 385, 394 (Canadian Supreme Court), Lamer J.

[2] Details and data on this have been surprisingly hard to obtain and to verify though apocryphally it seems beyond dispute. One only has to think about the massive transfer of tenanted properties from local councils to registered social landlords. The only real study of land ownership in the UK is K Cahill, *Who Owns Britain* (Edinburgh, Canongate Press, 2001). As vast amounts of land are still not registered, discovering who owns the freehold title for any piece of land is almost impossible. On his figures—and the book is a polemic—'between 1985 and 1997 up to 1 million acres, some of it immensely valuable development land, was transferred . . . through the medium of privatisation' (p 138). In support, he shows how—with what he thinks is reasonable accuracy—land held by the National Coal Board, electricity supplier, water generator and British Rail in 1962 totalled at least 1.17 million acres whereas now the utilities (water, electricity and rail) total only 0.5 millions acres (pp 139 and 147). Local authority land holdings in 1962 were estimated to hold just under 1 million acres (p 139) but by 2001 this had fallen to 65,000 acres (p 147)—but, since Cahill concedes, local authority land is exempted from land registration, his figures are also hard to verify.

At its most basic level, a protest needs a venue, somewhere it can take place. Several possible solutions present themselves. At one extreme, the law could take the view that groups may only stage protests on land they themselves own, the very idea rejected by Lamer J above. Adopting that position would obviously and inevitably restrict the group's options: neither the group nor any of its members might actually own any land. Even if they did, the protest may not be effective. If the land the protesters own is located out of the public eye and far away, what use is protesting about town hall corruption from a bedsit on a ring road? At the other extreme, the legal framework could permit a group to use whatever they land they wanted—no matter who owned it—for a protest. This, clearly, would have the effect of overturning centuries of private law jurisprudence. Another solution would be for the legal framework to allow but not entitle protest groups to reach agreements with landowners permitting them to use that land for a protest.[3] This position could be in addition to the first—that is that groups who own land have the alternative of using a third party's better placed land—or an alternative—so that groups or members who own their own land must use that land for a protest. Whichever approach is adopted—and domestic law broadly favours the former—is likely to be of limited value to most protesters: it would be a very benevolent, perhaps foolhardy, livestock farmer who permitted vegetarian groups onto his land to protest that meat is murder. These two solutions allow us more clearly to see that unless a group is granted an enforceable right to demand and require entry (rather than a Hohfeldian power to request entry) as against any landowner—whether public or private—to use the land for a protest, such as with publicly-dedicated and reserved 'protest spaces' as a minimum,[4] then private law principles of absolute title bring with them important ramifications for democratic participation in the public sphere.

The rules relating to land ownership are underpinned by several wider constitutional or public policy imperatives.[5] As Cass Sunstein notes, 'if people's holdings are subject to ongoing governmental adjustment, people cannot have the security, and independence, that the status of citizenship requires [and thus] . . . helps ensure deliberative democracy itself'.[6]

---

[3] This permission would almost certainly need to have been given expressly by the title-holder: it is unlikely that licence to occupy land belonging to another or occupying it under a lease would entitle the occupier to stage a protest. Thus a group given permission to use a farmer's field to camp overnight would not thereby be entitled to protest against his intensive farming techniques or his participation in a GM crop study.

[4] The term is not being used in the sense of 'free speech zones' in America which as critics suggest tend to be a contradiction in terms and resemble caged pens into which protesters are herded on pain of arrest; they are usually situated several hundred metres from the protesters' target. For example when President Bush visited South Carolina, in 2002, Brett Bursey sought to welcome him with a sign that read 'No War for Oil'. Standing among others who were waiting to greet the President without messages of dissent, Bursey was ordered by officials to remove himself to a designated protest zone three quarters of a mile away and out of sight of the President. When he refused, he was arrested, charged and later convicted of violating Secret Service restrictions on a person's presence where the President is temporarily visiting. There is considerable amount of literature: as a good overview article for much of the material in this chapter see T Crocker, 'Displacing Dissent: The Role of 'Place' in First Amendment Jurisprudence' (2007) 75 *Fordham Law Review* 2587 and the American Civil Liberties Union site: www.aclu.org/freespeech/protest/index.html (accessed 9 August 2008) generally. What is being suggested above is not that protesters use these zones to head off dissent when a President visits but that they be a permanent minimum provision in every town across the UK.

[5] There are echoes here in what follows of the debate about the relative public and private interests and concerns at stake in the tricky balancing act between rights of privacy and rights of free speech: see most recently D Mead, ' It's a funny old game—privacy, football and the public interest' [2006] *European Human Rights Law Review* 541.

[6] C Sunstein, 'Social and Economic Rights? Lessons from South Africa' John M Olin Law & Economics Working paper No 124 (2D series) (The Law School, University of Chicago, May 2001) p 2. See also J Harris, *Property and Justice* (Oxford, Oxford University Press, 1996) ch 15 and J Penner, *The Idea of Property in Law* (Oxford, Clarendon Press, 1997) generally for other discussions of the instrumentality of protecting the private holding of property.

Other justifications, both instrumental and deontological, present themselves: property ownership acts as a form of glue within a stakeholder society; the ability to exploit one's own capital provides the conditions for wider economic advances.[7] That said, there has been little exploration and certainly no attempt (within the UK at least) to locate the rules relating to land ownership within a wider framework of political pluralism: being able to use land for the purpose of protest and dissent serves wider and equally great (perhaps greater?) democratic imperatives. There is a strong case for arguing that at least some land should be available either to everyone or to no one for the purpose of protest (perhaps with some caveat for anti-democratic groups or messages). Otherwise we can easily envisage landowners only permitting protests or the voicing of democratic concerns of which they approve.[8] The demographic skew of landholding in the UK serves only to exacerbate this problem. The first few years of the new millennium saw the British countryside decked in signs extolling the virtues of the Countryside Alliance, the loose grouping that seeks to preserve the countryside and one of whose primary objectives was to oppose the ban on fox hunting. For three or four years drivers along the busy main road that connects Norwich to Southwold were greeted by a huge sign (some 8 metres by 5 metres) at the edge of a field, thanking the 409 000 who took part in the Countryside March in 2002. Drivers have yet to see one of any real size applauding the decision to ban hunting. General election campaigns over the last few years in the same area have seen trees and hedges swathed in blue 'Vote Conservative' posters the size of bed sheets.[9] A 'Vote Labour' sign of such prominence is as rare as spotting a white crowned sparrow in these parts: a bedroom window in a top-floor flat on a high street tends not to be such an attraction. The case that is made in connection with media ownership and political advertising on the television and radio can be made in the context of protest: in certain cases there is a public interest that requires rights and economic freedom be restricted for the greater good of wider access. In fact, as a minimum at the heart of any participative rationale would be a principle of equality or non-discrimination in access to land for the purposes of protest.

Before we embark on our detailed consideration of the law, let us lastly reflect on two further matters, both of which relate to the ownership of land, in order to appreciate the complex interplay of the public and the private within a political framework that recognises the participatory role that protest is capable of playing. The first is this. We will return to it in greater detail throughout this book. Title to land has knock-on effects elsewhere in the regulation of protest. Many of the criminal restrictions on protest depend first on someone having trespassed on land; that is entered land belonging to someone else without permission or been given permission to enter but remained there in excess of it.[10] Thus private law rules relating to land—ownership and control of it—are pivotal in the public regulation of

---

[7] See further the discussion in D Mead, 'Strasbourg Succumbs to the Temptation "To Make a God of the Right of Property": Peaceful Protest on Private Land and the Ramifications of *Appleby v UK*' [2004] *Journal of Civil Liberties* 98 and the works cited therein. Of course, it could be argued that the ability to own land is open to all so that the rules relating to land ownership support the democratic principle of equality. Like the doors of the Ritz being open to all, this is equality of opportunity rather than of treatment or of outcome.

[8] Such a framework would also require resolution of the question of who much land should be made available, chosen by whom and on what—if any—terms.

[9] On whether or not a protest banner was an advertisement and therefore required planning consent under the Town and Country Planning Act 1990 and the effect of Art 10 as a defence to proceedings brought for unlawful display, see *Butler v Derby City Council* [2005] EWHC 2835 (Admin) and to some extent *Westminster City Council v Haw* [2002] EWHC 2073 (Admin).

[10] For example, s 14A of the Public Order Act 1986 introduces the concept of a 'trespassory assembly' in anticipation of which the police may seek a banning order for a period of up to four days and for an area up to five miles. Organising or taking part in an assembly that is known to be prohibited is itself a criminal offence. Similarly, s 68 of the Criminal Justice and Public Order Act 1994 creates the new offence of 'aggravated trespass': where someone

protest through the criminal law.[11] This is exacerbated by our second point: in capitalist societies, notions of property rights, the doctrines of land law and even the very concept of land ownership from a socio-economic perspective are fraught, contested and entirely unegalitarian. The following contradiction seems inherent in any liberal capitalist democracy: on the one hand society values (or purports to value) public engagement with the polity by guaranteeing rights such as the right to peaceful protest whilst on the other hand shoring up the rights (largely) of a few to buy, to own and to bequeath great tracts of land, so removing them as places in which public debate and the expression of views can occur.[12] As John Rawls put it, '[t]he limited space of the public political forum, so to speak, allows the usefulness of the political liberties to be far more subject to citizens' social position and economic means than the usefulness of the other basic liberties'.[13]

This brings us to the first topic in this section: whether or not there is—or should be—a right of access to land in order to facilitate protest. The second topic is a discussion of place-specific restrictions on protest, over and above those that apply generally.

II. Rights of Access Over Land for the Purpose of Protest

This part provides an assessment from both a positive and a normative perspective of the case for an enforceable right of access onto land so as to hold a protest. This includes—if such should be the case—a consideration of the scope and content of that right. Our analysis needs first to distinguish between, on the one hand, 'public land', title to which is held by the state or another public body, and on the other, 'private land', title to which is held by private individuals or entities, such as companies. The fact that the law imposes different, usually more restrictive, burdens on public bodies than those it imposes on private bodies in all areas of decision-making, not just those relating to land (rather than there being something separate or different in the concept of property as held between the two) makes for two different regimes.[14] Simply put, private landowners may do whatever they choose with their own land (including disposing of it outright) unless expressly forbidden by law—such as by the restrictions imposed on landlords under the Rent Act 1977—whereas the reverse holds for publicly-held land: all public authority decisions, including those relating to land, require positive sanction by law. Though the end result is the same—someone is

---

trespasses on land and while doing so obstructs, disrupts or intimidates a lawful activity carried on by a third party on that or the adjoining land, that person has committed a crime.

[11] In the same way as the private feeds into the public, there are parallels with anti-social behaviour orders (ASBOs). We consider ASBOs in chapter seven. One of the main criticisms of the regime is that certain forms of behaviour are penalised by criminal sanction determined according to the lower, civil standard of proof. Another is that it requires police officers, when arresting to have knowledge of what constitutes a trespass, an area in civil law that perhaps few will have been trained in: J Driscoll, 'Protest and Public Order: The Public Order Act' [1987] *Journal of Social Welfare Law* 280, 295.

[12] Cahill estimates that in the UK fewer than 157,000 families (0.28% of the population) own 64% of the land area of the UK: above n 2 208. In 2001, the largest institutional owners were The Forestry Commission (2.4 million acres), the Ministry of Defence (750,000 acres), the Crown together with the Duchies of Cornwall and Lancaster and the sovereign's personally-owned land (677,000 acres), the National Trust (5500,000 acres), insurance companies and utilities (each with 500,000 acres), and the Church of England (135,000 acres): above n 2, 16–18.

[13] J Rawls, *Political Liberalism* (New York, Columbia University Press, 1993) 150.

[14] See J Rowbottom, 'Property and Participation: A Right of Access for Expressive Activities' [2005] EHRLR 186, fn 9, although it has been argued that there are two distinct regimes: see D Feldman, 'Property and Public Protest' in F Meisel and P Cook (eds), *Property and Protection* (Oxford, Hart Publishing, 2000).

excluded or denied access onto land so as to hold a protest—there is a considerable conceptual difference between public and private landowners deciding not to allow protester X onto their field to hold a demonstration. In the former case, the landowner must be able both to point to a specific lawful authority for that decision and be able to justify it if challenged, whereas the private landowner need provide no justification and her lawful authority boils down to 'because it's mine'.

In human rights terms, we can see also see this legal framework as a function of the difference between negative obligations—of restraint and forbearance—and positive obligations that require action in order to remain compliant with human rights obligations.[15] There is in fact a four-fold matrix of obligations.[16] The simplest, where it will be easiest for claimants to succeed, is the straightforward obligation of state restraint: there will be liability if the state itself positively interferes in the right to protest by, for example, banning a march or arresting those at a march where it does so disproportionately. The simple positive obligation on the state itself is best seen as a case where it should make its own land available for a protest. At the farthest extreme—the double positive obligation—the claim is that the state should positively have acted (perhaps by legislating to regulate the private sphere)—but did not—and the act it should have performed was to require a private party also positively to act—to take steps to facilitate access to land for the purposes of protest—and that party too did not.

A. Rights of Access Over Publicly-held Land

It is axiomatic that public land or government 'property' is held for the public good.[17] Before the advent of the Human Rights Act, even publicly-owned land created only limited duties on, say, councils as owner or controller, to make it available for the purposes of democratic participation by (for example) requiring them to grant permission for people to hold protests. As we shall see, the HRA is unlikely significantly to increase the availability of space that can be used for protest. Nonetheless, in those limited circumstances where obligations are imposed on state bodies, we can clearly see a functional link to the advancing or sustaining, at the very least, of a plural democracy.

(i) The General Historic Position

English law has never recognised a general, purely positive obligation on councils always to make their own space and land publicly available (by requiring them never to refuse permission), let alone contemplated a requirement that they provide local equivalents to Hyde Park's speaker's corner, whether for rent or free of charge, on a first-come-first-served basis.[18] The Ministry of Justice has awarded The Speakers' Corners Trust £15,000, as part of the Ministry's Innovation Fund. The Trust is aiming to create local sites across the United

---

[15] See generally A Mowbray, *The Development of Positive Obligations under the European Convention on Human Rights by the European Court of Human Rights* (Oxford, Hart Publishing, 2004).

[16] A negative duty of restraint on a state; a positive duty on the state itself to act; a positive duty on a state to ensure a private third party forbears from acting so as to violate a right; and a positive duty on the state to ensure a private third party itself performs an act.

[17] Laws LJ in *Tabernacle*, below n 119, at [38] called such a proposition 'elementary'.

[18] Such a requirement might involve them buying a farmer's field if they had no land left or available of their own. There would be nothing to prevent (say) a council providing such an open space subject to there being statutory authorisation to exercise discretion in that way.

Kingdom. It piloted a scheme in Nottingham leading to the unveiling of a permanent site in February 2009.[19] The only clear and definite means by which a council's reluctant hand can be forced, so as to require it to permit access to a venue for a political meeting, is one that is narrowly confined.[20] Under sections 95–96 of the Representation of the People Act 1983, election candidates are entitled to use free of charge (subject to paying expenses) state schools or publicly-owned meeting houses for the purposes of holding public meetings in furtherance of their candidature. This provision applies irrespective of the political views of the party seeking to use the room, even if they are abhorrent to the vast majority.[21] Other than that—so for party political meetings outside the strict confines of the election period[22] and for protest meetings per se—there is little that can be done by a group or individual to require councils or other state bodies to allow use of their premises for political purposes broadly defined.[23] By contrast, there is a long-standing negative obligation meaning that councils cannot simply decide to exclude private individuals by denying them access. This is surrounded by a fair deal of regulation. Even before the HRA came into force, a council's decision not to permit someone to use its land in the first place or to remove them if they are already present was capable of challenge under the ordinary principles of judicial review: namely that the decision was irrational, illegal or in some way procedurally improper.[24] We shall look at the first two in turn.[25]

(a) Irrationality

Arguing a decision is irrational creates a notoriously difficult hurdle for applicants. Since an irrationality challenge is one that goes to the merits of the decision reached, the test is designed to ensure that courts do not usurp the powers of primary decision-makers in areas of competence granted by Parliament. A decision is irrational if it is one that no other decision-maker, properly directed, would have come to: if it could be said of council B that they too would have refused access, the claim against council A will fail. The test has recently been described as assessing whether the body has acted outside the range of reasonable

---

[19] Source: www.justice.gov.uk/news/newsrelease260209a.htm, accessed 2 March 2009.
[20] See Bailey, Harris and Jones, *Civil Liberties Cases and Materials*, 5th edn (London, Butterworths, 2001) 433–437. As the works they cite show, the right is to hold a public meeting: this undefined term should mean 'to which the public have access' not a section of the public comprising baying acolytes since the aim of the section is to promote political engagement not simply political participation.
[21] *Webster v Southwark London Borough Council* [1983] QB 698, where the party concerned was the National Front, the forerunner of the British National Party (BNP).
[22] This includes a by-election: *Webster, ibid.*
[23] A measure of positive protection against those seeking to disrupt or disturb is provided for those holding meetings under s 97 of the same Act: it is an offence for any person at a lawful election meeting to act (or to incite others to act) in a disorderly manner for the purpose of preventing the transaction of the business for which the meeting was called together. For lawful public meetings outside an election period, the equivalent offence is one under s 1 of the Public Meetings Act 1908. See also s 43 of the Education Act 1986, which imposes positive duties on higher education bodies to take 'such steps as are reasonably practicable to ensure' freedom of speech on campuses.
[24] These public law remedies will be buttressed by contractual ones if an agreement for use of land has been reached. In *Verrall v Great Yarmouth Borough Council* [1981] QB 202, the Court of Appeal (Lord Denning MR) decided that the Labour-controlled council would not be permitted to renege on a contract between the previous Conservative administration and the National Front for them to hold their annual conference in the town. The National Front sued for breach of contract and was granted specific performance largely on grounds of the constitutional importance of free speech and assembly. The right in s.95 of the 1983 Act is a private law not public law one: *Ettridge v Morrell* (1986) 85 LGR 100, cited in Bailey, Harris and Jones, *Civil Liberties*, above n 20, 434.
[25] A decision will be procedurally improper where someone with an interest in the outcome has been allowed to participate in the process or if the decision-making process was unfair, what used once to be called a breach of natural justice.

124 *The Locus of Protest*

responses,[26] although—and this is so even outside the confines of the HRA—throughout the 1990s the courts developed the practice of subjecting those decisions that affect common law rights to more anxious scrutiny.[27] In essence it means that not only is the decision one that another reasonable decision-maker would have taken but was also one that can be justified—with the more substantial the interference, the greater the justification needed. The rights of assembly and of free speech are now well-established as being rights that inhere in the lineage of the common law, as we saw in chapter one, and as such are subject to more heightened review. That said, even that more intense human rights-centred sub-*Wednesbury* review has rarely led to success.

(b) Illegality

Illegality as a head of review looks to whether the decision is one that was within the powers of the body taking it. By contrast to private individuals, everything a statutory body such as a local council, NHS Trust or secondary school does and every act it performs needs positive authorisation (either express or by necessity implied) in the form of a statutory power.[28] Thus, decisions about publicly-owned land are qualitatively different to those taken in respect of privately-owned land.[29] It would be unlawful for a council—to choose just one—to reach a decision on access without the sanction of law. That said, the general discretionary framework created by the main legislative measure, section 120 of the Local Government Act 1972, is broad. It confers a general power to acquire and then to manage land for the benefit, improvement or development of their area.[30] There is thus little chance of a banning decision being struck down as ultra vires purely and simply because the council had no power at all—as occurred in *Attorney-General v Fulham Corporation*.[31] A decision may also be illegal as an abuse or misuse of power. We know from cases such as *Wheeler v Leicester City Council*[32] and *R v Ealing LBC ex p Times Newspapers*[33] that it will be a misuse of a statutory power for a council to use its discretion to manage the land so as to punish someone who has done no wrong or to make a decision in relation to use of its land that is primarily activated by ulterior political motives.[34] In *Wheeler* the issue was the

---

[26] *R v Ministry of Defence ex parte Smith and Lustig-Prean* [1996] QB 517.
[27] ibid.
[28] As creations of statutes, local authorities, schools and hospitals may only do such things permitted by statute—though not necessarily the one creating them—as well as anything calculated to facilitate or is conducive or incidental to the discharge of any of their functions: see *London County Council v Attorney-General* [1902] AC 165; *Ashbury Rly Carriage & Iron Co v Riche* (1875) LR 7 HL 653; and *Attorney-General v Great Eastern Rly Co* (1880) 5 App Cas 473.
[29] We should here distinguish land owned by statutory bodies and land owned by central government. Ministers—and thus their departments—as embodiments of the Crown are not creatures of statute and have capacity to do whatever a natural, private person could do. They are not confined therefore by statute or prerogative though as organs of government can only exercise that power for the public benefit and for identifiably 'governmental' purposes: *Shrewsbury and Atcham Borough Council v Secretary of State for Communities and Local Government* [2008] EWCA Civ 148.
[30] Other land ownership or management powers exist in the Open Spaces Act 1906. Though s 120(1)(B) talks explicitly about a power to acquire, it was held in *R v Sefton Metropolitan Borough Council ex parte BASC* [2001] Env LR 10 that by implication this encompassed a power to manage land once acquired for the same purposes.
[31] *Attorney-General v Fulham Corporation* [1921] 1 Ch 440.
[32] *Wheeler v Leicester City Council* [1985] AC 1054.
[33] *R v Ealing London Borough Council ex parte Times Newspapers* [1978] IRLR 129.
[34] See also *R v Somerset County Council ex parte Fewings* [1995] 1 WLR 1037. There a majority of the Court of Appeal decided that the power under s 120 of the 1972 Act did not permit councillors lawfully to ban stag hunting on its land if such a decision was based or significantly influenced by the councillors' collective moral perspective on hunting. Simon Brown LJ (dissenting) held that a 'majority of the council genuinely regarded hunting

legality of the Council's decision to ban Leicester rugby club from using a council recreation ground for training, after three Leicester players decided to tour South Africa during the apartheid era. The Council argued that in exercising its discretionary powers in relation to its own land, it was entitled to have regard to the need to promote good race relations as expressed in section 71 of the Race Relations Act 1976, especially in light of the large percentage of people of Asian or Afro-Caribbean descent living in Leicester. Lord Templeman commented that

> the laws of this country are not like the laws of Nazi Germany. A private individual or a private organisation cannot be obliged to display zeal in the pursuit of an object sought by a public authority and cannot be obliged to publish views dictated by a public authority ... The club having committed no wrong, the council could not use their statutory powers in the management of their property or any other statutory powers in order to punish the club ... this use by the council of its statutory powers was a misuse of power.[35]

In the *Ealing* case, the Divisional Court held it was unlawful for public libraries to refuse to stock newspapers, the printing of which was the subject of an acrimonious industrial dispute, where section 7 of the Public Libraries and Museums Act 1964 imposed a duty on 'every library authority to provide a comprehensive and efficient library service'. Watkins LJ observed that

> the ban imposed by the respondents was for an ulterior object. It was inspired by political views which moved the respondents to interfere in an industrial dispute and for that purpose to use their powers under this Act. Parliament, I am sure, did not contemplate such action as that to be within the power it conferred when it enacted s.7. I would go so far as to say that no rational local authority would for a moment have thought that such a ban was open to it to impose in discharge of its duty to service libraries. That the respondents took account of an irrelevant consideration has I think been clearly demonstrated.[36]

Thus, a decision by a council of one political persuasion to refuse permission to its rivals to hold public meetings would likely be ruled unlawful (as well as being irrational) as an abuse of discretionary power. Equally, if that governing party had a firm party policy on, say, the treatment of asylum seekers then it would, too, most likely be a misuse of power to ban a meeting by the 'Send them all back home' pressure group.[37] Could such a power be lawfully exercised 'for the benefit of the local area' (under section 120 of the 1972 Act) in an area of high racial tension or perhaps with a high influx of recent immigrants? As Sir Thomas Bingham MR said in *Fewings*, there is

> a categorical difference between saying 'I strongly disapprove of X' [which if it influenced a decision would render it unlawful] and saying 'It is for the benefit of the area that X should be prohibited'. The first is the expression of a purely personal opinion which may (but need not) take account of any wider, countervailing argument ... The second statement is also the expression of a personal opinion, but involves a judgment on wider, community-based grounds of what is for the benefit of the area. Both statements may of course lead to the same conclusion, but they need

---

over the common as a cruel and socially undesirable activity inimical to the best interests of their area' and since this was at least a matter they were entitled to consider in their discretion and to decide what weight to attribute to it (even if it was not something required of them to reflect upon) when exercising their power for the 'benefit of the area' the decision could not be said to be unlawful.

[35] *Wheeler*, above n 32, 1080–81.
[36] *Ealing*, above n 33, 133.
[37] This thus extends the case law found in *Webster*, above n 21, and *Verrall*, above n 24.

not. There is nothing illogical in saying 'I strongly disapprove of X, but I am not persuaded that it is for the benefit of the area that X should be prohibited'.[38]

Although it could be argued that it was for the benefit of the local area (assuming the local area equates to or at least includes its inhabitants), the outcome and reasoning in *Wheeler* would seem to pose an insurmountable hurdle. The 'Send them all back home' pressure group has done nothing wrong. We might equate them with the rebel rugby tourists to South Africa. A variety of views exist about the propriety of such a tour and about the likelihood of sporting engagement leading to the dismantling of apartheid barriers but in the absence of a ban, there was nothing per se unlawful about it. Even if the group applying to use the land was morally repugnant, if permission were refused the group might be able to argue that the ban was politically motivated so the council could ingratiate itself (yet further) with the local electorate.

Outside such obvious parameters, what about a council decision that is not tainted, partly or in whole, by using its powers to obtain electoral advantage or by some other sort of disguised political motivation?[39] How would the law respond where a council decides it will adopt a blanket policy of refusing permission for the use of council properties for all public meetings or demonstrations, outside the requirements of sections 95–96 of the 1983 Act? Of course, council landlords still need to point to a legal basis that entitles them to act or to decide. That would almost certainly be section 120 of the 1972 Act, of which section it has been said the draftsman 'would have been pressed to find broader or less specific language'.[40] Unless, in adopting the policy the council could be said to be defeating a legitimate expectation—derived either from a promise or an undertaking or from past practice[41]—or in following the policy it 'closed its ears' to those seeking that an exception be made,[42] it is unlikely that a council will have acted outside the law.[43]

(ii) The Impact of the Human Rights Act

What change, if any, might the HRA effect? It is beyond doubt that local councils—as well as schools, NHS hospitals, army bases and MoD sites—will be core public authorities under section 6 of the HRA.[44] They will be under an enforceable duty not to act incompatibly with

---

[38] *Fewings*, above n 34, at 1045.

[39] Although it is not a judicial review case, see *Porter v Magill* [2001] UKHL 67 for a discussion of blatant and dishonest misuse of public power for electoral advantage, in the form of gerrymandering.

[40] *Fewings*, above n 34, at 1045.

[41] Even if there were an explicit representation that premises could be used or the premises had consistently been used for meetings in the past, there is some doubt domestically whether the legitimate expectation thereby created is one recognised and therefore capable of protection in domestic law. Historically, courts have taken the view that while judicial review will enforce promises (or past practice) of procedural protection—fair hearings, giving reasons and legal advice—they have been reluctant to require public bodies to guarantee the continued existence of a substantive benefit, such (as here) a claim to a right to the use of land itself: see generally W Wade and C Forsyth, *Administrative Law*, 10th edn (Oxford, Oxford University Press, 2009) or P Craig, *Administrative Law*, 6th edn (London, Sweet and Maxwell, 2003).

[42] *British Oxygen Co Ltd. v Minister of Technology* [1971] AC 610 (Lord Reid).

[43] The Court of Appeal decision in *Redfearn v Serco (t/a West Yorkshire Transport Service)* [2006] EWCA Civ 659, in overturning *Showboat Entertainment v Owens* [1984] 1 WLR 384, closes off one other limited avenue for challenge. If a council refused permission for a meeting on council land where racial tension in the area was the reason given for its refusal, this might arguably have been a racially discriminatory decision contrary to the Race Relations Act 1975. *Showboat Entertainment* had established that less favourable treatment 'on racial grounds' could include any case where the race whether of the complainant or a third party was the effective cause of the detriment suffered by the complainant.

[44] As we saw in chapter two, a distinction is drawn between 'core' and so-called (but inaccurately) 'functional' public authorities with the latter only liable under the HRA when it performs acts of a public nature. The House

an individual's Convention rights—what we earlier called the duty of Convention compliance. Is then a failure to provide meeting rooms or some other suitable venue, outside the five-yearly month-long election period, or a decision not to allow any groups (or one in particular) onto council land to protest a breach of either of the rights contained in Articles 10 and 11? To succeed, applicants would need to clear several hurdles.

(a) Decisions to Ban from Council Land

The second type of decision is the easier insofar as it potentially involves a breach of the negative obligation in Article 11. Thus a decision to ban the use of council land could now be challenged not just as irrational, illegal or procedurally improper but also as a disproportionate restriction on the right of peaceful assembly in Article 11. The difficulty facing applicants is that the only real instance in which protesters have challenged a similar decision is *Rai v UK*, where the application was declared inadmissible.[45] The general policy of refusing permission to use Trafalgar Square for rallies about Northern Ireland unless they were entirely uncontroversial was upheld as proportionate given the need to prevent disorder. However, as we saw in chapter two, more recent cases such as *Öllinger, Aldemir, Galstyan, Oya Ataman* and *Balçik* all indicate a view on the part of the ECtHR that is more favourable to peaceful demonstrations and marches which might cause tension and heated exchanges, disorder and disruption but which are in essence and at heart peaceful.[46] Although none is a case involving a request to use council or state land—whereas *Rai* was—their underpinning rationale would surely influence domestic courts as and when council bans come before them in future? If, on the other hand, permission were given to one group then this would allow anyone denied access the opportunity to argue a breach of Article 14. Such a claim is parasitic and so is dependent on there being a free-standing claim under another Article. However, this does not mean that a claimant must also establish a violation of that other free-standing right: in claiming a violation of Article X linked with discrimination under Article 14, one needs only to show for the latter that the claim falls within the ambit or the sphere of another protected right, a considerably wider and fuzzier concept. Thus there was a violation of Article 14 in *Abdulaziz, Cabales and Balkandali v UK*,[47] where immigration rules imposed different requirements on those men and women seeking to enter the UK despite the ECHR not containing a right to enter. In one of the leading UK cases, *Ghaidan v Ghodin-Mendoza*,[48] where the survivor of a same-sex relationship claimed the right to succeed to the tenancy of the house he shared with his deceased partner, it was accepted by all parties that this engaged the Convention rights to respect to a home. In the words of Lady Hale,

> [i]t is common ground that one of the Convention rights is engaged here. Everyone has the right to respect for their home. This does not mean that the state—or anyone else—has to supply everyone with a home. Nor does it mean that the state has to grant everyone a secure right to live in their

of Lords in *YL v Birmingham* [2007] UKHL 27 has settled, though not without criticism, that contracted out bodies or bodies undertaking duties on behalf of a council are not 'public authorities' within s 6. The difference could become important if, for example, a group sought to protest outside and against the closure of a private care home that undertook certain housing tasks for local councils.

[45] *Rai v UK* (App 25522/94) EComHR inadmissibility decision 6 April 1995.
[46] *Öllinger v Austria* (2008) 48 EHRR 38, *Aldemir v Turkey* (App 32124/02) ECtHR judgment 18 December 2007, *Galstyan v Armenia* (App 26986/03) ECtHR judgment 15 November 2007, *Oya Ataman v Turkey* (App 74552/01) ECtHR 5 December 2005 and *Balçik v Turkey* (App 0025/02) ECtHR judgment 22 November 2007.
[47] *Abdulaziz, Cabales and Balkandali v UK* (1985) 7 EHRR 471.
[48] *Ghaidan v Ghodin-Mendoza* [2004] UKHL 30.

home. But if it does grant that right to some, it must not withhold it from others in the same or an analogous situation. It must grant that right equally, unless the difference in treatment can be objectively justified.[49]

Cases such as *Carson*[50] and *Mendoza* outline what should be a court's approach to the question of discrimination and justification, once it has been raised under Article 14.[51]

(b) Failing to Provide a Venue

As to the first type of decision, it is clear that the council is not in breach of the right to peaceful protest in its negative, restraining sense: it has done nothing to prevent the exercise of the right of the group to express itself or to associate. Nonetheless, again as we saw in the previous chapter, it is well established at Strasbourg that there is a positive, albeit weaker right comprised within the negative primary right contained in Article 11. This may in fact require the state itself to act even to the extent of requiring it to regulate activities between two private parties (which is not the case here).[52] So far, there has been no case on a footing with the instant example, so conclusions are hypothetical. We saw in *Plattform Ärzte für das Leben v Austria*[53] that an anti-abortion group alleged that they had been given insufficient police protection against pro-abortion counter-demonstrators set on disrupting their protest. On the facts no breach was made out as the Court concluded that Austria, through its police, had taken reasonable and appropriate measures to enable lawful demonstrations to proceed peacefully and had therefore complied with the duty imposed on it. The Court did not have to assess the expediency or effectiveness of the tactics adopted by the police in the circumstances of the case. States were not required to guarantee the right absolutely and they had a wide discretion as to the choice of the means to be used. The obligation is as to measures to be taken rather than as to results to be achieved. What is instructive here however is the Court's acknowledgement that '[g]enuine, effective freedom of peaceful assembly cannot, therefore, be reduced to a mere duty on the part of the State not to interfere: a purely negative conception would not be compatible with the object and purpose of Article 11'.[54]

Might groups in the local area be able to argue that absent some state provision, they had no effective freedom of peaceful assembly? This would accord with that element of the Court's jurisprudence that adjures that rights in the ECHR must be practical and effective, not theoretical and illusory.[55] It would also accord with the requirement in Article 1 that requires member states to secure to all within the jurisdiction the rights in the remainder of the ECHR.

---

[49] ibid, at [135].
[50] *Carson v Secretary of State for Work and Pensions* [2005] UKHL 37.
[51] (i) Do the facts fall within the ambit of one or more of the Convention rights? (ii) Was there a difference in treatment in respect of that right between the complainant and others put forward for comparison? (iii) Were those others in an analogous situation? (iv) Was the difference in treatment objectively justifiable, that is did it have a legitimate aim and bear a reasonable relationship of proportionality to that aim? (v) Was the difference in treatment is based on one or more of the grounds proscribed—whether expressly or by inference—in Article 14?: *Mendoza*, above n 48 at [134]
[52] *Plattform Ärzte fur das Leben v Austria* (1988) 13 EHRR 204. For a discussion of positive rights, see above text to n 15.
[53] ibid, at [32]–[38]. Technically, the Court judgment is concerned only with Art 13—the right to an effective national remedy—since the Commission had ruled that the Art 11 claim was inadmissible. That said, it is clear that the Court effectively revisited that issue since the tenor of the whole judgment is an assessment of whether or not there had been a violation of the positive right under Art 11.
[54] ibid, at [32].
[55] *Airey v Ireland* (1979) 2 EHRR 305 is probably the most well known, and the first of these cases.

The scenario portrayed above—a council banning a group from using its land to protest—is not on a par with the shopping centre cases, which we shall address below. These involve, it is said, more delicate questions of balancing competing private rights and proprietary interests of private citizens. Nonetheless, the more land that is privately owned (whether or not previously state-held) and placed beyond the reach of citizens claiming to use it for expressive purposes, then more pressing becomes the case to develop a non-discriminatory framework for publicly-held land to be made open on the basis that if the right to protest is to have any value at all, the greater becomes the burden on states to regulate private ownership.[56] It is to that subject—compelling landowners to allow protesters onto private land—that we will now turn.

B. Rights of Access Over Privately-held Land

Where land is in private hands, the position in law is very simple: no one can be compelled to allow anyone else onto their land or have access to it for any purpose, let alone to hold a protest or a public meeting. The nature of land ownership at common law is that it is all-defeating, trumping all other claims. Absolute title not only brings with it, but can be defined as, the right absolutely and arbitrarily to exclude anyone else unless there is either a contractual agreement to the contrary or statutory entitlement that dilutes that absolute right. This historic right is the golden thread that runs through the common law, reflected in that well-known aphorism that an Englishman's home is his castle.

The domestication of Convention rights has had no impact on this.[57] At Strasbourg, the leading—and so far only—case on the topic is *Appleby v UK*.[58] We shall consider the case critically shortly. For now, it will suffice to note that save in exceptional and limited circumstances, the Court has confirmed the right of landowners to exclude whomever they choose from their land. Article 11 will only very rarely impose a positive obligation on states to regulate domestic land law and property rights so as to promote or to guarantee the effective enjoyment of the right to communicate views to fellow citizens. In *Appleby*, a campaigning group was banned from setting up stalls, distributing leaflets and seeking signatures for a petition in a shopping centre. It applied to the Court, relying on Articles 10 and 11. The Court held that where the UK merely adhered to its historic common law position, whereby third parties cannot force reluctant owners to permit campaigning and protest activities on their land, this did not mean the UK, through its courts and legal system, would generally be in breach of the positive obligation inherent within Article 11.

(i) The Nature of Absolute Title and Categories of Private Land

It might repay us to unpack this a little more. The unqualified nature of absolute legal title means that individual university lecturers cannot be required to allow an environmental group to enter their back gardens to protest about their poor personal recycling record if they don't want them to. That much might be obvious and, one might hope, uncontentious

---

[56] Though of course, that merely postpones discussion (here in this book) and decision (in the courts) of the inevitable conflict when groups whose very raison d'être is the denial of rights and liberties equally seek to claim that right of open and free access: in other words, the very problem that confronted the US Supreme Court in *RAV v City of St Paul Minnesota* 505 US 377 (1992).
[57] So far Strasbourg law has had very limited impact on property law and relationships.
[58] *Appleby v UK* (2003) 37 EHRR 38.

but should it automatically be the case that that same group should be unable to stand in the car park of a multi-national conglomerate highlighting for its employees, suppliers and customers that company's unenviable record on pollution? The problem that we need to confront and that is implicit in these two scenarios is that land comes in different packages and can be classified or considered in several ways. It might not necessarily be appropriate to have a 'one size fits all' approach to regulating peaceful protest on private land.

Conceptually, we can distinguish private landholdings in one of several ways. We might first differentiate between different sizes of privately-owned land: the backyard of a residential house is obviously markedly different to hundreds of acres of land used to grow GM foods. Alternatively, we might reflect on the size of the private holding relative to any publicly-owned land in the area to see whether there is an adequate supply of land that is available for protest. That, though, assumes that citizens can force the state's hand to require access to protest, which may not be the case as we have seen. Next, we might categorise private land according to the power or impact that that holding has: we might contrast here a large country house, having acres of gardens used solely as a private residence, with an arms factory or fast-food outlet of a fraction of its size. Last, we might separate private land that has always been held privately from land which has been transferred by and from the contracting state into private hands under the guise of one of the various political measures undertaken in recent times.[59] Normatively speaking, those different typologies may justify imposing a regulatory regime under which different—perhaps graduated—obligations to permit protests or meetings are imposed on what appear all to be 'private' landowners.[60]

Clearly, size alone should not dictate how the law should respond when a peaceful protest on someone else's land occurs. Neither, in just the same way as, it is submitted, should the quirk of who owns the title. Generally we can probably assume that people do not decide to hold a protest on someone else's land purely because it is a sizeable chunk; their choice is far more likely the result of what that land holding signifies—who the owner is and what is being done on it. Seeing it in those terms will assist in resolving the problem. The other part of the resolution might be to ask whether, in the absence of a right of entry, the protest would be effective.[61] Thus there is no reason why a fast-food chain, an oil multi-national or an arms developer should per se be required to allow someone onto their own property so as to protest about the activities they conduct there, any more than someone should be allowed to stand in my kitchen to protest about my excessive consumption of power. However, our answer might well be different if the only place to protest was a mile away, where no workers, customers or suppliers of the concern would see. This is where the size of the land, relative to public land, may be important. As we shall see, even before the advent of the HRA, the common law in *DPP v Jones* recognised a limited right peacefully to protest on the highway.[62] Therefore if the fast-food chain, the oil multi-national or the arms developer were based on a main road, the group could easily and perfectly lawfully protest outside its gates. If it is located in the middle of a privately-owned industrial estate, miles from the road, the effect of any protest is considerably lessened. So far, the limited right

---

[59] I Harden, *The Contracting State* (Buckingham, Open University Press, 1992).
[60] We might also distinguish between land owned by natural persons—with autonomy and which are capable of being offended by the presence of protesters—and that owned by commercial companies.
[61] To some extent, this chimes with the approach adopted by the majority of the Strasbourg Court in *Appleby* albeit on the facts the Court might well have taken too narrow a view of what alternatives there were.
[62] *Director of Public Prosecutions v Jones* [1999] 2 AC 240.

established in *Jones* has been confined to the highway; the fact that it has not yet been extended in case law to all publicly-held land means, as we saw above, that it is by no means certain that a group will be able to require entry to other public land. An arms factory set amidst acres of national park would be isolated from any group being able to enforce the right of effective protest nearby. It is clear too that there is the world of difference in the use to which that land can be put, and thus in its impact and the power of its owner. It seems right too that a regulatory framework might seek to respond differently to that contrast. Here, admittedly, it is very hard to frame a workable rule or at least one that is clear and predictable, so as to be 'prescribed by law'. 'Impact', 'effect' and (worst of all three) 'power' are subjective terms: they are indisputably fact and context dependent. But there is surely a difference between my tipping paint down a drain and a paint manufacturer doing the same in the Thames—and it is not just scale or even culpability. If there is, should not the legal framework respond in a differentiated way?[63]

(ii) Quasi-public Land

One development in the attempt to create a sensitive legal framework governing access to private land has been to view some land as 'quasi public land', a loose term that tries to capture the essence of land that is in private ownership but with overtones of 'the public'.[64] It is more than, and different from, a hybrid form. The problem is that a proper definition usually eludes—perhaps is avoided by?—those using the term. 'Quasi-public' land can be thought of encompassing various subtly different holdings and uses, each of which might affect our thinking or the outcome that is proposed. The first is where despite being wholly privately owned, the land is being used to promote or to serve the greater public good, a rather nebulous concept: a good example might be a cinema or entertainment complex which enriches us culturally, socially and politically. The service being provided may be one that is paid for at cost—truly private—or may be subsidised or even fully funded by the state. The second type of use is where privately-owned land is used to provide a social good to the public under some form of arrangement with the state; provision which might complement, supplement or supplant the equivalent public sector provision. One type might be where a registered social landlord contracts with the local council to provide housing for the borough's homeless, needy or infirm in exchange for payment. This might discharge the council's duties, albeit that the council will remain legally liable to the public for providing that service.[65] Another might be where facilities or staff in a private hospital are used by an NHS Trust to treat the sick where capacity in the state sector has been reached.[66] Third and last, land might be considered quasi-public because it was once held publicly—such as a municipal theatre—but has been sold to a private developer or because it is held jointly in

---

[63] We might also see this as a clash of choices: between my choice to protest on farmer Giles's land and his choice not to let me. What is it about *his* choice that means it should always prevail? Why should absolute title here be an absolute given the added mix of public utility that surrounds the right to protest?

[64] See K Gray and S Gray, 'Civil Rights, Civil Wrongs and Quasi-Public Space' [1999] *EHRLR* 46.

[65] These facts fall between *YL v Birmingham City Council* [2007] UKHL 27 and *R (Weaver) v London and Quadrant Housing Trust* [2009] EWCA Civ 587. In the latter, it was decided that a registered social landlord terminating a tenancy, in HRA terms is a hybrid public authority performing an act not of a private nature under s 6 of the HRA, and thus liable under and bound by the HRA. That does not mean that the body itself is always liable under s 6—it is the act it performs that dictates its liability.

[66] There is something more 'public' about this than where someone pays privately and directly for treatment as of course will occur too.

private and public hands, such as under a private finance initiative (PFI) agreement.[67] Many hospitals and some schools have been built on publicly-owned land but with private capital. The result is that the buildings are now privately owned and operated for profit but are leased back to (say) the local primary care health trust for use in treating NHS patients free at-the-point-of-delivery.[68] Resolving these definitional and conceptual tensions is not a question that need detain readers of a general book on peaceful protest any longer; these are questions for public lawyers and land lawyers on another day. We need merely to note their existence. What is more important, given that little analysis of that question has occurred, is to analyse the case law, principles and rules. As with what we might call 'pure' private holdings, the legal position is quite simple: neither domestic law nor Strasbourg as part of the positive duty in Article 11 requires a state to force quasi-public landowners into allowing individuals onto their land for the purposes of protest. The only domestic or European case in point on the topic is the Strasbourg decision in *Appleby v UK*[69] and it is to that that we now turn.

(a) *Appleby v UK*

Three residents of Washington in the North-East of England were prevented from meeting in a privately-owned shopping centre in their hometown. They had wanted to impart information and ideas about a proposed local development plan, which they opposed. The plan related to the development of the only playing field in the vicinity of the town centre which was available for use by the local community. The applicants wished to protest so as to ensure the Council did not grant full planning permission to that proposal. The problem for the applicants was that a very large proportion of the new town centre (the Galleries) was located within an area now owned by a private company, Postel Properties Limited. The town centre was originally built by the Washington Development Corporation (WDC), a statutory body set up by private Act, and specifically charged with building the new centre. In 1987, WDC sold the centre to Postel. The owner of one hypermarket within the Galleries initially allowed the three to set up a stall, to seek petition signatures and to put up posters outlining their opposition to the plans. When they sought permission subsequently to collect a second petition, the owner rejected their request in these terms:

> the Galleries is unique in as much as although it is the Town Centre, it is also privately owned ... [Postel's] stance on all political and religious issues, is one of strict neutrality and I am charged with applying this philosophy ... I am therefore obliged to refuse permission for you to carry out a petition within the Galleries or the adjacent car parks.[70]

When Mrs Appleby, one of the three, had previously tried a similar tactic—setting up a stand, displaying posters and seeking signatures—in the entrance hall to the main shopping mall, Postel security guards had removed her.

---

[67] If a municipal theatre were sold off and private dwellings erected, it would be hard to categorise this still as anything but private land. That would not necessarily be the case if the theatre were sold off but were still to be run as a theatre albeit on commercial terms for private profit.

[68] Similar concerns arise with the vogue for expanding the educational academies scheme in which private investors 'sponsor' (usually) infrastructure development in exchange for greater say in running the school afterwards.

[69] *Appleby v UK*, above n 58, discussed D Mead, above n 7. Much of the detail of the case and the arguments presented is taken from this piece.

[70] Before the Chamber, the applicants gave evidence of groups which had been allowed to set up stalls within the Galleries. These included British Gas and the Royal British Legion. Even Sunderland Council was allowed to use the area to consult on the three leadership choices for the future of the Council. The judgment does not indicate why an Art 14 (discrimination) claim was not pursued by the applicants.

1. Reasoning and grounds The three applied to the ECtHR claiming that the UK was in breach of obligations it owed under Articles 10 and 11. This was despite the fact that the land was no longer owned by the state or a state entity.[71] This argument had two strands. First, the UK was in breach directly for failing, on the transfer from WDC, to impose on Postel an obligation to permit peaceful protest. Secondly, the UK was in breach of its positive obligations under those two articles. It had failed to put in place a legal framework which would have provided effective protection for the right of peaceful protest while at the same time balancing those rights against the rights of property owners. This, it was argued, would be in conformity with previous Strasbourg case law relating to positive obligations.[72] The legal framework that did exist—the law of trespass—required no balance to be struck between competing rights. Protection was given to property owners who were able to wield absolute discretion in granting access to their land; no regard was given to individuals seeking to exercise their individual rights. The applicants conceded that it would be for the government to indicate and to identify categories of 'quasi-public' land, but asserted that a tightly drafted definition (for example, excluding theatres) could be drawn up.[73] They argued this would permit a certain degree of protest and would not be out of line with jurisdictions such as the USA. There, concepts of reasonable access or limitations on arbitrary exclusion powers of landowners were being developed in the context of quasi-public land. The Government in turn accepted that positive obligations were capable of arising under Articles 10 and 11 but for three reasons denied that they arose on the facts. First, the effect on the applicants was not serious since they had other opportunities to collect signatures and to protest. Secondly, the burden, on the other hand, on the state of such a finding would be heavy. Local authorities, when selling land, would have to enter into walkways agreements with private purchasers so as to entitle the vendor authority later to regulate access by byelaw. Of course, private landowners might be reluctant to agree to such terms in advance when purchasing. Lastly, the applicants' contentions took no account of the legitimate objections that landowners might have to being required to allow protests when other avenues—the media and publicly-owned land—existed.

It was not a surprise that the Court did not find for the applicants on their first ground, the direct interference ground. The Court also decided that the UK had not failed to guarantee the positive obligation in the articles, the second ground. Although it accepted the functional importance of free speech in a healthy democracy, it decided that the balancing of individual interests with the general communal interest—required to be performed when deciding whether to impose positive obligations and whether there has been a breach—favoured not imposing liability here on the facts. First in the balance was Postel's right peacefully to enjoy its property under the First Protocol. Second was the fact that US case law provided no consensus view.[74] Third was the fact that Article 10 did not bestow any freedom of forum for exercising freedom of expression. The Chamber stated that

---

[71] In fact, rather than claiming that the UK failed to guarantee the right of peaceful protest (under Arts 10 and 11) the claim, as we shall see below, is more accurately summarised as a failure to guarantee the right not to be unreasonably denied access to privately held land for the purposes of protest

[72] See for example, *Stjerna v Finland* (1997) 24 EHRR 195.

[73] Presumably, it would also be for the government to establish the modalities of how the balancing of competing interests and rights should be drawn.

[74] The American position is by no means clear. In the seminal case of *Robins v Pruneyard Shopping* 447 US 74 (1980) the federal Supreme Court decided that a State could entertain a more expansive free speech constitutional guarantee, including as to granting limited and reasonable access rights over private property to hand out leaflets. The federal guarantee of free speech is a guarantee only against abridgment by the government, federal or State; thus, while statutory or common law may in some situations extend protection or provide redress against a

[w]hile it is true that demographic, social, economic and technological developments are changing the ways in which people move around and come into contact with each other, the Court is not persuaded that this requires the automatic creation of rights of entry to private property, or even, necessarily, to all publicly-owned property.[75]

The Chamber added that it might have taken a different view if Postel's bar had prevented the effective exercise of the right of free expression. Here, it was not the case that the bar had resulted in the destruction of the essence of that right. On their own admission, alternatives were available to the applicants. These included going door-to-door, using other available media and campaigning in the (admittedly) less used old town centre. The limit placed on the applicants was merely a ban on using the entrance areas and walkways of the Galleries. That being so, the Chamber decided that the applicants were not effectively prevented from communicating their views to their fellow citizens. This underplays the importance of autonomy and choice in determining content and forms of expressive activities as well as ignoring the fact that a chosen location may be 'uniquely positioned', have a 'close connection' or 'symbolic importance'.[76]

2. Analysis and comment   I have criticised the decision elsewhere, as have others.[77] In essence, the approach adopted by the Court erred in two ways when undertaking the balancing test. The first error was

> implicitly to hold as equal, in abstract terms, the value of Postel's property rights as a counterpoise to the applicants' rights under Article 10 and 11 ... Not only did it fail to consider (a) the crucial instrumental role that expressive activity can play within a democracy but it failed to recognise (b) the public nature of the seemingly private relationship between landowner and trespasser ... [with the result that] by adhering to a strictly delineated public/private (land) law dichotomy, the Chamber failed to require that law respond appropriately to paradigmatic socio-economic shifts in public ownership.[78]

The second error compounded the first. The court failed properly to weigh up the relative value of the applicants' claims to protest as against Postel's claim to property and any countervailing communal interests.

> The Chamber has unwittingly created [a logical impasse] by adhering to the straitjacket of public/private spheres. By espousing the absolute right of an owner to exclude, the Chamber has denied the need for a reasonableness test. However, only with a concept of reasonableness can there be any barometer against which to assess an owner's right to determine the implied licence to enter; only with the infusion of reasonableness can there be any 'balancing' exercise at all. But, it is this balancing requirement that lies at the heart of the positive obligations concept in Articles 10 and 11 and, indeed, at the heart of the exercise under Article 10(2) for direct breaches by the State.[79]

private corporation or person who seeks to abridge the free expression of others, no such protection or redress is provided by the Constitution itself; thus where union members tried to stage a picket in a shopping centre car park but were threatened with action by the owners, the Supreme Court held the workers had no First Amendment right to enter the car park: *Hudgens v NLRB* 424 US 507 (1976). As with free protest zones, there is a wealth of literature with a good overview being J Klear, 'Comparison of the Federal Courts' and the New Jersey Supreme Court's treatments of free speech on private property: where won't we have the freedom to speak next?' (2002) 33 *Rutgers Law Journal* 589.

[75] *Appleby v UK* (2003) 37 EHRR 38 at [47].
[76] J Rowbottom, 'Property and participation: a right of access for expressive activities' [2005] *EHRLR* 186, 189.
[77] See Mead above n 7, Rowbottom, *ibid*, and M Sanderson, 'Free speech in public places: the privatisation of human rights in *Appleby v UK*' (2004) 15 *Kings College Law Journal* 159.
[78] Mead, *ibid*, 103–4 and 106.
[79] Mead, *ibid*, 108–9.

The logical conclusion of the majority's position in *Appleby* would also mean there was nothing that could be done if a supermarket decided to ban any protester who had—unsuccessfully—opposed its development plans in a small town. This, of course, would not even be quasi-public land but purely private but should 'the law not now recognise that it would be invidious to permit [powerful] private parties . . . to punish objectors merely for exercising a constitutionally guaranteed right?'[80] Judge Maruste specifically rejected the majority view on the basis that it gave no consideration about how 'the privately-owned *forum publicum* was to be owned in the public interest' and the 'traditional rule that the private owner has an unfettered right to eject . . . without giving any justification and without any test of reasonableness . . . is no longer fully adapted to contemporary conditions and society'. The position adopted by the court undermines any notion of equal access to political institutions and to political participation, and thus of any Rawlsian idea of equal worth (and of dignity), by making access dependent on economic status and bargaining power. Is that really the way to sustain a democracy? It is clear that what is needed, as Rowbottom and others have argued, is in fact not an equal right, since that merely removes arbitrary discrimination—if the landowner chooses to permit entry to no one, then all can be said to have access equally—but a general right of reasonable access with limitations and safeguards for owners (such as compensation). Such a right 'aims to supply speakers and groups with the necessary resource for effective communication'.[81] It is clear that such a right should encompass both public and private land for the reasons set out earlier in this chapter: the artificiality of the distinction, the 'shifting sands of the historically clear public/private divide' and the 'major socio-economic changes in land ownership'[82] in the latter part of the twentieth century mean that matters such as type, nature, use and impact of the land, together with its value to protesters given their target, rather than ownership should be determinative. The right would need to be statutory: it is unlikely, given the historical attachment of the common law and the outcome in *Appleby* that a court would feel obliged—as a section 6 public authority itself—to mould and to develop the law not only of trespass (which would only provide a defence) but to forge a positive right to counter physical barriers.[83] The narrowness of the concept of 'public authority' under section 6 taken by the House of Lords in *YL* also indicates a lack of predisposition to expanding the boundaries of the state so that (if the general right were restricted to state bodies) greater access would be brought about. Since granting a right of access would involve, too, altering the property rights of owners (under the First Protocol) as well as, if the owner were a natural person, their privacy rights under Article 8,[84] then the right could never be absolute. In fact Rowbottom himself vacillates and asserts that 'the right of access would not apply to all private property'.[85] This seems sensible and fair: an equitable balance would presumptively

---

[80] Mead, *ibid*, 108. Rowbottom, above n 76, 187, cites *The Guardian* report (9 October 2004) of a trade union march to highlight low pay at Canary Wharf being cancelled after the owners of the estate obtained an injunction to prevent it.
[81] Rowbottom, *ibid*, 190 and see the discussion—and criticism—of American public forum jurisprudence at 192–3. It would also obviate any need to expand the definition of public land, perhaps by use of the term 'quasi public land' or even to conceptualise different regimes for public and for private land at all: see Rowbottom, *ibid*, 195–6.
[82] Mead, above n 7, 110.
[83] Rowbottom, above n 76, 197–9.
[84] Although companies can claim privacy—see *R v BSC ex parte British Broadcasting Corp* [2000] 3 All ER 989—such assertions are unlikely to hold great sway.
[85] Rowbottom above n 76, 199.

exclude property owned by natural individuals or—so as not to exclude the Earl of Buccleuch but to exclude the vast majority of residential land—holdings under a certain size. Protesters might be able to displace that presumption where they could demonstrate (say) a 'pressing social need' given the importance of the location to either their message or their means of communicating it. Clearly, other factors which would militate against an excessive intrusion might include: advance notice of intention to protest; the owner being able to prescribe time and duration conditions (though not so as to defeat the purpose of the protest) as well as limiting numbers and (perhaps) frequency; the provision of reasonable and equally effective alternatives; limiting the protest to peaceful communication and advocacy; limitations on content—but this is unlikely to hold up if the right not to exclude covers only companies or commercial concerns; and payment of reasonable expenses, but it seems unlikely, for the reasons Rowbottom sets out, that owners could claim compensation.[86]

(iii) The Countryside and Rights of Way Act 2000

The only erosion of the general common law rule—that unless owners of private land agree, they have an absolute right to refuse entry or access to others—is where legislation empowers third parties to overcome that refusal. Historically, the only legislation was that which authorised *public* bodies to enter without permission and then generally only for the purposes of detecting or preventing crime or for other public good, such as a child's welfare. In 2000, after over a century of campaigning, Parliament passed the Countryside and Rights of Way Act (the CROW Act) 2000. The detail of the legislative scheme need not concern us save to note that for the first time private individuals were given the right to enter someone else's land, against the landowner's will if need be, without need of a public right of way or some other defined path.[87] It is therefore a great inroad into the absolute title previously enjoyed by freeholders.

On its face there is little of relevance for the law of protest, concerned as it is with establishing what is usually but not entirely accurately referred to as the 'right to roam' over an estimated 1 million hectares of open land. The Act establishes a scheme of 'access land', land which has been mapped and shown as open country by the newly formed Countryside Agency or is registered common land.[88] Section 2 entitles

> any person . . . to enter and remain on any access land for the purposes of open-air recreation.

By virtue of section 2(1), they retain that right provided they do so

> without breaking or damaging any wall, fence, hedge, stile or gate'

and provided they observe the general and specific restrictions contained in selected other parts of the Act, notably Schedule 2. The question for us is then this: can someone claim the right to roam onto access land in order to stage a demonstration? The solution depends on two factors: is holding a protest using land 'for the purposes of open-air recreation' and is the protest an activity restricted by other sections and parts of the 2000 Act? As to the first

---

[86] ibid, 200–201.
[87] See generally A Sydenham, *Public Rights of Way and Access to Land*, 3rd edn (Bristol, Jordans 2007) chs 11–15.
[88] 'Open country' covers, broadly, land that appears to consist wholly or predominantly of mountain, moor, heath, or down.

issue, the Act—rather surprisingly—does not define 'open-air recreation'.[89] On its ordinary language, might it not be possible to argue that protest is or can be a form of recreation? There seems no reason to narrow the meaning only to include activities such as walking, bird watching, rock-climbing or orienteering. Protest—for some, for many maybe—is an activity that is enjoyed, that feeds the soul, that is creative and/or is a fillip from the humdrum of work and routine. Given the width attributed to section 3 of the Human Rights Act (as we saw in chapter two) in order to read and give effect to the phrase 'open-air recreation' in a Convention compatible manner, might it be interpreted as including elements of peaceful protest?[90] It is true that DEFRA guidance, specifically states, in relation to 'open-air recreation' that

> [e]xamples of activities which we consider are not forms of open-air recreation are political rallies, filming activities and professional dog walking. The right of access cannot in our view be relied on to undertake such activities, so consideration of the general restrictions in Schedule 2 is not relevant.[91]

As the Guidance admits, this though is not an authoritative interpretation; that is a matter for the courts. It is also true that Schedule 2 explicitly classifies some protest activity outwith the right of access. If someone commits aggravated trespass then that person no longer has any right to be on access land.[92] Neither does someone committing 'any criminal offence' or 'writing . . . a placard'.[93] Such a proscription is complicated by the separate problem of reading in or reading down 'standard' criminal offences so as to make them Convention compatible, as was done in *Connolly v DPP*, a case in which a protester sent photos of aborted foetuses by post.[94] We shall consider it in detail in chapter six. In other words, if X can argue that though the behaviour they have engaged in might be unlawful on the face of a section, they have not committed the criminal offence of Y since the Convention right of peaceful protest constitutes a 'lawful excuse' as envisaged and set out in the relevant Act. Thus as well as not having committed a criminal offence, they have not lost the 'right to roam' either. What is of interest is that nowhere in the Act, and certainly

---

[89] The term is also used in the National Parks and Access to Countryside Act 1949. Section 5 refers to 'the opportunities [areas] afford for open-air recreation' as one of the factors to be borne in mind in when designating an area of the country as a National Park. One of the few cases on either s 5 of the 1949 Act or s 2 of the CROW Act is *Meyrick Estate Management Ltd and Others v Secretary of State for Environment, Food & Rural Affairs* [2007] EWCA Civ 53. There the Court of Appeal was asked to determine how an inspector, conducting an inquiry into the designation of certain land within the New Forest National Park, should have approached the statutory test in s 5(2)(b) of the 1949 Act: 'opportunities for open air recreation', focussing on the first word.

[90] As we saw in chapter two, the key to interpretation under s 3, we learn from *Mendoza v Ghaidan* [2004] UKHL 30 is not the language that was chosen or not chosen; for Parliament to have imposed on the judges such an approach to utilising s 3 would have meant, in the words this time of Lord Rodger, it had 'devise[d] an entertaining parlour game for lawyers'. Judges would also need to ask: would it change the essence of the statutory scheme; would the urged for meaning be, in the words of Lord Nicholls, 'inconsistent with a fundamental feature of legislation'? Unlikely. Is it a decision that the courts are not equipped to make? Hardly. Will it have financial repercussions? Probably not. Will it have 'practical ramifications' for private landowners? That may be so in terms of security, order and policing.

[91] Information note on Schedule 2: General restrictions www.defra.gov.uk/rural/documents/countryside/crow/general-restrict.pdf (undated) accessed 20 January 2010.

[92] CROW Act 2000, Sch 2 para 1(q)–(r). We shall consider aggravated trespass in detail in chapter six. In essence it requires a defendant to be trespassing (as well as obstructing or disrupting a lawful activity) which makes this all rather circular since the CROW Act is about roaming not being deemed a trespass.

[93] ibid, paras (d) and (p); clearly the second can be circumvented by having with them a placard but not writing on it on the land. The inclusion of the first seems rather to render otiose the specific proscription of aggravated trespass.

[94] *Connolly v Director of Public Prosecutions* [2007] EWHC 237 (Admin).

not in Schedule 2 is there any specific mention of protest—and presumably not solely because of the difficulty of framing a definition or establishing criteria. That being so, despite what DEFRA believes, *expressio unius est exclusio alterius*. As Lord Millett put it in *Mendoza*,

> 'red, blue or green' cannot be read as meaning 'red, blue, green or yellow'; the specification of three only of the four primary colours indicates a deliberate omission of the fourth . . . Section 3 cannot be used to supply the missing colour, for this would be not to interpret the statutory language but to contradict it.

Might not the same be said, only in reverse, of the omission of protest from the list in Schedule 2 to the 2000 Act? It is clear that this will—and can—only be decided upon by the courts once, presumably, someone has been sued for trespass, or injunctive relief sought, after they protested on access land. So far as can be ascertained, no such cases have yet been brought.[95]

III. Place-Specific Restrictions on Protest

All the restrictions we have just been considering apply nationwide, irrespective of where the protest is taking place or where the land is located. In this second section, we shall consider the main ways in which protest is either not permitted in certain places or is regulated (and so restricted)—in scope or extent—in others.[96]

A. Wilful Obstruction of the Highway Without Lawful Excuse

Historically, one location where it was almost certain that a protester would be breaking the criminal law would be on the highway.

(i) The Offence

Arresting someone for wilfully obstructing the highway without lawful excuse is a trusted part of a police officer's armoury in dealing with and containing all forms of protest, not solely obstructive or intimidating direct action protest.[97] It will be an obstruction—certainly under pre-HRA precedent—for any part of the highway to be obstructed even if there is room to pass and re-pass on either side. What matters is that the part where someone else may choose to walk is obstructed: *Homer v Cadman*.[98] Equally, it is not a defence—by means of providing a lawful excuse—to argue that on all previous occasions when someone

---

[95] One last unanswered question is whether open access land becomes public space for the purposes of other legislation that regulates protest, such as s 14 POA 1986: see the DEFRA guidance and s 42 of the CROW Act 2000.

[96] We will not here, for obvious reasons, consider the impact of local byelaws or private Acts of Parliament.

[97] The place on which the protest is taking place must be, of course, a highway so illustrating yet again one of the themes of this book which we identified in the introduction: the importance of location or the rules relating to ownership of land. Thus, for example, all charges under s 137 were dropped against those protesting outside Carmel-Agrexco in west London after the police realised that the land outside the company's offices were owned by a private third party and so was not a 'highway': 'Agrexco UK Valentine's Blockade Case Dropped By Met Police', at: brightonpalestine.org/blog/?=138, filed 18 April 2007 (accessed 7 September 2007).

[98] *Homer v Cadman* (1886) 16 Cox CC 51, (Div Ct).

has held a meeting that has blocked the highway no one has been arrested nor that on those previous occasions the police attended and even facilitated free passage: *Arrowsmith v Jenkins*.[99] We saw in chapter three how prosecutions for the equivalent of section 137 were upheld as proportionate measures given the risk of disruption to the rights of others (including of traffic!).[100]

(ii) Strasbourg Law

Given the value laid by Strasbourg, as we have seen, on the right to peaceful protest and its fundamental status in any democratic society, for expressive communicative protests at least—meetings, marches, leafleting, petitioning, campaigning—there must certainly be some scope for utilising section 3 of the HRA to read and to interpret section 137 in a manner which only criminalises conduct which does actually obstruct. That conclusion is strengthened by the decision in *Patyi v Hungary*.[101] There one factor in the European Court's holding that there was a violation of the right to peaceful protest—where no more than 20 people were going to gather silently on the pavement opposite the Prime Minister's house—was the fact that 'the space in question was wide enough—approximately five metres—to allow other pedestrians to walk by during a demonstration'.[102] This might well be less so for protests which deliberately take the form of obstructive sit-ins on the highway—where the aim is not to persuade or to raise awareness but to stop the very thing that is being complained about from taking place—or other forms of direct action protest. Strasbourg case law has consistently come down against such forms as we saw in the four linked cases against Germany.[103] However, for other types of protest section 137 could be read down, simply, to read 'but no offence will be committed where the accused is exercising her right to peaceful protest under Articles 10 and 11'. Since that begs more questions, we might refine this to narrow the offence only to situations where there is

> actual physical obstruction rather than notional obstruction and where that obstruction is not only more than *de minimis* but is excessive—in both duration, numbers and impact—and is of such a nature as to occasion a serious identifiable risk to disorder or to the rights of others.[104]

In fact, the need to utilise section 3 to achieve such a Convention-compatible reading might be obviated under ordinary domestic principles. The offence is not made out if a protester has a lawful excuse; reasonable user will be a lawful excuse. This is a matter of fact for the magistrates and will depend on all the circumstances, including place, duration, purpose and whether it is an actual obstruction as opposed to a potential obstruction.[105]

---

[99] *Arrowsmith v Jenkins* [1963] 2 QB 561 (DC), there being no such concept in this regard of estoppel. The case before the Divisional Court (Lord Parker CJ giving judgment) revolved around the issue of wilfulness.
[100] Relevant cases would include *G and E v Norway* (App 9278/81 and 9415/81) EComHR inadmissibility decision 3 October 1983, *GS v Austria* (14923/89) EComHR inadmissibility decision 30 November 1992 and *S v Austria* (App 13812/88) EComHR inadmissibility decision 3 December 1990.
[101] *Patyi v Hungary* (App 5529/05) ECtHR judgment 7 October 2008.
[102] ibid, [41].
[103] *Arrowsmith v Jenkins* [1963] 2 QB 561.
[104] Such a reading would give effect to the thrust of cases such as *Galstyan, Balcik, Oya Ataman* and *Aldemir*—discussed above text to n 46—and re-asserts disorder not merely 'disruption' as the trigger. It would also add to the majority ruling in *DPP v Jones* [1999] 2 AC 240 (HL) where Lord Irvine, Lord Hutton and Lord Clyde, while holding that a non-obstructive static protest would not *per se* exceed the limited primary right to use and reuse the highway for passage (in the context of private law and trespass), refused to sanction as lawful protests that did cause a trespass and which were also obstructive.
[105] *Nagy v Weston* [1965] 1 WLR 280 (Court) 284 Lord Parker CJ.

(iii) Hirst and Agu

The most well known of the cases in which section 137 has been discussed in the context of a peaceful protest is *Hirst and Agu v Chief Constable of West Yorkshire*.[106] There, a group of animal rights protesters gathered in a busy but spacious pedestrian precinct outside a shop selling fur. Each was doing nothing more than peacefully seeking to communicate or to persuade, either by holding banners or by handing out leaflets. On appeal, by way of case stated, against conviction under section 137 the Divisional Court, unlike the Crown Court below, held that the question whether or not the user was reasonable was not restricted to obstructions that were incidental to the primary use of the highway to passing and to repass.[107] Glidewell LJ considered that the resolution of the reasonableness of an obstruction was the issue to be attended to in all section 137 cases, including, as here, a peaceful protest. He proposed a three-fold test:[108]

1. is there an obstruction that is more than de minimis?
2. was the obstruction wilful; that is deliberate or freely chosen?
3. was the obstruction without lawful authority or excuse? Was the activity engaged in first inherently lawful?[109] Only if it were did the second question—that of the reasonableness of the obstruction in all the circumstances mentioned in *Nagy*—arise.

This of course takes us a fair way, well before 1998, towards protecting the right of peaceful protest but leaves us short: nothing in the reasonableness test, as propounded by either Lord Parker or Glidewell LJ allows magistrates to balance the relative rights that come into play whenever there is a sit-down protest or some form of more extreme direct action. It is as close but as far apart as *Wednesbury* irrationality is from proportionality—the latter encompasses the former with some conceptual room to spare. It is for this reason that section 3 of the HRA—certainly when the factual matrix concerns peaceful persuasive or communicative protest such as took place in *Hirst*—ought still to have a significant role in developing the offence of wilful obstruction in a Convention-compatible fashion.

(iv) Birch v DPP

That there is still some way to go towards that better equilibrium can be seen in the mind of Rose LJ in the case of *Birch v DPP*.[110]

Birch was one of a group—protesting about a chemical reclamation plant—that sat down in the main road outside the company's offices. The group was warned they were obstructing the road, refused to move on and were arrested. Birch appealed his conviction under section 137 to the Divisional Court by way of case stated. There is clearly a great difference in legal terms between the facts in *Birch* and those in *Hirst*, yet the legal issue was the same—was Birch's action a reasonable user and thus lawful?[111] Yet Rose LJ held that

---

[106] *Hirst and Agu v Chief Constable of West Yorkshire* (1986) 85 Cr App Rep 143.
[107] The Crown Court considered itself bound by earlier authority *Waite v Taylor* (1985) 149 JP 551, which it interpreted as saying that where an obstruction occurred as a result of an activity that was not incidental to that primary purpose, the question of the reasonableness of the obstruction did not arise.
[108] *Hirst*, above n 106, 151.
[109] Thus, in the view of Glidewell LJ, unlawful picketing in furtherance of a trade dispute could not be a lawful obstruction.
[110] *Birch v Director of Public Prosecutions*, unreported High Court decision, 10 December 1999; *The Independent*, 13 January 2000, [2000] Crim LR 301.
[111] The main issue for the Divisional Court in fact related to the magistrate's decision to exclude evidence relating to B's allegations about the company's alleged unlawful activities—prevention of which crimes he hoped would found a lawful excuse for his obstruction or would show that his actions were a reasonable user of the highway.

so far from being on all fours with the present case, [Hirst] is plainly distinguishable. The question which there arose was whether the lawful activity of handing out leaflets was a reasonable activity providing a lawful excuse. In the present case, deliberately lying down in the road so as to obstruct the highway and traffic flowing along it was not, on its face, a lawful activity.[112]

This conclusion is asserted rather than being demonstrated or explained and in fact tends to circularity: B's activity was only unlawful if he wilfully obstructed the highway without lawful excuse yet that is the very same question that the Court was required to resolve. To some extent a solution to this conundrum is presented later in the judgment—by the conclusion that such behaviour would also constitute public nuisance.[113] While this may—although again there was not a great deal of explanation or reasoning especially to show why the same conclusion did not hold for *Hirst*—justify the holding that the activity itself was per se unlawful, we can see how it fails to take any account of the need to balance the various rights and interests and conflicting tensions that inhere in a situation such as this. Drawing on both *Hirst* and *Jones*, the Court's conclusion was that no one was permitted unreasonably to obstruct the highway and there was no right to demonstrate in a way which did obstruct the highway. In fact, it is probably consonant with the then Strasbourg jurisprudence as we saw in the four sit-in cases against Germany[114]—but again this is neither acknowledged nor shown. The argument that the sit-in obstruction was preventing an environmental crime was given short shrift too. While there might be circumstances in which preventing an actual, or imminently apprehended, breach of the peace or other serious offence, on or near the highway, would afford a lawful excuse for obstructing the passage along the highway of one or more vehicles, this was not Birch's claim. His related to the activities carried on at the business. There was no crime going on in the road—his activities might draw attention to the alleged crimes being committed but could not be said to be aimed at preventing them. His defence was not made out. This, it ought to be said, turns largely on what type of business was being complained about. It is surely easier to argue that an obstructive sit-in outside an arms manufacturer is aimed at (and may even prevent) say the crime of aggression or of genocide by ensuring that lorries delivering the weapons to air force bases cannot leave.[115] That said, the threat or likely crime would still probably not be sufficiently immediate or have a direct enough nexus to the action taken to prevent it.[116]

B. Exclusions on Grounds Related to National Security

(i) The Official Secrets Act 1911

Section 1 of the Official Secrets Act 1911 creates various offences in relation to 'prohibited places', defined in section 2 to include places such as dockyards, airbases and arsenals, but also a whole range of places declared by the Secretary of State to be so on the ground that 'information with respect thereto or the destruction or obstruction thereof or interference

---

[112] *Birch*, above n 110, at [8].
[113] *ibid*, at [25].
[114] *CS v Germany* (App 13858/88); *G v Germany* (App 13079/87); *Schiefer v Germany* (App 13389/89); and *WM and HO v Germany* (App 13235/87), all EComHR inadmissibility decisions on 6 March 1989.
[115] It would be, as John Spencer points out in his note in the *Criminal Law Review* (above n 110) prevention of crime—private defence—at common law rather than under s 3 of the Criminal Law Act 1967 which is predicated on a use of force to prevent crime: see *Blake v DPP* [1993] Crim LR 586.
[116] By analogy with *Blake* a case admittedly on s 5(2) of the Criminal Damage Act 1971, the immediacy of the crime being prevented would need to be clear.

therewith would be useful to an enemy'. Those sections are the only remaining parts of the 1911 Act not repealed and replaced by the Official Secrets Act 1989. Although section 1 is described in its margin notes as relating to 'Spying' its width is potentially much greater. It covers, for example, anyone who 'approaches ... or is in the neighbourhood of' any prohibited place for 'any purpose prejudicial to the safety or interests of the State'.

In *Chandler v DPP*, the House of Lords was asked to rule on the convictions of members of the Committee of 100, the non-violent demonstrations arm of CND.[117] The group had taken up positions demonstrating outside an RAF airbase, occupied at the time by the US Air Force, while some planned to enter the airfield and to sit in front of planes so as to prevent them taking off. The group was charged with conspiracy to commit breaches of section 1. The evidence at trial was that interfering with the ability of aircraft to take off was per se prejudicial to the interests or safety of the state. The group was refused permission to adduce evidence or to cross-examine so as to show that their beliefs were that their actions would not prejudice the state but would in fact benefit it. It was that issue that was one of the subjects of the appeal, appeals dismissed by both the Court of Appeal and the House of Lords. As Viscount Radcliffe put it,

> [w]hen a man has avowed that his purpose in approaching an airfield forming part of his country's defence system was to obstruct its operational activity, what if any evidence is admissible on the issue as to the prejudicial nature of his purpose? In my opinion, the correct answer is virtually none.[118]

Although clearly the impact of section 1 is limited by its connection to places linked in some way to the UK's defence and as such will not be a blanket cover-all for all protests—clearly animal rights protesters would be unlikely to fall foul of it—for those whose complaint is about the arms trade, it will become yet one more potential weapon to be used against them by the police. Its use in such protests and direct action seems now to have been overshadowed by reliance on the crime of aggravated trespass and criminal damage, if committed. These we will consider in chapter six.

(ii) Trespassing on a Designated Site

In 2005, a new criminal offence, trespass on a designated site, was created under sections 128–131 of the Serious Organised Crime and Police Act (SOCPA) 2005.[119] It is thus, locating this within one of the themes of this book, another example of the steady and gradual erosion of the divide between the public and private spheres in the regulation of protest. Prosecutions may only be brought with the consent of the Attorney-General: a 'designated site' means a site that is specified or described (in any way) in an order made by the Secretary of State, and designated for the purposes of this section by the order. The Secretary of State may, under section 128(3), only designate a site for the purposes of section 128 if it

(a) is comprised in Crown land; or
(b) is comprised in land belonging to the Queen or the Prince of Wales in their private capacities; or
(c) appears to the Secretary of State that it is appropriate to designate the site in the interests of national security.

---

[117] *Chandler v Director of Public Prosecutions* [1964] AC 763.
[118] *ibid*, 796.
[119] See the by-laws at the heart of *Tabernacle v Secretary of State for Defence* [2009] EWCA Civ 23 which restricted various activities, including camping, in Controlled Areas at Aldermaston, the atomic weapons establishment, on grounds inter alia of national security.

It is a defence under section 128(4) for a person charged with an offence to prove that he did not know, and had no reasonable cause to suspect, that the site in relation to which the offence is alleged to have been committed was a designated site. As a result of a series of designations, there is now a host of sites specifically protected in name against criminal trespass. On 1 April 2006, the first to be designated were 13 operational MoD sites, including many RAF bases that have been the subject of direct action protests against missions to Iraq: RAF Lakenheath, RAF Mildenhall and RAF Fairford as well as RAF Menwith Hill, home to the USA listening posts.[120] Later that same month a series of civil nuclear sites and power stations were added as a result of the automatic inclusion—by virtue of section 12 of the Terrorism Act 2006—of all licensed nuclear sites as designated sites, without any need for an order, alongside five nuclear defence (and research) sites such as the Rosyth Dockyard and Aldermaston. What has caused more furore was the addition on 1 June 2007 of 16 royal, governmental and parliamentary sites. These include Chequers, the Prime Minister's rural retreat, the main MoD building and Nos 10–11 Downing Street.[121] The fact that designation on national security grounds can be made by the Minister on a subjective basis—it merely need appear to her appropriate, not reasonably so—raises a concern about the width of discretion reposed in the Minister, though not one in human rights or judicial review terms.[122] However, as the Joint Committee in its Eighth Report of 2004–05 pointed out, when issuing any designation the Minister must at that time be acting compatibly with Convention rights including the right to peaceful protest—not just balancing and taking account of them.

> Although it may be possible to justify an interference with the rights, before making any designation the relevant Secretary of State would have to be able to show that any interference with rights under Articles 10 and 11 was a proportionate response to a pressing social need to advance one of the legitimate aims specified in Articles 10(2) and 11(2) respectively. If that could not be done, the designation would not be 'necessary in a democratic society' for a legitimate purpose within those Articles, and would amount to a violation of the Convention rights. This might be difficult, particularly as the offence of entering a designated site as a trespasser . . . does not involve the prosecution proving that the defendant knew or should have known of the designation, but instead imposes on the defendant the burden of establishing, by way of defence, that he or she did not know and had no reasonable cause to suspect that the site had been designated.[123]

The creation of these new offences was a response to a couple of very public intrusions at Windsor Castle and Buckingham Palace in the summer of 2003, as well as those in the more

---

[120] The Serious Organised Crime and Police Act 2005 (Designated Sites) Order 2005 (SI 2005/3447).

[121] The Serious Organised Crime and Police Act 2005 (Designated Sites under Section 128) Order 2007 (SI 2007/930), as amended (in relation to the map of Chequers) by SI 2007/1387. The full list includes in whole or in part the following: 85 Albert Embankment, London; Buckingham Palace, London; Ministry of Defence Main Building, Whitehall, London; Old War Office Building, Whitehall, London; St James's Palace, Cleveland Row, London; Thames House, 11 and 12 Millbank, London; The Chequers estate, near Aylesbury, Buckinghamshire; 10–12 Downing Street site as well as 70 Whitehall; Government Communication Headquarters, Harp Hill, Cheltenham; Government Communication Headquarters, Hubble Road, Cheltenham; Government Communication Headquarters, Racecourse Road, Scarborough, North Yorkshire; Government Communication Headquarters, Woodford, Bude, Cornwall; Highgrove House, Doughton, Gloucestershire; Palace of Westminster and Portcullis House site, London; Sandringham House, Norfolk; and Windsor Castle, Berkshire.

[122] Since any designation would be in the form of an order, it seems unlikely that issues surrounding accessibility—and thus prescription by law—would arise: cf the JCHR 4th report of session 2004–05 'Legislative Scrutiny 1st Report', para 1.134 available at: www.publications.parliament.uk/pa/jt200405/jtselect/jtrights/jtrights.htm (accessed 9 august 2008).

[123] www.publications.parliament.uk/pa/jt200405/jtselect/60/6005.htm#a25 (accessed 9 August 2008) para 2.68.

144 *The Locus of Protest*

distant past such as Michael Fagan in 1982.[124] Two reports recommended there be a new offence of criminal trespass 'into secure/specified (Royal/Government) premises'. It was agreed that a new offence was necessary for two reasons:[125]

- It would create a deterrent to intrusions at secure, sensitive sites. It had not been possible to secure prosecution (with an appropriate penalty) of any of the individuals who had carried out the high-profile intrusions at Buckingham Palace and the Palace of Westminster.[126]
- It would give the police a specific power of arrest of a trespasser at a sensitive site where no other apparent existing offence had been committed. This was something for which the police responsible for security at such sites had been lobbying.

(iii) Comment and Analysis

As we shall see, the range of public order offences is vast. Many already equate almost to criminalising a mere protesting presence. It is very hard to envisage, with the width permitted by the courts to the offence of aggravated trespass (under section 68 of the Criminal Justice and Public Order Act 1994), that the police could not already arrest those at designated sites for that offence or another relating to their conduct or behaviour rather than mere presence.[127] In short, aggravated trespass occurs where someone trespasses on land—in open air or indoors—and does something on that land that is intended to disrupt or obstruct someone from pursuing a lawful activity on that or on adjoining land or to intimidate someone so acting. Without knowing more about the detail of any of the intrusions that were the impetus for the new offence, it is hard to see how they would not also have been aggravated trespass. The new offence of trespass on a designated site now renders criminal simple common law/private law trespass without the need for there being any additional element to the actus reus which at least goes a little way towards redeeming the offence under section 68.[128] Aside from criminalising simply being on someone else's land, perhaps the only time that trespass on a designated site would fill a gap—or rather the gap left by section 68 alone—is where there is no one on the land (or land adjoining it) who is obstructed or disrupted: we know from *DPP v Tilly* that someone else needs to be physically present for that offence to be committed.[129] There is, it is submitted, the world of difference between protecting the Monarch in her own home and insulating the Prime Minister not just from criticism but from someone who may be trespassing as a precursor to a protest but who by definition has committed no other crime yet—since if they had, other powers of arrest would have been available to the police. To take such a measure by secondary legislation with no public consultation is worrying and it is to be hoped does not betoken a more cavalier attitude to the right to protest.[130] It seems hard to believe—if national security and the terrorist danger to the Prime Minister are the concern—that the police would

---

[124] For the background, this part draws on the explanatory memorandum to the statutory instrument to be found at: www.opsi.gov.uk/si/si2007/em/uksiem_20070930_en.pdf (accessed 17 December 2007).
[125] *ibid*, at para 7.1.
[126] This latter is a reference to the intrusions in 2004: explanatory memorandum above n 124.
[127] The explanatory memorandum concedes the minimal cost impact on the police by admitting that a 'very low number of arrests and prosecutions are anticipated': above n 124, para 8.2.
[128] In fact, the courts have held that trespass without more cannot constitute the offence under s.68: *Barnard v DPP* (CO/4814/98) unreported Divisional Court decision 15 October 1999, discussed [2000] Crim LR 371.
[129] *Director of Public Prosecutions v Tilly* [2001] EWHC Admin 821, Rafferty J.
[130] Explanatory memorandum above n 124, para 7.3. The focus of most of the concern seems to have been on ramblers accidentally wandering onto designated sites.

be unable to arrest someone simply for being on land at Chequers whom they genuinely consider a potential terrorist given the range of anti-terrorism offences now on the statute book.

The fact that specifying the sites—but not the creation of the offence itself—has been done by secondary legislation is a crucial factor when it comes to the right to protest under the HRA. As we have seen, whereas sections 3–4 do not empower judges to strike down incompatible primary legislation, secondary legislation—such as statutory instruments—is not so insulated from challenge. It is not difficult to imagine a challenge to the designation of the Chequers estate and the consequent power of arrest and risk of criminal prosecution—and facing 51 weeks in prison—merely for stepping a foot over the boundary, as too we could imagine for the various defence bases. If someone were arrested—such as the two peace protester grandmothers arrested in April 2006 after walking 15 feet across the sentry line at RAF Menwith Hill, deliberately to highlight the restrictions, as they saw it, on protest[131]—they could utilise section 7(1)(b) of the HRA to rely on their Convention right to peaceful protest under Articles 10–11 in any criminal legal proceedings brought.[132] It must be arguable at least that a prosecution for doing no more than stepping over a boundary during a protest is a disproportionate response to whatever social ill—danger to the Prime Minister and his family?—is perceived as being prevented by the outlawing of such behaviour per se in the first place.[133] Recall of course that the prohibition applies whether or not (say) the trespass was threatening or harassing or obstructive. Reading such a qualification—whether we call that 'reading in' or 'reading down'—might at least go some way towards ensuring the provisions are not (almost) patently incompatible.[134] The very fact that these powers exist might not mean that they are actually called upon: arresting someone for doing little more than stepping over a boundary is likely to be seen as disproportionate, whereas if the police waited until the protesters actually committed a further act, that ought to mean they would be arrested for the disruptive trespass or separate crime rather than for simple trespass on a designated site. Its very limited expected use may see it fall into desuetude, buttressing further the case that it is not necessary. That case is strengthened by the MoD's own admission, the veracity of which is unknown, that the list of royal and parliamentary/government sites had been chosen because they had been the scenes of regular protests.

> Persistent activity by protesters places them at risk of being mistaken for terrorists. It also unnecessarily diverts police resources . . . People will still be allowed to protest outside sites. This legislation is about keeping police focused on the job they are paid to do.[135]

---

[131] 'Helen and Sylvia, the new face of terrorism', *The Independent*, 6 April 2006. The pair were found guilty and given a conditional discharge (plus ordered to pay £50 costs) in October 2007: 'Women guilty in spy base case', *The Bradford Telegraph and Argus*, 10 October 2007, at www.thetelegraphandargus.co.uk/news/newsindex/display.var.1750994.0.women_guilty_in_spy_base_case.php (accessed 17 December 2007).
[132] If proceedings are dropped, then the problems of satellite litigation—at the heart of *Kebilene v Director of Public Prosecutions* [2000] 2 AC 326 (HL)—disappear such that someone charged but not prosecuted could seek judicial review relying on the 'sword' of s 7(1)(a) of the HRA.
[133] This is of course aside from any challenge to ensure the defence in s 128(4) is one imposing an evidential burden only.
[134] A not dissimilar approach was adopted to the powers of the Metropolitan Police Commissioner in *Papworth v Coventry* [1967] 1 WLR 663 (DC), discussed later in this chapter.
[135] Quoted in *The Independent*, 6 April 2006, above n 131. It has become customary to argue that there is a need to control and police large groups of protesters in case terrorists infiltrate and subvert them and use, say a peaceful march, to open fire on civilians. No evidence has ever been provided in support of such a claim.

C. Protest Around Westminster

As Shami Chakrabarti, the director of Liberty noted in the context of the two Menwith Hill protesters, 'just when politicians lament the demise of participatory democracy, they increasingly criminalise both free speech and protest'.[136] If that is so of an RAF base, it must apply with more force for Westminster, the heart of the UK's parliamentary democracy. Of course the right to peaceful protest needs properly to be tempered by and balanced against legitimate security concerns and the need to avoid damaging disruption to the day's business. MPs and members of the House of Lords, those working in the Palace of Westminster and citizens exercising the right to petition Parliament or informally raising matters of concern or merely observing Parliament at work should all be able freely to attend Parliament. It is true that in recent years, security at Westminster has been breached on several occasions. In May 2004, during Question Time on the floor of the house, the then Prime Minister Tony Blair was hit with two purple powder 'bombs' (in condoms) thrown by a pair of protesting Fathers4Justice members. In September 2004, a group of fox-hunt supporters was able to enter onto the floor of the Commons to protest against the Bill to outlaw fox-hunting with dogs, then making its way through Parliament. The group had managed, easily it seems with hindsight, to enter in the guise of workmen and with little by way of checks being made. Each was arrested and charged under section 5 of the POA 1986.[137] Whether the current framework properly guarantees the right to protest or sways too far in favour of security and order, responding too much to the faint possibility of disturbance and disruption is what we will consider now.

(i) Historical Overview

First, any framework needs to distinguish between activities designed to frustrate Parliament and activities designed to highlight something that Parliament should or could address, that is to say a peaceful communicative protest outside Parliament. Historically quite a complex legislative framework governed the area around Westminster but since 1986, there has been significantly less. Both the Tumultuous Petitioning Act 1661 and the Seditious Meetings Act 1817 were repealed in their entirety by the POA 1986, Schedule 3.[138] Nowadays, the primary control is exercised by the general rules for marches and assemblies contained in sections 12–14A of the POA 1986—which we will consider in chapter five— together with three place-specific measures. The first two—alongside in fact the general provisions in the POA 1986—have largely been superseded by the third, the ban on unauthorised demonstrations near Westminster. Although there are plans to repeal the third, while it is still in operation, the gaps it leaves for the first two to fill are very limited. First, both the Palace of Westminster and Portcullis House are included as designated sites under section 128 of SOCPA 2005 so that trespass on or in them is a criminal offence. Secondly,

---

[136] ibid.
[137] They were found guilty and given conditional discharges: *The Guardian*, 27 May 2005. In the same month, another Fathers4Justice protester dressed as Batman mounted the wall of Buckingham Palace and staged a protest. In February 2008, climate change activists from Plane Stupid staged a rooftop protest at Westminster opposing expansion at Heathrow airport.
[138] The 1661 Act allowed no more than ten persons at any one time to repair to the Queen or Parliament so as to present a petition. The 1817 Act broadly made it unlawful while either House was sitting for meetings of fifty or more to gather within a mile of Westminster 'for the purpose or on the pretext of considering of or preparing any petition, complaint, remonstrance, declaration or other address to the [Monarch] or to both Houses or either House of Parliament of alteration of matters of Church or State'.

under the annual sessional order both Houses direct the Commissioner of Police for the Metropolis to keep the streets leading to Parliament open.[139] The order has no freestanding legal force outside Parliament[140] but is given effect by directions made by the Commissioner pursuant to the general power contained in section 52 of the Metropolitan Police Act 1839.[141] Those directions have no free-standing power of arrest for their breach[142] though section 54(9) does make it a summary offence for anyone 'acquainted' with the directions willfully to disregard them. Thus, before 2005 the only action the police could take would have been (i) to issue summonses under either section 54 or under section 89 of the Police Act 1996 for obstruction of the police in the execution of their duty (the duty being to ensure free and easy access into Westminster)[143] or (ii) to carry out an arrest using their general powers relating to breach of the peace or for public order offences.

As the Clerk to the House commented in his memorandum to the Select Committee on Procedure in 2003, this meant that 'successive generations of Members are encouraged in the mistaken belief that its effect is to confer special and additional legal authority on the police in relation to the precincts of Parliament'.[144] For that reason, the Clerk along with the Metropolitan Police Commissioner and the Select Committee itself all recommended a formalisation of the position by means of legislation. That was done in Part IV of SOCPA 2005, the third measure. The sessional order has not been passed by the Commons since the 2005–06 session, although it is still passed by the House of Lords[145] and the Commissioner continues to issue directions under section 52, meaning that the police have been able to arrest for wilful disobedience provided the directions were made known to the protester before arrest.[146]

The leading case on section 52 is the pre-HRA case *Papworth v Coventry*[147] from the 1960s. The scope of the Commissioner's power under section 52 was narrowed significantly on grounds of vires (rather than on a rights basis) as a result of their successful challenge. A peaceful seven-person vigil was being held in Whitehall for an hour to call attention to the situation in Vietnam. The group stood stationary and spaced apart, each with a placard which, in sequence, made a message. Each was told that any assembly there was unlawful

---

[139] For details of the order, passed in the same form since 1842, see *Sessional Orders and Resolutions* The Select Committee on Procedure 3rd report of session 2002–03 HC 855 19 November 2003, at: www.publications.parliament.uk/pa/cm200203/cmselect/cmproced/855/85502.htm (accessed 8 January 2008). Is it disproportionate repeatedly to issue directions in the same form? Another factor behind the holding of disproportionality in *Patyi* (above n 101) was the repeat, mechanistic imposition of bans by the police.

[140] In *Papworth v Coventry* [1967] 1 WLR 663, 671 the Divisional Court accepted as 'clearly right the submission of [counsel for the defendant] that the sessional order . . . could have no effect outside the walls and precincts of the Houses of Parliament. It [c]ould have no extramural restrictive force, and would be incapable of creating any offence in respect of conduct in the area outside the precincts of parliament'.

[141] There is an analogous power in s 22 of the City of London Police Act 1839 for the Square Mile. There are also regulations governing the use of Trafalgar Square, the issue at the heart of *Rai* (above n 45) and see also Bailey, Harris and Jones, *Civil Liberties*, above n 20 429–31.

[142] Select Committee 3rd report above n 139 para 14 et seq. It is not clear from the case report in the *Papworth* case whether the protesters were arrested—mistakenly—under s 54 or arrested for another offence but charged and brought before the magistrates for the offence under s 54.

[143] There is no power of arrest attached to s 89.

[144] Select Committee 3rd report, above n 139, para 13 appended to the minutes of evidence taken on 2 July 2003.

[145] Personal email communication between the author and the Clerk to the House, 9 January 2008.

[146] There is still considerable confusion about the ambit of the sessional order. At the tail end of 2007, it was criticised by the leaders of the Police Federation (representing rank-and-file officers) after the power was set to be used to ban 10,000 officers who were planning to march through Westminster in protest at the proposed pay award: 'Police Anger at Commons march ban', *The Guardian*, 30 December 2007.

[147] *Papworth v Coventry* [1967] 2 All ER 41 (DC).

and, having been handed a copy of the section 52 direction, was asked to leave. The pavement was wide at the point where the vigil took place and there was no evidence of any obstruction of passage in and out of Parliament. The three who refused to move were arrested. On appeal by way of case stated, the Divisional Court concluded that the Commissioner's directions should be interpreted as to be limited to meaning 'such assemblies or processions of persons as are capable of causing consequential obstruction to the free passage of members to and from the Houses of Parliament or their departure therefrom, or disorder in the neighbourhood or annoyance thereabouts'.[148] The Commissioner's submitted meaning—that the directions should be read as they were worded so as to permit an officer to require all assemblies or processions in a large defined area surrounding Westminster to disperse—was ultra vires section 52. The power to give directions was limited to securing the objective of the sessional order, that is the free passage of Members, avoiding disorder in the House and preventing annoyance nearby. Under the HRA, the difference would be that if someone were arrested under section 54, then courts could be asked—utilising section 7(1)(b)—to assess not just the vires but the necessity and proportionality of restricting numbers around Parliament.

(ii) Serious Organised Crime and Police Act 2005

The third and greatest change to the general regime is contained in sections 132–138 of SOCPA 2005.[149] The effect of that Part is that demonstrators in the area around Parliament need to seek prior authorisation. Though neither the recital nor the side note refers to it, those sections were clearly intended to deal with the long-running one-man protest in Parliament Square being undertaken by Brian Haw against the Iraq War:[150] by mid-August 2009, he had been protesting for almost exactly 3000 days. The 2003 Commons' Select Committee on Procedure report *Sessional Orders and Resolutions* sheds some more light on the problem that needed confronting.[151] These tend to be access by members and the

---

[148] *ibid*, 46. Winn LJ added the additional quality of a likely breach of the peace.

[149] A private members bill (The Public Demonstrations (Repeal) Bill) to repeal the provisions was introduced into the House of Lords by Baroness Miller in November 2006 www.publications.parliament.uk/pa/ld200607/ldbills/012/2007012.pdf, accessed 10 January 2007. Following consultation—*The Governance of Britain: Managing Protest Around Parliament* (Cmd 7235, October 2007)—the Government stated that not only would it not pursue a harmonisation of powers concerning marches and assemblies but it committed itself to repealing ss 132–138 of SOCPA. The position would then revert to the general powers in the POA 1986 which we consider in chapter five: *The Governance of Britain—Constitutional Renewal* (Cm 7342 March 2008), both available via the Ministry of Justice Governance of Britain website governance.justice.gov.uk/ (accessed 9 August 2008). The White Paper accompanying the draft Constitutional Renewal Bill (laid before Parliament on 25 March 2008) invited Parliament to consider whether additional provisions might be needed to ensure free and open access or to prevent, for example, excessive noise disrupting the workings of Parliament. The Joint Committee on the draft bill produced its first report on 31 July 2008: www.publications.parliament.uk/pa/jt200708/jtselect/jtconren/166/16602.htm (accessed 9 August 2008). The proposed repeal, and consequential amendments to strengthen s 14 of the POA 1986 around Parliament, is contained in the Constitutional Reform and Government Bill laid before Parliament in July 2009

[150] His personal website is at: www.parliament-square.org.uk/index.htm (accessed 8 December 2006). As his website informs us 'Brian has been protesting in Parliament Square since 2nd June 2001. Initially he was campaigning against the economic sanctions on Iraq and the bombing of the country by the US and UK. After 11 September 2001, he widened his focus, directing his messages of peace against the 'war on terror', the terror that the US and UK have inflicted on Afghanistan and Iraq. He protests on behalf of those innocent people who suffer and die in other countries, as our governments seek to further their own economic, military, political and strategic interests around the world'. In December 2005, he was one of three people short-listed for the annual Human Rights of the Year award for '*outstanding commitment to justice by maintaining constant vigil outside parliament demanding respect for the human rights of those in other countries. For tireless and passionate defence of freedom of speech*'.

[151] Above n 139, paras 11–25

public, noise disrupting the work of Parliament, and 'long-standing and visually unattractive demonstrations'. As we saw, the combined effect of the sessional order and Commissioner's direction under section 52 was limited at very best. Further, as the Commissioner set out in his memorandum, the general power to impose conditions or to seek a ban of assemblies under sections 14 and 14A of the POA 1986 had large gaps.[152]

(a) Background

The Bill presented to Parliament in late 2004 bore little resemblance to the Act that was passed. Clauses 128–129 originally empowered officers to give directions based on the behaviour of someone in the designated area, namely within a 1 km radius from Parliament Square. The behaviour being 'punished' was that which reflected the concerns of the Select Committee: behaviour that has or could have the result of

- hindering any person from entering or leaving the Palace of Westminster
- hindering the proper operation of Parliament or
- spoiling the visual aspect or otherwise spoiling the enjoyment of members of the public of any part of the 1 km radius

An officer needed reasonably to believe both that the person was behaving in one of those three ways (or proposed to do so) and that it was necessary to prevent the causing of any one of those three results. Directions could include ceasing or not beginning the behaviour. That scheme was amended in Committee in the Commons and a whole new statutory scheme introduced into the House of Lords. That scheme was enacted in sections 132–138 of the Act and met with a greater level of approval from the Joint Committee on Human Rights.[153]

(b) The Statutory Scheme

Rather than being predicated on the (likely) effects of certain behaviour, the new scheme sets out a requirement of blanket authorisation in advance for 'demonstrations' within the designated area.[154] A failure to obtain one will likely result in criminal liability for its organisers and participants. The detail of the designated area was filled out, as is usual, by secondary legislation. The Serious Organised Crime and Police Act 2005 (Designated Area) Order 2005 came into force on 1 July 2005[155] and created a designated area the furthest point of which can be no more than 1 km from the Palace of Westminster.[156] Notable sites within it, as well as Parliament, are: Whitehall, Downing Street, the Home Office and New

---

[152] ibid, para 16. One of these—that the powers only applied to groups of 20 or more—was itself amended in the same Act so as to allow imposition of conditions on groups of only two or more: see chapter five below. The other reason given by the Commissioner was that the power in s 14 might not extend to entitling regulation purely on the ground of obstruction—though query whether that last comes within Art 11(2)?

[153] The original scheme was criticised by the JCHR in its 8th report of session 2004/5 on legislative scrutiny (HL 60/HC 388) dated 2 March 2005, paras 271–272, at: www.publications.parliament.uk/pa/jt200405/jtselect/jtrights/jtrights.htm (access 9 January 2008). Not least of these was that preserving the view was not a legitimate aim recognised in Arts 10(2) or 11(2)!

[154] Section 132(3) makes it clear that the authorisation requirements do not apply to public processions as defined under ss 11–13 of the POA 1986. It does not apply either to industrial action that is lawful under s 222 of the Trade Union and Labour Relations (Consolidation) Act 1992.

[155] Serious Organised Crime and Police Act 2005 (Designated Area) Order 2005 (SI 2005/1537).

[156] The map can be found at: www.met.police.uk/publicorder/images/Section_132_7_boundary.jpg (accessed 9 August 2008). The area measures at its furthest 1.25 km east-west and 1.75 km north-south.

Scotland Yard, as well as County Hall on the South side.[157] The authorisation provisions take precedence over the more general power to regulate and to impose conditions on public assemblies under section 14 of the POA 1986: section 14 of the POA 1986 cannot apply to demonstrations in the designated area that are also public assemblies.[158] Where authorisation is needed, section 133 sets out that any of the organisers or the sole demonstrator (when only one person demonstrates) must give written notice to the Metropolitan Police Commissioner. That notice should be given at least six days in advance unless it is not reasonably practicable to do so. In that case written notice must be given as soon as it is reasonably practicable, and in any event not less than 24 hours before the time the demonstration is to start. The notice must contain the date and time the demonstration will commence, its duration, the place where it is to be carried on, the name of the person giving notice and whether or not it will be a solo demonstration. Those who organise (or who participate in its organisation), take part in or carry on by themselves[159] a demonstration in a public place[160] in a designated area will be committing an offence if, when the demonstration starts, authorisation had not been given unless they can show they reasonably believed authorisation had been given: section 132(1)–(2).

Provided notice is given in correct form, the Commissioner is required to authorise the demonstration[161] (section 134) but may impose on the organisers or the participants such conditions specified in the authorisation and relating to the demonstration as in her reasonable opinion are necessary for the purpose of preventing any of the following:

(a) hindrance to any person wishing to enter or leave the Palace of Westminster or to the proper operation of Parliament;
(b) serious public disorder, serious damage to property or disruption to the life of the community;
(c) a security risk in any part of the designated area; or
(d) a risk to the safety of members of the public (including any taking part in the demonstration).[162]

In giving an authorisation and imposing any conditions, the Commissioner would be bound by the usual rules governing administrative decision-making—that decisions must be rational, legal and procedurally proper—as well as being bound as a public authority under section 6 of the HRA to reach decisions that were compatible with the demonstrators' rights under Articles 10 and 11. This, as the JCHR pointed out, would include the more limited positive obligation to facilitate the right to peaceful protest.[163]

Under section 134(5), the conditions may in particular impose requirements as to place, times and duration of the demonstration; numbers of demonstrators; number and size of banners and placards; and the maximum permissible noise levels. The Commissioner must give written notice of the authorisation and of any general conditions and particular

---

[157] H Fenwick, *Civil Liberties and Human Rights*, 4th edn (Abingdon, Routledge-Cavendish, 2007) 730.
[158] Section 132(6).
[159] Although 'organising' a demonstration does not include someone carrying on a demonstration by themselves, 'taking part in a demonstration' includes someone carrying on a demonstration by themselves, save in s 132(1) itself: s 132(7)(d)–(e)
[160] A public place means any highway or any place to which at the material time the public or any section of the public has access, on payment or otherwise, as of right or by virtue of express or implied permission: s 132(7)(b).
[161] It is not an ultra vires exercise of power for an officer of at least the rank of superintendent to authorise and to impose conditions on demonstrations if delegated by the Commissioner: *DPP v Haw* [2007] EWHC 1931 (Admin).
[162] Section 134(3).
[163] JCHR 8th Report on Legislative Scrutiny of session 2004–05, above n 153, at para 276.

modifications to details of the proposed demonstration to the person who gave the notice. Section 134(7) creates two further offences for either organisers or participants: knowingly failing to comply with a condition which is applicable to them or where they know or should have known that the demonstration is carried on otherwise than in accordance with the particulars of the demonstration set out in their notice. Again, there is a defence: if someone either fails to comply with a condition or diverges from one of the particulars, he must show that the failure or divergence arose from circumstances beyond his control, or from something done with the agreement, or by the direction, of a police officer. The most senior ranking officer present at the scene may impose additional conditions on the participants in or organisers of a demonstration or may vary any of the conditions already imposed if she reasonably believes that it is necessary, in order to prevent any of (a)–(d) above: section 135. Again, an offence will be committed where either organisers or participants knowingly fail to comply with a condition which is applicable to them and which is imposed or varied by a direction unless they can show that the failure to comply arose from circumstances beyond their control.[164]

(c) Analysis and Comment

In much the same way as the sections that immediately precede it (designating sites for criminal trespass), we can see that the need for authorisation does not depend on the quality, size or effects of the assembly that takes place but instead depends solely on its location. Thus it does not matter that a protest is taking place in the designated area but is not targeted at Parliament or politicians generally but at a publicly-listed pharmaceutical company whose AGM is taking place in Central London at the same time.[165] It does not matter that the demonstration will not commit trespass, or will remain peaceful or is just one person, a megaphone[166] and a placard; all that matters is that it takes place in a designated area.

The Joint Committee on Human Rights remained concerned by four matters.[167] One was a more philosophical objection: the clear shift from the historic common law position towards a system whereby demonstrations near Parliament were presumed to be unlawful.[168] As then Prime Minister Tony Blair memorably said in 2002: 'When I pass protestors every day at Downing Street, and believe me, you name it, they protest against it, I may not like what they call me, but I thank God they can. That's called freedom'.[169] As to the others, there were 'gaps in the provisions . . . which could make it difficult to ensure that they are operated in such a way as to avoid depriving people of the very essence of their rights or interfering disproportionately with them':

---

[164] Section 135(3)–(4).
[165] Thus 64 year-old Annabel Holt was moved on by police within moments after having started a protest outside GlaxoSmithKline's AGM in May 2006: 'Animal protests have kept firms out of UK, says Glaxo chief', *The Guardian*, 18 May 2006.
[166] With very few exceptions, it will always be a crime to use a loudspeaker (undefined) in a designated area and certainly not for the purposes of a protest: s 137. It was floated by the Government previously as to whether such use might be regulated by environmental pollution and nuisance legislation: see the response by Hazel Blears to the Select Committee on Procedure (above n 139) evidence 8 July 2003, Q.109.
[167] JCHR 8th Report on Legislative Scrutiny of session 2004–05 above n 153, para 276.
[168] A submission pointed out by the Human Rights Committee of the Cambridge Branch of the European Law Students' Association.
[169] Speech at the George Bush Senior Presidential Library, 7 April 2002, at: www.number10.gov.uk/output/Page1712.asp (accessed 9 August 2008).

(i) The provisions do not require the Commissioner to respond within a fixed time to notice given by a demonstrator. This could make it difficult or impossible to organise the demonstration in accordance with any conditions imposed by the Commissioner.
(ii) The meaning of 'demonstration' is uncertain.
(iii) The purposes in s 134(3)(b) above include 'disruption to the life of the community'. It is not clear how that relates to the permitted aims under Articles 10(2) and 11(2). In any case, if conditions were permitted only to prevent such risks when they were significant or substantial this would more easily satisfy the tests of pressing social need and proportionality.

A solution to (i) presents itself in the form of section 3 of the HRA. When taken with the positive obligation on (here) the Commissioner to facilitate and to guarantee an effective right to peaceful protest, section 3 might require words along the lines of 'and the Commissioner's notice must be given in good enough time to allow any demonstration of which notice has been given under section 133 to proceed' to be read into section 134(6).

1. What is a demonstration? As to (ii) there must clearly be uncertainty surrounding the use of 'demonstration' as the trigger incident. As has been noted elsewhere, it is the first time that UK law has sought to regulate protest defined in terms of 'demonstration'.[170] This does engage a much wider discussion about the meaning of protest: what is it about Brian Haw's protest that differentiates it from Mark Wallinger's Turner-prize winning exact replica installation—or are they both 'demonstrating' something, albeit that Wallinger is not necessarily 'protesting'? We can safely assumed that if Nigella Lawson stood on a plinth in Parliament Square to show us all how to make muffins, her cooking *demonstration* would not be of the sort contemplated by the Act—but why not? The uncertainty over the scope and coverage of the term might also sustain an argument that the restrictions are not 'prescribed by law'. In August 2005, *The Guardian* newspaper reported how one man was arrested after an impromptu Sunday 'Mad Hatter's Tea Party meets Speaker's Corner' picnic at Parliament Square featuring both a 'People's Commons' debate and a game of croquet.[171] Why, to look at another example, was the all-night drinkathon on the tubes, staged in part by those opposed to the ban on drinking on public transport introduced by the London Mayor, not viewed as a demonstration—as well, of course, as a revelling party?[172]

None of this is to suggest that it should have been so viewed, merely to ask on what basis the decision was reached. What has happened is that the police have constructed for themselves considerable discretion; practice seems to be that they distinguish between 'demonstrations' and publicity stunts, the latter not needing authorisation. The problem, as the Chair of the JCHR indicated, is that what occurs is 'inconsistent enforcement of the law entirely the opposite way round'.[173] As to (iii) it should be noted that the triggers of 'public disorder' and 'damage to property' are both subject to a seriousness test and no reason has been offered as to why those two should be singled out—although that is consonant

---

[170] Mead above p 59.
[171] 'Picknicking Protester Arrested Outside Parliament' *The Guardian*, 30 August 2005. www.guardian.co.uk/politics/2005/aug/30/houseofcommons.uk, and www.peopleincommon.org/reports.htm (accessed both 9 August 2008).
[172] 'Drinkers invited to parties on tube in protest at ban', *The Guardian*, 31 May 2008.
[173] Uncorrected evidence of the JCHR inquiry into Policing and Protest (9 December 2008) QQ 30–37. He gave the examples of a group of Conservative Party campaigners dressed as Father Christmas with Gordon Brown masks holding a banner outside Downing Street—a publicity stunt—whereas (as we shall see) reading out the names of those who have died in the Iraq war was a demonstration. www.publications.parliament.uk/pa/jt200809/jtselect/jtrights/uc40-i/uc4002.htm, accessed 9 January 2008.

with the triggers in section 14 of the POA 1986. That said, that does not justify why the triggers in section 134 and section 14 are not all treated equally. Indeed it is slightly counter-intuitive to require public disorder to be serious before the Commissioner can impose conditions but to allow conditions to be imposed for the merest hindrance to the proper operation of Parliament.

As with its use in section 14 and section 14A of the POA 1986, there must be serious concerns about the term 'community', again undefined. It is a rather nebulous concept, politically laden: does it mean the monolithic community, and so equate more with 'society' or 'people', or is it a reference to the sorts of communities claimed by distinct (usually minority or repressed) groups—the 'Muslim community', the 'gay and lesbian community'? If so, might not the demonstrators argue they are part of the 'protesting community' at odds with the counterposed 'other' community? Here we might sense it is being used to mean 'all other people save those seeking to protest' (perhaps the 'Saturday shopping community').[174] To that extent it has a distinct majoritarian flavour, at odds with the underlying thrust of the ECHR. As with section 14, there must also be some concern that 'disrupting the life of the community' is outwith the claw-backs of Article 11(2): section 134 also refers to disorder, which is specifically included in Article 11(2)—so disruption must be something different and lesser most likely. Though taking measures to prevent disruption might 'protect the rights and freedoms of others', it is by no means certain that the two are co-terminous and any gap would mean that the authorisation/condition system under section 134 did not meet a legitimate aim—and so would be unlawful.

2. Overbreadth and indiscriminate nature The scheme raises other serious concerns. It must be arguable either that designating such a large area—so as automatically to require authorisation—or imposing any conditions at all in many situations is ultra vires section 134 and so unlawful on traditional judicial review principles. It is hard to see how requiring authorisation for—or imposing conditions on—any demonstration at County Hall or outside the Home Office is capable of achieving at least three of the four aims of the Act in (a) to (d) above. At such a distance, hindering access to and from Parliament or its proper operation cannot really be the issue: if it were argued it were needed to ensure the Home Secretary was able to walk from the Home Office to Westminster to take her place as an MP then why not protect all Ministries that way? There was no need for legislation to minimise the risk of serious public disorder, serious damage to property or disruption to the life of the community since that it is ably covered by section 14 of the POA 1986. Indeed section 14A is the wider power to ban such a public assembly which is outwith the power in section 134 of SOCPA. The only caveat would be that the scheme under the 2005 Act is one of advance notice of assemblies and hence advance authorisation and conditions, whereas under the 1986 Act there is no need for advance notice and so conditions are more likely imposed to be on the spot by the most senior officer. But if advance notice and conditions are such a good idea then why limit it to an area around Parliament?

This is not to argue that the SOCPA scheme be extended nationwide, merely to acknowledge the strength of objections to the scheme that suspects an ulterior motive. The same argument applies to the last risk listed in section 134(3), the risk to the safety of the public including demonstrators. There is nothing that requires such breadth to the designated area

---

[174] On this see also P Fitzpatrick and N Taylor, 'Trespassers might be prosecuted: the European Convention and restrictions on the right to assemble' [1998] *EHRLR* 292, 298.

or, conversely, for the designated area to be limited at all—the public, and demonstrators, can be injured at assemblies anywhere. The only objective listed in section 134(3)—and thus as an aim of the Act—that bears any possible relationship both to the need for prior notice, authorisation and conditions and to the width of the designated area is the security risk. It bears out one of the worries expressed to the Select Committee on Procedure in 2003 that near-permanent demonstrations could be used as cover for terrorist activity directed at, say, Parliament or Downing Street.[175] While that may be a valid policing concern, it again fails to resolve the question of what exactly is so special about that small area of London that it needs to be singled out—and why does it require notice six days in advance? The Israeli Embassy is located in Kensington, still within London but a considerable distance from the designated area. Both the South African Embassy and UK offices of Shell, both historic sites of protest, are just outside the designated area. All three are therefore regulated by the ordinary law in section 14 of the POA 1986, where no advance notice is needed: the result is that regulation of demonstrations is largely done on the day by imposing conditions—albeit that for long term demonstrations the police could seek a banning order if the assembly were 'trespassory'. Secondly, is it appropriate to deal with terrorist threats by such a measure at all rather than by bespoke powers—again leading us to question whether we might lose more than we gain as we destroy hard-won historic rights to preserve our liberty?[176] This of course is not an argument going to the vires of the Order in terms of the parent Act but of the necessity, appropriateness and capability of the parent Act for achieving that objective at all. If the problem truly is that a demonstrating group could provide cover for terrorists (and there must be doubts over just a sole demonstrator) so surely could a large group of sightseeing tourists staring at Big Ben—yet they are not subject to SOCPA. It is not the fact that there is a demonstration but a large static group of people near Parliament that constitutes the threat and the worry.

If the Commissioner does seek to impose conditions on static demonstrations using the power in section 134(4) these must, again under standard public law principles, be carefully tailored. The problem is that the Act creates a matrix of permissible objectives allied to possible conditions. An overly broad—'blanket' even—set of conditions without thought to whether or not they were necessary or capable of achieving (say) unimpeded access to Westminster would be unlikely to have withstood challenge before October 2000, let alone be declared proportionate since then under the HRA. To make clear: if the Commissioner's fear is that there is a risk to safety, if challenged she would need to show why her reasonable opinion was that restricting noise levels was necessary to promote or to achieve greater safety.[177] Of course, such an issue is unlikely to arise. The width of section 134(3) and especially the catch-all of 'disruption to the life of the community' gives the Commissioner great latitude: what demonstration (assuming it is of sufficient size) would not cause

---

[175] This was also part of the Government's case before the Administrative Court in *DPP v Haw* [2005] EWHC 2051 (Admin), discussed in detail below fully.

[176] See the powerful admonition to this effect by Lord Hoffman in the Belmarsh case, *A v Secretary of State for the Home Office* [2004] UKHL 56 at [97] where he offered his view that 'the real threat to the life of the nation ... comes not from terrorism but from law such as these'.

[177] Professor Feldman makes the same point (at [14]) in his submission to the Joint Committee on the Draft Constitutional Renewal Bill: ' justifying an interference with a human right requires consideration, usually on a case-by-case basis, of the extent of the interference and the weight of the factors advanced by way of justification. A bright-line rule, such as a total ban on protests, is particularly likely to violate rights because it prevents context-sensitive assessment on a case-by-case basis of the impact of the restriction on a proposed assembly or demonstration': www.publications.parliament.uk/pa/jt200708/jtselect/jtconren/memo/551/ucm6602.htm (accessed 9 August 2008).

disruption—especially one which does not have to be serious? If not a major aim of a campaign, highlighting a political concern and making a point is nevertheless often best done by creating some level of inconvenience. Conditions may also be unlawful in ECHR terms if they—rather than the framework of the Act as we discussed above—are not sufficiently clear as to be prescribed by law.[178]

(d) Brian Haw's case

The provisions of Part IV were brought into force by Order on 1 August 2005.[179] Paragraph 4(2) of the Order stated that references in sections 132(1) and 133(2) to 'a demonstration starting' took effect as if they were references to 'demonstrations starting or continuing on or after 1st August 2005', a clear attempt to ensure that all demonstrations, irrespective of when they started, came within the ambit of the new regime, despite the apparently clear words to the contrary in the primary legislation.[180]

Those provisions came before the courts for interpretation as Haw sought, in advance, a ruling on the application of the new provisions to him.[181] At first instance, the Administrative Court decided (by a majority, Simon J dissenting) 'the construction point' and 'the Commencement Order point' unanimously in Haw's favour.[182] On its true construction SOCPA did not, as enacted, apply to Haw's demonstration because his demonstration started before the Act came into force. The majority was not convinced of taking a modern, purposive approach to the construction of a penal statute—that if the words failed to capture their obvious target, that was due only to inadvertence—and preferred instead to adopt one of strict constructionism. The second basis for the ruling was that in so far as the Order purported to alter and extend the provisions of the Act, as enacted, so as to apply

---

[178] *DPP v Haw* [2007] EWHC 1931 (Admin). There is no discussion in the Divisional Court's decision on the merits of the conditions other than to record that, having heard the evidence it was not unreasonable for the District Judge to conclude the conditions were unworkable. Mr Haw's counsel was described as having 'a field day' when cross-examining the police on them. The conditions, as varied, were: (at [14]–[15]) as follows:

'1. The site associated with your demonstration (including banners, placards etc) will not exceed three metres in width, three metres in height and one metre in depth. 2. The site should at no time prevent pedestrian movement along the footway. 3. Your property (including banners, placards etc) must be supervised at all times with diligence and care, in a manner that ensures that nothing can be added to your protest site without your immediate knowledge, or the immediate knowledge of a person nominated by you to care for your property whilst you are not able to do so. 4. You must not use articles in connection with your demonstration that would allow others to conceal items within them. 5. You must maintain your site in a manner that allows any person present to tell at a glance that no suspicious items are present. 6. If the numbers involved in your demonstration are to exceed 20 in total you must, where reasonably practicable, give six clear days notice of this fact to the operations office at Charing Cross Police Station. When it is not reasonably practicable to give six clear days notice, then give notice as soon as it is, and in any event no less than 24 hours before numbers are to increase to above 20. 7. If requested by a police officer in uniform you must confirm whether persons present are part of your demonstration or not'.

[179] The Serious Organised Crime and Police Act 2005 (Commencement No 1, Transitional and Transitory Provisions) Order 2005 (SI 2005/1521).
[180] Section 133(2) requires notice to be given six days 'before the day on which the demonstration was due to start' and s 132(1) only makes it an offence to demonstrate if there was no authorisation 'when the demonstration starts'.
[181] There have been a series of attempts at eviction and several court cases brought against Haw. In May 2006, 50 Metropolitan police officers mounted a night-time 'raid' to remove his display of placards, banners and messages of support. They also removed almost all of his personal possessions. He was left with only as much material and possessions that could fit into a 3 m square area so as to comply with the conditions the police had imposed under SOCPA, despite the fact that Haw was due in court a week shortly after appealing those very conditions, conditions which were ruled as being—and upheld as—unlawful in *DPP v Haw* [2007] EWHC 1931 (Admin).
[182] *Director of Public Prosecutions v Haw* [2005] EWHC 2061 (Admin) (Smith LJ and McCombe and Simon JJ).

its terms to demonstrations which began before the Act came into force, they were ultra vires and of no effect. The Order was not a transitional provision in connection with commencement but was an amendment to the original legislation.

The Court of Appeal (Sir Anthony Clarke MR giving judgment for the Court, with Laws and Hallett LJJ) found for the Secretary of State on the construction point and so overturned the Administrative Court decision. The Court rejected the idea that the deliberate distinction between the need for authorisation 'when the demonstration starts' in section 133(2) and other parts of sections 132 and 133, which refer to a demonstration 'being carried on', supported Haw's contention that the need to give notice was limited to those demonstrations starting after commencement. The majority in the court below had created 'a puzzle as to why Parliament should have wished to control demonstrations which started after the relevant commencement date but not demonstrations which started before'.[183] The Court declared that Parliament's intention was clear: 'to regulate all demonstrations within the designated area, whenever they began'.[184]

The Court downplayed the fundamental principle of doubtful criminality—that no one should be penalised save for when clear and express words have been used—by holding the construction of the Act to be clear. With respect, that is disingenuous: the clearer view must surely be Brian Haw's. In any event, if it were clear, why was there a need for a clarifying commencement order? Either it was a clarifying measure, and the principle of doubtful penalty would kick in, or it was an ultra vires attempt to expand the parameters of the section. The Court seems to elide clarity with ex post facto judicial confirmation of an *ab initio* meaning. The Court's preferred meaning meant that an ongoing demonstrator could only have complied with section 133(2) if he had given notice by 31 July 2005, a full day before there was any requirement on him to do so[185]—so anyone who gave notice on the day of commencement and who continued to demonstrate in Parliament Square on the same day, would have committed an offence, since they had not given the minimum 24 hours' notice. There must be question marks about retrospective punishment—under Article 7 and at common law—if demonstrators can be punished if they previously fail to do something at a time when there was no requirement to do it and nor was it a crime then to be demonstrating.

1. Comment and analysis There are two glaring omissions in the Court of Appeal decision. The first is the lack of any reference to or any discussion of the application of concepts such as freedom of assembly and the right to protest, or even just to the ECHR. The second is that there is no analysis whatsoever of the formula in section 3 of the HRA despite the fact that the Court, by its own admission, was dealing in interpreting and construing unclear Parliamentary words.[186] This case obviously engages the right of peaceful protest. That is

---

[183] The Court was assisted by a point put by the Metropolitan Police Commissioner, joined as a party, one not before the Administrative Court. The general system of regulating public assemblies (s 14 of the POA 1986) is disapplied by SOCPA to demonstrations to which it applies. Absent SOCPA, s 14 would have allowed conditions to be imposed on Haw's demonstration. It was inconceivable that Parliament would have repealed section 14 with respect to demonstrations which had already started, if it did not intend to apply the provisions of 132 to 138 of the Act to such demonstrations: *Haw, ibid*, [22]–[24].

[184] *Haw* [2006] EWCA Civ 532 at [18]–[19]. As the law was clear, once construed in context, the principle of doubtful penalty did not arise either: at [27]–[28]. The case is discussed by I Loveland, 'Public Protest in Parliament Square' [2007] *EHRLR* 252.

[185] Section 133(2) normally requires six days' notice but allows for a shorter period if it is not reasonably practicable to give notice but that period can never be less than 24 hours.

[186] Above n 184, at [17].

not to say that Mr Haw would have—or indeed should have—succeeded. The Court might well have concluded that a system of prior authorisation is compatible with the right. That is arguable—as we saw in chapter three (and which we shall presently revisit)—but to resolve that issue means first it must be addressed, an activity not engaged in by either the Administrative Court or the Court of Appeal in this case. Once Convention rights have been engaged, to decide a case simply by 'constru[ing the Act] in its context and having regard to the plain intention of Parliament as deduced from the Parliamentary language',[187] as was done here tells only half the story and performs only half the task in the new, *Mendoza* world. A sounder, more appropriate and more defensible opening by the Master of the Rolls could have been one along the following lines:

> This case raises fundamental questions about the right to protest in a free democratic society. It is accepted by Counsel for the Secretary of State that Mr Haw is engaged in a peaceful protest and so the fact that Parliament has legislated to require authorisations for those wishing to demonstrate in the area around Parliament takes us only so far along the path. As well as construing the provisions in the usual way, so as to ascertain the intention of Parliament, this Court is enjoined—if it be found that authorisation provisions do apply to demonstrations such as Mr Haw's—to consider two further propositions: whether or not there has been an infringement of the Convention right to peaceful assembly under Article 11 and if so, whether that infringement is one that is proportionate or necessary. If both of these are established in Mr Haw's favour, since this scheme of notice and authorisation is comprised in legislation expressing the will and intention of Parliament, then this Court must, having regard to the duty imposed on it under section 3 of the Human Rights Act 1998, ask whether it is possible to read and give effect to the terms of section 132 and section 133 'so far as it is possible to do so' compatibly with Mr Haw's Convention right to peaceful assembly and protest or, if such is not the case, to consider whether or not the grant a declaration of incompatibility under section 4 of the same Act.

Had that approach been adopted, how might the argument have proceeded? What do we learn from Strasbourg case law? Generally, received wisdom is that subjecting public assemblies to a prior authorisation procedure and (since they are less restrictive) a prior notification procedure does not normally encroach upon the essence of the right. If that is the case, states can usually impose sanctions on those who fail to comply lest the system otherwise break down.[188] That said, we saw in chapter three that this is not as clear-cut a position as is often thought.

(iii) Strasbourg Case Law

The leading case at the time of *Haw* was *Ziliberberg v Moldova*.[189] In this 2004 admissibility decision, a student challenged his conviction for 'active participation' in an unauthorised demonstration on the Great National Assembly Square in the capital, Chișinău. Not only had authorisation not been granted, it had not been applied for. There was no issue about the peacefulness of the demonstration. The Court rejected as manifestly ill-founded his claim that there had been a violation of his right peacefully to assemble. The Court had this to say about the challenge under Article 11:

---

[187] *Haw*, above n184, at [24] and also [17].
[188] *Rassemblement Jurassien Unité v Switzerland* (App 8191/78) (1980) 17 DR 93, 119, affirmed in cases such as *Bukta v Hungary* (App 25691/04) ECtHR judgment 17 July 2007 at [35] and *Ziliberberg v Moldova* (App 61821/00) ECtHR inadmissibility decision 4 May 2004.
[189] Above n 188: no paragraphing in original.

Where [meetings in public thoroughfares] are concerned, their subjection to an authorisation procedure does not normally encroach upon the essence of the right. Such a procedure is in keeping with the requirements of Article 11(1), if only in order that the authorities may be in a position to ensure the peaceful nature of a meeting, and accordingly does not as such constitute interference with the exercise of the right . . . [S]ince States have the right to require authorisation, they must be able to apply sanctions to those who participate in demonstrations that do not comply with the requirement. The impossibility to impose such sanctions would render illusory the power of the State to require authorisation. It appears that in the present case, the State imposed a sanction on the applicant strictly for his failure to comply with the prohibition on participation in unauthorised demonstrations.

The Court went on to assess the size of the penalty imposed. While it was at the lower end of the scale, it was relatively large in terms of Ziliberberg's income but it did not 'appear to be disproportionate to the legitimate aim pursued'. As we noted in chapter three, the apparent contradiction—that the system is both not an interference but is one that must be assessed for proportionality—is resolved by distinguishing the need to obtain an authorisation (and a fortiori, notification), which will not be an interference, and imposing punitive measures for failing to obtain one (or to request one or even to act in excess of authorisation granted?), which will be an interference needing assessment under Article 11(2) in the standard way.

Let us revisit the concerns we addressed in chapter three.[190] First, that distinction debars the court from ever assessing the severity of any authorisation. If a disgruntled protester reluctantly complies, there will be no challenge to a penalty imposed and so no opportunity for courts to assess what in fact could be excessive or disproportionate conditions. By not going behind the authorisation process, the judgment provides no incentive for states to construct measured and balanced authorisation schemes. It might be possible to argue that there is a difference between the actual and simple authorisation, which falls outside the purview of the Court's powers of review (as in *Ziliberberg*), and any conditions which might be attached to the authorisation, which does not and so is amenable to review on a proportionality basis. This might be stretching a point. Secondly, *Ziliberberg* does not sit especially comfortably with an earlier admissibility decision, *WG v Austria*.[191] There, the Commission seemed to be looking into the authorisation/notification system itself stating that 'in the present circumstances, the requirement of prior authorisation of his activities could be regarded as justified'. Thirdly, it seems a little short sighted to focus on the scale or level of penalties—with the implication that if they are not excessive, the system would be Strasbourg-proof.[192] The restriction is as much about being removed from a protest site as it is being fined a nominal amount, what in *Aldemir* the Court refers to as the 'chilling effect' of interference, use of force and subsequent prosecution.[193] In any event, translated into the UK, *Ziliberberg* may itself actually provide some comfort. Although Strasbourg was prepared to hold that a fine of about €3 was proportionate, the penalty under SOCPA can include imprisonment for up to 51 weeks or a fine at level 3 (£1000) or level 4 (£2500), depending on which offence is committed. Anything over a minimal fine would surely be

---

[190] Above pp 79–83.
[191] *WG v Austria* (App 15509/89) EComHR inadmissibility decision 30 November 1992.
[192] It was taken for granted that where domestic law imposed a penalty explicitly aimed at protecting public order, this would be in pursuit of the legitimate aim, the 'prevention of disorder'. The circularity of this or the ease with which it would be complied did not seem unduly to concern the Court.
[193] *Aldemir v Turkey* (App 32124/02) ECtHR judgment 18 December 2007, at [34].

disproportionate? Indeed, even a conviction with a nominal penalty or discharge still remains as a blemish on someone's record.

The greatest contrast is with the later judgment in *Bukta v Hungary* rather than the admissibility decision in *Ziliberberg*.[194] As we saw in chapter three, *Bukta* must mean that the SOCPA scheme is at least partially incompatible, requiring as it does normally six days' notice but a minimum of 24 hours. In its view,

> in special circumstances when an immediate response, in the form of a demonstration, to a political event might be justified, a decision to disband the ensuing, peaceful assembly solely because of the absence of the requisite prior notice, without any illegal conduct by the participants, amounts to a disproportionate restriction on freedom of peaceful assembly.[195]

Attempts to enforce SOCPA against demonstrators who give no or only a few hours' notice as a result of circumstances beyond their control are likely to be doomed to fail. Whether a court would 'read' section 132 as compatible or declare it incompatible under section 4 of the HRA raises the wider constitutional tensions and concerns about individual justice to one or other of the litigating parties as against the wider democratic balance that we identified in chapter two. What is as important is the view the Court seems to indicate towards the imposition of penalties on peaceful protests for technical infractions of procedural authorisation requirements. In an even greater departure from *Ziliberberg*, the Court in *Kuznetsov v Russia* decided that minor deficiencies (on the facts eight, not 10, days' notice was given) that do not cause problems for the policing of the event were not sufficient or relevant reasons for a subsequent criminal case.[196] The restriction, in the form of a prosecution, was thus not necessary or proportionate. The Court has been at great pains to stress the substance of the protest—its effects, its nature and its impact on others—as the determining factor. In *Bukta*, it reiterated the view it set out in *Oya Ataman v Turkey* in 2006 (decided after *Ziliberberg*) that

> where demonstrators do not engage in acts of violence, it is important for the public authorities to show a certain degree of tolerance towards peaceful gatherings if the freedom of assembly guaranteed by Article 11 of the Convention is not to be deprived of all substance.[197]

As there was no evidence to suggest that the applicants represented a danger to public order beyond the level of the minor disturbance which is inevitably caused by an assembly in a public place, the Court found the dispersal of the applicants' peaceful assembly could not be regarded as having been necessary. The Court took a similar view in *Aldemir v Turkey*, where—as with *Oya Ataman*—the police response was clearly excessive, brutal and violent.[198] However, both cases should not be so confined and marginalised. In *Aldemir*, a trade union demonstration was held. No prior authorisation was needed, only 72 hours' prior notice. The Court concluded that[199]

---

[194] *Ziliberberg* (App 25691/04) ECtHR judgment 17 July 2007.
[195] *Bukta*, above n 188, at [35]. The protest was designed to make the Hungarian Prime Minister aware of local feelings after he decided to attend an official reception to be hosted the following day by the Rumanian Prime Minister (during the latter's state visit)—Rumania's National Day, commemorating the annexation of Transylvania from Hungary.
[196] *Kuznetsov v Russia* (App 10877/04) ECtHR judgment 23 October 2008.
[197] ibid, at [37]; *Oya Ataman* (App 74552/01) ECtHR judgment 5 December 2006, at [41]–[42].
[198] *Aldemir*, above n 193.
[199] ibid, at [45]–[47].

160   *The Locus of Protest*

there [was] no evidence to suggest that the group in question initially presented a serious danger to public order [but it was] likely that they would have caused some disruption in a particularly busy square in central Ankara . . . In the Court's view, where demonstrators do not engage in acts of violence, it is important for the public authorities to show a certain degree of tolerance towards peaceful gatherings if the freedom of assembly guaranteed by Article 11 of the Convention is not to be deprived of all substance.

From this we might conclude that arrests and prosecutions of one-person demonstrations in Parliament Square, provided they themselves remain peaceful and only minimally disruptive would be unnecessary interferences, given the toleration needed. This might be so despite the fact that this makes any system of notice/authorisation very hard to police when that system itself might serve to guarantee the state's positive obligations towards counter-demonstrators and the public generally.

(iv) Evans and Blum v DPP

Brian Haw's was not a case about the substance of the authorisation scheme in sections 132–138. Throughout August 2005, there was a series of protests (followed by the inevitable arrests) against the new provisions themselves.[200] One has become something of a cause célèbre since it involved the prosecution of peace campaigners, Stephen Blum and Aqil Shaer and Maya Evans and Milan Rai.

Blum and Shaer were arrested on 1 August during a demonstration against the Act itself in Parliament Square organised by 'Stop the War'.[201] Opposite Downing Street, Evans and Rai read out a list of British soldiers and Iraqi citizens who had died in the Iraq war since the date of the invasion in 2003. Each pair was warned and invited to stop but neither did. Each was found guilty by the magistrates of the offence of either participating in an unauthorised demonstration or (in Rai's case) organising one contrary to section 132(1) of the Act. The week after Evans was found guilty, *The Guardian* newspaper reported that 'the Lord Chancellor branded as "ridiculous" yesterday the claims that the prosecution of a peace campaigner for reading out the names of British soldiers who had died in Iraq showed that free speech was threatened'.[202]

Their cases came before the Divisional Court (on appeal by way of case stated), which upheld the convictions of all four.[203] The Court concluded that there was nothing in Strasbourg case law, especially in *Ziliberberg*, that required a departure from the clear domestic position: authorisations were required for all demonstrations that took place on or after 1 August, absent which even a sole demonstrator would be guilty of the offence under section 132(1). There was no violation of the rights to peaceful protest under Articles 10 and 11.[204] The nub of their case was that despite the wording of sections 132–134, any court seised of the matter should consider the individual facts and circumstances of

---

[200] *The Guardian*, 2 August 2005.
[201] Also present among the 50 or so others was the then Prime Minister's sister-in-law, Lauren Booth: 'Activists Clash with police over ban on protests', *The Guardian*, 2 August 2005, at: www.guardian.co.uk/uk/2005/aug/02/houseofcommons.iraq (accessed 9 August 2008).
[202] *The Guardian*, 14 December 2005.
[203] *Evans and Others v Director of Public Prosecutions* [2006] EWHC 3209 (Admin).
[204] Before the District Judges in the Magistrates' Courts two lines of attack had been adopted by the defence. The first was to argue that s 3 of the HRA should be utilised to 'read down' s 132(1) so as to render it compatible which, otherwise, it was argued it was not. The second was to claim that under s 6 of the HRA both the conviction and prosecution of the protesters would be unlawful as a disproportionate interference with the right to peaceful protest by the state's prosecuting and criminal justice authorities. Only the second was pursued on appeal.

each demonstration so as to assess the proportionality of arrest, charge and conviction in Article 11 terms. Unless a court did pursue such an approach there would be a violation of the right. Waller LJ (with whom Lloyd Jones J agreed) followed what he thought was the *Ziliberberg* line: first that an authorisation procedure is normally compliant with the requirements of Article 11(1) and second that action or a process to enforce it will comply with Article 11; otherwise 'the impossibility to impose . . . sanctions would render illusory the power of the state to require authorisation'.[205] In his view, it was not absolutely clear whether the ECtHR was saying that there would be compliance with Article 11(1) or whether it was saying that the imposition of sanctions to compel compliance with the authorisation procedure was clearly justifiable under Article 11(2).

With respect, it is clear and it is here wherein the problem lies. In *Ziliberberg* the application was manifestly ill-founded because the penalty imposed was at the lower end of the scale of penalties; although €3 was heavy relative to the applicant's revenue, it did not appear to be disproportionate to the legitimate aim pursued. At its narrowest, it is clear that a court should at least assess the penalty that is actually imposed, and there is nothing in *Ziliberberg* that explicitly rules out taking a similar look at sanctions more generally, certainly at the proportionality of the conviction.

We looked above at some arguments for taking a much more rounded, inclusive approach to proportionality in the context of an authorisation system and many of those general criticisms of the framework apply here. However, the case does raise some discrete issues of its own. First, and this seems most obvious in the case of Evans and Rai, would be to argue that they were not taking part in a demonstration at all. The term, as we saw earlier in the chapter, is undefined and considerable doubt surrounds its penumbra. We might recall the discussion of 'demonstration' versus publicity stunt, and the instance of the political activists dressed up as Father Christmas.[206] In Evans's case it does seem a genuinely true argument that the application of the authorisation process to her activity was unforeseen and thus her arrest and conviction were not prescribed by law. Her activity was merely to read a list of names in a designated area. Why is that an offence but it is not (we must assume) an offence for a teacher at Westminster School to read out a list of names when taking the register? Clearly, the two differ but only in intent and purpose: if laws proscribe and permit behaviour based only on the actor's state of mind, that creates a concern.[207] Secondly, unlike the protester in *Ziliberberg* who was clearly exercising his Article 11 right to demonstrate by taking part in an assembly, all that Evans and Rai were doing was speaking: they were reading out a list of the dead. In so doing, they fell more under (or equally under) the ambit of Article 10. Although neither was arrested for exercising their rights to free speech but for failing to obtain authorisation, effectively they were prosecuted for failing to obtain state permission to speak their mind. Thirdly, what they were doing was not seeking to persuade or to cajole or to criticise but merely making public some factual information, the names of the dead in Iraq. Might it not be argued that a 'demonstration' is constituted by doing something more than individually or collectively seeking to present the truth?

---

[205] *Evans*, above n 203, at [29], quoting from *Ziliberberg* p 11 of the decision.
[206] See n 173 above.
[207] As we shall see, it is a criticism of some of the aggravated trespass cases that they criminalise behaviour largely on account of an intended result rather than what actually results.

IV. Police Powers in Relation to Protests on Land

The police and local authorities have various powers to regulate the use of land for the purposes of peaceful protest. They may impose conditions—or request a ban—on both marches and public assemblies under sections 12–14A of the POA 1986, as amended and widened by the Criminal Justice and Public Order Act 1994 and the Criminal Justice Act 2003. We shall consider these below in chapter five. The police also have various powers at common law to enter land in order to prevent—actual or imminent—breaches of the peace. Again, we shall consider these below in chapter seven. There is a fair deal of Strasbourg case law covering both of these scenarios, as we saw in chapter three. The caseload of the Court has yet to feature situations where the police take action against peaceful protesters, purely because they are trespassers. It is this that provides the focus of the last part in this chapter: under section 61 of the CJPOA 1994 the police may order trespassers—in certain conditions—to leave land, failing which they are liable to arrest.

A. Section 61 CJPOA 1994

(i) Statutory Scheme

These powers were originally introduced in section 39 of the POA 1986 to deal with that social ill of the late 1980s/early 1990s whereby convoys of travellers would set up camp on a farmer's field and remain until (and if) the farmer successfully obtained a court order seeking their removal for trespass.[208] What is now section 61 was designed to give the farmer a cheaper and easier mechanism of eviction. They could call in the police first to issue an order to leave and, if anyone failed to do so, then to arrest them. It is another means by which trespass—normally and historically a civil wrong—was criminalised and moved from the private into the public sphere. The scope of the section, though aimed 'at gipsies and travellers: persons with an unconventional nomadic life-style, living in caravans or trailers',[209] is potentially wide enough to encompass peaceful protesters. Before the senior officer present at the scene can direct anyone to leave,[210] she must reasonably believe that

- two or more persons are trespassing on land (narrowly defined)[211] and are present there with the common purpose of residing there for any period;[212]
- reasonable steps have been taken by or on behalf of the occupier to ask them to leave; and
- any one of those persons has caused damage[213] to the land or to property[214] on the land

---

[208] The power was not originally contained in the Bill but was introduced following 'the much publicised travels of the 'Peace Convoy' and other groups (described as mediaeval brigands)': Driscoll, above n 11, 295.

[209] *R (Fuller) v Chief Constable of Dorset* [2001] EWHC Admin 1057 at [1] (Stanley Burnton J).

[210] The direction can be communicated by either the senior officer or any constable at the scene.

[211] The section applies to common land but only applies to buildings that are either agricultural buildings or scheduled monuments: s 61(7) and s 61(9). It does not include land forming part of the highway unless it is also a footpath, bridleway, byway open to all traffic or a cycle track.

[212] Where the persons were not originally trespassers but became so at a later stage, the other conditions must have been satisfied after that time as well: s 61(2). The original s 39 referred only to those who had entered land as a trespasser and it was a defence for someone to show they did not originally enter as a trespasser i.e. the farmer has changed her mind and revoked the licence to enter and remain.

[213] This includes depositing any substance capable of polluting the land: s 61(9).

[214] As defined in s 10(1) of the Criminal Damage Act 1971: s 61(9).

or used threatening, abusive or insulting words or behaviour towards the occupier, a member of his family or an employee or agent of his OR that those persons have between them six or more vehicles on the land.

An offence will be committed where someone, who knows that a direction that applies to them has been given, fails to leave land as soon as reasonably practicable or leaves but returns as a trespasser within three months, beginning with the day on which the direction was given.[215] It is a defence for the accused to show either that she was not trespassing or that she had reasonable excuse for failing to leave as soon as reasonably practicable or for re-entering as a trespasser within three months.[216]

(a) Comment and Analysis

Section 61 is one of an array of offences where the crime is disobedience to a police order.[217] How, then, does the scope of section 61 leave peaceful protesters potentially exposed? Imagine a group sets up a peaceful vigil outside an arms factory or a GM farm. If this is on private land, unless it occurs with permission of the occupier, it will be per se a trespass: *Appleby* confirmed the historic common law rule that there is no right to force the hand of the reluctant landowner or occupier.[218] If the vigil is on the public highway, in light of *Jones and Lloyd v DPP* (which we will consider in detail in the next chapter) and the House of Lords holding that a static non-obstructive protest will no longer automatically constitute trespass, although the group is 'on land' under section 61(9), they will not necessarily be trespassing there.[219] Assuming the group is trespassing—whether or not they entered as trespassers—the remainder of the trigger conditions are easily satisfied.

The section is, on its face, wide in the following ways. First, the group does not even need to be trespassing as long as the senior officer 'reasonably believes' they are. An officer might argue that although the group was only using the highway for a peaceful non-obstructive protest, she still reasonably believed them to be trespassers. Because—again as we shall see—the House of Lords did not lay down a bright-line rule, whether or not such an activity is a trespass is not a question simply of law but of applying the law to the facts, it might still be reasonable to believe them to have exceeded the limits of what the House of Lords considered a reasonable (and thus non-trespassory) user of the highway. Although section 61(6) goes some way towards meeting this objection, it is a defence—that the group was not in fact trespassing—and imposes an evidential burden (at least) on the protesters which they may fail to satisfy. They could still be convicted without actually trespassing, as long as an officer reasonably believed them to be doing so.

Secondly, the occupier does not actually need to have asked the group to leave nor in fact need she have taken reasonable steps to do so. Again, all that is needed is that the senior officer reasonably believes the occupier has taken reasonable steps to do so.[220] Thirdly, the

---

[215] The offence is a summary one and brings with it a possible three-month term of imprisonment or a fine not exceeding level 4: s 61(4) and s 61(5).
[216] Section 61(6).
[217] D Bonner and R Stone, 'The Public Order Act 1986: steps in the wrong direction?' [1987] *PL* 202, 211.
[218] Above n 58.
[219] *Jones and Lloyd v DPP* [1999] 2 AC 240. As we shall see, there is no authority to equate other public land with the highway for these purposes so static non-obstructive protests on a public park or in the forecourt of the Town Hall will not necessarily be protected by the reasoning or outcome in *Jones and Lloyd* and so may well still be trespasses too.
[220] She may, for example, have been misinformed deliberately by the occupier or owner: Driscoll, above n 11, 295

damage that has to occur for the power to be triggered need not be serious or even more than minimal: it will include damage to single blade of grass.[221] It is almost impossible to conceive of a situation where this trigger is not met. Here, section 3 of the HRA might allow for a reading of damage, if not 'serious' or 'significant', that the 'damage must be of a type and extent in excess of that caused by the mere fact of trespass' or subtly different but stronger, the 'damage must be of a type and extent in excess of or attributable solely to a peaceful protest'. Only one of the protesting trespassers needs to cause damage or use threatening words etc as a result of which 'peaceful occupation of land may become criminal if only one of a number of occupiers misbehaves'.[222] That might require some fairly drastic 'reading in' or even 'reading out' but such a task would seem to be required by the thrust of *Ezelin* and its emphasis on 'reprehensible acts' and those recent cases we considered in chapter three which stress the need for tolerance in the face of peaceful protest.[223]

The last problem surrounds the need for the group to be 'residing'. Although the group needs to be present there as trespassers (or at least reasonably believed to be so) with a common purpose to reside, the Act is silent as to how long they must be present. The temporal qualifier 'any period' relates to the common purpose to reside and does not qualify (or fail to!) how long they need to have been present: the section does *not* say 'present there for any period with the common purpose of residing there'. In other words, the offence is made out as soon as a couple trespasses, no matter that they may only have stepped one foot over a boundary a few seconds previously, as long as they simultaneously share the common purpose to reside there 'for any period'. Further, the trespassing, protesting couple would only have to share the common purpose of residing momentarily for the offence to be made out; there is no minimum period of residence. Everything then turns on what it means to describe someone as 'residing', a notion left undefined in the Act. An essential element, as we have seen, in Article 10/11 restrictions is clarity and certainty so as to lead to predictable consequences, that is in terms of restrictions being imposed. If they are not sufficiently certain, they run the risk of being declared not prescribed by law: 'residing' here seems to fall into this category. The OED provides a series of meanings: to 'remain or continue *in* a certain place or position', to 'dwell permanently or for a considerable time, to have one's settled or usual abode, to live, *in* or *at* a particular place' and to 'settle; to take up one's abode or station'.[224] Common sense—if not section 3—would tend towards 'residing' as being more than just situational or locational but meaning living somewhere, treating somewhere as a home, underpinned by a state of mind—a decision to remain or to continue.[225] Implicit in the various dictionary meanings is an idea of (semi-) permanence; it means more than staying (being) somewhere but being somewhere with a view to staying (remaining) there: I would be a resident in my new home as soon as I walk through the door provided the intention to remain manifests itself. In that light, it seems unlikely that a short-term protest—seeking signatures outside an arms factory one afternoon or even a 9–5 vigil—would come within the ambit of section 61, whereas Brian Haw or the Greenham Common protests of the 1980s for the time being at least have settled at their respective

---

[221] *Gayford v Chouler* [1898] 1 QB 316.
[222] Driscoll, above n 11, 295
[223] *Ezelin v France* (1991) 14 EHRR 362 and above pp 106.
[224] dictionary.oed.com (accessed 4 March 2008).
[225] The meaning attributed by a court might be informed by its use in areas such as tax law or private international law though given the disparate subject matter, these are likely to be of limited assistance. The latter defines residence for jurisdictional purposes relating to serving a writ as 'settled or usual place of abode': see *High Tech International AG v Deripaska* [2006] EWHC 3276 (QB).

protest sites ... but what about a group that sets up a 24-hour camp or a week-long peace vigil, like the Lapplanders outside the Norwegian parliament in *G and E v Norway*;[226] where is the divide and how do we identify it?[227] Another way to obviate or to minimise the application of section 61 to peaceful protesters would be to utilise section 3 of the HRA to interpret 'common purpose' narrowly, as equivalent to motivation or to aim, rather than being akin to intention. That would rule out it being used solely to criminalise those whose wrongdoing is merely to be one someone else's land holding a protest—and so, it is submitted, compatible with Article 11. Effectively, it means posing the question 'what are you doing here?' to any trespassing group. Those whom it was intended the section should not capture (or whom it is necessary to exclude on Convention grounds) would quite properly answer 'protesting about X' or 'holding a vigil against Y', whereas a travelling group setting up camp could only honestly reply 'This is where we live for the time being'. Thus construed, the section provides a legitimate conceptual distinction between the two groups.

The HRA might also temper the application of section 61 to peaceful protest in other ways. First, by providing for a Convention-compatible reading of the defence in section 61(6): someone either not leaving or re-entering as a trespasser within three months could claim as a 'reasonable excuse' the right peacefully to protest. Secondly, Article 6 requires that any available defences are read so that defendants bear only an evidential—rather than a legal burden.[228] Lastly, where in relation to the third trigger condition a group is alleged to have used threatening, abusive or insulting language, it could be argued that the court read in a free speech defence—'unless such language is also merely the peaceful communication of a protesting viewpoint' or even 'though peaceful communication of a protesting viewpoint cannot also constitute threatening or abusive or insulting language'.

(b) *R (Fuller) v Chief Constable of Dorset*

There has been only limited reporting of cases in which section 61 has been an issue and in none of the three reported cases in England and Wales has its use in connection with peaceful protest been in question.[229] That said, what was established in *R (Fuller) v Chief Constable of Dorset* would be of direct relevance should section 61 be relied upon to direct trespassing protesters to leave land. There are two aspects worth further consideration. First, as a matter purely of domestic construction, it was implicit in the scheme that the trespassers had failed to comply with the steps taken by the occupier to ask them to leave *before* the power to give a direction under section 61(1) could lawfully be exercised.[230] For the

---

[226] *G and E v Norway* (App 9278/81) EComHR inadmissibility decision 3 October 1983.
[227] Is it possible to reside in two different places at the same time?
[228] The leading case is *R v Lambert* [2002] 2 AC 545 and as a recent example *R v Keogh* [2007] EWCA Crim 528.
[229] The three cases all involve the giving of directions to travellers to leave land: *Fuller*, above n 209, *R (O'Brien) v Basildon DC* [2006] EWHC 1346 (Admin) and *R v Ministry of Agriculture Farms and Fisheries ex parte Callaghan* (2000) 32 HLR 8.
[230] *Fuller*, above n 209, at [43]. His Lordship does appear here to distinguish s 61(1)(a) from s 61(1)(b): 'Whereas section 61(1)(a) applies to persons who have already been guilty of criminal or other misconduct, section 61(1)(b) applies to persons who may have been perfectly well-behaved. It seems to me that Parliament was unlikely to have intended to bring the criminal law to bear on such trespassers who had not refused to leave when asked'. One reading of that extract is that if a direction is given on the basis of s 61(1)(a) then the section need not be read as 'impliedly requiring that the trespassers have not complied with the occupier's request that they leave as a condition of the making of a direction by the police under the section'? That is not what Stanley Burnton J held, though, in so far as he did not distinguish the two limbs. It is strange that an officer does not have to specify which of the two limbs is being relied upon whereas for the three triggers in s 14 of the POA the reverse holds true: see *R (Brehony) v Chief Constable of Manchester* [2005] EWHC 640 (Admin), discussed below in chapter five.

offence to be made out by a failure to comply, the trespassers had to be afforded the opportunity to comply with a request to leave. Thus, where—as in the instant case—the police attended with the local authority owner and directed them to leave at the same meeting as they were told they were trespassers and asked by a borough official to leave, the direction was unlawful and so would be quashed. As Stanley Burnton J pointed out,

> It is difficult to see why section 61 should require the occupier to take steps to ask the trespassers to leave if their compliance with that request is irrelevant to the power to give a direction. In my judgement, it is implicit in section 61 that the trespassers must have failed to comply with the steps taken by the occupier to ask them to leave before the power to give a direction can lawfully be exercised. I do not think that Parliament should be taken to have intended to introduce the possibility of criminal sanctions to trespassers who comply with requests to leave.

This would also be the case if—again as took place—it was a direction to leave at some future date (two days' time) rather than being a direction to leave immediately. This was the natural construction and drew upon the wording of the offence created in section 61(4): failure to leave land 'as soon as reasonably practicable' knowing a direction has been given.

> In my judgement, the words in subsection (4) 'as soon as reasonably practicable' mean 'as soon as reasonably practicable after the giving of a direction'. If a direction may be given to quit at some time sufficiently in the future, say two days after the giving of the direction, it would be inappropriate to provide for an offence of failing to leave as soon as reasonably practicable: the offence would be a failure to leave by the time specified in the direction. Indeed, it would be quite wrong to render criminal a failure to leave as soon as reasonably practicable before the expiration of the time permitted by the direction.[231]

Secondly, was the direction compatible with various Convention rights? Given their status as a public authority and the duty of Convention compliance in section 6(1), it was clear that in choosing whether or not to issue a direction the police could not lawfully take a decision the result of which would be an infringement of Convention rights.[232] It was also accepted that the defence in section 61(6)(b) of 'reasonable excuse' for failing to leave land would include an infringement of Convention rights. However, and thirdly, turning to the scope of Convention rights and their application to the giving of directions, Stanley Burnton J held that giving a section 61 direction did not engage the right to a fair trial under Article 6 because someone arrested for failure to comply can challenge that arrest or prosecution before a court.[233] His Lordship was prepared to accept, though it was not raised or argued before him, that the defence in section 61(6) should be interpreted as raising an evidential burden only—the point raised above—so as to be compatible with cases such as *Lambert*.[234] The last point of note was this: although a local authority had to consider the Convention rights of trespassers living on its land when deciding whether or not to enforce its right to possession of that land, the police were not in the same position as a local authority. Though the police must not act in breach of Convention rights, in the absence of information to the contrary they are entitled to assume that a local authority seeking their assistance is not acting in breach of human rights.[235] A fortiori, in the private sphere the

---

[231] ibid, at [47].
[232] ibid, at [52].
[233] On the facts there were also arguments about the engagement of Art 8 and Art 1 of the First Protocol and would only arise for a protest akin to long-term encampment such as at Greenham Common: see [58]–[60] and [61]–[66].
[234] *Lambert*, above n 228.
[235] ibid, at [68]–[69].

police would be entitled to assume there is no breach of human rights by the private landowner, since by definition they owe no duties under section 6 to trespassing protesters.

V. Conclusion

This chapter has covered a topic that is usually sidelined—if it is covered at all—in civil liberties and human rights textbooks but resolution of the issues it throws up must lie at the heart of an *effective* right of peaceful protest.[236] We saw both that there was no right at all to force the hand of a reluctant private landowner, while only if a public body has acted irrationally or abused its power for political advantage would a protester denied access have any claim before the HRA, and that the HRA would only alter this for public land by providing the possibility of an action based on Article 11—but again, the chances of success were not overly high. In addition, we saw that certain land—most notably the area surrounding Parliament itself—is subject to greater regulation where protest is concerned. We also saw, in terms of the themes of this book, how one element of that regulatory framework—section 61 of the CJPOA 1994—although designed for one use is capable of being used to clamp down on those who express legitimate criticisms. That too is a concern.

As Rowbottom states, land 'is a crucial resource for such freedom as it provides the space in which speakers can meet with one another and reach a wide audience'.[237] The extent to which people are able to use that land for peaceful protest and other communicative activities is the subject of our next chapter.

---

[236] There is a good general discussion of some of the issues raised in this chapter at: www.liberty-human-rights.org.uk/pdfs/policy08/supplementary-evidence-to-jchr-protest-and-private-land-.pdf, accessed on 22 July 2009. This is Liberty's supplementary evidence to the JCHR inquiry 'Demonstrating respect for rights? A human rights approach to policing protest' (7th report of session 2008–09 23 March 2009) available at: www.publications.parliament.uk/pa/jt200809/jtselect/jtrights/47/4702.htm, accessed on 22 July 2009.

[237] Above n 14, 186.

5

Peaceful Persuasion and Communicating Dissent

In the introduction we saw how protest might be divided into several types. The next two chapters will look at the regulation and protection of just two. In this chapter we turn our attention to peaceful protests; those that are intended to communicate or to persuade (or at least whose effect is to do so), where any disruption is incidental or short-lived. The next chapter will consider protests that are intended to disrupt or to obstruct (or at least whose effect is to do so), that is direct action protest. Of course, fundamental to both is the availability of land, the issue we considered in the last chapter. Being able to exercise the right to protest *effectively* is dependent on finding a venue for the march, the meeting or the demonstration. If there is no right of access onto land or permission to enter, even the most innocuous, most peaceful, solitary persuasive demonstration runs the risk of being or becoming unlawful as a trespass.

I. Overview

Protests of this sort might take many forms, serve many functions and be directed at various targets, even simultaneously. Protesters might simply start a letter-writing campaign or a petition assisted now by technological advance. The fact that, say, a head office address is now more readily available on-line by a simple Google search, and the ease with which those details and of campaigns themselves can be passed on (via email or website) has changed the shape and tactics of protest immeasurably: facilitating cyber-protest is now something at the forefront of the international labour movement.[1] We noted in the introduction the new dimension of viral campaigns and social networking protests. Protesters, especially if they have ready access to funding, might choose (instead or also) to buy up media space to 'advertise' a political viewpoint or they might equally exercise shareholder power collectively or individually. Dissent may of course take the form of more traditional protest—holding a march, a rally, a demonstration or a vigil with hundreds involved, chanting and waving banners. In terms of functions and targets, some protests might be aimed directly at the political process, seeking public engagement with (most likely) the government of the day, some at the wider public while others might aim directly at the perceived 'wrongdoers', the polluting companies and the arms manufacturers, themselves. Each one may be seeking to cajole or to criticise, to

---

[1] 'Unions signal rise of the cyber-picket', *The Guardian*, 10 February 2000, at: www.guardian.co.uk/money/2000/feb/10/workandcareers.uknews (accessed 11 November 2008).

publicise an issue or raise its profile, to elicit greater support or even just to prompt the public into reflection. In each, the ultimate aim is that—usually by sheer weight of numbers and public outcry—the government or company is persuaded to change its policy.[2]

Law can respond to the communication of messages during a protest in one of two main ways. It can take a stance of 'content neutrality'—but which might allow for time, manner or place restrictions based on the form the communication takes (the number, the location, the date or duration or the medium)—or it can differentiate between different messages, tolerating some (effectively giving them the imprimatur of state support) and outlawing others. We shall see in this chapter that English law favours an approach that mixes the two. Where the law permits a march to be banned this must be done in blanket fashion—none or all must be banned, even those that do not threaten public disturbance. Against that, using abusive or insulting language which harasses or alarms (irrespective of the medium) is an offence. In general, English law tends to focus on effects rather than content—thus racist language is not forbidden, though it is if it incites racial hatred. One last obvious point before we commence our detailed study. The right of peaceful protest is likely to engage Article 10 as well as Article 11, either because the activity takes the form of actual speech—chanting on a march would be an obvious example—or is considered to be symbolic speech, such as erecting crosses on a roadside, symbolising the death of nature, to protest at a road building programme.[3]

II. Marching, Meeting and Holding Demonstrations: The Statutory Scheme in the Public Order Act 1986

One obvious way to show support for (or opposition to) a decision or policy or to highlight an issue or concern is to hold a meeting or to stage a march. There is a considerable degree of overlap between the two. Each can be regulated quite considerably—though with significant differences—by either the police or the local authority under the provisions of the Public Order Act (POA) 1986. The right to hold meetings and assemblies is usually said to be more fundamental to the exercise of free speech and peaceful protest than is the ability to hold a march[4]—which is why, as we shall see, there are still different regimes in place[5]—but is that really the case? Wouldn't more people see a march—and perhaps wonder what was going on—than would see a group meeting? Perhaps the difference lies more in our historical attachment to mass rallies, and their perceived epoch-changing capability, than it does to reality.

---

[2] Guaranteeing the right of peaceful protest might—as well as this public utility—serve a more ethereal, more basic yet intrinsically valuable function. Participating in protest is an important means of giving effect to individual autonomy and maintaining dignity in the face of seeming increasing political impotence. Where governments need formally to respond to the electorate only once every five years and where companies are largely responsive only to the market, many will feel they have little alternative but to become more politically engaged by protesting at corporate wrongdoing or governmental failings.

[3] *Moosman v Austria* (App 14093/88) EComHR admissibility decision 15 October 1991.

[4] Asserted in the 1985 White Paper, *Review of Public Order Law* (Cmnd 9510) para 5.3 that preceded the POA 1986 and in the statement by Leon Brittain, the then Home Secretary, introducing it into Parliament: Hansard, HC Deb 16 May 1985, vol 79 col 507.

[5] Assemblies are generally subject to lesser restriction and (away from Westminster) it is only public processions that require advance notice.

A. An Overview

One important point is worth emphasising first. Where none of the powers in the 1986 Act applies to a march or meeting—perhaps because the 'trigger' conditions for their exercise do not exist—that does not mean that regulating or controlling the march or meeting is a matter beyond the powers of the police. Aside from their statutory powers, the police can always fall back on their residual common law power to take action to prevent breaches of the peace. We shall return to this in chapter seven. There is a strong argument from principle that, where powers overlap—so that both statute and common law would entitle the police to act—they should rely, and should be deemed to rely, on the powers in the POA 1986 with the result that the statutory scheme governs the interaction. This was certainly the view of Lord Bingham in *Laporte*—at least when it came to seeking extensions of powers: these should be undertaken by Parliament, which can consult widely and is able to strike an appropriate democratic balance, not by judges on inter partes litigation.[6]

The statutory scheme vests considerable power in advance to local authorities and Chief Constables to impose bans or to officers on the spot or in advance to impose conditions. Given these are discretionary powers granted to state actors, it has always been possible to challenge a ban imposed in advance (or conditions if known about in advance) by judicial review, arguing that the powers have been exercised irrationally, illegally (perhaps for an improper motive?) or in a procedurally improper manner.[7] Historically, there was little realistic chance of success. The case usually cited is the unsuccessful challenge by Monsignor Bruce Kent of the Campaign for Nuclear Disarmament to a blanket ban (for 28 days, covering 786 square miles) on all marches in London. The decision was taken against a backdrop of inner-city disturbances and riots in the summer of 1981. In *Kent v Commissioner of Police for the Metropolis* it was argued that the blanket ban was unlawful: it unfairly punished those who posed no threat to order and who may have had legitimate grievances that they may wish to publicise, when it should instead have been used to restrict the activities of the likely misfeasors and real troublemakers, the National Front.[8] That argument was given short shrift by the Court of Appeal. In a judgment marked by considerable deference to the police and the Home Secretary, the court held that such decisions were intra vires unless the applicant could show there was no good reason at all for a ban.

The outcome was not surprising given the clear wording in the forerunner to the 1986 Act. The explicit scope of what is now section 13 is that a banning order operates to make it unlawful for *any* march—or any specified class of march—to take place in the prohibited area during the prohibited time. The blanket nature of such a ban might now—as we saw in chapters two and three—lend itself to charges of disproportionality, given its ill-targeted nature. That said, wide, general bans have been upheld at Strasbourg (in that applications have been declared inadmissible) in cases such *CARAF v UK* stemming from similar circumstances.[9] The fact that a ban targets all groups no matter what the threat—and incid-

---

[6] *R (Laporte) v Chief Constable of Gloucestershire* [2006] UKHL 55 at [52].

[7] Alternatively, protesters could set up (say) the illegality or irrationality of a condition as a collateral defence to any charges brought as occurred—on facts having no connection with a protest—in *Boddington v British Transport Police* [1999] 2 AC 143.

[8] *Kent v Commissioner of Police for the Metropolis, The Times*, 15 May 1981 (and see too *London Borough of Lewisham v Metropolitan Police, The Times*, 12 August 1977) though contrast the Illinois Court of Appeals decision in *Collin v Smith* 578 F 2d 1197 (1978). A good general account of the Skokie litigation can be found in A Sherr, *Freedom of Protest, Public Order and the Law* (Oxford, Blackwell Publishing, 1989) 193–200.

[9] *Christians Against Racism And Fascism (CARAF) v UK* (App 8440/78) (1980) 21 DR 138.

entally captures avowedly peaceful ones—does though serve the other equally valid public purpose of content neutrality. The measure is thus simultaneously discriminatory and non-discriminatory, on different bases. Presently, we shall see how such a case might be argued today under the Human Rights Act 1998 (HRA).

B. Advance Notice of Public Processions under Section 11 of the POA 1986

(i) The Meaning of 'Public Procession'

A 'public procession' is defined in section 16 with near circularity as 'a procession in a public place'. A 'public place' is itself defined in the same section as (in England and Wales)

> any highway or any place to which at the material time the public or any section of the public has access, on payment or otherwise, as of right or by virtue of express or implied permission.

Much has been written about the meaning of 'public place' in the context of public order law.[10] The fact that we are all 'members of the public' does not mean that when we enter land we do so *as* members of the public; otherwise as soon as any us was able to enter onto land, it would become public land. Instead, the words of Jowitt J in *Richard Williams* might assist us.[11] The test of 'publicness' is not dictated by the number of visitors or those who have access but by asking who, why and by what methods was access permitted to the premises or the land in the first place. Are people permitted to enter as they please or are they present there only because of some connection with those there already as owner or occupier or with the premises or land itself? It is possible that section 16 is capable of bearing quite a wide meaning. It makes clear that where the public or even a section of the public is able to enter land (whether or not anyone is actually present there is immaterial provided that the public or a section has access) not by right but by virtue only of express or even implied permission, that land is public land.[12]

There is very much less by way of explaining what constitutes a 'procession'. By implication from its absence it could be argued that this need not necessarily be a procession 'of people'. However, in *Flockhart v Robinson*, Lord Goddard CJ indicated a procession was more than 'a mere body of persons; it is a body of persons moving along a route'.[13] In *Kent*, Lord Denning, placing reliance on the Oxford English Dictionary, considered it was the 'act of a body of persons marching along in orderly succession'.[14] Given the different regulatory schemes for assemblies and processions, in very few cases the distinction between a static assembly and a procession might be important. But—as it is easier to impose restrictions on processions and since restrictions on processions encompass a wider scope—any group is likely to want to be classified as an assembly despite (perhaps) really being a procession. Is a group of people shuffling imperceptibly at snail's pace in circles outside the town hall a 'body of persons moving along a route . . . in orderly succession' or is it effectively a group of people standing and chanting? Similarly, it is clear that a lone protester walking or even

---

[10] Cases would include *Cawley v Frost* [1976] 1 WLR 1207; *Marsh v Arscott* (1982) 75 Cr App R 211; and *Williams (Richard) v DPP* (1992) 95 Cr App R 415.
[11] ibid, 419–20. This was not a case on the Public Order Act 1936—the forerunner of the 1986 Act—but about being drunk and disorderly in a public place.
[12] Under s 9 of the 1936 Act, a public place was limited to the 'highway and any other premises or place to which, at the material time, the public have or are permitted to have access whether on payment or otherwise'.
[13] *Flockhart v Robinson* [1950] 2 KB 498 (Div Ct) 502.
[14] *Kent*, above n 8.

marching cannot constitute a 'procession'; one individual cannot be 'a body' of persons ... but how many *are* needed? If restrictions are imposed, this seems another area ripe for challenge under the HRA as not being sufficiently certain and so not 'prescribed by law': would someone in a group of two have known in advance that they constituted a 'procession' and if so known, as we shall shortly see, that they needed to give advance notice of their plans?

(ii) What Does Section 11 Require and of Whom?

A framework that permits marches to be banned or conditions to be imposed really requires a system of advance notice in order to work properly. We have already seen that this might assist states in performing their positive duty to protect the right of protest: it allows the police more effectively (and more cheaply[15]) to plan for and contain public processions.[16] It thus might facilitate the right of protesters actually to protest. Section 11 of the POA 1986 provides such a police-managerial tool. The Green Paper preceding the 1986 Act also asserted that section 11

> might serve as the formal trigger for discussions between the police and organisers designed to agree the ground rules for a march [and] might in turn help to encourage organisers to assume more responsibility for policing their own people.[17]

But, as Sedley LJ noted, the applicability of section 11 is not determined or conditioned by whether the power to regulate a procession is available; the 'purpose of section 11 is to permit the policing of processions which pose no such threat [of disorder or intimidation] as well as of those which do'.[18]

Written notice must be given, at least six days in advance, of any proposal to hold a public procession that is intended

(a) to demonstrate support for or opposition to the views or actions of any person or body of persons,
(b) to publicise a cause or campaign, or
(c) to mark or commemorate an event.

If it is not reasonably practicable to give any advance notice, none is required but if it is reasonably practicable to give some notice, albeit not six days', then under section 11(6) whatever notice is reasonably practicable must be given. The requirement to give written notice does not apply where the procession is one that is commonly or customarily held in the police area[19] or is 'a funeral procession organised by a funeral director acting in the normal course of business'. That latter scenario clearly is not our concern. The written notice must, under section 11(3), specify when it is intended to hold the procession, its start time, its proposed route and the name and address of at least one of the proposed organisers. It must be delivered to a police station in the police area in which it is proposed the procession will start. Where a public procession is held each of the organisers will be committing an offence if either the notice requirements have not been met or there is a difference in

---

[15] H Fenwick, *Civil Liberties and Human Rights*, 4th edn (Abingdon, Routledge, 2007) 705.
[16] Previously, powers did exist under local Acts and by-laws: Sherr, above n 8, 68–9.
[17] Green Paper, para 71, quoted in D Bonner and R Stone, 'The Public Order Act 1986: Steps in the Wrong Direction?' [1987] *Public Law* 202, 217.
[18] *Kay v Commissioner of Police for the Metropolis* [2006] EWHC 1536 (Admin) at [9].
[19] The assumption is that as such marches will be known to the police, this allows them properly to police it: *ibid*, at [19].

date, time or route from those details given in the written notice.[20] It will be a defence for defendants to prove they did not know of, did not suspect and had no reason to suspect either the failure to satisfy the written notice requirements or the differences in date, time or route.[21] In that case, it is a defence to prove that the difference in date, time or route arose from circumstances beyond their control or from something done with the agreement of a police officer or by his direction.[22]

Under section 11(2), only those very few protest marches that are customarily or commonly held in the police area are exempt from the section 11 notice regime. Those processions remain undefined in the Act.[23] The requirement that organisers give whatever notice is reasonably practicable (even if that is no notice at all) if they cannot give six days' notice provides some flexibility where time is of the essence. It is worded so that those who wish to react suddenly where an urgent matter that has come to light may organise an ad hoc march. The Green Paper gave as examples

> a march to the embassy of a foreign power which had announced that one of its political prisoners was to be executed within 24 hours, or, on a more local level, a march against a factory closure or in favour of a pedestrian crossing outside a school after a fatal road accident.[24]

In this regard, domestic law is very likely to be seen as Convention compatible, in light of *Bukta v Hungary*.[25] There a violation of Article 11 was found because Hungarian law had a minimum period that admitted no exceptions.

(a) Organiser

It is important to emphasise that under section 11 only the organisers face the possible penalty of a fine under section 11(10); it is not an offence to participate in a public procession where no notice has been given. What it means to be an 'organiser' has generated very little case law. The main case is *Flockhart v Robinson* from the early 1950s, an appeal to the Divisional Court by way of case stated.[26] There, Lord Goddard CJ and Morris J (with Finnemore J dissenting) held that the defendant, at the head of a line of followers who marched through parts of central London, was the organiser of a political procession that came into being spontaneously at the end of a rally in Knightsbridge. At each traffic crossing the defendant held up his hands as a warning; at the first, the then loose group of followers closed up into a more orderly file so as to present a 'compact body marching in ranks in close formation'.[27] Throughout the march, the defendant gave orders as to stopping and starting and as to its direction and route. Lord Goddard CJ concluded simply and shortly

---

[20] Section 11(7).
[21] Defendants might be able to argue that 'prove' should be read, under s 3 of the HRA, as imposing an evidential burden only, in order to remain compatible with the fair trial guarantee and the presumption of innocence in Art 6(1) of the Convention: see *R v Lambert* [2001] UKHL 37 and *R v Keogh* [2007] EWCA Crim 528 in the context of the Official Secrets Act 1989.
[22] Section 11(8)–(9).
[23] The White Paper (above n 4, para 4.5) talks of 'processions of a religious, educational or ceremonial character'.
[24] Green Paper, para 68 (quoted in Bonner and Stone, above n 17, 216).
[25] *Bukta v Hungary* (App 25691/04) ECtHR judgment 17 July 2007, as interpreted in *Molnar v Hungary* (App 10346/05) ECtHR judgment 7 October 2008.
[26] *Flockhart v Robinson* [1950] 2 KB 498.
[27] ibid, 500. It was at that point, when the loose collection of individuals became a cohesive group, that the magistrates decided that a public procession of a political character came into being, spontaneously and without prior arrangement. This is an important point in the legal regulation, at a practical level, of public protest, although it is unclear from the report whether it became a procession at that point, having previously not been one, or that the existing procession became one with a political character.

that 'the person who organises the route is the person who organises the procession ... By indicating or planning the route, a person is ... organising a procession'.[28] Morris J was of a similar view. The defendant 'provided direction and leadership ... [He] marched at the head of the procession and gave words or signs of command that were obeyed ... giving the lead to those behind him'.[29] Influential was the finding that the defendant had earlier organised a lawful public procession in the City of London (rather than in the Metropolitan police area, as this one was). He issued instruments, marched at the head and gave verbal commands to the participants. Largely the same people were present at the later Knightsbridge march. For Finnemore J, the fact that the procession formed spontaneously and without any prior arrangement, as had been found as a fact by the magistrates, made it 'impossible to say that the defendant had organised' it.[30] Organising a procession means 'something in the nature of arranging, or getting up or planning a procession'.[31] It did not necessarily need 'people in a back room mak[ing] secret plans' in advance;[32] it could be organised on the spot on the street. Here however, the procession formed itself—thus it was self-organising—when its members moved into ranks and in close formation. The difference between the two approaches might be down to seeing a procession as an entity in itself—thus to be organised—separate from the movement of the people within and comprising it. If 'active participation' was held in *Ziliberberg* to be sufficiently certain as to meet the prescribed by law test, there is little reason to suppose a court not taking the same view of 'organising'.[33]

Section 11 of course was passed in different times: the changed and changing nature of protest 'groups' is a relatively modern phenomenon, in part due to the proliferation of means of communication and the mass availability of information in the internet age and in part due to more democratic forms of protest becoming the norm. It was designed, we can probably safely assume, to cover the leadership of formal groups: trades unions, pressure and protest groups and political parties. It is hard to envisage it covering many more modern protests which have tended to feature more individualised, more participatory, more localised forms, where approaches to tactics and goals are more democratic, 'bottom-up' driven rather than 'top-down' dictated.[34] Whether the section is apt to do so is certainly moot. One can imagine it being more difficult now to prove X organised (if we equate that perhaps to leadership?) a procession where groups are loosely aligned along cell-like lines, in which only a handful know a handful of other protesters. Would each person who passes on—via bulletin boards, by email, by word of mouth—details of a march being mounted 'as a show of strength against *Animal Experimenters plc* by storming from the Town Hall to their HQ next Monday lunchtime' be an organiser of the public procession that took place? On one view, each has only organised one more participant into coming, that is, ensured there is a good turn-out, not the substance or structure of the public procession itself; the actual 'organiser' is the one (or the cadre) who decided that there should be a march at all

---

[28] ibid, 502–3.
[29] ibid, 503–4.
[30] ibid, 505.
[31] ibid.
[32] ibid.
[33] *Ziliberberg v Moldova* (App 61821/00) ECtHR inadmissibility decision 4 May 2004, discussed in chapter three.
[34] In the context of 'organising' raves—and the impact of s 14—see *Baillie v DPP* [1995] *Criminal Law Review* 426. This is a very short note; there is greater detail in J Marston and P Tain, *Public Order: The Criminal Law* (London, Callow Publishing, 2001) 160–61.

and on what date and at what time. We might argue that even the person who took that decision not knowing if anyone will come (that being up to individuals down the line) was not 'organising' it? To hold those down the line as organisers would expose far more of them to prosecution than the ordinary meaning of 'persons organising' would appear to envisage. This is certainly consonant with the approach taken in *Flockhart* by all three judges. It is at least arguable, should a court be considering the case against all those along a chain of communication, that taking that wider reading runs the risk of restricting the Article 11 rights of that larger group: there would be a 'chilling effect' on participation if the legal position were that merely being a conduit for passing on details would incur potential liability. It would also be open of course to argue that an expansive meaning was not 'prescribed by law', as being too uncertain in advance.

In the High Court in *Kay*, Sedley LJ added a gloss on section 11 not warranted by the terms of the Act. He talks about the liability of those who organise a procession '*whether from the start or during its progress*' (emphasis added).[35] Section 11 is silent on this and given that it extends liability rather than limits it, it is certainly not an approach ordained by section 3 of the HRA. Of course effective policing can and must still take place ad hoc in response to changed conditions and circumstances but does this really require the imposition of criminal liability on those who take control of a fairly fluid, participant-led public procession (displaying the necessary collective intention) with a 'come on, let's go on City Hall!'?[36] The problem is that they face being fined unless they can prove they did not know of the failure to satisfy the written notice requirements *six days previously* and did not suspect or have reason to suspect that failure. Ignorance of the law of course provides no defence. To extend section 11, so that it captures not only those who organise in advance or at the outset but also those who take the lead, on the day, to provide some structure to an otherwise random collection of free wills, runs the risk that the penalty would not be prescribed by law, by virtue of its uncertainty. Would anyone who suddenly takes control— perhaps even to impose discipline on a procession that threatens to get out of hand—during such an event have considered themselves an 'organiser' such as that they should have given (ideally) six days' notice? Almost by definition, how could six days earlier that same person have predicted with sufficient certainty that if they did not at that time give written notice, in six days' time they would be arrested?

(b) Intention

One matter is clear. Section 11(1) only covers public processions that are intended 'to demonstrate support for or opposition to the views or actions of any person or body of persons', or 'to publicise a cause or campaign', or 'mark or commemorate an event'. This is irrespective, it must be added, of whether they actually do or are even capable of achieving it. As with so much in the law, it boils down to the meaning of intention. If a group meets for convenience at the Town Hall to march to the HQ of *Animal Experimenters plc* where they will hold a static demonstration, can it be said that the procession is being done with any of those intentions? Is it not their intention to move from A to B? Any publicity that accrues—bystanders asking what is going on—is not what the organisers (such as any exist) intend but is a by-product of the primary imperative, herding a large group from A to B.

---

[35] *Kay v Commissioner of Police for the Metropolis* [2006] EWHC 1536 (Admin) at [15].
[36] If liability is imposed for such utterances, this of course has implications for free speech as well.

(c) Kay v Commissioner of Police for the Metropolis

One of the few cases on the meaning and scope of section 11 arose from exactly one of these more participatory, ground-level types of protest, *Kay v Commissioner of Police for the Metropolis* decided by the House of Lords in November 2008.[37]

1. Background The issue was whether or not section 11 applied to Critical Mass, not an organisation but the name given to a recurrent event: some 140 or so mass bike rides that had been taking place since 1994 on every last Friday of the month in Central London, with similar events on the same day in many other cities throughout the world. The House of Lords reversed the decision of the Court of Appeal and upheld the High Court decision in favour of the cyclists.[38]

Critical Mass was accepted as being a spontaneous event with no advance planning or organisation as traditionally understood. It started at the same location (near the National Theatre) at the same time but

> it is in the nature of Critical Mass that there is no fixed, settled or predetermined route, end-time or destination; where Critical Mass goes, where and what time it ends, are all things which are chosen by the actions of the participants on the day.[39]

Numbers rarely fell below 100 and there were commonly 300–400, sufficient to make their presence felt by both passers-by and motorists. They were able to and did cause additional congestion but they kept moving and could legitimately say that they were part of the city's traffic.[40] From their observations, the police had identified two particular objectives in terms of location, venue and route: places where maximum disruption to vehicles could be caused and places where cyclists are considered to get a hard time from motor vehicles—making the Critical Mass event a form of 'payback'. The cyclists' main motivation, it was argued and set out in the group's website, was simply to celebrate or to promote cycling:

> There is no single aim of CM, although there is a shared wish to see less car-dominated cities and more people cycling. There are as many aims of CM as there are participants. Each individual comes there with his or her own idea of what it's about, and the sum of this makes up the mass.[41]

Kay brought the case, nominally on behalf of others, to clarify the legal position under section 11. A letter from the Metropolitan Police's Public Order Branch indicated their view that Critical Mass was not lawful 'because no organiser has provided the police with the necessary notification'. Having mis-stated the legal position—that the event was unlawful rather than its organiser acting unlawfully—it compounded this error by asserting that 'your participation in this event could render you liable to prosecution'.[42] Nonetheless, the Met's sentiment is clear: the Critical Mass bike rides needed six days' notice.

---

[37] *Kay* [2008] UKHL 69.
[38] *Kay* [2007] EWCA Civ 477 and [2006] EWHC 1536 (Admin) respectively.
[39] *Kay* [2008] UKHL 69, at [2].
[40] ibid, at [3]. As Sedley LJ noted in the Administrative Court ([2006] EWHC 1536 (Admin) at [6]) there was not complete agreement as to whether the choice of route was truly spontaneous but the point was academic.
[41] It then listed a variety of individual participants' aims. These included: raising the profile of cycling in towns and cities; campaigning for better provision for cyclists; raising awareness about pollution and other problems caused by cars; getting our own back at motorists; demonstrating opposition to car culture; causing disruption; feeling good about being safe on a bike on roads which are usually dangerous; creating a vision and experience of a possible future; and meeting friends and going for a beer later.
[42] *Kay* [2006] EWHC 1536 (Admin) at [10]

2. The case before the lower courts The common feature of the case before the Divisional Court and on the appeals was what the House categorised as the narrow issue: was Critical Mass a public procession that was 'commonly or customarily held', assuming the event had the necessary intention? The wider issue—did section 11 apply to an event and protest such as Critical Mass, typified by spontaneity with neither an organiser nor a fixed route capable of notification—was resolved by the High Court in favour of the Commissioner.[43] He had argued first that the question of who was the organiser could not be determined on an application such as this, and secondly that the route was a non-issue: if notice is required, a route has to be specified in it. There was no appeal on this.

The Divisional Court (Sedley LJ and Gray J) declined to hold that Critical Mass *collectively* (rather than its individual members) did not have any of the requisite intentions in section 11(1): that would be a matter for evidence should a prosecution ever be brought.[44] The Court did find that Critical Mass was a customarily or commonly held procession and so did not require notice. In its view,

> an unbroken succession of over 140 of these collective cycle rides, setting out from a fixed location on a fixed day of the month and time of day and travelling, albeit by varying routes, through the Metropolitan Police area, cannot by now sensibly be called anything but common or customary.

The Court of Appeal, by a majority, upheld the Commissioner's appeal:[45] the High Court had been 'insufficiently focused'[46] on the real question and had been overly swayed by the participants' collective intent. The analysis undertaken by Sedley LJ—that 'an event which has remained constant in form but has changed in intention may arguably cease to be common or customary within the meaning of section 11(2)'[47]—was wrong. Although no one feature was determinative, the court had underplayed the role and significance of a single, usual route.[48] The Court of Appeal's premise was this. A procession 'takes its regularity from an examination of all the features that make it up. A procession cannot . . . become common or customary if no route or end point is ever the same'.[49] The Court of Appeal was

---

[43] *ibid*, at [13]–[15]. Once the intention conditions set out in s 11(1) are met, it does not matter that there is no route or no organiser: the notice that is required must specify a proposed route and named organiser. The prior existence of a planned route or an organiser is not a condition precedent to the requirement of notice—they are assumed. Sedley LJ also rejected the argument that without a planned route or an organiser it was not reasonably practicable to give six-days' notice under s 11(1): the shorter period allowed in s 11(6) was 'to do with the practicalities of timing, not with the feasibility of giving the required details'. That said, for the police successfully to prosecute under s 11(7), they would actually have to find an organiser. This, because of the 'statutory assumption of a route and an organiser [which] represents a mismatch between what we have called the official mind and the way that Critical Mass works' might prove to be tricky: see Sedley LJ [2006] EWHC 1536 (Admin) at [15], and Leveson LJ [2007] EWCA Civ 477 at [35].

[44] It is clear the court would have been surprised if it could not be shown that Critical Mass intended to demonstrate support for or opposition to the views or actions or any person or body of persons or to publicise a cause or campaign. The analogy with a crocodile line of children marshalled in a group to school where the shared or dominant intention is simply to get the children to school safely, but where the organiser is also campaigning for better road safety and has arranged extensive publicity for the procession—and so falling outwith s 11(1)—was not one that found favour: [2006] EWHC 1536 (Admin) at [16]–[18].

[45] Sir Mark Potter P and Leveson LJ; Wall LJ dissenting.

[46] Sir Mark Potter at [70], *cf* Wall LJ at [63].

[47] *Kay* [2006] EWHC 1536 (Admin) at [22].

[48] There is certainly strength in the view of Wall LJ that by requiring routes to have a 'necessary element of repetition', Leveson LJ elevated route into the determinative feature, despite being at pains to suggest otherwise.

[49] *Kay* [2007] EWCA Civ 477 at [31] (Leveson LJ). In its view, there was clear disjuncture between s 11(2) and s 11(3). Section 11(3)—which sets out the matters comprising the notice (date, time, route and organiser)—does not define the proper construction of s 11(2) and so cannot decide whether or not a procession was customary or common.

concerned about the effective policing of processions (whether or not they threaten disorder) through advance planning. The ability to impose conditions or seek a ban would be undermined by the reverse scenario: a common end-point but no single fixed start.[50] No one would view that procession as commonly or customarily held even though there were identical features each month of time, date and destination.[51] It must be right that the High Court's focus on collective intention, as not only defining which processions are notifiable but also providing the measure for assessing which were customarily or commonly held, was mistaken.[52] There are good reasons why it cannot provide that definitional marker. As David Pannick QC argued, it would be unclear why a procession—held at the same time, date and route each week—was not one that was commonly held simply because it chose to publicise a different cause or campaign one week or after a while.[53] In deciding whether a particular procession is one commonly or customarily held 'it is necessary to have regard to its nature and quality as a procession, *including* the route which it follows'.[54]

3. The reasoning of the House of Lords Their Lordships, it would be fair to say, considered the whole thrust of the arguments to be misplaced. Lord Brown was clearly frustrated at 'wasting . . . time' by being asked to resolve the case in the 'straitjacketed way sought to be forced on us'.[55] Alone among the five, he decided the case on the basis of the wider issue, not on the basis of the ground of appeal. The real question was

> whether these cycle rides are prima facie notifiable processions at all within the meaning of section 11. And the answer is that they are not. Their very nature as impromptu rides to my mind takes them out of the section altogether. [Like the Commissioner] I too regard the random nature of the route taken as of central relevance in this case but it seems to me relevant to the altogether more fundamental and logically prior question whether the rides are in any event notifiable processions in the first place.[56]

Three of the remainder of the Committee offered strong obiter (as they must technically be) preliminary observations on that same question and on the issue more generally.[57] Lord Carswell offered no view.[58] Baroness Hale, for example, indicated her view that the case raised 'several important issues about the scope and coverage of section 11 of the 1986 Act [yet] reaches us on only one point which, on one view of the section, would not fall for decision at all'.[59]

We can discern several different strands to the reasoning on this point. First, that section 11 only extends to 'organised' processions and Critical Mass is the antithesis of that. There was never a time when anyone could have been said to organise one—the most that could be said is that someone once organised a gathering (undoubtedly itself a section 14 public

---

[50] On the necessary disjunction in purpose and scope between s 11 on one hand and ss 12–13 on the other, see Sedley LJ [2006] EWHC 1536 (Admin) at [9].
[51] The analogy though does not hold up: a protest that uses the same set-off point (but different route) goes some way towards obviating the problems of anticipation and planning since the police can at least track it as it veers off. In fairness to Leveson LJ, he himself recognised that: [2007] EWCA Civ 477 [29].
[52] *Kay* [2006] EWHC 1536 (Admin) at [20]–[22].
[53] *Kay* [2007] EWCA Civ 477 at [21].
[54] ibid, at [70] *cf* Wall LJ at [63].
[55] *Kay* [2008] UKHL 69 at [66] and [74].
[56] ibid, at [67].
[57] Lord Phillips at [22]–[26], Lord Rodger at [34], who talks of several 'untested assumptions [which] are, at least open to question' and at [41]–[43], Baroness Hale at [47]–[48] and [52]
[58] ibid, at [58].
[59] ibid, at [52].

assembly) from which 'inherently disorganised'—at least as to its route—processions took off.[60] This if course assumes that implicit in section 11—from construing the structure of section 11 as a whole, especially section 11(3)—covers only organised processions. This is buttressed by the further assumption that anyone organising a notifiable procession would be in a position to give the police advance notification of its proposed route.[61] It is by no means clear that section 11 should be so construed.

The second factor underpinning their view on the wider issue is one in fact that that first deals with: that a new Critical Mass would effectively be debarred from springing up. Counsel for the Commissioner had been forced to argue, so as to sustain his position on the 'customary or commonly held' narrow issue, that not only was section 11 drafted assuming processions would have a pre-determined route but section 11 impliedly required that that they *should* have one.[62] This would lead to one of two conclusions: either that processions without pre-determined routes meant automatic guilt for its organiser—meaning, as was conceded, that one would never take place again[63]—or such processions were outwith the requirements of section 11 *in toto*. Lord Rodger and Lord Phillips preferred this latter interpretation:

> [I]f Parliament had actually intended to use the Public Order Act 1986 to outlaw processions of that kind without a predetermined route, then it would not have done so by a side wind in a section creating a system of notification: it would have done so specifically[64]

as it had done under section 13 of the POA 1986. Of course, a third view might be open—processions without pre-determined routes meant automatic guilt for those who could properly be said to be organiser which, if the event is inherently disorganised will mean everyone escapes criminal liability. There is another concern if spontaneous protest marches without leaders, routes, plans or organiser within central London are outwith section 11. This was identified by Baroness Hale: they might be subject to sections 132–138 of the Serious Organised Crime and Police Act (SOCPA) 2005, while they remain in force.[65] That would mean potential liability for anyone organising but for participation too. Demonstrations that are also notifiable processions are exempt from the authorisation requirements. Holding Critical Mass to be a procession where advance notice was not needed would take them 'out of the frying pan of section 11 ... [but] ... thrust ... into the fire of section 132'.[66] The third factor was that notice is only required under section 11(1) of where there is a proposal to hold a procession and, as had been agreed, these impromptu rides involved no such antecedent 'proposal'.[67]

On the narrow issue before it (or, as Lord Phillips thought, an amalgam of two questions[68]) the House was unanimous: a fixed and known route was not an essential characteristic of a procession commonly or customarily held.[69] As Lord Carswell noted, holding

---

[60] Lord Brown at [68]–[69].
[61] ibid, at [72].
[62] ibid, at [41].
[63] ibid, at [23].
[64] Lord Rodger at [42], Lord Phillips at [24] and Baroness Hale at [48].
[65] We discussed these provisions in chapter four, above pp 148–157.
[66] *Kay* [2008] UKHL 69 at [53].
[67] ibid, at [23] (Lord Phillips).
[68] ibid, at [12]. These were (i) was the ride that took place each month the same procession and (ii) was it 'commonly or customarily held'?
[69] In the Court of Appeal, Wall LJ noted the absence of a fixed route is the common feature of Critical Mass: going off in different directions is 'what they commonly do' ([2007] EWCA Civ 477 at [54] and [57]) but, by extension though, so would having a different start and end point. That would rather leave s 11(2) in tatters.

otherwise could mean many Remembrance Day parades as well as many Orange Order parades in July in Northern Ireland might find themselves ineligible for the section 11(2) exemption.[70] On the natural meaning of the term, it was clear that the Critical Mass rides had enough common features as to be (a) the same procession albeit over different routes and (b) events that were 'commonly or customarily' held.[71] It had been argued that what was taking place was at best a series of monthly new one-off processions, each along a different route, such that none was 'common or customary'. The underlying statutory purpose did not gainsay that. It had been advanced that the whole scheme of the 1986 Act would be undermined if processions which did not follow the same route or end at the same place—despite having the same start—were absolved of the need to give advance notice, as the police would be unable to take precautions so preserve order and maintain traffic flow. Commonly or customarily held processions along the same route were exempt because the police would know all they needed to know already.

Lord Phillips advanced three reasons for this view. First, it is of value for the police to have advance notice of when and in what police area a procession is to be held, even if they do not know the route that it will follow. The history of Critical Mass shows the police are usually able to police it without difficulty. Secondly, most customary processions do follow the same route so that section 11 is not robbed of its utility. Thirdly, the key to the operation of section 11 was not whether a procession was likely to create a disturbance—many peaceful processions are captured by section 11(1). Section 11 requires notice for all demonstrative, publicising or commemorative marches irrespective of their likely effects, good or bad. The reason section 11(2) exempts certain ones is nothing to do with their impact but because either the police already know about them or because of the administrative burden of requiring notice of funeral processions. It is the ability to impose conditions or to ban under sections 12 and 13—once notice has been given—that has a link to disorder or 'inconvenience'.[72] The first reason must hold good. Why the Met started to police it in this way so late in the day is never answered. There is something vaguely troubling about the Court of Appeal finding that obliged the organisers of a protest, under the guise of statutory interpretation, to give notice when for over 10 years the police had never seen the need to rely on section 11. In his dissenting judgment, Wall LJ in fact implied that the police should have been estopped from relying on section 11.[73] Lord Phillips's second point seems beside the point. His third makes a strange bedfellow for Lord Rodger's comments. The possible interference with other traffic would be exactly the same whatever the motivation for the rides, yet section 11 only applies to public processions with certain intentions: those organising a mass bike ride simply for the sheer joy of cycling would not need to give advance notice. It followed, in his mind, that the essential purpose of section 11(1) cannot so much be to warn the police of possible interference with traffic as to warn them of a procession whose aim might provoke opposition and so give rise to public order problems.[74]

---

[70] *Kay* [2008] UKHL 69 at [61].

[71] Lord Phillips at [15]–[16] and [18]–[21], Lord Rodger at [35]–[36].

[72] In that regard Wall LJ in the Court of Appeal placed too much emphasis on what he called 'pragmatic policing' and practice to question whether there would be 'a qualitative or quantitative difference in public inconvenience or in the measure of policing, if the Critical Mass cycle ride followed an identified route': [2007] EWCA Civ 477 at [53].

[73] *ibid*, at [57]. None of the bodies responsible for public transport in London had thought it appropriate to invite the police to consider using s 11: at [56].

[74] *Kay* [2008] UKHL 69 at [29].

4. Comment So where does this leave section 11? Clearly 'commonly and customarily held' has taken on a much more expansive meaning, a meaning if not designed to be in tune with modern, plural loose protests groups then at least one that supports their rights. There is no danger that, where a group of people if not spontaneously forming only comes together so as to move off en masse in a 'follow my leader' protest, the person who happens to be at the front at any one time shouting 'turn left' will be liable as an organiser who has failed to give notice. Either it is one customarily or commonly held or—and this would apply on the first occasion—it is not even within section 11 at all. That was certainly Lord Brown's view and, if the matter came fully before the House, could have been the view of Lord Phillips, Lord Rodger and Baroness Hale too. Such a victory though would be short-lived. Even if a group such as Critical Mass is not required to give advance notice under section 11, it is almost certain that having met up (and become subject to section 14 of the POA 1986, which we shall address shortly) and moved off, they become subject to the power to impose conditions under section 12. The group would still constitute a public procession. Nothing in the judgment requires any different reading of section 12, which is framed very differently.[75] A reading of the speeches shows that Lord Phillips and Lord Carswell questioned whether Critical Mass constituted a public procession at all for the purposes of section 12—a very different question to whether the rides were subject to the notification process—but were prepared to accept that it did.[76] To decide they were not—should that question come before the courts—would mean an overturning of *Flockhart* and *Kent*, that we looked at at the start of the chapter. It cannot be that Critical Mass is not a procession simply because it featured bikes not pedestrians: both are active movements of people travelling on the highway along a route—albeit not a pre-ordained one—from A to B (unless it is crucial for a procession that as it travels it—not just the leader—knows its end point?) in some sort of order sharing a common objective, though that is by no means implicit in the term. Is it though implicit in the ordinary term 'procession' that there is an organiser? That seems to be the nub and the sticking point.

In Article 11 terms, is there an argument that section 11 imposes a disproportionate burden on protesters? Is the possibility of bringing criminal charges (rather than requiring notice) only against the organisers and not the participants a proportionate interference? Is it rationally connected to threat of disorder and to protect the rights of others where the risk of disorder comes from the procession, not the (absence) of notice from the organisers. Of course, notice allows the police to take measures but, as Lord Rodger pointed out, not all mass movements of people require advance notice and some that do not are more than capable of causing a disturbance to everyday life. We should note that in *Ziliberberg* the applicant was charged with 'active participation' in an unauthorised march. We can now see more clearly, in Convention terms, the failings of the reverse scenario posited by Leveson LJ in the Court of Appeal. There is clearly a social need to require organisers of one-off marches to give notice. Organisers of existing and regular (paraphrasing commonly or customarily-held) processions do not need to give notice because the police know of their existence and make provision. Processions that fall into that category but which change

---

[75] The issue of the route only appears as one circumstance to be considered before conditions can be imposed and, in any event, even an impromptu procession has a route—it is just one not agreed in advance.

[76] *Kay* [2008] UKHL 69 at [12] and at [58]. Lord Carswell abided by the acceptance by counsel for the cyclists that they were covered by s 11(1). Lord Rodger speaks of the questionable assumption that the ride constitutes a procession for the purposes of s 11 (at [34]), as does Baroness Hale at [47]. Lord Brown (at [68]) was prepared to accept the rides could properly be described as processions, without any mention of s 11 or s 12.

route (regularly or one-off does not matter) will already have had a policing decision taken about aspects such as officers to be deployed, back-up, prevention strategies. The possibility of responding properly and effectively to this change seems to be realistic; the only issue is whether the social need that requires such organisers to notify the police on each occasion is one that outweighs their individual rights to protest. That seems unlikely.

Last, in the High Court Sedley LJ made it clear that it was erroneous to talk of unlawful marches or protests or assemblies.[77] All that is created by sections 11–13 are criminal offences for *individuals* who breach certain aspects of the control regime for public processions. If everyone in the whole procession is acting unlawfully (perhaps willfully and without lawful excuse obstructing the highway) there are distinct powers to deal with that but these do not kick in merely because the organisers didn't give notice. As we shall see in chapter seven, this notion took a body blow in the House of Lords in *Austin*.[78]

C. Regulating Public Processions and Assemblies under Sections 12–14A of the POA 1986

(i) Public Processions

Public processions are regulated under section 12 and section 13 of the 1986 Act. Conditions may be imposed on public processions under section 12.

Having regard to the time or place at which and the circumstances in which any public procession is being held or is intended to be held and to its route or proposed route, if the senior officer reasonably believes that

(a) it may result in serious public disorder, serious damage to property or serious disruption to the life of community, or
(b) the purpose of [the organisers] is the intimidation of others with a view to compelling them not to do an act they have a right to do, or to do an act they have a right not to do,

then she may give directions imposing on the organiser or those taking part 'such conditions as appear to [her] necessary to prevent such disorder, damage, disruption or intimidation'. This may include (but is not limited to) conditions relating to the route or that prevent it from entering any specified public place. It could thus include directions as to numbers and duration, as well as start and end time. It could include conditions regulating noise levels, use of loudspeakers, what is chanted, what is worn and even carried, as Bonner and Stone note, extending to requiring that the names and addresses of all participants be provided, that every one visibly wear a name label and that no one wear disguise—provided each could be said to be necessary (or as we shall see, now proportionate) to the preventive task.[79] Although generally the senior officer would be the chief officer of police—who must give directions in writing—where persons are assembling with a view to taking part, then it is the most senior officer present at the scene (however junior and inexperienced she may be) who may impose conditions provided they also have the reasonable belief.[80]

---

[77] It was in response to the argument that Critical Mass could not rely on its own unlawful origins to give it a common or customary character.
[78] *Austin v Commissioner of Police for the Metropolis* [2009] UKHL 5. See also n 115 below.
[79] Bonner and Stone, above n 17, at 221.
[80] Section 12(2).

Under section 13 chief officers of police shall—that is, they must—apply to their local council for an order banning all public processions or class of public processions for up to three months if the trigger in section 13 is met. This is a reasonable belief that because of particular circumstances existing in any district or part thereof, the imposition of conditions under section 12 will be insufficient to prevent the holding of a public procession from resulting in serious public disorder.[81] The Home Secretary's consent is needed before any council ban, with or without modification, comes into effect. In London, the power to prohibit is vested directly in the Commissioner, rather than (say) the Mayor or London Assembly, but again with ministerial consent. Within London, this is a discretionary 'may' rather than a duty 'shall' as it is elsewhere in section 13 for anywhere outside the capital. Across England and Wales, in the period 2004–08, only eight public processions were banned (and in the same period there were 13 bans on assemblies under section 14A, which provisions we will consider below).[82]

So as to give teeth to these powers, several offences are created in sections 12–13. Those organisers and participants (and those who incite participation) who knowingly fail to comply with a condition imposed under section 12 or those who organise and participate in a public procession (and those who incite participation) knowing that it is banned under section 13 will be committing an offence. Those charged with knowingly failing to comply with a condition have a defence if they can prove that the failure to comply arose as a result of circumstances beyond their control.

These new sections contain several extensions to their precursors in the POA 1936. There, the power to impose conditions was reposed only in chief officers of police and then only in respect of serious public disorder. Despite general acceptance that the power had not been called upon very much by the police in the intervening 50 years (who had largely preferred to negotiate informal arrangements) as Driscoll comments, the provisions in the 1986 Act still enlarge the powers of the police to impose conditions on marchers.[83] Effectively because of its wording the 1936 Act permitted bans on processions only in boroughs and urban districts, not those in rural locations. That too, unsurprisingly, has been altered. Lastly, under the 1936 Act it was not an offence merely to participate in a procession known to be banned, only to organise it.

(ii) Public Assemblies[84]

Public assemblies in public places (defined as for processions) are regulated under section 14 and section 14A of the 1986 Act. There has been considerable change in this area in the

---

[81] Though in all likelihood it would encompass it, the Government rejected the proposal by the TUC, the (then) CRE and the Board of Deputies of British Jews for a power to ban marches on the ground they would incite racial hatred: Hansard, HC Deb 16 May 1985, vol 79 col 508 (Gerald Kaufman MP).

[82] Personal communication from Jonathan Batt, Public Order Section, Home Office, 21 October 2008: technically the data is for the period 2004 until October 2008 and covers only bans, all of which must pass over the Home Secretary's desk. This updates and corroborates Waddington's assertion that it is rare for the police to make use of the powers to ban or to impose conditions on marches at least: PAJ Waddington, *Liberty and Order: Public Order Policing in a Capital City* (London, University College London Press, 1994) 37–8. As Bonner and Stone suggest (above n 17, 227) a statutory requirement to record and report conditions imposed on marches and assemblies would improve transparency and accountability.

[83] White Paper, above n 4, para 4.19 and J Driscoll, 'Protest and Public Order: The Public Order Act 1986' [1987] *Journal of Social Welfare Law* 280, 285.

[84] The term 'assembly' is not wrapped up in protest and political participation (cf s 11(1)) and so s 14 and s 14A are capable of regulating supporters mixing after a game, rush hour commuters on the platform, shoppers queuing at the start of the sales and students gathering around Senate House for degree results.

last 20 years. A public assembly was originally defined, in section 16, as an assembly of 20 or more in a public place which is wholly or partly open to the air.[85] Under the POA 1936 there was no power to impose even conditions on assemblies in advance, only on public processions. The police had to wait and rely on discrete powers at common law such as the wider concept of preventing breach of the peace. The statutory power to impose conditions first came about in section 14 of the 1986 Act but even then there was no statutory power to ban large groups of people peacefully protesting. As the then Home Secretary announced to the House in 1985 on presenting the White Paper, 'the use of open-air assemblies is so fundamental to free speech and the right to protest that we think it would be quite wrong to confer any power to ban them'.[86] That position was altered by section 70 of the Criminal Justice and Public Order Act (CJPOA) 1994, which inserted section 14A of the POA 1986. This put static assemblies and processions on a largely similar footing by creating a power to ban 'trespassory assemblies', comprising 20 or more persons. The most recent change, in 2003, reduced to two the minimum number of participants that were needed to trigger the power to impose conditions on a public assembly; for bans, the number remained at 20.

The four triggers that activate the power to impose conditions on assemblies of two or more under section 14 are the same as under section 12 for processions.[87] Thus, having regard to the time or place at which and the circumstances in which any public assembly is being held or is intended to be held, if the senior officer (either at the scene or the chief officer in relation to an assembly intended to be held) reasonably believes that

(a) it may[88] result in serious public disorder, serious damage to property or serious disruption to the life of community, or
(b) the purpose of [the organisers] is the intimidation of others with a view to compelling them not to do an act they have a right to do, or to do an act they have a right not to do,

then she may give directions imposing on the organiser or those taking part such conditions relating to place, maximum duration or maximum number as appear to her necessary to prevent such disorder, damage, disruption or intimidation. Under section 14—where conditions only are imposed—organisers and participants (plus those who incite them) will commit offences if they knowingly fail to comply with a condition imposed, though it will be a defence to prove[89] that the failure arose from circumstances beyond their control.

For the power to ban under section 14A to become operative it requires the chief officer to have the reasonable belief that

---

[85] 'Partly open to the air' would not encompass a closed building with its doors open but would capture a football stadium: Marston and Tain, above n 34, 159. As they add, it might be important to ascertain the extent of the relevant place: what about an assembly in a marquee sited in a school field: is the 'place' the open air field or the closed marquee? Bonner and Stone, above n 17, 223 have also pointed out some of the problems here. What is the character of assemblies in a semi-enclosed shopping precinct? If there is overspill from an indoor meeting gathering outside to hear the speeches on loudspeaker is there a single assembly taking its character from the indoor assembly or does this single entity take its colour from its outdoor part or are there two severable assemblies?

[86] Above n 4, para 5.4. The police themselves were against a power of advance notice for and power to ban static assemblies: see too Driscoll, above n 83, 288.

[87] The figure was reduced from 20 by the Anti-Social Behaviour Act 2003.

[88] 'May' and so does not mean 'will' or even 'more likely than not': *R (Brehony) v Chief Constable of Greater Manchester* [2005] EWHC 640 at [20] (Bean J).

[89] See *R v Lambert*, above n 21. It must be shown that the conditions were actually communicated to those charged for charges to 'stick': *Brickley and Kitson v Police* (July 1988) *Legal Action* 21, cited in S Bailey, D Harris and S Jones, *Civil Liberties Cases and Materials*, 5th edn (London, Butterworths, 2001) 453.

(a) an assembly of 20 or more persons is intended to be held in the open air on land to which the public has no right of access or only a limited right of access
(b) that assembly is likely to be held without the permission of the occupier or is likely to conduct itself so as to exceed the limits of that permission or of the public's right of access; and
(c) it may result in either serious disruption to the life of the community or in significant damage to land, buildings or monuments of historical, architectural, archaeological or scientific importance.[90]

If so, then she may (not 'shall') apply to the local council for a banning order and the council may, with the consent of the Secretary of State, make an order either in the terms of the application or with such modifications as may be approved by the Secretary of State. Such an order can last for up to four days and span five miles, and prohibits all assemblies (that is, groups of 20 or more) which

- are held on land in the open air,
- to which there is no or only a limited[91] right of public access, and
- which take place without the permission of the occupier or which take place so as to exceed the limits of that permission or of those rights of public access.[92]

As with section 13, the power is buttressed by the creation of new offences: section 14B makes it an offence to organise, participate in (or to incite participation in) an assembly which that organiser, participant or inciter knows is prohibited by a section 14A order. Section 14C makes it an offence for someone to fail to comply with a uniformed officer's direction to stop and not to proceed to an assembly that the officer reasonably believes is likely to be prohibited by a section 14A order, and where the officer reasonably believes that the person is on her way to an assembly to which a section 14A order applies.

(iii) Analysis of the Statutory Regime

(a) The Statutory Triggers

First, let us look a little more closely at the four triggers which permit the police to impose conditions: serious public disorder; serious damage to property; serious disruption to the life of community (the 'effects' triggers); or an intimidatory purpose with a view to compelling others (the 'purpose' trigger). The Act's clear use of 'may result' signifies that the protest in question need not be the source of disruption or disorder.[93] Section 3 of the HRA might assist protesters in arguing that it be limited to those cases where disorder is caused rather than merely follows a procession or assembly.

None of the triggers is defined any further and their ambit is not especially clear or certain. The most contentious is 'serious disruption to the life of the community'. This creates serious concerns in both the context of 'domestic' law and under the case law and principles of the ECHR. We shall consider these below. There are also legitimacy concerns.

---

[90] Given the use of two separate terms 'significant' clearly bears a different—and slightly lesser—meaning than 'serious': the former has connotations of importance and being notable (OED) and the latter meaning 'Weighty, important, grave; (of quantity or degree) considerable, not trifling'.
[91] Section 14A(9) tells us that '"limited," in relation to a right of access by the public to land, means that use of it is restricted to use for a particular purpose (as in the case of a highway or road) or is subject to other restrictions'.
[92] Section 14A(5)–(6).
[93] Driscoll, above n 83, 286. Helen Fenwick makes the same point (above n 15, at 723) but asserts that the counter would be reliance on the common law principle set out in *Beatty v Gillbanks* (1882) 9 QBD 308—but would this not be seen as overruled by the later statutory intervention?

Such a wide term, when it is the trigger for imposing conditions on marches and assemblies by the police, fails to meet at least two of Feldman's four conditions for legitimacy of coerced toleration: overbreadth and lack of proper accountability for decision-making.[94]

We touched on the 'serious disruption to the life of the community' trigger when we looked at protests around Westminster in chapter four. How large is the community—if it is too large, we come dangerously near majoritarianism—who comprises it, and who decides? Is London a community? Is a borough? Is Oxford Street? It also has a rather oppressive 'them and us' flavour that is counter-intuitively at odds with human rights discourse and values. Might it even mean 'those not in the protesting community'—a worrying conclusion, surely? The Act takes us no further on these key issues. To the extent that the 'serious disruption to the life of the community' trigger does not obviously correspond to any of the permitted aims in Article 11(2), that part of the statutory scheme is one that is outwith the ECHR—or at least if the police sought to rely upon it, it would arguably be unlawful in ECHR terms. It may well be saved domestically by section 6(2)(b) of the HRA: the police were acting to give effect to provisions that cannot be read or given effect to in way that is compatible. The trigger closely resembles 'the rights of others' but recent case law (as we saw in chapter three[95]) has stressed the disjuncture of disorder from disruption and inconvenience, the latter two being necessary incidents of any protest that seeks to persuade or prompt reflection on an issue. Otherwise, as Gearty and Ewing state, the law only permits 'demonstrations that are so convenient they become invisible'.[96] The purposive fourth trigger (intimidation)—as Helen Fenwick makes clear—requires a reasonable belief as to both the intimidation and the coercion. One can occur without the other and if it does, the trigger is not made out.[97] As Jim Driscoll sets out, asking the police to evaluate purposes not effects will require the police to make 'essentially political judgements ... that may draw them into further conflict with sections of the community'.[98] Its inclusion—where any large group could be viewed as intimidatory based purely on size alone or, as Bonner and Stone posit, might be 'readily assumed . . . perhaps from the lack of sympathy with the group or its cause'[99]—may well have been as a result of actions during industrial disputes in the early 1980s, such as Wapping and the miners' strike. Such problems would have been better dealt with under bespoke trade union legislation, not in general public order law.[100] We know from *Police v Lorna Reid* that intimidation needs more than merely causing discomfort (on the facts, to those visiting the South African embassy), if for no other reason than that the trigger relating to serious disruption would be otiose.[101] Similarly, it must need more than persuasion, even aggressively: after all that is largely what protests are trying to do. But what about protests with mixed motives or even where, as is likely, some in the group want to intimidate and coerce while others merely to cajole and harass. Is the 'protest' imbued with the purpose of a section—and if so, need that be the majority or is it

---

[94] D Feldman, 'Protest and tolerance: legal values and the control of public-order policing' in R Cohen-Almagor (ed), *Liberal democracy and the limits of tolerance—essays in honor and memory of Yitzhak Rabin* (Ann Arbor MI, University of Michigan Press, 2000) 48 and 53.
[95] Above pp 106–109.
[96] C Gearty and K Ewing, *Freedom Under Thatcher Civil Liberties in Modern Britain* (Oxford, Oxford University Press, 1990) 121
[97] Fenwick, *Civil Liberties*, above n 15, 705.
[98] Driscoll, above n 83, 284.
[99] Bonner and Stone, above n 17, 225.
[100] Sherr, above n 8, 71.
[101] *Police v Lorna Reid* [1987] Crim LR 702.

enough if a 'fair few' have intimidatory intent? Can a march be intimidatory solely, say, as a result of what is worn or even displayed on banners, rather than what is actually said—or preferably—what is done? The section does not limit intimidation to threats to the person and so could conceivably cover threats to property or to business—and would still then be encompassed in Article 11(2) terms as 'protecting the rights of others'.

(iv) Comparing Processions and Assemblies and Comparing Bans and Conditions

Closer analysis of the sections shows that sections 12 and 14 confer a power to impose conditions (on both processions and assemblies)—'may give directions'—whereas for processions (outside London) section 13 imposes a duty—'shall apply'—to apply for a ban. In London, the Commissioner may decide to prohibit a procession. It still remains a power not a duty to seek a trespassory assembly banning order anywhere in the country under section 14A. Equally, the trigger in section 13—for a ban on a public procession—is the reasonable belief only of serious public disorder and not serious damage to property or serious disruption or intimidation. By contrast, as Helen Fenwick points out, the power (in section 14A) to seek a ban for a trespassory assembly is in part based 'not . . . upon the most grave risk [serious public disorder] but the least and most ill-defined, anticipation of serious disruption to the life of the community'.[102]

There is no minimum length of service to qualify as the senior officer at the scene; someone on their first day on the beat could, if they have a reasonable belief, impose conditions on those marching or assembling—though clearly such a scenario is less likely for the former because of the need under section 11 to give advance notice wherever reasonably practicable. The need for an officer to have 'reasonable belief' that the triggers exist must mean the hybrid test in policing cases (from different scenarios) such as *O'Hara* will operate:[103] the officer must herself have the belief that, say, the assembly will take place (the subjective element) and there must exist objective facts that would lead an outside observer to agree that, say, the assembly will result in serious disruption.[104] Similarly, the conditions that can be imposed are those that 'appear necessary' to the officer; mainstream public law principles would construe this as requiring an element of objectivity to the necessity.[105] It is inconceivable that a court would allow an officer successfully to argue 'the conditions seemed necessary to me even if no one else thought so'.[106] The banning power covers all public processions or class—neither the police nor the council can select which ones.[107] A blanket ban can be justified as preventing either the appearance of partiality/political bias (the police's worry) or actual discrimination but does mean that threats of violence or

---

[102] Fenwick, *Civil Liberties*, above n 15, 710.
[103] *O'Hara v Chief Constable of the Royal Ulster Constabulary* [1997] AC 286, as interpreted in *Raissi v Commissioner of Police for the Metropolis* [2008] EWCA Civ 1237.
[104] One way to reduce the chances of a s 14A banning order being made would be to reduce the likelihood of any of the three triggers being made out: if it could be said that there would not be 20 or more who would be meeting (perhaps because there will be several groups of 19). This raises, in a different way, the same issue at the heart of *Broadwith* (below).
[105] *Secretary of State for Education v Tameside Metropolitan Borough Council* [1977] AC 1014.
[106] This is aside from any HRA arguments or the common law principle that statutes affecting common law rights be strictly and narrowly interpreted that we discussed in chapter two: see cases such as *R (Morgan Grenfell) v Inland Revenue Commissioners* [2002] UKHL 21.
[107] The White Paper (above n 4, paras 4.12–4.14) proposed a power to ban a single march so as to prevent all marches being tarnished with the same brush as the banned one. The police—rightly it must be said—feared being asked to make political choices: Driscoll, above n 83, 287.

disorder from counter-protesters might lead to the peaceful march being banned. Although there is no case law, we can probably safely assume that whenever a protester has to 'prove' aspects of their defence, this will be read—under section 3 of the HRA—as one that imposes only an evidential burden, so as to remain—or become—compatible with the burden of proof requirements of Article 6(1).[108]

There are several differences between the regulation of processions on one hand and of assemblies on the other, and also between section 14 and section 14A. The scope of permissible conditions is much wider for processions than for assemblies. The former are limited only by the necessity of preventing (say) serious disorder. The power in section 14 has been interpreted restrictively: it will be ultra vires to seek to impose, using section 14 rather than section 12, conditions dealing with disembarcation and the route to a second demonstration from an assembly at a different place.[109] However, the Divisional Court in that case, *Jones*, did decide it would be lawful using section 14 to establish entry and exit points to an assembly provided these were contained within the designated assembly area. The extent of the power in section 14 is limited to being able to impose conditions that relate to place, maximum duration and maximum number of participants, a clear contrast with section 12. Whether it is a drafting error or deliberate choice, as a matter of technical interpretation section 14 contains no power to impose conditions as to the time or the date of an assembly, only its maximum duration.[110] On the face of the section, all an officer can require is that an assembly (say) 'last no longer than three hours' but without indicating which three hours. In part this may reflect the reality that, absent a power to require advance notice as there is for public processions in section 11, the police may well not know of a public assembly until it starts to form.[111] Being able to impose a condition—short of a ban—that an assembly meets tomorrow for two hours rather than today would be useful; it might provide a more proportionate alternative (assuming the police do have some advance warning) to seeking a ban under section 14A. On the other hand if such a power were 'read in', a group that had been directed to meet tomorrow not today could challenge that use of power as being ultra vires. There is after all the potential for criminal liability for knowing breach of conditions: would a court take a restrictive interpretation or presume that Parliament must have intended officers to be able to prescribe times as well as duration? This leads back to the principle of doubtful penalty, which we looked at in the context of Brian Haw's case in chapter four.

The difference in the extent of lawful conditions between section 12 and section 14 can be seen in this hypothetical scenario. A group marches to venue A so as to hold a sit-down protest.[112] If the senior officer at the scene reasonably believes that the procession may result, say, in serious disruption to the life of community, then she could require any of the

---

[108] See again *Lambert* and *Keogh*, above n 21.
[109] *Director of Public Prosecutions v Jones* [2002] EWHC 110. In any event, following *Director of Public Prosecutions v Hutchinson* [1990] 2 All ER 836 the High Court also held that as a matter of law it was possible to sever unlawful conditions from lawful ones (under both s 12 and s 14) so as to disregard the former. On the facts, textual and substantive severability was possible leaving the protester liable to the remaining lawful ones about the assembly which she had failed to obey.
[110] This may be a 'non-point': no argument was raised in *Jones*, above n 109, where a start time of 07:00 and end of 19:00 was listed as a condition.
[111] Waddington asserts this might also explain why so few bans on processions are sought: from the police point of view, it might be better to allow a march than for it to be banned and for the police then to confront a disorganised, disorderly ad hoc assembly: Waddington, above n 82, 60–61.
[112] Of course, if the group meets (say, at the railway station) before it marches that will also constitute a public assembly and possibly be subjected to ss 14/14A.

marchers to remove provocative clothing, forbid them from holding certain threatening placards or to refrain from certain offensive chants, if it appears necessary to prevent that serious disruption. Once the group stops and becomes an assembly, she could only direct that it meets at another venue for a shorter period with fewer people. That more limited power, as David Bonner and Richard Stone noted a good few years before the advent of the formal power to ban trespassory assemblies, could though be used effectively by the police to impose a practical ban.[113] The power to demonstrate for one hour no nearer than a mile from an animal experimentation breeding farm with a limit of one person will tend to render any right to protest of very limited real value. If the police use of section 14 to impose conditions results in what is in reality a ban—in effect subverting section 14A—this would (again) be an ultra vires decision.[114] The potential for this arises where the trigger conditions of section 14A do not apply—perhaps (as we shall see) because the assembly is not trespassory or because it numbers fewer than 20.

In *Austin*, at first instance, Tugendhat J reached some very surprising conclusions about the reach and scope of section 12 and section 14.[115] This included being able to rely on section 12 and section 14 even if officers did not have them in mind or purport to be exercising their powers under them; that section 12 includes a power to bring a procession to an end if it has started, even though it does not empower a ban; that section 14 includes a power to direct an assembly to disperse along a particular route and to detain those assembled in a particular place so long as necessary to effect that dispersal;[116] and that such conditions can be imposed as a result of the acts of disruptive others. The appeal was disposed of on other grounds so it was not necessary for the Court of Appeal to resolve these. That is regrettable as authoritative rejection of all these holdings is needed lest they resurface.[117]

Where conditions are imposed under section 14 (or, it is submitted, under section 12) in advance then the police are under a duty to identify which limb—the effects or the purposes (ie intimidation) and if the former, which one(s) of the three triggers.[118] An officer must then indicate the reasons for forming the belief, not in great detail but they must be

> sufficient to enable the demonstrators to understand why directions are being given, and to enable a court (if the matter goes to court) to assess, once the judge is presented with evidence as to the facts, whether the belief was reasonable or not.[119]

Under the normal principles of review of police discretion,[120] any conditions must be sufficiently clear so as to avoid being struck down for vagueness, and must evince an intention

---

[113] Bonner and Stone, above n 17, 222.
[114] D Feldman, *Civil Liberties and Human Rights in England and Wales*, 2nd edn (Oxford, Oxford University Press, 2002) 1063.
[115] *Austin v Commissioner of Police for the Metropolis* [2005] EWHC 480.
[116] Though compare *Jones*, above n 109.
[117] *Austin* [2007] EWCA 989 at [76] provides a useful summary of the lower court's holdings on these points and [80] and [83] provides a measure of rejection and doubt.
[118] *Brehony*, above n 88, at [18], reflecting cases such as *Ivanov v Bulgaria* (App 46336/99) ECtHR judgment 24 November 2005. There the finding of a violation of Art 11 was based on the fact that relevant and sufficient reasons had not been given to justify the ban on grounds of public order. Similarly, in *Stankov and Ilinden v Bulgaria* (Apps 29221/95 and 29225/95) ECtHR judgment 2 October 2001 the violation was founded partly on the fact that the ban of all pro-Macedonian meetings in an area of Bulgaria on grounds of national security and territorial integrity was held to be a violation as the reasons were not supported by evidence. *Stankov* was followed in *UMO Ilinden and Ivanov v Bulgaria* (App 44079/98) ECtHR judgment 20 October 2005 after Bulgaria continued the ban for a further five-year period.
[119] *Brehony*, above n 88, *ibid*.
[120] On which see *Holgate-Mohammed v Duke* [1984] AC 437.

to use the power for a purpose that is both capable of being achieved and one that is intra vires, not a disguised ultra vires purpose.[121]

One major difference between the banning provisions in section 13 and section 14A is the fact that the latter are dependent on trespass, an excess of permission. It therefore provides another example of the close link between public and private, in the field of protest, as well as the criminalisation of what were hitherto only civil wrongs, two of our themes in this book. We shall look at this in a little more detail shortly when we consider the case of *DPP v Jones*. It is not accurate, as Helen Fenwick asserts, that 'the power [in section 14A] is only to ban assemblies taking place on private land'.[122] Though it must be the case that it will largely—perhaps almost exclusively?—apply only to private land, nothing in section 14A so limits it. The triggers are, first, that I have no right or only limited rights of access and secondly, that I exceed the (limited) rights of access or permission to be there. Public land is not the same as open access land—I do not have at all times and in all situations a right to enter and remain on publicly-owned/held land and there are clearly occasions when I might exceed even the wide implied rights of access or permission to be there. A public library, while costing me nothing to enter—and not all public land is (for example, a council owned recreation centre)—will expressly or by implication attach conditions to my entry, such as silence and not eating. If I breach these, it must be the case that I become a trespasser on public land.

A major difference between section 14 and section 14A on the other hand is the minimum number of participants that will trigger the power. Since 2003, only two have been needed for the police to impose conditions on a 'public assembly'. The power to ban by contrast under section 14A depends on there being an 'assembly'. This is still defined in section 14A(9) as comprising 20 or more. The distinction between the two is likely to cause considerable confusion and difficulty in terms of practical policing and practical advice to protesting groups. Not only that, but how can two groups of 19 (each of which is thus outside section 14A) be distinguished from a single group of 38? There has surprisingly been no case law on this despite it seeming to be a sensible protest group tactic.[123]

(a) *Broadwith v DPP*

We may derive some assistance from the Divisional Court decision in *Broadwith v DPP*.[124] B, who wanted to protest about the breeding of cats for scientific research, was arrested and charged with taking part in an assembly and failing to comply with a condition contrary to section 14(5). The Chief Constable's written notice of conditions under section 14 permitted a group to assemble at point X but envisaged that some of them might wish to march to point Y, a little distance away, so permitted a further assembly there between 1:30 and

---

[121] Marston and Tain (above n 34, 161) discuss the conditions imposed in *Baillie v DPP*. A condition that the event must be licensed does not relate to the place—in the sense of location—but relates more to the use to which the place is put and thus 'is an attempt to enforce a different Act'. Conditions that related to place, number and duration but made each subject to advance police agreement were both vague and amounted, they say, to a condition to seek advance notice, something not required of organisers under s 14.

[122] Fenwick, *Civil Liberties*, above n 15, 710.

[123] We might recall how a key factor in holding the application in *Pendragon v UK* (App 31416/96) EComHR 19 October 1998 to be inadmissible was the fact that the (then) provisions did not affect groups of less than 20.

[124] *Broadwith v Director of Public Prosecutions* CO/4073/99, reported and noted [2000] Crim LR 924 DC. There is a Strasbourg case—*McBride v United Kingdom* (App 27786/95) ECtHR inadmissibility decision 5 July 2001—with very similar facts (a lone protester making their way from a protest site to another) but as the issue there related to arrest for breach of the peace, we cannot really derive anything useful from it.

4:00 pm only. B attempted to enter area Y at about 1:00 pm. He refused a direction to leave and to join the other protesters at point X and was arrested. One limb of his defence was this.[125] Section 14 is not directed at individuals but—at the time—at groups of 20 or more. B was not only not participating in a public assembly but was walking away from one; he was not in a group of 20 or more.

On that point, Rose LJ (with Alliott J agreeing) decided that B was taking part in a public assembly. It was inaccurate to describe B as not being part of an assembly simply because he was walking away from the other larger group: he had come with others by bus to Witney intending to demonstrate, had only a few minutes earlier been chatting to them, before covering his face and deliberately seeking to enter area Y and was doing so prior to the time when an assembly at Y was, in accordance with the notice, permitted. Secondly, as Rose LJ noted, although section 14 is aimed at groups, a group can only consist of individuals. It may be necessary according to the particular circumstances, in order to ensure that an assembly proceeds on permitted lines, to take steps in relation to controlling the movements of particular individuals. Were that not so, as the Chief Constable argued, demonstrators would be able to leave the main body of an assembly, without the police being able to control, for example, the route by which they chose to leave. Such an argument is to a large degree disingenuous: the width of the common law power to take action to prevent breaches of the peace would allow the police to regulate truly disturbing departures from the group, rather than those that merely didn't follow a pre-determined policing exit strategy. B's argument would also have obviated the value of imposing any conditions (or even one must assume a ban) since individual demonstrators would be able to circumvent any restrictions on the basis that they only applied to group of 20 or more. As the commentator in the *Criminal Law Review* put it, this aspect of the decision is to be welcomed. It must be a question of fact for the magistrates whether or not someone is a party to an assembly.

That said, and practical policing aside, the position is not as simple: the result was that B was considered to be part of a group of 20 or more some distance away. In reality there was no assembly of 20 or more at point Y at the relevant time—there was only B and a large group about 100 yards from him. Can it really be said that if I were to sit down at one end of a football pitch I would be in a 'group' with my friends at the other end? Here, on the facts—and they are important—the matter is simplified: B split away but was 'clearly' still at one with them despite the distance. What, though, if individuals turned up separately (perhaps having pre-arranged it) and sought to enter point Y? This is the point on which Rose LJ was mistaken. There would no power to prevent a group of 10 or so from doing exactly that—B's mistake was in ever going near to his protesting friends in the first place. This is the 'problem' of the arbitrariness of the 20 figure, clear as that is, now 'rectified' by the reduction to two. In that sense, the decision is now largely academic in relation to conditions. As soon as protester No 1 is joined by protester No 2, each is subject to any section 14 conditions either imposed in advance or on the spot.

---

[125] The other went to the lack of clarity in the Chief Constable's notice. This permitted a 'further assembly' at point Y. It was contended by B that this could only apply to those who had also first assembled at point X. That is, the same group was permitted to hold—but also restrained from any deviation in holding—two consecutive assemblies at two different points but anyone not a member of both was not so restrained. Since B was present at only the second assembly, a fact conceded, the conditions did not apply to him. As this was a penal statute, any lack of clarity, ambiguity or width should be resolved in his favour. The Court found against B on this point: the notice signed by the Chief Constable was totally clear in relation to the prohibition upon the presence of an assembly at point Y prior to 1:30 pm. The notice prohibited any subsequent and second assembly of twenty or more irrespective of membership until that time.

One wider HRA issue remains more for section 14A bans. The lack of clarity in how a collection of possibly disparate individuals comes to be seen as a group leads to concerns with the prescribed by law test. Someone such as B should, before they are arrested, have been able to predict that the law would apply to them. That is they should know with sufficient clarity that they would be considered part of a group of 20 (even two) or more. How can anyone know for sure if they are subject to the constraints of section 14 and section 14A if the test is so fact-specific? Marston and Tain highlight the anomaly:

> [I]n *Broadwith*, a person sought to walk down a proscribed road on his own and this was an offence whereas [as we shall see] in *Jones*, a group of over twenty was permitted to use a restricted route so long as their activity was reasonable.[126]

(v) The Extent of the Banning Power under Section 14A

One other important issue surrounds the drafting of section 14A for trespassory assemblies. This is the seeming disjuncture between the power to obtain a ban—in section 14A(1)—and the extent of the prohibition contained in section 14A(5). The result is that assemblies—of 20 or more—might be banned that do not in fact create serious (or any) disruption to the life of the community or significant (or any) damage to historical etc. buildings. Let us see why this might be.

The power to ban in section 14A(1) depends on the reasonable belief that each of the three triggers exist at some point *in advance*. These are (a) an assembly of 20 or more persons is intended to be held in the open air on land to which the public has no right of access or only a limited right of access; (b) that assembly is likely to be held without the permission of the occupier or is likely to conduct itself so as to exceed the limits of that permission or of the public's right of access; and (c) it may result in either serious disruption to the life of the community or in significant damage to land, buildings or monuments of historical, architectural, archaeological or scientific importance. No trespassory assembly, within the meaning of that phrase, need actually ever be held to trigger the power to ban. It may be that no more than five people ever do meet, for example. However, once a ban is in place section 14A(5) prohibits only those assemblies—that is groups of 20 or more—that meet on land in the open air to which the public has no right of access or only a limited right of access *and* which take place in the prohibited circumstances, that is to say, without the permission of the occupier of the land or so as to exceed the limits of any permission of his or the limits of the public's right of access.[127] The third trigger for obtaining a ban (serious disruption or significant damage) is omitted from the scope of the prohibition. In other words, a ban can be granted on reasonable belief that a specific protest meeting may create serious disruption but the ban will prohibit all protest meetings that number more than 20 and which trespass on land in the open air whether or not they do cause serious disruption or significant damage or threaten it. This is so even if the first meeting, the targeted meeting, is cancelled or their existence or the threat they posed was beyond the contemplation of the

---

[126] Marston and Tain, above n 34, 162.
[127] To that extent Lord Irvine must be wrong (*DPP v Jones and Lloyd* [1999] 2 AC 240, 252) when he states that an order of that kind may be obtained only in respect of land 'to which the public has no right of access or only a limited right of access'. In fact s 14A(5) tells us that an order only operates to *prohibit* an assembly on such land, a subtly different point. It is possible for an order to be made that covers more land than that (ie land to which there is in fact unlimited right of access) provided (s 14A(1)) the chief officer reasonably believes there is no right of access or only a limited right.

Chief Constable at the time she sought the ban. Its organisers and participants would face prosecution under section 14B.

Was this a drafting fault? Both the other triggers in section 14A(1) are referred to in section 14A(5) but serious disruption/significant damage is not. It might be argued that its omission reflects the exigencies of practical policing: it is simple enough to count numbers to see if a banning order applies to a group that is in the process of assembling and also to determine whether or not the land is in the open air—but is it any easier for an officer to assess whether that group is engaged in trespass (ie is on land without permission or is acting in excess of any permission) than it is to assess whether serious disruption is going to be caused? It might in fact be easier to assess the latter—if in a field miles from anywhere with no obvious historical, architectural, archaeological or scientific importance—than to assess whether a group has been given permission to be there by a farmer but has exceeded the area he allocated to them or the time he said they could stay. The point is that there is no obvious reason for exempting from extant banning orders those groups of up to 19, or those groups which meet inside, or those groups which have permission to be where they are, without also exempting those groups whose presence will clearly cause no harm.

Even statutory wording as clear as section 14A(5) is ripe for a fairly radical reading under section 3 of the HRA on that basis, should anyone involved in such an assembly be prosecuted. One alternative would simply—but drastically—be to add a new subsection (c) to section 14A(5) so that it reads

> and which does result in either serious disruption to the life of the community, or where the land, or a building or monument on it, is of historical, architectural, archaeological or scientific importance, in significant damage to the land, building or monument.

The other would be to consider that protests which do not cause serious disruption or significant damage to buildings, land or monuments are not, as a matter of law, ones that exceed the limited rights of public access: that is they are not trespassory assemblies and so cannot be ones that are prohibited. If that were so, the offences in section 14B and section 14C would not apply: a protester cannot 'know' an assembly is prohibited if, in fact, it is not.

The reasoning, in Article 11 terms, would be that it was disproportionate to punish those who organise or participate in protest assemblies merely on the basis of size and an excess of permission without there also being some tangible damage or social cost attributed to the protest. Any other reading makes too large an inroad into the right of peaceful protest by unduly restricting the rights of like-minded citizens to assemble. This would be in line with the thrust of more recent cases such as *Balçik*[128] and *Oya Ataman*,[129] which as we saw in relation to section 11, stress the need for tolerance of peaceful mass protests where people commit no 'reprehensible acts' (*Ezelin v France*).[130] Even aside from a transformative section 3 reading, based on section 14A(1) and its trigger conditions it seems clear that the legislative aim was only to capture (that is to ban) those who organise and take part in protests numbering 20 or more and that assemble on land in the open air either without permission or that

---

[128] *Balçik v Turkey* (App 0025/02) ECtHR judgment 29 November 2007.
[129] *Oya Ataman* (App 74552/01) ECtHR judgment 5 December 2006.
[130] We must assume this means violent and non-peaceful rather than it being reprehensible merely to break the law ie not to provide the required notice. Such an approach would add nothing further. While it is not clear from her text if Helen Fenwick (*Civil Liberties*, above n 15, 725) takes the contrary view, this would also lead to a self-serving justification: it would allow states to require notice and for any protester who did not do so, to mean they were unable to rely on their peaceful protest as a defence to a charge because of their unlawful or criminal 'reprehensible' behaviour in not doing so.

exceed that permission, and where it is likely that one of two listed consequences—serious disruption to the life of the community or significant damage to historically, architecturally, archaeologically or scientifically important land, buildings or monuments—will transpire. To hold otherwise flies in the face of what we might presume was Parliament's intention.

(a) *DPP v Jones and Lloyd*

Some of the arguments rehearsed above are echoed in the leading case on trespassory assembly *DPP v Jones and Lloyd*.[131] This is still one of the few House of Lords decisions on protest generally. The scope of the offences created in section 14B and section 14C came under the spotlight and, since they are parasitic upon a meeting being a 'trespassory assembly' and thus being prohibited, the scope of the power to regulate peaceful protest by categorising it as a trespassory assembly did so too.[132]

1. Background Jones and Lloyd were arrested on the grass verge abutting one of the three main roads that creates a triangle around the historic site at Stonehenge. They were part of a larger group that was protesting peacefully and non-obstructively about the fact that Stonehenge had effectively been out of bounds during the Summer solstice.[133] An inspector concluded the group constituted a trespassory assembly and warned that they were stationed within an area covered by the order and that if they continued, they were liable to arrest for taking part in a trespassory assembly knowing it to be prohibited, contrary to section 14B(2). Most of the group dispersed; Jones and Lloyd remained and were arrested. They appealed against their convictions before the magistrates to the Crown Court. They succeeded largely on the basis that they were not 'being destructive, violent, disorderly, threatening a breach of the peace or, on the evidence, doing anything other than reasonably using the highway'. The Divisional Court, on an appeal by way of case stated, reinstated the convictions and so they appealed directly to the Lords. The issue for the House (and for the Divisional Court below) was the definition and scope of the *trespassory* element of the crime: if a group of 20 or more engages in a peaceful non-obstructive protest, does that remain within—or does it exceed—the public's limited right of access to and over the highway?

By a majority the House (Lord Irvine, Lord Hutton and Lord Clyde; Lord Slynn and Lord Hope dissenting) held that the common law had developed to a stage where it could be said that as well as the primary right of access, that of passing and re-passing—as well as matters obviously incidental to it—there was a right to reasonable user of the public highway.[134]

---

[131] *DPP v Jones and Lloyd* [1999] 2 AC 240. Commentary on the case is considerable and various: see especially G Phillipson and H Fenwick, 'Public protest, the Human Rights Act and judicial responses to political expression' [2000] *PL* 627. It is subjected to considerable criticism by Fenwick, *Civil Liberties* above n 15, 711–20 and almost wholesale endorsement by G Clayton, 'Reclaiming public ground: the right to peaceful assembly' (2000) 63 *Modern Law Review* 252. See also N Taylor and B Fitzpatrick, 'Freedom of assembly' (1999) 4 *Journal of Civil Liberties* 253 and their consideration of the Divisional Court decision: 'Trespassers might be prosecuted: the European Convention and restrictions on the right to assemble' [1999] *European Human Rights Law Review* 292.

[132] It should be noted that the offence in s 14C, where someone fails to comply with a direction not to proceed, is more likely made out: it requires only an officer reasonably believing that someone is on their way to an assembly to which a s 14A order applies—so they might not in fact be doing so—and reasonably believing that the the assembly is likely to be one that is prohibited by that order—and again, it may on the facts not be.

[133] So as to protect the ancient druid site, for two years' running a s 14A ban had been obtained, covering the few days either side of the June summer solstice with its centre at the site.

[134] At common law a highway comprises any land (and so includes roads, carriageways, bridleways and footpaths) to which the public have access and over which there is a public right of way. There was some discussion in the case about the qualifying word 'public' before highway in the certified question. It was agreed that it was otiose. By definition highways are public in terms of dedication and use if not in terms of ownership of the land from or

This would include a limited right to use it for the purposes of peaceful, non-violent and non-obstructive protest. Such a protest by a group of 20 or more would not exceed the limited rights of public access to the highway (see section 14A(5)) and so could not constitute a trespassory assembly. This in turn meant that someone being in or at such a meeting could not be taking part in a trespassory assembly knowing it to be banned. Broadly the dissenting minority followed the line adopted by the Divisional Court (McCowan LJ and Collins J): at common law, an assembly on the highway, however peaceable, per se exceeds the limits of public rights of access. These are limited to passing and re-passing and matters obviously incidental or ancillary thereto (such as stopping to tie a shoelace or asking directions). Anything more was an excess of the right for which use of the highway was dedicated. Peaceful protest was neither incidental nor ancillary.

2. The reasoning in *Jones and Lloyd* More detailed analysis of their Lordships' reasoning as well as the outcome will allow us to assess whether domestic law properly and fully accords with the right to peaceful protest under Article 11.[135] The case is as much about its limitations as about its seeming extent. As Fenwick adverts, even the majority view does not establish a clear-cut right of peaceful protest on the public highway, nor more generally on public land, let alone anywhere else. In that she must be right—or more right than those who laud the decision as ushering in a 'broad common law right'[136] or as an 'endorsement of the right to peaceful protest on the highway'.[137] For all five Law Lords, the 'right' was limited by the fact that no use of the highway would be lawful if it impeded the primary right to pass/re-pass: any obstruction or non-peaceful use would be incompatible with that primary right, as would any other 'unreasonable use'. Despite the judgment largely being framed in the language of rights, what the House confirmed was, in Fenwick's eyes, more akin to a classic English liberty of peaceful assembly—there was only a 'right' to use the highway, even for peaceful protest, in a way that is reasonable (or, as she stresses, since it was at the heart of even the majority decision, in a way the tribunal of fact considers reasonable) and certainly no duty on others to respect, promote, guarantee.[138] Even the majority gave presumptive pre-eminence to the 'right' to use the highway (a right if it exists at all is one purely of common law derivation) rather than construing peaceful protest as the Dworkinian trump, rarely to be defeated. It is clear that all five (obviously the minority) considered that it would be open to magistrates in future to hold that even a peaceful demonstration exceeded the boundaries of reasonable user, if by dint of duration or weight of numbers or other circumstances the assembly became (unduly?) obstructive.[139] Given

---

over which they are carved. The finding in the case is equally applicable to highways over land where the subsoil land is vested in the hands of private landowners as it is to highways over land where the subsoil is vested in public authorities.

[135] Although the case was decided by the House after the HRA came into force, this was the only one to do so: the Divisional Court decision was in 1997. The House of Lords decision was reached on the basis of the old common law position, that of very limited ECHR influence. Had prosecutions been brought after 2000, the reasoning would have been rather different in that it would at least have had to acknowledge the public authority status of the police and prosecuting authorities under s 6 of the HRA.

[136] E Barendt, 'Freedom of assembly' in J Beatson and Y Cripps (eds), *Freedom of Expression and Freedom of Information* (Oxford, Oxford University Press, 2000) 3.

[137] Clayton, above n 131, 252.

[138] Fenwick, *Civil Liberties*, above n 15, 713.

[139] As Fenwick (*ibid*, 717) notes the House here was not even seeking to protect property owners from actual physical detriment to the value or use of their land a factor which at least it could be argued underpinned the two nineteenth-century cases on which the whole House relied (see below).

196 *Peaceful Persuasion and Communicating Dissent*

this seeming congruity, what differences were there between the majority and minority views?

1. The two groups took a very different view of the scope of the historic cases concerning trespass on the highway and perhaps on the extent to which 'older' cases need a measure of modern re-evaluation.
2. The minority conceptualised the case entirely differently from the majority. Lord Slynn and Lord Hope saw it as primarily (perhaps exclusively) concerned with private rights of property and of an individual's rights over and in relation to land. Lord Irvine, Lord Hutton and Lord Clyde to a very limited—but significant—degree saw the case as more about the public sphere, human rights and individual/state interaction.
3. The extent to which landowners, especially private landowners whose land was subjected to a public right of way (or highway), would be able to prevent long-term squatting and peace camps.
4. The relevance of the offence of wilful obstruction of the highway without lawful excuse, contrary to section 137 of the Highways Act 1980, and the need for symmetry between these two areas.

We will look at the speeches structured around those four points before turning to consider the decision in terms of Convention compatibility.[140]

(i) All five revisited the two nineteenth-century cases that established the extent of the public's common law right to use the highway, on which the Divisional Court based its decision, *Harrison v Duke of Rutland*[141] and *Hickman v Maisey*.[142] The division between the majority and the minority on this decided the outcome. Lord Irvine, Lord Hutton and Lord Clyde took the view that these cases establish a wider proposition than merely that the public have the right to pass and re-pass. Instead they are, in Lord Irvine's words,

> authority for the proposition that the public have the right to use the public highway for such reasonable and usual activities as are consistent with the general public's primary right to use the highway for purposes of passage and repassage.[143]

Limiting the primary right only to cover that which is incidental or ancillary 'would be to place an unrealistic and unwarranted restriction on commonplace day-to-day activities' as there was in truth very little that could be so described. The 'rigid approach' (of the minority)

> would have some surprising consequences. It would entail that two friends who meet in the street and stop to talk are committing a trespass; so too a group of children playing on the pavement outside their homes; so too charity workers collecting donations; or political activists handing out leaflets; and so too a group of members of the Salvation Army singing hymns and addressing those who gather to listen.[144]

---

[140] Clearly the speeches of the minority cannot be in that they upheld the convictions of the pair. Both judges seemed clearly (and mistakenly) to view the fact that peaceful protests were largely tolerated as on a footing with a legally enforceable right. Secondly, if they were wrong on that, each considered that English law complied with Art 11 since that article was subject to qualification in Art 11(2) even though at no time did they assess the proportionality of the absolute rule they were proposing be maintained, a rule which favours the rights of landowners absolutely to exclude over the rights of people peacefully to protest.
[141] *Harrison v Duke of Rutland* [1893] 1 QB 142 (CA).
[142] *Hickman v Maisey* [1900] 1 QB 752 (CA).
[143] *Jones*, above n 131, at 255. See also Lord Clyde at 279–88 and Lord Hutton at 287, 291–2.
[144] *Jones*, above n 131, at 254 (Lord Irvine).

In contrast, Lord Slynn and Lord Hope took a much narrower, more static approach to those same cases: Lord Hope interpreted the words of Lord Esher MR in *Harrison*—that the rights included 'any reasonable or usual mode of using the highway as a highway'—as not being intended to include acts done by people who were not in the ordinary sense of the term passing and re-passing along the highway:

> the principle . . . is that the highway is for passage, and such other uses as may be made of it as of right must be capable of being recognised as a reasonable and usual mode of using the highway as such.[145]

The argument, he decided, that in the late twentieth century the law should be developed so that assemblies that were not obstructive and otherwise lawful were deemed reasonable and usual uses of the highway was not reconcilable with either law or principle.[146]

(ii) The case was decided wholly without reference to the ECHR but had resort been needed, their Lordships thought it would have led to the same result. As Lord Irvine said, English law would not 'comply with the Convention unless its starting-point is that assembly on the highway will not necessarily be unlawful . . . [M]ere toleration does not secure a fundamental right'.[147] We shall see presently whether this is an accurate distillation.

Lord Hutton was the only member of the five to give any real prominence to a discussion of the case from a rights perspective. It was one of three factors behind his conclusion that in certain circumstances rights over the highway might encompass the right to hold a peaceful assembly—though even then he shrouded the 'right' in caveats: it must not cause an obstruction to anyone using the highway and must otherwise be a reasonable user.[148] The common law recognised a right for members of the public to assemble together to express views on matters of public concern as one of the fundamental rights of citizens in a democracy. Further, the common law should now recognise that the right will be unduly restricted unless it can be exercised in some circumstances on the public highway.[149]

Lord Clyde also accepted that there was a public right of assembly but one hedged with restrictions and limitations at both common law and in Article 11(2). He was certainly not prepared to affirm as a matter of generality that there was a right of assembly at any place on a highway at any time, even under the more qualified position that using the highway for that purpose was only lawful if reasonable, peaceful and non-obstructive. That opened 'a door of uncertain dimensions into an ill-defined area of uses which might erode the basic predominance of the essential use of a highway as a highway'.[150]

Lord Irvine dwelt much less on this angle. Both he and Lord Clyde, although they may have framed parts of their speeches in the language of rights, analysed the case largely from a common law perspective and based their decision on the development of those common law cases on trespass. Neither considered the functional role of peaceful assembly even in the limited way that Lord Hutton did. There is, in their speeches (as in the speeches of Lord Hope and Lord Slynn), no appreciation of the fact that contextuality is all,[151] no recognition

---

[145] Lord Hope at 274 and see Lord Slynn at 261–4.
[146] Lord Hope at 274.
[147] *ibid*, 259.
[148] *ibid*, 287; the other two were his re-evaluation of the nineteenth-century cases and the need for symmetry between trespassory assembly and obstruction of the highway.
[149] *ibid*, 287–8. In reaching this conclusion he drew on the well known dicta by Lord Denning MR in *Hubbard v Pitt* [1976] QB 142, 178 and Otton J in *Hirst and Agu v Chief Constable of West Yorkshire* (1987) 85 Cr App R 143, 151, that we considered in our introduction.
[150] *Jones*, above n 131, 281.
[151] *R (Daly) v Secretary of State for the Home Department* [2001] UKHL 26 at [28] (Lord Steyn).

that neither nineteenth-century case featured a protest but instead was concerned with protecting a landowner's commercial or social interests,[152] and no understanding that property rights too do not operate *in vacuo*.[153] As Helen Fenwick points out, 'it appeared to make no difference whether a group of people were meeting to engage in political protest or to look at an interesting shop window'.[154] In Lord Irvine's mind, the public highway was a public place

> which the public may enjoy for any reasonable purpose, provided the activity in question does not amount to a public or private nuisance and does not obstruct the highway by unreasonably impeding the primary right of the public to pass and repass: within these qualifications there is a public right of peaceful assembly on the highway.[155]

Similarly, both Lord Hope and Lord Slynn considered there was no need to resort to the ECHR: in domestic law section 14A was not ambiguous and neither was the common law of trespass uncertain.[156] Lord Hope accepted that it was arguable that a restriction on assembly even on the highway may interfere with the right of assembly in some situations, but was not satisfied that there was such a violation here either by the law relating to access to the highway as it stands, or in its application to the facts of this case. The Convention did not require an

> attempt to reform the private law relating to trespass on which section 14A relies in order to mitigate the effects of its application to trespassory assemblies which are held in breach of an order obtained under that section.[157]

(iii) The minority was very concerned about what Lord Hope called 'a fundamental rearrangement of the respective rights of the public and of those of public and private landowners'.[158] Lord Slynn thought that acceding to the defendants' argument would involve giving to members of the public the right to wander over or to stay on land for such a period and in such numbers as they choose so long as they were peaceable, not obstructive, and not committing a nuisance. As Lord Hope put it,

> [i]t is not difficult to see that to admit a right in the public in whatever numbers to remain indefinitely in one place on a highway for the purpose of exercising the freedom of the right to assemble could give rise to substantial problems for landowners in their attempts to deal with the activities of demonstrators, squatters and other uninvited visitors. It would amount to a considerable extension of the rights of the public as against those of both public and private landowners which would be difficult for the courts to control by reference to any relevant principle... The proposition that the public are entitled to do anything on the highway which amounts in itself to a reasonable user may seem

---

[152] *Hickman* is clearly about preventing damage to the owner's horseracing business and *Harrison* about preventing interference with the owner's pastime of shooting grouse. A close reading of the latter shows that the trespasser was not a direct action protester concerned with animal welfare but had a an ongoing 'annoyance' with the Duke: *Harrison*, above n 141, 150.

[153] On this last point see the short discussion and material referred to in Fenwick, *Civil Liberties*, above n 15, 718.

[154] Fenwick, *Civil Liberties*, above n 15, 714.

[155] *Jones*, above n 131, 257.

[156] *ibid*, 265 and 277 respectively.

[157] *ibid*, 278. This must be wrong. At Strasbourg level, if a state chooses to frame its law so that it results in a violation of the right, it does not matter that the interference with a right stems from the application of the criminal law, the civil law or from an interdependent fusion of the two. He did make a valid point that giving the public greater rights over land including private land was being discussed in a case to which no landowner was party and so unable to defend their interests, the more so given their rights to peaceful enjoyment of possessions under the First Protocol.

[158] *ibid*, 276.

at first sight to be an attractive one. But it seems to me to be tantamount to saying that members of the public are entitled to assemble, occupy and remain anywhere upon a highway in whatever numbers as long as they wish for any reasonable purpose so long as they do not obstruct it.[159]

By failing to locate their reasoning in a wider functionalist perspective about the role and value of free speech and peaceful assembly, the minority crucially misconceptualised the case. In effect, they equated what the appellants were doing with 'squatting, putting up a tent, selling or buying food or drinks'.[160] It was true that the appellants' case made the purpose of the non-passing use of land immaterial but there is nothing in the views of Lord Irvine, Lord Hutton or Lord Clyde that would make it lawful to remain on land in such circumstances, limited as the right was by the requirement of reasonableness in terms of numbers, duration and place. Unreasonable use that was obstructive of the primary right would still not be permitted.

Lord Hope's and Lord Slynn's concerns are easily allayed. Lord Irvine rejected the idea that his 'broader modern' test materially realigned the interests of the public and landowners. The law of trespass would continue to protect those private landowners who owned the subsoil against unreasonably large, unreasonably prolonged or unreasonably obstructive assemblies upon highways—and of course would continue to protect private landowners absolutely if the protest strayed or started on private land, not on the highway. The new test would not afford carte blanche to squatters or other uninvited visitors whose activities would almost certainly be unreasonable or obstructive or both. As the reasonableness of the user and its being consistent with the primary right to pass and re-pass took into account size, duration and the nature of the highway on which it took place, the test of reasonableness would be strictly applied by magistrates where narrow highways (such as footpaths or bridle-paths) went across private land where even a small gathering would be likely to create an obstruction or a nuisance.[161] For Lord Clyde the test of fact, circumstance and degree required a careful assessment of the nature and extent of the activity in question. If the purpose of the activity became the predominant purpose of the occupation of the highway, or if the occupation became more than reasonably transient in terms of either time or space, then it might come to exceed the right to use the highway.[162]

(iv) Lord Irvine and Lord Hutton were also influenced by the desirability of promoting the 'harmonious development' of the criminal law: as a result of their ruling, the offences under sections 14A–14C would be broadly aligned with the offences of wilful obstruction of the highway without lawful excuse contrary to section 137 of the Highways Act 1980.[163] The minority didn't see the two systems as analogous and starkly rejected any need for symmetry: the approach of and language chosen by Parliament, that is its link to private law concepts of title, made the lack of symmetry inevitable. In any event, the private law and

[159] ibid, 276.
[160] ibid, 264 (Lord Slynn).
[161] ibid, 257. To stipulate in the abstract any maximum size or duration for a lawful assembly would be an unwarranted restriction on the right defined. There was no principled basis for limiting the scope of the right by reference to the subjective intentions—premeditated or spontaneous—of the persons assembling: what matters is its objective nature. Similarly, there was no basis for distinguishing highways on publicly owned land and privately owned land. The nature of the public's right of use of the highway could not depend upon whether the owner of the subsoil is a private landowner or a public authority although if the owner is a council or highway authority, Arts 10 and 11 will impose greater burdens on them directly.
[162] Although he agreed that the Crown Court reached the correct conclusion, Lord Clyde was troubled that the evident determination by the two defendants to remain where they were seemed to make it look as if they were intending to go beyond their right and to stay longer than would constitute a reasonable period.
[163] Jones, above n 131, 258–9 and 287–91 respectively. We looked at s 137 in chapter four above.

public law were concerned with different spheres of interaction and depended upon entirely different concepts.[164] Again, we see the nature—and effect—of the misconceptualisation of the case.

3. Analysis of *Jones and Lloyd* from an ECHR perspective In Convention terms, clearly the outcome is welcome—even if the House of Lords did not in reality recognise a right to peaceful assembly as a positive right rather than residual Diceyan liberty. The result accords with what surely would have occurred at Strasbourg.

It is hard not to compare the couple in *Jones* with the successful three applicants in *Steel and Others v UK* (decided just six months previously) albeit the arrests there were for breach of the peace.[165] The arrests of Jones and Lloyd were clearly a restriction on the right of peaceful protest but prescribed by the law contained in sections 14A–14C. Although the UK would have been able to make a case that the measures (both the section 14A order and the subsequent arrest for disobeying it) were aimed at preventing disorder and protecting the rights of other highway users (and owners of the subsoil), it is very likely that the ECtHR would have considered this was a disproportionate restriction. The words of the Court in *Steel* seem equally applicable here:

> [T]he Court sees no reason to regard [the protest by the 3rd to 5th applicants] as other than entirely peaceful. It does not find any indication that they significantly obstructed or attempted to obstruct those attending the conference, or took any other action likely to provoke these others to violence. Indeed, it would not appear that there was anything in their behaviour which could have justified the police in fearing that a breach of the peace was likely to be caused.[166]

That being so—although it would have to be noted in the absence of a domestic court decision on the matter—the European Court held that there was a violation of Article 10 (and of Article 5(1)) because the measure was not necessary.[167]

What do we learn about the state of the law from the reasoning of the House of Lords? From a purely domestic point of view we might note two matters. First, if it confers a right to assemble at all, the decision does so only in a limited way and in relation only to the highway. Secondly, *Jones* changes the shape of the administrative, regulatory power in section 14A.

Let us develop that first point. It does not establish such a right over any other public land, that is land owned by the state—such as a council playing-field, school hall, police station or NHS car park—or dedicated to some other public use, though its rationale might appear to support such an extension as would section 6 of the HRA. If we equate public ownership with ownership by a section 6 public authority, then councils, schools, the police and NHS trusts are not only under a duty not to restrict access disproportionately but might even be under a positive duty to facilitate peaceful protest in some way. We considered this in some detail in chapter three. However, if Jones and Lloyd had been seeking to exercise their rights over private land, the inevitable finding of trespass in domestic law would clearly have been supported at Strasbourg, as it was in *Appleby v UK*.[168] If either the (topsoil) land on which the protest was taking place was owned privately or the land surrounding the highway had been privately owned, and the group had spilled one inch from the highway, each of those acts would have

---

[164] *ibid*, 265 (Lord Slynn) and 277 (Lord Hope). Fenwick makes a compelling case that the outcome preferred by the minority would have meant the inevitable overruling of *Hirst*—a matter that neither Lord Hope nor Lord Slynn addressed, adverted to or even realised: Fenwick, *Civil Liberties*, above n 15, 716.
[165] *Steel and Others v United Kingdom* (1998) 20 EHRR 603.
[166] *ibid*, at [64].
[167] *ibid*, at [110]–[111] (and [64]–[65]).
[168] *Appleby v United Kingdom* (2003) 37 EHRR 38.

been an actionable trespass. It would, in section 14A(5) terms, have meant that the assembly was taking place on land to which the public had no right of access and was taking place without permission or so as to exceed any permission. Unless, in the second situation, the Strasbourg court was prepared to base a decision on the transient, perhaps unintended nature of the trespassory incursion, it would in all likelihood have followed *Appleby*.

Turning to the second point, we can see how obtaining a section 14A banning order was simpler pre-*Jones*. Any assembly of 20 or more on the highway necessarily exceeded the public's right of access, thereby satisfying the limb in section 14A(1)(a). Now an officer must reasonably believe that the assembly is likely to conduct itself so as unreasonably to obstruct the highway bearing in mind all the circumstances alluded to above such as time, size, duration. That must be a much harder matter to show and so greatly reduces the chances of obtaining a section 14A order without which no prosecutions under section 14B or section 14C can even be started.[169]

More importantly, can we conclude that the House of Lords has brought home the right of peaceful protest? Even the speeches by those in the majority do not suggest, let alone provide wholesale support for, a particularly extensive right of assembly. The decision is still primarily located in the realm of land law, property ownership and associated rights. The presumptive right is still that of passage and the right to protest peacefully is still subject to the activities not being an unreasonable and obstructive intrusion into that. The law of trespass 'will continue to protect private landowners [of the subsoil] against unreasonably large, unreasonably prolonged or unreasonably obstructive assemblies upon these highways'.[170] If, on a narrow footpath 'the right to use the highway would be highly unlikely to extend to a right to remain, since that would almost inevitably be inconsistent with the public's primary right to pass and repass',[171] the difficulty in ECHR terms is this. No article in the Convention confers on the public a right to use the highway for passing and re-passing.[172] It is at best a social *interest* and thus a legitimate aim under Article 11(2), which can only trump the primary right—the right of peaceful assembly under Article 11(1)—if it is necessary and proportionate to do so.[173] Despite attempting to realign the law, Lord Irvine merely indicates how far English law had to go: 'our law will not comply with the Convention unless its starting-point is that assembly on the highway will not necessarily be unlawful'. That is not, with respect, how Strasbourg would approach the question, improvement as it is on the previous position.

The starting point, the working presumption, must be that peaceful assembly on the highway will always be lawful unless shown not to be by reason of a necessary and proportionate restriction to achieve one of the legitimate aims in Article 11(2). Although Lord Clyde did not incline to the view that a peaceful non-obstructive assembly would necessarily exceed the

---

[169] In light of the Lords' judgment in 1999, the local police for the Stonehenge area decided not to pursue an application and have not done so since.
[170] *Jones*, above n 131, 258.
[171] ibid, 256 (Lord Irvine).
[172] Unless it were claimed that the right to liberty of movement contained in Article 2, Fourth Protocol included a positive right to move by whatever means and to whatever destination one chose. In any event, the UK is not a party to the Fourth Protocol and so that argument could not be run under the HRA or at Strasbourg should any cases be brought against the UK.
[173] Ironically, Lord Hope (at 278) might more accurately sum up the position when he adds to the mix the property rights of the owners of the subsoil; at least they do have separate extant rights that clash with the right to assemble. However, as those owners have already lost the right absolutely to control access to their (subsoil) land when the (topsoil) land was dedicated as or made into a public highway, any claim that the assembly interferes with their title and rights of ownership must pail somewhat.

public's right of access to the highway, in that it could (but would not always) constitute a reasonable user and thus not a trespass, he was not prepared 'to affirm as a matter of generality that there is a right of assembly at any place on a highway at any time'. In any event he was not persuaded that the present case had to be decided by reference to public rights of assembly.[174] If he is saying there is no right—that is such activities do not engage Article 11—rather than that such claims will always defeat the public interest, his stance is fundamentally out of line with Strasbourg's approach generally to the qualified rights in Articles 8–11. One way to produce greater comity with the ECtHR would be for courts, as section 6 public authorities bound horizontally by the HRA, to interpret and develop the common law so that the 'reasonable' user test is taken to connote 'proportionality'. That would allow the right of peaceful protest under Article 11 to be balanced against the interests of others in using land as a highway.

The majority view in particular is open to criticism in terms of the Strasbourg foreseeability test. The advantage of the approach preferred by Lord Slynn and Lord Hope is simplicity and clarity: there is no right in any circumstance to protest or to assemble on the public highway. In trying to accommodate the historic concerns of English private land law with a new rights-based approach, has the position been made less certain and less predictable? Lord Clyde was keen to emphasise that this was a decision on its facts. The new expanded 'right' is predicated on assemblies being reasonable and non-obstructive, issues left to the primary determiners of fact—magistrates in the main—to decide, bearing in mind matters such as the space occupied or duration. If, as Lord Clyde indicated, a reasonable user can become an unreasonable user over time—perhaps because of how long the group remains or because its size increases—then how, and on what basis, is a protester to predict in advance the point that their assembly will become an unlawful one, by virtue of it becoming a trespass?[175] We reach an age-old dilemma: the Lords' judgment could have been framed with precision, as section 14 is, to give numbers of those permitted assemble. That would certainly have reduced the chances of a successful challenge based on the 'prescribed by law' limb of Article 11(2) but would have rendered it more susceptible to challenge on grounds disproportionality; blanket rules tend to. Why would it be as necessary to restrict to, say, 10 the number who could assemble in Trafalgar Square as it is on a footpath in the country? Taking the route of flexibility, as the House of Lords has done, leaves open a domestic challenge under the HRA for someone arrested for knowingly taking part in a trespassory assembly, on the basis that they had no idea that 15 people on the pavement in a High Street for half an hour at Saturday lunchtime would be seen to be an unreasonable and obstructive use.[176] Either prosecutions on individual facts will still need to be brought to establish parameters or the law needs to be applied judiciously and cautiously by officers on the street in their discretion if the 'right' established by *Jones* is to be secured.

At Strasbourg, as we have seen, very few applications relating to demonstrations have been upheld on the ground that the restriction was not prescribed by law. In *Mkrtchyan v*

---

[174] *Jones*, above n 131, 281.
[175] *ibid*, 281: 'The test [of whether the right of access has been exceeded] then is not one which can be defined in general terms but has to depend upon the circumstances as a matter of degree. It requires a careful assessment of the nature and extent of the activity in question. If the purpose of the activity becomes the predominant purpose of the occupation of the highway, or if the occupation becomes more than reasonably transitional in terms of either time or space, then it may come to exceed the right to use the highway'.
[176] Of course, if such a view were taken by Strasbourg or even domestically under the HRA, swathes of criminal law would be incompatible—the reasonableness of force in self-defence, the reasonableness aspect in recklessness—and so it is unimaginable a court finding for the appellants on this basis.

Armenia[177] the law was imprecisely formulated. In *Stefanec v The Czech Republic*[178] the interpretation of domestic law that had been undertaken so enlarged the scope of a criminal statute as to make it impossible to foresee its applicability to the applicant's situation. However, in *Rai, Allmond and Negotiate Now! v UK* we can witness the latitude allowed the UK. As we saw in chapter three, this featured a challenge to a decision not to permit any meetings or demonstrations in Trafalgar Square that related to Northern Ireland.[179] Regulations made in 1952 provided that permission was required, inter alia, to organise, conduct or take part in any assembly, parade or procession or to make or give a public speech or address in Trafalgar Square.[180] The refusal of permission to the applicants was in accordance with government policy on the exercise and structuring of permission under the 1952 regulations, a policy announced to the House of Commons in a Ministerial statement in 1972. The European Commission affirmed a position it had previously adopted that

> a law which confers a discretion is not in itself inconsistent with the requirement of foreseeability inherent in this concept, provided that the scope of the discretion and the manner of its exercise are indicated with sufficient clarity to give the individual protection against arbitrary interference.

On the facts, the Commission concluded that although the power to regulate the Square was not subject to defined restrictions, the policy was formally and publicly announced and there had been numerous refusals subsequently. The fact that exceptions were made for rallies that were 'entirely uncontroversial and non-partisan' was not problematic either, despite the fact that it must be difficult for anyone to know in advance if a rally is going to be uncontroversial. The Commission iterated that in its view the 'scope and manner of the exercise of the power to regulate assemblies in Trafalgar Square [were] indicated with the requisite degree of certainty to satisfy the minimum requirements of the criterion of "prescribed by law"'.

(vi) The Effect of the Human Rights Act on Sections 12–14A

The HRA expands in substantial terms the basis on which conditions or bans on either marches or assemblies can be challenged, even if it does not necessarily enhance the likelihood of success, that being largely a function of Strasbourg case law on peaceful protest. The first is the greater opportunities, in terms of modalities, it affords protesters who wish to challenge decisions. The second goes to the substance of the various triggers.

(a) Bans and Conditions Must Now be Proportionate

Anyone upon whose planned march or assembly restrictions have been imposed may use the sword and shield of section 7(1) to argue a breach of Convention rights.

Section 7(1)(a) allows a protester pro-actively to mount a challenge on Convention grounds by seeking judicial review of the police's or the council's decision to to impose a ban or conditions, hoping to have them declared unlawful. There would clearly be no issue over the public authority status of the decision-maker, whether police officer, council or Home Secretary giving consent: each would be a quintessential core public authority, exercising a core governmental function, bound by the section 6 duty imposed on all

---

[177] *Mkrtchyan v Armenia* (App 6562/03) ECtHR judgment 11 January 2007.
[178] *Stefanec v The Czech Republic* (App 75615/01) ECtHR judgment 18 July 2006.
[179] *Rai, Allmond and Negotiate Now! v UK* (App 25522/94) EComHR inadmissibility decision 6 April 1995.
[180] These were made pursuant to primary legislation in 1926, which empowered the making of such regulations as is considered 'necessary for securing the proper management of [any] park and the preservation of order and prevention of abuses therein'.

public authorities. Section 7(1)(b) allows protesters to wait until they are prosecuted for (for example) knowingly being in breach of a condition and then to rely on its illegality, in Convention terms, collaterally in those legal proceedings as a defence to the charge. In both cases the protesters would clearly be victims.

Irrespective of the statutory wording, all restrictions on marches or on assemblies—as a ban or conditions clearly are—will require justification in Article 11(2) terms by whichever body has imposed them or agreed to them. In effect, the move from a residual, liberty-based system to one based on positive rights brings a shift in the burden of proof. States bodies— what we now call public authorities—must now explain why it was necessary to restrict the right to peaceful protest in these circumstances on this occasion, and must provide an objective basis for doing so. There must be a rational connection between the ends and the means, the means chosen must be the least restrictive necessary and must in any event be balanced.[181] Failing that, the decision will be unlawful. We know from *Gough* that decision-makers must tailor their responses to individuals and to individual circumstances.[182] The mechanistic application of conditions may also render a decision unlawful in Article 11 terms for being disproportionate: ie the reasons given for taking the measure would not be seen as relevant or sufficient.[183] The domestication of the right of peaceful protest involves the courts adopting a proportionality test to gauge the necessity and thus the lawfulness of any ban or condition. This is not something required by the terms of the POA 1986 itself: as we have seen, none of the sections has a 'pressing social need' test as one of its triggers.[184] If the triggers are reasonably believed to exist, officers may impose conditions as appear necessary to prevent disorder, damage, disruption or intimidation. At common law, this was not especially onerous; it did not mean for example 'the least necessary' or 'only those conditions that properly balance the rights of protesters against the interests of others in order'. The change effected by the HRA is that necessity must be read as proportionate. We can see the difference in approaches—if not in result—by comparing *Kent v Commissioner of Police for the Metropolis*[185] with *R (Brehony) v Chief Constable of Greater Manchester*.[186]

In *Kent*, as we saw earlier, the Court of Appeal rejected the claim that a ban on all processions within Greater London (save for religious and May Day festivals) in response to disorders and riots in Brixton was unlawful, even though its unforeseen consequence meant a CND march could not be held. The decision is one marked for the considerable discretion and deference allowed to the police. The standard test was that of *Wednesbury* review—flagrant irrationality or illegality—and the statutory power was so widely drawn as to exclude

---

[181] *R (Huang) v Secretary of State for the Home Department* [2007] UKHL 11. Might protesters subjected to a blanket ban be able to claim it discriminates not—clearly—between different view points (since all are treated equally) but between protesters and others groups with the potential for disturbance and disruption and disorder? If protesters could show that large groups of football fans were never banned from marching from the train station through a city centre on Saturday afternoons in the run up to Christmas—or even teenage drinkers were never banned from mingling outside the town's pubs the same night (assuming they both constitute a trespassory assembly)—then there is at least the start of a complaint. Clearly, it will be resolved by the court's decision on a choice of comparator: would it be all other protest groups (all banned) or all larger groups in the town centre on a Saturday? On this see the discussion in *Rai*, above n 179. Waddington notes how one reason behind the rare use of the banning power by the Met was their concern that they would be asked to explain how the London Marathon takes place every year without the need for such heavy-handed regulation: Waddington, above n 82, 59.

[182] *Gough v Chief Constable of Derbyshire* [2002] EWCA Civ 351 at [68].

[183] *Patyi v Hungary* (App 5529/05) ECtHR 7 October 2008.

[184] Technically, the proportionality test should be applied to the Art 11(2) legitimate aims—so far as they exist on the facts –not to or not solely to the triggers in ss 12–14A.

[185] Above n 8.

[186] *R (Brehony) v Chief Constable of Greater Manchester* [2005] EWHC 640.

any challenge premised on the fact that the Commissioner had not directed his mind when he imposed such a wide ban; it was not for the court to re-assess the Commissioner's view of likely risk. It was for the applicant to show there were no reasonable grounds on which the Commissioner could have come to the view he did on the likelihood of the CND march causing serious disorder.

By contrast, in *Brehony*, every Saturday for four years a group (Victory to the Intifada) had been protesting outside Marks and Spencer about the company's links to and (the group maintained) implicit support for Israel. The shop was in a pedestrianised area in the city centre. The group urged a public boycott of the shop and hoped to do so by handing out literature, having a petition to sign alongside banners and placards. From the summer of 2004, a pro-Israel group had started a counter-demonstration. In the run-up to Christmas 2004 the Chief Constable wrote to Mr Brehony, representing the group, and informed him of his decision, taken under section 14, to impose conditions on the protest. The police viewed this as necessary to prevent serious disruption or serious disorder and did take account of the need to ensure that a balance was struck between the rights and freedom of the protesters and those living and working close by. For a six-week period, the protest was to be limited to 20, could only take place for three hours from midday and was no longer to be located outside the shop. Instead it was to take place about half a mile away from the city centre in an area that was well-frequented. The police considered that the conditions still provided the group with the right to demonstrate peacefully and facilitated the right of freedom of speech under Article 10. It was over this that the group was in dispute with the police. In their view it was disproportionate: it was clear that the new venue significantly reduced the impact of a demonstration in close proximity to the Marks & Spencer in the city centre.

Bean J held that this decision was neither irrational at common law (even bearing in mind the heightened human rights context) nor was it disproportionate under the HRA. Key factors were: the conditions were for a limited period; they covered both the group and the counter-demonstrators; and they did not prevent the group from putting its message over, albeit not in the location or to the audience that it had previously chosen. The conditions were therefore those that intruded and interfered the least while seeking to achieve the legitimate aim of preventing disorder on the busiest shopping days of the year.[187] The court did not really engage in a consideration of lesser alternatives or, as would seem to be required by Article 11, impose any real burden on the police to displace the presumption that the right should continue to be enjoyed and to show good reason why it should not.[188]

(b) Utilising Section 3 of the Human Rights Act

Section 3 of the HRA requires courts to read sections 11–14A 'so far as possible' in a manner that renders them Convention compatible within the parameters set in cases such as

---

[187] There was some argument about what seems to have been a one-off animal rights demonstration outside another city centre shop about the same time. This, comprising about five people, was allowed to go on. Bean J did not consider that the fact that this demonstration was permitted invalidated or rendered disproportionate the decision in respect of *Brehony*. 'On the contrary, it demonstrates that the police were looking at proposed demonstrations on their facts. It is not clear whether the animal rights demonstration was notified to the police in advance; but even if it was, a demonstration consisting of five people is much smaller than the demonstrations that were organised by the claimant's group. There does not appear to have been a counter-demonstration, and the 11 December episode appears to have been a one-off occasion' (at [24]). Whether this would remain so in the light of *Ollinger v Austria* (2008) 48 EHRR 38 seems moot, as we shall see below.

[188] We considered earlier that aspect of the judgment relating to the giving of reasons for the decision and for the choice of trigger.

Ghaidan and *Re S*.[189] We have just seen how this will effectively mean that 'necessary' as the qualifier for the trigger conditions in section 12 and section 14 be read as 'necessary and proportionate'. It would also mean that even a general ban on marches should still be worded as narrowly as possible—in time and place—so as to capture the targeted procession and as few others collaterally as possible. Similarly, as Helen Fenwick suggests, the power to ban all marches could be interpreted as a power

> to ban all marches espousing a particular message ... Alternatively, the words 'or any class of public procession' ... could be utilised to afford leeway to include potentially disruptive marches (using 'disruptiveness' as the method of defining their membership of a class) and therefore to exclude marches expected to be peaceful.[190]

Might a court—so as to protect peaceful protest—read 'life of the community' as being a community in which peaceful protest is not seen as anti-social but as intrinsically good and pathologically healthy and thus part of the community not divorced from or antithetical to it? Its very public utility and value is what bestows on peaceful protest its communal spirit. To take up on another point we encountered earlier, might the word 'result' be given a causative link not just one that is temporal or incidental? This would limit the triggers to cover only those protesters who are the source of serious disruption or serious disorder. That would avoid penalising those who do not themselves act reprehensibly, something emphasised by the ECtHR in *Ezelin*.[191] That leads us to our last point. The extent to which a court must undertake that balancing exercise—and thus the actual effect of the ECHR on sections 11–14A—will be determined by Strasbourg case law.

(vii) ECHR Jurisprudence on Marches and Assemblies

As we saw at the start of chapter three, bans or restrictions on marches, rallies or assemblies historically comprise over half the workload for Strasbourg on the question of peaceful protest. A clear majority of all violation findings also arises from interferences with rallies and assemblies, with very few involving marches. We also know that many cases result in a finding against the applicant because the measure is one deemed necessary in the interests of preventing disorder—and 'serious public disorder' is of course one of the three express triggers in section 12 and in section 14 that permits the police to impose necessary (now proportionate) conditions.

There have been very few cases at Strasbourg against the UK that deal with restrictions on marches or demonstrations; most have been concerned with breach of the peace, in some guise. The only two have been the inadmissibility decisions in *CARAF v UK*[192] and *Rai, Allmond and Negotiate Now! v UK*,[193] both discussed in some detail in chapter three.[194] Very few of all the cases brought involve challenges to restrictions or bans imposed in advance or at the scene. Mostly, they concern claims about the violent police response to a

---

[189] *Mendoza v Ghaidan* [2004] UKHL 30 and *Re S* [2002] UKHL 10.
[190] Fenwick, *Civil Liberties* above n 15, 729–30.
[191] *Ezelin v France* (1991) 14 EHRR 362.
[192] Above n 9.
[193] Above n 179.
[194] Three more cases have been brought against the UK challenging the exercise of the power under ss 14–14A but do not feature peaceful protest: *Chappell v UK* (App 12587/86) EComHR inadmissibility decision 14 July 1987, *Pendragon v UK* (App 31416/96) EComHR inadmissibility decision 19 October 1998 and *Gypsy Council v UK* (App 66336/01) ECtHR inadmissibility decision 14 May 2002. The first two involved challenges to the ban on using Stonehenge at the summer solstice and the third concerned the decision to ban an annual gypsy horse fair.

peaceful assembly;[195] requiring permits or authorisation or notification;[196] or challenges to penalties imposed after participating in a meeting or a march or where other consequences attract as a result of behaviour at a march or assembly.[197] Many have an unknown result, were struck out or were declared inadmissible on procedural grounds, such as failing to exhaust local remedies or the absence of a victim.[198] In some a violation was found because the reasons given were not relevant and sufficient[199] or the law was not sufficiently certain.[200] The only cases that might help shed light would be *CARAF, Rai, Heikkila v Finland*,[201] *Güneri v Turkey*,[202] *Öllinger, Plattform Ärzte für das Leben v Austria*,[203] *Rassemblement Jurassien et Unité Jurasiènne v Switzerland*,[204] *S v Austria*[205] (the prohibition of a demonstration on ground of likely excessive noise), *Stankov v Bulgaria*[206](and its successor *UMO Ilinden v Bulgaria*[207]) and *Patyi v Hungary*.[208]

(a) Limited Protection for the Right

It was true a few years ago that we could identify a radical line of cases and a more conservative, deferential line which did 'exhibit an unwillingness to examine the proportionality of bans to the threatened risk with any rigour'.[209] As Helen Fenwick noted, this second, minimalist line is largely drawn from 'prior restraint' admissibility decisions in cases featuring bans and conditions on assemblies and marches, whereas the first strand—that would 'prohibit the application of criminal sanctions to peaceful protests as a result of blanket bans'—stems from Court decisions in *Steel* and *Ezelin*, less directly on the point. Thus, until recently, it was fairly clear that Strasbourg was not especially sympathetic to those whose march or meeting had been banned or been hedged with conditions. As we shall see—and we saw in chapter three—the past few years has brought a welcome wind of change.

Most of the deferential line of cases were manifestly ill-founded, what Helen Fenwick called (of *CARAF*) 'relatively elderly [admissibility] decisions strongly affected by the

---

[195] This would include cases such as *Oya Ataman v Turkey*, above n 129 (though distinguished on its facts in *Çiloğu v Turkey* (App 73333/01) ECtHR judgment 6 March 2007 where by five votes to two no violation of Art 11 was found), *Balcik v Turkey* above n 128; and *Aldemir v Turkey* (App 32124/02) ECtHR judgment 18 December 2007.
[196] *Andersson v Sweden* (App12781/87) EComHR inadmissibility decision 13 December 1987, *Ziliberberg v Moldova* (App 61821/00) ECtHR inadmissibility decision 24 May 2004, *Bukta v Hungary* (App 25691/04) ECtHR judgment 17 July 2007.
[197] Such as *Ezelin* above n 191, *McBride v UK* (App 27786/95) ECtHR inadmissibility decision 5 July 2001, *Piermont v France* (App 15773–4/89) ECtHR judgment 3 December 1992, *Galstyan v Armenia* (App 26986/03) ECtHR judgment 15 November 2007 and *Salduz v Turkey* (App 36391/02) ECtHR inadmissibility decision 28 March 2006.
[198] See respectively *Guliyev and Ramazanov v Azerbaijan* App 34553/02 EctHR judgment 19 June 2008 and *Direkci v Turkey* (App 47826/99) ECtHR inadmissibility decision 3 October 2006.
[199] In cases such as *Christian Democratic People's Party v Moldova* (App 28793/02) ECtHR judgment 14 February 2006 and *Ivanov v Bulgaria* (App 46336/99) ECtHR judgment 24 November 2005.
[200] See p 86–88 above.
[201] *Heikkila v Finland* (App 25472/94) EComHR inadmissibility decision 15 May 1996.
[202] *Güneri v Turkey* (Apps 42853/98, 43609/98 and 44291/98) ECtHR judgment 12 July 2005.
[203] *Plattform Ärzte für das Leben v Austria* (1991) 13 EHRR 204.
[204] *Rassemblement Jurassien et Unité Jurasiènne v Switzerland* (App 8191/78) EComHR inadmissibility decision 10 October 1979.
[205] *S v Austria* (App 13812/88) EComHR inadmissibility decision 3 December 1990.
[206] *Stankov v Bulgaria* (App 29221/95 and 29225/95) ECtHR judgment 2 October 2001.
[207] *UMO Ilinden v Bulgaria* (App 44079/98) ECtHR judgment 20 October 2005.
[208] *Patyi v Hungary*, above n 183.
[209] Fenwick, *Civil Liberties*, above n 15, 724 et seq.

margin of appreciation doctrine'.²¹⁰ The exception is *Plattform Ärzte* but we can dispose of that speedily: a claim that Austria was in breach of its positive obligation to protect the right of protest is a long way from the sorts of case we are considering here. In *CARAF, Rai, Heikkila, Rassemblement Jurassien* and *S v Austria*, the state was successfully able to argue that its ban or restrictions were necessary in the interest of preventing disorder, at the very least. *CARAF* was factually similar to the domestic case of *Kent* that we considered above: a general ban on marches in London aimed at prohibiting a proposed march by the National Front also meant that CARAF could not stage a counter-march to protest. The ban was made under the equivalent of section 13 (section 3 in the old Public Order Act 1936)—necessary to prevent serious public disorder. The European Commission accepted the UK's argument that the ban served the legitimate aims of preserving public safety, preventing disorder or crime and protecting the rights and freedoms of others and concluded that the restriction was necessary.

> A general ban of demonstrations can only be justified if there is a real danger of their resulting in disorder which cannot be prevented by other less stringent measures. In this connection, the authority must also take into account the effect of a ban on processions which do not by themselves constitute a danger for the public order. Only if the disadvantage of such processions being caught by the ban is clearly outweighed by the security considerations justifying the issue of the ban, and if there is no possibility of avoiding such undesirable side effects of the ban by a narrow circumscription of its scope in terms of territorial application and duration, can the ban be regarded as being necessary ... The situation ... at the relevant time ... was characterised by a tense atmosphere resulting from a series of riots and disturbances, having been occasioned by public processions of the National Front and counter-demonstrations in connection therewith ... Whilst it was clear that the applicant association had wholly peaceful intentions it is nevertheless true that its statutory purposes were expressly directed against the National Front policies and it could therefore not be excluded that the proposed procession could also give rise to disorder ... In these circumstances it was not unreasonable for the competent authorities to prohibit all public processions other than customary ones during the relevant two months.²¹¹

As we have seen, *Rai* featured a challenge to the blanket policy of refusing permission to hold rallies about Northern Ireland in Trafalgar Square unless they were 'entirely uncontroversial'. Again the decision was upheld as proportionate—so as to prevent disorder and protect the rights and freedoms of others—and the application was declared inadmissible as manifestly ill-founded.²¹² This was the case in which, on the question of necessity, the Commission clearly preferred the ex post facto government justification rather than the contemporaneous view of the Metropolitan Police Commissioner: on being informed of the group's intentions, he considered it would create no danger to public order. The applicants had argued that there was no real risk of disorder, that other groups had been granted

---

²¹⁰ ibid, 709.
²¹¹ *CARAF*, above n 9, (1980) 21 DR 138 at 150–1. Factors borne in mind by the Commission were that large-scale deployments had not previously been able to prevent grave damage to persons and property; more National Front marches were imminent; the possibility of circumvention justified a ban across London; and that CARAF was not restricted from marching two days after it had originally planned, once the ban ended, or indeed anywhere outside London at the same time as the ban. A claim under Article 14—that CARAF was being discriminated against by being treated the same as groups that did represent threats to public order—was also rejected as manifestly unfounded. It was accepted by all that CARAF did not advocate violence but the issue, the Commission considered, was the objective likelihood of violence ensuing rather than whether this was a result subjectively intended by the group. It was clear the authorities considered the group as involving a risk of disorder, and they did not thereby deliberately or arbitrarily put it in a category of demonstrations with which it had nothing to do (at 152).
²¹² The case is discussed in some depth in chapter three at pp 101.

permission and there was the possibility of avoiding any trouble by using stewards and co-operating with the police. The Commission concluded that the decision to grant permission to three other groups fell within the UK's margin of appreciation, without saying why, and that for a fourth group trouble had actually occurred, giving sustenance to the government's view. It was furthermore not a blanket prohibition on holding a rally but only on use of a high-profile location.[213] This seems to disregard two factors. First, there are very few similarly situated places in London that would be available, the parks being the only probable ones. Second, the rally could lawfully have taken place spontaneously at a nearby location without—as an assembly—needing permission either then or now (and even processions only need notice rather than permission)[214] yet still have caused disorder that would have been harder to control and manage. Logically, allowing the rally to be held at a venue where permission and thus prior notice was needed would have facilitated more effective policing, but this presumably would have been a matter, in the Commission's view, for the UK's margin of appreciation.[215]

Several other cases indicate a steep hill for protesters whose marches or meetings have had conditions imposed or have been banned. In *Heikkila*, the Commission declared inadmissible applications by a group arrested for obstruction after they refused to obey a police instruction to move on.[216] The group wanted to stage a protest against a motor race and tried to do so outside the town hall where a civic reception was being held. The Commission decided that the claim under Article 10 was manifestly ill-founded; the group had not been prevented from attending an earlier demonstration at another location and the order to cross the street at the town hall was necessary to prevent disorder and in the interest of public safety. In *S v Austria* an 11-hour demonstration (from midday to eleven o'clock at night) planned as a means to protest about repression in Austria was banned![217] The Commission declared the application under Article 11 manifestly ill-founded and so upheld Austria's claim that it was proportionate to ban it in order to prevent disorder and to protect the rights of others. What is of interest is the basis of that view. The ban was put in place on the expectation of excessive noise and the likelihood of seditious slogans being shouted. Recent past history predicted both and the organisers had expressly stated there would be noise but that it would end by 10 o'clock at night, that is after 10 hours. Only the excessive noise aspect was upheld by the Austrian Constitutional Court. The Commission made reference to the margin of appreciation: it was not disproportionate

> to [prevent excessive noise] by the prohibition of the demonstration rather than by its subsequent dissolution. Having regard to the previous experience it was in no way unreasonable or arbitrary

---

[213] We considered this critically *ibid*. It would seem that blanket bans on protest do not per se fall foul of the necessity principle at Strasbourg but there will be close scrutiny of the reasons relied on to justify the interference and the significance of that interference, see *Stankov*, above n 118, at [92]: 'an automatic reliance on the very fact that an organisation has been considered anti-constitutional –and refused registration—cannot suffice to justify under Article 11(2) of the Convention a practice of systematic bans on the holding of peaceful assemblies'.

[214] The only exception in recent times is the need for authorisation for demonstrations in the vicinity of Westminster.

[215] The application under Art 14 was rejected on the basis that Negotiate Now! had not been subjected to any discernible difference in treatment in comparison to other groups also refused access to Trafalgar Square rather than, as was argued, there being discrimination based on whether or not a group voiced views that were contrary to government policy. Again, as with most questions of discrimination, the more pertinent comparator might not have been other groups concerned with Northern Ireland who largely had been banned and those who had been given permission were politically unaffiliated, but with all other political/protest groups many of whom may well have been permitted to meet and to assemble.

[216] Above n 201.

[217] Above n 205.

to assume that the proposed demonstration would also lead to excessive noise. This assumption was supported, in particular, by the text of the applicant's notification to the authority and his subsequent admission that the noise should be loud enough to be heard by an inmate of a prison.

Rassemblement Jurassien is one of the more well-known Article 11 cases. It involved two short-term, temporary bans on all political meetings within a single municipality imposed by the executive council in the Canton of Berne at a time of heightened separatist tension and possible violence.[218] As a result both applicants, pro-Jura separatist organisations, were prevented from organising political meetings on two separate occasions. To that extent it is not dissimilar to *Rai* or *CARAF* whereby one 'innocent' group was prevented from meeting or demonstrating as a by-product of the imposition of restrictions on all groups. The result in *Rassemblement Jurassien* was the same: the application under Article 11 was declared inadmissible. Bearing in mind the state's fairly broad margin of appreciation, the decision to ban all such meetings—for a limited time and in a limited area—was not disproportionate given the foreseeable danger affecting public safety and order and the fact that the decision as to what means were to be employed to prevent it was often taken at short notice at a time of considerable tension. The applicants had argued that the decisions were disproportionate: there had been no consideration of the possibility of intervening against counter-demonstrators so as to prevent at *that* time any serious clashes that might occur rather than by precipitously banning all-comers. The ban was therefore excessive and not tailored towards the least restrictive measure or the 'true' cause of any violence that might have occurred. The Commission disagreed.

(b) A New Expansionism?

On the other hand several judgments by the ECtHR (the majority having come since the turn of the decade) rather than admissibility decisions by the Commission provide support for those wishing to argue that bans or restrictions on marches and meetings violate the right of peaceful protest. We shall consider each—*Öllinger v Austria, Cetinkaya v Turkey, Stankov v Bulgaria, Güneri v Turkey, Makhmaduv v Russia* and *Patyi v Hungary*—in turn.[219]

In *Öllinger*, we might recall, the Court held as unlawful the prohibition of a public meeting designed to clash with, and be a counter-demonstration to, a long-standing SS commemoration ceremony on All Saints' Day in the municipal cemetery in Salzburg. The ban struck the wrong balance; the Austrian authorities had attached too much weight to the rights of other cemetery goers under Article 9 freely to manifest the religion and to commemorate their own deceased relatives and too little to the group's right to protest. We saw in chapter three how the case might take Strasbourg jurisprudence under Articles 10–11 in new directions.[220] Two points here are worth noting. First, the Court was not convinced by Austria's argument that taking preventive measures was not a viable alternative that would have allowed both meetings to take place. Öllinger had argued that if the state had ensured a police presence sufficient to keep the two assemblies apart this would have preserved his own right while simultaneously offering sufficient protection for the rights of the

---

[218] Above n 204.
[219] *Öllinger*, above n 187; *Cetinkaya v Turkey* (App 75569/01) ECtHR judgment 27 June 2006; *Stankov*, above n 118; *Güneri v Turkey* (Apps 42853/98, 43609/98 and 44291/98) ECtHR judgment 12 July 2005; *Makhmaduv v Russia* (App 35082/04) ECtHR judgment 26 July 2007 and *Patyi* above n 183.
[220] Above pp 111–114 and D Mead, 'Strasbourg discovers the right to counter-demonstrate: a note on *Öllinger v Austria*' [2007] EHRLR 133.

cemetery's visitors. In doing so, the Court bucked the trend. Most cases largely abdicate responsibility for assessing this aspect of a claim under the guise of a state's broad margin of appreciation, allowed because of their close contact with events on the ground. It is easy to see how taking a stance of that nature might have led to a different outcome in one of the section 14 cases we considered above, *Brehony*. Why could the police there not have limited the numbers to five or so for both groups, policed it properly or taken action against the one threatening violence or trouble and so allowed both to continue in the same venue? It is true that the venue in *Öllinger* did not feature a city centre at a busy time of year but the events did take place in a cemetery likely on All Saints' Day to be heavily populated. Secondly, it is clear that the decision marks a departure from cases such as *Rai*, *CARAF*, *Rassemblement Jurassien*, *S v Austria* and even *Chorherr v Austria*,[221] in each of which the threat of disorder or violence from third parties had been enough for the court to hold bans on all parties, even innocent non-violent groups, to be lawful.

Although not a ban on a march as such, in *Cetinkaya v Turkey* the Court decided that convicting someone merely for participating in an 'illegal assembly'—not for what they or anyone had said or because of violence but because the state had de facto construed it as unlawful—was a violation of Article 11.[222] C had been present at a press conference—for which under Turkish law no prior authorisation was needed (contrasted with meetings)—at which a statement was read out, condemning the authorities' inertia at pursuing those responsible for a suspected arson attack that killed 39 intellectuals, poets and artists. The police later that day decided the conference constituted an illegal open-air assembly of 800 people. C among others was convicted and fined for his participation in that meeting without any consideration of whether the meeting had remained peaceful. The Court at Strasbourg took the view that the conviction was akin to a general ban on the content of assemblies and meetings save where sanctioned by the state and as such defeated the democratic principles underpinning Articles 10 and 11. Sweeping measures to suppress freedom of assembly and freedom of expression, save where there was incitement to violence or rejection of democratic principles, did a disservice to democracy and often even endangered it.[223]

Cetinkaya reflected in that way the earlier case of *Stankov* (and its successor *UMO-Ilinden*). There a general seven-year ban on meetings by a group (denied authorisation because of its unconstitutional status) to commemorate events of historic importance to Macedonians was held to be a violation. First, automatic reliance on the fact that the group was considered anti-constitutional and so denied registration did not suffice to justify under Article 11(2) a practice of systematic bans on peaceful assemblies.[224] Secondly, in the absence of any evidence indicating that its meetings were likely to become platforms for promoting violence and rejecting democracy or without a real foreseeable risk of violence or incitement, a ban was not justified and the state had overstepped its margin of appreciation.[225]

Güneri continues this line.[226] A regional mayor, inter alia, banned outdoor meetings in a town due to be visited by officials from the Democracy and Peace Party. Account was taken of the tense political and terrorist situation (as also existed in *Rai*, *Rassemblement Jurassien* and *CARAF*, all declared inadmissible) but since advance notice of the contents of any

---

[221] *Rai* above n 179; *CARAF*, above n 9; *Rassemblement* above n 204; *S v Austria*, above n 205; and *Chorherr* (1994) 17 EHRR 358.
[222] *Cetinkaya*, above n 219.
[223] ibid, at [29].
[224] *Stankov*, above n 118, at [92].
[225] ibid, at [103] and [111].
[226] Above n 219.

speech was given to the governor, and permission could be required of potential organisers, the decision was disproportionate for the second reason in *Stankov*.

Part of the reason for the finding of a violation in *Makhmaduv* was a failure to produce any evidence substantiating the claim of a terrorist threat, said to be behind the decision to withdraw permission for an assembly. However, as M's meeting was the only one cancelled and the only one directed at Moscow's policies—whereas public festivities organised by Moscow were not banned despite the supposed threat—this meant the ban on grounds of preventing disorder and crime and protecting the rights of other was arbitrary and not justified. Although under sections 13 and 14A, targeted bans—on the basis of content—are not possible, the case would have relevance in domestic law under section 12 and section 14 where conditions are imposed on one march or assembly but not on another and the reason given can clearly be seen to be undermined by the reality. In *Patyi*, a group no more than 20 strong planned a protest in front of the Prime Minister's house, standing silently in line on a five-metre-wide pavement. The Court decided the prohibition on that protest was disproportionate: there was no evidence of violence and no likely danger to public order. There was not likely to be a significant impeding of traffic or pedestrians. The reasons given were therefore neither relevant nor sufficient.[227]

These cases all indicate a far more favourable stance from Strasbourg with outcomes more disposed to ensuring that peaceful protest—with its democratic rationale and participatory underpinnings—takes place unless to do so would undermine that very same democracy or incite violence.[228] They stress the need for criminal sanctions to be tailored to individual activity and behaviour. They make a strong case for arguing that the offences under sections 12–14C—linked as they are to knowing participation and organisation and not to other culpability—should be narrowly interpreted, so as only to punish those who are not peaceful in both intention and in fact. Helen Fenwick suggests a route by which this might occur;[229] it is the same reading of section 14A(5) as we looked at earlier.[230] She rejects it because it would mean 's.14A effectively ceased to bestow a power to impose blanket bans' but is wrong to do so. The error underpinning her reasoning is to conflate the power to impose a ban (section 14A(1)) with its effects, that is what the ban prohibits (section 14A(5)). It is that second matter that is being revised not the first, leaving the power to seek blanket bans unadulterated.

One simple solution would be to give the 'serious disruption to the life of the community' trigger as narrow a reading as possible, even to the extent of it becoming redundant. For disruption to be so 'serious' as to trigger the power, it would have to exceed the sorts of disruption that occurred in *Aldemir*, *Galstyan* and *Bukta*. In *Aldemir v Turkey* the Court considered that 'any demonstration in a public place may cause a certain level of disruption to ordinary life and may encounter hostility'.[231] In *Galstyan v Armenia* the Court found it 'hard to imagine a huge political demonstration at which people express their opinion not generating a certain amount of noise'.[232] In *Bukta*, there was no evidence to suggest a

---

[227] *Patyi*, above n 183.
[228] It is not all one-way traffic. In *Molnar v Hungary* (App 10346/05) ECtHR judgment 7 October 2008 the Court concluded that peaceful dispersal of a fairly large demonstration (which blocked a central road bridge in Budapest) was lawful. The protest was allowed to continue for several hours and the protesters' complaint—about a disputed election result—did not demand a response whereby no notification was given.
[229] Fenwick, *Civil Liberties*, above n 15, 728.
[230] Above pp 193.
[231] *Aldemir v Turkey* (App 32124/02) ECtHR judgment 18 December 2007 at [42].
[232] *Galstyan v Armenia* (App 26986/03) ECtHR judgment 15 November 2007 at [16].

danger to public order 'beyond the level of the minor disturbance which is inevitably caused by an assembly in a public place' thus bringing into play the need for tolerance towards peaceful non-violent demonstrations.[233] These must cast considerable doubt on a case such as *Brehony*.[234] There 'disorder' or 'the rights of others' (in Article 11(2) terms) was little more than traffic congestion and the inability to get around the shops speedily, compatible as it may have been with earlier cases such as *WG v Austria, GS v Austria* and *G and E v Norway*.[235]

III. Showing Support for Causes and Campaigns

Supporters of particular causes and those seeking particular political outcomes will want to demonstrate, to publicise that support and to convert others. This may of course take place by means of a mass show of support—in a march or at a meeting as we have just seen—but it might also take the form of groups or individuals conveying their protest message by some other communicative activity to those it hopes to persuade or convert.

A. Choice of Clothing

(i) Wearing Political Uniforms in Public Places under Section 1 of the POA 1936

One way that a group—and the individuals within it—may wish to show solidarity with or opposition to a cause is through similar clothing, perhaps highlighting the issue being campaigned about. In most cases, the choice of what to wear is a matter for the group or the individual but in very few it may be regulated.[236] This would be where a protester's choice of clothing falls under the wide proscription on wearing 'political' uniforms in public contained in section 1 of the Public Order Act 1936. It is an offence in a public place[237] or at a public meeting[238] to wear a uniform signifying association with any political organisation or with the promotion of any political object. Prosecutions require the consent of the Attorney-General. Any Chief Constable (or in London the Commissioner) may, with the Home Secretary's consent, permit or make its wearing subject to conditions if satisfied that its wearing on a ceremonial, anniversary or special occasion will not likely involve a risk of public disorder.

---

[233] *Bukta*, above n 25, at [37].
[234] *Brehony*, above n 88, [2005] EWHC 640.
[235] *WG v Austria* (App 15509/89) EComHR inadmissibility decision 30 November 1992; *GS v Austria* (App 14923/89) EComHR inadmissibility decision 30 November 1992; and *G and E v Norway* (Apps 9278/81 and 9415/81) EComHR inadmissibility decision 3 October 1983.
[236] In some American States, wearing political clothing—badges, T-shirts slogans—on election day in or near polling stations is banned as unlawful campaigning. Several voters have been turned away: see First Amendment centre news, 'Issue of what not to wear emerges as voters go to the polls', 27 October 2008, at: www.firstamendmentcenter.org/news.aspx?id=20789 (accessed 20 July 2009).
[237] This includes the highway and any other places or premises to which at the material time the public have or are permitted to have access whether on payment or otherwise: s 9. We discussed this above n 12.
[238] A meeting held for the purpose of discussing matters of public interest or for the purpose of expressing views on such matters held in a public place or any meeting which the public or a section thereof are permitted to attend whether on payment or otherwise: s 9.

214 *Peaceful Persuasion and Communicating Dissent*

The origin of section 1 is fairly clear. The 1930s were a time of considerable unrest on two-linked fronts: first was the economic dislocation of the Great Depression and the second was political, the pan-European rise in extremist nationalism. In England, these two came together in the clashes between Jews and Oswald Mosley's 'Blackshirts' in the East End of London. Section 1 is a product of its time—the need to deal with the threat from the Blackshirts and to minimise support for Mosley, both so as to dampen tension. Prohibiting the wearing of political uniforms in public can be justified for their internal and external contributions: it prevents easy identification of like-minded people (and so is aimed at destroying cohesion and morale and communications) and by minimising the impression of strength, it reduces the chances of garnering support.

There has been little case law on the scope and meaning of section 1. It is a provision that is little called upon by the police as a weapon in the context of peaceful protest.[239] Probably the most significant case is the Divisional Court decision in *O'Moran v DPP; Whelan v DPP*,[240] an appeal by way of case stated arising from what was worn at a traditional Irish Republican funeral ceremony. Eight members of the IRA attended dressed in berets and dark glasses and gave a rifle salute. The question for Lord Widgery CJ was whether all the constituent elements of the section 1 offence had been made out. He concluded that

(i) 'Wearing' implies some article of apparel being worn. It could not include a badge but did not need to cover the whole or major part of the body.
(ii) Being worn 'as a uniform' required proof by evidence in the usual way that in its association a black beret worn in isolation has been recognised and known as a uniform. It did not necessarily require proof of previous use where, as here, the berets and sunglasses were worn by all eight as a group as a uniform in order to indicate that the group was together and in association:

> the simple fact that a number of men deliberately adopt an identical article of attire justifies ... the view that that article is a uniform if it is adopted in such a way as to show that its adoption is for the purposes of showing association between the men in question.[241]

(iii) 'To signify association' required either evidence that it had been used in the past as a uniform of a recognised association that was capable of identification in some manner (even if that organisation cannot be specified) or by judging from events and circumstances when it was worn.

The problem that surrounds this offence is its ambit and breadth. On one hand, there is a clear case for the 'content-neutral' approach of section 1 that outlaws all political uniforms rather than targeting only certain groups, leading to challenges based on Articles 14 and 11 combined. On the other, ostensible neutrality usually shrouds an increase in 'on the spot' police discretion in maintaining order. The offence is not linked, as many other public order offences are (as we shall see), to concepts of violence, disruption, or causing offence or fear. That might well make it susceptible to challenge on human rights grounds

---

[239] In 2001, there were seven, in 2002, eight and in 2003 eleven defendants taken to court: source *Number of defendants proceeded with against at magistrates courts for various offences by police force area in England and Wales 2001–2003*, Home Office RDS, supplied personally under an FoI request in 2005. Sherr, above n 8, 144–5 relates most of the pre 1970s cases.

[240] *O'Moran v DPP; Whelan v DPP* [1975] QB 864 (DC).

[241] *ibid*, 873–4, although he later refers to the adoption of a 'similar style' dress so as to show mutual association. Lord Widgery CJ distinguished here between say police officers or soldiers, with their universally recognised uniforms, and those such as the accused wearing something without what might be a track record of association.

relating to freedom of expression and privacy. Strasbourg case law clearly identifies the wearing of clothing as aspects of both: choosing how to express oneself is integral to moral autonomy.[242] We now have a clear Strasbourg ruling on the matter in the context of protest/political expression: 'deciding to wear the red star in public must be regarded as his way of expressing his political views. The display of vestimentary symbols falls within the ambit of Article 10'.[243] In that case, *Vajnai*, it was the blanket ban on wearing the red star— a symbol with multiple meanings, not just one linked to or evincing support for totalitarianism—that was disproportionate for its breadth and its indiscriminate nature.[244] That is not to say wearing similar political clothing should be unrestricted but the legal response should as a minimum be tailored to effects or results rather than being predicated on the wearer's purpose, alone or in combination.

Might defendants pray in aid the second limb of section 1? Even though that only applies to ceremonial, anniversary or other special occasions, it permits political uniforms to be worn where there is no likely risk of public disorder.[245] Defendants might utilise section 7(1)(b) of the HRA to set up the disproportionality of the restriction (in Article 8 and 10 terms) collaterally as a shield. A court might be asked to read in a qualification to section 1 so as to ensure that it only criminalised conduct or activities to the extent necessary to guarantee one of the social goals and interests in Article 8(2) or Article 10(2). In the abstract, the only relevant ones would be preventing disorder or crime or perhaps the rights of others— but each would require evidence of effects not the wearer's purpose. The prosecution might find some difficulty in arguing that there existed a pressing social need—linked to preventing either disorder or causing offence—that required the prosecution and conviction of those wearing uniforms purely because they have political undertones, political significance or political solidarity. If a uniform is intrinsically offensive or even threatening (an SS knife?) then other means present themselves to contain and to deal with potential harm. This was another factor behind the Court's holding in *Vajnai*: that Hungary has a number of offences aimed at suppressing public disturbances provoked by the wearing of the red star.[246] It seems unlikely that the application of section 1 to peaceful protesters has survived the HRA.

Aside from that human rights concern, other concerns surrounding section 1 also present themselves. What does it mean to call something a 'uniform'? Must it be uniform—that is, the same—or must it be sufficiently similar as to leave no doubt that wearers subjectively wish to be seen as being in solidarity? To some extent, this was addressed by Lord Widgery CJ in *O'Moran* but as we also saw in his judgment, he interchanged 'identical' with 'similar' within a couple of lines. There is the world of difference: is an environmental protest group of seven all wearing overcoats in the seven different colours of the rainbow wearing a 'uniform'? What about a large group of animal rights protesters all disguised as different endangered animals? What about a group of nine anti-globalisation protesters all wearing a mask and clothing to represent one of the leaders of the G8 group of economic nations? As one of my undergraduates asked: does this mean that all Labour Party delegates who wear the

---

[242] In *Sahin v Turkey* (App No 44774/98) (2007) 44 EHRR 5 (Grand Chamber) the claims under Arts 8 and 10 were treated as raising no different issues to that under Art 9 and so failed but not because the University ban on wearing Islamic headscarves failed to engage either Article. See too *Kara v UK* (App No 36528/97) EComHR inadmissibility decision 22 October 1998.
[243] *Vajnai v Hungary* (App 33629/06) ECtHR judgment 8 July 2008 at [47].
[244] ibid, at [52]–[55].
[245] Against that would be posited *expressio unius est exclusio alterius*.
[246] *Vajnai*, above n 243, at [55].

traditional red tie while waiting outside the annual conference are liable to arrest? Lord Widgery CJ was content that the offence was made out solely by the wearing of berets without anything more extensive being worn.

In *O'Moran*, there was no discussion of what constitutes 'political'. It was rightly assumed on the facts that the association between the men was political in nature, concerned as it was with the creation of a free independent Irish state or at least ridding Ulster of British occupation. There was no discussion of what constitutes a 'political objective', the second limb of the offence under section 1. That latter issue raises a question of much wider import. Section 1 of the Terrorism Act 2000 defines terrorism as, inter alia, using or threatening serious violence for the purpose of advancing a political cause. In our context—as with terrorism—it must obviously encompass much more than party politics but must stop some way short of encapsulating the idea that every act is political, if not directly, then indirectly or by default: every time I do my shopping at a supermarket not at the corner shop I prop up capitalist consumerism not localised communitarianism. It presumes at the very least some sort of engagement with the polity but—on our definition of protest[247]—since all protest activity is 'political' (even if merely to support or reinforce the need not to change policy or a decision) it would seem unavoidable that protesters wearing uniforms will be doing so to 'signify [their] association ... with the promotion of any political object'.

Concluding that the reach of section 1 extends to all protesters in groups in the same clothes might be tempered by requiring a causative link between the uniform and the political objective promoted—effectively asking 'is wearing *this* uniform by *these* people today crucial to conveying the political message, without which the political message (ie political objective) would not be achieved?'—or arguing that the crucial question is 'was the wearer's primary objective to promote or "merely" to show support or strength in numbers?' Even that seems tenuous: those marching through Skokie, Illinois in the 1970s in their American Nazi uniforms may well have argued that was their aim but—in such numbers—the resulting intimidation and fear (or disorder and disruption) would create the conditions whereby their political goals might be more easily realised.[248]

(ii) Other Issues Thrown Up by a Protester's Choice of Clothing in Public

We might deal briefly with two further issues. First, section 60(4A) of the CJPOA 1994 (as inserted by section 25 of the Crime and Disorder Act 1998) allows uniformed officers to require the removal of any items which, it is reasonably believed, are being worn wholly or mainly for the purpose of concealing the wearer's identity. Anyone who fails to do so when required commits an offence. The power is contained within the controversial part of the 1994 Act that permits blanket stops and search without reasonable suspicion in anticipation of violence, section 60;[249] the removal power kicks in only if a 24-hour authorisation order has been made by an officer of inspector rank or above. However, as the Administrative Court made clear in *DPP v Avery*,[250] despite its location within section 60, the removal power does not attract the safeguards that apply to stops and search contained in sections

---

[247] Above pp 58.
[248] Sherr provides a good discussion of the various actions, above n 8, 193–8.
[249] It is similar in that regard to s 44 Terrorism Act 2000 which was the section at issue in the unsuccessful challenge in *R (Gillan) v Commissioner of Police for the Metropolis* [2006] UKHL 12, discussed below in chapter seven.
[250] *Director of Public Prosecutions v Avery* [2001] EWHC Admin, [2002] Cr App R 31, noted D Ormerod and D Tausz [2002] *Crim LR* 142n.

2–3 of PACE and Code of Practice A, as the power is not in essence about stops at all. Citizens who refuse to remove, say, a mask where an officer fails to provide their name and station cannot then argue—as was successfully done in *Osman* in the context of a search—that that failure rendered the request as being one outside the officer's duties and thus unlawful.[251]

The second is contained in section 13 of the Terrorism Act 2000: the prohibition on wearing items of clothing in a public place in such a way or in such circumstances as to arouse reasonable suspicion that the wearer is a member or supporter of a proscribed organisation. This is currently of limited relevance: no peaceful protest group has yet been proscribed. That said, even proscribed groups might engage in persuasion and advocacy— that is protest—as well as violence and threats, and section 13 is parasitic simply on the group being outlawed not on its activities or the activities of the accused. Further, as we shall see in the next chapter in some detail, the definition of 'terrorism' in section 1 of the 2000 Act is wide enough to cover *some* protesting activities if they take the form of direct action, such as activists causing damage to a GM crop field. If that group were then proscribed— by the Secretary of State using Part II of the 2000 Act on the basis she believes the group is concerned in terrorism—then wearing anything that might reasonably create the suspicion of membership or support of such a group is a crime.

There has been only one reported case under section 13 and that is from Scotland. In *Rankin v Murray* someone left the Belfast-Troon ferry and was spotted openly wearing a ring inscribed with the initials 'UVF', well known as an abbreviation of the proscribed Ulster Volunteer Force.[252] The High Court of Justiciary held that even if it were established that the appellant had received the ring as a gift, regularly visited Northern Ireland, and was not a member or supporter of the said organisation, these facts did not negative the actual suspicion of the officers nor the objectively reasonable basis for that suspicion. It implicitly rejected counsel's view that section 13 should not be construed so as to criminalise, in the wearing of apparel, conduct which might be regarded as simply foolish or as a display of bravado or that merely indicated an interest in the organisation in question. The statutory side note 'uniform' to section 13 did not have the effect of restricting the offence to the wearing of some distinctive comprehensive attire. Carrying or displaying a single article may, if done in a relevant way or in relevant circumstances, be sufficient to arouse reasonable suspicion of the specified kind. Neither did it matter that the defendant did not know of the proscription—as here was alleged—as long as he was aware of what (here) the initials represented. On this basis, woe betide Mr and Mrs Anderson giving their daughter Isobel Rachel a coming-of-age bracelet engraved with her initials!

B. Placards and Language

Clearly, clothing may contain an explicit communicative message—the most well-known perhaps being the 'Fuck the Draft' t-shirt, at the heart of *Cohen v California*[253]—as well as the implicit or sub-conscious communication by a uniform through its long-standing use or association with any given group or cause. Largely though protesters will want to get their message across using more explicit and more direct forms of communicative media to

---

[251] *Osman (Mustapha) v Southwark Crown Court* [1999] *Crown Office Digest* 446 for a section 60 stop and search.
[252] *Rankin v Murray* (2004) SLT 1164 (High Court of Justiciary).
[253] *Cohen v California* 403 US 15 (1971).

218 *Peaceful Persuasion and Communicating Dissent*

signal support or opposition: banners, placards, speeches or chants. Protest of this sort is subject to regulation by various means. At the forefront is probably the interplay of three sections in the POA 1986, sections 4, 4A and 5.[254] These provisions reflect similar, albeit differently framed, proscriptions in the 1936 Act.

(i) Outline of the Operation of Sections 4–5 of the POA 1986

All three sections involve the key concept of using 'threatening, abusive or insulting words or behaviour' or 'distributing or displaying any writing, sign or visible representation which is threatening, abusive or insulting'.[255] Subject to what is set out below, all three can be committed in public or in private but where the threatening, abusive or insulting words or behaviour is used (or writing etc distributed or displayed) inside a dwelling and B is also inside that (or another) dwelling then no offence is committed.[256] None is dependent on the notion of 'breach of the peace', a keystone of the 1936 regime, which made it unlawful to use threatening abusive or insulting words with intent to provoke a breach of the peace or where a breach of the peace was likely to be occasioned.[257]

Section 4 relates the threatening, abusive or insulting words or behaviour to violence. It occurs where A uses 'threatening, abusive or insulting words or behaviour' towards B or distributes or displays 'any writing, sign or other visible representation which is threatening, abusive or insulting' towards B,

(i) where A intends to cause B to believe that immediate unlawful violence will be used against him or another by any person or
(ii) where A intends to provoke the immediate use of unlawful violence by B or by another or
(iii) where B is likely to believe that such violence will be used or will be provoked.[258]

By virtue of section 6(3), A must intend their words, behaviour, writing, sign or visible representation to be threatening, abusive or insulting or be aware that they may be so.

Sections 4A and 5 link the threatening, abusive or insulting words or behaviour to causing harassment, alarm or distress to a third party. Section 4A occurs where A uses 'threatening, abusive or insulting words or behaviour, or disorderly behaviour' or distributes or displays 'any writing, sign or other visible representation which is threatening, abusive or insulting' thereby causing—and intending to cause—harassment, alarm or distress to B or any other person.[259] Section 5 is made out where A uses 'threatening, abusive or insult-

---

[254] Offences committed under s 5 are subject to the 'on the spot' penalty fine regime created in Part I of the Criminal Justice and Police Act 2001. All three offences under ss 4–5 are also subject to the regime of racially and (since 2001 by virtue of s 39 of the Anti-Terrorism Crime and Security Act 2001) religiously aggravated crimes contained within ss 28–33 of the Crime and Disorder Act 1998.

[255] Since changes effected in 2005 by SOCPA, it is no longer a requirement for an arrest under s 5 that the person has been warned to stop and they do not or they re-engage 'immediately or shortly after'.

[256] The change from the old position was effected, according to the White Paper, above n 4, para 3.8, because of the supposed difficulties in prosecuting miners during the strike in 1984–85 who from NCB property threatened working miners on the public highway.

[257] See on this, as on much else, DGT Williams, *Keeping the peace: the police and public order* (London, Hutchinson, 1967) ch 7.

[258] *R v Horseferry Road Metropolitan Stipendiary Magistrate ex p Sidiatan* [1991] 1 QB 260 tells us that 'such violence' means the immediate (i.e. sufficiently proximate in time and place) use of unlawful violence so that even where A does not intend to be violent, the offence can still be made out if B considers it likely that immediate unlawful violence will be used or be provoked.

[259] In *Rogers v DPP* (unreported Divisional Court decision 22 July 1999), a case discussed by Richard Stone in his *Textbook on Civil Liberties*, 6th edn (Oxford, Oxford University Press, 2006) 263, the Court decided that it did

ing words or behaviour, or disorderly behaviour' or distributes or displays 'any writing, sign or other visible representation which is threatening, abusive or insulting' within the hearing or sight of someone likely to be caused harassment, alarm or distress. Section 5 does not require anyone actually to be harassed, alarmed or distressed. A must, though, intend their words or behaviour or the writing, sign or other visible representation to be threatening, abusive or insulting or must be aware that they may be so or (as the case may be) must intend his behaviour to be, or must be aware that it may be, disorderly.[260]

There are two defences available to those charged under either section 4A or section 5. The first is where A can prove that their threatening abusive or insulting words or behaviour were used or took place inside a dwelling and they had no reason to believe that the words or behaviour would be heard or seen outside dwelling.[261] The second is if A proves their conduct was reasonable. A third defence, open only to those charged under section 5, is for A to prove they had no reason to believe that anyone within hearing or sight was likely to be caused harassment alarm or distress. Sections 4A and 5 introduce in the actus reus an extra element to that contained in section 4, disorderly behaviour. This must mean something different to and less than abuse, threats or insult.[262] We might well question whether the term—with its connotations of what right-thinking, properly-conducted people would (not) do—sets out with sufficient clarity to allow protesters (and in fact anyone) to know what is and is not permitted. If so, charges and prosecutions of protesters would then fall foul of the 'prescribed by law' test in Article 11(2).[263]

(ii) Analysis of the Case Law under Sections 4–5 of the POA 1986

The three sections, and their forebears, have generated a wealth of case law. Some expand the law while others have acted as brakes and limiters. We have also had some decisions under the HRA which shed more light, both specifically and generally, on the interplay between domestic regulation and a more rights-based approach. Section 5 has become one of the mainstays of public order policing in the UK, called upon to deal with low-level disorder and offensive conduct, usually characterised by abuse and threats, often with violence, late in the evening or early morning at weekends in city and town centres. It seems not to be overly used as a means to police protest.[264]

---

not matter, for charges under s 4A, that there was no evidence that a protest group was aware either that their target was at home or that he could experience their allegedly disorderly behaviour. It was enough to infer the relevant intention from the group's mass presence outside a mink farm, from their activities and a common intention to disapprove of the farmer's activities and from a confrontation with the police.

[260] Section 6(4). This was described as 'an awareness of a possibility' by Auld LJ in *DPP v Norwood* [2003] EWHC 1564 (Admin) at [17].

[261] Whether this means the defences must be 'proved' to the higher legal burden or lower evidential burden and the related issue of compatibility with Article 6 was discussed but not decided in *Norwood*—though Auld LJ swayed to the former: [19]–[20] and [38].

[262] Bonner and Stone, above n 17, 208.

[263] This, of course, is similar to the successful argument in *Hashman and Harrup v UK* (2000) 30 EHRR 241 in the context of binding over to be of good behaviour. The prosecution of a protester in New Zealand for behaving in a disorderly manner and the extent of the free speech protection in the New Zealand Bill of Rights Act 1990 was the issue for resolution by the Supreme Court in *Brooker v Police* [2007] NZSC 30, discussed A Geddis (2008) 8 *Oxford University Commonwealth Law Journal* 117.

[264] See D Brown and T Ellis, *Policing low-level disorder: police use of section 5 of the Public Order Act 1986* (HORS 135, 1994). The limited use and reliance on s 5 to quell disorder during protests may well be a result of the continuing availability of powers that depend on the more flexible, less certain concept of breach of the peace at common law, discussed below in chapter seven.

(a) The Need for Someone to be Harassed, Alarmed or Distressed?

A key element to the former main public order power—section 5 of the POA 1936—was the link between using threatening words and either intended or likely breach of the peace. That is no longer the case. With its emphasis on likely *physical* reaction, it was long established under the old section 5 that speakers must take their audience as they find them. In *Jordan v Burgoyne*[265] the defendant was charged with using insulting words whereby a breach of the peace was likely to be occasioned. Jordan's inflammatory speech suggested that 'Hitler was right . . . our real enemies . . . were not Hitler and the National Socialists . . . but world Jewry and its associates'. The Divisional Court took the view that, as the basis of the legislation was maintaining public order, it did not matter that ordinary reasonable persons would not commit breach of the peace. A speaker must take his audience as he finds it, even if a body of hooligans were present with the express intention of preventing the speech. The new offences are premised on likely *mental* reaction, a point noted by McCullough J,[266] but there is no reason why the *Jordan* principle should not apply equally well to likely harassment alarm or distress. This possible explanation would be tempered by the need still to prove mens rea. Under section 4A, could it be said that someone really intended to harass someone else if they foresaw such a reaction as being unlikely, based on their own (ir)rational assumptions about a sympathetic audience? Even the lesser offence under section 5 still requires an intention or at least awareness that, for example, the words used are threatening: *DPP v Clarke* tells us that this is to be assessed subjectively whereas in contrast the reasonable conduct defence is judged objectively.[267] There is little room there for a 'reasonable man' or even a '*talem qualem*' approach.[268]

We shall return in chapter seven to one of the matters raised in *Jordan*, as well as in a host of others, the heckler's veto: against whom and on what basis should the police take action when a threat to the peace exists? Sherr compares *Jordan* with *Beatty* (which we will consider in detail later) and—not unjustifiably—notes that courts tend to base their decisions on their preference for the views of the audience or the speaker. Despite being 'first in the field' Jordan was criminally liable:

> while one might not wish to query the essential wisdom of backing the Salvation army [in *Beatty*] and not Colin Jordan, the lack of a meaningful peg on which to hang such decisions in a less discriminatory manner becomes obvious'.[269]

In HRA terms, the *Jordan* approach sets up two problems. First, it subjectifies the effects of insulting speech, meaning there is less room—perhaps no room at all—for the more objective, proportionality standard required under Article 10(2). It also creates uncertainty, unpredictability and inconsistency in the criminal law, dependent as it is on the (non-)reaction of a specific crowd—and thus may fall foul of the prescribed by law test under Article 10(2).[270]

It will be no defence for protesters charged under section 5 (at least) to argue that the only other person in hearing range or sight was a police officer and so was not 'a person likely to

---

[265] *Jordan v Burgoyne* [1963] 2 QB 744.
[266] *DPP v Orum* [1989] 1 WLR 88, 95.
[267] *DPP v Clarke* [1992] Crim LR 60 (DC).
[268] Although as Tony Smith has pointed out, the measure of the ordinary reasonable woman does or can play a role in deciding whether a word is insulting or behaviour is abusive: ATH Smith, *Offences against public order* (London, Sweet and Maxwell, 1987) 14.
[269] Sherr, above n 8, 82.
[270] On which, see similarly *Hashman and Harrup*, above n 263.

be caused harassment alarm or distress'. First, case law indicates no one actually needs to be caused harassment alarm or distress at all.[271] Secondly, it was held in *DPP v Orum* that a police officer as a matter of law can be caused harassment, alarm or distress.[272] This marked a change from earlier cases predicated upon the fact that officers would not respond to harassing threatening or alarming words or behaviour by causing a breach of the peace themselves—the constituent element in the 1936 Act. Despite this, if the only person on the scene is an officer, that fact alone should considerably lessen the chances of a conviction: the Court in *Orum* went on to note that since this was a question of fact for the jury, given an officer's training and experiences, it was unlikely in fact for an officer actually to be harassed, alarmed or distressed. The reality that the only person hearing offensive chanting or witnessing graphic posters is a police officer is unlikely. It would almost certainly mean the protest had not achieved its aim of challenging or changing public opinion. Case law does not seem to have resolved whether or not a co-protester can be someone 'likely to be harassed alarmed or distressed'. Again this must be a matter of fact for the magistrates and realistically the chance of someone testifying is low. That said, it must be possible for a co-protester—despite broad general agreement with a group's aims and even methods—to become distressed by a particular image chosen to make a point at a meeting. It must be open to doubt that the conviction of someone who uses abuse or insult where the only person harassed is a co-protester has been the victim of a proportionate restriction on their free speech.

(b) The Meaning of Insulting, Offensive and Abusive

It was no defence, before the HRA, to a charge under section 5 that the words or images were accurate or truthful.[273] Whether that should remain so is open to question: the essence of free speech is to challenge existing dogma or established viewpoints and what better way to do so than with 'the truth'—accepting of course the contestability of most truths? Can it really be maintained that, giving the words their ordinary English meaning, someone can be insulted or abused let alone threatened by an accurate but graphic representation of an aborted foetus? We might usefully heed Lord Scott's dissent in the *Pro-Life* case, made admittedly in a slightly different context. The group challenged a ban on its party election broadcast that had been instituted on the ground that it was 'offensive to very large numbers of viewers'. His analysis was that

> voters in a mature democracy may strongly disagree with a policy being promoted by a televised party political broadcast but ought not to be offended by the fact that the policy is being promoted nor, if the promotion is factually accurate and not sensationalised [and relevant to a lawful policy on which its candidates are standing for election], by the content of the programme. Indeed, in my opinion, the public in a mature democracy are not entitled to be offended by the broadcasting of such a programme. A refusal to transmit such a programme based upon the belief that the

---

[271] *Norwood*, above n 260, at [34]. Under s 4 the presence of another is needed when threats are made: *Atkin v DPP* (1989) 89 Cr App R 199. Proportionality might mean a new approach to the former.

[272] *DPP v Orum*, above n 266, overturning *Marsh v Arscott* (1982) 75 Cr App Rep 211 a case decided under the old s 5 with its trigger of breach of the peace not harassment, alarm or distress.

[273] *Lewis v Director of Public Prosecutions*, unreported Divisional Court decision in 1995 quoted in Bailey Harris and Jones, *Civil Liberties*, above n 89, 492. A group of anti-abortion campaigners outside an abortion clinic displayed graphic images of aborted foetuses covered in blood and tried to argue that as they were accurate representations of the results of an abortion they could be neither insulting nor abusive. It would not be beyond the realm of imagination for charges at common law for outraging public decency to be brought, given the result in *R v Gibson* [1990] 2 QB 619. There an artist was successfully prosecuted for exhibiting earrings made from frozen foetuses.

programme would be 'offensive to very large numbers of viewers'... would not, in my opinion, be capable of being described as 'necessary in a democratic society... for the protection of... rights of others'. Such a refusal would, on the contrary, be positively inimical to the values of a democratic society, to which values it must be assumed that the public adhere.[274]

Brutus v Cozens establishes that the word 'insulting' at least (though there is no reason to separate this from the other two) should be given its ordinary English meaning.[275] This ushers in the possibility of some notion of reasonableness into the area. The House of Lords allowed an appeal (under the old section 5) following an anti-apartheid demonstration that took the form of leafleting, whistling and a sit-in on court during a tennis match at Wimbledon. Lord Reid gave the leading speech. He concluded that the meaning of 'insulting' was not a matter of law. It should be given its ordinary meaning as a question of fact for the jury so that 'vigorous... distasteful or unmannerly speech or behaviour [was] permitted so long as it [was] not threatening... abusive... or insulting'.[276] Of the two contemporary uses listed by the Oxford English Dictionary, the meaning of insult is to 'assail with offensively dishonouring or contemptuous speech or action; to treat with scornful abuse or offensive disrespect; to offer indignity to; to affront, outrage'.[277] This should provide some clear limits to its use as a regulator of certain socially undesirable conduct, let alone of peaceful protests.

Though we can easily imagine what an insulting (or abusive or threatening) banner or placard might contain—'We know where you live and we'll hunt you down, fox hunt scum'—the section has been called upon to excess if Lord Reid's words are to be taken at face value.[278] How else can we explain it being relied upon to crack down on anti-abortion protesters—displaying photos of aborted foetuses seen as capable of 'insulting' a police officer as a father and being seen as abusive[279]—or to arrest those protesting about a motorway

---

[274] *R (Pro-Life Alliance) v BBC* [2003] UKHL 23 [98].

[275] *Brutus v Cozens* [1973] AC 854.

[276] The Divisional court was wrong therefore to view insulting as including 'behaviour which affronts other people and evidences a disrespect or contempt for their rights, behaviour which reasonable persons would foresee is likely to cause resentment or protest such as was aroused in this case'.

[277] www.oed.com/, accessed on 27 October 2008. The other is: to manifest arrogant or scornful delight by speech or behaviour; to exult proudly or contemptuously; to boast, brag, vaunt, glory, triumph, esp. in an insolent or scornful way.

[278] Can I be insulted—affronted, debased—purely by hearing unwelcome or outrageous views and thus knowing that someone subscribes to them even if personally hearing them uttered has no effect on me? Is insulting the right word for that presumed moral complicity where A makes known his abhorrent views to B presuming (or at least this is what B assumes) B will agree or will not object. Is it insulting to hear someone so abuse, in our opinion, the right to free speech? All of these do seem to mark the start of a slippery slope if 'insulting' is to remain the test, though it is possible to see the first as implied by the Strasbourg ruling in *Wingrove v UK* (1997) 24 EHRR 1 at [45].

[279] *DPP v Clarke* (1991) 94 Cr App Rep 359 DC although the acquittals were upheld by the Divisional Court on the basis that none of the defendants intended the displays to be threatening, abusive or insulting or were aware that they might be so. Contrast *DPP v Fidler* [1992] 1 WLR 91 in which the Divisional Court concluded the court below was wrong to decide there was no case to answer where there was no evidence showing two anti-abortion protesters had issued threats or been abusive though plenty of evidence that a nearby group, to which they were attached, had done so. The result is that the prosecution did not have to prove an act or threat of actual physical violence to or towards any person as an essential ingredient or element of the offence and could be made out by showing conduct which evidenced a disrespect and disregard for the distress likely to be (and in fact) caused to others. On this and other anti-abortion cases involving s 5 see Bailey Harris and Jones, above n 89, 490–93. For example in *Morrow and others v DPP* [1994] Crim LR 58 the Divisional Court upheld convictions based on the fact that shouting slogans, waving banners and preventing entry to an abortion clinic could constitute distressing and disorderly conduct.

extension who obstructed the view of a surveyor through his theodolite[280] or against those supporting a united Ireland? Gearty and Ewing tell us of an arrest under section 5 of the 1986 Act for the insulting offence of having an 'Ireland: Twenty Years of Resistance' poster that featured four youths stoning an army armoured car.[281] Simon Brown LJ has even considered—though without the benefit of argument on the point—that disrupting an angling competition by throwing sticks into the water, sounding air-horns and 'seeking verbally to persuade' anglers to stop fishing might be capable of being regarded as abusive or insulting.[282] It is time for the HRA to reclaim the right to utter 'the contentious ... the unwelcome and the provocative'[283] so as to minimise the operation of section 5 in the field of peaceful protest.

Whether it will be applied on the beat in a proportionate, rights-sensitive fashion seems open to question. In 2006, a leading Christian fundamental evangelist and campaigner was arrested and charged under section 5 after he handed out leaflets at a gay and lesbian Mardi Gras which talked of a 'lifestyle that led to hell' and compared homosexuality with incest. Charges were dropped later by the Crown Prosecution Service (CPS).[284] In 2008, a teenager was warned to get rid of a sign proclaiming that Scientology was not a religion but a dangerous cult 'as it breached the Public Order Act'. The CPS was reported as having advised that it was neither abusive nor insulting.[285] In both, the worry was the chilling effect on the right of peaceful protest of police behaviour at the scene and at the time even (especially?) where no one was ever prosecuted—let alone found guilty.

(c) The Reasonable Conduct Defence

The specific 'reasonable' conduct defences under both section 4A and section 5 ought to mean greater protection for peaceful protest. Surely it must always be 'reasonable' conduct peacefully to exercise a Convention right? That must be all the more so if the reasonable conduct defence is interpreted under section 3 of the HRA as connoting proportionality and thus compatible with the right of peaceful protest?[286] Even if someone is vituperatively expressing views that are hostile to the mainstream or that arouse anger and inflame the passions, this is no more than engaging or entering into debate and so supports the public utility and functional justification of free speech in the first place. Another route to the same destination might be to argue that reasonable people not only hold different views on politically or socially contentious matters but appreciate that others do. They are cognisant of the role of the individual dissenter as a '"place holder" for the values and goals which we

---

[280] *Chambers and Edwards v DPP* (1995) COD 321. In causing 'harassment', no element of apprehension about one's safety was required, and so could be made out by showing annoyance or inconvenience. The words 'disorderly behaviour' should be given their ordinary meaning. There need not be any element of violence, present or threatened for there to be disorderly behaviour.

[281] Gearty and Ewing above n 96, 122–3. They also report t that s 5 was used 'to curb ... a craze for obscene T-shirts and hats in Skegness'.

[282] *Nicol v DPP* Unreported Divisional Court decision 10 November 1995 CO/1382/95, Lexis transcript, no page numbering or paragraphs in original.

[283] *Redmond-Bate v DPP* [2000] HRLR 249 at [20] DC Sedley LJ, noted Connolly [1999] *J Civ Lib* 382.

[284] See the comment piece by George Monbiot: 'I'm pleased the case against this ranting homophobe was dropped', *The Guardian*, 3 October 2006; though, as he indicates, had charges been brought under other legislation such as the PFHA 1997, the prosecution might have succeeded.

[285] BBC news website 23 May 2008: news.bbc.co.uk/1/hi/england/london/7416425.stm (accessed 25 May 2008).

[286] On this, see *Norwood* text to n 314 below.

think [are] central to a properly ordered civic structure'.[287] Reasonable people are robust and tolerant of others and their views and appreciate the wider public utility or value of peaceful protest; it is thus 'reasonable' for A to 'insult' B for the greater good of society. This is not quite what Geddis refers to as the 'transformative' approach to section 5 (as contrasted with the dominant 'pro-civility' discourse), though it draws on it. Geddis proposes that people should 'learn to tolerate such offence in the name of a vibrant . . . public discourse'.[288]

In the context of different legislation, the case of *Connolly v DPP* casts some light on such an approach.[289] C was charged under the Malicious Communications Act 1988 after she sent graphic images of aborted foetuses through the post to three pharmacies. Broadly speaking, section 1 makes it an offence for A to send to B something conveying an indecent or grossly offensive message or something which is wholly or partly indecent or grossly offensive if (one of) her purpose(s) is to cause distress or anxiety to the recipient. Connolly attempted to argue that section 1 should be read subject to an implied free speech defence, utilising Article 10. On this she was successful; Dyson J was prepared to accept that it was possible to interpret section 1 of the 1988 Act in a way which is compatible with Article 10, either by giving a heightened meaning to the words 'grossly offensive' and 'indecent' or by reading into section 1 a provision to the effect that the section will not apply where to create an offence would be a breach of a person's Convention rights, ie a breach of Article 10(1), not justified under Article 10(2).[290] These would be two other approaches to ensuring the compatibility of section 5 with the right to peaceful protest. However, on the facts he held that the conviction was not a disproportionate restriction on her rights; the intended recipients were sent grossly offensive photographs of abortions at their place of work. They were not targeted in the hope that they might alter the public position on the morning after pill or abortion generally, as would have been the case with elected politicians or others who had taken up a public position and could be expected to contribute to political debate.[291] Neither were they doctors who routinely performed abortions, less likely to find the photographs grossly offensive than the pharmacist's employees.

(d) The Triptych of *Percy, Hammond* and *Norwood*

There have been three significant decisions on section 5 of the 1986 Act under the HRA.[292] We can see the importance of assessing the proportionality of any restriction (prosecution or arrest) gauged in terms of content of the message, the circumstances of its transmission or its effect on the likely (or actual) audience. They also allow insight into the use of section 7(1)(b) as a shield. The first two, *Percy v DPP*[293] and *Hammond v DPP*,[294] appear at first blush to sit ill alongside each other. The third is *Norwood v DPP*.[295] All three were appeals

---

[287] A Geddis, 'Free speech martyrs or unreasonable threats to social peace?—'insulting' expression and section 5 of the Public Order Act 1986' [2004] *PL* 853.
[288] *ibid.*
[289] *Connolly v Director of Public Prosecutions* [2007] EWHC 237 (Admin).
[290] *ibid*, at [18].
[291] *ibid*, at [31]–[32]. One matter that Dyson J thought relevant was that this was 'hardly an effective way to promote' the cause. That, it is submitted, is a matter of choice for the protagonists and not for a court when considering the necessity of a restriction. This would be quite a worrying aspect if it were taken more generally.
[292] Each is discussed generally by Geddis, above n 287.
[293] *Percy v DPP* [2001] EWHC Admin 1125, noted [2002] Crim LR 835.
[294] *Hammond v DPP* [2004] EWHC 69 (Admin).
[295] *Norwood v DPP* [2002] EWHC 1564 (Admin).

by way of case stated. In each—even the successful appeal in *Percy*—it is probably true to say that too great a weight was placed on the public's peace of mind.[296]

1. *Percy v DPP*   Lindis Percy is a long-standing protester against the arms trade, war and US foreign and military policy. She daubed 'Stop Star Wars' across the US flag and waved it outside a US Air Force air base in East Anglia.[297] She also placed it onto the road in front of a US service vehicle and trod on it. She was convicted under section 5 of the 1986 Act of using threatening, abusive or insulting words or behaviour likely to cause harassment, alarm or distress. The District Judge had concluded first that there was a social need 'to prevent denigration of objects of veneration and symbolic importance for one cultural group', and secondly that a criminal prosecution and subsequent conviction under section 5 were a proportionate response so as to achieve that end.

Her appeal against conviction was upheld by the Divisional Court: insufficient weight had been given to her Article 10 right freely to express herself. The Divisional Court, while it agreed with the first point as being one that was open to the judge to find, disagreed with the balancing act undertaken. It outlined other considerations pertinent to any future disposition. At first instance the only factor considered, hence the appeal succeeding, was the first: the availability of alternative means to voice her views. Others included whether or not the behaviour had gone beyond legitimate protest; whether or not it had been disproportionate and unreasonable rather than being *merely* the expression of an opinion on an issue of public interest (emphasis added); the knowledge of the perpetrator of the likelihood of the effect on witnesses; and the relevance of the flag (or other venerated symbol) to the content of or the transmission of the protest message—was it a gratuitous and calculated insult?

The reasoning is open to some criticism. Asking whether the behaviour had gone beyond legitimate protest has a degree of both circularity and elusiveness; the legitimacy of the protest (that is 'was it lawful?') is the outcome of the balancing assessment being undertaken first by the authorities and then the court. Asking whether the protest and behaviour was proportionate and reasonable misses the point and views the question through the wrong end of the lens. The real target of the court's inquiry should always be the response to that expression and communicative behaviour; while it is always reasonable to exercise a Convention right, sometimes it may also be reasonable and proportionate to interfere. Last, it is difficult to see the relevance in terms of HRA reasoning—founded as it is on rights being exercisable freely unless it is proportionate to restrict them for a sound legitimate aim—of a matter such as 'the knowledge of the perpetrator of the likelihood of the effect on witnesses'. How does a perpetrator's mental state as to consequences tell us anything about assessing the balance of the state's response? In any event, this is superfluous in that it goes to the mens rea contained in section 6(4).

Percy is not technically a case where courts revisit statutory terms and consider them anew through the prism of section 3. It is a case in which a higher court reviewed the outcome before the lower court by assessing in Article 10 terms the process by which the District Judge reached his conclusion on the merits of the charge.[298] Because he had only

---

[296] Geddis, above n 287, 867.
[297] On the similar issue of flag burning as protected First Amendment speech in the USA see *Texas v Johnson* 491 US 397 (1989).
[298] In that sense, *Dehal v CPS* [2005] EWHC 2154 (Admin), noted V Bettinson [2006] *Web Journal of Current Legal Issues* offers a new and better view. Again, this was an appeal by way of case stated but before a single judge as an urgent case. Charges had been brought after an insulting poster was displayed outside a Sikh temple by

taken account of that one factor and not the full range later elucidated, he had not conducted a proper Article 10 balancing exercise and so it could not be said it was proportionate to convict. As Geddis notes, we do not know whether the protest was actually reasonable and nor do we learn much about how future cases might be disposed of. The guidelines are opaque and circular, albeit, as he indicates, designed to factor in the (now) extra value of free speech and whether this should outweigh the upset caused.[299] To that extent it stands as more compatible with Article 10 than either of the other two cases to follow it.

2. *Hammond v DPP* A contrasting result was reached in *Hammond* a few years later. Hammond was an evangelical Christian convicted under section 5 after preaching one Saturday afternoon in a pedestrianised part of a town centre. As part of his campaign to convert others, he used a sign bearing such exhortations as 'Stop immorality' 'Stop Homosexuality' and 'Stop Lesbianism'. That afternoon, a crowd of some 30–40 gathered. Some became overtly hostile, angry and aggressive: mud was slung at Hammond and water was poured over his head. Someone else tried to wrestle his sign away, in the course of which struggle someone else was struck by it. Hammond was arrested and convicted of displaying an insulting sign within the sight of someone likely to be caused harassment alarm or distress. Again, we come up against the ordinary English word 'insulting'. The magistrates reasoned as follows:

1. The words displayed on the sign were in fact insulting and caused distress to persons who were present.
2. Hammond was aware that those words on the sign were insulting. He admitted this at the scene to the arresting officer and he had travelled that day on the bus having covered the sign with a black plastic sack while travelling in light of a similar reaction in the past.[300]
3. The restriction on Hammond's right to freedom of expression had the legitimate aim of preventing disorder in view of the reaction of people in the crowd to the appellant's sign.
4. There was a pressing social need for the restriction and the restriction corresponded to that need; the words on the appellant's sign were directed specifically towards the homosexual and lesbian communities, implying that they were immoral and there was a need to show tolerance towards all sections of society; the sign was displayed in the town centre on a Saturday afternoon provoking hostility from members of the public.
5. The interference with the appellant's right to freedom of expression by prosecuting him was a proportionate response in view of the fact that the appellant's behaviour went beyond legitimate protest,[301] was provoking violence and interfered with the rights of others.

---

someone upset at its approach to how dogma was taught. In upholding the appeal, Moses J held that the important factor upon which the Crown Court should have focused was the justification for bringing any criminal prosecution at all. However insulting, however unjustified what D said, a criminal prosecution was unlawful as a result of s 3 of the HRA and Article 10 unless and until it could be established that such a prosecution was necessary in order to prevent public disorder. There was no such finding or any justification whatever. In short, there was no basis for the Crown Court concluding that the prosecution was a proportionate response to D's conduct.

[299] Geddis, above n 287, 861.
[300] It was not satisfactorily explained why that showed an awareness of the insulting nature of the signs and not a fear of retribution or an attack.
[301] See the discussion immediately above in the context of *Percy*.

The Divisional Court upheld the conviction.[302] In the view of May LJ, though 'not without hesitation', the magistrates' decision—that factually the sign was insulting, that H's conduct (even bearing in mind his Article 10 right) was not reasonable and so the arrest, charge and conviction was a proportionate response—was not one which it could be said it was not open to them to reach.[303] Although, as he noted, the words were short and the language 'not ... intemperate', the clear deciding factor was that the words on the sign was directed specifically at gays and lesbians, implying they were immoral. To assimilate such a group with immorality meant the words went beyond legitimate expression, protected under Article 10 and—as this was also a manifestation of a religious view—beyond what was permitted under Article 9 as well.

What counts for the difference in outcome between this case and *Percy*? There is a fine but discernible line between the two. In both, the language and terms used were not per se insulting or abusive but the difference lies in the chosen target and likely audience. Lindis Percy was attacking US policy, a policy that was freely chosen, and was only indirectly attacking individual servicemen and women by her 'desecration' of the flag; it was the medium of her message that was insulting. Hammond's attack was contained within his message and was a direct one on private individuals, some (many?) of whom might have been in his audience; individuals defined by membership of a group according to a matter quintessentially of private life, sexual choice. It was also the case that his chosen targets were themselves members of a protected minority group, if not deserving of protection under Article 14 (given they had no rights at stake on which the Article could bite) then at least beneficiaries of its assumed well-intentioned largesse.[304] An application to Strasbourg by Hammond's daughter and his executors (after Hammond himself died) was declared inadmissible on the ground that the applicants were not victims and so did not have standing within Article 34.[305] As Geddis points out, the speaker was left with no effective way of expressing his beliefs about the issue of same-sex relationships. Whatever one's view on these and other contested matters, for the law to adopt the position whereby 'society will not tolerate the public expression of his core beliefs' must be a worrying position.[306]

3. *Norwood v DPP*   Can we say the same about the applicant in *Norwood*? Mark Norwood was the regional organiser of the BNP. He was convicted under section 5 after he displayed a threatening, abusive or insulting party poster in the window of his first-floor flat. The A3 poster was clearly visible to passers-by, thus within the hearing or sight of a person to whom it was likely to cause harassment, alarm or distress. The poster bore the words 'Islam out of Britain' and 'Protect the British people' together with a photograph of one of the twin

---

[302] The House of Lords refused leave to appeal on the ground that no point of law of public importance arose. This does seem strange in light of the fact that the CPS dropped charges against Stephen Green for basically doing the same at the Cardiff Mardi Gras: above n 284.

[303] In each, one issue was whether the protester's language or conduct was intentionally insulting, a question of fact for the tribunal and reviewable only on Wednesbury-perversity grounds. Whether Geddis is right (above n 287, 872) that under s 6 of the HRA the Divisional Court should be conducting its own proportionality review 'rather than subcontracting it to the lower court' opens up a much wider constitutional debate.

[304] Again, it is the language and the attack that distinguishes this case from *Redmond-Bate* above n 283, discussed in more detail in chapter seven. Was Hammond in the words of Sedley LJ, 'being so provocative that someone in the crowd without behaving wholly unreasonably, might be moved to violence ... [or] was the threat of disorder or violence ... coming from passers-by who were taking the opportunity to react so as to cause trouble'?

[305] *Fairfield, Tredea and Cox v United Kingdom* (App 24790/04) ECtHR inadmissibility decision 8 March 2005.

[306] Geddis, above n 287, 865.

towers of the World Trade Center in flames on 11 September 2001 and a crescent and star surrounded by a prohibition sign.[307] He appealed to the Divisional Court.

Auld LJ decided that on the evidence of the content of the poster and of the circumstances of its display, the District Judge was entitled to find that the first limb of the aggravated section 5 offence was made out, namely that the appellant had displayed the poster intending it to be, or being at least aware that it might be, insulting. The words of the poster alone, and even more so when considered alongside what it depicted, were clearly racially directed and racially insulting.[308] The poster was a public expression of attack on all Muslims in this country, urging all who might read it that followers of the Islamic religion here should be removed and warning that their presence here was a threat or a danger to the British people. It could not, on any reasonable basis, be dismissed as merely intemperate criticism or protest against the tenets of the Muslim religion, as distinct from an unpleasant and insulting attack on its followers generally.[309] As to the harassing, alarming or distressing effect, the terms of the poster and the circumstances and location of its display were, as matter of plain common sense, capable of causing harassment, alarm or distress to those passing by who might see it. Such would be the reaction of any right-thinking member of society concerned with the preservation of peace and tolerance and the avoidance of religious and racial tension, as well as to any follower of the Islamic religion. In this it was irrelevant how people actually felt—what mattered was what was likely.[310] Auld LJ held it was plain from the wording of section 5(1) that the prosecution does not have to prove that the display of the poster in fact caused anyone harassment, alarm or distress. In fact, it is not as clear under sections 4–5 as it is under sections 1–3 that no one need witness the words or behaviour: these latter offences specifically state that 'no person of reasonable firmness need actually be or likely be present at the scene'. There is the world of difference between a situation where no one did witness the insulting words but it is presumed that any witnesses *would* be harassed, alarmed or distressed and the situation here where someone did witness it and they were not harassed, alarmed or distressed but it is still presumed that AN Other hypothetical onlooker would be.

Lastly, the Court elided arguments based on Article 10 with those based on the reasonableness defence in section 5(3).[311] The only way in which Convention arguments intrude (aside perhaps from questioning the nature of the reverse burden of proof) was when asking whether conduct was objectively reasonable, having regard to all the circumstances: Article 10 has no bearing on the insulting quality of the words or behaviour or on whether

---

[307] No issue was made about this also being an aspect of his spatial privacy, the exact opposite of the problem that arose in the New Zealand case *Brooker* (above n 263) where the protest took place outside the house of a police officer and was designed to vex and annoy her as she tried to sleep. There the balance between the right to protest and the 'victim's' right of privacy was the deciding issue between the majority and minority. If privacy enters the protest equation, as it might well do post-*Pretty* and its acknowledgment of autonomy as an aspect of Art 8, the matrix has the potential to take on a whole new dimension.

[308] The offence was religiously aggravated under ss 28 and 31 of the Crime and Disorder Act 1998, that is the offence was motivated (wholly or partly) by hostility towards members of a racial or religious group based on their membership of that group. On the meaning of 'racial group' under this legislation see now *R v Rogers* [2007] UKHL 8.

[309] *Norwood*, above n 260, at [33].

[310] *ibid*, at [34]. The complainant said that he had felt quite sick when he had seen the poster and had thought that it would cause offence. Two police officers gave evidence that they considered the poster to be in bad taste and inflammatory, that it left a 'bad taste' and that, having worked in London, one of them knew the distress and racial feeling 'this sort of material' could stir up: at [9]. See in this context the short discussion about third party insults above n 278.

[311] *ibid*, at [37]–[40].

it was intentional.[312] Abusive or insulting remain ordinary English words, untainted by Article 10 concerns. In that, *Norwood* follows *Hammond*. The 'reasonable conduct' defence is construed as impliedly containing notions of proportionality, whereas in *Percy* the whole basis was a review of the balancing exercise undertaken, an approach specifically disavowed in the other two cases. In *Norwood*, Auld LJ reiterated as having general application two of the factors thought relevant by Hallett J in *Percy*, namely: whether the accused's conduct went beyond legitimate protest and whether the behaviour had not formed part of an open expression of opinion on a matter of public interest, but had become disproportionate and unreasonable. This circularity takes us no further towards a reasoned resolution.

It was also assumed that 'in most cases' conduct would be objectively unreasonable where it had already been proved (as it would have to be for a defence to be raised) that the conduct was intentionally insulting or the defendant was aware that it might be.[313] This rather misses the point of reasonableness in its reincarnation as proportionality. Furthermore, many statements and much behaviour can be deliberately insulting without there being a pressing social need for them to be repressed. Obviously, the nearer one gets to truly insulting words—rather than a 'Troops Out' poster, for example—then the less likely it will be that the public and private interests in a right of free speech outweigh the private and social interests in silence. That might well be the case here—given that rights under Articles 9 and 17 are also in play[314]—but with respect, it deserves greater elucidation and explanation than is proffered by Auld LJ. He candidly admitted that though analysis was always fact-dependent, it was 'difficult to envisage' cases where intentionally insulting language was at the same time reasonable. He is making a point of general application, not one reserved for dealing with and confronting the odious views of neo-Nazis. It is not so hard to imagine such words or behaviour where it could properly be said that it would only be reasonable—proportionate—to clamp down if there was a real risk of disorder resulting. The problem is this. Effectively in his mind, section 5—including the reasonableness defence—strikes the correct balance required by the domestication of Article 10. If that were so, we are not much further forward than in 1997: expressive conduct, even on a matter of political importance on which views are mixed, can be restricted if it is intentionally insulting (in ordinary language) without disturbing the Article 10 equilibrium.

There is one last point, seemingly lost in the analysis of reverse burdens and Article 6. The question of burden *is* important and not solely as an aspect of a fair trial. Where free speech rights are engaged—as here—then in Convention terms, the right may only be restricted where it is shown *by the state* to be proportionate. If domestic law continues to adhere to the view that section 5(3) creates a defence, that it is only within section 5(3) that proportionality plays a role and that defences must be proved—whether that be a legal or evidential burden—by defendants, there is a serious risk that judicial analyses will go off Convention track very swiftly.[315] Even on the approach adopted in all three cases, the defendant has to 'prove' the reasonableness of her conduct—or, better put, the disproportionality of her conviction—once insulting conduct or words have been shown whereas the looking-glass of the ECHR

---

[312] Auld LJ at [37] *cf Hammond* (at [21]), May LJ and *Connolly* [2007] EWHC 237 (Admin) at [18] (Dyson LJ).
[313] *ibid*, at [39]. On the facts the Divisional Court concurred with the lower court that the defendant's conduct was not reasonable, bearing in mind too Arts 9 and 17.
[314] In fairness, Norwood's application to Strasbourg was declared inadmissible on the basis that displaying the poster was an act within Art 17, so grave an attack was it on the values proclaimed under the ECHR, and thus outwith protection of either Art 10 or 14: *Norwood v UK* (App 23131/03) ECtHR inadmissibility decision 16 November 2004.
[315] This is the same point, broadly, as was made in argument by Keir Starmer QC in *Percy*: above n 293, [19].

presumes all speech and protest to be lawful and performed with proportionate regard for wider social concerns unless shown otherwise. It is to Strasbourg case law that we now turn.

C. Strasbourg Case Law on Peacefully Communicating Dissent and Showing Support

It is unfortunate that the merits of *Hammond* were never aired, given both its similarity to *Percy* domestically and the fact that Strasbourg case law places a high stock on free speech by 'rewarding' it with a narrow margin of appreciation.

Peaceful protest that we could loosely categorise as taking a 'communicative' form has a good track record before the Court.[316] None has really resembled *Hammond* insofar as the objects of attack have been governments, other official bodies or state policy.[317] These groups should always expect greater levels of protest and to have to tolerate greater levels of criticism—meaning that restrictions on the right to peaceful protest will be harder to defend—than would be the case if the target was a private individual.[318] In *Kandzhov v Bulgaria*, the Court put it thus:

> In a democratic system, the actions or omissions of government and of its members must be subject to close scrutiny by the press and public opinion. Furthermore, the dominant position which the government and its members occupy makes it necessary for them—and the authorities in general—to display restraint in resorting to criminal proceedings and the associated custodial measures, particularly where other means are available for replying to the unjustified attacks and criticisms of their adversaries.[319]

Intuitively, protests against other private entities, such as companies, are less likely to be offered the wide shroud of protection under Article 10 or Article 11.[320]

Provided there are not calls to arms, clear incitements to violence and disorder or a rejection of democratic principles, the Court has taken the view that where a state cracks down on dissent, this is likely to be disproportionate. Good examples where findings of a violation have been made include *Piermont v France* (the complicating factor there being that the speaker was a German MEP visiting French Polynesia and New Caledonia) and *Guneri v Turkey*, where the applicants, banned from entering certain towns as part of a plan to meet local people, were officials of the Democracy and Peace Party.[321] *Osmani v*

---

[316] D Mead, 'The Right to Peaceful Protest Under the European Convention on Human Rights—A Content Study of Strasbourg Case Law' [2007] *EHRLR* 345.

[317] The cases it most resembles would be *Chorherr* and *Öllinger*, both discussed below.

[318] That approach would be consonant with those media cases under Art 10 that enshrine what is in effectively a public figure defence in defamation: see for example *Castells v Spain* (1992) 14 EHRR 445.

[319] *Kandzhov v Bulgaria* (App 68294/01) ECtHR judgment 6 November 2008 at [73].

[320] In any event, purely private gripes and concerns, what Bedau called 'personal hand-washing', we have defined as being outwith our concept of 'protest': see chapter three.

[321] *Piermont v France* (App 15773-4/89) ECtHR judgment 27 April 1995; and *Guneri v Turkey*, above n 202. In *Guneri*, the Court at [79] also talks of 'potentially harmful consequences [of speech] that would justify their prohibition'. This is rather open-ended and provides little by way of guidance for framing discretion and laws. Other cases that show the generally favourable way in which Strasbourg treats those who merely peacefully want to communicate, to persuade or to cajole include *Incal v Turkey* (App 22678/93) ECtHR judgment 9 June 1998; *Cetinkaya v Turkey*, above n 219; *Ataman v Turkey*, above n 129; *Karakaya and Piroglou v Turkey* (Apps 37581/02 and 370/02) ECtHR judgment 18 March 2008; *Duzgoren v Turkey* (App 56827/00) ECtHR 9 November 2006; and *Kuznetsov v Russia* (App 10877/04) ECtHR judgment 23 October 2008. We might contrast *Arrowsmith v UK* (App 7050/75) (1978) 19 DR 5. There the Commission reported there to be no violation of Art 10 for someone convicted of incitement to disaffection. The Incitement to Disaffection Act 1934 served the twin legitimate aims of protecting national security and preventing disorder in the army.

Turkey[322]—where the application was declared inadmissible as manifestly ill-founded—further reinforces the divide between what Strasbourg deems acceptable protest, and language—and what is beyond the pale. There the Mayor of Gostivar was convicted of stirring up national and racial hatred for his role in speaking at and organising a public meeting at which he defended the use of the Albanian flag and used inflammatory language such as 'we're going to reply to a slap with a slap'. The Court concluded that the prison sentence was not disproportionate, and served a variety of legitimate aims, given his encouragement of armed resistance and riot.

Although not a traditional 'protest' case, *Verein gegen Tierfabriken (VgT) v Switzerland* is instructive for the recognition of the value and role of communicative (protest) activity.[323] The European Court declared that a ban preventing the association—not a political party—from transmitting a commercial that had a clear political character (about the meat industry) was disproportionate: it limited without demonstrably good enough reasons an individual's ability to participate in debate on matters of public concern. Last, we might reflect on the lessons from *Öllinger v Austria*,[324] a case we considered in some depth in both chapter three and earlier in this chapter. Although it featured a ban on a counter-meeting, planned to coincide with an SS commemoration ceremony, it has more general import. Strasbourg decided the ban was disproportionate because the Austrian authorities struck the wrong balance: too much weight was attached to the rights of other cemetery visitors (under Article 9) to have undisturbed peace on All Saints' Day when paying respects to their dead relatives and friends, and too little to the rights of Öllinger. This provides a welcome corrective to the lack of an extensive counter-demonstration jurisprudence at Strasbourg. It must cast doubt on that line of cases, culminating in *Chorherr v Austria*,[325] that uphold decisions to arrest someone who is engaging in peaceful communicative activity solely on the ground of perceived risk to order or threats from third parties. When choosing a military ceremony in Vienna for his demonstration against the Austrian armed forces, Chorherr must have realised that it might lead to a disturbance requiring a measure of restraint. In the light of that, the ECtHR decided the restriction on his rights under Article 11 was justified and proportionate. The contrast in terms of outcome with *Öllinger* is marked; if anything Öllinger's situation was weighted even more against him.

> [A]s the Court correctly identified, the matrix of rights included [the former SS group] Comradeship IV's right to meet and Öllinger's right to counter-protest. In *Chorherr* the Court did not even need to balance Chorherr's right to protest against a third party's right to counter-protest or even to balance it against another right since, on the facts, neither of those two countervails existed. Thus, where Chorherr failed, one could legitimately expect Öllinger to have done so too.[326]

That he did not must indicate a shift in thinking at Strasbourg that remains unacknowledged in the judgment.

The case of the third to fifth applicants in *Steel v UK*[327] also illuminates well the regressive nature of *Chorherr*.[328] Their protest outside an arms conference in central London—distributing leaflets and holding banners—led to their arrest so as to prevent a breach of the

---

[322] (App 50841/99) ECtHR inadmissibility decision 11 October 2001.
[323] *Verein gegen Tierfabriken (VgT) v Switzerland* (2002) 32 EHRR 4.
[324] *Öllinger v Austria*, above n 187, discussed Mead above n 220.
[325] *Chorherr v Austria* (1994) 17 EHRR 358.
[326] Mead above n 220, 139–40.
[327] *Steel v UK*, above n 165.
[328] We considered this above text to n 165 in our discussion of *DPP v Jones*.

peace. After a seven-hour detention they were released by the magistrates and, when no evidence was called at an adjourned hearing, all charges were dropped. At Strasbourg, these three were successful in claiming both a breach of Article 5(1)(c) and of Article 10—though it should be noted that the key was the absence of a domestic decision. The arrests and detention were a disproportionate interference with their rights under Article 10 for the same reason as underpinned its decision on Article 5. There was

> no reason to regard their protest as other than entirely peaceful. It does not find any indication that they significantly obstructed or attempted to obstruct those attending the conference, or took any other action likely to provoke these others to violence. Indeed, it would not appear that there was anything in their behaviour which could have justified the police in fearing that a breach of the peace was likely to be caused.[329]

The likelihood of actual obstruction or disruption is what seems to separate *Chorherr* from *Steel*. Whether or not a state's response to perceived threats of disruption from third parties—the so-called heckler's veto—should be to restrict peaceful protest is an issue we will turn to when we look at breach of the peace and the role of the police in chapter seven.

One of the few peaceful communicative/expressive protest cases to have been rejected at Strasbourg on substantive grounds is *JK v Netherlands*.[330] We looked at this in chapter three. A protester was removed from Amsterdam railway station after unfurling a 'No Olympics' banner aimed at Amsterdam's candidate as host of the 1992 Olympics. This was done without permission from the railway authorities. Her application under Article 10 was declared inadmissible as manifestly ill-founded. Prior permission was viewed as necessary to prevent disorder, she was not prosecuted and she was not prevented from protesting elsewhere. Some comment is necessary: there was no evidence that any disorder was taking place—so far as can be seen from the short report, the target of the applicant's ire was a train carriage of official delegates en route to Lausanne for an Olympic meeting. It is often highly influential that alternative means to protest exist, as we considered in chapter three, but the decision removed from the applicant the choice as to venue—and presumably means—unless it was state sanctioned. That is not to say that the state should not be able to control such matters but should only be able to do so on clear evidence of the likelihood of disorder.

Similarly, there is now doubt cast on the notion that where applicants fail to obtain permission to protest then any application is inadmissible—or perhaps not even an interference. Cases such as *Bukta* and *Ataman* seem to indicate some leeway here.[331] Both might call for a revision of a decision such as *JK*. There is now a wealth of case law that indicates the police should seek to protect the right to protest and should only step in when it becomes clear that the protesters represent a real danger to public order, and that does not include traffic disruption. A case in point is *Ataman* in which the Court held that

> in the absence of violent acts on the part of the demonstrators, it is important that the public powers demonstrate a certain tolerance of peaceful gatherings so that the freedom of assembly as guaranteed by Article 11 is not deprived of all its meaning.[332]

---

[329] ibid, at [64] and [110].
[330] *JK v Netherlands* (App 15928/89) EComHR inadmissibility decision 13 May 1992 and *Arrowsmith*, above n 321. *Moosman v Austria* (App 14093/88) resulted in a friendly settlement before the Commission (9 July 1992) for a complaint based on the removal, ordered by a member of the regional government, of crosses from private property adjoining a road construction project, symbolising the death of nature.
[331] Both discussed above pp 108.
[332] *Ataman*, above n 129, [42].

IV. Conclusion

This chapter has considered the main ways in which protest—when it takes the form of a peaceful, expressive communication of ideas and views—is regulated and lawfully protected. It offers a snapshot of the more traditional, central forms.

One tactic reportedly being used by those seeking to pressurise a company as part of a campaign is either to set up spoof websites based on that company's logo or to use the protest group's own site to display spoof items or products. Satirical cyber-protests such as these are very likely to interfere with the company's intellectual property rights, especially copyrighted logos and slogans (eg 'Coke Is ShIt'?) There have been no reported cases in the UK or under World Trade Organization rules but France has seen several where companies such as Esso have taken proceedings against Greenpeace for infringing copyright.[333] Contrariwise, the offences of incitement to disaffection and sedition still exist at common law or on the statute book, but it is generally accepted that there is no place for charges to be brought nowadays simply for airing views, even contemptible ones or those seeking political change.[334] While it is *just* possible that a protester, while not being violent themselves, could fall foul of the prohibition against intentionally or calculatingly 'raising discontent or disaffection among Her Majesty's subjects or to promote feelings of ill-will and hostility between different classes',[335] the scope of sedition at common law was significantly narrowed in *Choudhury*.[336] This required not only an incitement to violence or public disturbance but that the violence, disturbance resistance or defiance should be against 'constituted authority'.

Equally, we have not considered the regulation of political (or advocacy) advertising whereby protesting groups or individuals—as well as formal political parties—try to buy space in the media. If the advertisement is in the written media there is no regulation save the general laws we considered elsewhere in this chapter and throughout the book. Thus, a single page protest spread in a newspaper or magazine could as easily fall foul of section 5 of the POA 1986 as would taking an offensive banner on a march. Similarly, as we shall see in chapter eight, private law rules on libel might come into play, as conceivably could the provisions about harassing conduct contained in the Protection from Harassment Act 1997 if the copy is repeated.[337] Political advertising in the broadcast media is treated

---

[333] *SA Societé Esso v Association Greenpeace France* judgment of the Parisian Court of Appeal 4th chamber 16 November 2005. An earlier action involving the same two parties was *SA Societé Esso v Association Greenpeace France*, judgment of the Parisian Court of Appeal, 14th chamber 26 February 2003, noted: 'France: Appeals Court overturns ruling on use of trademarks in online protests' (2003) 3 *World E-Commerce & Intellectual Property Report* 9; 'France: Appeals Court allows use of marks in Internet-based protests' (2003) 3 WEC & IPR 5; H Obhi, (2003) 4 *World Internet Law Report* 28–31; 'France: Appeals Court overrule allows use of trademarks in internet-based protest' (2003) 4 World ILR 8; (2002) 2 WEC & IPR 6; (2002) 3 World ILR 11. See also 'France: Danone prevails in trademark case, fails to win condemnation of ISP' (2001) 1 WEC & IPR 12 and (2001) 2 World ILR 11 and 16.

[334] See generally Williams, *Keeping the Peace*, above n 257, ch 9, M Supperstone, *Brownlie's Law of public order and national security*, 2nd edn (London, Butterworths, 1981) ch 11 and Sherr, above n 8, 107–10. Treason, as it involves the use of or display of force (say) to seek changes in established law or religion or to usurp the government cannot be committed by peaceful protesters—though of course, their use of force may be minor. In any event, treasonable protest is likely to overlap with several more clearly defined tailored offences.

[335] *R v Burns* (1886) 16 Cox CC 355.

[336] *R v Chief Metropolitan Stipendiary Magistrate ex parte Choudhury* [1991] 1 QB 429.

[337] In *Thomas v News Group Newspapers* [2001] EWCA Civ 1233 a series of stories about a female black police officer was held capable of constituting harassment under the 1997 Act . Thus is it possible for the substance of reports and articles to constitute harassment as well as (or more obviously) this being so as a result of how a story was obtained.

differently.[338] Broadly speaking, section 321 of the Communications Act 2003 provides for a ban on political advertising on TV or on radio. The aim is to try to ensure that wealth alone cannot skew political debate as it might if access to disproportionate air time were allowed solely on the basis of being able to afford to pay. The Minister on the Second Reading of the Bill made a statement under section 19 of the HRA (so far the only one made) that in her view the Bill was not compatible with the Convention right of free speech—based on the Strasbourg decision *Verein gegen Tierfabriken v Switzerland*[339]—but that she wished Parliament in any event to proceed. In that light, it was a surprise that the House of Lords upheld the ban as being proportionate, the exact opposite conclusion of the ECtHR. *Animal Defenders International* was factually indistinguishable from the *Tierfabriken* case: an animal rights organisation wanted to have broadcast a short piece condemning the treatment of certain animals by commercial companies. The House decided the ban was a proportionate response given the anti-democratic concerns outlined by the Minister; what Lord Bingham called the need to create a level playing-field for debate.[340] Lord Scott, alone, did consider that its absolute nature and its width might mean the ban in certain cases could overreach and thus be disproportionate.[341] In the view of the House, the full strength of the argument from democracy had not been fully explored at Strasbourg and the duty contained in section 2 of the HRA was not slavishly to follow but to take account. It was within Parliament's discretionary area of judgement to decide how to frame the law.[342] It remains to be seen how the ECtHR will treat section 321 as and when it comes before it. *VgT* has been confirmed by the Grand Chamber.[343] This followed a finding of a violation on similar facts—albeit a mainstream political party rather than an interest group, in the run up to an election—in *TV Vest v Norway*.[344]

We have considered how the Public Order Act 1986 can be used to regulate both marches and static assemblies, treating all large groups the same. Sections 12–14A contain no notion of the political dimension to protest and confers no special treatment; protests are all lumped in with football crowds or those on a station concourse awaiting a delayed train. We saw too how police discretion is at the heart of the exercise of the right in practice and that the very scheme of the Act involves them in politically controversial judgements when, for example, officers are asked to assess intimidatory purpose in sections 12–14A. Bonner and Stone highlight the dangers that lie in the vague line between serious disruption—the trigger under the Act—and a degree of inconvenience.

> One can accept fairly readily, subject to an opportunity to challenge the reasonableness of police belief, the need to intervene over route, location, numbers, etc., where serious public disorder or damage to property is in issue or where there is a clear intimidatory purpose, since none of these

---

[338] A good discussion of the topic can be found in H Fenwick and G Phillipson, *Media Freedom and the Human Rights Act* (Oxford, Oxford University Press, 2006) 1012–36.
[339] *Verein gegen Tierfabriken v Switzerland* (2002) 34 EHRR 4, cf *Murphy v Ireland* (2004) 38 EHRR 13 (a ban on religious advertising was not disproportionate), noted A Geddis, 'You Can't Say 'God' on the Radio' [2004] EHRLR 181.
[340] *R (Animal Defenders International) v Secretary of State for Culture, Media and Sport* [2008] UKHL 15 at [28].
[341] ibid, at [42].
[342] Query the relevance of the ban to commercial concerns whose adverts allude to or make 'political' claims about matters on which in the UK there is all-round agreement (such as global warming) given the trigger condition of 'political controversy in the UK' under s 321(3)(g) for the matter to be political under the Act: C Knight 'Monkeying around with free speech'(2008) 124 LQR 557, 560.
[343] *Verein gegen Tierfabriken v Switzerland (No 2)* (App 32772/02) ECtHR (Grand Chamber) judgment 30 June 2009.
[344] *TV Vest v Norway* (App 21132/05) ECtHR 11 December 2008.

are part of peaceful protest. But the [serious disruption to community] trigger empowers interference with peaceful protests exhibiting none of those deplorable characteristics. Some degree of inconvenience, discomfort or annoyance to others is an almost inevitable consequence of any protest of significant size. There may be a danger that the police, faced with conflicting demands to use or not to use this power may accord too much protection to business and community convenience at the expense of freedom of speech and assembly, especially with respect to unpopular causes and non-establishment groups.[345]

Whenever a protest takes the form of a march or a demonstration, we must take account not only of the European dimension in the form of the ECHR but EC law as well. The decision not to ban a demonstration was held by the European Court of Justice as capable of being challenged as a restriction on free movement of goods. On the facts, the result was complete closure for 30 hours of the Brenner Pass that links Austria and Italy. Though the decision was in principle in breach of EC law, there was an objective justification: Austria was pursuing the aim of protecting the protesters' rights under Article 11. Given the state's wide margin of discretion and the fact that the objective could not be achieved by measures less restrictive of the right of free movement of goods, the decision not to seek a ban struck a fair balance between the competing rights of the traders and protesters.[346]

We also saw—largely though our discussion of section 5 of the POA 1986—how domestic law regulates the content of expressive messages during protests. The impact here of the HRA and Article 10 has been rather limited. Courts have not really adopted a view of section 5 that (using section 3 of the HRA) they should read in a requirement that prosecutions should only succeed if it is shown that the language or behaviour is not only seriously disruptive or disorderly but is also of such a type or quality that its value (either to society or to the speaker) is outweighed by the need to protect hearers and society from such utterances (if ever they should be). It even seems under section 5 that the likelihood of avoiding prosecution varies inversely to the popularity of the message or subject-matter. The more a protester needs or wants to challenge accepted views or values, the more likely it is they will have to do so in the face of intransigence or positive support and so will engender the sorts of feelings that section 5 seeks to prevent from occurring. This is what Geddis calls the audience veto whereby the right to express oneself is 'entirely dependent on the internal feelings of irritation generated' in the audience.[347] Indeed, there might even be strangely an inverse relationship between the spread of the communication and any likely Article 10 defence: if

[345] Bonner and Stone, above n 17, 226 (footnotes omitted).
[346] Case C-112/00 *Eugen Schmidberger Internationale Transporte Planzuge v Austria* [2003] ECR I-5659, noted M Humphreys, 'Free Movement and roadblocks: the right to protest in the Single Market' (2004) 6 *Environmental Law Review* 190 (*cf* Case C-265/95 *Commission v France* [1997] ECR I-6959, where farmers violently disrupted the flow of agricultural produce into France following which the police were reluctant to intervene). The same result—albeit on a slightly different factual matrix and with a different approach and analysis to that in *Eugen Schmidberger* —was reached by the House of Lords in *R v Chief Constable of Sussex v International Trader's Ferry* [1999] 2 AC 418. This was a judicial review of the Chief Constable's decision to reduce police protective cover for those exporting live animals from a port in the county and who faced intense opposition from animal rights protesters. Given the drain on the county's resources, the police turned back livestock transporters on days when no cover was made available on grounds that they otherwise feared breaches of the peace. Even if the Chief Constable's decisions constituted 'measures' restricting free movement (which was doubted) the wider requirements of public policy, such as the need to maintain public order, were, under EC law, capable of justifying the restrictions, provided the steps taken were proportionate. Limiting the number of days of police cover was not disproportionate in the light of the available resources and his duty to police the whole county. The House of Lords decision and issues are discussed by I Hare and C Barnard 'Police discretion and the rule of law: Economic Community rights versus civil rights' (2000) 63 *MLR* 681 and the Court of Appeal decision is discussed 'The right to protest and the right to export: police discretion and the free movement of goods' (1997) 60 *MLR* 394.
[347] Geddis, n 287, above, 121.

a protester sends to just one other person (the pharmacist in *Connolly* for example) an offensive protesting message, she cannot lay claim to her free speech having some wider functional value or utility as she might have been able to had she stood on a street corner with a loud speaker blaring out.[348]

The European Court made reference to the notion of audience sensitivity in *Vajnai*, the 'red star' case. While acknowledging the ubiquity of the red star as a symbol of terror such that victims and survivors might find the condoning of its use disrespectful, the Court added that

> such sentiments, however understandable, cannot alone set the limits of freedom of expression. Given the well-known assurances which the Republic of Hungary provided legally, morally and materially to the victims of Communism, such emotions cannot be regarded as rational fears. In the Court's view, a legal system which applies restrictions on human rights in order to satisfy the dictates of public feeling—real or imaginary—cannot be regarded as meeting the pressing social needs recognised in a democratic society, since that society must remain reasonable in its judgement. To hold otherwise would mean that freedom of speech and opinion is subjected to the heckler's veto.[349]

As currently interpreted and constituted, what Geddis calls a 'pro-civility' discourse pervades not just section 5—as he asserts—but sections 12–14A too, even in light of *Jones*. The state can

> legitimately require that anyone wishing to espouse or discuss matters of general public or political interest respect the sensibilities of others and act in a fashion which preserves a measure of decorum in society as a whole. Shaping or conditioning of the realm of public discourse in this fashion reflects a communitarian ethos; the rights of individual speakers should not be allowed to trump the wider collective social interest in establishing standards that govern what is an acceptable contribution to the public debate over matters of common current importance.[350]

Such a position is of course self-fulfilling and self-insulating. If we are not exposed to, do not expect to be exposed to, and indeed are protected by law from being exposed to, such views, we will continue to feel insulted when we are. Each protest that is silenced is one more that reinforces the status quo to which we have been sensitised. There is an important alternative message that the state could send and which, if repeated, could reinforce a wholly new mindset, one that is behind the ECHR's message of tolerance. It is this that Geddis calls the transformative approach.[351] After all, without my tolerating others why should my views—at some later date—be tolerated? Democratic civic membership must presume on my part values and ideals—about ends and means—that are contested and further must presume too that this is not a one-way street. This leads in to a much wider agenda of public education about rights, and about the role and value of protest generally. We will return to this matter in our concluding chapter.

---

[348] I am grateful to one of my undergraduate students Tom Lenihan for this insight.
[349] *Vajnai v Hungary*, above n 243, at [57].
[350] Geddis, above n 287, 869.
[351] *ibid*, 870.

6

Taking Direct Action

I. Introduction and Overview

Previously we considered the framework surrounding communicative protest, broadly described: marches and assemblies that try peacefully to persuade and to demonstrate dissent. The focus of this chapter is the regulation of a more modern phenomenon, albeit one with an historical pedigree[1]: direct action protest. At the extremes the difference is clear. We can easily contrast someone who suspends a 'Peace Now' banner from their bedroom window with those members of Reclaim The Streets who in July 1996 dug up the tarmac on parts of a central London motorway, replacing it with trees and turf for children to play on.[2] It may though be difficult to discern a clear boundary as communicative protest merges and blurs with obstructive protest.

A mass sit-in outside the entrance to an airbase, with people holding and waving 'War Is Bad' banners or chanting while sitting peacefully in the road would clearly be a 'communicative protest' as would symbolically at least the very act of creating a blockade. However, blockading personnel trucks is also quite obviously a direct action protest. The driving force behind the protesters' choice of that method of 'communication' was not so as to engage with the political process or to ask citizens to reflect on the state's defence policy. Instead the protesters were aiming at preventing the very activity complained about from taking place, albeit temporarily. The difference between this type of protest and a stall in a pedestrian precinct on a Saturday morning petitioning for signatures or distributing leaflets is clear. Both are obstructive but in the first this is largely an unintended incident of a process of engagement with people and politicians and is largely symbolic; it does not have—as the second does—obstructing or disrupting the targets of protesters' ire as a freestanding tactic of coercion. Direct action protests do not seek to convert or to proselytise but seek by their actions to change or bring an end to some existing socio-economic activity in line with their own moral viewpoint.[3] Protesters—rather than protests—that are violent (certainly) or

---

[1] We could trace its lineage through the suffragette movement back to and beyond the Levellers and Diggers in the 1600s.

[2] B Seel and A Plows, 'Coming Live and Direct—strategies of Earth First!' in B Seel (ed), *Direct Action in British Environmentalism* (Abingdon, Routledge, 2000) 120 and generally.

[3] Helen Fenwick and Gavin Phillipson in their typology further distinguish between persuasive protest—where the activity obstructed is not the activity complained of—and direct action protest by sub-dividing the latter into primarily symbolic and symbolic protest with no or minimal disruption on the activity in question; protest that actually physically obstructs or that actually interferes with the activity in question; protest that intimidates those participating in the activity in question; forceful physical obstruction such as resisting police attempts at removal from a sit-in; and violent protest: see H Fenwick and G Phillipson, 'Direct action, convention values and the Human Rights Act' (2001) 21 *Legal Studies* 535, 540–41.

which use force (quite possibly) will largely be outwith any protection for 'peaceful' protest under Article 11 and Article 10, as outlined in chapter three.[4] As we shall see in this chapter, the Westminster Parliament has increasingly been paying attention to Fenwick and Phillipson's third type of protest: one that seeks to intimidate in order to dissuade, say, investors in or lenders to those who run animal experimentation laboratories or those who are employed at abortion clinics.

This chapter follows a similar format to the previous one. It will identify the framework of rules that governs and regulates direct action. These we can sub-divide as follows: the possibility that direct action might fall within the definition of terrorism; crimes of violence and damage; aggravated trespass; harassment; and discrete types of intimidation and disruption such as computer hacking, malicious communications and interfering with contractual relationships so as to cause harm. Strasbourg principles and jurisprudence (covered in detail in chapter three) will be synthesised so that we may see how domestic law has been—or might be—affected by the domestication of the right to peaceful protest.[5] The analysis of this here will be shorter for one good reason: Strasbourg is singularly unsympathetic not only to direct action but also to protests that create only incidental or marginal disruption. We might consider again *WG v Austria*.[6] The conviction of an anti-nuclear campaigner for using the road without authorisation was upheld as justified. He had set up a stall and distributed environmental protest leaflets. In the eyes of the authorities, he was using the road for the purposes of an assembly and to impart information. The EComHR concluded that the requirement for authorisation was justified on the facts and in the circumstances to ensure security and to prevent disorder (the free flow of traffic), and so a punishment for failing to obtain an authorisation was also justified as part of the enforcement package.

Although, as we saw in chapter three, there has been a marked move by the Court—in cases such as *Oya Ataman*[7]—towards demanding tolerance of disruptive protests, this has only gone so far. There has still not been a single direct action protest case to have succeeded on its substantive merits. The only successful cases have been where a restriction has not been prescribed by law, such as in *Hashman and Harrup v UK*.[8] The contrast between the treatment of the 1st and 2nd applicants in *Steel v UK*—direct action, obstructive protest; no violation—and the 3rd to 5th leafleting outside an arms fair (held as disproportionate) makes the point well.[9]

---

[4] As we saw in chapter three, the case law of the ECHR distinguishes between violent protests and protesters who are violent; only the latter lose protection of Art 11: *Ezelin v France* (1992) 14 EHRR 362.

[5] The question of land ownership still remains pivotal to the location and success of any direct action protest. Whether a group is holding a march or trying to handcuff themselves to a JCB, the same questions about rights of access to land hold true. We shall see again how the reality of protest is shaped by the interplay of various factors: the socio-economic demography of land ownership; political decisions regarding public space; the scope of private, common law remedies relating to land and the increasing criminalisation of trespass such as aggravated trespass under s 68 of the Criminal Justice and Public Order Act 1994 (CJPOA).

[6] *WG v Austria* (App 15509/89) EComHR inadmissibility decision 30 November 1992.

[7] *Oya Ataman v Turkey* (App 74552/01) ECtHR judgment 5 December 2006.

[8] *Hashman and Harrup v United Kingdom* (2000) 30 EHRR 241.

[9] *Steel v United Kingdom* (1998) 28 EHRR 603.

II. Direct Action Protesters As Terrorists

We touched on the socio-legal phenomenon of constructing deviance in our introduction. The literature on the creation of folk devils and moral panics is well-known and extensive.[10] The most obvious is the media's portrayal of the religious fanatic, the Islamist extremist terrorist, but increasingly we read about eco-terrorists such as those at the annual climate change camps in the United Kingdom.[11] This book is not the place to debate the appropriateness of such labelling, the knock-on effects for political and legal discourse and the simplistic dichotomising that such value-laden terms bring. Instead though, we do need to focus on the definition of terrorism in domestic law to see whether or not direct action might be viewed as terrorist activities.[12]

Certain types of protest activity might well be under the wide definition of 'terrorism' in section 1 of the Terrorism Act 2000 even if that is far removed in the public psyche from the 7 July suicide bombers in London and the Shankill Butchers of the 1970s. This would clearly be a concern to those seeking a shift in agriculture policy away from GM crops, or those who want greater limits imposed on the availability of abortions, or those trying to stop arms exports to belligerent and tyrannical regimes. Section 1 sets out what constitutes terrorism. Importantly it does not itself create a free-standing offence of 'terrorism'; it is a definitional catalyst for a range of other offences and powers dotted throughout the panoply of anti-terrorist legislation from 2000 to 2006. These include: fund-raising for the purposes of terrorism (sections 14–18 of the 2000 Act) and possessing an article where there is a reasonable suspicion it is possessed for the purposes of terrorism under section 57. Terrorism is the use or threat of action

(a) designed to influence the government or to intimidate the public or a section of the public
(b) made for the purpose of advancing a political, religious or ideological cause and
(c) where the action (used or threatened)
  (i) involves serious violence against a person,
  (ii) involves serious damage to property,
  (iii) endangers a person's life, other than that of the person committing the action,
  (iv) creates a serious risk to the health or safety of the public or a section of the public or
  (v) is designed seriously to interfere with or seriously to disrupt an electronic system.

Let us take those in turn. In the main, protests by means of deliberately chosen 'serious violence' can be ruled out as being peaceful within Article 11. That much is clear on current Strasbourg case law and so would not be protected any further under the HRA than before, although protests where 'serious violence' occurs are not automatically removed from protection under Article 11 if the violence arises from the acts of third parties. The use of

---

[10] See above p 17 and also "Ministry of Justice lists eco-activists alongside terrorists" *The Guardian* 26 January 2010.
[11] There was extensive discussion of this in the broadsheet media itself in relation to the events at Heathrow in the summer of 2007 and Kingsnorth power station in August 2008.
[12] See C Walker, *Blackstone's Guide to the Anti-Terrorism Legislation* 2nd edn (Oxford, Oxford University Press, 2009) and H Fenwick, *Civil Liberties and Human Rights*, 4th edn (Abingdon, Routledge-Cavendish, 2007) ch 14.

'involve' in two of the five triggers does undoubtedly widen the scope of the offence, since it ties the actor to the act to a much lesser degree. It is conceivable that 'terrorist activity' could include cases where the actor does not cause or intend the consequence of serious violence ... it just happens to be the result. In those cases, as we saw in chapter three, the protection of Article 11 is not lost; the potential for disparity between Article 11 and section 1 is all the wider since terrorist activity can be the mere threat to 'involve serious violence'. Could this even go so far as to encompass threats that cannot be carried out?

We can see how other examples of direct action protest could potentially be encompassed under (ii)–(v) above. A group marches into farmer Brown's field and rips up several acres' worth of GM crops being grown under licence—or of course just threatens to do so—or indeed their actions merely 'involve' that serious damage! This will fall four-square within (ii)—though query the meaning of 'serious'.[13] Another group, while staging a vigil outside an abortion clinic, decides to hold up banners announcing: 'Murderers. We know where you live. We'll repay the debt'. This is not so clear. The action—murder or maiming—that is threatened (unless this is the actual act of carrying a placard?) is one that would obviously endanger someone's life—and also creates a risk to health! An animal rights protester bombards a research laboratory with hoax emails or delivers a virus into its pc system. The design—does this mean 'fashioned' or 'planned'?[14]—seriously to interfere with an electronic computer system is again clear. For each, it still needs to be shown that the remaining two limbs are made out: there must be a design to influence the government or to intimidate the public or a section of it and the purpose must be to advance a political, religious or ideological cause. It can almost be assumed that the second would be made out by any protest—that is its purpose after all and was one of the four qualities we ascribed it in trying to define it[15]—given the undefined width of 'political'.[16] The first limb might cause prosecutors some difficulty. Clearly, the immediate target of some protests might not be the government but private industry and so cannot be said to be aimed or planned (if we assume 'designed' is synonymous with these) to influence the government. Might they be designed to intimidate the public or section thereof? On this the Oxford English Dictionary provides for a modern use of intimidate as 'to force to or deter from some action by threats or violence' so greatly increasing is scope.[17] That said, it might be more accurate to think of it being designed to *influence* the public—to convince them to lobby for better environmental regulation or limits to the trade in arms—or to highlight a perceived inequity in the law.

Let us be clear. None of this is either to approve or to gainsay the moral defensibility of any form of obstructive, coercive, intimidatory direct action. It is merely to record that those types of protest activity are far removed from what we would normally associate with terrorism and all that that entails. Once a protester is construed (and constructed) as a terrorist and arrested for a terrorism-related offence, the time limits for detention without charge are greatly increased from 96 hours to (currently) 28 days. Control orders may be imposed on suspected terrorists under the Prevention of Terrorism Act 2005—in

---

[13] This clearly creates a potential problem for all those who buy the Greenpeace magazine and all its active members who own spades under ss 14–18 and s 57. The burden of disproving the article is possessed for a non-terrorist purpose is on the defendant but will surely be, following *R v Lambert* [2001] UKHL 37, read as meaning an evidential not legal burden so as to remain compatible with Art 6(1).

[14] If the latter meaning is adopted, this at least has something approaching a mental element rather than attributing terrorism to what takes place or what results from the action as the others do.

[15] See above p 58.

[16] We adverted to this briefly in chapter five at p 216.

[17] www.dictionary.oed.com/ (accessed 25 November 2008).

admittedly relatively narrowly prescribed circumstances—and the possibility at least arises for the Secretary of State to proscribe a direct action protest group on the grounds that it is concerned in terrorism.

Legislation passed in the shadow of terrorism can lead to policing decisions later being made in its full glare. Anti-terrorism legislation has meant certain protesters being subjected to stop and search without the need to show reasonable suspicion, under the blanket authorisation provisions contained in section 44 Terrorism Act 2000.[18] Anti-terrorism legislation brought to public attention the notorious case of Walter Wolfgang, a matter that would be comedic were it not a tragedy. Although the full details have never been made public, there was wide media coverage when this 82-year old was ejected from Labour's annual conference in 2005, after heckling the Foreign Secretary over the Iraq war. He was prevented from re-entering by Sussex Police using 'terrorism powers'.[19] At the same conference another attendee wearing a T-shirt proclaiming 'Bush Blair Sharon to be tried for war crimes torture human rights abuse' was stopped and searched. The form filled out by the police officer stated, under grounds for intervention, 'carrying plackard [sic] and T-shirt with anti-Blair info'. The purpose of the stop and search was stated as 'terrorism'.[20] We saw in chapter four how the spectre of terrorism informs and structures legal responses to 'normal' legitimate peaceful protest: we read of the two grandmothers from Yorkshire described by *The Independent* as 'the new face of terrorism' after they were prosecuted for trespassing a few feet over the boundary at Menwith Hill after it was listed as designated site.[21] One of the reasons given for requiring authorisation around Westminster was the worry that even solo protests could be used as subterfuge by determined terrorists. This mindset is prevalent also when it comes to direct action. Partly the reason Heathrow succeeded in obtaining an injunction against climate change protesters in 2007 was the worry about the deployment of officers away from dealing with possible terrorist threats.[22]

III. Crimes of Violence and Damage

As well as bespoke 'protest' or 'direct action' crimes—such as failing to give notification of a public procession under section 11 of the POA 1986 or aggravated trespass (to come in this chapter)—protesters also run the risk of offending against the ordinary law of the land. We have met some of these crimes before: wilful obstruction of the highway without lawful excuse would be a good example as this captures those who double park their cars as well. Those engaging in deliberately obstructive, disruptive or intimidatory direct action are more likely to commit general crimes than those who seek to persuade or to show solidarity en masse.[23] This section cannot hope properly to explore all possible 'ordinary' crimes

---

[18] We shall consider this in chapter seven.
[19] BBC News on-line 28 September 2005, news.bbc.co.uk/1/hi/uk_politics/4291388.stm; www.noliberties.com/stories_ww.htm; 'When a slogan equals terrorism', Marcel Berlins, *The Guardian*, 3 October 2005; www.guardian.co.uk/politics/2005/oct/03/terrorism.immigrationpolicy (all accessed 25 November 2008).
[20] Berlins, *ibid*.
[21] Above pp xx.
[22] *Heathrow Airport Ltd v Garman* [2007] EWHC 1957 (QB) at [112]. See too '"Bullying" BAA tries to scare off protesters', *The Observer*, 11 January 2009.
[23] Several of these are subject to the provisions of ss 28–33 of the Crime and Disorder Act 1998, which deal with racially and religiously aggravated crimes.

in any depth. Instead, its aim is more modest: to identify the most likely offences and to seek to locate this within the context of direct action.[24]

A. Crimes of Violence and Harm

The fact that a protest becomes or even starts off violently will not automatically debar its participants from claiming the protection of Article 11. An assembly or protest can be 'peaceful' under the ECHR even if violence occurs; what matters is whether organisers and individual participants had 'peaceful' intentions at the outset.[25] It is a right secured to all those acting peacefully—that is not intentionally violently—even if some of the group did intend there to be violent trouble. The key, in *Ezelin* at least, was the absence of 'reprehensible' acts on the part of the individual concerned.[26] More recently in *Ziliberberg v Moldova*, the Court stated that

> an individual does not cease to enjoy the right to peaceful assembly as a result of *sporadic* violence or other punishable acts committed by others in the course of the demonstration, if the individual in question remains peaceful in his or her own intentions or behaviour (emphasis added).

As we consider the various crimes below, we should bear in mind that the right of peaceful protest could still provide a shield, under section 7(1)(b), for direct action protesters to seek collateral defensive protection if charges are brought if they themselves were not actually violent. This might be especially so where domestic law confers criminal liability for violence imputed to all participants in a group or to threats but no actual violence. The question would then become one of the proportionality of any conviction.

Sections 1–3 of the Public Order Act 1986 create three specific public order crimes. They replace the common law crimes of riot, rout, unlawful assembly and affray, abolished following a Law Commission recommendation in 1983.[27] The three are riot, violent disorder and affray. As well as being the means for the police to control demonstrations and protests, they provide the basis for much control and order maintenance outside pubs and bars and in city centres on Saturday nights and near football grounds on match days. The three vary in degrees of seriousness and in minimum numbers required but each is linked in some way to violence or threats and there being a person of reasonable firmness at the scene fearing for their personal safety. Each can occur in either public or private.

Riot is committed by each person who uses unlawful violence for a common purpose and who intends to use violence or is aware that their conduct may be violent[28] provided that

(i) 12 or more are present together using or threatening unlawful violence for a common purpose and
(ii) the conduct of them all together is such as would cause a person of reasonable firmness at the scene to fear for their personal safety.[29]

---

[24] Greater detail will be found in any standard criminal law text or practitioners' work.
[25] *CARAF v United Kingdom* (App 8440/78) (1980) 21 DR 138 at [4].
[26] *Ezelin v France*, above n 4, at [53].
[27] The Law Commission, *Criminal Law Offences Relating to Public Order Law* (Report No 123, 1983). On the old common law offences see DGT Williams, *Keeping the Peace* (London, Hutchinson, 1967) 236–50 and R Card, *Public Order Law* (Bristol, Jordans, 2000) ch 3.
[28] The mental element is contained in s 6(1). The maximum sentence for riot is 10 years.
[29] It is immaterial under s 1(2) whether or not the 12 use or threaten unlawful violence simultaneously. The common purpose may be inferred from conduct: s 1(3).

Violent disorder is committed by each person who uses or threatens unlawful violence for a common purpose and who intends to use or to threaten violence or is aware that their conduct may be violent or may threaten violence [30] provided that

(i) three or more are present together using or threatening unlawful violence for a common purpose and
(ii) the conduct of them all together is such as would cause a person of reasonable firmness at the scene to fear for their personal safety.[31]

Affray is committed by each person who uses or who threatens unlawful violence towards another[32] and who intends to use or to threaten violence or is aware that their conduct may be violent or may threaten violence and where their conduct is 'such as would cause a person of reasonable firmness at the scene to fear for [their] personal safety'.[33]

We will not go into great detail but instead will focus on some general points.[34] None of the three needs someone actually to be put in fear for their personal safety; the measure is a hypothetical person, objectively judged. The fact that people were present—and witnessed the threats or the violence—will not necessarily determine that a person of reasonable firmness would have been caused to fear.[35] Neither does any offence require a third party actually to have been present at the scene—see section 1(4) for riot, section 2(3) for violent disorder and section 3(4) for affray. This is a strange omission for a series of sections dedicated to controlling public order, as too is the fact that it can be committed in private.[36] Richard Card has questioned, in view of the range of other offences against the person or against property, 'whether there would be a significant gap in the law if the three offences did not exist'.[37] The Law Commission's view was that there was a certain and added seriousness to mob violence or threats given the increased sense of exposure sensed by members of the public in such situations and the difficulties of policing such groups. As Card counters, that would be logically more defensible if it were not possible for an individual to commit affray and for only three to commit violent disorder and in neither case for anyone actually either to fear violence or even to be present. We can easily see—although evidential matters and policing discretion may indicate otherwise—how even charges of riot might possibly be brought against a group of twelve direct action protesters. The reference to unlawful violence as part of the actus reus of all three offences means (section 8) 'any violent conduct'. It covers for both riot and violent disorder (but not for affray) not just violent attacks on others—or threats to do so—but also violent conduct towards property. Thus where a group of three or more rampage through an animal experimentation laboratory or an abortion clinic, in the still of night, smashing up the equipment—or scrawling on the walls that they will return to do so in daylight—the constituent elements of violent disorder have been made out.

Using that example, let us make two final HRA points. The first concerns the term 'violent' and the second 'unlawful' but both ultimately involve the same analysis: the extent of

[30] The mental element is contained in s 6(2).
[31] It is immaterial under s 2(2) whether or not the three use or threaten unlawful violence simultaneously.
[32] The omission of this qualification from the two more serious offences indicates that they can be committed by using or threatening violence against property.
[33] For affray, a threat cannot be made by words alone—s 3(3).
[34] For a detailed consideration, see Card, above n 27.
[35] At common law, an essential element was the presence of innocent third parties: see the cases referred to in A Sherr, *Freedom of protest, public order and the law* (Oxford, Blackwell Publishing, 1989) 88–9.
[36] As Sherr (*ibid*, 95) notes, this is another example of the privatisation of public order.
[37] Card, above n 27, 83.

Article 11 protection for riot, violent disorder and affray. First, the omission of any definition of 'violence' or 'violent' in the relevant part of the Act means, as Card notes, that it will be for the arbiters of fact to decide if, say, a group of football fans pushing and shoving the chairman of the club, in an effort to secure his resignation, are using 'violent conduct'. Similarly this would be the case towards the director of an arms factory or the farmer in his GM crop field. He refers to *Dino Services v Prudential Assurance Co Ltd*—albeit itself circular—for his view that 'violence is a strong word that should not be watered down'.[38] This must be all the more so under section 3 of the HRA and its requirement of Convention-compatible readings if possible. We have seen that Article 11 is capable (albeit unlikely it would have to be conceded) of protecting even certain forms of direct action protest. This might mean that section 3 of the HRA required the reading in of 'serious' as a qualifier or more radically 'and then go on to commit it' after 'who threaten unlawful violence'. Equally, Strasbourg cases in which the non-peaceful nature of an assembly has been an issue have involved violence to persons; the peaceful quality of the protester is lost where A intends violent actions towards B. It is not certain that the European Court would conclude that those who intend violence towards property or possessions would also cease to be protected (though it would have to be conceded that such behaviour might well also be 'reprehensible', in the words of *Ezelin*.) If that were so, it would be open to argument—under the HRA—that a prosecution for violent disorder when the accused had only made threats against property belonging to another, which that other did not even witness and did not know about, would at least engage the right of peaceful protest, if not constitute a disproportionate restriction on it. Another line of attack might be to argue that prosecuting someone for riot or violent disorder where they themselves were not actually violent towards another was an abuse of process, based on Article 11, given the existence of countless alternative charges.

The second point is this. Violence must also be 'unlawful'. All defences and justifications provided elsewhere by law will constitute an excuse. Alongside the use of lawful force—by officers making arrests—might the right of peaceful protest also found a legitimate reason for threatening what would otherwise be unlawful violence? The problem with this, as we have seen, is that Strasbourg has so far not looked favourably on direct action and has removed all protection for activity that is not peaceful. It might provide a defence, as above, for those who only threaten violence. It might do so even more in cases—such as our example above—where protesters are said to have committed the crime, on the ordinary reading of the legislation, even though no one was present in fact to be or feel threatened, or the person present did not fear for their safety (even though a person of reasonable firmness would have done). It is hard to see how charges of riot are a proportionate response in light of the right.

A related crime is putting someone in fear of violence under section 4 of the Protection from Harassment Act (PFHA) 1997.[39] What has been added by section 4 that was not covered before at common law as assault or as affray under section 3 of the POA 1986? The offence is made out by someone whose

---

[38] ibid, 87. In *Dino Services* [1989] 1 All ER 422 (CA) 426 Kerr LJ indicated his view that violence 'is intended to convey . . . the use of some force . . . which may be minimal . . . if accentuated or accompanied by some physical act which can properly be described as violent in its nature or character'.

[39] Its value rests as much in the link to restraining orders available to courts under s 5. Defendants may be restrained from any activity so as to protect either the victim or any other person from further conduct which either amounts to harassment or which will cause a fear of violence. Breach of an order granted under s 5 is without reasonable excuse itself a separate crime.

course of conduct causes another to fear, on at least two occasions, that violence will be used against him [provided] . . . he knows or ought to know that his course of conduct will cause the other so to fear on each of those occasions.

The test for the mental element in section 4(1) is set out in section 4(2): would a reasonable person in possession of the same information think the course of conduct would cause the other so to fear on that occasion? There are three defences set out in section 4(3):

(a) his course of conduct was pursued for the purpose of preventing or detecting crime;
(b) his course of conduct was pursued under any enactment or rule of law or to comply with any condition or requirement imposed by any person under any enactment; or
(c) the pursuit of his course of conduct was reasonable for the protection of himself or another or for the protection of his or another's property.

At first sight, the scope of the actus reus means that affray provides the better opportunity for prosecutors: there is a wider range of defences under section 4 of the PFHA and section 4 requires threatening behaviour on at least two occasions. It is the mental element that might lend support to the use of section 4. For affray, it must be shown that D was aware his conduct may threaten violence—a test that lends itself to subjectivity, albeit shrouded with recklessness—whereas under section 4 the test is whether D knew or ought to know it would cause fear, judged by the objective 'reasonable person' test.

Protesters who threaten others—alongside possible affray or use of section 4 of the PFHA (if there is a course of conduct)—run the risk of committing common assault. This is a summary offence under section 39 of the Criminal Justice Act 1988. An assault is any act by which a person intentionally or recklessly causes another to apprehend the application of immediate[40] and unlawful force, no matter how minor that force might be.[41] Assault can thus be committed by threatening words[42] (provided they cause the necessary apprehension of force or violence[43]) and also by silence alone, such as by repeated silent phone calls to women.[44]

Where common assault extends to actually inflicting harm, this is technically two separate offences: common assault and battery charged as 'common assault by beating'[45] under section 39, or the more serious offence of assault occasioning actual bodily harm under section 47 of the Offences against the Person Act 1861. Battery is the intentional and reckless application of unlawful force to another.[46] In truth, there is little difference

---

[40] In fact 'at some time' not excluding the immediate future: *R v Gaetano Constanza* (1997) 2 Cr App R 492.

[41] *Director of Public Prosecutions v Parmenter* [1992] 1 AC 699, 740; and *Archbold Criminal Pleading, Evidence and Practice* (London, Sweet and Maxwell, 2006) paras 19-166 and 19-172.

[42] In *Constanza*, above n 40 (stalking over a prolonged period) the Court of Appeal held that an assault could be committed solely by words even if no physical harm had occurred provided it could be proved that the victim had a fear of violence 'at some time'.

[43] The fact that D doesn't inflict any force on V means there is no battery but it will still be an assault if V is caused to fear she will be battered. Thus shaking fists at V even if it is physically impossible to make contact or something will prevent it will be an assault (*Stephens v Myers* (1830) 4 C & P 349) unless the words used in the assault make it clear there is no intention to batter: *Turberville v Savage* (1669) 1 Mod Rep 3.

[44] *R v Ireland; R v Burstow* [1998] AC 147. See now the summary offence under s 127 of the Communications Act 2003 discussed below pp 295.

[45] *Director of Public Prosecutions v Little* [1992] 1 All ER 299.

[46] In *R v Donovan* [1934] 2 KB 498 (CA), actual harm was defined as 'any hurt or injury calculated to interfere with the health or comfort . . . It need not be permanent but must no doubt be more than merely transient and trifling'. It covers even the slightest force, such as by touching (*Cole v Turner* (1704) 6 Mod Rep 149) directly or indirectly. Force can be applied by hitting or throwing an item (*Pursell v Horn* (1838) 8 Ad & El 602; *R v Savage* [1992] 1 AC 699). Again, there might be some argument that including within the category of assaults even de minimis touching during a protest would require an adjustment to the common law (by the court as a s 6 public authority) to bring domestic law back into line Convention rights under Arts 10 and 11. Alternatively, it might be argued that to prosecute or even convict a protester for such a minimal intrusion would be to impose a disproportionate restriction

246 *Taking Direct Action*

between common assault and actual bodily harm other than the types of injury sustained and the consequent length of sentence; the mental element is the same—intention or recklessness.[47] Common assault by beating does require the infliction of force, however minor, to the person of another, whereas 'actual bodily harm' under section 47 can include psychological harm.[48] Where the harm caused is more serious, other charges are available. These include unlawful wounding (that is breaking of the skin) or causing grievous (that is really serious[49]) bodily harm with intent, contrary to section 18 or section 20 of the Offences against the Person Act 1861.[50] There could of course be charges of murder or manslaughter if death resulted: in the United States, anti-abortion protesters have shot doctors who perform terminations.

B. Crimes of Damage

One of the reasons Card doubted the need for the three new offences was the existence of more mainstream offences that criminalise the destruction of property, the issuing of threats and causing physical harm to others.[51] They are reinforced by the inchoate offences of attempt, of aiding and abetting and of conspiracy (which again we shall only touch upon) as well as other crimes that regulate inter-personal relations generally such as (particularly) blackmail.[52] We shall consider any civil remedies that victims of protest may have in chapter eight.

on the right of peaceful protest under the ECHR (or that in bringing charges, the CPS was acting ultra vires s 6 of the HRA by acting in a disproportionate fashion).

[47] The Crown Prosecution Service Legal Guidance (http://www.cps.gov.uk/legal/l_to_o/offences_against_the_person/ accessed 2 February 2010) distinguish the two.

[48] In *Ireland*, above n 44, the House of Lords held that the victims of the repeated silent phone calls were in immediate fear owing to the nature of the telephone contact: they were afraid as they did not know what the caller would do next and the silence was capable of being as frightening to the victims as threats would have been.

[49] See the CPS Guidelines (above n 47) on this.

[50] The offence under s 18 is one of specific intent. Under s 20 the prosecution need prove only that the defendant intended to cause (or actually foresaw) some harm: *DPP v Smith* [1961] AC 290 (HL).

[51] There is a range of fairly discrete offences that have been used or are capable of being used against direct action protesters depending on the form their protest takes. We will look at public nuisance, sending malicious letters or making annoying calls together with computer hacking and misuse later in this chapter. Another similar offence would be bomb hoaxes contrary to s 51 of the Criminal Law Act 1977. Place or activity specific crimes of a general nature would include: having in a public place an offensive weapon without lawful authority or reasonable excuse, contrary to s 1 of the Prevention of Crime Act 1953; entering a prohibited place for a purpose prejudicial to the safety or interests of the state contrary to s 1 of the Official Secrets Act 1911 (see *Chandler v DPP* [1964] AC 763, a mass trespass by members of CND at an airbase); unlawfully climbing on Stonehenge contrary to the Stonehenge Regulations 1997 (SI 1997/2038) (see 'Flintstones fined for Stonehenge stunt', at www.thisiswiltshire.co.uk/display.var.1755708.0.flintstones_fined_for_stonehenge_stunt.php, 11 October 2007, relating to two Fathers4Justice protesters); and contaminating or interfering with goods with the intention inter alia of causing public alarm and anxiety, harm or economic loss contrary to s 38 of the Public Order Act 1986. The general catch-alls of vagrancy contrary to s 4 of the Vagrancy Act 1824 and outraging public decency at common law (*Knuller v DPP* [1973] AC 435 and *R v Gibson* [1990] 2 QB 619 (CA)) remain. All of the foregoing takes no account of offences under local authority bye-laws or under place specific legislation such as ss 54 and 60 of the Metropolitan Police Act 1839 or s 28 of the Town Clauses Act 1847 (causing obstruction and nuisance in the street). On the latter two see Williams, *Keeping the Peace*, above n 27, 230–35.

[52] A group of hard-core direct action protesters was convicted of conspiracy to commit blackmail (contrary to s 21 of the Theft Act 1968) after they dug up the corpse of the mother-in-law of the owner of a farm that bred guinea pigs for animal experiments. Theft—the dishonest appropriation of property belonging to another with the intention permanently to deprive them of it (s 1 Theft Act 1968)—is easier to envisage. Releasing animals from an experimentation laboratory at night, taking away the equipment necessary to perform abortions, grabbing and throwing away the keys for a lorry transporting arms are all capable of constituting theft. Protesters entering a building intending to carry out such a theft would likely commit the more serious offence of burglary under s 9 of the Theft Act 1968.

Intentionally or recklessly destroying or damaging property belonging to another—such as pouring paint stripper over cars belonging to BAA executives for their role in transporting live animals for experimentation[53]—without lawful excuse is a crime under section 1 of the Criminal Damage Act 1971.[54] It can include even minor damage: the test is whether the property has suffered permanent or temporary either physical harm or impairment of its use or value.[55] There is little case law on the meaning of 'damage' and it is largely seen as a question of fact for the magistrates or jury. Given the increasing criminalisation of trespass—sometimes triggered by damage (as is the power to order removal under section 61 of the Criminal Justice and Public Order Act (CJPOA) 1994)—protesters should be aware that grass may be damaged by trampling on it[56] and that using mud to write graffiti, even though it could be washed off, could also be damage.[57] Preventing a farmer using her tractor by wheel clamping it or even by attaching oneself to it is unlikely to amount to criminal damage. This merely deprives her of the use of the tractor without intruding into the integrity of the property,[58] whereas removing part of a machine, so that it cannot work, may damage the machine (even if the part if not damaged) because its use is impaired.[59] A development site subjected to fly-tipping can still be 'damaged', as its use and value are impaired, even if it is in the same state below, for no other reason than the costs of clean up.[60] In *Hardman*, water-soluble paint was used to outline dead bodies—to represent those who died at Hiroshima. They were washed off by the local authority even though if it had rained, that too would have been the result. Criminal damage had occurred because the owners of the property had incurred expense.[61] The fact that any damage is remediable does not prevent it being damage. In 2005, a union official was arrested—though charges were dropped three months later—after he placed a wreath on top of one placed by the British National Party at a Holocaust memorial service.[62]

The 'lawful excuse' defence is developed in section 5. At the time of the act or acts alleged to constitute the offence, did the defendant believe first that the property was in immediate need of protection (it being material whether a belief is justified or not if it is honestly held) and secondly that the means of protection adopted or proposed to be adopted were or would be reasonable having regard to all the circumstances?

Blake v DPP is a protest case that turned on the defence in section 5.[63] As part of his protest against the Gulf war, a vicar defaced a pillar outside the House of Commons with a

---

[53] 'Macaque business puts airlines on back foot': *The Guardian*, 28 May 2005.
[54] Arson will be the charge for anyone damaging or destroying property by fire. 'Animal Rights Extremists in Arson Spree', *The Guardian*, 25 June 2005 gives details of arson attacks allegedly perpetrated by the ALF on those who have at best tangential connections with animal research: the house previously owned (but sold 18 months previously) by a lawyer employed by Fisons, a pharmaceutical firm, and property belonging to the finance director of a small brokers who raised funds for a company that was also a customer of Huntingdon Life Science. Section 2 creates the offence of making threats to commit criminal damage while s 3 penalises the possession of articles or material that are intended to be used to commit criminal damage.
[55] *R v Whiteley* (1991) 93 Cr App Rep 25 (CA); *R v Fiak* [2005] EWCA Crim 2381.
[56] *Gayford v Chouler* [1898] 1 QB 316.
[57] *Roe v Kingerlee* [1986] *Criminal Law Review* 735 (DC).
[58] *Drake v Director of Public Posecutions* [1994] Crim LR 855 (DC).
[59] *R v Fisher* (1865) LR 1 CCR 7, 35 LJMC 57; *Getty v Antrim County Council* [1950] NI 114.
[60] *Henderson v Battley*, Unreported Court of Appeal decision, 29 November 1984.
[61] *Hardman v Chief Constable of Avon and Somerset* [1986] Crim LR 330.
[62] 'BNP wreath charge for union man', *The Guardian*, 23 February 2005 (and 'BNP wreath charge dropped', 25 May 2005)
[63] *Blake v Director of Public Prosecutions* [1993] Crim LR 586 (DC). See too *R v Hill* (1988) 89 Cr App R 74 (CA): intending to cut the wire to an airbase, so as to enter in order to persuade the USAF to leave, was an act that was too remote to decrease the risk of Russian nuclear attack thereby to protect local private property.

marker pen. Part of his defence was that he was protecting property in the Gulf states belonging to another. He appealed to the Divisional Court by way of case stated. Though both limbs of section 5 seem on their face to be subjectively worded—that D believed the means were reasonable, not that they actually were so—previous case law had taken a more objective stance, so that the means did need to be objectively justified.[64] Here the Divisional Court concluded that the vicar's conduct objectively viewed was too remote and so was not capable of protecting the property of another.[65] For completeness—as for unlawful violence in sections 1–3 of the POA 1986 and in the context of section 5 of the POA 1986 (discussed in chapter five)—the obvious point can be made. This is that exercising the Convention right of peaceful protest can provide a lawful excuse. Although violent direct action does not engage Article 11 (or 10) where protesters have violent intentions, the fact that criminal damage under section 1 of the 1971 Act can result from entirely peaceful protest or protest that is no more than minimally disruptive or damaging—muddy graffiti—must leave the door open to claims of disproportionality and thus to a compatibility challenge collaterally under section 7(1)(b) of the HRA if protesters are charged.

C. Inchoate Offences

Even if criminal damage or assault is not committed, it may still be possible to prosecute everyone in a group of direct action protesters who had intended, planned or agreed to do so, or who had urged others to do so, or who had tried but failed to do so. This is because the inchoate crimes of conspiracy, incitement and attempt (and even attempted incitement!) widen the criminal noose further, removing it yet further from actual committing any offence and actually causing direct harm. As such, charges against protesters for inchoate offences might be thought riper for challenge—or defence—utilising section 7(1) based on the right of peaceful protest. We shall keep our consideration brief.[66]

Incitement at common law was abolished by section 59 of the Serious Crime Act 2007, being replaced by the various offences of 'encouraging or assisting an offence' in sections 44–46 of that same Act. At common law, it did not matter that the offence was not committed, or that a different offence was committed or even that it could not be committed provided A intended that it should. Conspiracy is largely now also a statutory offence, though certain common law conspiracies still exist. Under section 1 of the Criminal Law Act 1977, conspiracy to commit (say) criminal damage occurs where A agrees with B that a course of conduct should be pursued which, if the agreement is carried out in accordance with their intentions, either will necessarily amount to or will involve the commission of criminal damage by A or B or would do so but for the existence of facts which render its commission impossible. It requires a joint intention that A and B pursue the agreed course of conduct. The offence is made out at the time of the meeting of minds. It does not matter that the plan is never executed or even put into effect, and the conspiracy continues so long as the

---

[64] See *R v Hunt* (1989) Cr App R 74. As John Spencer says in his comment on *Blake* (above n 63) the objective element is 'is difficult to reconcile with the terms of the section'. Whether a reading contrary to the statutory wording could withstand a challenge under s 3 of the HRA for a narrower more Convention compatible reading is a matter of conjecture . . . but seems unlikely.

[65] The Court also rejected his argument that he believed God was able to—and did—consent to his use of a marker pen. Belief in the consent of another is also a lawful excuse under s 5(2)(a).

[66] See generally Card, *Public Order Law* (above n 27) ch 17 or *Archbold*, above n 41, ch 34.

consensus or agreement subsists.[67] Conspiracy can be charged alongside the substantive offence, as a failsafe, and is a very common piece in the prosecutor's toolkit when dealing with all sorts of protests. Criminal attempt under section 1 of the Criminal Attempts Act 1981 takes places where A, with intent to commit a substantive indictable offence, does an act that is 'more than merely preparatory' towards the commission of that offence. Thus there cannot be an attempt to commit a summary offence, such as aggravated trespass under section 68 of the CJPOA1994. We discuss this in detail below and see how case law in that case has made the distinction redundant. Charges of attempt can be brought, again, even if it is impossible as a matter of fact to commit the substantive offence.[68]

D. Defences

All general criminal law defences are available to protesters. Let us concentrate in turn on the three most likely: prevention of crime (one aspect of what is usually referred to as public defence), defence of property and self-defence (or another) against attack (aspects of private defence).[69] That last has recently been put into statutory form in section 76 of the Criminal Justice and Immigration Act 2008.

Section 3 of the Criminal Law Act 1967 allows reasonable force to be used to prevent a crime.[70] In *R v Jones*, a group of direct action protesters argued that the section 3 defence should be available to them after they were charged with criminal damage.[71] The group had broken into an air force base and damaged fuel tankers and bomb trailers. They argued their actions were necessary to prevent the crime of aggression, contrary to customary international law. The House of Lords was asked to decide if the term 'crime' in section 3 of the 1967 Act was limited to domestic offences or whether it could encompass international criminal law? The House accepted that the crime of aggression—defined by Lord Hoffman as the 'unlawful use of war as an instrument of national policy'[72]—was sufficiently well established as a crime in customary international law. Its core elements were understood with sufficient clarity to permit lawful prosecution and punishment at all relevant times. The House accepted too—as it had been by the parties—as a general principle that customary international law is without the need for any domestic statute or judicial decision part

---

[67] *R v Hobbs* [2002] 2 Cr App R 324 (CA).
[68] *R v Shivpuri* [1987] AC 1.
[69] See generally Card, *Public Order Law*, above n 27, chs 18–19. These all have origins in common law. Even where there has been statutory intervention, it is thought that the common law continues to run in parallel: *R v Cousins* [1982] QB 526.
[70] As both Spencer (above n 63) and Card (*ibid*, 770) note, in their comments on the case of *Blake*—where the Court rejected the vicar's defence under s 3 on the basis that using a marker pen was not using force—it is strange that s 3 permits the use of force to prevent a crime but not less serious conduct.
[71] *R v Jones* [2006] UKHL 16, case comment by C Walker [2007] *Crim LR* 66. Two of the defendants were originally freed after jurors failed to reach a verdict: 'Freed activists accused of US bomb carrier damage face retrial', *The Guardian*, 16 September 2006. It was their subsequent re-trial that led to the House of Lords decision. A similar argument was raised in the unsuccessful ECHR case *Drieman v Norway* (App 33678/96) ECtHR inadmissibility decision 4 May 2000) but sidelined because the ECnHR deferred to the national Supreme Court on question of the legality of whaling and the interface between domestic/international law. See also *Hutchinson v Director of Public Prosecutions* (unreported, *The Independent*, 20 November 2000): there was no customary rule of international law the effect of which would be to render it unlawful to produce or develop nuclear weapons and certainly not one of sufficient clarity to provide a s 3 defence to charges relating to cutting the fence at a weapons establishment. Scotland has seen similar protests and issues, discussed S Neff, 'Idealism in action: International Law and nuclear weapons in Greenock Sheriff Court' (2002) 4 *Edinburgh Law Review* 74.
[72] *Jones*, above n 71, [44].

of the law of England and Wales. The protesters had argued that it followed that crimes recognised in customary international law were without more recognised and enforced by the domestic law of England and Wales. The House did not agree: crimes established as offences under customary international law *may* become assimilated into domestic criminal law but that this was not automatic. In the absence of an express provision to the contrary, the terms 'crime' or 'offence' in a domestic statute were ordinarily treated as referring to a crime or an offence committed in the domestic sphere against a common law or statutory rule. The word 'crime' in section 3 was therefore to be understood as referring only to domestic criminal offences, whether created by statute or at common law; despite the protesters' contesting otherwise, the crime of aggression was not one known on the English domestic plane.[73]

The House has fairly clearly closed the door to any international law defence, though Lord Bingham came to the view obiter that war crimes may well be recognised domestically (as well as under customary international law) as an offence 'triable and punishable under the domestic criminal law of this country irrespective of any domestic statute'.[74] That would mean that protesters could mount a section 3 defence based on preventing war crimes, not acts of aggression, assuming sufficient proximity and that the prevention was reasonably necessary. In 2007, a jury acquitted two protesters charged with conspiracy to commit criminal damage (to B-52s at an airbase), the pair having argued that it was reasonable to prevent war crimes and property damage in Iraq.[75] Of course, the real problem facing many direct action protesters is the need for the targeted activity to be a crime (whether or not under domestic law). Much of the regulation of, say, environmental issues is administrative in origin so that any unlawfulness of the GM farmer will be breach of EC rules, of international treaties or licence provisions, possibly committing tort or other civil wrongs but few if any of the farmer's wrongs will be criminal. Even if any could be said to be they may well be too remote in time or place for the prevention of crime defence to be run, on which see below in the context of private defence of property.

Protesters might also rely on self-defence (of oneself or another) from an unlawful act though its close overlap with the use of reasonable force to prevent a crime means, for our purposes, we need dwell little upon it. Both self-defence and using reasonable force under section 3 require the use of force which is no more than 'reasonably necessary'[76] in the circumstances as the defendant believed them to be.[77] The threat or danger must be reason-

[73] Three main reasons were given. The first was constitutional. Assimilation of customary international law crimes into domestic law was not automatic. It was not now for the courts but for the democratically elected Parliament to create new offences: statute is the sole source of the power to impose a criminal penalty upon conduct not previously regarded as criminal: Lord Bingham at [28]–[29], Lord Hoffman at [60]–[62] and Lord Mance at [102]. The second was an amalgam of logistics and justiciability: a charge of aggression against an individual presupposed state culpability and so would call for a review of the exercise of prerogative powers in the conduct of foreign affairs and the deployment of the armed forces. Since the courts would not, save exceptionally, inquire into such areas, it would be incongruous for them without specific statutory authority to treat the crime of aggression as a domestic crime: Lord Bingham at [30], Lord Hoffman at [63]–[67] and Lord Mance at [103]. The last was that it would be anomalous to do so where the International Criminal Court Act 2001 had deliberately excluded the crime of aggression when giving domestic effect to other crimes recognised under international law: Lord Bingham at [28] and Lord Mance at [104].
[74] At [22].
[75] 'Fairford two strike blow for anti-war protesters after jury decide they were acting to prevent crime', *The Guardian*, 26 May 2007. The pair were those who had taken the preliminary issue to the House of Lords in *Jones*, above n 71, Phil Pritchard and Toby Olditch.
[76] *Palmer v R* [1971] AC 814.
[77] See *R v Gladstone Williams* [1987] 3 All ER 411 (CA): even if the belief was mistaken and that mistake was unreasonable.

ably imminent and must be of a nature which could not be met by more peaceful means.[78] The major difference is that section 3 of the 1967 Act only avails itself to those suffering from or seeking to prevent crime:[79] where the harm suffered by V is not a crime but is only, say, a trespass they must rely on self-defence or the common law private defence of property. Thus, landowners can use it to rid themselves of someone unlawfully on their land. However, both self-defence and defence of property need an unlawful act—whether criminal or civil wrong—before they are available.

In *Bayer v DPP*, charges of aggravated trespass were brought against a group that had attached themselves to tractors to prevent GM crop planting.[80] The GM field bordered a wetland bird reserve. The protesters argued private defence of property, that is damage by pollen distribution, animal transfer and soil transfer to the surrounding land, the natural environment, animals and other crops. The defence succeeded before the District Judge. On an appeal by way of case stated, the question for the High Court was whether the finding that the defendants' actions were reasonable in the defence of property was one that was properly open to the court. The Divisional Court (Brooke LJ and Silber J) upheld the appeal. At common law the private defence of property was only available where

(a) force was used to defend property that was under threat of actual or imminent damage which constituted or would constitute an unlawful or criminal act; and
(b) objectively the force that had been used was reasonable in all the circumstances bearing in mind the facts as the defendants honestly believed them to be.[81]

As a matter of law, here private defence of property was simply not available to the defendants: they knew quite well that there was nothing unlawful about the drilling of GM maize on the land, even if the seed might be transferred by one means or another to the neighbouring land. They acted as they had because they believed strongly that the seed represented a danger to neighbouring property and they knew that the law would not help them because what was going on was not unlawful or criminal.

The defence of necessity—sometimes elided with duress of circumstances—is not yet accepted as a general defence to crimes and even if it were, its tenets (and whether

---

[78] *Attorney-General's Reference (No 2 of 1983)* [1984] QB 456 (CA).
[79] Most arrests of protesters will necessarily involve the infliction of some measure of force and so will constitute as a minimum the crime of 'common assault by beating' . . . unless excused because the officer has a lawful power to arrest under s 24 of PACE. Where protesters are arrested unlawfully—perhaps because there was no reasonable suspicion, perhaps because the arrest was a violation of a Convention right orperhaps because they were not told of the ground of arrest (s 28 of PACE)—then they have the right to use reasonable force under s 3 or self-defence at common law to evade the assault on themselves. The problem is that this can largely only be determined *ex post facto* so the danger is that if they are mistaken they themselves will have assaulted an officer in the execution of her duty, contrary to s 89 of the Police Act 1996. Powers of arrest for private citizens such as private security guards at road extension or outside an animal research laboratory (rather than constables) are more limited under s 24A of PACE. There is no power to arrest where no offence is shown actually to have occurred and so they are exposed more easily to civil claims by protesters for wrongful arrest—or charges for assault.
[80] *Bayer v Director of Public Prosecutions* [2003] EWHC 2567 (Admin). Aggravated trespass is an offence s 68 of the Criminal Justice and Public Order Act 1994, which we shall consider below.
[81] The Court contrasted this with the statutory defence contained in s 5(2)(b) of the Criminal Damage Act 1971. This latter is dependent only on (a) a belief that the property was in immediate need of protection and (b) the means of protection adopted being reasonable having regard to all the circumstances.

excusatory or justificatory)—through no personal fault being left with no choice but to commit crime X—are likely to mean it will avail little to any protesters charged.[82]

IV. Aggravated Trespass

The offence of aggravated trespass was created in Part V of the CJPOA 1994.[83] It has been amended and extended in the intervening years. Sections 68–69 were aimed primarily at controlling the activities of fox-hunt saboteurs. As with section 61 of the same Act (empowering the removal of trespassers on land which we looked at in chapter four) and section 14A of the POA 1986 (trespassory assembly, covered in chapter five), these two sections criminalise trespass. One of the themes of this book has been to chart the change from the position where historically the state rarely concerned itself with the regulation of ostensibly civil law matters between private landowners and third parties on their land without consent. Remedies historically and normally were damages or injunctive relief.

The offence under section 68 is made out where

(a) persons are engaging in, or are about to engage in, a lawful activity on land whether or not (since 2004) that land is in open air;[84]
(b) D trespasses on that same or on adjoining land (again now whether or not in the open air); and
(c) in relation to that lawful activity D does there anything which she intends to have the effect of

   (i) intimidating those persons or any of them so as to deter them from engaging in it;
   (ii) obstructing it; or
   (iii) disrupting it.[85]

The section has generated a good deal of case law. Both it and section 69 (which we will look at presently) have become major weapons in dealing with protest. In police and prosecu-

---

[82] For recent case law discussions, see *R v Shayler* [2002] UKHL 11 and *Re A (Conjoined Twins)* [2001] 2 WLR 480 (CA), and for academic discussion C Clarkson, 'Necessary action—a new defence' [2004] *Crim LR* 81 and S Gardner, 'Direct action and necessity' [2005] Crim LR 371.

[83] A good albeit dated study of the policing of aggravated trespass and the use of the offence in practice, especially in the context of fox hunt protest and environmental action, can be found in T Bucke and Z James, *Trespass and Protest: Policing under the Criminal Justice and Public Order Act 1994*, HORS 190 (London, Home Office, 1998) 33–57 and ch 5. Part V of the 1994 Act created a series of new offences, which were implicitly aimed at different sorts of perceived social ills or lifestyles. Some sections made it easier to move on groups of travellers (ss 61–62) while another regulated raves, that is music performed in the open air predominantly characterised by the 'emission of a succession of repetitive beats'. Whether that allows for a proper distinction between Moby at Glastonbury and Mozart at Glyndebourne seems moot.

[84] Amendment made by Sch 3, Para 1 of the Anti-Social Behaviour Act 2003. Before 20 January 2004, the trespass had to take place in the open air. Thus protesters can now be arrested for aggravated trespass if they disrupt a company AGM or where students disrupt their University Senate: ' "Lancaster Six" to challenge trespass convictions', *The Guardian (G2* education section) 9 March 2006, at: www.guardian.co.uk/education/2006/mar/09/highereducation.uk1, accessed 11 August 2009.

[85] Section 68 creates a single offence committed by either intimidation, disruption or obstruction. An information alleging that a defendant intended to intimidate so as to deter, to disrupt or to obstruct was not void for duplicity; there was no need for a separate charge: *Nelder v DPP*, Unreported Divisional Court, 3 June 1998. It must be asked whether one can actually disrupt (rather than obstruct) an activity that has not yet begun, even if the reason for it not beginning was the protester's own direct action? See the example in Bucke and James, above n 83, 52.

tion terms it is a fairly simple offence—albeit one with a distinctly low conviction rate, at least in its formative years.[86]

A. The Constituent Elements of Aggravated Trespass

Let us now dissect the elements that make up the section 68 offence and its attendant case law in more detail.

(i) Requires an Act Over and Above the Simple Trespass

Nothing in section 68 prevents prosecutions being brought against protesters whose activities, aside from any trespass, are lawful; what matters is their trespassory and disruptive nature. That said, trespass alone cannot constitute the necessary act implied by 'does there anything' in (c) above.

In *Barnard v DPP*, a group of 15 had trespassed onto an open-cast mine in order, it was alleged, to intimidate, disrupt or to obstruct the mining operation carried out there.[87] The magistrate dismissed the informations as not disclosing an offence known to law; no further act on the part of the defendants was alleged other than their unlawful entry onto land, which was intended to have the necessary effect. The prosecutor appealed by way of case stated. Laws LJ agreed the magistrate was right in holding that section 68 required proof not only of trespass on land but of two further elements:

(i) the doing of some distinct and overt act beyond the trespass itself; and
(ii) the intention that this second act would be to intimidate, obstruct or disrupt.[88]

The magistrate also refused leave to amend the informations. The proposed amendment, setting out the necessary second act as 'unlawful occupation in company with numerous others', was no improvement. Continued occupation is still a mere trespass made no worse by dint of the numbers involved—as is also the case, we must also accept, irrespective of its length. Counsel for the defendants conceded that there might be circumstances in which unlawful occupation in company with others could amount to the second act required. Laws LJ accepted this was so or at least did not close the door on it. He has been criticised for denuding a constituent element of the offence of any content. There is some truth in that but we should also bear in mind that he continued:

> [I]n such a case I doubt whether a bare allegation of occupation would be satisfactory. At least I think it should be supported by some further particulars of what it is said the defendant was actually doing. The starting point is that the second act required by the statute must, in my judgement, be distinct and overt. Occupation may, in reality, in some cases amount to no more than the initial trespass. If the case being made were that the second act was constituted by the Respondents distinctly

---

[86] Bucke and James, above n 83, 53 citing a rate of about 50% compared to about 80% overall in the magistrates' courts.
[87] *Barnard v Director of Public Prosecutions* CO/4814/98 unreported Divisional Court, 15 October 1999, discussed [2000] Crim LR 371.
[88] To that extent we should be cautious about the earlier Divisional Court case, *Lucy v Director of Public Prosecutions*, unreported, 22 November 1996 (Staughton LJ and Tucker J) noted at (1997) 73 P & CR D25. A group entered a quarry to hold a demonstration about continued mining. The only activity they engaged in was to stand on top of a 60-feet-high pile of stones. Staughton LJ concluded there was plainly a positive act by the appellants made with the intention of preventing the owners carrying out quarrying work: 'To load . . . on to the lorries while there were protesters on top of the pile . . . would present a considerable danger to health and safety'.

remaining on the land in force and thus intimidating those lawfully engaged there, then I would expect to see something more than mere occupation with others pleaded in the information.[89]

The more valid criticism is that he paid no attention to the constitutional element and the rights dimension to the case: we might say of Laws LJ (as was said of *Winder*) that he was engaged 'simply on the mechanistic interpretation of the section'.[90]

(ii) Requires Someone Else to be Present

For the offence to be made out, someone must be physically present on the land at the time of the distinct, overt second action intended to disrupt the lawful activity being carried out, someone whose lawful activities can be or are capable of being disrupted, intimidated or obstructed.[91]

In *DPP v Tilly*, the Divisional Court heard two linked appeals by way of case stated.[92] In both protesters had destroyed GM crops being grown by farmers in fields. Rafferty J held that a successful prosecution did require someone to be present on the land, or adjoining land, and engaging in or about to engage in a lawful activity at the time of the alleged disruptive act. The section was clear and unambiguous.[93] As she made clear, dealing with counsel's arguments about what 'activity' meant,

> whether one can indulge in an activity present or absent is not the point. The point is whether in the context of this section one can, absent from an activity, endure the obstruction or disruption of it, or potentially be intimidated or be intimidated in the performing of it. I have no hesitation in concluding that presence is necessary before an offence under this section can be made out. [The section] contemplates and is designed penally to mark a situation in which people are meant to be intimidated, or cannot get on with what they are entitled to do. Thus, to suffer inconvenience or anxiety they must be present.[94]

As favourable as this decision is to direct action protesters, it again takes no account of any wider rights perspective. Given the result, it may well have been that the HRA would have made little difference—and indeed the weight of Articles 10 and 11 is against supporting direct action protesters—but for Rafferty J not even to allude to it, even if just to confirm that her 'mechanistic' (Fenwick and Phillipson) statutory interpretation approach was supported by it, seems strange.[95]

Her verdict largely renders the provision nonsensical. As counsel for the Crown Prosecution Service put it in argument, it would mean that the offence is committed if crops are destroyed while the farmer is ploughing his field but not if they are destroyed after he and his tractor have passed outside his gate. It would also exclude cases where a protester damages the farmer's gate so as to make it impassable, even though on any sensible

---

[89] Laws LJ seemed also to accept that if s 68 could be made out by mere mass trespass, that rendered otiose the power in s 69 to direct trespassers to leave land. This kicks in if two or more persons are trespassing on land in the open air 'and are present there' with the common purpose of intimidation, obstruction or disruption and. That second 'contemplates a state of affairs in which a s 68(1) offence will not necessarily have been committed': *Barnard*, above n 87.
[90] Fenwick and Phillipson, above n 3, 552. We shall consider *Winder* below
[91] The key time is not the time the trespass took place.
[92] *Director of Public Prosecutions v Tilly* [2001] EWHC Admin 821, [2002] Crim LR 128.
[93] Save for the fact that, as Rafferty J noted at [19], each of the three limbs to s 68(1)—intimidation, disruption or obstruction—should be read disjunctively despite there being an 'or' only between the second and third.
[94] *ibid*, at [25]–[26].
[95] It would appear to follow however the staged test propounded by Lord Woolf CJ in *Poplar Housing v Donohue* [2001] EWCA Civ 595.

approach that would too disrupt many of the farmer's lawful activities. It would presumably mean that the offence could not be committed if the protesters disrupted an automated activity—the timed spraying of fertiliser, for example—even though rendering the crop-sprayer out of action would surely disrupt the activity of growing crops? To these points—though the third was not made at trial—she replied (though without specifying) that '[a]lternative and well-established statutory provisions exist to catch circumstances in which wrong-doing occurs without the presence or the imminent presence of the aggrieved'.[96] This of course is true—and we should welcome this exhortation for judicial restraint—but it is moot whether it is appropriate as a limiter.

Similarly, as long as someone is present, nothing in section 68 limits aggravated trespass only to those cases where the disruption, obstruction or intimidation is aimed or targeted at the activity the protesters find abhorrent. It would be committed by a group which disrupts those operating the staff canteen at a vivisection laboratory or intimidating the security guards running the staff car park at an NHS hospital where abortions are performed. Although the balance of Strasbourg case law is largely not favourable to intimidatory protests—though of course (as we shall see) section 68 covers protests that are not actually intimidatory, only intended to be so—the same is not true certainly of disruptive and possibly obstructive protests. The former connotes the activity can and is still undertaken; the latter that it does not. That being so, protesters could convincingly argue (using section 3 of the HRA) that section 68 should be read down as to cover only disruption (certainly) and obstruction (possibly) to activities that are central, not peripheral, to the protesters' ultimate objectives. The section could then be read 'in relation to any lawful activity which persons are engaging on *which activity it is the aim of the person ultimately to disrupt*' or perhaps 'in relation to any lawful activity *taken as a whole* which persons are engaging on'. It could not be said that the ultimate aim—or some similarly worded phrase—of the protesters was to disrupt the mealtimes of animal researchers or to cause chaos in a hospital car park.[97] The peripherality too might be sufficient to bring the protesting activity within the scope of Article 11 protection, so allowing for section 3 in the first place.

Both appeals technically concerned only disrupting lawful activities, not obstructing them, let alone intimidating someone from performing them. Clearly someone must be physically present in order to be intimidated into being deterred from continuing a lawful activity. That does not, despite what Rafferty J asserted, always follow for obstruction or disruption.[98] It is not a contortion of language to argue that A can be engaged in an activity without physically being present and for B's acts to constitute a disruption or obstruction to it. It must all depend on what 'the aggrieved' (using the words of Rafferty J) is doing and what exactly the protesters are obstructing or disrupting. I am currently in my study typing out this chapter; I am currently engaged in the activity of research. Before I started work, I mixed a cake for my wife's birthday. It is currently baking in the oven in my kitchen. I would also say I am 'engaged'[99] in the activity of cake-making: it is an ongoing activity, one not currently needing personal engagement and attention but one which for its achievement I was

---

[96] *Tilly*, above n 92, [26].
[97] This construction is supported by the view taken about peripheral illegality in cases such as *Hibberd v Director of Public Prosecutions*, unreported 27 November 1996 (Staughton LJ and Tucker J) noted [1997] *Current Law Yearbook* 1251.
[98] Let us assume one cannot obstruct an activity yet to be begun but can only disrupt it, the point we suggested above. Many activities might have no one present if they have not yet started: does this mean they cannot be disrupted?
[99] The meaning in the OED closest to that used in s 68 is 'to enter upon or employ oneself in an action'.

required to undertake some activity at the outset and to complete it I will have to perform others (removal from the oven, icing) later. I need not be doing it myself personally all the time nor even be in the same place as the activity all the time but I am carrying it out, with help from the oven. Someone can be engaged in an activity without being present throughout it: I would surely be engaged in playing cricket even if I am in the pavilion waiting to bat?

Looked at in this way, the problem is less one of what 'engaging in' or 'activity' means and more one of what it means to talk about being 'on land'. Land, in section 68, comprises no sense of boundary and finality, no 'end point'. Does it mean field, legal title, house, room? Can I be engaged in baking from my adjoining study? The larger the land—and let us assume farmers have large holdings—the more likely there will be an offence on it or the adjoining land: the larger the land, the more likely it is that someone will be present. In both appeals it is noticeable that the information in the first referred to land 'namely Starve Acre Field' and the other to land 'namely Lime Farm'. Prosecutors would be advised to refer to land at its maximum and leave defendants to argue that being in the farm house having a cup of tea meant the farmer could not be present in the bottom field several hundred acres away. A reading down under section 3 of the HRA would of course help here—but that presumes there is a potential incompatibility, not something we can take for granted in the context of direct action and Strasbourg's treatment of it.

(iii) Requires Protesters to be Trespassing

The third element to the offence—and perhaps most obviously—is that protesters can only be convicted if they trespass on land belonging to another. This, simply put, will be so if protesters either enter or remain on land (perhaps having been permitted originally to enter) where they have no entitlement to do so. It might also occur as a result of what is carried out there: someone might have permission to be there but not to undertake the activity in question.

This highlights yet again another consideration of this book: the crucial role played in the public regulation of peaceful protest by private law concepts stemming from ownership and title to property. Where protesters enter private land belonging to someone else where they have no permission (or licence) to enter—either express or implied[100]—that will be a trespass *ab initio*. This is not problematic. There are two areas that are. We shall consider these in turn.

First is the case where permission to enter was originally granted, including cases where a group is allowed onto land for one purpose—even if that is to protest—but that is revoked. Common law is clear. Even express permission (and certainly an implied licence) to enter can be revoked by a clear countermand to leave, such as a 'no protesters' or 'protesters keep out' notice.[101] A limited express licence to enter or to remain on one part of a property does not extend to permission to roam at will. A protester who exceeds whatever original permission was granted will become a trespasser at the time the excessive activity is

---

[100] Even uninvited visitors on legitimate business (perhaps even those who think they have legitimate business) will have an implied licence to walk up someone's path to ring the bell. If express permission to remain or to enter is not given or the implied permission is revoked, the visitor only becomes a trespasser after a reasonable period to allow her to retrace her steps and to leave unless they seek to assert their right to remain, at which point they are trespassers. This is the combined effect of *Robson v Hallett* [1967] 2 QB 939 and *Davis v Lisle* [1936] 2 KB 434. At common law, reasonable—perhaps now in the light of Art 3 and Art 8 'proportionate'?—force may be taken to evict a trespasser as an aspect of private defence (see above p 251).

[101] See *Robson v Hallett*, above n 100. Mere abuse might not be sufficient to counter an implied licence: *Snook v Mannion* [1982] Crim LR 601. It was a question of fact for the tribunal to decide if the words (here 'Fuck Off' to police officers seeking to breathalyse the defendant) constituted a rebuttal of a licence or were just vulgar abuse.

first engaged in, allowing for a reasonable period to leave.[102] A recent Scottish protest case, albeit that there are significant differences between Scottish and English private law, illustrates this. In *McAdam v Urquhart*, a group appealed against their convictions under section 68 after they disrupted the sowing of GM seeds in a farmer's field.[103] One limb of their ultimately unsuccessful defence was that since they had been permitted by the farmer to protest there, they could not be 'trespassing'. The farmer's permission had in fact been relayed to them by a police officer, who then escorted them onto the land. It was after this that the group made its protest by sitting in front of a tractor. The High Court of Justiciary held that it was clear the group was at the time trespassing on that part of the field on which they chose to sit down. The lower court was correct to conclude that at best, they had a conditional licence—to be present on the land so as to protest—provided they did not interfere with the sowing process. Once that condition was broken they could no longer claim to be present on the land with the consent of the owner or anyone else.[104]

The second problem relates to the thorny issue of public land and the highway. The easy answer is given by sections 61(9) and 68(5). The term 'land' is undefined—and thus encompasses much publicly-owned or publicly-dedicated land—save for the specific exclusion of all highways and roads that do not also constitute

(i) a footpath, bridleway or byway open to all traffic within the meaning of Part III of the Wildlife and Countryside Act 1981 or
(ii) a restricted byway within the meaning of Part II of the Countryside and Rights of Way Act 2000 or
(iii) a cycle track under the Highways Act 1980 or the Cycle Tracks Act 1984.

In other words, aggravated trespass cannot be committed on highways or roads unless they are also footpaths, bridleways, cycle tracks and most byways. That answers the first limb, 'what public land can be trespassed upon?' but the second 'what is considered to be trespass?' depends on what is a lawful use of such land.

That was, we might recall, the issue for determination in *DPP v Jones and Lloyd*.[105] How far lawful use extends will depend on the use to which the land has been dedicated. It is certainly true that in *Jones and Lloyd* the House of Lords (by a majority) extended the previous position, that the scope of the right to use the highway was limited to passing and re-passing. The House was prepared to countenance peaceful, non-violent and non-obstructive protest as being within the rights of reasonable user of the highway, although the majority speeches do not really expand upon that formula. Despite that seemingly favourable outcome, in our previous chapter we doubted that this constituted recognition of a right to protest. In the context of aggravated trespass, for those highways that do constitute 'land' under section 68, it might though mean fewer protesters are caught as fewer will be seen as trespassing. The difficulty lies in imagining a scenario falling four-square within section 68 that also falls within Lord Irvine's protective definition of peaceful, non-violent and non-obstructive

---

[102] *Robson v Hallett*, above n 100.
[103] *McAdam v Urquhart* 2004 SLT 790.
[104] The Court made the interesting point that permission at any one time to stand or be on one part of the field should not be equated with unqualified permission to stand or be on every part of the field,. Thus while the charges included reference to trespassing on 'a field at Tullich', it was quite sufficient if at the time of the alleged offence the Crown proved trespass on a part of the field so specified. An alternative view would be that if permission is granted, then this extends to all land unless it is clearly and expressly limited by the licensor. We can again see how private law law concepts continue to shape the public law regulation of trespass.
[105] *DPP v Jones and Lloyd* [1999] 2 AC 240 (HL).

protest. The factual matrix in *Jones* was far removed from the sorts of cases that form the bread-and-butter of a court's case load under section 68. Even the majority view leaves little room to doubt that intimidatory, obstructive or disruptive protests on the highway would not also constitute trespass on the highway. That said, direct action of the type we have been considering—GM crop or anti-war protests—is not of itself unpeaceful or violent (many in fact are avowedly not so); often the only obstruction offered is to those engaged in the activity rather than, as is implicit in *Jones*, to other users of the highway.

Aggravated trespass may occur even if the trespass is not initially disruptive provided it becomes so sometime later. In *Lucy v DPP* the owners of a mine had made it clear, following advance publicity of a demonstration, that no mining would be carried out on the day, but later changed their minds.[106] The protesting group was arrested under section 68(1)(c). The first limb of their unsuccessful appeal was the argument that they could not have intended to disrupt any activity when they entered as trespassers as, at that time, they had reasonably believed no activities would be carried out that day. Staughton LJ held against them on that point. It would have been clear soon thereafter and in any event section 68 covers 'not only a person who enters the land knowing that she is a trespasser, but also a person who remains on land as a trespasser and knows that activities are being disrupted'.

(iv) Requires the Other Activity to be Lawful

Several cases have addressed the alleged unlawfulness of the activity said to be disrupted, obstructed or from which someone was deterred by intimidation. Lawful activities—against which the protest takes place—are those that may be engaged in on the land on that occasion without committing an offence or trespassing on land.[107] Clearly, unless the activity complained about is a specific crime or itself involves trespass then it is one that is lawful.

There is a drafting infelicity in the use of 'may' in 'may be engaged in . . . without committing an offence'. Any and all activities can—'may'—be performed without also constituting an offence: forcing a knife into someone's chest will not be murder or an assault if it is done during the course of heart surgery. The more germane question is surely whether at the time it *is* an offence. This of course cuts both ways: protesters would be arguing that the activity complained of *may* involve commission of a crime—even if at the time it does not do so—whereas those who are being disrupted would argue that the activity would never necessarily involve commission of a crime and thus it can always be said that they 'may' engage in it without committing a crime. On this in the Divisional Court in *Ayliffe*, Waller LJ concluded that the proper meaning of the phrase must be that

> Parliament cannot be presumed to have intended to make it an offence [under section 68] for a person to disrupt an activity being carried on unlawfully, simply because, if carried on in another way, the activity could be carried on lawfully.[108]

Thus 'may engage' should be taken as meaning 'was lawful, was permitted when it was being carried out'. He preferred this construction to that put forward by prosecuting counsel that

---

[106] *Lucy v DP*, above n 88.

[107] Section 68(2). To that extent the criticism made in S Bailey, D Harris and S Jones, *Civil liberties cases and materials*, 5th edn (London, Butterworths 2001) 520 about the ambiguous nature of 'lawful' seems misplaced. The authors ask whether those performing the putatively lawful activity must point to a specific legal right to act in that way or need they only show that the activity has not been expressly forbidden, on the basis that the common law permits us to do whatever we like provided it is not prohibited.

[108] *Ayliffe v DPP; Swain v DPP; Percy v DPP* [2005] EWHC 684 (Admin) [51]–[52]. The matter was not taken on appeal to the House of Lords in the combined appeal with *Jones* [2006] UKHL 16.

the phrase meant 'if the activity engaged in at a particular moment were unlawful, provided it might have been engaged in lawfully, the activity would be lawful'.

Other cases have shed more light on the nature of the lawful activity complained about. Peripheral or collateral (perhaps even de minimis) breaches of the criminal law will not affect the overall lawfulness of the activity where the 'unlawful' activity does not go to the heart of what the actual object or target of the protest was; what might be called the central activity.[109] *Hibberd v DPP* was an appeal by way of case stated.[110] It was alleged that someone using a chainsaw to fell trees as part of land clearance scheme for a road expansion project was in breach of health and safety regulations, rendering it an 'unlawful' activity. This, it was argued, meant that the disruptive activity—Hibberd refusing to leave his protesting position in a tree—could not be an offence under section 68. His appeal was dismissed. The activity in question that was being disrupted was the clearance of land and the felling of trees, which had been properly authorised and was lawful. The fact that a breach of the regulations had occurred did not make the activity as a whole unlawful.

In *Nelder v DPP*, the Court took a similar view.[111] Although some of the huntsmen at the time of a disruptive protest were trespassing, and so were acting unlawfully, the protester's intention had been to disrupt a lawful hunt. As the hunt had permission to be on all the surrounding land, only a section having trespassed, in general the hunt was still lawful. Both decisions favour practical managerial policing: it will be easier for officers on the spot to assess the legality of a trespassing protest group than to assess the legality of the activity itself. As Bailey, Harris and Jones comment: 'How will an officer know . . . whether someone is trespassing unless he has the express information from the landowner?', though of course this must apply with equal force to the protesters as well as their targets . . . save that officers might reasonably assume if protesters are on land belonging to anyone else then they will not be there with the owner's permission.

We have already considered whether or not protesters charged, say, with criminal damage could point to alleged unlawfulness in international law to found a defence based on section 3 of the Criminal Law Act 1967, using reasonable force to prevent a crime.[112] We saw they could not. A similar issue has arisen under section 68: can the activity being disrupted be an unlawful one solely by virtue of its violating international law? *R v Jones* under section 3 of the 1967 Act was in fact a combined appeal with *Ayliffe v DPP*, the latter a question about the extent of 'offence' in section 68(3) of the 1994 Act.[113] A group was charged with aggravated trespass having entered a military port, in protest at the war in Iraq, and disrupted the loading of vessels bound for the Middle East. The same reasoning and outcome was reached as for disposing of the *Jones* appeal under section 3.[114] The Court held

---

[109] This supports the view suggested above that s 68 should not be read as to make it a crime to disrupt the operation of the car park at an abortion clinic rather than the performing of abortions.

[110] *Hibberd v DPP*, above n 97. A similar argument, albeit reasoned entirely differently by the High Court of Justiciary, was tried in the Scottish case of *McAdam v Urquhart*, above n 103. The issue was an alleged breach of conditions and consent by farmers and others engaged in GM crop trials.

[111] *Nelder v Director of Public Prosecutions*, unreported Divisional Court, 3 June 1998, *The Times*, 11 June 1998, noted Bailey, Harris and Jones, *Civil Liberties*, above n 107, 520.

[112] The only difference is that references are to 'offence' under s 68(3) and not to 'crime' as is the case in s 3 of the 1967 Act.

[113] *R v Jones and Others; Ayliffe v DPP* [2006] UKHL 16. Several groups were charged under s 68 in respect of different unlawful trespasses. The leading speeches were by Lord Bingham and Lord Hoffman. Lord Carswell and Lord Rodger agreed with the disposal and reasoning as did Lord Mance with only a little more elaboration.

[114] Defendants in other prosecutions under s 68 have tried to rely on general criminal law defences, each without success: see for example *Bayer v DPP*, above n 80, where the defendants argued the common law private defence of property.

that the defendants had no defence under section 3. There was no basis for asserting that any war crimes had been committed on British soil and there was no connection between the protesters' acts and the speculative possibility of crimes being committed. Their underlying purpose had been to protest, not to prevent crime.

(v) Requires Only a Limited Connection in Time Between the Protest and the Activity

There is no need for the disrupted activity even to be going on at the time the protest occurs. Aggravated trespass can be committed against those who are 'about to engage in' a lawful activity. Those who intend protesting about an activity that has not yet begun can still be arrested, such as when protesters enter field A with spades ready to disrupt the planting of GM crop seeds that is about to start in field B. How distant in time 'about to' covers is moot. Here, surely, is a case for a narrow reading under section 3 of the HRA so as to promote compatibility between domestic law and Articles 10–11, such that it is a paraphrase for 'on the verge of'. Such a plea though (again) might flounder on the limited (if any) protection of direct action protest at Strasbourg level such that there is no incompatibility for section 3 to 'cure'. Resort to section 3 may not be needed. On traditional principles of statutory interpretation it is surely true that the mischief aimed at in section 68 is obstruction or disruption of someone else's lawful activities, not their preparations for such activities.

Section 68 is made out not by the performing of an intimidatory, obstructive or disruptive act but by performing any act with an intimidatory, obstructive or disruptive intent. This difference in wording is crucial. Even this fairly extensive provision has been widened by case law. The result of *Winder v DPP* is that the protest activity engaged in need not be one that is even capable of intimidating, disrupting or obstructing.[115] As long as at the time it is performed, the protester intends it should have that effect and the activity can be said to be more than 'merely preparatory' to that end, the offence is committed. The case has been heavily criticised by commentators.[116] Some fox-hunt saboteurs decided to protest and gathered in a field. They were armed with citronella that they intended to spray, when within range of the hunt, to put the dogs of the scent. They started to run towards a second field where the hunt was actually taking place. They were arrested at that point and charged with aggravated trespass. Their appeal (by way of case stated) against conviction by the magistrates was dismissed by the Divisional Court (Schiemann LJ and Smedley J). The appellants were trespassing on land. At the time, fox-hunting with dogs was a lawful activity. Running across the fields towards the hunt was accepted as not being a disruptive activity. Nonetheless, the group had the general intent of disrupting the hunt as and when they reached it and, though they were still some way away when they were arrested, they had done an act—viz carrying and making ready for use some citronella—that was more than 'merely preparatory' to the eventual intended disruption.

The case pre-dates the HRA. Although the ECtHR does not look favourably on direct action, it is hard to think of a comparable Strasbourg case where protesters have been convicted not for disruption but for wanting and being prepared to do so. It is instructive that there is no understanding, let alone acknowledgement, in the judgment of the importance or even the relevance of the right to protest. Although one cannot attempt a summary offence—such as aggravated trespass—unless the section specifically provides for that, the

---

[115] *Winder v Director of Public Prosecutions* (1996) 160 JP 713 (DC).
[116] D Mead 'The Human Rights Act—A Panacea for Peaceful Protest' Part II (1999) 4 J Civ Lib 7, 15–17; Fenwick and Phillipson, above n 3, 551 and 561.

Divisional Court has manufactured an inchoate offence in the guise of the substantive offence. If attempted aggravated trespass were possible—and the language of the judgment is in terms of attempt—we would need to ask what more is needed to commit it? Buying citronella? Driving to the field? Parking the car? Getting out and entering the field? The judgment comes very near to imposing criminal liability on the basis of intention, not deeds. The remoteness issue was sidelined by the Court but what would—and should—have been the result if the hunt had that day been cancelled or the citronella cans were empty? To find such protesters guilty would be nonsensical—and prosecuting them would clearly achieve no social or public objective—yet there is nothing in section 68 or in the judgment that would indicate otherwise. The protesters were guilty because they had done something while simultaneously also intending their actions would, at some stage in the not too distant future, result in disruption to the lawful activities of someone else on the same or adjoining land. The Court provides no guidance for future protests on how far back in time or how disjoined the disruption needs to be from the protesters' actions for liability not to attract. That uncertainty is enough to question whether or not the convictions could be said to be 'prescribed by law'—and it certainly seems an appropriate plea in any future case.

The width of section 68 is of concern also because it has knock-on effects elsewhere in the law of protest. Convictions for aggravated trespass have been taken without much more to found the necessary evidence of likely future harassment such as to allow claimants to obtain injunctive relief under section 3 of the Protection from Harassment Act 1997.[117] It also has the potential further to erode any gains made in *Jones and Lloyd* for trespassory assemblies under section 14A. We considered earlier how *Jones* might alter the view that a court would take of the trespassory element to section 68, leaving fewer activities as trespass. Let us look at the reverse position, how aggravated trespass affects section 14A. The speeches of the majority provide no clear steer on the link between the otherwise (un)lawfulness of the activity and (un)reasonable user of the highway.[118] If a group of 20 or more on a footpath open to all has done something that is more than merely preparatory to disrupting a farmer planting GM seeds—carrying spades and forks for use when they get to the field—it has almost certainly committed aggravated trespass under *Winder*. Not only that, the group may well be in danger of breaching any trespassory banning order for having used the highway in excess of its limited rights to do so.

B. Preventing Aggravated Trespass by Giving Directions

There is a separate offence created in section 69. It is clearly intended to buttress section 68 but the interpretation of the two sections has meant an expansion of both with a much less clear delineation between them.

Under section 69(1), the senior officer present at the scene[119] may direct someone to leave land if she reasonably believes

---

[117] See *EDO Technology Ltd v Campaign to Smash EDO* [2005] EWHC 837 at [66].
[118] Above p 258. See Lord Irvine at 255 and 257 and Lord Clyde at 280–81. Lord Hutton made no mention of unlawful behaviour
[119] Is the 'scene' the couple of metre squared area where the direction is given, where perhaps only a couple of officers are placed or the 100 acre GM crop field in which perhaps 20 officers might be spread? This is a similar question to what constitutes the extent of 'land' that we looked at above n?. What if there are two sergeants present at the scene—is the senior the longest serving? See the example given in Bucke and James, above n 83, 45.

(a) that a person is committing, has committed or intends to commit . . . aggravated trespass on land . . .;[120] or
(b) that two or more persons are trespassing on land . . . and are present there with the common purpose of intimidating persons so as to deter them from engaging in a lawful activity or of obstructing or disrupting a lawful activity.[121]

It is an offence to fail to abide by a direction. Knowing that a direction has been given which applies to them, if a person fails to leave the land as soon as practicable or, having left, enters the land again as a trespasser within three months, they commit an offence.[122] There is a defence in section 69(4) if the defendant can show either

(a) that [she] was not trespassing on the land, or
(b) that [she] had a reasonable excuse for failing to leave the land as soon as practicable or, as the case may be, for again entering the land as a trespasser.

There has been only one reported section 69 case, *Capon v DPP*, an appeal to the Divisional Court by way of case stated.[123] A hunt had chased a fox to a hole on a farm. A small group of fox-hunt protesters trespassed on the land so as to observe (and to record on video) the digging out of the fox so as to ascertain whether the hunt committed any separate crimes. A brief exchange took place between all three appellants, in turn, and the senior police officer at the scene. All three were arrested for aggravated trespass under section 68 but were later charged under section 69. The Crown Court convicted them of failing to leave after a direction under section 69 had been given. This was despite the Court not only finding the group not guilty of aggravated trespass but that it was doing all it could to avoid any disruption, the integral aspect of the section 68 offence. The Court found there was sufficient evidence for the officer reasonably to believe that the three were committing the section 68 offence, based upon his discussion with the Master of the Hunt, and found that his words constituted a direction within section 69, which the three knew had been made. Their failure then to leave constituted the offence.

The Divisional Court (Lord Bingham CJ and Dyson J) resolved the matter in four stages. First, there was evidence before the Crown Court to support the contention that the officer had a reasonable belief of aggravated trespass. Secondly, the officer's words were sufficient to amount to a direction within section 69(1). The words to the first appellant, within the hearing of the other two 'You either leave the land or you're arrested' and the repetition of the mantra 'Are you leaving the land?' to the other two were deemed by the Lord Chief Justice to be imperative rather than questioning.[124] There was no requirement to make any reference to the relevant statutory power or even to make clear which land should be left. Thirdly, there was evidence to support the conclusion that all three knew that a direction had been given, as there was no contrary indication that any had not understood what the officer had said. Lastly, none of the three had a reasonable excuse for failing to leave. That

---

[120] Given, as we have seen, the elastic connection between the protest activity and (say) the obstruction (it need only be intended and the obstructed lawful activity need not have commenced) the fact that s 69 refers to an intention to commit aggravated trespass further removes the connection between the two.
[121] 'Land' and 'lawful activity' have the same meaning as in s 68: see s 69(6), although there is no qualification to the 'lawful activity' as there is in s 68 that it must be taking place on the same or adjoining land.
[122] Section 69(3).
[123] *Capon v Director of Public Prosecutions* CO/3496/97 unreported Divisional Court decision.
[124] It is worth reading this exchange, set out in full in D Mead, 'Will peaceful protesters be foxed by the Divisional Court decision in *Capon v DPP*?' [1998] *Crim LR* 870, as it gives a flavour of how vague the language can be for a Court still to consider it a 'direction'. The transcript evinces a worrying lack of understanding on the part of officers of the limits and parameters of their powers to police and to regulate peaceful protest.

they were not, in the event, committing aggravated trespass would not found a reasonable excuse. Neither the belief that the officer was not entitled to give the direction nor staying on the land in an attempt to establish what offence they had actually committed were reasonable excuses.

I have criticised this decision elsewhere.[125] First, it must be very difficult to 'know' (within section 69(3)) that a direction has been given if the police are permitted such wide and uncertain language as this. It is a drafting flaw that a direction need not be accompanied by any clear indication of what response is required and no indication of what consequences might flow from failure. This means it may fall foul of the 'prescribed by law' test under Article 10 and 11, which requires certainty and foreseeability, such that under section 3 of the HRA the word 'direction' might need to be read as including a warning that failure to leave will itself be an offence. There is the world of difference between understanding what an officer has said and knowing that officer has given a direction.

Secondly, the police are permitted two bites of the cherry. They may first arrest ostensibly on reasonable suspicion of aggravated trespass, as they did here, but provided they also warn—even in vague terms—that someone should leave the land then they may later proceed under section 69. *Capon* provides a lawful basis for deprivations of liberty and for intrusions into the right of peaceful protest where no actual substantive offence has been committed, perhaps where none can be committed, provided an officer reasonably believes it will. In that it is not dissimilar to many domestic offences save that section 69 was introduced, we can sensibly assume from the existence of section 68, to provide a refuge, a halfway house for protesters from immediate arrest.

This is our third concern: the line between section 68 and section 69 is obfuscated. The decision in *Capon* emasculates section 68. When and why would the police arrest for aggravated trespass where they cannot arrest under section 69, given that both carry the same possible sentence? Equally, we might ask what, in light of *Winder*, is the point of section 69? As Fenwick and Phillipson comment, section 69 was surely apt (if not intended) to cover precisely the set of circumstances that arose in *Winder*.[126] By extending the ambit of section 68 to encompass acts provided they are more than preparatory, the Divisional Court has also extended the ambit of section 69, a section predicated upon an intention to commit the substantive offence under section 68 in the future. It would mean that section 69 could presumably be utilised at an even earlier stage than the arrests of Winder and his group under section 68.

Our fourth and last point to note is that the Court's restrictive approach to the 'reasonable excuse' defence provides little by way of a let out for protesters.[127] It is something of an irony that the more convinced a group is of its innocence and so tries to argue its corner at the site, the more likely will be their eventual conviction under section 69(3). The irony is heightened if, as here, the group actually is innocent. Might a defence of a reasonable but ultimately mistaken belief (thus in fact resembling the police case here) that animal cruelty was being perpetrated succeed . . . or even honest belief, as applies for preventing crime under section 3 of the Criminal Law Act 1967?[128] Of course, now those charged under

---

[125] Mead, above n 124.
[126] Fenwick and Phillipson, above n 3, 551.
[127] Whether the burden of proving the defence is a legal or an evidential one has yet to be tested let alone decided. The latter is more likely compatible with the right to a fair trial and the presumption of innocence in Art 6 of the ECHR, by virtue of s 3 of the HRA: see *Lambert* above n 13.
[128] See above p 250.

section 69 could argue that their Convention right to peaceful protest founded the reasonable excuse, heralding some judicial analysis of Strasbourg case law and the proportionality test and its application to the facts. This is sadly absent from the reasoning of Lord Bingham, which is without even a passing reference to the constitutional dimension and human rights implications of the decision.

V. Harassment and Intimidation

One prominent development in the law and regulation of protest at the start of the twenty-first century has been the increasing reliance—by private companies—on injunctions to try to prevent protesters harassing them, their directors, their employees and their contractors and suppliers. Much of this explosion in case law stems from the passing, in 1997, of the Protection from Harassment Act (PFHA). This part will consider how the law responds to direct action protest that seeks to intimidate or to harass others from pursuing an activity, often economic, that the protesters object to. We will call this the targeted activity. We will see here most markedly the overlap and blurring between public law (criminal or administrative) and private law (contractual or tortious) regulation—with a shift from the former to the latter and the consequential shift in the allocation of risk and financial cost of enforcement. We shall pick these themes up again in our concluding chapter.

A. Harassment Under the PFHA 1997

The PFHA, it is fairly clear from the parliamentary papers, was brought in to deal with the specific problem of stalkers, at a time when a few high-profile cases had made the news.[129] Despite that, there are now many reported cases of it being used against protesters. Given, we might safely assume, many injunctions are not formally reported, its 'real' use is likely to be much more. The PFHA is a strange mix of the criminal and the civil, with the former free-riding on the back of breach of the latter in parts.

One by-product of claiming that protesters are engaged in harassment, of inestimable value to target companies, is that this greatly extends the ambit of private law protection and jurisdiction. Obtaining an injunction against protesters on grounds that they are trespassing only protects the company's interests in or over their own land, whereas a PFHA injunction has the potential effectively to insulate companies and individuals from protests over a much wider area than that—the public highways that surround it, routes to and from work—a remedy the scope of which would be beyond the court's powers if only trespass were alleged.

(i) The Statutory Scheme

Anyone who harasses another is, by virtue of section 2, committing a summary offence punishable by up to six months imprisonment, or may, by virtue of section 3, be liable in

---

[129] The precursor was a Private Member's Bill, introduced by the then Opposition Labour MP Janet Anderson on which, with some differences, the Government-sponsored Bill was based. The PFHA 1997 passed onto the statute book in the last few months of John Major's Conservative administration.

the civil courts for statutory harassment, a new private law cause of action. Under section 3 damages (including for anxiety and financial loss) may be awarded, though, in the context of protest, the more likely remedy sought will be an injunction. This, it is clear, is a civil remedy—sought by an individual and between two private parties—and thus the lower, civil standard of proof, rather than the criminal standard, applies.[130] It also means that rules of civil procedure—such as (broadly) the admissibility of hearsay evidence—apply. This is even more of a worry where, as we shall see, breach of an anti-harassment injunction granted under section 3 might lead to arrest and prosecution. An injunction can be granted in favour of anyone who is subjected to a course of harassing conduct, actual or apprehended. Under section 3(5A), a third party (C) may apply for an injunction in cases where A harasses B with the aim of persuading C not to do something they are entitled to do or to do something they need not do. Where an injunction is granted and 'the [claimant] considers that the defendant has done anything which he is prohibited from doing by the injunction', then the claimant may apply for the issue of a warrant for arrest under section 3(3).[131] Furthermore, where an injunction has been granted for the purpose of restraining the defendant from pursuing any conduct which amounts to harassment, the defendant will be guilty of the separate offence created in section 3(6) if 'without reasonable excuse [she] does anything which [she] is prohibited from doing by the injunction'. This is triable either way and carries a maximum penalty on indictment of five years.

(ii) The Need for a Harassing Course of Conduct

Section 1 forbids someone from pursuing a course of conduct which amounts to harassment of another and which she knows or ought to know amounts to harassment of another. A second limb, section 1(1A), was inserted by section 125(2)(c) of SOCPA 2005 and came into force on 1 July 2005. It states that

a person must not pursue a course of conduct—

(a) which involves harassment of two or more persons, and
(b) which he knows or ought to know involves harassment of those persons, and
(c) by which he intends to persuade any person (whether or not one of those mentioned above)—

   (i) not to do something that he is entitled or required to do, or
   (ii) to do something that he is not under any obligation to do.

This change introduces two subtly distinct concepts: what might be called secondary harassment and group harassment. Secondary harassment is where X harasses a third party, not themselves the direct or real object of X's ire, in the hope that the harassment of X will

---

[130] *Hipgrave v Jones* [2001] EWHC 2901 (QB). It was plain that the criminal standard of proof was ill suited to the degree of flexibility that was required in civil proceedings for the grant of an injunction. Furthermore, the criminal standard focused unduly on the rights of the defendant and its application would thus pay insufficient regard to the fact that the rights of the claimant under the ECHR were engaged. See too *EDO Technology Ltd v Campaign to Smash EDO* [2005] EWHC 837 (QB) at [47]–[49]: the standard is the civil standard and not the criminal standard of proof, merely because under the PFHA criminal penalties may attract to breaches. However, in *Heathrow Airport v Garman* [2007] EWHC 1957 (QB) at [78]–[80] Swift J accepted that the criminal standard should apply because the nature of the hearing was in effect final in nature rather than interlocutory. There must be some strength to the defendants' other argument: an order under s 3 gives rise under the PFHA to a regime for the imposition of criminal penalties, effectively a hybrid criminal-civil system rather like ASBOs. See further Fenwick, *Civil Liberties*, above n 12, 789–96.

[131] Sections 4–5 provide more detail. Only if the application is on oath and only if the judge has reasonable grounds for believing that the defendant has done anything which he is prohibited from doing by the injunction should a warrant be issued.

persuade Y, the real target. Thus, a campaign of harassment against selected employees could be harassment of them all, or harassment of a company's suppliers could be harassment of the company if the aim were to persuade the company to stop its targeted activity.[132]

Taken with new section 7(3)(b), section 1(1A) also provides an easier route to claim group harassment. A single instance of harassing behaviour cannot constitute harassment under the PFHA; it needs at least one repetition, what is called a 'course of conduct'. If it is being alleged that the harassment is of the same person—section 1(1)—then 'course of conduct' means, under section 7(3)(a), harassment of that person on at least two occasions. If what is alleged is group harassment of two or more under section 1(1A), then 'course of conduct' means under section 7(3)(b) 'conduct on at least one occasion to each of those persons'. This change was brought in to deal with decisions such as *Banks v Ablex Ltd*, an employment case in the Court of Appeal.[133] Under the original provisions, the same person had to be the victim on each occasion when the alleged harassment occurred.[134] A single incident of harassment to each member of a group could not constitute statutory harassment to any of them.[135] Thus a cleverly targeted campaign by a group of protesters with each only harassing one person once—or one protester harassing several people but only once—would not have fallen foul of the rules. This change does mean that the larger the group claiming to have been harassed the greater is the number of harassing incidents needed, as each must suffer harassment at least once.

On a strict reading of section 1(1A) and section 7(3)(b), where two or more people are claiming harassment under the PFHA, though there need be only one harassing incident per claimant, anyone not yet harassed cannot lay claim to the protection of the PFHA. That said, where not everyone in a group, say, of employees has yet been targeted all is not lost. It may still be possible for a representative claim for injunctive relief to be brought on behalf of all of them. It is also possible to claim injunctive relief based on 'apprehended harassment'. Although statutory harassment is defined as a course of harassing conduct, in order to obtain an injunction under section 3 there is no requirement of a second incident, provided such a second incident is 'apprehended': it can be granted on the evidence of one incident and apprehension, if not restrained, of a second, that is 'provided there is some conduct giving rise to the apprehension that there will be a breach of section 1'.[136] This obviates the need for a repeat before action can be taken or (in the case of a workforce) obviates the need for all to have been harassed provided in either situation that it is reasonably apprehended all will be.

---

[132] See the Explanatory Notes to SOCPA 2005 at www.opsi.gov.uk/acts/en2005/ukpgaen_20050015_en.pdf, accessed 10 September 2007: 'the sort of behaviour which will engage the new offence is activity involving threats and intimidation which forces an individual or individuals to stop doing lawful business with another company or with another individual' (at para 304). It is important to note that what we are calling secondary harassment needs harassment of two or more targets, as a means to persuade third parties, not merely of one—as is the case under the s 1 as originally drafted but which does not encompass secondary harassment. Explanatory Notes to the Bill as introduced at 1st Reading can be found at: www.publications.parliament.uk/pa/cm200405/cmbills/005/en/05005x—.htm, accessed 12 August 2009.

[133] *Banks v Ablex Ltd* [2005] EWCA Civ 173, but see *R v Williams (Michael)*, unreported Divisional Court, 28 July 1998, [1998] CLY 954.

[134] *ibid*, at [20]. That cannot be entirely correct: even under the wording of the old s 1, provided the harassment took place to X at least twice, it should not matter that it also took place to Y and Z.

[135] See *Animal Welfare—Human Rights: protecting people from animal rights extremists*, paras 81–82, at: police.homeoffice.gov.uk/news-and-publications/publication/operational-policing/humanrights.pdf, accessed on 7 September 2007.

[136] *Bayer v Shook* [2004] EWHC 332 at [21] and *EDO Technology* [2005] EWHC 837 (QB) at [62]. Could it be argued that s 3 of the HRA requires a different approach to the word 'apprehended' so as to avoid an incompatibility with the right of peaceful protest with injunctions being granted on the basis of one protest incident?

A course of conduct need not involve conduct on separate occasions. It has included a series of short telephone calls, all recorded within five minutes and listened to in succession.[137] It does also need a link or nexus between the two incidents, to reflect the use of the word 'course' but two spontaneous and unplanned incidents would not preclude a finding that they were part of a course of conduct; conduct could be spontaneous and unplanned and at the same time highly repetitious.[138] What comprises a 'course of conduct' is far from clear. Is a single spread-out harassing event—having a vigil with placards outside someone's house all day—which was witnessed on at least two occasions (eg driving off to the shops at 9:00 am, returning from a meal at night) by the same person count as a course of conduct? That seems to be one continuous incident. Different would be where two different and separate incidents of harassment occur during that day-long vigil, say, chanting obscenities and then blocking the car. Both raise issues surrounding the 'prescribed by law' test as well as calling for, whether under section 3 of the HRA or otherwise, a reading that precludes their inclusion.

(iii) The Meaning of Harassment

Given the consequences that attach, potential defendants really need to know what a 'harassing' course of conduct is so that they might avoid it. What does the PFHA tell us? We learn very little about the qualities or tests that would be applied to determine whether behaviour would be harassing or even capable of being harassing. First, in terms of the mental element, section 1(2) merely informs potential protesters that

> the person whose course of conduct is in question ought to know that it amounts to harassment of another if a reasonable person in possession of the same information would think the course of conduct amounted to harassment of the other.

Secondly, there is no definition of harassment save that under section 7(1) it can *include* alarming a person or causing them distress—but is obviously not limited to that. Whether something is 'harassment' is a matter of fact for the tribunal.[139]

Immediately there are questions over the compatibility of the new offence and new tort of harassment—if used to clamp down on legitimate protest—with the rights contained in Article 10 and Article 11. In the absence of some indicia about permitted and proscribed behaviour, how can an arrest or an injunction—obviously a restriction or interference with those rights—have been foreseen with sufficient certainty to meet the 'prescribed by law' test so as to allow protesters to predict that their behaviour was or would be considered harassment? There has been a dearth of case law on the meaning of the term. Rather, like

---

[137] *Kelly v DPP* [2002] EWHC 1428. Three separate and distinct calls constituted a course of conduct—the time interval being just one factor—and the mischief at which the crime of harassment was aimed was repetitious conduct with an intention to cause fear. There could be no offence under s 4 as this requires the causing of fear on more than one occasion. In *Lau v Director of Public Prosecutions* [2000] 1 FLR 799 (but contrast *Pratt v Director of Public Prosecutions* [2001] EWHC Admin 483)—not a protest case—the Court held (at [15]) that though of course there need be only two occasions, the 'the fewer the occasions and the wider they are spread the less likely it would be that a finding of harassment can reasonably be made . . . but one could conceive of circumstances where incidents, as far apart as a year, could constitute a course of conduct and harassment. In argument [counsel] put the context of racial harassment taking place outside a synagogue on a religious holiday, such as the day of atonement, and being repeated each year as the day of atonement came round. Another example might be a threat to do something once a year on a person's birthday'.
[138] *Hipgrave*, above n 130.
[139] *The Church of Jesus Christ of the Latter Day Saints and Others v Price* [2004] EWHC 3245 (QB) at [181].

the proverbial elephant, harassment is something judges will know when they see it. Lord Phillips MR in *Thomas* (not a protest case) thought that section 7 did not purport

> to provide a comprehensive definition of harassment. There are many actions that foreseeably alarm or cause a person distress that could not possibly be described as harassment. It seems to me that section 7 is dealing with that element of the offence which is constituted by the effect of the conduct rather than with the types of conduct that produce that effect. The Act does not attempt to define the type of conduct that is capable of constituting harassment. 'Harassment' is, however, a word which has a meaning which is generally understood. It describes conduct targeted at an individual which is calculated to produce the consequences described in section 7 and which is oppressive and unreasonable.[140]

We can add the comments of Beatson J in *The Church of Jesus Christ of the Latter Day Saints v Price*:

> Alarm and distress are, as the wording of s.7(2) shows, not requirements. Alarm and distress are states of mind included within a broader concept of harassment. The archetypal case of harassment may involve distress, but it may also be harassment to wear out a person, to beset that person, or to constantly trouble, annoy or pester him or her. [P]ersistent telephone calls are as a matter of fact, capable of being harassment, even apart from the content of those calls.[141]

More recently, in the House of Lords in 2006, Lord Nicholls intimated that

> Where . . . the quality of the conduct said to constitute harassment is being examined, courts will have in mind that irritations, annoyances, even a measure of upset, arise at times in everybody's day-to-day dealings with other people. Courts are well able to recognise the boundary between conduct which is unattractive, even unreasonable, and conduct which is oppressive and unacceptable. To cross the boundary from the regrettable to the unacceptable the gravity of the misconduct must be of an order which would sustain criminal liability under section 2.[142]

That was said in the context of holding an employer vicariously liable for the alleged harassment of one employee to another. It is arguably of limited relevance in our context, given the presumed desire on the part of the House to limit the practical ramifications of their decision: exposure to a possible multiplicity of unfounded speculative claims years later.

There has been more recently a judicial hardening to harassment. Treacy J in *Broughton* listed as synonyms 'threatening or menacing [behaviour] . . . [feeling] alarmed, distressed, threatened or frightened' and specifically rejected irritation, distaste, upset, unwelcome intrusion and loss of enjoyment.[143] Against this, and in support of the 'prescribed by law'

---

[140] *Thomas v News Group Newspapers* [2001] EWCA Civ 1233 at [29]–[30]. We also know that whether a hypothetical reasonable person would think the conduct was harassing (and whether it was reasonable to pursue the course of conduct) are to be judged objectively without reference to any relevant peculiar personal characteristics, conditions or traits (such as schizophrenia): *R v Colohan (Sean Peter)* [2001] EWCA Crim 1251. It is the essence of harassment that it normally needs a positive act not an omission—*Morris v Knight* [1999] CLY 3682—and so breaking off normal social contact and intercourse or 'sending someone to Coventry' cannot be harassing behaviour.
[141] Above n 139.
[142] *Majrowski v Guy's and St Thomas's NHS Trust* [2006] UKHL 34 [30]. Baroness Hale (at [66]) considered that courts would be able to draw sensible lines so as to recognise harassment only as 'genuinely offensive and unacceptable behaviour'. The words of Lord Nicholls were interpreted by Gage LJ in *Conn v Council of the City of Sunderland* [2007] EWCA Civ 1492 [11]–[12] as meaning that the touchstone for recognising what is the statutory tort of harassment was 'whether the conduct [was] of such gravity as to justify the sanctions of the criminal law'. This therefore meant that even the civil wrong impliedly contains a mental element—knowing or ought to know (judging by the standards of what the reasonable person would think) that their course of conduct amounts to harassment of another.
[143] *University of Oxford v Broughton* [2008] EWHC 75 (QB) at [32]–[33].

point made above, we might reflect on the words of Swift J in *Heathrow Airport Ltd v Garman*.[144] The context was an environmental protest by a protest group known as Plane Stupid, opposed to airport expansionism and seeking reductions in air travel. The plans included holding a Climate Camp outside Heathrow one August week, at the height of summer, with educational workshops but also obstructive direct action. Swift J had to assess whether there was any evidence of harassing behaviour by any of the group or its supporters so as to found an injunction. The claimants had argued that causing annoyance or inconvenience would suffice whereas the protesters stressed the need to fear for safety. The Court found there was no evidence that those involved with Plane Stupid or those acting in concert with them had committed harassing behaviour in the past and so declined the application for an injunction. In so holding she stated:

> [H]arassment cannot . . . be confined to conduct which would place the victim in fear of violence. Neither in my view can it be right that harassment is confined just to conduct that will cause alarm and distress. Quite where the line is to be drawn and whether a particular type of conduct can properly be considered to amount to harassment will depend on the particular facts and circumstances of the incident in question. It is not a matter that can—save in a clear case—be predicted in advance. All I am able to say at this stage is that the fact that the actions of protestors will or may cause annoyance and inconvenience to the travelling public (whether by a blockade or any other form of action) does not necessarily mean that their conduct will amount to harassment. It may do. It may not.[145]

In 2005, as we saw, secondary harassment became proscribed so that single acts of harassment towards suppliers A and B so as to persuade C no longer to conduct, say, animal experiments would meet the course of conduct test. This extension was met with criticism from the Joint Committee on Human Rights (JCHR). The Government's express case was that it was not

> intended to catch lawful lobbying or peaceful protesting. A person distributing leaflets outside a shop about which they are protesting, for example, would not be caught unless they were to actually threaten or intimidate the person to whom they were handing out the leaflet and that person felt harassed, alarmed or distress.[146]

That sets out a much narrower scenario than was eventually proscribed by section 1A. The JCHR took issue with the necessity of the measure. It accepted there was a pressing social need to protect people going about their lawful business and private lives against harassment and disruption on account of their beliefs or lawful activities but was less convinced

> that the measures . . . can be said to be proportionate to that aim. Nothing in the clause limits the offence or the power to grant injunctions to the situations which are primarily envisaged as the object of the measures. The very wide formulation of the prohibited purpose (persuading a person not to do something he or she is entitled or required to do, or persuading him or her to do something he or she is not under an obligation to do) is capable of covering any political activity. There seems to us to be a danger that the provisions could be used to inhibit ordinary political demonstrations, particularly as it would be possible to treat a single episode of harassment towards each of a number of different people as a course of conduct.[147]

[144] *Heathrow Airport Ltd v Garman* [2007] EWHC 1957 (QB).
[145] *ibid*, at [99].
[146] Explanatory notes to SOCPA above n 132 at para 304.
[147] JCHR Fourth Report of session 2004–05, 24 January 2005 HL 26/HC 224, para 1.118 www.publications.parliament.uk/pa/jt200405/jtselect/jtrights/26/2604.htm, accessed 10 September 2007.

(iv) The Statutory Defence

The extent to which anti-harassment injunctions are available in the field of protest should have been limited. Section 1(3) provides three defences to criminal charges or to civil actions by excusing a course of conduct that would otherwise have been harassing. The defendant must show that the pursuit of the course of conduct was

for the purpose of preventing or detecting crime

pursued under any enactment or rule of law or to comply with any condition or requirement imposed by any person under any enactment, or

reasonable in the particular circumstances.[148]

The prevention of crime defence, that we have discussed in relation to aggravated trespass[149], was one of the preliminary issues explored thoroughly in *EDO Technology Ltd (EDO) v Campaign to Smash EDO (Preliminary Issues)*.[150] It was accepted by the defendant arms protesters (though it was the contentious issue for the House in *R v Jones*) that 'crime' was restricted to those crimes that were offences under domestic law. The defendants alleged that the claimants—arms designers and manufacturers—sold arms to the UK and USA governments which were used for military operations in Iraq (which the claimants did not deny). It was also alleged there was evidence that the arms had been used for crimes of aggression and crimes under both the Geneva Conventions Act 1957 and the War Crimes Act 2001. In the High Court, Walker J decided that section 1(3)(a) should be interpreted subjectively rather than objectively: a defendant did not need to show either that it was reasonable to think a crime was occurring or would occur or that the conduct was reasonably or objectively capable of preventing it. A failure to use any words indicating a test of reasonableness in that particular subsection when it had been used elsewhere plainly suggested that no such test was intended.[151] Logically, too, it would render the subsection otiose. If all prevention of crime defences had to be reasonable, they would by definition also satisfy the test in section 1(3)(c). This latter defence would still be wider than the preventing crime defence but in reverse, there would be no case where that defence captured and excused conduct where section 1(3)(c) would not also do so.[152] It was also unnecessary for the defendants to prove that an offence was actually committed. All that needed to be established is that any course of conduct was pursued for the purpose of preventing crime. A

---

[148] This is, unsurprisingly, objective in its nature, without any recognition or allowance for the standards or characteristics of the defendant himself: *Colohan* above n 140.

[149] See *R v Jones*, above n 71.

[150] *EDO Technology Ltd (EDO) v Campaign to Smash EDO (Preliminary Issues)* [2005] EWHC 2490, at [27]–[38] (Walker J).

[151] The opposite conclusion was reached in a case decided three weeks later: *KD v CC Hampshire* [2005] EWHC 2550 [144]. There the High Court—admittedly not in a protest case—decided it was clear that the draftsman's deliberate omission of 'necessity' or 'proportionality' from the language of the Act did not preclude a reading, by virtue of s 3 HRA of such terms. Thus s 1(3)(a) could not be read as providing an entirely subjectively worded defence based on preventing or detecting crime. Such an outcome allowed the Court to find that a policeman who for his own gratification had obtained from the victim of a serious sexual assault information about her sexual activities over and above what was needed to investigate the crime could not rely on s 1(3)(a) in defence to a claim for harassment and battery. Of course there, the questioning engaged the woman's Article 8 rights and so brought s 3 of the HRA into play in relations to s 1(3)(a). *EDO Technology* was not referred to by the court or in argument and of course Arts 10–11 are there pulling the court in the reverse direction.

[152] Walker J recognised that this interpretation may mean that s 1(1) of the PFHA would be disapplied in the case of harassment by a schizophrenic who is under the delusion that someone is about to commit murder but that any rectification would have be done by Parliament.

course of conduct might be pursued for the purpose of preventing crime, even if, as it turned out, no crime was actually committed (or even contemplated), so long as the course of conduct was genuinely pursued for the purpose of preventing crime.[153] It was also available to prevent what might be termed third party crimes, that is where the crime that was sought to be prevented was not being committed by the person subjected to the harassment.[154] The availability of alternative means to prevent crime is not determinative of the defence under section 1(3)(a).[155]

This wide interpretation was countered to some extent by the restrictive approach adopted to the meaning of 'preventing crime'. Defendants did not have complete freedom to mount a section 1(3)(a) defence. They still had the burden of proving that the harassment was intended to prevent a crime that was both specific, in the sense that a particular victim or victims and a particular danger could be identified, and immediate or imminent.[156] Preventing (here) war crimes meant thwarting, forestalling or bringing an immediate stop to them. It did not cover longer term measures to prevent them by highlighting the issue and hoping that the resulting public pressure might dissuade the company from continuing its business, as was conceded by counsel for the defendant protesters was their purpose. It had been argued by the protesters that to take any other approach might mean that a defendant would specifically have to identify the victim location and time of the crime it was hoped to prevent and that this would prove impossible. To meet that objection, Walker J gave his view about the possibility that section 1(3)(c)—with its balancing test and 'reading in' of proportionate protection of rights—may act to exculpate harassing behaviour on such a basis.

There is a strong case that the defences in either section 1(3)(b) or section 1(3)(c) might apply to protests—though both presuppose a favourable disposition by Strasbourg towards direct action such as to render it not only engaged by but also protected under Article 11. This so far has not been forthcoming and without a significant shift in approach by the domestic courts to counter this—again not yet evident—what follows is academic. Let us assume nonetheless that peaceful direct action—or some forms of it if not entirely obstructive but on the cusp of strong persuasion and intimidatory—are capable of protection as aspects of the right to peaceful protest.

First, protesters are pursuing their otherwise harassing conduct under (that is permitted by) an enactment, the HRA: Article 11 grants to them the right to go about peaceful protests. In section 1(3)(b) it is clear that the three limbs are disjunctive 'pursued under any enactment *or* rule of law *or* to comply with any condition or requirement imposed by any person under any enactment' (emphasis added). The last limb, which refers to conditions or requirements imposed by an enactment, does not qualify the first but instead provides a further opt-out defence. Thus a protester does not need to show, in order to satisfy the subsection, that she had to pursue the course of conduct so as to protest peacefully (ie that no other means were open) or even—which it is submitted is the likelier interpretation—that she was under a duty imposed by statute to act as she did. For that, the subsection would have to read '... pursued under any enactment *or* rule of law *so as* to comply with any condition or requirement imposed by any person under any enactment' (emphasis added). She

---

[153] *EDO Technology (Preliminary Issues)* [2005] EWHC 2490 at [40] (Walker J).
[154] ibid, [44]: where a claimant is being exposed to harassment to prevent the crimes of others, then the public good may require that there be an inroad on the claimants' ability to seek relief for harassment.
[155] ibid, [54].
[156] ibid, [53].

needs merely to show that the activity and course of conduct is one permitted to her under any other Act. It does not even require her to show that it is permitted under any Act and not prohibited by any other.

Secondly, section 1(3)(c) must be capable of applying to those protests that are peaceful albeit not welcomed by their targets. It must always be 'reasonable' to exercise a human right especially one so enmeshed in our democratic plural and participatory system of government. This must be the more so given the domestication of the right to peaceful protest in the HRA with its parliamentary imprimatur of support. Vindication of such a line was given in the early days of the PFHA by Eady J in *Huntingdon Life Sciences v Curtin and Others*.[157] HLS, a well-known and long-targeted animal research centre, had been granted an injunction under the PFHA to prevent activities of animal rights protesters that they said were detrimental to their business and which amounted to harassment of it and its employees. In agreeing to the variation of the injunction sought by one of the defendants the British Union for the Abolition of Vivisection and removing them from its terms, Eady J commented that the PFHA was clearly not intended by parliament

> to be used to clamp down on discussion of matters of public interest or upon the rights of political protest and public demonstration which was so much part of our democratic tradition. I have little doubt that the courts will resist any such wide interpretation as and when the occasion arises, but it is unfortunate that the terms in which the provisions are couched should be thought to sanction any such restrictions.

The fact that section 1(3)(c), at least since 1998, contains an implicit balancing act between competing fundamental rights—on the one hand that of freedom of expression and on the other corporate rights relating to property under the First Protocol and of individuals under Articles 3 and 8—to be struck by the court on any application, was confirmed in the *EDO (Preliminary Issues)* case we considered above.[158] Walker J held that the role of the court is to ensure that 'legitimate protest is not stigmatised as unlawful' such that it will be 'impossible for the claimants to succeed if their claim would amount to a disproportionate interference with freedom of expression including the expression of protest'.

The scope of the reasonableness defence in human rights terms was subject to considerable qualification in *DPP v Moseley, Selvanayagam and Woodling* involving criminal charges under section 2.[159] Although the court accepted the appropriateness of undertaking a balancing exercise between the protection of the victim and the right to peaceful protest, it also held that it could never be reasonable, as a matter of law under section 2, to pursue a course of conduct clearly in breach of an injunction without exceptional circumstances. The example given was the need to rescue a person in imminent danger. In general, conduct that constituted harassment for the purposes of the Act could not be reasonable and such action could not be justified merely because the defendant believed it to be reasonable. The avenue of redress for a disgruntled defendant was to make an application to set aside the order rather than setting up its 'reasonableness', or rather the reason-

---

[157] *Huntingdon Life Sciences v Curtin and Others*, unreported High Court, *The Times*, 11 December 1997, discussed K Kerrigan (1998) 3 *Journal of Civil Liberties* 37.

[158] Above n 150 [25], following the approach adopted by Hallett J to s 5 of the POA 1986 in *Percy v DPP* [2001] EWHC Admin 1125.

[159] *DPP v Moseley, Selvanayagam and Woodling*, unreported High Court decision, 9 June 1999, *The Times*, 23 June 1999, an appeal by way of case stated. The case is discussed by E Finch, 'Legitimate protest or campaign of harassment—protestors, harassment and reasonableness' [1999] *Web Journal of Current Legal Issues* 5 and K Kerrigan (1999) 4 *J Civ Lib* 390.

ableness of action in breach of an order, as a defence to any criminal proceedings subsequently brought.[160]

In the case, a small group was involved in peaceful protests outside a mink farm and occasionally within its boundaries. The owner obtained an ex parte injunction against one of the three specifically prohibiting her, and anyone else receiving notice of its terms, from entering his farm, neighbouring property, or the highway adjoining the farm, on the ground that it was conduct causing harassment to the farm owner and his family. Notwithstanding the injunction, the defendants continued their protest in the restricted areas and informations, pursuant to the PFHA, were subsequently laid in the magistrates' court. The stipendiary magistrate determined that, although the defendants' conduct amounted to harassment and was also in breach of the injunction, when the nature and purpose of the protest was weighed against the impact upon the owner as a victim, the defendants had established the defence of reasonableness under section 1(3)(c). The High Court overturned this. The case was declared inadmissible by the ECHR on the ground that the restraining order was necessary to prevent crime or disorder and/or to protect the rights of others as was a conviction for breaching an ex parte injunction. Doing so deprived someone of the chance as a matter of law of arguing reasonable conduct.[161] The protester had acted in full knowledge of the injunction and had done nothing to have it discharged or varied. Fenwick comments that the most striking feature is 'the acceptance that a central issue in a criminal trial can be pre-determined in civil proceedings, particularly uncontested ex parte proceedings... The matter clearly raises Article 6 issues; it comes close to obtaining a conviction "on the papers"'.[162]

(v) The Impact of the PFHA on Protesters

The words of Eady J in *Curtin* have largely gone unheeded. Case law has increased the opportunities for those 'harassed' by protests to call in aid section 1 and (now) section 1A. Many of the cases though are procedural rather than substantive in nature. Let us now turn to consider some of the main ones to see if we might elicit some general principles.

(a) Companies Cannot be Harassed

In *DPP v Dziurzynski* Rose LJ (with Gibbs J agreeing) held that Parliament had not intended to make harassment directed at a limited company a criminal offence.[163] The legislative history—with its origins in attempts to protect vulnerable people, usually women, from 'stalking'—largely supported the conclusion that 'person' did not mean a corporation. It was significant that in section 4(1) the word 'him' was used, and in section 5(2) the word 'victim' was used. Rose LJ decided that the decision by the Court of Appeal in *Huntingdon Life Sciences v Curtin*,[164] holding the reverse, was not binding because 'it was not a decision reached as a consequence of argument on both sides. An ex parte injunction was being

---

[160] We might contrast here the approach to satellite criminal justice proceedings taken by the House of Lords *R v DPP ex p Kebilene* [1999] 4 All ER 801.
[161] *Moseley, Selvanayagam and Woodling v UK* (App 57981/00) ECtHR inadmissibility decision, 12 December 2002.
[162] Fenwick, *Civil Liberties*, above n 12, 793.
[163] *Director of Public Prosecutions v Dziurzynski* [2002] EWHC 1380 at [31]–[32].
[164] *Huntingdon Life Sciences v Curtin*, unreported Court of Appeal, 15 October 1997 (Thorpe LJ and Schiemann LJ).

granted'. It was also not a criminal case but an application for an injunction. In the civil sphere, *Daiichi Pharmaceuticals v Stop Huntingdon Animal Cruelty (SHAC)* followed *Dziurzynski* in the criminal sphere and dealt with *Curtin* in the same way as Rose LJ did.[165] Thus an injunction will not be available to a company, not being a person within section 1 and therefore not within the ambit of protection offered by that section. Section 7(5), inserted by section 125(7)(b) of the SOCPA 2005, makes it clear that references to 'person' mean references to a person who is an individual. As Jillaine Seymour notes, this does not leave 'harassed' companies without a remedy. Their central concern—as opposed to their employees, directors and suppliers—is interference with business, an interest (as we shall see) in most cases protected by the economic torts.[166]

(b) The Need for an Identifiable Target?

Individuals who allege they are being or have been harassed will be able to claim injunctive relief. In fact, not all those who have been or are being harassed need sue: civil procedure rules (CPR 19.6) permit representative claims by, say, one or a few employees on behalf of all employees, provided they share the same interest in the action.[167] The shared interest is usually simply asserted as being an interest in not being harassed by GM protesters or animal activists.[168]

The problem, as Seymour identifies, is that this judicial approach suffers from a failure to explain why they share an interest.[169] Specifically, without assessing each and every employee, director or supplier, how can it properly be said that each has and does suffer from harassment? If the representative group is 'all employees of Animal Experimenters plc at the Newtown site', it is inevitable that it will encompass some (many?)—unless the work force is small—who have not yet been harassed (that is, subjected to a course of conduct). All may of course apprehend harassment—which is enough to give rise to a claim for injunctive relief under section 3—but that would presuppose knowledge by B of the harassment suffered by A, something which would need to be shown on evidence by B . . . yet B might not be before the court on a representative action. Similarly, they could only be existing victims—rather than apprehended victims—if they both knew of the incidents affecting others and were as a result caused anxiety or distress (a form of secondary harassment or harassment in lieu?) . . . but again this needs to be shown.[170] The real problem in this area is that representative actions are allowed by judges on the assumption that all employees both know of and suffer from the harassment of a colleague: as Field J asserted in *Avery* 'the letters caused a great deal of concern, distress and upset not only to the recipients but . . . also to other Emerson employees'.[171] The same must hold—and be multiplied—should claims be brought on behalf of customers.

As to the scope of protection for injunctive relief, the courts have been willing to grant injunctions in fairly wide terms covering large groups and categories of people. In

---

[165] *Daiichi Pharmaceuticals v Stop Huntingdon Animal Cruelty (SHAC)* [2003] EWHC 2337.
[166] J Seymour, 'Who can be harassed? Claims against animal rights protestors under section 3 of the Protection from Harassment Act 1997' (2005) 64 *Cambridge Law Journal* 57, 60.
[167] Civil Procedure Rules 1998 (CPR) r 19.6.
[168] See Owen J in *Daiichi*, above n 165, at [22].
[169] Seymour, above n 166, 61–62.
[170] The fact that these need proving—and the fact that the nature of representative actions denies this opportunity yet presupposes it exists—is not something directly addressed by Seymour.
[171] *Emerson Developments Ltd v Avery* [2004] EWHC 194 at [7].

Broughton[172] animal rights protesters wanted to prevent construction of a new science research centre and laboratory in Oxford, as they were opposed to the live animal experimentation that would take place there once it was built. In July 2004, all the contractors on the project resigned, as a result of a campaign of intimidation including (it was alleged) bomb threats and threats falsely to publicise convictions for sexual offences, made to directors of the various (sub-)construction companies. The University then sought an injunction to protect itself and those engaged on the building works so that construction could be recommenced. The first case concerned the continuation of a temporary injunction.[173] The protesters complained that the original injunction—in favour of unnamed 'protected persons' categorised by their association with the University—made it insufficiently clear to them what they were permitted to do and against whom they were lawfully able to protest. In the criminal sphere, *Dziurzynski* had made it clear that a single charge alleging harassment of a group of employees was bad for duplicity, as they did not constitute a close enough knit group.[174] Grigson J distinguished *Dziurzynski*, as it involved a prosecution for criminal harassment not, as here, deciding whether or not to continue (or to grant) a civil injunction.

> The purpose of this injunction is to prevent harassment as defined by the Act taking place. To that end, the restraint is designed to prevent acts which may, if continued, constitute the full offence. It would be pointless otherwise. If the Claimants had to wait for the full offence to be committed, they could rely upon the Criminal Law but the Criminal Law acts retrospectively. A civil injunction is prospective. Necessarily an injunction is designed to catch acts which are less than the full offence. Consequently the Courts have the power to grant injunctions in wide terms to prevent the harassment of a class of persons, for example, the employees of contractors or sub-contractors, so that they may go about their lawful business.[175]

Arguing that anonymity meant it was impossible for the protesters to comply was met with this rejoinder:

> First . . . the notion of 'accidental harassment' which is in effect what [counsel] complains about is absurd. Second . . . in none of the other reported cases involving various members of the Animal Rights movement have the protesters had the slightest difficulty in identifying contractors, sub-contractors and their employees. Not only has there been no difficulty, the details of such people have been publicised on web-sites and they have been the target of harassment. If a protester can identify a person as a suitable target of harassment, he or she can equally identify those who are protected by injunction.[176]

---

[172] *Chancellor of the University of Oxford v Broughton* [2004] EWHC 2543 (Admin) and [2006] EWHC 1233 (Admin). See also *Hall v Save Newchurch Guinea Pigs Campaign* [2005] EWHC 372. The Court of Appeal decision in *Broughton* [2006] EWCA Civ 1305 revolved around two minor procedural issues: (a) should the lower court have accepted an undertaking from one of the defendants rather than subjecting him to an injunction?; and (b) should the lower court have struck out the claim against another defendant on the ground that as a member of one of the unincorporated associations subject to the injunctions, to allow proceedings to continue was an unnecessary proliferation?

[173] The power to grant injunctions is given in s 37(1) of the Supreme Court Act 1981 where it is 'just and convenient'. But, by virtue of s 12(3) of the HRA, where what is being sought is interlocutory or temporary injunctive relief that will have an impact on the Convention right of free speech, then the test is whether or not the applicant is likely to establish at trial that publication should not be allowed. 'Likely' is used in the sense set out by Lord Nicholls in *Cream Holdings v Banerjee* [2004] UKHL 44, [22].

[174] *Dziurzynski*, above n 163.

[175] *Broughton* (2004) above n 172, at [39]. The fact that the defendants were anonymous at this stage did not deprive any of the protesters of their rights to a fair trial under Article 6 of the ECHR. If proceedings were brought later for breach of the injunction, the alleged victims would have to be identified.

[176] *Broughton* (2004) above n 172, at [43].

276 *Taking Direct Action*

In the criminal sphere, prosecutions under section 2 for harassment must make clear the individual targets with sufficient specificity as to identify them—or at least must avoid charging someone with 'harassing employees of Animal Experimenters plc'. Although authorities such as *DPP v Dunn*[177] established that members of a close-knit definable group could be the victims of a single act of harassment, applying that test in *Dziurzynski*, Rose LJ concluded that the employees of the targeted company were not a sufficiently closely-knit group:

> The authorities . . . have been concerned with a very small number of people. In the case of *Dunn* they were husband and wife. For my part, I have no difficulty with the concept that a family living together at the same address, or it may be unrelated persons living together at the same address, may properly be regarded as a close knit group. Every case must be determined as one of degree by reference to the particular circumstances. But, for my part, I simply do not accept that 60 persons, whose only common feature is that they work for the same employer, are a close knit group.[178]

(c) The Protesters Need Not be Individually Named[179]

Ordinarily, 'you cannot have an injunction except against a party to the suit'.[180] Injunctions can normally only be granted against those who are already named parties to extant proceedings. This is for good reason: only if someone is already being sued, and thus already a party, do they have a right to be heard before relief is obtained. However, instances where injunctions have been granted against non-parties so that they are enjoined and bound are on the increase in protest cases. They fall into one of two categories: relief against parties by description and representative claims under CPR 19.6.

In *Broughton*, Grigson J relied on *M Michaels (Furriers) v Askew*[181] to hold that an injunction could be granted against unknown and unidentified members of loosely formed unincorporated associations where that was necessary to do justice in the case. This was so if, using the words of Dunn LJ in *Askew*,

> a number of unidentified person are causing injury and damage by unlawful acts of one kind or another, and there is an arguable case that they belong to a single organisation or class which encourages action of the type complained of, and their actions can be limited to that organisation.

So for example, in the *Heathrow* case, the injunction granted (admittedly not one based on the PFHA but on possible breach of airport byelaws and/or nuisance) bound (i) all persons who are and/or are acting as officers, activists and/or supporters of and/or in the name of the unincorporated association known as Plane Stupid; and (ii) all persons acting in concert with any of the above persons for the purpose of disrupting the operation of Heathrow Airport.[182]

---

[177] *Director of Public Prosecutions v Dunn* [2001] 1 Cr App R 352
[178] *Dziurzynski*, above n 163, at [42].
[179] See generally J Seymour, 'Injunctions enjoining non-parties: distinction without a difference?' (2007) 66 *CLJ* 605.
[180] *Iveson v Harris* (1802) 7 Ves Jun 251, 257 and *Re Wykeham Terrace, Brighton, Sussex, ex parte Territorial Auxiliary and Volunteer Reserve Association for the South East* [1971] Ch 204, 208 (Stamp J). Both cases are referred to in Seymour *ibid*.
[181] *M Michaels (Furriers) Ltd v Askew*, unreported Court of Appeal, 23 June 1983 (Dunn and Purchas LJJ), *The Times*, 25 June 1983.
[182] *Garman*, above n 130, at [118]. Of category (ii) Swift J adopted the approach of Holland J in *Huntingdon Life Sciences v SHAC* [2007] EWHC 522 at [15]: 'For practical purposes the Order would be ineffective from the standpoint of HLS and unfair from the standpoint of the Defendants if "non-SHAC" protestors when within any such Exclusion Zone could claim immunity from the Order. It follows, by way of example, that if Uncaged's

If a claimant tries to restrain harassment by suing an unincorporated association (and so not a legal person) such as a pressure or campaigning group—as well as, or as an alternative to, individual protesters (named or not)—this will only be possible in one of two situations.[183] In the *EDO Technology* case these were stated as: first where such a course was authorised by express or implied statutory provisions—which was not the case under the PFHA—or secondly where there was an individual before the court capable of being sued and about whom it could properly be said she was a representative of the association.[184] The latter will only be appropriate where there is not a divergence of interests between members of the association.[185] Thus where the evidence shows that not all protesters in a group share the same view about, say, using unlawful means to achieve their ends, a representative order would not be suitable.[186]

Whatever difficulties there were in attributing liability in harassment cases to a large group of like-minded protesting individuals and groups were alleviated considerably by another change to the PFHA. Section 7(3A) was introduced by section 44 of the Criminal Justice and Police Act 2001. It increases the protective ambit of the 1997 Act by bringing into the fold those who do not themselves harass but who stand behind the actual harassers. Under section 7(3A),

> a person's conduct on any occasion shall be taken, if aided, abetted, counselled or procured by another—
>
> (a) to be conduct on that occasion of the other (as well as conduct of the person whose conduct it is); and
> (b) to be conduct in relation to which the other's knowledge and purpose, and what he ought to have known, are the same as they were in relation to what was contemplated or reasonably foreseeable at the time of the aiding, abetting, counselling or procuring.

As a result, where A urges (or counsels) B to harass C, the director of an animal research laboratory, or shows B where C lives and B then engages in a course of harassing conduct, that harassment is as much harassment undertaken by A as it is by B and with the same mens rea. The Government viewed section 7(3A) as dealing with, by criminalising, 'collective

---

members are minded to demonstrate within an Exclusion Zone, then, good intentions notwithstanding, arguably they too become "Protestors" so as to be bound by the Order'. In precisely the same way, in the view of Swift J, the order would be ineffective and unfair if persons not acting in the name of Plane Stupid could claim immunity from it.

[183] Previously injunctions had been granted against unincorporated protest associations regardless of whether there was a representative individual as well before the court and seemingly without a great deal of argument about the legal propriety of such a course. In some cases it was just assumed: see as examples *Huntingdon Life Sciences Group Plc v SHAC* [2003] EWHC 1967, *Phytopharm Plc v Avery* [2004] EWHC 503 and the *Newchurch* case, above n 172.

[184] *EDO Technology* [2005] EWHC 837 at [40]–[43]. Gross J concluded that 'Smash EDO' was a sufficiently identifiable group as to be an unincorporated association. Relevant factors—drawing on *Monsanto v Tilly* [2000] Env LR 313 (CA)—were that it had a telephone number and at least one e-mail addresses; it conducted fund-raising and published a newsletter; it holds protests; it conducted legal workshops; and it held itself out as a group of people campaigning with the purpose of removing EDO from Brighton and/or shutting it down through 'raising awareness and direct action. There was no evidence the second defendant 'BOOB' was even an association rather than a mere slogan.

[185] See Stuart-Smith LJ in *Monsanto v Tilly*, above n 184, at [42] when distinguishing the unreported case of *United Kingdom Nirex Ltd v Barton, The Times*, 13 October 1986.

[186] See, by way of example, the analysis by Swift J of the different protest groups in *Garman*, above n 130, at [62]–[74]. Whether or not a protester who was not made a party to the proceedings but was the subject of a representative order could properly be made the subject of a power of arrest see *Garman* at [103] and the cases referred to therein: *Huntingdon Life Sciences Group plc v SHAC* [2007] EWHC 522 *RWE npower Plc v Carroll* [2007] EWHC 947 (the Radley lakes litigation) and *SmithKline Beecham plc v Avery* [2007] EWHC 948.

harassment'. In its response to the 2001 consultation, the Government considered that section 7(3A) created a form of harassing joint enterprise: 'it is an offence for a group of people to collude with each other to cause harassment, alarm or distress where each of the perpetrators only undertakes one act of harassment'.[187]

That, it is submitted, is not quite what the subsection says—people can aid and abet or counsel or procure without themselves actually committing any harassment at all. That is not 'joint and several liability', in civil law terms, which the Government appears to believe its 2001 amending clarification created. At the very least, there must be a strong case—though section 7(3A) is silent—for utilising section 3 of the HRA, so as to reduce the scope of both criminal and civil liability, to 'read in' the fact that A must know (or at least be reckless as to the fact) that B will harass C—otherwise many innocent third parties could be seen as aiding others in harassment. That would prevent liability being attributed to A for B's state of mind but would not obviate the fact that section 7(3A) is drafted more widely than could be justified by a desire simply to capture those who collude, the Government's stated aim. We might ask why it was needed at all, at least in the criminal sphere, given the existence of the inchoate crimes we considered earlier in the chapter. In the civil arena, it is quite clear that the new section goes much further than was needed to deal with the perceived mischief alluded to in the government's response to the consultation.

Injunctions under the PFHA 1997 (and otherwise) are capable of being enforced against 'true' third parties, that is enforced against a group wider than those enjoined and bound by its terms, whether that be named individuals, representative defendants or parties bound by description. First, an injunction can be enforced against those who have specific enough knowledge of its terms and exact provisions. Secondly, its terms can be enforced against those deemed to be acting in concert with a named or identified party—though there is no clear line on what this means.[188]

(d) Procedural Protection for Protesters

There are several matters of concern here, and one links directly from what has just been said. Whatever procedural rights and guarantees that a defendant party has when an injunction is being sought, none is afforded to those not actually before the court yet enjoined by its terms: ie representative claims under CPR 19.6 or those identified by description. Yet, for those the full weight of the order will come down on them and breach without reasonable cause will constitute a separate crime. There are clear Article 6 issues here.

The protection that parties are entitled to is limited in any event. Since the process is civil, evidentiary rules are more relaxed and the standard of proof is lower. It is very likely to include hearsay evidence from private investigators employed by the target company. Yet, as we have just seen, once granted—on this lesser standard—breach can turn a protester into a criminal. This is very much the point that Helen Fenwick was making earlier, commenting on *Moseley*, where she talks of it verging on 'obtaining a conviction "on the papers"'.[189] It is likely the application will be heard without notice, something designed deliberately by claimants so as not to tip off the protesters and thereby provoke them into

---

[187] *Animal Rights Extremism: Government Strategy Responses to the Consultation Document* (Home Office, December 2001) para 2.1. This does not appear any longer to be available at the Home Office webpages, though the March 2001 consultation document is: www.homeoffice.gov.uk/documents/animal-rights-extremism-270401?view=Binary, accessed 12 August 2009.

[188] See for example the discussion in *Moseley* and the note by Finch, both above n 159.

[189] Fenwick, *Civil Liberties*, above n 12, 793.

any sort of pre-emptive 'strike', and in private. These aspects were strongly criticised by the JCHR in its March 2009 report *Demonstrating respect for rights? A human rights approach to policing protest*.[190] Costs, too, are likely to be an issue and a significant burden for most protesting defendants such as to mean many will not be able to right their corner.[191]

(e) Protest Exclusion Orders: Balancing the Right of Peaceful Protest and the Protection of Legitimate Businesses

In several protest cases, injunctions granted by the courts on the basis of actual or apprehended harassment have included protest exclusion zones of considerable size.[192] Courts have also imposed restrictions on what protest activities will be permitted, for how long, when and by whom.[193] What is worrying about some of these cases is the ready assumption that demonstrations and assemblies will per se constitute harassment and intimidation. In one of the many applications concerning harassment during the protracted construction of the Oxford research laboratory site, Treacy J was asked to create a second designated protest site as a *quid pro quo* of extending a protest exclusion zone. He rejected the application in these terms:

> In my judgement any demonstration or protest permitted at Point Y or on the pavement opposite Point Y would be likely to have the effect of harassing those entering the site. As paragraphs 7 and 9 of Mr Broughton's 6th witness statement make plain, the purpose of having a presence near or at Point Y would be so that the protesters could 'interact with those using and visiting the laboratory'. In my judgement, interaction, even by a limited number of people, is likely to have the effect of amounting to intimidation and harassment.[194]

The *Broughton* litigation provides an insight into the extent. It will also allow us to see how the requirements of peaceful protest and proportionality were approached. The cumulative effects of the orders granted by Grigson J in 2004 and extended in 2006 by Holland J were that any protest—save a procession that was lawful within sections 11–12 of the Public Order Act 1986—within an exclusion zone somewhat larger than 50 metres from the construction site was banned save that 50 people were permitted to protest at one spot for four hours on a Thursday afternoon.[195] The orders also banned the taking of photographs by

---

[190] Seventh report of session 2008–09 (23 March 2009) www.publications.parliament.uk/pa/jt200809/jtselect/jtrights/47/4702.htm (accessed on 12 August 2009) paras 96–110.
[191] Evidence from Dr Peter Harbour (from the Save Radley Lakes campaign) to the JCHR in its investigation into policing and protest (see above) available at www.publications.parliament.uk/pa/jt200809/jtselect/jtrights/47/47we33.htm, accessed 12 August 2009.
[192] Following *Burris v Adzani* [1995] 4 All ER 802, 810. The Court there accepted that both the High Court and County Court, in the context of matrimonial harassment and non-molestation, had the power to grant interlocutory injunctions in wide terms to restrain conduct that was not in itself tortious or otherwise unlawful, if that was reasonably necessary for the protection of a plaintiff's legitimate interest. Courts therefore have power to impose exclusion zones when granting non-molestation injunctions restraining harassment of the victim by the defendant, provided no unnecessary restraint was placed on the defendant. Though both *Burris* and *Broughton* involved applications for an exclusion zone in interlocutory proceedings, exclusion zones have been granted as final relief: see *Price*, above n 139, at [194]–[201] and *Silverton v Gravett*, unreported High Court decision, 19 October 2001, involving protesters against furriers.
[193] Courts have even held that it may be proportionate—in Art 10 terms—to grant injunctions restraining publication of even truthful information abut a third party victim *R v Debnath* [2005] EWCA Crim 3472. However, as the case concerned a jilted former lover taking revenge by falsely circulating stories as well, it was one in which protest was not an issue. The instrumentality of Arts 10 and 11 was not canvassed or discussed.
[194] *Broughton* (2008), above n 143, at [23].
[195] It will not always be the case that a claim to restrict the numbers or frequency of what we might call ordinary protest will be sanctioned by judicial order: see as a contrary example, *EDO Technology* [2005] EWHC 837 at [84] (Gross J): 'What has been objectionable in this case are certain of the protestors' activities; not the frequency of the protests or the numbers of those involved'.

protesters, seen as a means to identify and thus to start to intimidate those connected with the project,[196] and publication of any material that might lead to the identification of a 'protected person'. A further injunction banned the use of megaphones and amplification at parts of the permitted protest site.[197] The University's claim for a zone totalling 1000m by 600m was 'inordinately large, impossible readily to identify and owed nothing to the present issues save that everything within it was University property'. It was also more difficult to police. Holland J drew up the zone to balance interests of safety, noise, disturbance and the legitimate interests of both sides and to keep the restrictions to the minimum level that were also consonant with the protection needed. He rejected, for example, an additional buffer zone, claimed as being necessary to prevent protesters loitering near the site and monitoring traffic and being able to identify workers and University employees, as he could not see how this could be justified. Whatever the size of the zone, nothing could prevent lawful uses of the surrounding roads and the opportunity to observe, provided that did not amount to demonstrating or protesting. At each stage in the various cases, it was clear that each aspect of the orders should be kept under review so as to ensure the balance continued to be struck appropriately and fairly. Hence, at one of the hearings a ban on amplified noise in one part of the zone was relaxed, as there was no clear evidence of complaints about its use.

In the *Newchurch* case, injunctions were granted in relation to the guinea pig breeding farm operated by the Hall family.[198] Evidence had been presented of an unremitting campaign of intimidation—'a form of terrorism'[199]—being waged that included threats to and attacks on pubs where the Hall family drank, the golf club where Mr Hall was a member and those who employed members of the Hall family.[200] Named groups and individuals, anyone acting in concert with any one named group or individual who also had knowledge of the order and anyone else given notice of the order was forbidden from pursuing a course of conduct which amounted to harassment of a large unnamed amorphous group. This included employees and tenants at the farm, proprietors, employees and shareholders of the contractors and their families, servants or agents and anyone visiting the farm. Lawful protesters were limited to 25 in number on Sundays between 12 pm and 3 pm. This did give preference to the argument that Sunday was the only day on which protesters would largely be free rather than the claimant's argument to keep their Sundays free from disturbance. The protected persons were granted the protection of a 100-metre exclusion zone around their houses or premises. Each was thought to be a fair balance between competing inter-

---

[196] This was later set aside: the defendants had successfully argued that both the police and the University took photos and the protesters, in turn, might wish to do so to record any untoward incidents that affected them.

[197] This was despite an acknowledgement that if the Thursday protest were lawful, how could people register their views over the noise of traffic?: see *Broughton* (2006), above n 172, at [24]–[28].

[198] See p 17 above for detail. In about two and a half years (January 2003 until the summer of 2005) Staffordshire police received reports of more than 460 incidents at the farm or other related targets: *The Guardian*, 24 August 2005.

[199] *Newchurch*, above n 172, at [75] (Owen J).

[200] The argument that it would be an abuse of the process of the court to grant such a wide injunction when sufficient other public order powers had been made available to the police by Parliament was met with this rejoinder from Owen J: 'the availability of such powers has not enabled the police to prevent the unlawful activities directed at the claimants and their associates. The unlawful activities of the protesters can be described as a guerrilla campaign. They usually take place at night, over a wide area, and directed at a wide range of targets. The reality is that notwithstanding the level of police involvement ... the police have been unable to prevent unlawful intimidation, harassment, criminal damage and arson. I do not consider that to invoke the jurisdiction of the court under the Protection from Harassment Act 1997 amounts to an abuse of process in such circumstances'. Quite how and why the matter would be made better by the granting of an injunction is not explained.

ests and rights. The Court rejected an application for an exclusion zone of roughly 200 km in area, as not being reasonably necessary for the protection of any of the protected persons.

Various issues that relate generally to the impact on the right to protest of a broadly-worded statutory right not to be harassed were discussed in the *EDO Technology* case.[201] The managing director of EDO, an arms manufacturer and supplier, sought an interim anti-harassment injunction against various protesters and campaign groups. Counsel for the protesters had argued that an anti-harassment injunction should rarely, if at all, be used in the context of protest for the fear of its stifling effect; perhaps only where there was a concerted campaign against individuals and the campaigning groups had the avowed intention of, inter alia, employing unlawful means. Section 3 of the HRA, it was argued, meant that absent violence or the threat of violence, freedom of speech and assembly were not to be restricted and unless the 'harassment' did involve alarm and distress, it was difficult to justify restricting freedom of expression and assembly. While Gross J acknowledged that the PFHA had been passed to deal with stalkers and that there was understandable concern that it should not be used to clamp down on rights of protest and expression, there came a point when protest and expression might cross the line into harassment.

> I cannot accept that it would be right to read into the Act fixed limits as to its applicability, whether as to categories of cases or inflexible threshold requirements. So, for instance, while it must be likely that most restrictions on freedom of expression or assembly would result from a risk of violence or the threat of violence, 'harassment' is not confined to acts which place the victim in fear of violence ... The right not to be harassed is not or not only a right not to be placed in fear of violence or subjected to violence. So too, it would be inappropriate to read 'harassment' as *confined* to conduct which alarms or causes distress, though again, ordinarily, it must be unlikely that conduct which does not amount to that will be restrained by interim injunction.[202]

The evidence was of a concerted campaign. This had included obstruction of the highway, aggravated trespass and criminal damage and, at the least, seriously arguable instances of harassment: targeting of directors' homes or neighbourhoods and intimidation of employees. In the court's view, those who suffered infringement of their lawful rights were entitled to the protection of the law.[203] The protesters argued that the police were—or should have been—able to control any protests using the criminal law, so rendering otiose reliance on a civil injunction. The court, following the line adopted in *Broughton*,[204] concluded that the purpose of a civil injunction under the PFHA was the prospective prevention of acts which, if allowed to continue, could amount to offences that would be dealt with retrospectively by the criminal law. This does rather seem to underplay the reach of the criminal law in this area, especially attempts to commit (say) criminal damage or even the statutory offence of harassment under section 2. What this does allow is easier criminalisation by the backdoor: breach of a civil PFHA injunction, granted on the lesser standard of proof using rules of civil procedure, will itself also constitute a crime.

Other cases decided under the HRA have explicitly acknowledged the need to take account of the rights of protesting defendants under Articles 10 and 11 and the fact that the grant of an injunction—whether interim or final—will inevitably place a considerable restriction on what might not in fact be unlawful activities. The problem facing protesters in such cases is that, as we have seen, Strasbourg has never upheld the rights of protesters

---

[201] Above n 117.
[202] *ibid*, at [61].
[203] See also *Monsanto v Tilly*, above n 184.
[204] Above n 143.

engaged in direct action protest on substantive grounds.[205] In many of the Strasbourg cases there was evidence of a much lower degree of harassment than in most of the cases we have looked at here, yet the applications were all either declared inadmissible or were unsuccessful on proportionality grounds. What the courts strive to protect is peaceful communicative activity, whether in the form of demonstrating or chanting, while restricting the ability of protesters to engage in any activity where there is sound evidence (from past activities or from a group's press statements or website publicity about its intentions) that it will cause obstruction or intimidation—or perhaps any more than is a by-product of a peaceful, communicative protest. This is not always the case. We might recall the comment by Treacy J in *Broughton* (2008).[206] Similarly, despite a relaxation by the relevant council, a High Court injunction banned protesters from engaging in any activity 'in connection with opposition to or protest against' the construction of a bypass at Linslade in Buckinghamshire.[207]

There has been in certain cases a noticeable shift in favour of protests that are not threatening or menacing, effectively defining it out from harassment. In *Broughton* (2008), Treacy J said this, in relation to an application to obtain an exclusion order insulating Oxford graduation ceremonies from the animal rights protest outside:

> None of the evidence shows that the shouting or chanting taking place intermittently during the various ceremonies was of itself threatening or menacing. The evidence shows that chants of 'Stop the Oxford animal lab' or 'Oxford University—a place that tortures animals', were typical of the sort of chants being used. The University's witnesses speak of the effect of the chanting being to reduce the enjoyment of, and the sense of, a solemn occasion. They speak of irritating and distasteful noise. They speak of an unjustifiable intrusion by noise which ruined or spoilt the ceremony ... Nowhere in the University's evidence does any witness speak of feeling harassed, alarmed or threatened. The language is all in terms of irritation and the loss of enjoyment. The members of the audience ... did not appear to be alarmed, distressed, threatened or frightened by what was going on intermittently outside.[208]

Of course, this might easily be circumvented by claimant witnesses attesting to being harassed and on a representative claim, the choice of witnesses can more easily be managed.

In the *Garman* case, as we have seen, Swift J refused to grant an injunction against Plane Stupid or its members/activists on the basis that there was no evidence of previous harassing behaviour at any of the previous Climate Change camps or sit-ins (such as at the Drax power station) and the evidence that there was to be a blockade of Heathrow over August, and thus apprehended harassment, was weak.[209] The only evidence of past behaviour adduced before the court was a blockade of BAA's Heathrow offices and playing loud music outside the home of BAA's chief executive when, in all likelihood, he was away. The injunction that was granted—on the balance of convenience—was premised on likely widespread unlawful disruptive protest and action that would breach airport byelaws and constitute nuisance.[210] Even then its terms were such that the judge hoped

> should not affect the peaceful and lawful activities associated with the climate camp. It is targeted solely and specifically at a group of persons who are intent upon disrupting the operation of the airport, irrespective of the rights of passengers and others to go about their lawful activities. The

---

[205] As we saw in chapter three, the only direct action case in which a violation was found was because the law—as it happens UK law—was not framed sufficiently clearly to meet the 'prescribed by law' test under Art 11(2): *Hashman and Harrup v United Kingdom* (2000) 30 EHRR 241.
[206] Above n 143.
[207] 'Protesters Win Over Bypass Injunction', *The Guardian*, 2 February 2002.
[208] *Broughton*, above n 143, at [32]–[33].
[209] *Garman*, above n 130, at [99].

purpose of the injunction is to enable the airport to continue to function and to permit those responsible for security at the airport and elsewhere to focus on their prime concern of protecting the public from the risk of terrorist attack.[211]

The unacknowledged problem that underpins many harassment cases is this. One party is being restrained in order to protect or to guarantee the lawful activities of others when the activities of that first group may themselves not be unlawful: after all, injunctive relief under *Burris v Adzani* is available even to restrain activities not in themselves 'tortious or otherwise unlawful, if such order was reasonably to be regarded as necessary for the protection of a plaintiff's legitimate interest'.[212] Two examples will allow us to see this point though in neither has research produced the actual wording of the order. In one case, granted in favour the company running Drax power station in August 2006, an injunction banned 'unauthorised' people from using an adjacent public footpath.[213] In another, Mohammed Al-Fayed was able to obtain from Stanley Burnton J an injunction restraining shouting and preventing certain groups from using the Brompton Road in Kensington, where Harrods is situated.[214] We saw earlier in *Broughton* that the terms of the injunction banned, with a very limited exception, the exercise of the very right of protest brought home in the HRA and banned absolutely another perfectly lawful activity, taking photos.[215]

Why *should* the rights of protesters in those cases lose out? They too have a legitimate interest in pursuing activities that are not only lawful but are expressions of view and peaceful protest guaranteed by the ECHR. This is thrown into stark relief by the words of Grigson J in *Broughton*.

> The right of freedom of expression is not to be exercised in a vacuum created by the assumption that only the views of the animal rights movement are correct. Those who believe that experimentation on live animals is both morally and scientifically justified also have the right of freedom of expression. Further such people and those who, in the broadest sense, work for them have the right to respect for their private and family life, their homes and correspondence under Article 8. Whilst [a law–abiding protester] has the right to express his views, another citizen has an equal right not to listen to [them]. [A law-abiding protester] has no right to coerce an unwilling citizen to receive [their] opinions. Freedom of expression entitles you to publish your views on a website. It does not entitle you to incite others to commit criminal offences. Further, when considering the infringement upon [a law-abiding protester's] right to express himself, the Court must keep in mind that … it does not prevent [a law-abiding protester] (or anybody else) expressing his views. He may do so to his heart's content. What it does restrict is to whom and where he expresses those views. A similar consideration applies in respect of his right to peaceful assembly and freedom of association. A right to freedom of peaceful assembly does not entitle a citizen, by means of a mass protest, to stop the lawful activities of others. A protest may impinge on others rights temporarily, but actions designed to prevent permanently others exercising their lawful rights cannot be regarded as a reasonable exercise of civil rights and consequently the Courts may act to restrain them.[216]

[210] *ibid*, at [109]–[116].
[211] *ibid*, at [120].
[212] *Burris v Adzani*, above n 192.
[213] 'Power station protesters arrested' BBC News on-line 1 September 2006 at: news.bbc.co.uk/1/hi/england/north_yorkshire/5300560.stm, accessed 22 July 2009.
[214] Details supplied by Stephanie Harrison, counsel for the protesters, at a Liberty/Norton Rose seminar: 'The right to protest', 5 May 2009.
[215] Above n 172.
[216] *ibid*, at [80]–[82]. Grigson J decided that injunctive relief was necessary to enable the claimants to go about their lawful business. The restrictions were proportionate: they were limited, they did not significantly impinge on the rights of the protesters; and there was no other way to achieve the protection of the claimants from tortious and criminal activities.

Here is the rub. Equally, and conversely, an anti-harassment injunction 'stops the lawful activities of others', a peaceful protest and, if it is a final order, is 'designed to prevent permanently others exercising their lawful rights'. It is rarely if ever from this perspective that the courts view the complex intertwining of interests that are enmeshed in such scenarios.[217] Nothing that has been said above seeks to excuse the activities of some, the many or even a few who commit violent intimidation or are on its periphery, but it is a valid criticism if—as is possible under *Burris*—injunctive relief is granted where there has as yet been no wrongdoing.[218] Imagine an injunction granted under section 3 ordering protesters

> not to impede or prevent access to or egress from Greengage Farm or to obstruct or interfere with the operation of the farm and its business or with any person acting in the execution or his or her duty in relation thereto.

That would debar a direct action protester from changing tactics and trying peacefully to persuade farmworkers to seek other jobs if in so doing they stood outside the farm gates, blocking the way in for a few minutes while they attempted to engage the workers in conversation. The reasonableness of that conduct would not, as *Selvanayagam* establishes,[219] constitute a defence to any charges under section 2 or arrests for breach of the injunction. It is here that the real interference with peaceful protest comes about.

B. Unlawful Harassment Outside Someone's Home: Sections 42–42A of the CJPA 2001

Harassing someone outside their home exposes protesters to the separate regime contained in sections 42–42A of the Criminal Justice and Police Act 2001, as amended by SOCPA 2005. The regime takes what is becoming an increasingly common approach in this area, one we met when we considered aggravated trespass: section 42 empowers the police to give directions, where knowing failure to comply is a summary offence. These powers run alongside the PFHA or, in those increasingly unlikely cases where the PFHA is unable to respond, section 42 may provide the only option.[220] It might well also be possible to charge someone in that case with watching and besetting, contrary to section 241 of the Trade Union and Labour Relations (Consolidation) Act (TULRCA) 1992, which we cover below.

---

[217] A similar point was made of the judicial approach to privacy and free speech cases in the early days of the HRA: G Phillipson, 'Judicial reasoning in breach of confidence cases under the Human Rights Act: not taking privacy seriously?' [2003] *European Human Rights Law Review* Supplement (special issue privacy) 54.

[218] In *Price*, above n 139, the Mormon church was able to restrain another Minister (in the Church of England (Continuing)) from persisting with his campaign of harassment and nuisance. This was despite the fact that he had not used or incited violence nor used profane or foul language. Local residents and visitors to Mormon properties had been disturbed, intimidated, alarmed, and offended by the behaviour. The case report includes amongst his activities: haranguing members of, and visitors to, Mormon establishments around the country; shouting outside temples during services and activities; prolonged, loud proselytising outside on the highway outside Mormon missions; making inappropriate and offensive comments to church members and the general public about Mormon beliefs and practises; making uninvited visits to Mormon missionaries' homes; and making thousands of unwanted telephone calls to Mormon missionaries.

[219] Above n 159.

[220] In light of *Rimmington* [2005] UKHL 63 (see below text to n 250) since s 42 is statutory, it would 'trump' criminal charges for public nuisance being brought against those who stage (mass) pickets outside private houses, envisaged as a possibility by Scott J in *Thomas v NUM* [1986] Ch 20.

(i) The Statutory Scheme

Under section 42 the most senior-ranking officer at the scene may give a direction to the defendant (D) where D is present outside or in the vicinity of any premises used by any individual victim (V) as his dwelling[221] and the officer believes, on reasonable grounds, both that

(a) D is present there for the purpose (by his presence or otherwise) of representing to V or another individual (whether or not one who uses the premises as his dwelling), or of persuading V or such another individual that
   (i) he should not do something that he is entitled or required to do; or
   (ii) he should do something that he is not under any obligation to do; and
(b) D's presence (either alone or together with that of any other persons who are also present)
   (i) amounts to, or is likely to result in, the harassment of V; or
   (ii) is likely to cause alarm or distress to V.[222]

The direction can be given orally and may be given to each of several persons individually or all together. D may be required to do whatever the officer may specify such as she considers necessary to prevent either (or both) the harassment of V or the causing of any alarm or distress to V.[223] The direction might include—but is not limited to—a requirement that someone simply leave the vicinity of the premises (either immediately or after a specified period of time) or that they leave (either immediately or after a specified period of time) and not return within a period specified by the officer, not being longer than three months.[224] A direction may make exceptions to any requirement it imposes and those exceptions might be subject to such conditions as the officer thinks fit. These could include conditions as to

(a) ... the distance from the premises at which, or otherwise as to the location where, persons who do not leave their vicinity must remain; and
(b) ... the number or identity of those authorised by the exception to remain in the vicinity.[225]

Knowingly failing to comply with a direction is a summary offence, as is, if directed not to do so, returning within three months in order to represent to, or persuade V not to do something they are entitled to do or to do something they are not required to do. Thus D who is directed to leave and not to return within three months, commits no offence if she does leave and stays away or, if she returns, as long as she only does so for a non-persuading purpose.

---

[221] Section 42(6)(a). Dwelling bears the same meaning as in s 8 of the POA 1986: 'any structure or part of a structure occupied as a person's home or as other living accommodation (whether the occupation is separate or shared with others) but does not include any part not so occupied and for this purpose 'structure' includes a tent, caravan, vehicle, vessel or other temporary or movable structure'. As the authors of Bailey, Harris and Jones, *Civil Liberties*, above n 107, at 420 point out, would this catch the republican outside Buckingham Palace or the government critic outside Downing Street? The word 'vicinity' is not defined at all. Section 3 of the HRA, and perhaps even general principles of statutory interpretation (given the mischief aimed at was harassment in one's home) should mean that a narrow test is adopted, equating to little more than 'outside the front gate' and certainly nowhere near as wide as 'in the environs or neighbourhood' as that could catch protesters several hundred yards away.
[222] Section 42(1).
[223] Section 42(2)–(3).
[224] Section 42(4).
[225] Section 42(5). The power to give a direction excludes any power to direct a person to refrain from conduct that is lawful under s 220 of the Trade Union and Labour Relations (Consolidation) Act 1992, right peacefully to picket a work place: s 42(6)(b).

D who does not leave commits an offence there and then even if later she returns again for a non-persuading purpose. D who does return so as to persuade only commits an offence at that later date—assuming it can be established that it was the same person on both occasions and that the three-month deadline had not passed. At a practical level, there must be significant doubts about how the police could ever check the former.

(ii) The Scope of Section 42

Where section 42 has the upper-hand over the PFHA as a policing measure is that the trigger is not a course of conduct; that is there is no need for a repetition of harassing behaviour. Officers can direct protesters (on pain of arrest) to leave and not to return for up to three months on the basis of a single incident of harassment—still undefined—outside or in the vicinity of someone's house. Since these are not judicially-sanctioned banning orders,[226] one major problem with permitting the police to act in this way is that considerable power resides in their hands based on their own reasoned assessment of anything untoward occurring. Of course, this applies across the board in the policing context and this is not necessarily to suggest that these directions be given by, say, magistrates on evidence but it is worth re-iterating this general concern.

Taking the section in turn, we can see that a direction can be given on reasonable belief—not proof—that a protester is present outside the home of (say) a GM farmer[227] in order to persuade them to desist and on reasonable belief not even that their presence is actually harassing them, merely that it is likely to do so. All of this represents a cumulative divorcing of the power to give a direction from any actual social harm being caused. D's intention or actual purpose (since these are different) is, on the clear face of the section, something officers need not be concerned with when deciding to give a direction, provided they reasonably believe that D's purpose in being present is to persuade. The potential for interfering with free speech and the right of protest is self-evident, as is the fact that we have here another policing power that overlaps with several others. Section 5 of the POA 1986 would be the most notable as well as sections 1–3 of the PFHA 1997.[228] None of this is to be welcomed.

(iii) The Three-Month Return Rule

The three-month return rule, introduced by section 127(2) of SOCPA 2005, only heightens these concerns. Under section 42 as originally worded, an officer could only direct someone to leave the vicinity of a dwelling; they could not direct them not to return. It was doubted that an officer could thereby direct someone to stay away for anything other than a relatively short period.[229]

---

[226] Contrast football banning orders and terrorist control orders. The latter are not really comparable in effect but are football banning orders significantly more draconian?

[227] This jurisdictional fact must, following *Khan v Commissioner of Police for the Metropolis* [2008] EWCA Civ 723, be one that is true: it will not be enough, we must assume, for the police to show they reasonably believed that the property was a dwelling belonging to the victim.

[228] The power has seen little use: Home Office data (supplied under a personal FoI request) show that in the three-year period 2001–03, only 14 people were proceeded against in the magistrates courts in England and Wales, five of which were in Staffordshire in 2003: personal communication from Home Office RDS within the Office for Criminal Justice Reform. The novelty of the new provisions might account for (some of) the data.

[229] See the Explanatory Notes to the Bill para 317 at www.opsi.gov.uk/acts/en2005/ukpgaen_20050015_en.pdf (accessed 10 September 2007).

The view of the JCHR on the new three-month power was that since people were permitted to return, provided it was not for the purposes of harassment, the seemingly draconian interferences with Articles 9(2)–11(2) of the ECHR were probably justifiable.[230] This is not entirely true. Someone may return not in order to harass but still be caught. What the section criminalises and thus seeks to prevent is someone returning within three months with the purpose set out in section 42(1)(b): of representing to V or another individual (whether or not one who uses the premises as his dwelling) or of persuading V or such another individual that he should not do something that he is entitled or required to do, or that he should do something that he is not under any obligation to do. The new section does not also refer back to section 42(1)(c). It should. This is the paragraph that sets out those matters that should result, or be reasonably believed to result, in order for a direction to be made in the first place, namely likely harassment or likely causing of alarm or distress. Thus protesters will commit a criminal offence if, having been warned not to return, they do so within three months merely to engage in peaceful communicative persuasive protest even if they do not cause or intend harassment, alarm distress or intimidation. Protesters will commit a criminal offence even if the persuasion on their return is directed at a wholly new activity of the householder. Thus an anti-abortion protester subjected to a section 42 direction could not return within three months to persuade a doctor to sell her shares in an arms manufacturer or to vote for a different political party or even, so it would seem, to persuade her not to do something as innocuous as keeping an unsightly broken down car outside her home.

The drafting of section 42 raises considerable concern that it creates an unnecessary restriction on the right of peaceful protest by its over-capture of protest activity and its over-protection of third party rights, troubled as they may have been by the harassing nature of the original protest. At the very least section 3 of the HRA could be utilised so as to limit the application of section 42(7A)—which criminalises the return—to cases where the returning protester does cause—or perhaps returns in order to cause?—harassment, alarm or distress or, to cater for our examples, they return so as to persuade V on the same topic (if such a thing could be defined and identified!) in respect of which they were originally directed to leave. Given that harassment is no longer a form of limiter but under the PFHA has become a wide empowering provision, even better would be to qualify that to allow protesters to return so as to persuade, provided the harassment, alarm or distress was not excessive or put someone in fear. Free speech, after all, encompasses the airing of views that are confrontational or that disarm and worry us. In order to give the direction to leave in the first place, harassment, alarm or distress (or a reasonable belief of it) was required— the absence of those qualifying states gives the police greater powers if someone returns than they had at the outset. Someone could be penalised on returning for doing something that would not have been enough originally to have entitled the police to give a direction . . . not to return! Whether it would be said, of section 3 of the HRA here, that this would cross the boundary of legitimate judicial activity is moot, but it would certainly present a more balanced, Convention-compatible outcome.

(iv) Other Peaceful Protest Concerns

There are at least two other aspects of the section that would appear suitable for intervention under section 3 of the HRA, all constitutional objections aside in respect of the second.

---

[230] JCHR Fourth Report of session 2004–05, 24 January 2005 HL 26/HC224, para 1.118 www.publications.parliament.uk/pa/jt200405/jtselect/jtrights/26/2604.htm#a21, accessed 10 September 2007.

First, we must assume that any references in section 42 to 'necessary' directions and conditions are to be read down as meaning proportionate. This was certainly the view the House of Lords took of the same term in section 10 of the Contempt of Court Act 1981, in relation to journalists' sources.[231] Equally, such directions as an officer 'sees fit' must assume that officers only see fit to impose conditions that are proportionate restrictions on the right of peaceful protest. Secondly, it is strange that there is—unlike in, say, section 69 of the CJPOA 1994 (aggravated trespass directions) as we saw above—no defence that permits a protester with a reasonable excuse to return within three months. Such a defence could be read in to provide a measure of protection for peaceful protest where, in our example above, a protester returns to seek to persuade a householder on an entirely new matter or where all they do is return to try to persuade peacefully, without harassment. The same objective would be obtained by the reading of section 42(7A) suggested above.

(v) Section 42A

As if this width were not enough, section 42 was extended yet further in 2005 by the creation of a free-standing offence of harassment of a person in his home, one that is independent of a refusal to comply with a direction.[232] The summary offence under section 42A largely follows section 42. It is made out where:

(a) D is present outside or in the vicinity of any premises that are used by V as his dwelling (as defined in section 8 of the POA 1986);
(b) D is present there for the purpose (by his presence or otherwise) of representing to V or another individual (whether or not one who uses the premises as his dwelling), or of persuading V or such another individual that they should not do something that they are entitled or required to do; or that they should do something that they are not under any obligation to do;
(c) D intends his presence (either alone or together with any other person) to amount to the harassment of, or to cause alarm or distress to, V; or knows or ought to know that his presence is likely to result in the harassment of, or to cause alarm or distress to, the resident;[233] and
(d) the presence of D (either alone or together with any other person) amounts to the harassment of, or causes alarm or distress to, V (the resident in the dwelling) or to any person in V's dwelling or another person in another dwelling in the vicinity of V's dwelling or is likely to result in the harassment of, or to cause alarm or distress to any such person.

Section 42A therefore entitles an officer to arrest a protester or a group of protesters without issuing a direction. Nothing in the CJPA prevents an officer relying on section 42A if section 42 has previously been used: if a direction is given and D refuses to leave, section 42A allows an officer to arrest. What would a court conclude where a section 42 direction is given and moves are being made to leave yet someone is still arrested under section 42A? It is to be hoped that a court (whether or not using section 3 of the HRA) would disapprove. To hold otherwise would have echoes of the double bite of the cherry that we identified above in relation to sections 68 and 69 of the CJPOA.[234] We should safely be able to assume the officer would no longer be empowered to arrest in that case either. If so, the cynic might wonder whether saving perhaps ten seconds of an officer's time—by obviating the need for a direction at all—was a matter Parliament should have been attending to.

---

[231] *Ashworth Hospital Authority v MGN Ltd* [2002] UKHKL 29.
[232] Inserted by s 126 of SOCPA 2005.
[233] The test here under s 42A(4) is largely the same as that in the PFHA: would a reasonable person in possession of the same information think that D's presence was likely to have that effect?
[234] See text to nn 125–126 above.

What was the thinking behind section 42A in the first place? The combined Home Office/DTI strategy paper on animal rights extremists explains.

> One of the operational difficulties with [section 42] is that it does not cover the situation where a complaint is made about the presence of protestors outside a person's home, but the protestors disappear before the police arrive or the police are not able to give a direction as they do not have the ability to enforce it at the scene. We are therefore proposing to make it an offence to protest outside homes in such a way that causes harassment alarm or distress to residents. The proposal would not affect the right to picket peacefully at a work place . . . This means that the police will be able to deal with protestors after the event, which will address the difficulties of having to enforce a direction at the scene of the protest.[235]

That provides a ingenuous solution to two non-problems or, if they are problems, to which section 42A is not the solution. First, presumably without the police being on the scene, the added difficulty of identification comes to the fore. If the police do not know who has disappeared, what benefit will a new substantive offence provide? Secondly, the fact that the police cannot enforce it at the time presents a rather misleading case for the new offence: section 42 could be enforced after the event, just as section 42A can, by an arrest at a later stage for failure to obey a direction. Again, providing a new offence is not going to make another crime more enforceable; this is a function of policing priorities, adequate personnel and tactics. What this new offence—or indeed section 42 for that matter—adds to the armoury that was not already comprised within, say, section 5 of the POA 1986 has not been made out. Although section 5 requires on one hand harassment, alarm or distress as likely effects and also for there to be threatening, abusive or insulting words or behaviour, it is almost impossible to imagine how someone can be harassed (section 42A) without also seeing or hearing something threatening, insulting or abusive. This must be all the more so given, as we have seen, the latitude allowed by the courts (pre-HRA at least) to that phrase.[236] The possible sentence under section 5 of the POA 1986 is less than under section 42A, but that was not, according to the government, its main worry in introducing the changes. It cannot be that section 42A now provides the advantage of easier arrest. It used to be the case that section 5 required, in a similar way to section 42, a warning to stop that was ignored before an officer could arrest but SOCPA (the same legislation that introduced section 42A) removed this requirement. Since 2005 those suspected of committing an offence under section 5 of the POA 1986 can be arrested without warrant and without warning, as can those harassing someone outside their dwelling under section 42A.

The view of the JCHR on the proposed section 42A was that it was less likely to give rise to an unjustifiable interference with the rights to free expression and to peaceful protest (than was extending the PFHA to include single acts of harassment to more than one victim) on the basis that it was less extensive, limited as it was to harassment of people in dwellings.[237] While that may be so, the considerable overlap with section 5 of the POA 1986 must give rise to *some* questions about the necessity for yet another crime on the statute book.[238] We shall pick up this theme in our concluding chapter, and it was alluded to in our introduction.

---

[235] *Animal Welfare–Human Rights: protecting people from animal rights extremists*, paras 77–79, at: police.homeoffice.gov.uk/news-and-publications/publication/operational-policing/humanrights.pdf, accessed on 10 September 2007.
[236] See chapter five above p 221.
[237] JCHR Fourth Report, above n 230, paras 1.114–1.116.
[238] Given the extremely low number of prosecutions under s 42 (see above n 228), it seems impossible to conclude otherwise.

C. Watching and Besetting

There is considerable overlap between the different means to control and regulate harassment and intimidation. One more is the summary offence of watching and besetting contrary to section 241 of TULRCA 1992.[239] This can apply in situations that are similar to those in which both sections 42–42A of the CJPA 2001 and also the PFHA 1997 are used. Laws prohibiting the intimidation at which it is aimed first appeared in section 7 of the Conspiracy and Protection of Property Act 1875. Section 241 of TULRCA simply re-enacts the offence in a consolidating statute. As the title of the Act shows, its origins lie in the sphere of industrial relations, stemming from a time of political fear of organised labour and considerable regulation of combinations and collective action.

(i) The Statutory Scheme

Section 241 is headed 'Intimidation or annoyance by violence or otherwise'. Under it,

> 'a person commits an offence [if], with a view to compelling another person to abstain from doing or to do any act which that person has a legal right to do or abstain from doing, wrongfully[240] and without legal authority [she]
>
> (a) uses violence to or intimidates that person or his spouse or civil partner or children, or injures his property,
> (b) persistently follows that person about from place to place,
> (c) hides any tools, clothes or other property owned or used by that person, or deprives him of or hinders him in the use thereof,
> (d) watches or besets the house or other place where that person resides, works, carries on business or happens to be, or the approach to any such house or place,[241] or
> (e) follows that person with two or more others in a disorderly manner in or through any street or road.

(ii) Scope of the Offence

There have been very few reported cases under section 241 though there were more under its predecessor. As with all the offences we are considering, it is impossible to assess from that the extent of its utility and efficacy in controlling either industrial disputes or protests. In one of those few cases, an appeal against conviction—by way of case stated—was based in part on an argument that section 241 was limited to industrial disputes. That was

---

[239] A detailed discussion can be found in R Card, *Public Order Law* (Bristol, Jordans, 2000) 399–406.

[240] It seems now firmly established that this means unlawful, that is the activity under s 241(1) should constitute a separate crime or tort: see Card, *ibid*, 402 and the cases cited therein such as *Ward, Lock & Co v The Operative Printers' Society* (1906) 22 TLR 327 and *Thomas v National Union of Mineworkers (South Wales Area)* [1985] 2 All ER 1. In *Ward, Lock & Co* the Court of Appeal had established that there was no such tort as 'watching or besetting man's house' even if done with a view to compelling another; watching or besetting was only wrongful if combined with other conduct (for example, obstruction or violence) such that the whole conduct amounts to a nuisance. By contrast, in *J Lyons & Sons v Wilkins* [1899] 1 Ch 255, seven years earlier, the Court of Appeal held that watching or besetting of the plaintiffs' premises with a view to compelling the plaintiffs not to do acts which it was lawful for them to do was capable in law of amounting to a private nuisance.

[241] As Card points out, 'watches' is an ordinary English word so its meaning and occurrence is a question of fact whereas 'besetting' is an archaic term meaning, according to the Shorter OED 'surround with hostile intent, besiege, assail on all sides; occupy and make impassable; close round, hem in' (above n 239, 402). In *Ward, Lock—* under the former law—Moulton LJ asserted that watching and besetting is only wrongful if combined with other conduct such as obstruction and violence.

rejected. The court upheld the conviction of an environmental protester who had locked himself into a crane on a motorway extension project, thereby hindering the use of the crane.[242] The Divisional Court concluded that the legislative history of the section and Parliamentary intention was that it should not be artificially confined in its application to cases involving industrial action. As John Spencer commented, TULRCA 'is a funny place in which to find a general criminal offence such as section 241 is held to create'.[243] In the context of animal rights protest, it is doubtful what more is captured by section 241 than has not more recently been criminalised by section 146 of SOCPA, intimidating someone connected with an animal research organisation, which we shall consider presently in detail.

Section 241 creates a series of different offences, some wide, some overlapping and each subtly different. For example, section 241(1)(b) is made out where D persistently follows V from place to place,[244] whereas section 241(1)(e) requires two or more people to follow V but it need not be persistent provided it is disorderly. That is a question of fact for the magistrates or jury. Both clearly differ from section 241(1)(a), which refers to violence, injury to property or intimidation. There are clear overlaps with the POA 1986 and with section 4 of the PFHA 1997. In *R v Jones*, the Court of Appeal held that intimidation included: 'putting persons in fear by the exhibition of force or violence or the threat of force or violence; and there is no limitation restricting the meaning to cases of violence or threats of violence to the person'.[245] As Richard Card points out, this would now include *threats* to injure property, significantly extending the ambit of section 241(1), which on its face only refers to actual injury to property. He poses a few more questions of the case and the drafting of the section (which now need to be read in light of the pro-Convention slant provided by section 3 of the HRA). Does D's threat to break a contract with V count as intimidation under section 241 as it can for the tort of intimidation? Must the intimidation succeed in putting someone in fear or need it only be likely to do so?

It must be assumed that the defence of 'without lawful authority' would encompass lawfully exercising the Convention right of peaceful protest under Articles 10 and 11, in the same way as we considered for section 5 of the POA 1986 in chapter five. If so, then a conviction under section 241 should only withstand challenge—and a charge should only have been brought—if it can be said to be a proportionate restriction on those rights. Of course, as with all such arguments in relation to direct action, its likely success is dependent on and limited by the dismissive view taken at Strasbourg of such protests.

(a) *Fidler v DPP*

In any event, the need to rely to any great degree on the HRA was reduced considerably by the decision in *Fidler v DPP*.[246] There Nolan LJ and Rougier J came to the view that 'watching' and 'besetting' for the purpose of persuasion or dissuasion as opposed to coercion or compulsion did not amount to an offence. Presumably, though this was not before the court, that conclusion would hold for any other behaviour outlawed by section 241(1). To

---

[242] *Todd v Director of Public Prosecutions* [1996] *Crown Office Digest* 111 (DC). The short report does not make clear which subsection of s 241 was operative but the facts would indicate it could only be s 241(1)(c).
[243] Case note [1996] *Crim LR* 344.
[244] Persistent does not imply repeated or more than once: see Card, above n 239, 401 and the discussion of *Smith v Thomasson* (1891) 16 Cox CC 740 (DC), in which D followed V, a co-worker, through three streets after a picket.
[245] *R v Jones* (1974) 59 Cr App R 120, 125, quoted in Card, above n 239, 400.
[246] *Fidler v Director of Public Prosecutions* [1992] 1 WLR 91 (DC).

that extent there is little disparity between section 241 and the right of peaceful protest: peaceful persuasion and communication is outwith the ambit of the offence, and coercive or obstructive protest is largely outwith the protection of Article 11. The case concerned two groups, with opposing views on abortion, protesting outside an abortion clinic. The defendants were part of the group seeking to dissuade women who came to the clinic from having lawful terminations. They were arrested and charged inter alia under the pre-cursor to section 241. The case was dismissed by the magistrates on the basis that there was no evidence that the defendants watched and beset the clinic with a view to preventing the women from having abortions. The Divisional Court upheld the approach of the magistrates:

> There was no evidence that anyone was either prevented, or likely to be prevented, or intended to be prevented from performing or undergoing an abortion in the strict sense of being rendered unable to do so. The long-suffering police were in control of the situation. It seems plain enough that the purpose of the anti-abortion group in watching and besetting the clinic was to stop abortions from being carried out there, but it is equally plain that the means employed to implement this purpose were confined to verbal abuse and reproach and shocking reminders of the physical implications of abortion. Physical force was neither used nor threatened. The evident purpose of the demonstrators' behaviour was to embarrass and shock and shame those concerned into abstaining from abortion. In my judgement, the justices were right to find that this purpose, thus implemented, was a purpose of dissuasion rather than one of compulsion.[247]

Some play is made by Nolan LJ of the role of the police in keeping order and control—Would the offence be found more easily committed were that not the case, insofar as compulsion (which counsel for the DPP accepted meant 'to urge irresistibly', 'to constrain', 'to oblige' or 'to force'[248]) would more easily happen?

VI. Other Criminal Measures to Control Direct Action

Those who throw themselves into direct action run the risk of acting unlawfully in a host of other ways. They may be liable in civil proceedings because they have committed one or more of the economic torts—where liability is imposed for intentionally inflicted economic loss such as inducing or procuring a breach of contract, conspiracy to injure, causing loss by unlawful means[249]—or because they have trespassed on land, interfered with goods or committed nuisance at common law. We shall consider various tortious wrongs that protesters—mainly direct action protesters—run the risk of committing in chapter eight when we consider the rights and duties of private parties.

The focus of this next part will be on the alternative: their actions may leave them open to prosecution. They might have obstructed the highway unlawfully—which we considered in chapter four—or committed the crime of public nuisance. Hacking into computers or barraging someone with offensive material by post raise specific criminal issues as does, currently only for animal rights protesters, interfering with lawful business, a crime introduced in sections 145–146 of SOCPA 2005. We will look at all these in turn.

---

[247] ibid, 97.
[248] ibid, 97.
[249] We shall consider these briefly in chapter eight on private law remedies and rights.

A. Public Nuisance

Committing public nuisance is both a crime at common law and a tort. However, the effect of the House of Lords decision in *Rimmington* will be that the offence should increasingly fall by the wayside in the battle to police direct action protest.[250]

Rimmington had been found guilty of committing public nuisance after posting hundreds of packages containing crude and coarse racially offensive, insulting and even threatening or obscene material to members of the public, themselves either members of a racial ethnic minority or who were perceived to support ethnic minorities. His campaign was prompted by a racially motivated assault upon him by a black man some 10 years previously. The actus reus of the offence was set out as:

> doing an act not warranted by law, or omitting to discharge a legal duty, where the effect of the act or omission is to endanger the life, health, property or comfort of the public, or to obstruct the public in the exercise of rights common to everyone.[251]

The mens rea is that D must know or should have known that the act or omission would cause a substantial injury to a significant section of the community.[252] It could apply where, for example, a group of direct action protesters lays siege to the roads surrounding a GM crop farm,[253] or infects an arms manufacturer's website with a computer virus, or makes a hoax bomb call to an abortion clinic leading to immediate evacuation.[254] The House also confirmed the continued existence of the offence at common law; it was for Parliament not judges to abolish an existing offence. It was also sufficiently clear and precise enough not to fall foul of the rule against retrospective penalties in Article 7 or at common law. That said, the caveat added by the House will likely cause the crime of public nuisance to fall into desuetude. Where Parliament has provided a discrete offence to deal with the conduct in question, the Lords ruled, prosecutors should use those statutory offences in preference to common law nuisance unless there was a good reason not to do so. Procedural hurdles and bars or limits on penalties would not generally constitute a good reason, so the circumstances in which resort to charges for public nuisance was needed were likely to be very rare.

Two factors are likely to mean that its use before the courts in public order and protest cases will diminish. First, the range of other offences that covers the sort of conduct usually seen in such protests—such as harassment, aggravated trespass, obstructing of the highway, computer misuse or sending malicious communications—would require direct action protesters to be rather inventive to concoct an activity that was not otherwise an offence but which was a public nuisance as defined in *Rimmington*. Secondly, the actus reus is narrower in terms of its target and effect. Rimmington's conviction was overturned as his conduct lacked an essential ingredient of the crime: his campaign did not cause common injury to the public or a sufficiently large section of it. An individual act of private nuisance could not become a criminal public nuisance merely by reason of the fact that the act was one of a

---

[250] *Rimmington* [2005] UKHL 63, a combined appeal.
[251] The offence can no longer be made out simply by an act the effect of which is to endanger public morals: see *R v Shorrock* [1994] QB 279.
[252] *Rimmington*, above n 250, Lord Bingham at [40] and Lord Rodger at [57].
[253] Similarly in *R v Clarke (No. 2)* [1964] 2 QB 315 although obstructing the highway will only constitute the offence of public nuisances if that user is unreasonable in all the circumstances. The law here is broadly in line with the law under s 137 of the Highways Act 1980: see chapter four above p 140.
[254] See *R v Madden* [1975] 3 All ER 155 CA though we should now bear in mind the Malicious Communications Act 1988 and s 237 of the Communication Act 2003 that we consider below.

294   *Taking Direct Action*

series; individual acts causing injury to several different people rather than to the community as a whole or a significant section of it could not amount to the offence of causing a public nuisance, however persistent or objectionable the acts might be.[255]

B. Malicious Communications and Computer Misuse

Direct action protesters who want to disrupt a target business might choose to hack into the company's IT system or bombard its computer systems with spam email or flood its phone lines[256] so that communications systems crash and become temporarily (or permanently) unworkable or unusable.[257] Such action is very likely to fall foul of the criminal law on hacking or those laws that relate to the content of material sent by post or by email.[258] There is a two-fold scheme under the Malicious Communication Act 1988 and the Communications Act 2003 for those who, as a part of a protest, decide to send various messages or information to a target whether by email, fax or phone.[259] There are important differences between the 1988 and 2003 Acts, but first let us consider them separately.

(i) Malicious Communications

Section 1 of the Malicious Communication Act 1988, as amended, creates the summary offence of sending[260] to someone else either

    (a) a letter, electronic communication[261] or article of any description which conveys—

        (i) a message which is indecent or grossly offensive;
        (ii) a threat;[262] or

---

[255] That said, the activity need not itself be unlawful provided it constitutes a disruption or an interference. A disturbance or annoyance caused by lawful use of the highway can still constitute public nuisance provided that it is borne in mind that 'every annoyance is not a nuisance. The annoyance must be of a serious character and of such a degree as to interfere with the ordinary comforts of life': *Lyons v Wilkins*, above n 240, 271 (Chitty LJ).

[256] 'Auditors under fire over animal rights' *The Guardian* 20th February 2003. According to this report, a mole at the auditors for Huntingdon Life Science, the global accountancy firm Deloite and Touche, passed on the contact details for 135 senior managers to 8000 activists who began to 'bombard email addresses and disable mobile phones with basic phone-jamming software capable of dialling a number 500 times an hour'.

[257] See *Animal welfare-human rights* (July 2004), above n 135, para 45. Other relevant offences might include sending a bomb hoax letter (covered by s 51(1)(b) of the Criminal Law Act 1977) or ordering good and services in the name of a third party without their consent—another tactic with items (fast food) being delivered to or services (taxis) ordered from target companies—which is covered by the offences of obtaining goods and services by deception under the both the 1968 and 1978 Theft Acts.

[258] Those who choose to protest by sending material by post might find themselves caught by the much wider definition of terrorism in s 1 of the Terrorism Act 2000, discussed above p 239. Though not every parcel will create 'a serious risk to health', sending razor blades and used toilet paper as well as say syringes and excrement would well do so.

[259] Section 85 of the Postal Services Act 2000 makes it an offence to send by post any article that is likely to injure 'postal operators' or which is obscene or indecent. In *R v Kirk* [2006] EWCA Crim 725, an anti-vivisectionist was convicted under s 85 after he sent a package to a research laboratory bearing a swastika and addressed to 'the sons and daughters of Dr Joseph Mengele' at 'an Auschwitz laboratory'. The Court of Appeal upheld his conviction: obscene and indecent were ordinary English words. There had been no misdirection of the jury on the meanings.

[260] Sending means 'delivering or transmitting and to causing to be sent, delivered or transmitted': s 1(3).

[261] This includes (a) any oral or other communication by means of an electronic communications network and (b) any communication (however sent) that is in electronic form: s 1(2A).

[262] There is a defence in s 1(2) for those who send threats: they need to show both that the threat was used to reinforce a demand made on reasonable grounds; and that the sender believed, and had reasonable grounds for believing, that the use of the threat was a proper means of reinforcing the demand. Section 43(2) of the CJPA 2001 amended the previous subjectively worded defence making it harder for a protester to argue that she believed her demand and the use of force to back it up was reasonable, whether or not objectively others would have done so.

(iii) information which is false and known or believed to be false by the sender; or

(b) any article or electronic communication which is in whole or part, of an indecent or grossly offensive nature.

It must be sent with the purpose that it should 'cause distress or anxiety to the recipient or to any other person to whom he intends that it or its contents or nature should be communicated' or that should be one of its purposes.

Section 127 of the Communications Act 2003 creates two summary offences. Section 127(1) makes it an offence to send or to cause to be sent 'by means of a public electronic communications network a message or other matter that is grossly offensive or of an indecent, obscene or menacing character'. Section 127(2) makes it an offence either to send (or to cause to be sent) 'by means of a public electronic communications network a message that [the sender] knows to be false' or 'persistently [to make] use of a public electronic communications network', in both cases for the purpose of causing 'annoyance, inconvenience or needless anxiety' to another.

The House of Lords in *Collins* analysed the different rationales behind the two legislative schemes.[263] The object of section 127 was not to protect against receipt of unsolicited messages which the recipients might find seriously objectionable, that being the purpose of section 1 of the 1988 Act. Instead, it was 'to prohibit the use of a service provided and funded by the public for the benefit of the public for the transmission of communications which contravene the basic standards of our society'.[264] Thus under section 127 it does not matter that the communication is not heard—only that the system is misused. Where the communication is by letter—whether sent by post or delivered by hand—or is by telephone or email but not on a *public* electronic communications network—then section 127 cannot apply.[265] Although both Acts cover indecent or grossly offensive material being sent or communicated, material that is obscene is covered only by section 127 and so again must be sent via a *public* electronic communications network for it to be an offence.[266] Similarly, persistently contacting someone for the purpose of causing annoyance, inconvenience or needless anxiety to another is only a crime under section 127 and then only if done on a *public* electronic communications network. Sending letters every day for that purpose would not be caught, though that may well constitute harassment under the PFHA 1997. If the letters were indecent or grossly offensive, they might be caught by section 1 of the 1988 Act; thus sending or putting through the letter-box indecent or grossly offensive articles

---

[263] *Director of Public Prosecutions v Collins* [2006] UKHL 40.

[264] *ibid*, at [7]. Thus, the offence under s 127(1) was complete when the message was sent by the defined means by someone intending the words to be offensive or aware that they may be; it did not matter that the message was never received or was received by someone who was not deeply offended: Lord Bingham at [8], Lord Carswell at [21], and Lord Browne at [26]. Given the underlying different rationale for s 1 of the 1988 Act, based on legislative history, it seems clear that liability under that section will only be made out where the message is received and the recipient finds it indecent or grossly offensive, a question of fact to which should be applied 'the standards of an open and just multiracial society' (at [9]).

[265] Public electronic communications network is one that is open (subject to commercial arrangements) to the general public rather than a network that is closed (an internal office network). One protester targeting a co-employee by the work email or phone would not be covered by s 127. I am grateful to my colleague Daithí Mac Síthigh for assisting my understanding of the minutiae of digital communications law.

[266] Query the relevance of s 2 of the Obscene Publications Act 1959 (is the letter, email or phone call going to deprave and corrupt? Is sending it 'circulating' or 'distributing' it?) or at common law for outraging public decency or conspiracy to corrupt public morals. These wider offences might well be committed by protesters not when they target companies for emails and post but on placards or banners during marches and demonstrations, which we covered in chapter five.

such as human excrement or aborted body parts with the purpose of causing anxiety or distress is likely to be an offence, but only under the 1988 Act. Likewise, issuing threats—unless they are also menacing—is a crime only under the 1988 Act.

(a) *Connolly v DPP*

The offence under section 1 of the 1988 Act, as mediated by the right of free speech under Article 10, was before the courts in a protest case, *Connolly v DPP*.[267] A practising Catholic posted photographs of aborted foetuses to various pharmacists as part of her protest and education campaign about the rights of the unborn child. She was found guilty of the crime under section 1(1)(b): she had sent indecent or grossly offensive material intending to cause, or with the purpose of causing, distress or anxiety to the recipients. She appealed to the Divisional Court by way of case stated. Part of her argument before both the Crown Court and the Divisional Court was that a conviction would be a disproportionate restriction on her right freely to communicate and manifest her political and moral views under Articles 9 and 10. Dyson J held first that the phrase 'indecent or grossly offensive' did not bear a special meaning such that communications of a political or educational nature fall outside its ambit, as had been argued by her counsel. The fact that a communication is political or educational in nature cannot have any bearing on whether it is indecent or grossly offensive.[268] In other words, political or educational material is not per se decent and inoffensive. 'Indecent' and 'grossly offensive' were ordinary English words and so were matters of fact for the tribunal; the Crown Court's decision on the matter could only be overturned if it could be said that no court acquainted with the ordinary use of language could have reached the same view. That was not the case here.

Connolly's second argument was that section 3 of the HRA required section 1 of the 1988 Act to be read in a Convention-compatible manner so far as it was possible to do so. Dyson J held it was clear that Article 10 was engaged and, as the expression of a political message, was of a kind that was regarded as particularly entitled to protection by Article 10.[269] He offered two complementary routes to achieve that objective. First, he accepted that it was possible to interpret section 1 of the 1988 Act in a way which was compatible with Article 10 by giving a heightened meaning to the words 'grossly offensive' and 'indecent' (to counter to some extent the point made above). Alternatively, he was prepared to read into section 1 a provision to the effect that the section would not apply where to create an offence would breach a person's Convention rights; that is, to convict someone would result in a disproportionate restriction on free speech.[270] He then turned to the balancing test required under Articles 10(2) and 9(2) so as to assess whether this was the case. The restriction clearly met the 'prescribed by law' test. Although the aim of the Act, focused as it was only on distress or anxiety, could not be said to be the protection of health,[271] it did protect the rights of others not to be sent material of a kind as to be caused distress or anxiety. Quite

---

[267] *Connolly v Director of Public Prosecutions* [2007] EWHC 237 (Admin).
[268] *ibid*, at [9] although the nature of the communication might shed light on the defendant's mens rea in so far as it might indicate a purpose either to cause or not to cause distress or anxiety.
[269] *ibid*, at [14].
[270] *ibid*, at [18], and contrast the limited analysis of free speech by the Court of Appeal in *Kirk*, above n 259, at [11]–[12]. There, it was assumed and accepted that since Art 10 is a qualified right, the restrictions imposed by s 85 of the Postal Services Act 2000 are permissible.
[271] *Connolly* [2007] EWHC 237 (Admin) at [22]. Dyson J was very clear on this. What was relevant was not what aim would be served by convicting D, nor whether D's aim was to injure health.

what those 'rights' were is not entirely clear.[272] This was not an absolute position but the Court held that the restriction—in the form of the prosecution and conviction—was therefore proportionate.

> Just as members of the public have the right to be protected from such material (sent for [the purpose of causing distress or anxiety]) in the privacy of their homes, so too, in general terms, do people in the workplace. But it must depend on the circumstances. The more offensive the material, the greater the likelihood that such persons have the right to be protected from receiving it.[273]

Equally important in his view was the identity (perhaps status) of the recipient and the instrumental connection between the message (either its contents or the medium) and what might be said to be the sender's ultimate objective. The fact that the three recipients were employed by pharmacists selling the 'morning after pill' was not of itself sufficient to deny to them protection from receiving grossly offensive photographs of abortions at their place of work. They were more akin to ordinary members of the public than a doctor who regularly performed abortions (who would be less likely to find the photographs grossly offensive) or a politician receiving such photographs in her office in Westminster.[274] Both, in His Lordship's view, might well be deserving of lesser protection such that it might be less proportionate to convict in such cases. Nor were the recipients here targeted in the hope that they might alter the public position on the morning after pill or abortion generally, as would have been the case with elected politicians or others who had taken up a public position and could be expected to contribute to political debate.[275]

The most that Mrs Connolly could have hoped to achieve was to persuade those responsible in the pharmacies for their purchasing policies to stop selling the 'morning after pill'. But it was always likely that the photographs would be seen by persons who had no such responsibility, and it was by no means certain that they would be seen by the persons who had that responsibility. In any event, even if the three pharmacies were persuaded to stop selling the pill, it is difficult to see what contribution this would make to any public debate about abortion generally and how that would increase the likelihood that abortion would be prohibited.

The decision provides a more sensitive and nuanced approach to the offence under section 1 and, I would suggest, to similar communicative offences that protesters might commit. The holding here, that the offence may or may not be committed by sending the same item with either a different motive—when one item may be a form of expression and the other a gratuitous parcel designed to offend—or to different people, politicians (and the like) or ordinary people who have no influence or public position, is one that has much to commend it. This more measured response does provide a sound answer to why Ms Connolly's rights should here lose out to someone else's interest in not being offended but

---

[272] *ibid*, at [28]. The Court recognised this was wider than merely Convention rights. This is rather circular and self-fulfilling: if an Act prohibits conduct X this creates a 'right' in other not to be subjected to it. Dyson J relied heavily on *Chassagnou v France* (1999) 29 EHRR 615 at [113] and *R (Pro-Life Alliance) v British Broadcasting Corp* [2003] UKHL 23 at [91] (Lord Scott) and [123] (Lord Walker).

[273] *Connolly* [2007] EWHC 237 (Admin) at [28]. There is no real analysis of what sort of 'right' this might be in the workplace; clearly it cannot be that aspect of Article 8 that relates to respect for the home but it may well be comprised within either a wider spatial concept of privacy, following *Niemitz v Germany* (1993) 16 EHRR 97 or autonomy-based following *Pretty v United Kingdom* (2002) 35 EHRR 1.

[274] *Connolly*, above n 267, at [29].

[275] *ibid*, at [31]–[32]. One matter that Dyson J also thought as relevant was that this was 'hardly an effective way to promote' the cause. That, it is submitted, is a matter of choice for the protagonists and not for a court when considering the necessity of a restriction. This would be quite a worrying aspect if it were taken more generally.

would not always do so. There is, strangely, likely to be an inverse relationship between the extent of circulation and the chances of a successful Article 10 defence: the more a sender tried to minimise offence, distress and anxiety by restricting the number of people who saw the photographs, the less likely it is that they would be able to argue they were trying to engage with the public.[276]

(ii) Computer Misuse

Protesters who interfere with or hack into a target company's computer system run the risk of committing offences under section 1 of the Computer Misuse Act 1990.[277] The summary offence of unauthorised access to computer material is committed if someone causes a computer to perform any function with intent to secure access to any program or data held in any computer where, at the time when she causes the computer to perform the function, the access she intends to secure is unauthorised and she knows this to be the case.[278] Under section 3 it is also an offence for someone to do any act which knowingly causes an unauthorised modification of the contents of any computer where in doing so they intend to impair the operation of any computer; to prevent or hinder access to any program or data held in any computer; or to impair the operation of any such program or the reliability of any such data.

(iii) Obtaining and Misusing Personal Information Relating to Directors, Shareholders and Employees

Sending material by post to say the homes of directors of an animal research laboratory (or even harassing them outside their home) requires knowledge of their address, perhaps publicised on a website so other protesters can follow suit. This would be an actionable breach of confidence by the protesters, almost certainly before 1998 but for certain now, following the development of the 'reasonable expectation' of privacy test in cases such as *Campbell*.[279] There has been considerable movement on this in recent years in response to such targeting.

Since April 2002 when sections 723B–F of the Companies Act 1985 came into force company directors, secretaries and permanent representatives of certain foreign companies in Great Britain have been able to apply to the Secretary of State for what is known as a confidentiality order.[280] This prevents their usual residential address being made available for public inspection on the register if they feel that making it available for inspection by the public creates or is likely to create a serious risk that they or a person living with them will be subject to violence or intimidation. In the two years since its introduction (2002–2004),

---

[276] I cannot lay claim to this insight—my thanks are due to a former undergraduate student Tom Lenihan.

[277] See N MacEwan, 'The Computer Misuse Act 1990: lessons from its past and predictions for its future' [2008] *Crim LR* 955. If the activity is an unauthorised interception of a communication in the course of its transmission by a public telecommunications system that would also constitute an offence under the Regulation of Investigatory Powers Act 2000.

[278] Section 2 creates the specific offence of unauthorised access to computer material with intent to commit or facilitate the commission of further offences. It is no defence for D to argue that they had authorised access to the computer rather than to the data or information and D needs specific authorisation to that particular piece of data not just to similar data: *R v Bow Street Metropolitan Stipendiary Magistrates' Court ex parte USA (No 2)*; sub nom *Re Allison* [2000] AC 216.

[279] *Campbell v MGN* [2004] UKHL 22. Of course if the company—or a counter-interest group—did the same, it would be exposed to claims by protesters.

[280] These sections were inserted by s 45 of the CJPA 2001.

over 3,000 confidentiality orders had been granted.[281] The position is now covered by various aspects of the consolidating Companies Act 2006.[282] Sections 240–246 deal with what is called 'protected information', that is directors' (and ex-directors') residential addresses.[283] The effect of these sections is that home addresses do not become a matter of public record as of right; a company must not use or disclose protected information unless a director consents.[284] Section 1088 basically reflects—and widens—the old confidentiality order system by empowering the Secretary of State to make regulations requiring the registrar, on application, to make an address on the register unavailable for public inspection. The Companies (Disclosure of Address) Regulations 2008 (revised from July 2007) were laid in draft before Parliament in November 2008.[285]

Though shareholders are required to provide an address as a public record available for inspection, there has never been a requirement for them to provide a home or residential address but the fear is that too few are aware of this latter.[286] *The Guardian* reported how pharmaceutical giant GlaxoSmithKline became the first company to obtain an injunction on behalf of its 170 000 small investors to prevent an unknown group of animal rights activists publishing their names and addresses on a website if they did not sell their shares.[287] Under the 2008 draft Regulations, a company can apply on behalf of its shareholders—as well as its directors and bankers (as chargees)—to keep addresses from the public register.[288]

Employees and suppliers are the least easily protected. There is no requirement that their names let alone addresses be published, as there is for directors and shareholders under company law, but if they are published the only remedy would be to sue under the HRA for breach of confidence (privacy by any other name) or to seek an injunction under the PFHA. Costs here would be a problem for the individuals.

C. The Impact of Animal Rights Direct Action Protests on Commercial Relationships

Instead of merely targeting animal research companies and their employees and directors to get them to change tack, a more recent protesting tactic has been to exert pressure on those who supply goods and services—whether or not connected with the research—and on those

---

[281] *Animal welfare-human rights* (July 2004), above n 135, at p 20.
[282] See G Morse et al, *Palmer's Company Law Annotated guide to the Companies Act 2006* (London, Sweet and Maxwell, 2007) 221–5.
[283] Section 163 requires now that a company's register of interests contain a service address for directors rather than a residential address though each company must keep its own register of residential addresses (s 165).
[284] The provisions were drafted as an opt-in scheme but at report stage in the House of Lords it became an opt-in scheme for directors who wishes their home addresses to be on the public register: Morse above n 282.
[285] www.opsi.gov.uk/si/si2008/draft/ukdsi_9780111470220_en_1, accessed 7 January 2009. These are due to come into force in October 2009. Part 3 governs s 1088 applications to make an address unavailable for public inspection by an individual on grounds of serious risk of being subjected to violence or intimidation. Suppliers of goods and services—unless they are also chargees—who may well be at risk and employees are not covered.
[286] *Animal welfare-human rights* (July 2004), above n 135, para 94.
[287] The move came after the anonymous campaigners wrote to some of the company's 170,000 small investors warning them to sell their shares within the next two weeks or face identification: 'Glaxo gains injunction against animal activists', *The Guardian*, 10 May 2006 (and also 12 May 2006). The newspaper report does not make clear the basis for the High Court injunction. Neither Westlaw nor Casetrack has any details of the case.
[288] It is an offence under s 119(2) of the Companies Act 2006 to make disclosures of details of members from the register to another knowing or having reason to suspect that the other person will use to for a purpose that is not a proper purpose.

who provide the companies with finance so as to persuade or intimidate them into ending the relationship. For example, in February and March 2003 animal rights activists turned their attention to the accountants Deloitte & Touche who audited the books of Huntingdon Life Science. The Stop Huntington Animal Cruelty newsletter reported in a one-week period:

> throwing concrete slab through glass front door of Deloitte & Touche offices in Nottingham; Deloitte & Touche receive 200,000 emails in a mass global email action; office occupations at Deloitte & Touche office in Liverpool; home demos on two Deloitte & Touche directors in the West Midlands; [Animal Liberation Front] spray paint at Deloitte & Touche director's house; Deloitte & Touche offices spray painted in Italy.[289]

The 'systematic way in which animal rights extremists have [acted] with the calculated aim of disrupting organisations carrying out licensed animal research procedures'[290] led Parliament to add to the raft of legislation already on the statute book.

Sections 145–146 of SOCPA 2005 criminalise what were previously only torts—mostly but not exclusively the economic torts—in private law.[291] We will look at these latter more extensively immediately below.

(i) Interfering with Contractual Relationships so as to Harm Animal Research Organisations

The crime of interfering with a contractual relationship, in section 145,[292] is made out where A

(a) intends to harm[293] an animal research organisation;[294] and
(b) does an act or threatens that he or somebody else will do an act that either amounts to a criminal offence or is a tortious act causing B to suffer loss or damage of any description; and
(c) in circumstances in which that act or threat is intended or likely to cause B[295]

   (i) not to perform any contractual obligation[296] owed by B to a third person (C) whether or not such non-performance amounts to a breach of contract (which term includes any other arrangement; or
   (ii) to terminate any contract B has with C; or
   (iii) not to enter into a contract with C.[297]

---

[289] Quoted by Royce J in *Chiron Industries v Avery* [2004] EWHC 493 QB at [7].
[290] Explanatory Notes to the Serious Organised Crime and Police Bill above n 132 para 533.
[291] Neither of the two sections was in the Bill at 1st Reading—both were introduced at Report Stage in the Commons: see JCHR Fifteenth Report of session 2004/5 31 March 2005, HL 97/HC 496, para 2.1, at: www.publications.parliament.uk/pa/jt200405/jtselect/jtrights/97/9702.htm, accessed 10 September 2007.
[292] Acts done wholly or mainly in contemplation or furtherance of a trade dispute are exempt: s 145(6)–(7) SOCPA 2005.
[293] 'Harm' means to cause the organisation to suffer loss or damage of any description, or to prevent or hinder the organisation carrying out any of its activities: s 145(5).
[294] Defined in s 148 of SOCPA as someone who (1) is the owner, lessee or licensee of premises constituting or including a place specified in a licence granted under s 4 or s 5 of the Animals (Scientific Procedures) Act 1986, a scientific procedure establishment designated under s 6 of that Act, or a breeding or supplying establishment designated under s 7 of that Act; or (2) employs or engages under a contract for services, anyone who is the holder of a personal licence or a project licence granted under s 4 or s 5 of the 1986 Act or who is a person specified under s 6(5) or s 7(5) of that Act.
[295] Section 145(1).
[296] Section 145(4) states that 'contract' includes any other arrangement (and 'contractual' is to be read accordingly).
[297] Sections 145(2) and 145(4).

In all likelihood, A is a direct action protester, B is a supplier or in some other commercial relationship with C, the animal research organisation.

(a) The Statutory Triggers

The seeming width of the offence becomes narrower when we consider the first trigger in section 145, the need for what is called 'a relevant act'.[298] The protester must have committed either a crime or a tort causing loss or damage to B, or have threatened to do so.[299] First, since they could have been arrested for whatever discrete crime(s) they are alleged to have committed as 'relevant acts', this new power really only entitles the police to arrest in two situations: for threats to commit either crimes or certain torts (or that someone else will do so)—though for the former in many cases these might be covered by aspects of existing inchoate offences—or for the actual commission of those torts that cause any loss or damage to B. The tort need not be committed by A against B or be actionable by B against A, provided A has committed a tort and this causes B to suffer loss or damage of any description. In this, the Explanatory Notes to the Act appear to be incorrect, since they assume B is the victim of the tort or crime.[300] It is of no consequence for the criminal liability of A under section 145 that anyone else (whether that is either C or the animal research organisation itself) suffers loss or damage if B does not. Secondly, the offence is not made out if A's only relevant tortious act is one that is actionable on the ground that it induces another person to break a contract with B.[301]

The Government's thinking on this was that—under section 145 at least—no offence would be committed by those peacefully advocating or representing that one person should cease doing business with an animal research organisation, even if that means ending a contractual relationship, since such protests and expressions of opinion are not capable of causing loss or damage to the person at whom they are addressed.[302] Section 145 does not really give effect to that welcome desire. In fact it seems to be its reverse. If it is B (the supplier) who is induced to break its contract with any another person, whether or not that contract is with the animal rights organisation (though this is clearly the thrust of the provision), the exemption does not apply. Here, B is almost inevitably going to suffer loss and damage by being sued by the other party.[303] However, if A induces the animal research organisation itself to break its contract with B—a supplier—no offence can be committed by A—though A would still be liable in damages for one of the main economic torts, inducing or procuring another to breach a contract with a third party. The first trigger to the offence is potentially very wide indeed. Provided A commits a tort, provided B thereby suffers loss or damage and provided A's intention was to harm an animal research organisation, the

---

[298] All of what follows depends on establishing that A has the necessary intention to harm an animal research organisation.
[299] The reference in the Act is clearly to a tort: other private law or civil wrongs would not trigger the offence. Most obvious in this regard is if a protester publishes true information about a bank or its directors and employees, such as their addresses. This would be an actionable wrong but since there is no known tort of breach of privacy, only the equitable wrong of breach of confidence (*Wainwright v Home Office* [2003] UKHL 53), this would not apply—though it may well be the economic tort of causing loss by unlawful means—see below.
[300] Explanatory Notes to the Act, para 372, available at: www.opsi.gov.uk/acts/en2005/ukpgaen_20050015_en.pdf (accessed 11 August 2009).
[301] Section 145(3).
[302] Explanatory Notes, above n 300, para 372.
[303] If there is no contract, the exemption for inducing breach of contract cannot apply but B may still take the relevant step of not entering into a contract as a result of A's tort, so meaning A is criminally liable.

contractual relationship (actual or potential) that is affected can be between B and any one else, not the animal research organisation.

The second trigger is that A's crime or tort needs to be intended or likely to cause B to fail to perform a contractual obligation owed to C (whether or not a breach of contract), to withdraw from a contract with C or to decide not to enter into a contract with C. It would thus capture cases where protesters target a potential or existing supplier of goods and services, a potential or existing customer or a potential or existing employee (who of course have or will have, if taken on, a contractual relationship with their animal research employer) by engaging in tortious activities that are intended or likely to affect the relationship (actual or future) between B and C, the animal research organisation. It is irrelevant that B chooses (or why B chooses), say, not to enter into a contract; what matters is that A intends this or their actions make it likely. The fact that B was never going to contract with C will not provide an escape route for A. If B chooses in any event not to enter into a contract with the animal research organisation—for example B decides lending it money does not make sound business sense for lack of adequate security—although A's actions would not be to be likely to cause B to act—since B was going to do so anyway—A did intend B so to act, and that is all that is needed to make out the section 145 offence. In this, we can see very clear similarities with aggravated trespass under section 68 of the CJPOA 1994, especially following the decision in *Winder*.[304]

(b) Scope

Let us consider a few select protest scenarios to see where—and how—section 145 fits in. A is an animal rights protester who wants to stop Big Bank making any further advance to Animal Experimenters plc in the hope that without the loan the company and its business will collapse. To that end, A may trespass on Big Bank's land or interfere with the bank's property—such as its post. A may issue defamatory statements or commit malicious falsehood by spreading false rumours about the sex life or sexual offences of one of its directors. A may threaten the bank's employees thereby committing assault. A may commit nuisance against the bank by picketing it or bombarding it with emails designed to jam its computer and communication system. A may harass the banks employees and directors at common law[305] or under the PFHA 1997 by holding vigils outside their homes. Each of these would very easily constitute torts.[306] A of course might also commit one of the economic torts: conspiracy; procuring or inducing a breach of contract *by* Big Bank (Animal Experimenters breaking their contract with B having been specifically removed by section 145(3)(b)); or the new tort of causing loss by unlawful means established by the House of Lords in *Mainstream Properties*.[307] Any actionable, unlawful wrong perpetrated by

---

[304] *Winder v DPP* above p 260.
[305] Under the principle established in *Thomas v NUM* [1985] 2 All ER 1
[306] We shall consider various torts when we look at private law remedies available to deal with protest in chapter eight.
[307] *Mainstream Properties v Young; OBG v Allan; Douglas v Hello!* [2007] UKHL 21. The House rejected the unified theory comprising 'unlawful interference with contractual relations' (a super-tort comprising both procuring breach of contract and unlawful interference) in favour of two separate torts: procuring breach of contract alongside the wider tort of 'causing loss by unlawful means'. This latter encompassed unlawful interference and subsumed intimidation as well. Procuring breach of contract is dependent on a third party's primary wrongdoing—breaching its contract with X—whereas causing loss by unlawful means is primary rather than accessory liability. These two torts though separate could overlap and in the right circumstances the same activity could give rise to concurrent liability.

A against B—even where B suffers no direct loss—which interferes with B's freedom to deal with C and where A intends to cause loss to C will be actionable at the suit of C. Here it adds very little: where a protester commits any other free standing separate tort against Big Bank so as to harm Animal Experimenters economically this will cause loss by unlawful means, the new actionable tort. But this, as we saw, is how section 145 works in any event.

(c) Peaceful Protest Issues and Concerns

Several issues warrant further comment. First, section 149 contains the possibility that the Minister may extend protection to cover targets other than animal research organisations.[308] This power to extend is worrying. The Secretary of State may do so if she is satisfied that a series of acts has taken place and that

> those acts were directed at persons or organisations of the description specified in the order or at persons having a connection with them, and
>
> if those persons or organisations had been animal research organisations, those acts would have constituted offences under section 145 or 146.

There is nothing in section 149 to limit this to animal research-type organisations and so it is easy to imagine if a 'series (!) of acts' has taken place directed towards GM crop research centres or farms or towards abortion clinics or towards arms manufacturers, there being a political or popular clamour for extension. Second, many 'relevant acts' in section 145 will also constitute offences exposing the perpetrators to arrest in any event. Issuing threats is also a crime, as we have seen, at common law or under the Offences Against the Person Act 1861. As the JCHR indicated when considering the Bill, to what extent is this new power necessary, in Articles 10–11 terms? The Committee noted

> the extensive list of offences and police powers already available against intimidatory forms of protest published as an annex to *Animal Welfare—Human Rights: protecting people from animal rights extremists* . . . [but was] not so far persuaded that any of the specific examples of intimidation which have so far been relied on by the Government to justify the need for the new power is not already a criminal offence under existing provisions.[309]

The third is not a problem of duplication but a lacuna resulting from the wording of section 145. We have already considered how for the first trigger B must suffer loss caused by A's tortious act but this need not actually be actionable by B. The real problem is that B, who suffers loss, must also be the one in a contractual relationship with C which is then broken, to use the simplest example. Simply put, if A commits a tort not against Big Bank—by hosting a website *BigBankDefraudsCustomers.com*—but defames its directors or harasses its employees then what contract are those directors or employees going to break? Though it is not necessary under section 145 for that contract to be with the ultimate target, Animal Experimenters, there needs to be a contract between the employees and some other party that is then intended to be or likely to be broken. It is possible that the employees might

---

[308] Might the fact that s 145 is limited to animal rights protesters give rise to the possibility of a discrimination challenge under Article 14? That the power might possibly be extended would not show that the restriction just to animal rights protesters was proportionate: the minister would have to show, on the historic evidence, that there was a pressing social need to limit the scope currently just to one type of protest.

[309] JCHR Fifteenth Report of session 2004–05, above n 291, para 2.4. The document referred to *Animal Welfare—Human Rights* is above n 135.

refuse to work—and thus be in breach of contract with the Bank itself, causing it to pull finances on Animal Experimenters, so causing it 'harm' within section 145(5). This will be a matter of circumstance—it seems all the more likely that a family-run limited company will respond to unlawful action taken against its employee/director/owners than it would be to expect a multi-national bank to respond to a threat made once to a cashier at a high street branch.[310] In any event, there are likely to be cases where there is no separate contract—extant or putative. Little might turn on this: if there are gaps as a result of a restrictive reading of section 145 this will increase the role and relevance of section 146 which we will turn to presently.

The fourth area of concern was highlighted by the JCHR in its report on the Bill.[311] It is that of uncertainty, bringing problems under both Articles 10–11 (for the prescribed by law test) and with a knock-on effect for Article 5. For the arrest of a protester to be lawful under Article 5(1), the deprivation of liberty must be one that is prescribed by law. The Committee considered that the well-known uncertainty in the scope and extent of the economic torts was compounded by their being criminalised under section 145. The chilling effect was also a concern. Although certain types of non-intimidatory peaceful protest would remain outwith the ambit of the economic torts and so outwith the scope of new offence, many protesters might be dissuaded from, say, urging a boycott of companies which trade with animal research organisations or airlines which transport live animals for fear that those activities might be captured. If that were so, the Committee's view was that the restrictions would be disproportionate.[312]

The next matter is linked and relates to the dependence of section 145 on the separate commission of a tort; aside from (yet again) the merging and blurring of boundaries between public and private, for this new offence to be parasitic on the vagaries and potential width of (say) the new tort of harassment under section 2 of the PFHA is a worry. There is no guarantee or clear and explicit indication on its face that section 145 was not intended and should not be used to criminalise peaceful protest—though of course the section could be interpreted so as not to do so by using section 3 of the HRA.

Last, and in a similar vein, it might also be thought to be disproportionate to criminalise (admittedly) unlawful activities by A which cause any loss or damage to B, however small or trivial, and which are aimed at C, the real target and which need in turn, as well as suffering *any* loss or damage, be prevented or hindered in any way in carrying out *any* of its activities. There is no need for the loss to be 'serious' 'substantial' even 'not insubstantial' and the activities prevented or hindered need not be key or significant to its core business.

(ii) Intimidating Those Connected with Animal Research Organisations

As if section 145 were not sufficient, section 146 creates the crime of intimidating someone connected with an animal research organisation. The focus of section 145 is an actual or potential contractual relationship between B and C (usually but not necessarily) an animal research organisation. The ambit of section 146 is ostensibly wider. Its focus is not solely on those who have contractual relationships but instead is directed at an archetype situation where animal rights protester A, because of B's relationship or position to C the animal

---

[310] If this were so, the offence will be more likely committed if the victim is a partnership or sole-trader, since the corporate veil rule would not apply.
[311] JCHR Fifteenth Report of session 2004–05, above n 291, para 2.5.
[312] *ibid*, para 2.7.

research organisation, threatens B with an unlawful act in the hope this may influence B's freedom of lawful action.[313]

(a) The Statutory Scheme

The crime under section 146 is as follows:[314]

(1) A commits an offence if, with the intention of causing a second person (B) to abstain from doing something which B is entitled to do (or to do something which B is entitled to abstain from doing)

   (a) A threatens B that A or somebody else will do a relevant act, and
   (b) A does so wholly or mainly because B is a person falling within (2) below.

(2) A person falls within this subsection[315] if he is—

   (a) an employee or officer of an animal research organisation;
   (b) a student at an educational establishment that is an animal research organisation;
   (c) a lessor or licensor of any premises occupied by an animal research organisation;
   (d) a person with a financial interest in, or who provides financial assistance to, an animal research organisation;
   (e) a customer or supplier[316] of an animal research organisation;
   (f) a person who is contemplating becoming someone within (c), (d) or (e);
   (g) a person who is, or is contemplating becoming, a customer or supplier of someone within (c), (d), (e) or (f);
   (h) an employee or officer of someone within (c), (d), (e), (f) or (g);
   (i) a person with a financial interest in, or who provides financial assistance to, someone within (c), (d), (e), (f) or (g);
   (j) a spouse, civil partner, friend or relative of, or a person who is known personally to, someone within any of (a) to (i);
   (k) a person who is, or is contemplating becoming, a customer or supplier of someone within (a), (b), (h), (i) or (j); or
   (l) an employer of someone within (j).

(b) Scope

We can see that many of the incidents of harassment that the police had to deal with, and to which those involved with animal experimentation were subjected, at protests such as *Newchurch* and the new Oxford research laboratory would now be separate crimes under section 145 or more likely under section 146 as acts of intimidation. The difference is that harassment needs a course of conduct under section 2 of the PFHA before it becomes a crime whereas just one instance would suffice under sections 145–146. Sections 145–146 thus for provide a speedier response for dealing with intimidatory harassment of those connected with animal research at one or two or more removes (ie secondary and tertiary targets) such as suppliers, customers, financiers and their friends and employers, although this has become easier under the PFHA with the introduction of section 1A in 2005. At

---

[313] In that aspects of it are not dissimilar to watching and besetting under s 241 TULRCA 1992 which we considered above.
[314] The section does not apply to acts done wholly or mainly in contemplation or furtherance of a trade dispute: s 146(7)–(8) SOCPA 2005.
[315] *ibid*, s 146(6): the Secretary of State may amend the list by order so as to include any description of persons framed by reference to their connection with an animal research organisation, or any description of persons for the time being mentioned in that subsection.

its furthest the web of protection is cast incredibly widely. Rather like the parlour game 'Three degrees of separation', it is entirely possible it could cover most of the UK. If we work backwards from (k), it protects those who are not yet (but who hope to become) suppliers to or customers of friends of those who provide financial assistance to someone considering becoming a supplier or customer to someone contemplating becoming (a) a customer or supplier of an animal research organisation; or (b) a person with a financial interest in, or who provides financial assistance to, an animal research organisation; or (c) a lessor or licensor of any premises occupied by an animal research organisation. The house that Jack built has nothing on section 146 of SOCPA!

There is clearly quite an overlap with section 145 in that many of those falling within section 146(2) do so because they have a contractual relationship with an animal research organisation. Many of the concerns in respect of section 145 arise here too—such as its parasitic nature, the uncertain extent of many torts as a relevant act, whether a new crime was needed at all and if so, did it need to penetrate so far away from the intended target? That said, wherever it stops one can imagine determined intimidatory protest being commenced against those left out of the protected circle.

There is one last matter. The definition of 'relevant act' in section 146(5) includes 'a tortious act causing B or another person to suffer loss or damage of any description'. This is different in two ways to that found in section 145: first, it excludes the caveat attached to section 145 by section 145(3)(b)—the exclusion of acts by A which are actionable on the ground only that it induces another to break a contract with B. This should not matter: the offence under section 146(1) concerns what B may lawfully do and as B is not entitled to break a contract with C, if she does, the trigger in section 146(1) is not made out in any event. If B does not enter into a contract with C, something B is entitled to do, there is then no loss to B. That though identifies the second difference: unlike section 145, the relevant act—and so the offence—under section 146 can include a tort that causes loss to others, not just the immediate victim. This, we can recall, lay behind the government's assertion that section 145 would not unduly restrict non-intimidatory campaigns and boycott. There must be doubt that this is the case under section 146. After all, C the animal research organisation <u>could</u> suffer loss or damage—recall it does not have to be sizeable—and can be of any description as a result of tort perpetrated on B where B itself suffers none. C may have entered into agreements with D and E dependent on B providing a service to C which B had 'promised' in a situation where C and B had no contract (thus no unlawful breaking by B) but a reasonable expectation that one would be concluded. A's threats persuade B to renege. C suffers loss when sued by D and E.

VII. Conclusion

Evidence at least is that participation in and support for more direct forms of action is on the increase in the UK.[317] Regular reading of the papers or watching the news provides

---

[316] A person is a customer or supplier of another person if he purchases goods, services or facilities from, or (as the case may be) supplies goods, services or facilities to, that other; and 'supplier' includes a person who supplies services in pursuance of any enactment that requires or authorises such services to be provided: *ibid*, s 146(4).

[317] Verifiable evidence is hard to come by. In their study of Earth First!, for a 10-year period 1992–2001, Doherty, Plows and Wall show quite a considerable increase in the number of actions per year, reaching a high in

apocryphal data—though how much is due to the media creating, shaping and driving dissent and opposition is open to question.[318] With it has emerged what Lord Hoffman has referred to as the new phenomenon of litigation as the 'continuation of protest by other means', by which protesters invite courts to adjudicate on the merits of their opinions and provide themselves with a platform from which to address the media.[319] In his view, committing crimes so as to bring the issue of the lawfulness of government policy before the courts was something to be specifically disavowed: it would be inconsistent with the UK's traditional respect for conscientious civil disobedience. Aside from the fact that the specific issue in *Jones*—the legality of the Iraq war—was not in fact a minority, side-lined position, taking such a line does rather accentuate the traditional (bi-)partisan nature of domestic politics. It underplays the difficulties of publicising, certainly at the outset, counter-hegemonous viewpoints: where is the scope for such discourse given that politics is increasingly fought at and over the centre-ground?

From Swampy, the environmental tree dweller and tunnel-digger in the 1990s, the issues may have changed but in most cases targets have just been added to or the focus shifted. Now it is hunt saboteurs who are acting lawfully as they try to monitor illegal fox-hunts across the UK.[320] In December 2008, as part of a protest against airport expansion—rather than road building—and to highlight the need for urgent action on climate change, over 50 members of the group Plane Stupid cut through a perimeter fence at Stansted. Chaining themselves to fencing near a runway caused the airport to be closed for five hours. In January 2009, as this part is being written, the participants received sentences of between 50 and 90 hours Community Service as punishment for committing aggravated trespass. The change, as Doherty Plows and Wall note, from say the anti-nuclear movement of the 1960s and 1980s and the anti-apartheid protests of the 1970s is that 'until the 1990s, direct action was a tactic used by movements, not the defining feature of a movement'.[321]

There is, though, the world of difference, as we saw in the introduction, between different types of direct action, between, say, a campaign of throwing bricks through the windows of animal researchers—or even killing doctors who perform abortions—and the almost symbolic obstruction of workers as they arrive at an arms factory, where the linked arms of the protesters drop to allow anyone to enter once their point has been made and observed. The problem is the middle ground and how law should respond and treat it. The Plane Stupid protest at Stansted is a good case in point. They committed criminal damage—but not to the targets of their ire, as did the defendants in *Jones* when they took hammers to bombers and trailer trucks.[322] All the 'Suffrajets' did was cut through the fence to stage what was always going to be a reasonably shortlived protest highlighting what they see as the stark choice facing the world and in fact trying to save it: one of the protesters calculated that each

---

1999 of about 300: B Doherty, A Plows and D Wall, ' "The preferred way of doing things": the British direct action movement' (2003) 56 *Parliamentary Affairs* 669, 671.

[318] See on this the illuminating discussion in K Milne, *Manufacturing Dissent: Single-Issue Protest, the Public and the Press* (London, Demos Publishing, 2005) and her case that much of the growth in single-issue campaigns can be attributed to press support at a time of falling circulation.

[319] *R v Jones and Others; Ayliffe v DPP*, above n 113, at [90]–[93].

[320] That does not mean they are now immune from harassment injunctions. The Crawley and Horsham hunt went to court in 2007 to try to obtain injunctions under the PFHA 1997 to prevent filming on public roads and loitering on footpaths: SchNEWS issue 637, 27 June 2008 at: www.schnews.org.uk/archive/news637.hrm, accessed 1 July 2008. The case was dropped in July 2009: 'Call off the hounds' SchNEWS issue 684, 17 July 2009 at: www.schnews.org.uk/archive/news684.php, accessed 12 August 2009.

[321] Doherty et al, above n 317, 671.

[322] *Jones*, above n 71.

member on the runway prevented about 41.5 tonnes of CO^2 emissions from the 57 cancelled flights.[323] Their protest was never going to, nor was it ever intended to, bring an immediate stop to all flights from the UK or to lead the Government to change its mind over plans to increase Stansted's capacity by 10 million passengers a year, at a time when it is estimated that aviation already accounts for 13 per cent of the UK's climate impact and is growing.[324] This protest highlights the important supporting and catalysing role that forms of obstructive protest can play within, and as an adjunct to, the democratic process. Sometimes democracy and debate need a jump-start and a wake-up call.

We have seen in this chapter that domestic law and more so Strasbourg case law tends not to operate such a nuanced approach, preferring instead the more monochromatic distinction between peaceful marches, assemblies and large-scale demonstrations seeking peacefully to persuade and to communicate on the one hand and on the other, all other forms of protest. This is partly a function of the way in which legislation is framed, partly of its interpretation by judges and partly of its application by the police. At Strasbourg level, there has been, as we have seen, an inclination to confer quite considerable protection on 'peaceful protest' but given that in the past direct action protests, even those that effect only minimal and temporal disruption or obstruction, such as *Drieman v Norway*[325] (the Greenpeace anti-whaling protest) or *G v Germany*[326] (the sit-in outside the US military barracks) have met without success there is no reason to think that domestic law is out of kilter needing re-alignment. The only direct action protest to have succeeded before Strasbourg is *Hashman and Harrup v UK*.[327] There the Court held that the binding over imposed on the fox-hunt saboteurs violated Article 11 not because it was disproportionate but because it was not prescribed by law. Requiring someone not to act *contra bonos mores* was not sufficiently certain—given that the test was whether other right-thinking members of society would agree—as to indicate to the protesters what behaviour was or was not permitted in the future.

We did see in chapter three that the past few years has seen a softening in attitude at Strasbourg towards obstructive protests that create short-lived inconvenience and only indirectly—because of their nature—cause disturbance and disruption. These would be cases such as *Öllinger, Aldemir, Galstyan* and *Oya Ataman*.[328] We learn that 'any demonstration in a public place may cause a certain level of disruption to ordinary life and may encounter hostility'[329] (but also that those organising demonstrations 'as actors in the democratic process, respect the rules governing that process by complying with the regulations in force'). In *Bukta v Hungary*, the Court was clearly swayed by the fact that there was no evidence to suggest a danger to public order 'beyond the level of the minor disturbance which is inevitably caused by an assembly in a public place'.[330] In both *Oya Ataman* and *Balçik* the Court stressed that where demonstrators

---

[323] J Garman, 'Today's protesters, tomorrow's saviours', *The Guardian*, 'Comment Is Free', 8 December 2008. www.guardian.co.uk/commentisfree/2008/dec/08/plane-stupid-stansted, accessed 9 January 2009.
[324] *ibid.*
[325] *Drieman v Norway* (App 33678/96) ECtHR inadmissibility decision 4 May 2000.
[326] *G v Germany* (App 13079/87) EComHR inadmissibility decision 6 March 1989.
[327] *Hashman and Harrup v United Kingdom* (2000) 30 EHRR 241.
[328] *Öllinger v Austria* (2008) 46 EHRR 38; *Aldemir v Turkey* (App 32124/02) ECtHR judgment 18 December 2007; *Galstyan v Armenia* (App 26986/03) ECtHR judgment 15 November 2007; and *Oya Ataman v Turkey* (App 74552/01) ECtHR judgment 5 December 2006.
[329] *Aldemir*, above n 328, at [42].
[330] *Bukta v Hungary* (App 25691/04) ECtHR 17 July 2007, at [37].

do not engage in acts of violence, it is important for the public authorities to show a certain degree of tolerance towards peaceful gatherings if the freedom of assembly guaranteed by Article 11 of the Convention is not to be deprived of all substance.[331]

However, unless there is an even more marked shift, it is likely that this will be confined to protests where it is third parties who are affected rather than the targeted company or institution itself, and confined too to more formal protests and demonstrations in the shape of marches, meetings and rallies. We are unlikely in the near future to see a similar softening in attitudes towards direct action as a whole.

As the JCHR pointed out, the extension of the PFHA to encompass secondary harassment of third parties is as apt to capture quintessentially peaceful protest, symbolically obstructive protest and even obstructive protest that causes moderate and relatively little harm as it is to capture intimidation. We encountered similar concerns, for example, when we looked at the new offence of interfering with contractual relationships. We need look no further than *Winder* or *Capon* and the judicial interpretation of sections 68–69 to see how courts bear responsibility for the considerable growth in the extent of regulation, or Swift J in *Garman* not rejecting outright the argument that harassment might encompass mere inconvenience or annoyance. We might also reflect on the conclusion reached in *Selvanayagam* that acting in breach of a civil injunction is per se unreasonable, so depriving defendants as a matter of law from arguing the reasonableness of their action as a defence to charges of harassment.[332] Against these of course might be placed decisions more disposed to direct action protest—or at least comments—such as in *Curtin* or *Tilly*.

The police share the blame for constricting the ability protesters have to engage with the public by being overly zealous in (mis)applying the law. As well as dealing with 82-year-old heckler Walter Wolfgang at the Labour Conference using terrorism powers, which we considered earlier in the chapter, there were verifiable media reports of plans to use section 44 of the Terrorism Act 2000 as part of the policing of the Climate Change camp at Heathrow in August 2007.[333] A letter in *The Guardian* highlighted a real concern.[334] John Wilding, a pensioner, was on his way to Heathrow to a rally about the third runway. Three of his group were wearing T-shirts inscribed with 'Stop Airport Expansion'. They were stopped. Heathrow by-laws, he was told, permitted access to the bus station only to air passengers or those meeting them. 'Oddly only members of the party wearing t-shirts appeared to be in breach of these by-laws', he wrote. The group was questioned and forbidden to have access to the airport for 24 hours on threat of arrest; in one case 'T shirt' was even recorded as the reason for the stop. There has been a furore annually over the policing of the climate change camps, especially the most recent at Kingsnorth power station in Kent in 2008. Protesters have accused the police of unprovoked unwarranted aggression and the police in turn have defended their tactics as proportionate to the threats to and attacks on them. In December 2008, the Home Office Minister responsible for policing was forced to apologise for misleading Parliament. He had previously justified the £9.5m cost of the operation (in which the police were alleged to have confiscated toilet rolls and board games) as proportionate

---

[331] *Balçik v Turkey* (App 0025/02) ECtHR judgment 29 November 2007, at [51]–[52], *Oya Ataman*, above n 328, at [41]–[42] and *Bukta*, above n 330, at [37].

[332] *DPP v Moseley, Selvanayagam and Woodling* above n 159.

[333] 'Police to use terror laws on Heathrow climate protesters', *The Guardian*, 11 August 2007, referring to documents produced by the Met Police for use in the *Garman* case. See too 'Angry parents say air protest girls were held in solitary for 36 hours', *The Observer*, 8 October 2006.

[334] *The Guardian* letters page, 3 June 2008.

by pointing to the fact that 70 officers had themselves been injured. It transpired that no injuries were recorded as sustained in clashes with demonstrators; six were bitten by insects![335]

There is in this area an official assumption that increasing statutory regulation will 'solve' the problem of direct action protest. There is some evidence here of success, though whether the expansion of the legal regime has caused what is said to be a massive decline in action such as targeting the homes of animal researchers cannot be known.[336] It could as easily be attributable to changes in police responses and to changes in public attitudes, exemplified by the growth in support for Pro-Test, a group whose members are prepared to stand up publicly in support of animal testing and research. It seems in fact, looking at the matter more generally, that an increase in legislation will not assist save at the margins and peripheries. Much was made in the run up to SOCPA 2005 of the need for new offences to deal with a 'tiny minority of animal rights extremists who are behind an illegal campaign of intimidation'.[337] As we noted in our introduction, if the campaign is 'illegal', their conduct must already be against the law. If so, why are newer and greater powers needed—why are they not being arrested and stopped? It cannot be for lack of an offence—how else could they be acting 'illegally'?—so the 'problem' must be one relating to enforcement—identification of the wrongdoers, insufficient resources for the police, lack of witnesses, poor training in new offences. None of these problems, though, will be rectified by creating another crime or series of crimes. In short, the problem is not insufficient law but how it is applied. There is support for this in figures showing the use made by the police of various offences commonly committed by direct action activists.[338]

Our remaining substantive chapters will consider the regulation of protest from two further perspectives. Rather than structuring our analysis around the nature and type of the protester, chapters seven and eight will focus on the other protagonists. First, we will look at the position of the police and then we shall assess how commercial targets might be able to prevent or restrict protest. We shall see not only how these sets of powers and remedies overlap and complement each other but, since the first is based in public law and the second in private law, we shall also see that their inter-relationship creates tensions, if not outright conflict.

---

[335] 'Minister Vernon Coker apologises for misleading MPs over injuries' 'Those Kingsnorth injuries in full: six insect bites and a toothache', *The Guardian*, 15 December 2008. The policing of the event is the subject of a formal legal challenge.
[336] 'Sudden decline seen in attacks by animal rights extremists', *The Guardian*, 30 June 2007.
[337] Foreword to the Joint Home Office/DTI 2004 consultation paper *Animal Welfare—Human Rights* above n 135, accessed 18 September 2008.
[338] See p 19 above.

7

Preventive Action by the Police

Chapters four, five and six considered how the law responds to different types and forms of protest as well as how law controls its location. Amongst other matters, in those chapters, we examined the powers the police have in advance to prevent protest or after the event to arrest those who take part. This chapter builds on that as we reflect more broadly on preventive action and decision-making by the police. The police have been given considerable power by Parliament and judges, through the common law, to take action to restrict and to manage protest and disorder. Some of these are specific to protest while others are general but have been used or manipulated to govern protests. We will not revisit powers such as that in section 69 of the Criminal Justice and Public Order Act (CJPOA) 1994, the power to give directions in respect of suspected aggravated trespass, or section 42 of the Criminal Justice and Police Act 2001, giving directions in respect of harassment in the vicinity of someone's home. We looked at these preventive powers in some detail in our last chapter. This chapter should be read alongside the next, which draws together—and supplements—some of the earlier material on private law remedies.

I. The General Duties of the Police

Before looking at the powers of the police, we should consider their duties. Alongside the general common law duties of preventing and detecting crime, maintaining order and keeping the peace, the police are now under the specific statutory duty contained in section 6 of the Human Rights Act 1998 (HRA). It is beyond doubt, as we saw in chapter two, that the police will be a core public authority. All officers are thus obliged—at both macro-levels and micro-levels, that is policy/strategy and operational/on-the-street—to act in a manner that is compatible with Convention rights. This means, as is now well known, in the context of the right of peaceful protest that officers should not act or take decisions that disproportionately restrict that right. The matrix of rights at any one protest scenario is more complicated. Alongside the rights of protesters under Article 10 and Article 11 the police will also need to bear in mind, as we shall see in the next chapter, the property rights of companies (under the First Protocol to the ECHR) as well as quite possibly the privacy rights—in the broadest sense—under Article 8 of the targets of protest. To this mix of rights must of course be added the general, wider social interests reflected in the wording of the legitimate aims in Article 10(2) and 11(2) which can offset, where it is necessary to do so, the primary right.

Pre-HRA case law, arising from challenges to policing decisions but based on traditional common law principles of judicial review, should now be treated with some caution. In particular, there is considerable doubt that a case such as *Phoenix Aviation*[1] or *CEGB*[2]—on the scope of the duty on what we now refer to as public authorities, the police or local councils, to respond to potentially unlawful or disruptive protests—would be decided the same way for the same reasons today. In the first case, various councils had decided to ban live animal exports from their airports or harbours because of the disruption caused by protesters. The Divisional Court (Simon Brown LJ and Popplewell J) held that under the statutory scheme regulating these transport links, the councils had no discretion to distinguish between different lawful trades. Had they such a discretion, they would in any event have been acting unlawfully to exercise their discretion in the proposed manner.

> Even, however, if the port authorities are to be regarded as having a discretion to determine which legal trades to handle, then in our judgment they could not properly exercise it here in favour of this ban. One thread runs consistently throughout all the case law: the recognition that public authorities must beware of surrendering to the dictates of unlawful pressure groups. The implications of such surrender for the rule of law can hardly be exaggerated. Of course, on occasion, a variation or even short-term suspension of services may be justified. As suggested in certain of the authorities, that may be a lawful response. But it is one thing to respond to unlawful threats, quite another to submit to them—the difference, although perhaps difficult to define, will generally be easy to recognise. Tempting though it may sometimes be for public authorities to yield too readily to threats of disruption, they must expect the courts to review any such decision with particular rigour ... None of [the councils] it appears, gave the least thought to the awesome implications for the rule of law of doing what they propose. None considered the inevitable impact upon the future conduct of the protesters—that their ever more enthusiastic activities would concentrate upon an ever smaller number of outlets. None seems even to have considered the legitimate interests of all those whose livelihood depends upon this lawful trade.[3]

As we have seen, Strasbourg does not look especially favourably on direct action (that is, directly disruptive protest) such that at first glance *Phoenix Aviation* would not be out of line. However, what is instructive is that the case was disposed of on a crucial distinction between lawful and unlawful protest. Simon Brown LJ commenced by saying that some of the protest was lawful; some was not.

> The precise point at which the right of public demonstration ends and the criminal offence of public nuisance begins may be difficult to detect. But not only is all violent conduct unlawful; so too is any activity which substantially inconveniences the public at large and disrupts the rights of others to go about their lawful business.[4]

As a statement of current doctrine, it is no longer the case that substantial inconvenience and disruption does render a protest unlawful—or, even more accurately, render a protester acting unlawfully. That premise wrongly sites the line such that *Phoenix Aviation* is not necessarily 'good law' in the HRA-era.

Similarly, the broadly abstentionist position adopted in the *CEGB* case—even if it did favour the protesters who were disrupting site inspections at a potential nuclear plant in Cornwall—cannot now be seen as the last word, even if it does follow a long line of cases on constabulary independence.[5] If there were a challenge to a Chief Constable's decision not to intervene in a similar case featuring clashes of rights and interests—bearing in mind the

---

[1] *R v Coventry City Council ex parte Phoenix Aviation* [1995] 3 All ER 37 (DC).
[2] *R v Chief Constable of Devon and Cornwall ex parte Central Electricity Generating Board* [1982] QB 458 (CA).
[3] *Phoenix Aviation*, above n 1, 62 (Simon Brown LJ).
[4] *Phoenix Aviation*, above n 1, 41.
[5] Such as *R v Commissioner of Police of the Metropolis, Ex parte Blackburn* [1968] 2 QB 118.

positive duty comprised in Article 11 (see below)—the High Court would be hard pushed, given the democratic imprimatur of the HRA, to maintain its line that the decision was not one that could be overturned or interfered with by a court and thus to refuse mandamus. Another difficulty of course with this non-interventionist stance is that, unlike local councils and Ministers, the mechanisms of democratic control and account are much more limited when it comes to the police.[6] This is another reason why it is important to distinguish between the powers to impose conditions and to impose a ban on marches and assemblies under sections 12–14A of the POA 1986.

The duty of the police is complicated and, frankly, unenviable. Just like the state as it seeks security against counter-terrorism, there is an inescapable contradiction in the policing of protest: the police are both the guarantors of the right of peaceful protest and the greatest threat to it—and in fact increasingly its targets. This Janus head, as Leigh and Lustgarten call it,[7] means the police must balance all the competing tensions and concerns so as to ensure not only that any restrictions on protest are ones that are proportionate—ie necessary, with relevant and sufficient reasons, and, other less intrusive alternatives having been ruled out, the most minimal to achieve the aim—but that any competing rights are given effect to as well. Of course, these other rights too can be limited on proportionality grounds including, in rather circular fashion, the fact that they can be limited so as to give effect to the right to peaceful protest.

In short, under section 6 the police are obliged to guarantee the full extent of the qualified right to peaceful protest, the turns, the gaps and the limits of which we assessed in chapter three. We saw that implicit in the full protection of Article 11 is a positive duty, a duty of commission. It might not be enough for the police to argue that they did nothing to interfere with, say, a march or demonstration. The duty might well extend to facilitating whatever protest is planned: by ensuring adequate resources and by maintaining disruptive counter-protesters at a distance. It might even be argued that the positive duty to guarantee and facilitate protest should extend (unless it would be disproportionate to do so) to arresting violent or disruptive counter-demonstrators first lest the heckler's veto come into effect. We shall see that domestic law does not yet quite accord with that position.

II. Stop and Search Powers

A. General Powers Dependent on Reasonable Suspicion

A major weapon in the police armoury to prevent crime, disorder and disruption is the general power to conduct stops and searches in public places. It is contained in Part I of PACE. This is not a general stop and search power. It is not a stop to search for evidence or for questioning and nor is it a general power to detain; it is limited to situations where officers reasonably suspect they will discover stolen or prohibited articles. Prohibited articles

---

[6] D Feldman, 'Protest and tolerance: legal values and the control of public-order policing' in R Cohen-Almagor (ed), *Liberal democracy and the limits of tolerance—essays in honor and memory of Yitzhak Rabin* (Ann Arbor MI, University of Michigan Press, 2000) 48 and 53. Proper accountability is the third of Feldman's criteria for the legitimacy of rules that enforce toleration.

[7] I Leigh and L Lustgarten, *In from the cold: national security and parliamentary democracy* (Oxford, Oxford University Press, 1994) 12–16.

includes offensive weapons—articles made or adapted for use for causing injury to persons or intended for such use—and articles made or adapted for use or intended for use in connection with property offences, such as theft and burglary, or in connection with committing criminal damage. To that extent, it is—or should be—of limited use during purely peaceful protests, though of course officers <u>might</u> reasonably suspect (rightly or wrongly) that many of those involved, especially direct action protests, will be carrying offensive weapons or articles intended for use in committing criminal damage. By far the greatest restriction on the power is the substantive one of 'reasonable suspicion' in section 1(3), fleshed out PACE Code of Practice A.

That is not to say that the power is not relied on, perhaps even relied on to excess. There is credible evidence of excessive use of stop and search, whether under section 44 of the Terrorism Act 2000 (considered below) or under PACE, at the Kingsnorth Climate Camp in the summer of 2008.[8] A judicial review challenge by 11-year-old twins to the exercise of the PACE power is underway; Keene LJ has given permission for a full hearing on the merits.[9] There were newspaper reports of up to 10,000 protesters corralled into airport-style 'checkpoints' for blanket stops and searches before entering the camp.[10] The operation cost £5.3m and involved 1400 officers from across the United Kingdom. Almost by definition, blanket searches defy explanation on 'reasonable suspicion' grounds. A Liberal Democrat report into the policing, presented to Parliament in March 2009, indicated that the police seized more than 2,000 items. This included a clown outfit, cycle helmets, tent pegs and board games. The confiscation of the camp's supply of soap was justified by police 'because protesters might use it to make themselves slippery and evade the grip of police'.[11] An official inquiry into the policing at Kingsnorth, specifically stop and search, concluded that the use of the power by Kent police was 'disproportionate and counterproductive'. There was clear evidence too of breakdowns in communication, poor public order training, misunderstandings about legal powers, outdated intelligence—as well as the blanket stop-and-search tactic backfiring by 'stoking up' those attending.[12]

There has also been evidence of excessive use of another preliminary investigative power, contained in section 50 of the Police Reform Act 2002.[13] If a constable in uniform has reason to believe that a person has been acting, or is acting, in an anti-social manner (within the meaning of section 1 of the Crime and Disorder Act 1998, which we look at later in this chapter) he may require that person to give his name and address to the constable. It is an offence to fail to do so or to give false details. Liberty claims the power is being used to intimidate protesters and in some cases identity details were demanded as a condition of allowing protesters to leave cordons, such as that at the G2O demonstrations on 1 April

---

[8] 'Police to use terror laws on Heathrow climate protesters', *The Guardian*, 11 August 2007, referring to documents produced by the Metropolitan Police for use in the *Garman* case that we considered in our previous chapter. See too 'Angry parents say air protest girls were held in solitary for 36 hours', *The Observer*, 8 October 2006.

[9] 'Court says police can be challenged on 'stop and search' powers', *The Guardian*, 6 May 2009.

[10] There were in fact a total of 8, 218 searches carried out but only 2,000 stop-and-search forms—fewer than 25%—were legible: 'Kingsnorth report criticises "counterproductive" policing tactics', *The Guardian*, 22 July 2009.

[11] 'Protesters fought the law but the law fought back ... very very loudly', *The Guardian*, 12 March 2009.

[12] The inquiry was undertaken first by the National Police Improvement Agency and then South Yorkshire police: 'Kingsnorth report criticises "counterproductive" policing tactics', *The Guardian*, 22 July 2009.

[13] Liberty evidence to JCHR supplementary inquiry into policing and protest pp 6–7 (May 2009) available at: www.liberty-human-rights.org.uk/pdfs/policy-09/liberty-s-written-evidence-to-the-jchr-re-policing-and-protest.pdf, accessed 24 July 2009.

2009 in the City of London. As they ask, what justification is there for a criminal offence of failing to give a name and address when stopped on mere suspicion of committing a non-criminal act, when it is not a criminal offence to fail to give a name and address in respect of suspicion of criminal offences?

> The fact that this provision is used by the police to request names and addresses of peaceful protesters makes this provision all the more worrying. Not only does the offence turn the already blurred distinction between civil and criminal law on its head but its misapplication to peaceful protesters poses a threat to freedom of speech and freedom of assembly.[14]

B. Stop and Search Without Reasonable Suspicion

The requirement of reasonable suspicion has been omitted from two other stop and search powers, an omission of some considerable contention. These two are: stopping and searching in anticipation of violence, contained in section 60 of the CJPOA 1994; and stopping and searching where it is thought 'expedient for the prevention of acts of terrorism' in section 44 of the Terrorism Act 2000. Both follow a similar format: a senior officer issues a written authorisation entitling any officer for a limited, but renewable period, to stop and search anyone within the authorised area without them needing to suspect they will find anything.

Under section 60 the authorisation must be given by an inspector (or higher rank) who must reasonably believe that within any locality in her police area

(a) incidents involving serious violence may take place and that it is expedient to give an authorisation to prevent their occurrence; and
(b) persons are carrying dangerous instruments or offensive weapons without good reason.[15]

It lasts for 24 hours. Uniformed officers may then stop and search pedestrians and anything carried by them or any vehicle or its driver for offensive weapons or dangerous instruments as they see fit, whether or not they have any grounds for suspecting the person or vehicle is carrying such weapons or article.

Under section 44, the authorisation must come from an officer of at least the rank of Assistant Chief Constable, or a Commander in either the City of London or the Metropolitan Police. It lasts for 28 days but can be renewed on the same basis by the same officer or by someone who could originally have authorised it. Under section 46(3)–(7), authorisations need confirmation by the Secretary of State within 48 hours. The test under section 44(3) for Assistant Chief Constables or Commanders to give an authorisation is whether they consider it 'expedient for the prevention of acts of terrorism'. Any uniformed officer then may stop vehicles—so as to search drivers, passengers, the vehicle itself or anything in or on it or being carried by the driver or a passenger—and pedestrians so as to search either them or anything carried by them. The power may only be exercised for the purpose of searching for articles of a kind which could be used in connection with terrorism, and it may be exercised whether or

---

[14] ibid.
[15] Although we have seen that courts might be prepared to 'read in' to that phrase (under s 3 of the Human Rights Act) the right of peaceful protest, effectively as an exculpation, where violence is anticipated, it is unlikely that the right under Article 11 would be engaged so there would be nothing to read in, domestic law being entirely compatible. That said, of course—an individuals' right to peaceful protest is not lost by the protest as a whole becoming violent, provided (using the words in *Ezelin v France* (1992) 14 EHRR 362) the protesters themselves are not acting reprehensibly.

not the officer has grounds for suspecting the presence of articles of that kind or that the person searched is a terrorist. Section 47, unlike the similar provisions in the CJPOA 1994, creates separate free-standing offences: failing to stop when required to do so, or willfully obstructing a constable exercising the power to stop and search.

(i) Gillan

The power conferred by section 44 was considered by the House of Lords in a protest case in 2006, *R (Gillan) v Commissioner of the Police for the Metropolis*.[16] A student who wished to protest outside an arms fair in London and a journalist who wanted to film the protests were both stopped and searched—for a time somewhere between five and 30 minutes—by officers purportedly exercising the section 44 power. Nothing incriminating was found on them or in their rucksacks and camera bag respectively, so each was released. They challenged these searches on both common law and on ECHR grounds but failed before the Lords on all counts.[17]

The leading speech was given by Lord Bingham. The House decided that a stop and search under section 44 was not a deprivation of liberty and so did not engage Article 5 and thus did not need justification under Article 5(1).[18] Searches did engage Article 8—as well as Articles 10 and 11 on the instant facts—but were justified as proportionate.[19] Given the width of section 44, in particular Parliament's deliberate choice of the word 'expedient' rather than 'necessary',[20] and provided the constraints which had been put in place by the scheme were adhered to[21]—as they had been here[22]—there was nothing unlawful about the

---

[16] *R (Gillan) v Commissioner of the Police for the Metropolis* [2006] UKHL 12. There is an excellent case note, C Walker [2006] *Criminal Law Review* 751. See too D Moeckli, 'Stop and Search under the Terrorism Act 2000: A Comment on *R (Gillan) v Commissioner of Police for the Metropolis*' (2007) 70 *Modern Law Review* 659.

[17] Lord Hope, Lord Scott and Lord Brown dealt with the possibly discriminatory impact of such a stop and search power, something not raised in argument: see *Gillan*, [2006] UKHL 12 at [40]–[47], [68] and [81]–[92].

[18] See Lord Bingham, *ibid*, at [25]: 'the procedure will ordinarily be relatively brief. The person stopped will not be arrested, handcuffed, confined or removed to any different place. I do not think, in the absence of special circumstances, such a person should be regarded as being detained in the sense of confined or kept in custody, but more properly of being detained in the sense of kept from proceeding or kept waiting. There is no deprivation of liberty.' His Lordship based his view on the line of cases stemming from *Guzzardi v Italy* (1980) 3 EHRR 333. There had been some academic discussion about what was the correct view: see D Mead, 'The likely effect of the Human Rights Act on everyday policing decisions in England and Wales' (2000) 5 *Journal of Civil Liberties* 5, 10–13.

[19] On this, Lord Bingham provided little by way of reasoned explanation. At [29] he asserted, leaving aside the lawfulness of the search (yet to be established), there was 'little question that [a search] is directed to objects recognised by article 8(2). The search must still be necessary in a democratic society, and so proportionate. But if the exercise of the power is duly authorised and confirmed, and if the power is exercised for the only purpose for which it may permissibly be exercised (ie to search for articles of a kind which could be used in connection with terrorism: s 45(1)(a), it would in my opinion be impossible to regard a proper exercise of the power, in accordance with Code A, as other than proportionate when seeking to counter the great danger of terrorism'.

[20] It had been argued that s 3 of the HRA required a restrictive meaning such that s 44 authorisation could only lawfully be granted if the decision-maker had *reasonable grounds* for considering that the powers were *necessary and suitable, in all the circumstances*, for the prevention of acts of terrorism.

[21] Lord Bingham in *Gillan* [2006] UKHL 12 at [14]. He lists the 11 constraints as follows: 'First, an authorisation under section 44(1) or (2) may be given only if the person giving it considers (and, it goes without saying, reasonably considers) it expedient "or the prevention of acts of terrorism". The authorisation must be directed to that overriding objective. Secondly, the authorisation may be given only by a very senior police officer. Thirdly, the authorisation cannot extend beyond the boundary of a police force area, and need not extend so far. Fourthly, the authorisation is limited to a period of 28 days, and need not be for so long. Fifthly, the authorisation must be reported to the Secretary of State forthwith. Sixthly, the authorisation lapses after 48 hours if not confirmed by the Secretary of State. Seventhly, the Secretary of State may abbreviate the term of an authorisation, or cancel it with effect from a specified time. Eighthly, a renewed authorisation is subject to the same confirmation procedure. Ninthly, the powers conferred on a constable by an authorisation under sections 44(1) or (2) may only be exercised to search for articles of a kind which could be used in connection with terrorism. Tenthly, Parliament made

legislative scheme or the searches that were conducted under it. The system was governed by clear and publicly-accessible rules of law. Although reasonable suspicion was not required, this could not extend to meaning a general power to stop and search those who were obviously not terrorist suspects. By implication, such a search—if it could be 'proved' would be ultra vires. The power existed to ensure that a constable was not deterred from stopping and searching a person whom he did suspect as a potential terrorist by the fear that he could not after the event show reasonable grounds for his suspicion.[23] The 'not . . . unattractive submission'[24] was made that the authorisation was unlawful for being excessive in its geographical ambit; it covered the whole metropolitan police area. This was countered by the fact that security intelligence indicated a spread of terrorist targets throughout London; the powers could be used to nip any such activity in the bud by 'early, disruptive police action . . . divorced from the actual point of attack'.[25] Similarly, while it could be argued that the continuous re-authorisation on a rolling blanket basis (which was only revealed during evidence and discovery of documents in the cases) had become a 'routine bureaucratic exercise and not [an] informed consideration' as required under the Act, it complied with the terms of the Act. In the words of the [independent reviewer] it 'remained necessary and proportional to the continuing and serious risk of terrorism'.[26]

(a) Analysis

Gillan means little can be done if a protester is stopped under section 44 unless she is, as Lord Bingham stated, 'obviously not a terrorist suspect'.[27] Since terrorists tend not to have emblazoned on them their terrorist allegiances, such a qualification is what Strasbourg terms 'theoretical and illusory not practical and effective'.[28] Given too the seemingly near-permanent threat to the UK[29] the stance taken by the House of Lords is unlikely to diminish the incidence and availability of the power randomly to search without reasonable suspicion that section 44 confers. However, in light of *Gillan* the Association of Chief Police Officers (ACPO) drew up new guidance or 'practical advice' on the use of section 44. The power 'should never be used to conduct arbitrary searches. Officers should always use objective criteria to select people for search. Criteria could be related to the individual themselves; to the location the person is in; or a combination of the two'.[30] However, none of us—and we are all potential protesters—will know whether such a search has been authorised. Officers are entitled to keep this aspect of the empowering scheme secret: it

---

provision in section for reports on the working of the Act to be made to it at least once a year, which have in the event been made with commendable thoroughness, fairness and expertise by [the independent reviewer of terrorism legislation]. Lastly, it is clear that any misuse of the power to authorise or confirm or search will expose the authorising officer, the Secretary of State or the constable, as the case may be, to corrective legal action'.

[22] Those constraints help ensure the legality of the scheme in both common law and ECHR terms since they established 'sufficient safeguards to avoid the risk of the power being abused or exercised arbitrarily': see Lord Brown, *ibid*, at [76].

[23] Lord Bingham, *ibid*, at [35].
[24] Lord Bingham, *ibid*, at [17].
[25] Walker, above n 16, 754.
[26] Lord Bingham [2006] UKHL 12 at [18].
[27] *ibid*, at [35].
[28] *Airey v Ireland* (1979–80) 2 EHRR 305 at [24].
[29] Confused, perhaps as Clive Walker points out (above n 16, 754), with vulnerability?
[30] National Policing Improvement Agency, *Practice Advice on Stop and Search in Relation to Terrorism* (2008) p 14 at: www.npia.police.uk/en/docs/Stop_and_Search_in_Relation_to_Terrorism_-_2008.pdf, accessed 11 April 2009.

would 'stultify a potentially valuable source of public protection to require notice of an authorisation or confirmation to be publicised prospectively'.[31] How are ordinary citizens—protesters or not—to know at any given time or in any given place whether an authorisation is in place so as to know whether, if they went say to Oxford Street, they would be liable to a stop and search without any reasonable grounds being shown?

Both of these aspects, it was argued forcefully by counsel for the claimants, are integral to the principle of legality at both common law and under the ECHR.[32] The House of Lords took a peculiarly narrow view of law. By contrast with the general power in the Police and Criminal Evidence Act (PACE) 1984, what legitimises and empowers officers to search is not solely section 44—or even at all—but an authorisation granted under it. To confer the status of 'law' on the former but to consider the latter merely the implementation[33] of it brings an unreal and unnecessary artificiality to the notion of law. That such stops are not even considered to engage Article 5—nor perhaps even Article 8[34]—is also a conclusion not without its critics. As Clive Walker points out, *Gillan* is part of a 'continuing trend ... which is to deny its applicability to detentions which occur during police operations where detention is not the primary aim—such as search powers ... and such as operations to keep the peace'.[35] Sadly, we shall see later in this chapter how this has been continued and extended. Helen Fenwick must be correct in asserting that the situation confronting the two protesters in *Gillan* was qualitatively different from that confronting Signor Guzzardi, and so doubting the reliance placed on *Guzzardi* by the House: 'Gillan and Quinton were completely detained i.e. they could not move appreciably from the spot on which they were stopped and searched. Had they sought to do so, they would probably have been arrested'.[36]

(b) The Intrusion of Anti-terrorism Powers

Gillan evinces a more worrying trend: reliance on anti-terrorism powers to deal with common or garden protest. This normalisation of abnormal powers has been noted and discussed by, among others, Dame Mary Arden writing extra-curially[37] and we came across it ourselves in the previous chapter when we considered the arrest of Walter Wolfgang at the Labour Party conference in 2005.[38] We can see very clearly from the policing of protest at RAF Welford in the Spring of 2003, in the build-up to and start of the Iraq War, how the police made great use of these supposedly extra-normal powers, designed for an entirely different scenario. A Liberty pamphlet entitled 'Casualty of War: Eight Weeks of Counter-Terrorism in Rural England' highlighted the police tactics.[39] It identified a series of moves, which it criticised heavily. These included the creation of exclusion zones around the base, using section 69 of the CJPOA 1994 (directions linked to aggravated trespass), and confiscation of cameras pursuant to section 19 of PACE 1984. As the pamphlet continues, that

---

[31] *Gillan* [2006] UKHL 12 at [35] (Lord Bingham).
[32] Set out in the speech of Lord Bingham, *ibid*, at [32] and more fully at [2006] 2 AC 307, 310–16 and 329–32.
[33] Lord Bingham, *ibid*, at [33].
[34] Lord Bingham considered that an ordinary superficial search of the person and an opening of bags, of the kind to which passengers uncomplainingly submit at airports, for example, could scarcely be said to reach the level of seriousness needed to engage the operation of the Convention: *ibid*, [28].
[35] Walker, above n 16, 755. As he points out, it was regrettable that no reference was made to the decision in *Murray v MoD* [1988] 2 All ER 521 (HL), where there was no doubt that holding an occupant for 30 minutes pending a house search by soldiers in Northern Ireland was a detention.
[36] H Fenwick, *Civil liberties and human rights*, 5th edn (Abingdon, Routledge-Cavendish, 2007) 1131.
[37] M Arden, 'Human rights in the age of terrorism' (2005) 121 *Law Quarterly Review* 604, esp 625.
[38] Above p 241.
[39] www.liberty-human-rights.org.uk/issues/pdfs/casualty-of-war-final.pdf, accessed 12 November 2007.

only allows seizure of material where the police are lawfully on premises and they reasonably believe that this is either evidence of an offence or has been obtained in consequence of committing one. In a 50-day period (from 21 February to 11 April 2003) 995 stops and searches were made using either section 44 of the Terrorism Act or section 60 of the CJPOA 1994.[40] We shall develop some of these matters in the conclusion to this chapter.

III. Preventing Breaches of the Peace

The mainstay of public order policing is the common law power to arrest or take action short of arrest so as to prevent breaches of the peace, either those actually occurring or reasonably apprehended to do so. Alternatively, the police might seek a binding over order from the magistrates. Being bound over to keep the peace is not dependent on a previous arrest or a criminal offence having taken place.

Much has been written about the origins, scope and development of this ancient power, in fact duty. We shall not dwell overly on all of this.[41] Instead, we shall focus on its pre-emptive use as a means to impose control on peaceful protest and peaceful protesters in advance of any trouble. There has been a considerable amount of case law under the HRA. There is considerable potential for the common law power and the statutory powers under sections 12–14A of the POA 1986, which we considered in chapter five, to overlap and duplicate each other. This causes a measure of concern. Unless the powers run completely in parallel (in which case the common law must be taken to have fallen into desuetude, on similar lines to prerogative power[42]), there is a strong policy argument that where statutory powers are capable of governing a public order or protest situation, the police should not also be able to call upon the common law, perhaps to avoid or skirt statutory protection.[43] If there is a gap in section 14 being available—perhaps because (before 2003) there were not 20 or more protesters at the scene—the common law should not be taken to fill that gap. Parliament has spoken and decided on a particular, balanced democratic framework to regulate the event. It is implicit too in the speech of Lord Bingham (at least) in *Laporte* that the common law should not be used to undermine or to relegate the statutory safeguards.

> It would, I think, be surprising if, alongside these closely defined powers and duties, there existed a common law power and duty, exercisable and imposed not only by and on any constable but by and on every member of the public, bounded only by an uncertain and undefined condition of reasonableness.[44]

Lord Bingham's concern might not be so much the residual common law power per se as the residual common law power being exercised on the basis of what is reasonable. We shall consider this below.

---

[40] *ibid*, p 9. In fact contrary to the Liberty report (p 19), the written answer from Bob Ainsworth MP (Hansard HC 28 April 2003, vol 404 col 219) on which the Liberty report draws does not state that 'the vast majority [were] made under s.44'.
[41] See generally DGT Williams, *Keeping the peace: the police and public order* (London, Hutchinson, 1967) ch 4; D Feldman, *Civil liberties and human rights in England and Wales*, 2nd edn (Oxford, Oxford University Press, 2002) and K Kerrigan, 'Breach of the Peace and Binding Over—Continuing Confusion' (1997) 2 J Civ Lib 30.
[42] *Re De Keyser's Royal Hotel* [1920] AC 508.
[43] Though it is not the best example and a little way from analogous, this is the approach to the crime of nuisance at common law favoured by the House of Lords in *Rimmington* [2005] UKHL 63.
[44] *R (Laporte) v Chief Constable of Gloucestershire* [2006] UKHL 55 at [46] and also at [52].

A. The Meaning of a 'Breach of the Peace'

What is now the fairly well-settled definition of a breach of the peace comes from the Court of Appeal decision in *R v Howell*. It occurs when 'harm is actually done or likely to be done to a person or, in his presence, his property or is put in fear of being harmed through an assault, affray, riot, unlawful assembly or other disturbance'.[45] In *R v Chief Constable of Devon and Cornwall ex p CEGB* Lord Denning MR put it differently. A breach of the peace occurs 'whenever a person who is lawfully carrying out his work is unlawfully and physically prevented by another from doing it'.[46] This is clearly wider, conferring greater power but its standing as a correct summary of the law has been consistently doubted. As Collins J put it in *Percy v DPP*, neither Lawton nor Templeman LJJ in the *CEGB* case agreed with those observations. Indeed it was implicit that each considered violence or a threat thereof to be a constituent element. Collins J concluded that 'breach of the peace is limited to violence or threats of violence as set out in [*Howell*] and any observations which may indicate something wider ought not to be followed'.[47] Lord Denning's dicta were declared to be 'erroneous'.[48] Thus 'mere' noise and disorder will not be enough.[49]

Nonetheless, as Helen Fenwick notes, 'the fact that as eminent an authority as Lord Denning could offer such a radically different definition from that put forward . . . a year earlier epitomises the disturbingly vague parameters' of the concept.[50] In her view, the concept is overly broad and ill-defined in three ways. It is not limited to either violence or even threats of violence to people; it is not dependent on a finding of free-standing unlawful behaviour; and since it clearly encompasses third parties as the source of the violence or harm, it would entitle arrest or action short of arrest against protesters who do not themselves breach the peace. Richard Stone adds a fourth objection: the test of whether someone is in fear of harm is factual; there is no requirement that the fear be a reasonable one.[51]

Whether domestic law was sufficiently clear as to allow protesters to foresee, to a degree that is reasonable in the circumstances, the consequences which any (continued or repeated) protest might entail so as to satisfy the 'prescribed by law' test was one of the issues before the ECtHR in *Steel v UK*.[52] If it did not, it would mean that arrests for, or to prevent, a breach of the peace were not 'lawful' under Article 5.

---

[45] *R v Howell* [1981] 3 All ER 383 (Watkins LJ). As we saw in chapter five, unlawful assembly at common law has been abolished, and has now largely been replaced by the offence of violent disorder contrary to s 2 of the Public Order Act 1986. There is some support for the contention that future violence or harm is not itself a breach of the peace albeit that it still entitles the police to arrest: see *Lewis v Chief Constable of Manchester*, The Independent, 23 October 1991 (CA), quoted in S Bailey, D Harris and B Jones, *Civil liberties cases and materials*, 5th edn (London, Butterworths, 2001) 464.

[46] *CEGB*, above n 2, 471.

[47] *Percy v Director of Public Prosecutions* [1995] 1 WLR 1382 (DC) 1393–4. His Lordship also made it clear that it is clear that harm to property will constitute a breach of the peace only if done or threatened in the owner's presence because the natural consequence of such harm is likely to be a violent retaliation. The House of Lords accepted the *Howell* definition in *Laporte*, above n 44, at [28] (Lord Bingham).

[48] *Percy*, ibid, 1395.

[49] *Redmond-Bate v Director of Public Prosecutions* (1999) 7 BHRC 375 (DC) at [9] (Sedley LJ).

[50] Fenwick, *Civil Liberties*, above n 36, 753.

[51] R Stone, 'Breach of the Peace: the case for abolition' [2001] 2 *Web Journal of Current Legal Issues* and also see K Reid and D Nicolson, 'Arrest for Breach of the Peace and the European Convention on Human Rights' [1996] Crim LR 764, 767–8.

[52] *Steel v United Kingdom* (1998) 28 EHRR 603.

The various applicants made three points.[53] First, if an individual could commit a breach of the peace when he or she behaved in a manner the natural consequence of which was that others would react violently (which as we shall see seemed to be supported in cases such as *Percy*) it was difficult to judge the extent to which one could engage in protest activity, in the presence of those who might be annoyed, without causing a breach of the peace.[54] Secondly, the power to arrest whenever there were reasonable grounds for apprehending that a breach of the peace was about to take place granted too wide a discretion to the police. Thirdly, as we have just seen, there were conflicting decisions in the Court of Appeal, *Howell* and *ex p CEGB*. The Court was satisfied that the legal rules provided sufficient guidance and were formulated with the required degree of precision.

> The concept of breach of the peace had been clarified by the English courts over the last two decades, to the extent that it is now sufficiently established that a breach of the peace is committed only when an individual causes harm, or appears likely to cause harm, to persons or property or acts in a manner the natural consequence of which would be to provoke others to violence. It was also clear that a person may be arrested for causing a breach of the peace or where it is reasonably apprehended that he or she is likely to cause a breach of the peace.[55]

B. Preventing Breaches of the Peace—An Overview

At common law the police have considerable, cumulative power to take steps to bring actual breaches of the peace to an end or to prevent imminent and reasonably suspected breaches from occurring. The first is the power to enter premises without warrant. Secondly, while there is no substantive offence of breaching the peace in domestic law at least,[56] those committing or about to commit a breach of the peace can be arrested so as to prevent it continuing or ever taking place. Thirdly, the police may take action short of arrest—such as ordering protesters to stop or to move on—and those who refuse may be arrested for obstructing the police in the execution of their duty to keep the peace.[57] Lastly, the police may seek a binding over order from the courts requiring protesters to keep the peace or to be of good behaviour. We shall consider all of these in turn during which discussion we shall also address this question: Against whom should the police properly act—against the provocative but ultimately peaceful protester, or against the person who has become irate and whose hackles are up and who threatens to become violent as a result of the provocation? This is the question of the so-called heckler's veto.

---

[53] ibid, at [52].
[54] This has echoes of the divide between what Andrew Geddis calls the 'pro-civility' and 'transformative' discourse surrounding s 5 of the POA 1986: see chapter five above p 236.
[55] *Steel*, above n 52, at [55] effectively endorsing *Howell* and relying on *Albert v Lavin* [1982] AC 546. See also *McLeod v United Kingdom* (1999) 27 EHRR 493 at [42] in similar terms. The omission of any mention of imminency or immediacy in the last line was relied on by counsel for the police in *Laporte* as we shall see.
[56] *R v County Quarter Sessions Appeals Committee, ex parte Metropolitan Police Commissioner* [1948] 1 KB 260. In *Steel*, above n 52, at [49] and [86] the ECtHR considered 'breach of the peace' to be an offence for the purposes of the Convention so bringing into play the extended protection in Art 6 as well as being relevant to Art 5(1).
[57] Section 89 of the Police Act 1996. It is in fact the duty of all the Queen's subjects to maintain her peace throughout the realm.

C. Entering Property to Prevent Breaches of the Peace

The power to enter private property without warrant in order to 'deal with or prevent' a breach of the peace has expressly been preserved by virtue of section 17(6) of PACE. The key case in the context of protest and free speech is *Thomas v Sawkins*.[58]

(i) Thomas v Sawkins

The case dates from the 1930s, another time of economic unrest and disruption. The case established that the police have the power at common law to enter and remain on private premises against the wishes of the occupier for the time (whether or not they own them) if they reasonably anticipate that a breach of the peace might otherwise occur. A widely-advertised public meeting was being held at a venue that had been hired privately for the occasion. The police had specifically been refused entry by the organisers.[59] It had previously always been assumed—albeit never established—that the police only had that power where a breach was actually taking place. Lord Hewart CJ in the Divisional Court decried that as an unheard-of proposition of law. Instead he thought there was

> quite sufficient ground for the proposition that it is part of the preventive power, and, therefore, part of the preventive duty, of the police, in cases where there are such reasonable grounds of apprehension as the justices have found here, to enter and remain on private premises. It goes without saying that the powers and duties of the police are directed, not to the interests of the police, but to the protection and welfare of the public ... [A] police officer has *ex virtute officii* full right so to act when he has reasonable ground for believing that an offence is imminent or is likely to be committed.[60]

On the topic of trespass, his view was that 'it was remarkable to speak of trespass when members of the public who happen to be police officers attend, after a public invitation, a public meeting'. Avory J did note that permission to enter someone else's property seemingly granted to all by widely disseminated advertising and invitations can always be revoked by those with the right to do so, here the hirers. He then added the caveat that it was quite different to say they might withdraw the invitation from officers 'who might be there for the express purpose of preventing a breach of the peace or the commission of an offence'.[61]

Mostly the reasoning took the form of unsubstantiated analogy. Avory J saw no distinction between the duty of a constable to prevent a breach of the peace and a magistrate's

---

[58] *Thomas v Sawkins* [1935] 2 KB 249 (DC). During a meeting (being held in a South Wales public library) protesting about the Incitement to Disaffection Bill of 1934, Thomas attempted to remove Inspector Parry by placing his hand on the latter's shoulder. At that point Sergeant Sawkins brushed Thomas's hand from his superior officer. The private prosecution of Sawkins for assault turned on whether the police had any right to be at the meeting. If they did not, the police would be trespassers and so Parry would not have been acting lawfully in trying to break up the meeting.

[59] That a breach of the peace can occur on private land without either any spillover onto public land or affect on third parties outside the land was established by the Court of Appeal in *McConnell v Chief Constable of Greater Manchester* [1990] 1 All ER 423.

[60] *Thomas v Sawkins*, above n 58, 254–5. Avory J was of the view that 'no express statutory authority [was] necessary where the police have reasonable grounds to apprehend [or] reasonable grounds for believing that, if they were not present, seditious speeches would be made and/or that a breach of the peace would take place' (at 256–7).

[61] In fact, Avory J considered that an invitation could be withdrawn 'from any particular individual who was likely to commit a breach of the peace of some other offence'. This leaves open the question, as David Williams pointed out, whether the conveners of a public meeting can withdraw an invitation from someone who either does or is likely to heckle: DGT Williams, *Keeping the peace*, above n 41, 147.

power to bind over to be of good behaviour.[62] Equally, just as a constable on hearing an affray in progress in a house may break in to suppress it and to arrest, he also has a right to break in to prevent an affray which he has reasonable cause to suspect may take place on private premises.[63] Conflating a power to enter to suppress an affray with a power to enter to prevent one is in conflict with a pervasive principle of the common law. This is the difference between punishment and prevention, 'a distinction ... on which freedom of speech [and] freedom of public meeting are founded'.[64] In the mind of Lawrence J, just as constables in the execution of their duty to preserve the peace are entitled to commit an assault, they are equally entitled to commit trespass.[65] For both issues the case turned on its particular facts, especially the fact that this was a public meeting that was extensively advertised and to which the public were invited.[66]

(a) Analysis

The decision, the reasoning and the analysis displayed by all three judges have been subjected to a weight of criticism. Goodhart commented wryly about the lack of any direct authority on the point in textbooks or case law, such that the previous year Home Office legal advice was quite the opposite.[67] David Williams in *Keeping The Peace* dedicates a whole chapter to preventing breaches of the peace on private premises.[68] First, the emphasis the Court placed on its status as a 'public meeting' might have meant that the ratio would not apply to private meetings on purely private premises. This could have been its one saving grace—conceptually flawed as this would have been at common law[69]—but even this has been shown not to be the case. Although neither is concerned with public order but with marital disputes, in both *Lamb v DPP*[70] and *McLeod v Commissioner of Police for the Metropolis*[71] the domestic courts upheld the right of the police to enter or to remain on private residential premises to deal with breaches of the peace. In the first an actual breach of the peace was taking place and in the second one it was reasonably anticipated. Secondly, what exactly needs to be apprehended so as to justify the police entering is of uncertain width. Both the Lord Chief Justice and Avory J considered that the police were entitled to enter so as to prevent not only future

---

[62] *Thomas*, above n 58, 256. As Goodhart notes, the analogy does not hold up. First, binding over powers derive their authority from statute. Secondly, they are an exercise of judicial not executive power: AL Goodhart, 'Thomas v Sawkins: A Constitutional Innovation' (1936) 6 *Cambridge Law Journal* 22, 26.
[63] *Thomas*, ibid, 255–6.
[64] Goodhart, n 62, 30.
[65] *Thomas*, above n 58, 257. This was based on two nineteenth-century Irish cases *O'Kelly v Harvey* (1882) 10 LR Ir 285 and *Humphries v Connor* (1864) 17 Ir CLR 1. Goodhart again shows the differences: 'Because an officer may in a public street remove a provocative emblem from a person's coat, it does not necessarily follow that he is entitled to enter that person's home' given the particular protection afforded private property: Goodhart, above n 62, 27.
[66] *Thomas*, above n 58, 255 and 257.
[67] Goodhart, above n 62, 25.
[68] DGT Williams, *Keeping The Peace*, above n 41, ch 6 and pp 142–9.
[69] It should not have been the nature of the meeting that determined the rights of third parties to enter and to remain but whether or not that third party had licence to remain when it would otherwise have been a trespass to do so.
[70] *Lamb v Director of Public Prosecutions* [1990] Crim LR 58.
[71] *McLeod v Commissioner of Police for the Metropolis* [1999] 4 All ER 553. When the case reached Strasbourg (*McLeod*, above n 55), the ECtHR upheld the domestic ruling as in accordance with law—both the concept of breach of the peace and its application here being sufficiently clear and predictable—and only found for Mrs McLeod on the ground that the police decision to enter and remain was unnecessary, in Art 8(2) terms. Had the police verified the court order, they would have discovered Mr McLeod had no right to enter and take property and they should not have remained once it became clear Mrs McLeod was not there since the risk of disorder or crime dissipated.

breaches of the peace but any offence such as, but not limited to, sedition.[72] Clearly as one of the 'sweeping assertions of Lord Hewart's courts'[73] in the 1930s, this grants an incredibly wide power to the police, one in fact still not even reflected in PACE. The third criticism was a glaring omission but one which has now been remedied. This was the failure to define or even to indicate roughly what is meant by 'breach of the peace'. Williams's last complaint has a modern-day ring: the decision 'once again presents the danger of selective and unfair action by the police'. This was rather prescient. There was much evidence of violence at Fascist meetings in the 1930s, where stewards were accused of using unnecessary force to evict hecklers, which could truly be said to be a breach of the peace warranting summary and speedy police intervention to keep order—but none was forthcoming.

One striking aspect of the case—one that resonates with one of the main themes of this book—is the adoption of a counter-orthodoxy in relation to the control of entry onto land. We have seen—and in *Appleby* the ECtHR has confirmed[74]—that a private landowner is able to restrict entry to all-comers without any need to balance (say) the importance of free speech against the right of property. Yet, in *Thomas v Sawkins* the Divisional Court was not prepared to countenance an absolute right in the hands of those in possession for the time being, the organisers of the meeting, to exclude anyone arbitrarily and without justification. What confers on the police this pre-eminence was never discussed or explained. That is not surprising, it would have to be conceded, for the 1930s, but it has set down a marker that has been followed and adopted uncritically since then. To this unsatisfactory mix we can add the fact that the Court did not at any stage discuss the value and role of free speech and the extent to which—if at all—it should lose out to claims of the public good and public safety. Although that approach would not have been out of line 75 years ago, it is in short yet another case where the conceptualisation of the issues largely determined the outcome. *Thomas v Sawkins* is a case entirely fought out on a battleground of private rights of exclusion and public rights of access by the police without any acknowledgement of what we would now call a human rights/free speech dimension.

(b) The Impact of Articles 10 and 11?

There is no reason to assume that the domestication of the ECHR, had the HRA been passed in the 1930s, would necessarily have led to a different outcome. There is no Strasbourg case that closely resembles what took place in *Thomas*. Clearly the facts engage Article 10 and 11. The chilling effect on all those at the meeting of police officers not only entitled to enter but actually remaining would be enough to constitute an interference or a restriction. The issue would almost certainly fall to be decided as an assessment of the proportionality of a rule that compels protesters to let officers remain against their (the protesters') will solely because there is a reasonable anticipation of breach of the peace (quaere any offence). In terms of legality, 'breach of the peace' has not been found wanting at Strasbourg as being too uncertain.[75] There is no doubt that it would be successfully argued that the police

---

[72] *Thomas*, above n 58, 255 and 256 respectively, though Avory J seems later to qualify this by focussing on sedition: see 256–7.
[73] Williams, *Keeping The Peace*, above n 41, 147.
[74] *Appleby v United Kingdom* (2003) 37 EHRR 38, which we discussed in detail in chapter four.
[75] *Steel*, above n 52. Even the widest meaning attributable to the Court—where there is talk of preventive action for 'any offence'—would not make this any the less 'lawful' for being any the more arbitrary: someone affected, even under such a wide power, would be able to foresee and to predict with sufficient certainty the consequences of the rule. It does make it more susceptible to challenge on grounds of proportionality: blanket or wide rules while clear tend not to be sufficiently discriminating in their reach.

presence could be in the interests of public safety or capable of preventing crime (if there is violence or trouble) or of protecting the rights of others (in the meeting to counter-demonstrate). Thus it would be capable of meeting one of several legitimate aims. It would be accepted that it is always proportionate—though the level or type of response might not be—for the police to enter once violence has broken out. This would probably be so for an actual, on-going breach of the peace (a wider concept, as we have seen).

Whether or not it would be so—and would always be so—where there is only a threat, or an anticipation, or a suspicion that physical violence or a breach of the peace might erupt is not as clear cut. Certainly, it would neither always nor never be proportionate; proportionality is heavily fact- and context- dependent. It is possible to envisage a court holding that a proportionate response would involve the police remaining outside the premises, prepared to respond but only doing so when violence—or (wider) a breach of the peace—does erupt or perhaps is clearly on the verge of doing so. Taking such a stance would really only hold if the police could wait nearby; if the meeting took place in rooms on a grand estate, it might take 15 minutes for the police to seek to bring calm if they were required by law to wait outside. Then it might be proportionate for a proper police presence to be on the private land but not in the meeting. In both, the dampening effect on hotheads would reduce the likelihood of trouble to such an extent as to render disproportionate any attempt on the part of the police to be allowed to enter 'just in case'. To some extent, the Strasbourg decision in *McLeod*, even though it relates to a wholly different scenario, provides support.[76] The ECtHR upheld a wife's claim (on a marriage break-up) that in positioning themselves on her driveway, the police—who had hoped to bring calm so as to effect a more peaceful removal of possessions by the husband—had disproportionately breached her rights under Article 8. This must all be heightened in the context of the right of peaceful protest and its well-known wider public or functional utility. Without any requirement of acting in the last resort or that all other attempts have been tried and failed—or will demonstrably not succeed—a right in the hands of the police to enter and remain at a political meeting 'merely on the ground that some disorder is probable, [means that] . . . the right of public meeting becomes an illusory one'.[77] Taking that line would also fit with that line of cases, such as *Oya Ataman*—albeit on very different scenarios—which stress the need for certain levels of tolerance by the authorities, in the absence of violence, if the right of peaceful protest is not to be denuded of all meaning.[78]

D. Powers of Arrest to Prevent Breaches of the Peace

Like all citizens, police officers may arrest where a breach of peace is committed in their presence, where they reasonably believe that a breach will be committed in the immediate future, or where a breach has been committed and they reasonably believe that a renewal is threatened.[79] We shall consider at what point the law permits the police to arrest and against whom they may lawfully act. The difficulty surrounding the lack of a precise definition (as

---

[76] *McLeod v UK*, above n 55.
[77] Goodhart, above n 62, 28 presciently reflecting the *Airey* test (above n 28) that rights must be 'practical and effective not theoretical and illusory'.
[78] *Oya Ataman v Turkey* (App 74552/01) ECtHR judgment 5 December 2006.
[79] *Howell*, above n 44, 426, though Glanville Williams takes the view that where renewal is reasonably expected, this too should be 'immediate': G Williams, 'Dealing with Breaches of the Peace' (1982) 146 *Justice of the Peace Notices* 199 and 217.

was argued in *Steel*) creates a predictability problem for those deprived of their liberty by the police when they arrest to prevent breaches of the peace. As Reid and Nicolson put it, the discretion that inheres in an officer's 'speculative judgement' as to whether X is put in fear of harm is 'particularly unpredictable as officers must assess a subjective state of mind'.[80]

(i) The Scope of the Power

Where a breach of the peace is not taking place but is anticipated, even greater caution must be exercised: the effect will be a deprivation of liberty for those acting provocatively or threateningly but perfectly lawfully. In *Bibby v Chief Constable of Essex*,[81] Schiemann LJ held that the legal position surrounding arrests for anticipated breaches of the peaces could be distilled, from cases such as *Foulkes v Chief Constable of Merseyside*,[82] *Redmond-Bate v DPP*[83] and *Nicol v DPP*,[84] as follows:

1. There must be a sufficiently real and present threat to the peace coming from the person who is to be arrested to justify the extreme step of depriving of their liberty someone who is not at the time acting unlawfully.
2. Their conduct must be unreasonable and must clearly interfere with the rights of others.
3. The natural consequence of their conduct must be violence from a third party, violence which must not be wholly unreasonable.

It is crucial that the power be exercised only in the clearest circumstances. The police must therefore see where the threat to the peace comes from, although as the authors of Bailey, Harris and Jones ask, 'should there be a requirement of "unlawfulness" in any activity before it triggers a power of arrest?'[85] In one of the few protest cases, *Kelly v Chief Constable of Hampshire*, the Court of Appeal was clearly of the view that the (un)lawfulness of and as between the parties at least was irrelevant.[86] A hunt saboteur, K, was holding the reins of X's horse. K and X were in a heated altercation. K was arrested to prevent a breach of the peace. It transpired that a few seconds before the officers appeared on the scene, X had assaulted K with his whip. The question for the officer

> did not depend on who started the altercation or who was responsible for the apprehended violence . . . the law does not require the constable to go into the rights and wrongs of the matter at that stage . . . The rights and wrongs as between the parties come later.

Lloyd LJ added, obiter, that if the officer had seen the assault, that too would not have been relevant. *Kelly* predates all those other cases except *Foulkes*. That said, nothing in *Bibby* requires the arrestee to be acting unlawfully: unreasonableness does not presume unlawfulness and neither does being threatening.[87] It is, though, inconceivable that it would not be

---

[80] Reid and Nicolson, above n 51, 769.
[81] *Bibby v Chief Constable of Essex* (2000) 164 JP 297 (CA). It was not a protest cases but featuring a bailiff trying to levy distress.
[82] *Foulkes v Chief Constable of Merseyside* [1988] 3 All ER 705 (CA) 711. The case involved not a protest but a family dispute.
[83] *Redmond-Bate v DPP* (1999) 7 BHRC 375 (DC).
[84] *Nicol v Director of Public Prosecutions*, unreported Divisional Court decision, 10 November 1995: *The Times*, 22 November 1995, (1995) 160 JP 155, [1996] Crim LR 318.
[85] Bailey, Harris and Jones, *Civil liberties* above n 45 467.
[86] *Kelly v Chief Constable of Hampshire Constabulary*, unreported, *The Independent*, 25 March 1993, quoted in Bailey, Harris and Jones, above n 45.
[87] Indeed as is pointed out (in Bailey, Harris and Jones, *ibid*) in *Maguire v Chief Constable of Cumbria* (unreported, 26 April 2001) the Court of Appeal in a case after *Bibby* upheld arrests as lawful where the behaviour was 'lawful but provocative'.

decided differently now: that line of cases that culminates in *Bibby* does emphasise the need for an unreasonable violent response to the arrestee's unreasonable protest: surely, the rights and wrongs as between the parties go to that very question?

(ii) Case law

Reported cases where protesters have actually been arrested for committing a breach of the peace—or for being about to—are relatively rare. More common are those cases where a protester is arrested for obstruction after they refuse to obey a request from the police to move on or to stop their protest.

(a) Duncan v Jones

The most prominent of these is probably the restrictive decision of the Divisional Court in *Duncan v Jones* in 1936.[88] Like *Thomas v Sawkins*, it dates from the turbulent inter-war period. It was in fact decided only five months later with (again) Lord Hewart presiding as Lord Chief Justice. The case has been heavily criticised 'as noteworthy today for the vacuity of its reasoning as for its long term deleterious effect on civil liberties'.[89] Nonetheless, throughout the second half of the twentieth century it broadly dictated the extent to which officers were able to detain by arrest so as to prevent putative breaches of the peace. Recent times have seen some liberalising movement in favour of the right of peaceful protest, a move quite clearly influenced by Strasbourg case law—although it would be fair to say that legal position is marked by a degree of opacity. These later cases, some involving obstructive direct action, throw into sharp relief the problem of the 'heckler's veto': against whom should the police act when trouble is threatened between two warring or just opposing factions? Against the side that throws the first stone? Against the side whose presence provides the flashpoint? Against the side that is easier to police and to contain—either because of size or threat? Against the side which is acting 'unlawfully'? We shall consider these in turn.

Katherine Duncan, from the National Unemployed Workers' Movement, was about to address a meeting in a south London street opposite the entrance to an unemployed training centre. The meeting had been advertised as concerned with defending the right to free speech and public meeting.[90] Duncan was about to mount a box to speak when she was told that a meeting could not be held there but it could be held some 175 yards away. Duncan then said: 'I'm going to hold it', stepped on to the box, and started to address those present. At that point Inspector Jones took her into custody. She submitted without resistance. Duncan was charged with unlawfully and wilfully obstructing an officer when in the execution of his duty under the precursor to the current law. It was accepted that no one present at the meeting committed, incited, or provoked a breach of the peace. However, a year before Duncan had also spoken at a meeting at the same venue after which there was a disturbance inside the training centre. She had, it was alleged, made repeated attempts to hold meetings there since that time.

---

[88] *Duncan v Jones* [1936] 1 KB 218. There is an excellent discussion of the political backcloth and the underlying tensions behind these key cases, as well as the legal and political personalities, in K Ewing and C Gearty, *The Struggle for Civil Liberties: Political Freedom and the Rule of Law in Britain 1914–1945* (Oxford, Oxford University Press, 1999) esp 252–70 and 289–95.

[89] Ewing and Gearty, above n 88, 265.

[90] It is impossible to tell from the case but as Ewing and Gearty show (*ibid*), this was a test case that had been waiting to happen for a couple of years since the so-called Tenchard Ban (on public meetings in the vicinity of Labour Exchanges) was promulgated in November 1931, a ban with doubtful legal provenance and intra vires status.

In the course of a remarkably short judgment, totalling just over two pages, the entire case was misconceptualised by all three judges.[91] Lord Hewart CJ put it thus:

> There have been moments during the argument in this case when it appeared to be suggested that the Court had to do with a grave case involving what is called the right of public meeting. I say 'called,' because English law does not recognise any special right of public meeting for political or other purposes. The right of assembly, as Professor Dicey puts it, is nothing more than a view taken by the Court of the individual liberty of the subject. If I thought that the present case raised a question which has been held in suspense by more than one writer on constitutional law—namely, whether an assembly can properly be held to be unlawful merely because the holding of it is expected to give rise to a breach of the peace on the part of persons opposed to those who are holding the meeting—I should wish to hear much more argument before I expressed an opinion. This case, however, does not even touch that important question.[92]

That being so, it was no surprise that the Court unanimously decided that where officers reasonably apprehend a breach of the peace it is their duty to take steps to prevent it, such as here by requiring that the meeting move. If, while taking any of those steps, they are wilfully obstructed, then the offence is made out. The Court concurred with the deputy-chairman of the quarter sessions (which had heard the first appeal) that there was evidence on which Jones could reasonably base an apprehension, viz the previous disturbance that was not only 'post the meeting but was also propter the meeting' and so causally connected to it.[93]

Underlying the judgment is an implicit acceptance of the realities and exigencies of policing on the ground: it is always easier to police a single person whose words or behaviour might cause a disturbance than it is to take action against the large group stirred to action as a result. Let us though discount that—a matter not voiced in the case, or cases, but underpinning many of them—and consider *Duncan* from a doctrinal perspective.

(b) *Beatty v Gillbanks*

What was the leading case until then, *Beatty v Gillbanks*, involved clashes between the Skeleton Army and the Salvation Army in the West Country. It is sidelined in *Duncan* as a 'somewhat unsatisfactory case' and is dealt with by highlighting not the tenor of the judgment but the limiting words of Field J (with which Cave J concurred):[94]

> Now I entirely concede that every one must be taken to intend the natural consequences of his own acts, and it is clear to me that if this disturbance of the peace was the natural consequence of acts of the appellants they would be liable, and the justices would have been right in binding them over.

There is some truth in the distinction being drawn but it does not justify or account for the departure from the principle established in that case. In *Beatty*, clearly the disturbance was going to come from the counter-opposition, the Skeleton Army. It is then clearer—perhaps?—that the Salvation Army could not be liable even for the natural consequences of its

---

[91] In *R (Laporte) v Chief Constable of Gloucestershire* [2006] UKHL 55 at [151], Lord Mance says of the case 'the facts are either reported or were investigated in so limited a way that the merits or demerits of the result are difficult to address'.

[92] *Duncan v Jones*, above n 88, 223. Humphreys J regarded it as a 'plain case [which] had nothing to do with the law of unlawful assembly ... The sole question raised by the case is whether the respondent, who was admittedly obstructed, was so obstructed when in the execution of his duty' (at 223). Singleton J was of the view that '[a]uthorities in other branches of the law do not carry the matter any further' (at 224).

[93] Lord Hewart CJ, *ibid*, at 223.

[94] *Beatty v Gillbanks* (1882) 9 QBD 308, 314.

actions if those natural consequences are an antagonistic violent reaction from their opponents. This is the essence of what Field J goes on to say, something omitted by Lord Hewart CJ in *Duncan*:

> But the evidence set forth in the case does not support [that] contention; on the contrary, it shews that the disturbances were caused by other people antagonistic to the appellants, and that no acts of violence were committed by them. What has happened here is that an unlawful organization has assumed to itself the right to prevent the appellants and others from lawfully assembling together, and the finding of the justices amounts to this, that a man may be convicted for doing a lawful act if he knows that his doing it may cause another to do an unlawful act. There is no authority for such a proposition, and the question of the justices whether the facts stated in the case constituted the offence charged in the information must therefore be answered in the negative.[95]

The difference is that in *Beatty* a rival group was threatening trouble and violence—in response to the defendant's words—whereas in *Duncan* any disturbance or violence was going to come from those in the training centre to whom she was indirectly speaking and whom Duncan was trying to stir into political action. Does the likely reaction to a speaker's words by her own sympathisers or her own audience (which may or may not have been violent or disturbing) justify imposing restrictions on the speaker as a result? It is entirely consistent to argue that action should only be taken against those who are (or perhaps are obviously about to become) violent but never against those merely who express a view, no matter how forcefully or even how inflammatory.

Cases since then—until *Redmond-Bate v DPP* in 1999[96]—have largely followed the *Duncan* rather than the *Beatty* line. What does follow from these consequent cases is that they each involve—in some degree—more than peaceful communication and instead take the form of (mildly) obstructive or disruptive direct action targeted at the objected-to activity. That said, there is an unfortunate lack of consistency in the case law during the 1990s—so much so that it must be questionable if the legal position was sufficiently clearly set out as to make an outcome predictable to any potential protester. In others words, in ECHR terms any restrictions (arrests or binding over orders) could not be said to be 'prescribed by law' within Article 11.

(c) *R v Morpeth Ward Justices ex p Ward*

R v Morpeth Ward Justices ex p Ward[97] was a judicial review of a binding over decision rather than an appeal by way of case stated. Protesters came out of woods into a field shouting, waving and running amongst shooters, getting between them and their target, pheasants. There was no evidence of any act by the group which either physically harmed anybody who was present or their property, or which was likely to cause such harm in a direct sense, or which put anyone in the shooting party or any of the beaters in fear of such harm being done. It was agreed that there was no violence, only shouting and the creation of a general disturbance. Some members of the shooting party felt 'irritated [and] wanted to retaliate' but were dissuaded by the police. In fact the only evidence of a threat came from one of the members of the shooting party who said 'If you don't move, I'll hit you'.[98] Yet it was the protesters who were rounded up and subject to criminal intervention.

---

[95] ibid, 314–15.
[96] *Redmond-Bate*, above n 83.
[97] *R v Morpeth Ward Justices ex parte Ward* [1992] 95 Cr App R 215.
[98] ibid, 217.

The issue was whether there was evidence entitling the magistrates to find that a breach of the peace had been committed by the protesters or to justify a finding that there was a risk of a breach of the peace on a future occasion. Brooke LJ (with Mann LJ agreeing) had this to say:

> [S]o long as the Queen's peace is put at risk by the disorderly activities of the person against whom the justices are invited to exercise their bindover powers, then it is not necessary to show that that person put anyone in bodily fear if his disorderly conduct would have the natural consequence of provoking others to violence ... on the facts of this case, because provocative disorderly behaviour which is likely to have the natural consequence of causing violence, even if only to the persons of the provokers, is capable of being treated as conduct likely to cause a breach of the peace, then it would be quite impossible to say that the justices were perverse in finding that there was a risk that the applicants were likely, unless bound over, to cause a breach of the peace.[99]

Clearly, a legal framework is entitled to respond differently where A's lawful activity is disrupted and where A's natural response might well be (low-level) violence or force—even where B's activity is not per se unlawful (shouting, running and waving all being lawful) and is only unlawful because it obstructs what we might call the incumbent lawful activity.

(d) *Nicol v DPP*

We can see this too in *Nicol v DPP*.[100] There a group of six to 10 protesters attempted to disrupt an angling competition of some 40 or so anglers and were bound over. Their behaviour consisted of throwing sticks and twigs at the anglers' lines and into the water where the anglers were fishing, sounding air-horns, and seeking verbally to persuade the anglers to stop fishing. No violence took place and no threats were made. Three police arrived and those who did not heed their warnings to stop were arrested. The magistrates found that the consequences of the appellants' conduct would almost certainly have been a breach of the peace: by preventing or frustrating the lawful conduct of the anglers, the likelihood was that some or all of the anglers present would resort to forceful means of removing or restraining the appellants. This resulting confrontation would almost certainly have resulted in acts of violence or disorder, provoked by the protesters, from the anglers that would give rise to a breach of the peace.[101] The two who refused to be bound over to keep the peace were committed to custody. They appealed, by way of case stated, to the Divisional Court. The issue for our purposes was this. Can defendants who attempt to disrupt lawful activity by peaceful means and without otherwise acting unlawfully be guilty of conduct likely to cause a breach of the peace if a breach of the peace may be committed, if at all, by those whose lawful activity the defendants seek to disrupt?

Simon Brown LJ, with Scott Baker LJ agreeing, rejected the submission that only conduct that would otherwise constitute an offence under section 4A of the POA 1986 is in law capable of resulting in a binding over order.[102] It would be odd if someone seeking a binding over order, which requires graver consequences to be proved than does section 4A—imperilling of the Queen's Peace—but which provides an altogether less draconian penalty, had

---

[99] ibid, 219–21.
[100] *Nicol*, above n 84. The following passages are taken from the Lexis transcript.
[101] There was clear evidence that two anglers commented to the police that they themselves would shortly take violent action to remove the protesters.
[102] This argument was based on a narrow reading of the words of Channel J in *Wise v Dunning* (1902) 1 KB 162, 179—itself an erosion of the wide principle set out in *Beatty* (above n 94)—that a breach of the peace 'although an illegal act, may be the natural consequence of insulting language or conduct.'.

in addition to prove misconduct which itself necessarily contravenes section 4A. It also followed from *Duncan* that a conviction for obstruction could arise from someone acting perfectly lawfully where that conduct, if persisted in, created the risk of a breach of the peace. That being so, it would be illogical if a lesser penalty—binding over—attracted the need to establish actual criminal conduct rather than some lesser conduct, provided 'always that its natural consequence is to provoke others to violence'. There was no need to prove unlawfulness on the part of protesters before the power to bind over or (pace *Duncan*) to arrest for obstruction. There were three caveats: first the defendant must be acting unreasonably, secondly (if this is different) the violence provoked must not be unreasonable, and thirdly (if, again, this be additional) the protester's conduct must interfere with the rights of those stirred to respond.[103]

The difficulty with this approach is that it is (at a minimum) circular and (at worst) devoid of any substantive meaning as to be useful as an analytical tool to resolve real life conflicts. Simon Brown LJ drew on the comment on the *Ward* case by Professor John Smith in support of his concluding riders.[104]

> In these cases we have to distinguish between the person who is simply carrying on a lawful activity (the actor) and the person who is trying to stop that lawful activity (the protester). It seems that the conduct of the protester can be prevented by binding over but, presumably, only if it is unreasonable. If the mere presence of the protester in a place where he is entitled to be were so provoking to the actor as to be likely to cause him to act violently, the positions would seem to be reversed. It is now the actor who should be bound over. He is trying to prevent the protester from doing what he is entitled to do—and this time he is the one who is behaving unreasonably.

It is not per se unreasonable, nor even unlawful, to throw sticks into a pond or a river— AA Milne was a famous advocate of 'poohsticks' and many dog walkers will do this daily. Nor so, without more, is it to sound an air-horn or to seek to persuade someone of that their views or conduct are morally wrong. What—it must be assumed—makes it so is the intention, the motive, the desire behind the throwing of the sticks or the sounding of the horn. Is it always 'unreasonable' to stop A from undertaking a lawful act—here fishing?

What we might consider the difference to be is where B *prevents* and where B *persuades*. That difference—however small—surely justifies the imposition of a restriction on B, such that they cannot continue. But—and here is the crux—the effect of that restriction (whether that be an arrest, binding over or merely a demand to stop) is to prevent B doing something she is lawfully entitled to do, absent any restriction. In other words, someone is going to be prevented from doing something they would, absent any interference, be entitled to continue doing. But what is it about B's protest that justifies the interference or restriction with his rights, and his choice? In most walks of life, we can identify one person's activity as preventing those of another: my decision to take over a park to play football might prevent someone else playing cricket or having a picnic and vice versa. This requires normative resolutions, something avoided by the Court in *Nicol*.

That leads to another dimension in the case, that of balance. That something is unreasonable does not mean it is not proportionate; these two are, as Lord Steyn sets out in *Daly*, conceptually quite different.[105] None of this was a matter of concern for Strasbourg when

---

[103] *Nicol*, above n 84, no paragraphs in original. It is not entirely clear from this passage by Simon Brown LJ whether there are two separate hurdles or only that an interference with another's rights will render conduct unreasonable but not vice versa.
[104] J Smith, *R v Morpeth Ward Justices ex parte Ward* [1992] Crim LR 497, 499.
[105] *R (Daly) v Secretary of State for the Home Department* [2001] UKHL 26 at [23] et seq.

it came to consider the *Nicol* case itself.[106] It declared the application inadmissible on the ground that the committal served the twin aims of preventing disorder and protecting the rights of others (as well as maintaining the authority of the judiciary) and was not disproportionate given the risk of provoking disorder or violence from others. There is no engagement even at Strasbourg level with balance and why the 'rights' of fishermen should trump those of the protesters. Indeed, what 'rights' the fishermen had, in either domestic law or under the ECHR, was never explained, let alone their legal basis shown.

(e) *Percy v DPP*

We can see elements of balance in *Percy v DPP* but largely the difference that accounts for the finding in favour of the protester lies in the fact that her activities were at best only marginally obstructive and in reality only symbolically so.[107]

Percy was a serial trespasser onto a US air base as a means to demonstrate her opposition to the US Air Force using Royal Air Force bases as military air bases.[108] At no stage was violence used or even threatened and no property was damaged. Each time she was escorted off without incident. The justices found, on the civil standard of proof, that her repeated presence on the base could have provoked military personnel to react violently. Percy refused to be bound over and was committed to prison for contempt. Her appeal, before Balcombe LJ and Collins J, was successful.

Collins J held that although violence or threats were constituent parts of the power to bind over, the violence could come from a third party. It did need a real risk of a breach of the peace (rather than a mere possibility)[109] and required that a natural consequence of the defendant's conduct (which itself did not have to be either disorderly or a breach of the criminal law) if persisted in would be actual danger to the peace in so far as it would provoke others to violence.[110] In this, it is wider than both *Ward*—where, to recall, Brooke LJ talked of 'disorderly conduct [having] the natural consequence of provoking others to violence'—and *Nicol*, with its holding of unreasonableness and that the protest must interfere with someone else's rights. Nonetheless, and this is the contrast, Percy was successful. The case largely turned on its facts. There was no evidence of violence being provoked and the finding that her conduct could have provoked trained personnel to violence was highly improbable, unsupported by evidence and vague. The Court did rule that a civil trespass itself could not amount to a breach of the peace but it could be imagined that civil trespass might produce violence as its natural consequence, such as continued incursions in the face of expressed threats to use violence to remove the trespassers.[111]

(f) *Redmond-Bate v DPP*

The case which subtly shifted the balance is *Redmond-Bate v DPP*, a case that involves an arrest for wilful obstruction of an officer in the execution of his duty.[112] It does, though,

[106] *Nicol and Selvanayagam v United Kingdom* (Case 32213/96) EComHR decision 11 January 2001 (inadmissible).
[107] *Percy v Director of Public Prosecutions* [1995] 1 WLR 1382, noted Spencer [1995] *Crim LR* 714.
[108] She also had the aim of challenging the legality of bye-laws which forbade any incursion into military bases on grounds that they were ultra vires: see the outcome of a case involving one of her co-protesters, *Bugg v Director of Public Prosecutions* [1993] QB 473.
[109] *Percy*, above n 107, 1396. We considered Lindis Percy's conviction under s 5 of the POA 1986—the 'no to star wars' protest—in chapter five above pp 225.
[110] ibid, 1392.
[111] ibid, 1396.
[112] *Redmond-Bate v DPP* (1999) 7 BHRC 375 (DC). Sedley LJ gave the judgment of the Court, Collins J agreeing. The case is discussed by K Connolly [1999] J Civ Lib 382.

involve someone protesting in 'traditional' form rather than engaging in even slightly obstructive or disruptive activity. Three Christian fundamentalists preaching on the steps of Wakefield Cathedral drew a crowd of 100 or so people, several of whom demonstrated hostility. An officer requested that they stop, made out of fear for a breach of the peace. The three refused. Each was arrested for breach of the peace, and subsequently charged with wilful obstruction. One of the three appealed by way of case stated to the Divisional Court where she was successful. For the Court, the underlying question was whether it was reasonable for the officer to arrest Ms Redmond-Bate in the light of what he perceived to believe, viz that the appellant was about to cause a breach of the peace.

The narrow disposal of the case was based purely on interpreting—and in one case—revisiting, domestic authorities such as *Beatty*, *Wise* and *Duncan* that we have already looked at. The test for whether it was objectively reasonable for the arresting officer to fear an imminent breach of the peace was one that must be decided by the court in light of what he knew and perceived at the time rather than on the basis of whether it was *Wednesbury* reasonable. The critical question was to assess where the threat came from 'because that is where the preventive action must be directed'. Can it be said that the defendant is responsible for the threat to the peace or is somebody else? Thus *Beatty* and *Wise* could be differentiated because

> the reactions of opponents would in either case be unlawful, but while in the first case they were the voluntary acts of people who could not properly be regarded as objects of provocation, in the second the conduct was calculated[113] to provoke violent and disorderly reaction.[114]

Similarly, where the case differed from *Duncan* and resembled *Beatty* was

> in the source of the threat to public order: in the former case, on the Justices' findings, it was the appellant herself; in the present case the critical issue, if there was a true threat of breach of the peace, was where the threat was coming from.[115]

In holding that lawful conduct could, if persisted with, lead to a conviction for wilful obstruction, the Court concluded that the Crown Court had misdirected itself in law on the basis of the authorities. Instead, Sedley LJ held that it is

> only if otherwise lawful conduct gives rise to a reasonable apprehension that it will, by interfering with the rights or liberties of others, provoke violence which, though unlawful, would not be entirely unreasonable that a constable is empowered to take steps to prevent it.[116]

We can see that *Nicol* has been extended to include liberties as well as rights, so rendering the discussion about whence comes the 'right' to fish redundant. We might, though, note that by so construing it, we are led inevitably into the same normative—but circular—discussion about clashes of liberties—better Hohfeldian privileges?—and no-rights to stop it, whether that be fishing or the liberty of throwing stones. While Sedley LJ accepted the difficulties of ex post facto review of on-the-spot policing decisions, in the eyes of the Court the question for each officer was whether there was a threat of violence and from whom it stemmed.

---

[113] We must assume calculated is here being used in its less usual form—intended—rather than as a synonym for likely since that latter would not provide the differentiation between the two cases: in both violent was likely to be provoked.
[114] *Redmond-Bate*, above n 112, at [6].
[115] ibid, at [7].
[116] ibid, at [16].

> If there was no real threat, no question of intervention for breach of the peace arose. If the appellant and her companions were (like the street preacher in *Wise v Dunning*) being so provocative that someone in the crowd, without behaving wholly unreasonably, might be moved to violence he was entitled to ask them to stop and to arrest them if they would not. If the threat of disorder or violence was coming from passers-by who were taking the opportunity to react so as to cause trouble (like the Skeleton Army in *Beatty v Gillbanks*), then it was they and not the preachers who should be asked to desist and arrested if they would not.[117]

On the facts, the situation perceived by the officer did not indicate he had apprehended a breach of the peace, much less a breach of the peace for which the three women would be responsible.

Redmond-Bate goes a long way towards protecting forceful, unwelcome but peaceful communication, advocacy and protests, certainly, and *Percy* provides comfort—on its facts at least—for those whose protesting activities go beyond that but do not extend as far as deliberate or provocative interference with the targeted activity itself. Might more be needed? As public authorities under section 6 of the Human Rights Act 1998 (HRA), courts must develop and mould the common law to meet the perhaps changing requirements of Strasbourg: this is the notion of indirect horizontal effect that we have encountered before. It is also clear—from the case of *Steel v UK* at least at Strasbourg level—that the police may only arrest someone engaged in peaceful protest (on breach of peace grounds) where that is a proportionate response to the perceived threat. Certainly where the form the protest takes is communicative or persuasive—as was the case for the 3rd to 5th applicants in *Steel*—arrests are likely to be seen as unnecessary restrictions on the rights contained in Articles 10 and 11.[118]

E. Powers Short of Arrest to Prevent Breaches of the Peace

The House of Lords established in *Albert v Lavin* that officers

> in whose presence a breach of the peace is being or reasonably appears to be about to be committed has the right to take reasonable steps to make the person who is breaking or threatening to break the peace refrain from doing so; and those reasonable steps in appropriate cases will include detaining him against his will.[119]

The police and in fact all citizens have the power to take preventive action short of arrest in anticipation of a breach of the peace. This small and discrete area of public order law has been reviewed twice by the House of Lords. First was *R (Laporte) v Chief Constable of Gloucestershire*, a case arising out of the policing of the protests against the second Iraq

---

[117] *Redmond-Bate*, above n 112, at [18].

[118] *Steel v UK* (1998) 28 EHRR 603. It is worth recalling that even for the 1st applicant—detained for 44 hours—the Court split 5:4 on the question of proportionality and did not define her obstructive and disruptive behaviour outside the realm of Art 10. Arrests to prevent actual or anticipate breaches of the peace will necessarily involve deprivations of liberty and so also require justification under Art 5(1), most likely Art 5(1)(c). In *Steel*, the ECtHR held that though under domestic law 'breach of the peace' is not an offence, the autonomous meaning given under the ECHR means it is: at [48].

[119] *Albert v Lavin* [1982] AC 546 (HL) 565 (Lord Diplock), perhaps refined by Lord Bingham in *Laporte* (below n 120) at [29]: 'Every constable, and also every citizen, enjoys the power and is subject to a duty to seek to prevent, by arrest or other action short of arrest, any breach of the peace occurring in his presence, or any breach of the peace which (having occurred) is likely to be renewed, or any breach of the peace which is about to occur'.

War,[120] and then *Austin v Commissioner of Police for the Metropolis*, concerning the policing of the May Day disturbances in central London in 2001.[121]

Two of the questions that arise are markedly similar to that for arrests—what level of immediacy triggers the ability to take action and against whom can they act?—but there is a third: what action short of arrest can the police lawfully take? In *Albert v Lavin*, as we saw above, there was reference to 'reasonable steps'. We shall see that cases have included being ordered to move on or to disperse (*Duncan v Jones*[122] and *O'Kelly v Harvey*[123]) or being ordered not to proceed (*Moss v McLachlan*[124]), being rounded up and detained (*Austin*), removing provocative items of clothing (*Humphries v Connor*[125]) or even plans to confiscate insulting banners (during protests at the Olympic torch being carried through London en route to Beijing).[126]

(i) Laporte

Laporte was a test case brought by one of a group of protesters in a convoy of coaches that was stopped and searched en route to a protest at RAF Fairford in Gloucestershire and then ordered back to London under police escort. Fairford was the site from which US B-52 bomber missions to Iraq were launched on 21 March 2003.

(a) Background

Ms Laporte sought judicial review of the Chief Constable's decisions to prevent the group from travelling to the demonstration and then to turn it around, arguing they were unnecessary, disproportionate restrictions on the rights contained in Articles 10–11. The Chief Constable's evidence was that he had information that the coach passengers were likely to cause a breach of the peace at the demonstration. The previous month had seen a serious demonstration by a group calling itself Wombles (White Overalls Movement Building Libertarian Effective Struggles). This began peacefully but escalated into serious disorder and an incursion into the base. The period leading up to the demonstration in question saw 50 arrests made. The demonstration had been well publicised and officers had made plans to enable the protest to take place peacefully and to minimise the risk of serious public disorder. There was going to be a three-hour rally at the main gate with estimated numbers ranging from 1000 to 5000. Officers were instructed to intercept the coaches before they reached the base and, pursuant to an authorisation under section 60 of the CJPOA 1994, to search the coaches and the passengers. The senior officer in charge clearly and very specifically considered that a breach was not imminent and so directed that the passengers were not to be arrested at that point. The search led officers to conclude that some, but not necessarily all, passengers intended to cause a breach of the peace at the demonstration and ordered

---

[120] *R (Laporte) v Chief Constable of Gloucestershire* [2006] UKHL 55, discussed in Fenwick, *Civil Liberties*, above n 36, 757–62, A Smith, 'Protecting protest—a constitutional shift' (2007) 66 *CLJ* 253 and A Ashworth, 'Public order: police powers to control demonstration' [2007] *Crim LR* 576.
[121] *Austin v Commissioner of Police for the Metropolis* [2009] UKHL 5.
[122] *Duncan v Jones* [1936] 1 KB 218.
[123] *O'Kelly v Harvey* (1883) 14 LR Ir 105.
[124] *Moss v McLachlan* [1985] IRLR 76.
[125] *Humphries v Connor* (1864) 17 ICLR 1.
[126] Commander Bob Broadhurst, Metropolitan Police, *BBC News At Ten*, 3 April 2008 and taken from 'Envoy will carry Olympic torch' *BBC News On-Line*, 3 April 2008, at: news.bbc.co.uk/1/hi/uk/7328447.stm, accessed 4 April 2008.

them all to return to the coaches. The police escorted the coaches back to London so as to prevent the passengers from disembarking until then.

(b) The Journey Through the Courts

The case reached the House of Lords after both the Divisional Court and Court of Appeal found that the decision preventing participation in the demonstration had been necessary and proportionate, but that the forcible return to London was unlawful since there had not been an immediately apprehended breach of the peace sufficient to justify even transitory detention. May LJ in the Divisional Court (Harrison J agreeing) took the view, first, that as a matter of law action short of arrest could be lawful in situations where—because of the lack of immediacy of any breach—arrest would not:[127] 'imminence is thus relevant to the lawfulness of preventive measures of this kind, but the degree of imminence may not be as great as that which would justify arrest'. Although the police could not act indiscriminately, 'there may be circumstances in which individual discrimination among a large number of unco-operative people is impractical'.[128] Secondly, the enforced return was an unjustified deprivation of liberty not protected by either Article 5(1)(b) or 5(1)(c).

The Court of Appeal ((Lord Woolf CJ, Clarke and Rix LJJ) largely followed the approach of May LJ on the first limb: the case was

> very much on all fours with the decision in [*Moss v McLachlan*] which we would endorse. If the police had done no more than direct the passengers to reboard the coach and instructed the driver not to proceed to Fairford, this would have been an appropriate response that was both necessary and proportionate.[129]

On the second limb, the Court looked at the case solely from the perspective of the common law—and did not need to revert to Article 5—holding that the passengers were 'virtually prisoners': the action taken went well beyond anything held to be justified by the existing common law authorities given it had not been shown there were no less intrusive measures that could have been taken.[130]

By contrast, the House unanimously held for Ms Laporte on what was the first ground: the decision to stop her from proceeding to Fairford was unlawful so the Chief Constable's cross-appeal—on the issue of the escort back to London—failed too. Their Lordships were persuaded by various factors. The Chief Constable had the option of utilising the powers in sections 13–14 of the POA 1986 (query section 14A, which needs a trespass) but had chosen only to issue a section 12 direction prescribing the time, place of assembly and procession route. The police tactics on the day and preparations in advance were informed by an assessment that the protesters would include hard-line activists intent on violence and entry to the base. The progress of the coaches was monitored. Influential was the senior officer's assessment about two hours before that there was not an imminent breach of the peace.[131] The coaches were stopped about five kilometres from the edge of the base. The searches found some articles capable of being used in protest that would be less than peaceful, but not all owners were identified and not all passengers were questioned.[132] Shortly thereafter,

---

[127] *Laporte* [2004] 2 All ER 874 (DC) at [39]–[41].
[128] ibid, [41].
[129] *Laporte* [2005] QB 678 (CA) [45].
[130] ibid, at [52]–[55].
[131] This is set out in full, [2006] UKHL 55 at [10].
[132] Items seized included: some dust and face masks, three crash helmets, hoods, five hard hats, overalls, scarves, a can of red spray paint, two pairs of scissors, a safety flare and five polycarbonate home-made shields.

the coaches began their escorted journey back to London, with passengers not even being allowed to stop to use motorway services. The senior officer justified the decision to turn the coaches around on the past history of the groups involved which satisfied him that hardcore members were on the coaches, on intelligence sources and on the articles seized and found. He considered that on arrival at the base a breach of the peace would have occurred. If the coaches had been permitted to continue

> the protesters on the coaches would have been arrested upon arrival ... a breach of the peace then being 'imminent' ... I therefore concluded that I faced a choice of either allowing the coaches to proceed and managing a breach of the peace at RAF Fairford, arresting the occupants of the coaches in order to prevent a breach of the peace, or turning the coaches around and escorting them back away from the area ... I could not discount the potential risk that some peaceful protesters were caught up in the decision not to allow coaches to proceed, but it was not possible to be certain who had brought the articles onto the coach and who were intent on direct action.[133]

In essence the dispute between the parties was narrow: to what extent was the interference with the right of peaceful protest—both in stopping the coaches and in not allowing them to continue—lawful? The Chief Constable accepted that the burden of justifying the interference rested with him, requiring him to show the interference was both 'prescribed by law'—that is, warranted under domestic law—and necessary. It was argued by the claimant that the interference was both premature and indiscriminate and as a result, in both cases, disproportionate.[134] The House held unanimously that the decision to stop the coaches and to prevent all the protesters (save for three who were speaking at the demonstration) from continuing to the demonstration exceeded what was lawfully permissible at common law.[135] That was enough to dispose of the appeal. As we shall see, the speeches offered views on the necessity of the intervention and on what was called the causal nexus: could and should the police have acted indiscriminately against all the coach passengers?

(c) The New Test of Imminence

All five members of the House decided that the test of lawfulness for action to deal with or to prevent a breach of the peace—actual or reasonably apprehended—was the imminence of it occurring, not the reasonableness of the response.[136] The Chief Constable had proposed, relying largely on the picketing case *Piddington v Bates*,[137] that the police may (and in fact must) do whatever they reasonably judge to be reasonable to prevent a breach of the peace. Questions of imminence would be relevant to what is reasonable. The House unanimously rejected this sliding scale approach. Moreover, it held that the same test should

---

[133] *Laporte* [2006] UKHL 55 at [13].
[134] *ibid*, at [38].
[135] The case could be seen as one in which the ECHR does nothing to aid our understanding or the reasoning: the decision to stop and turn the coaches around was on that was, purely and simply, an unlawful excess of policing power at common law—effectively ultra vires the police since they were only permitted to act when a breach of the peace was imminent. The case though was argued and, largely, resolved around an ECHR framework centring on the 'prescribed by law' test in Article 11.
[136] Lord Bingham, *ibid*, at [45]–[51] esp [50], Lord Rodger at [66], Lord Carswell at [101], Lord Brown at [114]–[115] and Lord Mance at [141].
[137] *Piddington v Bates* [1961] 1 WLR 162, an extempore judgment of Lord Parker CJ in the Divisional Court. Counsel for the police also relied on the judgment of Cooke J (as he then was) in the New Zealand case *Minto v Police* [1987] 1 NZLR 374 and *Moss v McLachlan* [1985] IRLR 76, Skinner J. Lord Bingham described *Piddington* (at [47]) as 'an aberrant decision [that] showed no recognition that the police, in this context, enjoyed no powers not enjoyed by the private citizen, and the test applied was inconsistent both with earlier authority and that later laid down authoritatively in *Albert v Lavin*'.

apply to all policing decisions taken to prevent or to quell a breach of the peace, whether that was an arrest or action short of arrest. Reasonableness and proportionality *would* have a role to play, but at the stage of determining the propriety of the police response such as whether or not to arrest. As Lord Mance put it, 'even when a breach of the peace is reasonably judged imminent, the police must still take no more intrusive action than appears necessary to prevent it'.[138]

Differing justifications were proffered for the uniformity of the imminence approach. In Lord Bingham's mind, there were five reasons:[139]

(i) It would be surprising if, alongside the closely defined powers and duties in the POA 1986, there existed a common law power and duty, exercisable and imposed not only by and on any constable but by and on every member of the public, bounded only by an uncertain and undefined condition of reasonableness.
(ii) Aside from the possible exception of *Piddington v Bates*, there was little trace of a broad reasonableness test in any of the authorities.
(iii) Contrary to counsel's contention, no general test of reasonableness was to be read into what was at the time section 24(7) of PACE: 'Had Parliament intended to confer a power of anticipatory arrest whenever it was reasonable to make an arrest, it would have laid down that rule'.
(iv) *Albert v Lavin* laid down a simple and workable test readily applicable to constable and private citizen alike, one that recognised the power and duty to act in an emergency to prevent something which is about to happen. There is very unlikely to be doubt about who to take action against, since this will be apparent to the senses of the intervener.
(v) There was also little support in the authorities for the proposition that action short of arrest may be taken to prevent a breach of the peace which is not sufficiently imminent to justify arrest.

Lord Rodger considered it a matter of principle. Reformulating the common law by means of reasonableness, not imminence, would 'weaken the long-standing safeguard against unnecessary and inappropriate interventions by the police—and indeed, in theory at least, by ordinary citizens'.[140] The duty to keep the peace is an 'exceptional' one; the common law is primarily concerned with punishment of wrongdoing or its deterrence. It tends not to step in beforehand to prevent people committing offences. Lord Brown took a similar stance, worried that the approach of the lower courts involved too great an inroad on liberty:

> Civil rights must be jealously guarded and ... prior restraint (pre-emptive action) needs the fullest justification. This critically was where the Divisional Court and the Court of Appeal went wrong. On their approach the police are under a duty to take reasonable steps to prevent a breach of the peace from becoming imminent (rather than which is imminent). The duty they postulate would allow for reduced imminence for lesser restraint (i.e. for preventive action short of arrest) on some sort of sliding scale.[141]

---

[138] *Laporte* [2006] UKHL 55 at [114].
[139] ibid, at [45]–[50]. He does in fact offer a sixth (at [51])—but this is more concerned with distinguishing *Moss v McLachlan* on the facts rather than sustaining his position on the imminence test—and an aside that any extension to police powers to control demonstrations should be by Parliament not courts: at [52].
[140] ibid, at [66] and see too [62].
[141] ibid, at [114]–[115].

Lord Mance thought the reasonableness test too broad and too flexible. It would give

> the police (and theoretically any citizen) very extensive power—indeed in the case of the police an active duty—to regulate the behaviour of other citizens in advance in a way which would duplicate a number of statutory powers in this field, would be uncertain in its practical impact and could have a potentially chilling effect on freedom of assembly and expression. The requirement of imminence is relatively clear-cut and appropriately identifies the common law power (or duty) of any citizen including the police to take preventive action as a power of last resort catering for situations about to descend into violence.

All five agreed that a breach of the peace was not imminent at the time of the stop. This was largely on the basis of the police's own evidence and nothing had happened in the interim to make it more so.

The House divided on whether or not the senior officer's view on likely imminence should be conclusive. Lord Rodger and Lord Carswell appear to defer to the view of the officer on the ground.[142] Lord Bingham, Lord Brown and Lord Mance, had they needed to, would have subjected even that view to some scrutiny.[143] In doing so, they emphasised that one factor in determining the imminence of any threat, and thus the necessity of dealing with it, was the level of likely police response, albeit also clearly recognising what Lord Bingham called the 'danger of hindsight' and the difficulties facing officers on the ground.[144] Lord Brown considered it was not open to the police on the facts to take the view that a breach of the peace was imminent.[145] First, the 120 coach passengers had by then been searched and deprived of such objects as were calculated to threaten the peace. Secondly, the eight 'Wombles' present had been identified and one other passenger arrested for an earlier offence at Fairford. Lastly, the police had extensive forces and carefully laid plans for guarding against any disorder whether on arrival at Fairford, during the subsequent procession, or at the bell-mouth area opposite the air-base gate. Lord Mance echoed that last point.[146] There were 'very extensive precautions in place at Fairford to meet and park vehicles and to channel and control, and counter any threat of disorderly conduct by, protesters arriving on them' and there was no reason to think that police plans were inadequate to meet any likely eventualities, given that they had catered for the possibility that as many as 10,000 protesters would arrive, when at the time of the stop there were only about 3,000.

> If the coaches had been allowed to continue to Fairford, any disturbance (if any) would only have been likely some time after their arrival and then only in circumstances and at a time which could not be predicted at Lechlade. If and when any occurred or was about to occur, the actual or likely trouble-makers would be likely to be identifiable at that time. The respondent's submission that indiscriminate action had to be taken against all 120 passengers at Lechlade faces the justified objection that the suggested difficulty in identifying particular trouble-makers and the suggested

---

[142] Lord Rodger (*ibid*, at [71], echoed by Lord Carswell at [104]) indicated that 'on the basis of the information and advice available to him, Chief Superintendent Lambert considered that a breach of the peace would occur if the coaches and the protesters reached Fairford. It was only just over three miles away-a few minutes by coach. In these circumstances, if Mr Lambert had concluded that a breach of the peace at Fairford was imminent, I might have been disposed to accept that'. Lord Carswell (at [105]) made play of the justified and considerable suspicion on the part of the police in light of the identity of some of the passengers, what was found and the refusal of many to gives a name or an address.
[143] Lord Bingham, *ibid*, at [53], Lord Brown at [118] and Lord Mance at [142].
[144] *ibid*, at [55] and see also Lord Rodger at [90] and Lord Carswell at [106].
[145] *ibid*, at [118].
[146] *ibid*, at [142].

need for indiscriminate action only arose because the action taken was premature-taken at a time when a breach of the peace was not imminent.

(d) Analysis

It is clear that *Laporte* marks a significant change in judicial approach to what is permissible when it comes to policing peaceful protest. In rejecting the sliding scale—whereby imminence was needed to arrest but either less imminent violence or even mere unreasonable action was tolerated as the trigger or criteria for police involvement—in favour of the uniform test of imminence, the court has provided a clear signal to the limits of tolerable pre-emptive action.[147]

1. The meaning of 'imminence' That said, there is only limited clarity on what it means to say that a breach of the peace is imminent. Lord Bingham, Lord Carswell and Lord Brown considered it meant something is 'about to happen'.[148] Lord Rodger also talks of it 'going to happen in the near future',[149] though not necessarily in the next few seconds or next few minutes.

> That would be an impossible standard to meet, since a police officer will rarely be able to predict just when violence will break out. The protagonists may take longer than expected to resort to violence or it may flare up remarkably quickly. Or else . . . the breach of the peace may be likely to occur when others arrive on the scene and there is no way of . . . predict[ing] exactly when the violent reaction provoked by the protests would occur.[150]

Lord Mance on the other hand preferred to formulate it contextually rather than by a ticking clock: 'imminence [could not fall] to be judged in absolute and purely temporal terms, according to some measure of minutes'.[151] However, three Law Lords were prepared to grant some flexibility in the operation of the imminence test, recognising relevant circumstances. For Lord Mance 'what is imminent has to be judged in the context under consideration and the absence of any further opportunity to take preventive action may thus have relevance'.[152] Lord Rodger, while still upholding the view that a breach had to be 'about to happen', stressed that changes in technology and in policing practice might mean that officers could intervene at an earlier stage.

> The police officer's view of the matter will depend on the information he has and on his assessment of that information . . . [T]oday, officers on the ground can be supplied by radio with information about what lies round the corner or what people are doing a few miles down the road. Armed with such information, they may have good reason to anticipate that people in front of them are intending to take part in a breach of the peace, or are likely to become involved in one, a short time later or a short car ride away. Intervention to prevent that breach of the peace may therefore be justified. A fortiori, a senior officer at the centre of a police operation, receiving reports from his officers on the ground, plus intelligence and advice on how to interpret the data, may have good reason to appreciate that a breach of the peace is 'imminent' or 'about to happen', even though that

---

[147] Consequently it must 'cast doubt upon the propriety of some of the other mainstays of public order law' such as *Duncan* (above n 88) and *Piddington* (above n 137): Smith, above n 120, 254.
[148] *Laporte* [2006] UKHL 55 at [49], [100] and [114].
[149] ibid, at [66] and [68].
[150] ibid, at [69].
[151] ibid, at [141].
[152] ibid.

would not be apparent to officers lacking these advantages. The precondition for intervention remains the same but the test has to be applied in the conditions of today.[153]

For Lord Carswell it was

> rational and principled to accept that where events are building up inexorably to a breach of the peace it may be possible to regard it as imminent at an earlier stage temporally than in the case of other more spontaneous breaches.[154]

The absence of any clear guidance on what it means to say a breach of the peace is imminent, though not surprising, means that protesters may well still be arrested and are likely still to need to resort to litigation to establish that they were arrested or escorted away peremptorily. It must surely be a moot point how much the threat of damages—either at common law or under section 8 of the HRA—provides a realistic inhibitor on the working practices of the police during protests. They might well prefer to take their chances after the event in exchange for diffusing—and defusing—what appears to them to be a credible threat of violence and disorder. This, as we have seen throughout this book, is all too often the way at sites of protest—the damage is done, the chilling effect imposed at the scene. Damages after the event—unless exemplary—are unlikely to compensate for the loss of the right to protest en masse and in combination with others. Indeed, damage is also done—but unquantifiably—to those remain. Their numbers are diluted as a result of (to be proved later) unlawful police action, their strength is diminished—for the TV cameras—and their cause appears to be one supported by a handful of people rather than by hundreds.

2. Police strategy and tactics   More positively, for protesters in future, the police will be taken to task if they fail to target more closely those likely to cause violence and disorder, fail to develop (even) more flexible and responsive policing strategies in their use of powers to prevent breaches of the peace and if they act in too peremptory a fashion. Even assuming that some on the coaches were intent on (or were not averse to) causing damage and injury, at the time that any of them were intent on doing so—it being clear that none had tried when the coaches had been stopped—there would have been a full police presence, 'in close attendance well able to identify and arrest those who showed a violent propensity or breached the conditions to which the assembly and procession were subject'.[155] There is also clear criticism of the rigidity of the 'pre-set' or 'preconceived' plan—in directing the stop and the return—without considering any less drastic alternative.[156] Lord Carswell made it clear that when it became apparent that the 'Wombles' were in a very small minority and that the vast majority of those on the coaches posed no threat 'it was incumbent on the police to review their strategy in relation to these coaches'.[157]

3. The status of *Moss v McLachlan*   The House of Lords in *Laporte* divided on what now should be the status, in terms of both reasoning and outcome, of *Moss v McLachlan*.[158] This

---

[153] ibid, at [67].
[154] ibid, at [102].
[155] Lord Bingham, ibid, at [55], Lord Rodger at [88] and Lord Carswell at [105] and Lord Mance at [152]–[155]. As Lord Rodger pointed out at [89], 'the forces assembled to deal with an anticipated demonstration of up to 10,000 protesters would surely have been able to prevent any breach of the peace which the eight known Wombles were planning.'
[156] See Lord Rodger, ibid, at [88].
[157] ibid, at [105].
[158] *Moss v McLachlan* [1985] IRLR 76.

342 *Preventive Action by the Police*

has been a long-term bête noire for protesters, dating from the turbulence of the miners' strike in the mid-1980s. Skinner J in that case endorsed the decision to turn back, on threat of arrest, convoys of striking miners en route to pickets and mass demonstrations in the Nottinghamshire coalfields (but at least 1½ and as much as five miles distant). This is considered by many to have so extended the common law on dealing with anticipated breaches of the peace as to leave the police a virtually unconstrained and untrammelled power. The police arrested for obstruction a group of 60–80 who refused to turn back (and in fact tried to break through the cordon), on the basis that they feared a breach of the peace would otherwise occur. Any indication in *Moss* that the gauge for assessing the lawfulness of police intervention was reasonableness was rejected unanimously in *Laporte*.[159]

However, a majority of the House (Lord Bingham, Lord Rodger and Lord Brown) was still prepared to concede that the outcome in *Moss* was one that was just justifiable and permissible on the basis of imminence—though at the extreme limits—rather than reasonableness.[160] Lord Bingham explicitly rejected the view taken in the Court of Appeal, that the instant case was 'very much on all fours' with *Moss*.[161] There 'four members of one belligerent faction [were] within less than five minutes of confronting another belligerent faction, and no designated, police-controlled, assembly point separated them from the scene of apprehended disorder'. Whereas in the instant case, '120 passengers, by no means all of whom were or were thought to be Wombles members, were prevented from proceeding to an assembly point which was some distance away from the scene of a lawful demonstration'. Lord Brown was the most critical. It was '(just) sustainable on what is certainly one possible view of the facts' and at the 'furthermost limits of any acceptable view of imminence, and then only on the basis that those prevented from attending the demonstration were indeed manifestly intent on violence and were not . . . quite possibly intent only on peaceful demonstration'.[162]

What is preserved from *Moss* by *Laporte* is the finding that the basis of the apprehended threat need not be known personally to the arresting officers. As Reid and Nicolson ask, is it not implicit in the test that the arrestors witnessed the facts giving rise to their anticipation rather than, as was clear in *Moss*, having read about previous trouble in the press or watched it on television?[163] Any argument (implied by the reference in *Howell* to 'such a

---

[159] Skinner J said that the 'imminence or immediacy of the threat to the peace determines what action is reasonable' (*ibid*, at 79). This 'significant modification to the law' (*Laporte* [2006] UKHL 55 at [63]) was what prompted Lord Rodger to call the reasoning 'flawed' (at [71]) and so, effectively, wrongly decided. As Lord Bingham too pointed out (at [42]) Skinner J 'cited with approval the observation of Lord Parker CJ in *Piddington v Bates* that the police must anticipate a real, not a remote, possibility of breach, preferring that test, if different, to the 'immediate future test' put forward in *R v Howell* [1982] QB 416 (CA) 426.' To that extent, the House of Lords must be taken as endorsing the approach in *Peterkin v Chief Constable of Cheshire* unreported, *The Times*, 16 November 1999, discussed by Fenwick, *Civil Liberties*, above n 36, 756.

[160] See Lord Bingham in *Laporte* [2006] UKHL 55 at [51], Lord Rodger at [71], Lord Carswell at [102] and Lord Brown at [118]. Lord Mance (at [150]) did not specifically uphold the outcome. The sprinkling of 'reasonableness' rather than imminence or immediacy within the judgment may have led to a material misdirection at common law. Under the Human Rights Act judicial scrutiny of such factual and legal issues should now be closer than is suggested in the case. As he concluded, the 'effect of the police action in *Moss v McLachlan* was to preclude any mass demonstration or picket at any of the four neighbouring collieries, on the basis of a general apprehension of a breach of the peace there because there had been breaches of the peace at collieries in the Nottinghamshire area in the previous days or weeks.' It must be assumed—by implication—that the unreported decision in *Foy v Chief Constable of Kent* (20 March 1984, noted Fenwick, *Civil Liberties*, above n 36, 756) where the courts upheld a decision by the police to turn back striking miners at the Dartford Tunnel some 200 miles from their eventual destination is no longer sustainable, if ever it was before.

[161] *Laporte* [2005] QB 678 at [45].
[162] *Laporte* [2006] UKHL 55 at [118].
[163] Reid and Nicolson, above n 51, 769.

Preventing Breaches of the Peace 343

breach') that the future breach must be committed in the presence of arresting officer rather than as in *Moss*, merely be committed in 'close proximity in time and place' is one too that seems now to have been relegated to the passage of time.

(e) *Laporte*: the obiter issues

Although its holding of imminence as the litmus test was sufficient to dispose of the appeal, the House did go on to consider two further questions. The first was this: assuming a breach of the peace is imminent, against whom may the police lawfully take preventive action? The second was whether the decision to stop the coaches and to turn the passengers around was a disproportionate restriction on the right to peaceful protest in Article 11.

The first lays to rest one further criticism of *Moss*. The fact there was no 'requirement that there was anything about these particular miners to suggest they might cause a breach of the peace' meant 'a number of individuals were lawfully denied their freedom of movement and assembly apparently on no more substantial grounds than that other striking miners had caused trouble in the past'.[164] These two can be viewed as raising the same question from the opposing perspectives of the common law and the HRA. In fact the two were elided, as Lord Bingham says: 'It was wholly disproportionate to restrict [the claimant's] exercise of her rights under articles 10 and 11 because she was in the company of others some of whom might, at some time in the future, breach the peace'.[165] It is to these we shall now turn.

1. Taking preventive action against 'innocent' third parties Their Lordships, in differing detail, address the issues thrown up when the police act against innocent protesters. This may be either as part of a collective round-up (as here) or where officers take action against protesters who do not themselves breach the peace but who cause others to do so, usually by provoking them into violence.[166]

Given the disposal of the case on other grounds, what follows is obiter. Again, there is a divergence of views in the speeches, and the analyses undertaken are not entirely convincing, coherent or doctrinally sound. Not all of Their Lordships addressed the first aspect, the arrest of innocent parties in connection with apprehended breaches of the peace by others. Lord Carswell did not do so. Lord Rodger rejected the need for any causal nexus between those affected by any measure taken by the police and the potential breach of the peace in extreme and unavoidable cases. His speech can be seen as approval of collective arrests.

> In some circumstances a requirement [that the police restrict themselves to those who are or who are likely immediately to act unlawfully] . . . would make it impossible for police officers to discharge their primary duty to preserve the peace. In a case like the present, therefore, provided that there was no other way of preventing an imminent breach of the peace, under the common law a

---

[164] Fenwick, *Civil Liberties*, above n 36, 756.
[165] *Laporte* [2006] UKHL 55 at [55]. Arguing that it was disproportionate because it was premature rather replicates the issues surrounding the imminence test: it was premature because there was no hint of disorder when the coaches were stopped and no reason to apprehend that there would be an immediate outburst of disorder even at the designated drop-off points in Fairford and the designated assembly area. As a result, it was also indiscriminate because the police could not at that stage identify those (if any) of the passengers who appeared to be about to commit a breach of the peace.
[166] All expression on this latter issue was obiter. It was never an issue that Ms Laporte or any non-Wombles member might tempt third parties into violence. It is for that reason, we must assume, that Lord Bingham did not address the matter.

police officer could stop a coach load of protesters from proceeding further, even although those on board included entirely peaceful protesters. The proviso is, however, vital.[167]

Clearly, if there were another way, the action would be unlawful as being unnecessary and indiscriminate.

Lord Mance was prepared to assume the existence of a principle by which B, if asked to desist from entirely lawful and innocent conduct but refused, could be restrained or arrested for obstruction in order to prevent A causing a breach of the peace. It was unnecessary for the appeal, he continued, to conclude how far it survived at common law or under the ECHR. That principle though was 'confined to rare situations where [it is] the only way to avoid a reasonably apprehended and imminent breach'.[168] He added that wherever possible, the focus of preventive action should be on those about to act disruptively not on innocent third parties. Lord Bingham did consider that 'it was wholly disproportionate to restrict [Ms Laporte's] exercise of her rights under articles 10 and 11 because she was in the company of others some of whom might at some time in the future breach the peace'.[169] Although this seems to be a corrective to Lord Rodger's view on the matter of indiscriminate action based only on the reasonably suspected proclivities of a few, we should not forget that Lord Bingham's word are confined to the facts. They are not a general pronouncement of law. Lord Brown sides with Lord Bingham but again only on the facts:

[E]ven if [the police] had both regarded and been entitled to regard a breach of the peace as imminent (whether [at the stop or at the base]) it is difficult to see how at common law he would have had the power and duty to take action against those he had no reasonable grounds to apprehend were intent on violence.[170]

Thus as an assertion of *law*, we have only the pronouncements of Lord Rodger and Lord Mance. These, on closer inspection, are not made out by the cases they call in aid. Only one of the ECHR cases cited in fact deals with the exact issue in the instant case. The application of that one, *Chorherr* (referred to by Lord Rodger and Lord Brown) must be in doubt, as we considered in chapter three, in view of *Öllinger*.[171] If, as a matter of European Law, as *Öllinger* seems to indicate, it is no longer true to assert, as Lord Mance did, that 'a policeman may take preventive action against a person who by interference with the rights and liberties of others is likely to provoke violence'[172] then a fortiori, the police cannot act against wholly innocent protesters who are not even acting provocatively.

Let us assume—though this is not to accept—that *O'Kelly v Harvey*, an Irish case from the 1880s—central to the obiter reasoning of all bar Lord Bingham (who was silent on the

---

[167] Laporte [2006] UKHL 55 at [84] (Lord Rodger).
[168] ibid, at [147]–[149]. He based this in part on the general duty to prevent breaches of the peace which, by extension, might entitle police officers to require B to desist as part of B's general duty of assistance. He cited *O'Kelly* (above n 123) and ECHR cases such as *Christians Against Racism and Fascism (CARAF) v UK* (App 8440/78) (1980) 21 DR 138 and *Ziliberberg v Moldova* (App 61821/00) ECtHR inadmissibility decision 4 May 2004. Support here was drawn from *Ezelin v France* (1991) 14 EHRR 362 where the EComHR at [34] said 'generally speaking, an individual does not cease to enjoy the right to freedom of peaceful assembly simply because sporadic violence or other punishable acts take place in the course of the assembly, if he himself remains peaceful in his intentions and behaviour'. The ECtHR at [53] said 'the freedom to take part in a peaceful assembly-in this instance a demonstration that had not been prohibited-is of such importance that it cannot be restricted in any way, even for an avocat, so long as the person concerned does not himself commit any reprehensible act on such an occasion'.
[169] Laporte [2006] UKHL 55 at [55].
[170] ibid, at [129].
[171] Öllinger (2008) 46 EHRR 38 and D Mead, 'Strasbourg discovers the right to counter-demonstrate—a note on Ollinger v Austria' [2007] EHRLR 133.
[172] Laporte [2006] UKHL 55 at [145].

matter)—remains good law on dealing with groups.[173] There is still a clear difference between it and the instant case. Harvey was a Justice of the Peace and O'Kelly was a nationalist Member of Parliament. The previous day a placard appeared summoning local Orangemen to assemble and oppose a public meeting at which O'Kelly and his group, the Land League, would be present. Harvey knew of the placard and believed on reasonable and probable grounds that the only way of preventing a breach of the peace when the Orangemen arrived was to order the nationalists to separate and disperse. When they failed to leave, he laid his hand on O'Kelly in order to do so. O'Kelly sued for assault and battery. The Irish Court of Appeal held that, if made out, these averments would constitute a sufficient defence to the action. Law C explained the position. Taking necessary steps to stop and disperse a meeting, even if those assembled and ordered to disperse were doing nothing unlawful, was justified where there were reasonable grounds for believing: first that there would be a breach of the peace if they continued so assembled; and secondly that there was no other way in which the breach of the peace could be avoided. A magistrate did not need to defer action until a breach of the peace had actually been committed; her paramount duty is to preserve the peace unbroken by whatever means available, meaning she may, and in part must, intervene the moment she has a reasonable and bona fide apprehension of a breach of the peace being imminent.

> Even assuming that the danger to the public peace arose altogether from the threatened attack of another body on the plaintiff and his friends, still if the defendant believed and had just grounds for believing that the peace could only be preserved by withdrawing the plaintiff and his friends from the attack with which they were threatened, it was, I think, the duty of the defendant to take that course ... [as long as] he had reasonable ground for his belief that by no other possible means could he perform his duty of preserving the public peace.[174]

In *Laporte*, it was not asserted, nor could it ever have been, that the coach party, as a group separate and apart from its members, was likely to cause them to react adversely, if not actually being provocative towards others. It would only have been those few Wombles, had they arrived at Fairford, who would have caused trouble and disorder. The Land League meeting on the other hand as an entity could conceivably said to be so, so justifying its dispersal en masse and arrest of anyone who objected. It is also a case decided a century before the HRA heralded what in *Redmond-Bate* Sedley LJ called a 'constitutional shift'.[175]

2. Taking preventive action where disruption and threats emanate from third parties
Lord Bingham is the only one of the five Law Lords not to offer a view on the heckler's veto. There is considerable common ground among the other four but with subtly different emphases.

All the remaining judges agreed that where A's behaviour is likely or liable to provoke in others a violent reaction, whether or not A intends to be provocative, even if A is otherwise acting lawfully, this entitles the police to act and require A to desist.[176] Further (according to Lord Rodger) lawful and proper conduct by A may be liable to result in a violent

---

[173] *O'Kelly v Harvey* (1883) 14 LR Ir 105.
[174] ibid, 109–10, 112.
[175] *Redmond-Bate*, above n 112, at [13].
[176] *Laporte* [2006] UKHL 55 Lord Rodger at [75], Lord Carswell at [96], Lord Brown at [120] (though for him in addition A had to be acting unreasonably and the targets of the various disruptive activities could not reasonably have been expected to put up with them) and Lord Mance at [145], who adds the caveat that the interference must be with someone else's rights or liberties, as per *Nicol* (above n 84).

reaction from B, even though it is not directed against B. If B's resort to violence can be regarded as the natural consequence of A's conduct, and there is no other way of preserving the peace, a police officer may order A to desist from his conduct, even though it is lawful. If A refuses, she may be arrested for obstructing a police officer in the execution of his duty.[177] Lord Brown was at pains to distinguish that line of cases where A provokes a breach of the peace as what might be termed a natural consequence, and cases where a citizen's lawful conduct, perhaps in the exercise of their own right of free speech, is adjudged by a constable likely to provoke imminent violence in others—violence which would be 'not merely unlawful but wholly unreasonable'.[178] In those latter cases, plainly the constable's duty if he can is

> to protect the citizen's rights and to control, and if necessary arrest, those behaving unreasonably—summoning if need be the support of other officers and/or members of the public. But if he cannot, can he instead require the citizen to desist and, if he refuses, arrest him? In my judgement the answer to that question is that—save perhaps in extreme and exceptional circumstances—he cannot ... The police's first duty is to protect the rights of the innocent rather than to compel the innocent to cease exercising them.[179]

On the facts, it followed that turning back, as part of a pre-set plan, a group that was intent on peaceful protest rather than provoking others or acting so as to cause violence in others was premature, given the precautions in place at Fairford. The decision to rely only on section 12 of the POA 1986 indicated the police thought they could manage. Any argument that tried to illustrate the logistical difficulty of making mass arrests at Fairford was diluted by the fact that the Chief Constable, by deciding not to seek an order under section 13 of the 1986 Act, had judged the demonstration to be controllable.[180]

We have seen too that the common law power was used here in a way that was very indiscriminate in its target. Both went to show the disproportionality of the measures in ECHR terms. At the very least, it is clear that the strong adjuration about restraint from Sedley LJ in *Redmond-Bate* now has (obiter) support in the House such that we might formally start to consign to the past cases such as *Duncan v Jones* and to *Wise v Dunning*. In fact, it might even seem to herald an age that is even more restrictive of police activity than *Redmond-Bate*. Lord Brown, for example, takes great pains to stress that where

> a citizen's lawful conduct, perhaps in the exercise of his own right of free speech, is adjudged by a constable likely to provoke imminent violence in others, violence which would be 'not merely unlawful but wholly unreasonable' ... if he cannot [control, and if necessary arrest, those behaving unreasonably], can he instead require the citizen to desist and, if he refuses, arrest him? In my judgement the answer to that question is that—save perhaps in extreme and exceptional circumstances—he cannot.[181]

---

[177] ibid, at [78] relying on cases such as *O'Kelly v Harvey* above n 123; *Nicol* above n 84; *Redmond-Bate*, above n 112; and *Chorherr v Austria* (1993) 17 EHRR 358.
[178] *Laporte*, at [123].
[179] ibid, at [123]–[124]. The only counter-argument was along these lines: if a constable's ultimate duty is to preserve the Queen's peace and in doing so he can call upon citizens to assist him (on pain of arrest should the citizen refuse) then why should not an innocent protester be required to stop protesting so as to avert the peace being broken in the first place?
[180] *Laporte*, above n 176 at [55] Lord Bingham.
[181] *Laporte*, above n 176 at [123]. We saw above (n 179) that the 'extreme and exceptional circumstances' refers to the fact that there might be an argument that the officer should be able to call upon all citizens to perform their duty to preserve the Queen's peace and if they should fail—i.e. desist—then to arrest them.

It is clear from the speeches that the focus of the police's activities should be on those about to disrupt—perhaps by provoking—and not on 'innocent' persons. If those latter are to be the focus, then that should be only if there are no other possible means of avoiding an imminent breach. To that extent the case chimes well with the decision of the Strasbourg Court in *Öllinger*, a case only put before the House of Lords in general terms and not as overturning or casting doubt on the extent of *Chorherr*, which was cited and formed part of Their Lordships' reasoning.[182]

(f) Reflection

Let us not overplay *Laporte*. As Andrew Ashworth comments, had the police not been honest enough to reveal either that they did not need to invoke section 13 or the fact that a breach was not imminent, who knows what the courts might have concluded.[183] The police still have considerable power to intervene whenever and wherever a breach of the peace is imminent, a test with extensive flexibility built in. Those who have been arrested will at least have the chance to challenge that in court, using Article 11 as a shield under section 7(1)(b) of the HRA or arguing that the arrest was unlawful at common law. If instead a protester is directed away or a group is ordered to disperse, a problem arises. For those who refuse, the police are faced with the choice of arrest for obstruction—which too can be challenged—or letting the protester proceed. Where, however, someone is ordered to turn back or to desist and they accede, a situation we must assume is commonplace, that shifts the onus of proving that the police action is unlawful onto citizen protesters. That would be a challenge either at common law for want of immediacy or under Article 11 for being disproportionate on grounds of prematurity and indiscrimination. Even if officers at the scene take a broad—and ultimately mistaken—view that what is unfurling is an immediate threat to the peace, the chances of that being successfully shown in court are, we must imagine, remote. It is here—on the ground, at the scene, in practice—that the law plays out and where the common law power to take preventive action will be most sorely felt and where, away from the judicial gaze of five members of the House of Lords, the law is least likely to constitute an effective constraint.

There is, within the speech of Lord Bingham at least, the nascent acceptance of the 'undesirability of the duplication of legal powers; [s]pecifically . . . where another power . . . is more precisely defined than the breach of the peace power, then there is no need for the latter power to remain available'.[184] Nonetheless, we should not overestimate what Lord Bingham says. In Fenwick's view, had the decision gone the other way, this would 'have continued to render much of the Public Order Act 1986, as amended, effectively redundant, since it would continue to be unnecessary in most circumstances to rely on sections 12 and 14'.[185] She continues:

---

[182] *Öllinger*, above n 171, and *Chorherr*, above n 177, both discussed by Mead above n 171.
[183] Ashworth, above n 120, 578. As he points out, Lord Rodger ([2006] UKHL 55 at [71]) might have been disposed to accept the police view had it been that a breach *was* imminent.
[184] Stone, above n 51. Stone provides a range of statutory powers that could fill the gap were breach of the peace abolished, such as the various offences under ss 4–5 of the POA 1986. Given the range of other—usually statutory offences—might it not be possible to argue that it is never (or only rarely) 'necessary [in a democratic society]' to arrest or take action where breach of the peace at common law is the underpinning concept?
[185] Fenwick, *Civil Liberties*, above n 36, 762.

the statutory scheme is still highly likely to be marginalised. If a large group of protesters appears to the police to contain some unruly or aggressive or potentially aggressive elements, the police appear post-*Laporte* to retain very broad powers to intervene.[186]

The problem is not solely the one she portrays—a large group infiltrated by a potentially violent cadre—but also this. The statutory scheme can still be marginalised, since sections 12 and 14 are only triggered where the police reasonably believe that '*serious*' public disorder, damage to property or disruption to the life of the community may result.[187] The power at common law by which the police may take action to prevent breaches of the peace—even with the uniform imminence test—is dependent on the *Howell* formula being made out. That does not qualify the harm or damage. All that is needed is harm 'actually [to be] done or is likely to be done to a person or in his presence to his property'.[188] The problem is not whether the test should be 'imminence' or 'reasonableness'—though clearly the latter greatly enables police action—but becomes one of transposing the common law power from domestic disputes and post-pub scuffles into the public arena of peaceful protest without the need for the police to show any measure of likely harm. The fact that, under Article 11 as was accepted in *Laporte*, the police can only act proportionately—as well as reasonably—provides only a partial counter to this. The statutory scheme is also 'more precise, more detailed and more complex; it appears to present the police with a greater challenge in terms of defending their actions at a later point'.[189]

Our last point is this. The case sends out a strong message to the police that officers should properly police protests, giving full recognition to the rights of protesters to be present and to the public role such protests can play. The police should have in place (assuming of course that they are aware) proper and full plans both to avoid and to cater for trouble and should not make mass arrests away from the scene, either because they have failed to plan properly or because it is just simpler, less fraught or more (cost) effective. They should also be responsive to and flexible in the face of developments as the protest takes shape and comes to fruition. The proper police response to the threat of trouble or violence presenting itself is either to arrest—where it can be said there is an imminent threat of a breach of the peace—or divert protesters away, again where the threat is imminent. Where it is not, the police should allow protesters to proceed and then arrest (or divert) at the site only those who present an immediate threat and only then when they do so.[190]

---

[186] *ibid*, 763.
[187] It is the last of these three—disruption to the life of the community—that, as Fenwick notes (*ibid*, 754), means the statutory power can be utilised on wider grounds than for breach of the peace. However, despite the minimum number of participants for the police to be able to impose conditions on a static assembly being reduced in 2003 from 20 to two, for a static trespassory assembly to be banned (under s 14A) there still needs to be 20 or more people: see s 14A(9). Common law powers to take action to prevent breaches of the peace can be triggered by any number and, given the scope of the common law power, could extend to what would in effect be a ban by ordering mass dispersal of a meeting, as occurred in *O'Kelly v Harvey*, above n 123.
[188] *Howell*, above n 45, 427.
[189] Fenwick, *Civil Liberties*, above n 36, 755.
[190] To some extent the Court's holding in *McBride v United Kingdom* (App 27786/95) ECtHR 5 July 2001 gainsays this. There the Court declared inadmissible an application from M who had been arrested to prevent a breach of the peace. M had been walking on what she alleged was the public highway (there was some dispute on this) en route from an anti-arms trade demonstration towards an arms fair, some 10–15 minutes distant. Domestic proceedings were brought (*cf* the 3rd–5th applicants in *Steel v UK* (1998) 28 EHRR 603). The Strasbourg Court held, in light of the English court's findings that the police had reasonable cause and that there was a very real, high risk of violence at the arms fair, that it was not disproportionate to arrest M, to 'remove from the scene of the demonstration' and detain her for about 90 minutes (p 6 of the decision).

(ii) Austin

A matter discussed obiter in *Laporte* in some of the speeches but ultimately left unresolved was what action, if any, the police could lawfully take against third parties where it was known that not all were—or even could be—troublemakers, or even causing or provoking trouble. In *Austin v Commissioner of the Police for the Metropolis*, the House of Lords was asked to decide that question head-on, albeit framed under Article 5(1) of the ECHR rather than at common law.[191]

(a) Background and Overview

The case arose from a challenge by two people detained within a police cordon for about seven hours at Oxford Circus during the anti-capitalism disorder in central London on May Day 2001. The endorsement of the technique, known colloquially as 'kettling', by the House early in 2009 led to it being used a few months later as part of the strategy for containing and dealing with the protesters in the City of London at the G20 summit. It was during this operation that an innocent by-stander, returning home from work, was assaulted by an officer and died from a heart attack moments later. This, at the time of writing, is the subject of an independent police investigation.

Austin breaks new ground domestically and, as interpretation of the ECHR, internationally. As Lord Hope pointed out, the Strasbourg Court has not had to address attempts by states to exert control over a potentially disorderly and dangerous crowd in the context of Article 5(1).[192] In short, their Lordships formulated a new test for deprivation of liberty based on the underlying motive and intention of the person doing the detaining. I have analysed the case in some detail elsewhere; what follows provides a distilled overview.[193]

(b) Facts

About 3,000 people were held within a 2,000 square-metre cordon on May Day 2001. The police had information that a mass rally against capitalism and globalisation was planned for later that afternoon at Oxford Circus. Quite violent disorder took place in other parts of the capital as it had over the past two years at demonstrations in London. Deliberately, the organisers had given no advance notice and had not co-operated with the police. Just after 2 o'clock, officers began to pen people in—irrespective of any outward signs or propensity to demonstrate—by refusing to allow the vast majority to leave. It was an on-the-spot response to the arrival, on the hour, of considerable numbers of people, taking the police by surprise. Ultimately, many were forced to remain until the evening in conditions which rather speedily and obviously became fairly intolerable. It was accepted at trial that the cordon was only established as crowd-control measure, to facilitate a controlled dispersal from the area, over what was initially hoped to be a two-hour period, when it was safe and practical to do so. A few hundred were released within the hour. The delay was due to the behaviour within the cordon of a sizeable minority, who did not co-operate or who became actively hostile and violent towards the police, and a large number outside who did not accept control by the police. Austin was a demonstrator. She continued to make speeches

---

[191] *Austin and another v Commissioner of the Police for the Metropolis* [2009] UKHL 5.
[192] *ibid*, at [23].
[193] D Mead, 'Of kettles, cordons and crowd control—*Austin v Commissioner of Police for the Metropolis* and the meaning of deprivation of liberty' [2009] *EHRLR* 376. See too D Feldman, 'Containment, deprivation of liberty and breach of the peace' (2009) 68 *CLJ* 243.

via a megaphone. She was well aware that the protest was not expected by anyone to end without serious violence even though she remained peaceful throughout. Saxby was in London on business so became embroiled totally innocently. Each presented themselves to an officer but was refused permission to leave. There was no suggestion that either was violent and neither threatened to become so or to breach the peace. It was accepted that Austin and Saxby acted lawfully throughout. They brought test cases claiming damages at common law for false imprisonment and under section 8 of the HRA for deprivation of liberty contrary to Article 5.

(c) Journey Through the Courts

In the High Court, Tugendhat J dedicated over 600 paragraphs to holding first that the claim for false imprisonment was defeated by the defence of necessity, and secondly that the deprivation of liberty was justified under Article 5(1)(c).[194] The Court of Appeal (Sir Anthony Clarke MR giving judgment) founded its decision on two bases. First, preventing a breach of the peace constituted a good defence to the common law claim for false imprisonment (subsuming the defence based on necessity).[195] In exceptional circumstances a police cordon was lawful to contain third parties not themselves threatening an imminent breach of the peace, where no other alternative strategy or action was possible to avoid it.[196] This was the matter discussed obiter by the House of Lords in *Laporte*.[197] Secondly, Article 5(1) was not engaged on the facts either at the outset or any time thereafter.[198] This second basis was the sole ground of appeal to the House of Lords.[199]

On this, the House aligned itself with the Court of Appeal: it disposed of the case simply by holding that Article 5(1) was not engaged. As Lord Hope put it, measures of crowd-control undertaken in the interests of the community will fall outside Article 5 so long as they are not arbitrary: they must be resorted to in good faith, they must be proportionate and they must be enforced for no longer than is reasonably necessary.[200]

---

[194] *Austin* [2005] EWHC 480 (Admin) at [574]–[578] and [512]–[566] respectively. Fenwick, *Civil Liberties*, above n 36, 763–71 contains a detailed summary of the 150-page High Court judgment. Claims under Arts 10 and 11 were rejected (at [598]–[608]) and not pursued on appeal. The right to peaceful protest had not been restricted. Austin was able to continue using her megaphone within the cordon for an hour or so at which time she had planned to leave in any event to collect her baby from the childminders. Thereafter she was in fact detained but 'in fact enjoyed all the opportunities which she wanted to enjoy to exercise her rights of freedom of speech and assembly. She was not prevented in any way from exercising those rights as she wished' ([2005] EWHC 480 (Admin) at [601]).

[195] *Austin* [2007] EWCA Civ 989 at [73]. Although it was only obiter, the Master of the Rolls (at [74]–[84]) did address ss 12–14 of the Public Order Act 1986. He was concerned lest it be thought that the Court of Appeal was reaching the same conclusion as Tugendhat J. We considered some of these aspects in chapter five above pp 189. He also highlighted the desirability that the common law and statutory positions should be reviewed 'to see whether it would be possible to make clear provisions appropriate to cover a case of this kind in the future' (at [84]).

[196] ibid, [2007] EWCA Civ 989 at [56]–[62]. Although this aspect of the Court of Appeal decision was not appealed, the precedent it sets—since it is not inconsistent with the House's later holding—remains strong.

[197] The Master of the Rolls distilled the essence of the obiter dicta of Lord Rodger, Lord Brown and Lord Mance: *Austin* [2007] EWCA Civ 989 at [35]–[36] The relevant extracts from and analysis of the House of Lords' speeches in *Laporte* are to be found at [38]–[42] of the Court of Appeal judgment.

[198] ibid, [2007] EWCA Civ 989 at [102]–[104].

[199] Before the House of Lords, it was accepted by both sides that determining whether the detention was an unlawful deprivation of liberty contrary to Art 5(1) would also resolve whether it was also a lawful exercise of breach of the peace powers at common law: *Austin* [2009] UKHL 5 at [11].

[200] *Austin* [2009] UKHL 5 at [37] though the qualification of the interests of the community is to be found at [34].

(d) Reasoning

That conclusion was described by Lord Neuberger as 'on the face of it, surprising'.[201] What persuaded the House to conclude that being held for seven hours in a police cordon without food or water, without shelter or suitable clothing on a wet, windy day unable to leave even though, of most members individually, there was no suspicion that that they themselves had done anything wrong, was not in fact a deprivation of liberty? Although the House made reference to standard Article 5 cases on the nature of 'deprivation'—such as *Guzzardi*[202] or *Engel*[203]—its novelty is not in applying that test to a new scenario but reinterpreting the test so as to hold that what was truly determinative is the purpose or motive behind the cordon.[204] Account must be taken not just of the standard factors (duration, type, nature, effects and manner of implementation), to see if the threshold between depriving of liberty and restricting movement has been crossed, but also the intentions of the police in implementing the strategy.[205]

In Lord Hope's mind, without a binding European view on the matter,[206] reading certain Strasbourg cases[207] what pervades the whole ECHR—not just those articles obviously subject to qualification such as the rights in Articles 8 to 11—is the notion of balance and proportionality.[208] Thus it was open to take a more textured and contextualised approach to Article 5, in which motive and purpose were key factors.

> I would hold therefore that there is room, even in the case of fundamental rights as to whose application no restriction or limitation is permitted by the Convention, for a pragmatic approach to be taken which takes full account of all the circumstances . . . But the importance that must be attached in the context of article 5 to measures taken in the interests of public safety is indicated by article 2 of the Convention, as the lives of persons affected by mob violence may be at risk if measures of crowd control cannot be adopted by the police. This is a situation where a search for a fair balance is necessary if these competing fundamental rights are to be reconciled with each other. The ambit that is given to article 5 as to measures of crowd control must, of course, take account of the rights of the individual as well as the interests of the community. So any steps that are taken must be resorted to in good faith and must be proportionate to the situation which has made the measures necessary. This is essential to preserve the fundamental principle that anything that is done which affects a person's right to liberty must not be arbitrary. If these requirements are met however it will be proper to conclude that measures of crowd control that are undertaken in the interests of the community will not infringe the article 5 rights of individual members of the crowd whose freedom of movement is restricted by them.[209]

---

[201] *ibid*, at [51].
[202] *Guzzardi v Italy* (1981) 3 EHRR 333 at [92]–[95].
[203] *Engel v Netherlands* (1979–80) 1 EHRR 647 at [56]–[59].
[204] See also *Austin* [2007] EWCA Civ 989 at [98]–[99] and [103]–[104].
[205] *Austin* [2009] UKHL 5: see Lord Scott at [39], Lord Walker at [47] and Lord Neuberger at [54] and [63].
[206] Thus there is no role for s 2 of the HRA to play *strictu sensu* so no 'mirror principle' and nothing to depart from.
[207] Such as *O'Halloran and Francis v United Kingdom* (2007) 46 EHRR 397; *Soering v United Kingdom* (1989) 11 EHRR 439; and *N v United Kingdom* (2008) 47 EHRR 885. Their relevance is discussed below.
[208] *Austin* [2009] UKHL 5 at [27]. See too Lord Neuberger at [55]. The Court of Appeal too was greatly influenced by the infusion of proportionality into Art 5: see *Austin* [2007] EWCA Civ 989 at [93]–[94] and [106].
[209] *Austin* [2009] UKHL 5 at [34]. When he uses the word 'infringe' Lord Hope must be taken as meaning 'engage': see [37] where he adds a further fourth qualification (to the lack of arbitrariness and the need for both good faith and proportionality) that crowd control measures should not be enforced any longer than necessary. This must be implicit in their proportionality. See also Lord Neuberger at [60]: 'In [a case such as the instant one] it seems to me unrealistic to contend that article 5 can come into play at all, provided, and it is a very important proviso, that the actions of the police are proportionate and reasonable, and any confinement is restricted to a reasonable minimum, as to discomfort and as to time, as is necessary for the relevant purpose, namely the prevention of serious public disorder and violence'.

What swayed both the House of Lords and the Court of Appeal was the fact that the situation was indistinguishable, in their view, from cases where football fans were detained outside a stadium to avoid crowd violence or motorists on motorways were detained after a crash blocked the road.[210] In their view, no one would consider these to be deprivations of liberty.

(e) Analysis

The case is open to considerable criticism on several fronts, notably at a doctrinal and policy-level. Perhaps most strange is the analysis provided by Lord Walker. In the first few paragraphs of his speech, he referred to Lord Hope's 'very guarded' conclusion on the matter, and indicated his own preference for caution. He then demonstrated that cases such as *Engel* and *Guzzardi* do not list 'purpose' as a relevant factor, something more generally relevant to determining whether a deprivation of liberty is protected under Article 5(1)(a)–(f).[211] But, without further reasoning or explanation, he nonetheless felt able to conclude that it was essential to pose this simple question:

> [W]hat were the police doing at Oxford Circus on 1 May 2001? What were they about? . . . They were engaged in an unusually difficult exercise in crowd control, in order to avoid personal injuries and damage to property . . . The aim of the police was to disperse the crowd, and the fact that the achievement of that aim took much longer than they expected was due to circumstances beyond their control.[212]

1. Doctrinal divergence? Let us consider the doctrinal point. Both premises that underpin the judgment—that proportionality could and should play a role in deprivation of liberty cases, and the idea that motive and purpose were significant in determining whether or not Article 5(1) was even engaged—do not accord with the view the Strasbourg Court is likely to take, based on precedent, when Ms Austin's application reaches it.[213] First, in none of the leading non-paradigmatic (that is non-incarceration) Article 5 cases has such an approach been adopted or even contemplated by the Strasbourg Court.[214] None of the eclectic, almost random cases selected by Lord Hope—*Soering v UK*,[215] *N v UK*[216] and *O'Halloran v UK*—is an Article 5 case. In none of the works on the ECHR is there any discussion of the European Court taking an approach to 'deprivation of liberty' premised on balance.[217] It has played a role, quite properly, in Article 5 cases but at the stage when the

---

[210] *Austin* [2009] UKHL 5, Lord Hope at [23] and Lord Neuberger at [58]. He added to this mix the example of a deranged or drunk gunman on the loose in a building. What is more worrying is the self-serving reasoning he employs at [64]: the unlikelihood of the cordon being protected by Arts 5(1)(b) and (c) supported a conclusion that the cordon was outwith Art 5(1) in the first place.

[211] *ibid*, [2009] UKHL 5 at [43]–[44]. He also doubted the continued relevance of some other key Article5 cases such as *Nielsen v Denmark* (1988) 11 EHRR 175 and *X v Germany* (1981) 24 DR 158.

[212] *Austin* [2009] UKHL 5 at [47]. It is hard to know what 'further remarks' of his Lord Hope earlier said (at [38]) he endorsed.

[213] There is greater discussion of all these points in Mead above n 193

[214] See *Guzzardi*, above n 202; *Amuur v France* (1993) 22 EHRR 533 [37]–[49]; *HL v United Kingdom* (2005) 40 EHRR 32 at [89]–[94]; and *Engel* above n 203.

[215] *Soering*, above n 207, at [89]

[216] *N v UK*, above n 207, at [44].

[217] That view is borne out by consideration of the relevant chapter in P Van Dijk, F von Hoof, A van Rijn and L Zwaak (eds), *The Theory and Practice of the European Convention on Human Rights*, 6th edn (Antwerp, Intersentia, 2006) and of Harris, O'Boyle and Warbrick, *The Law of the European Convention on Human Rights* (Oxford, Oxford University Press, 2009) 123–9, of Clayton and Tomlinson, *The Law of Human Rights* (Oxford, Oxford University Press, 2001) paras 10.80–10.89 and of J Murdoch, *Article 5 of the European Convention on*

'lawfulness' (that is, the arbitrariness) of any deprivation is being assessed in terms of the limitations under Article 5(1)(a)–(f). Here the Court is assessing alternatives—have 'less severe measures been considered and found to be insufficient to safeguard the individual or public interest which might require a person be detained'?[218]—and is thus acting as a brake on states, not as a facilitator as the decision in *Austin* portends.

The decision is also out of line with domestic Article 5 cases, such as those decided in the context of control orders, *JJ*, *MB* or *EE*.[219] In none of these or in *Gillan*[220] did the House of Lords approach the question as one of balance. It is instructive that Lord Hoffman, one of two dissentient voices in *JJ*, is the only member of the House of Lords also cited in the speeches in *Austin*, and then from those two or three passages that discuss the prison/incarceration paradigm.[221] There is in fact some support for a conclusion at odds with what was decided in *Austin* in his words elsewhere in *JJ*,[222] as well as in those of Baroness Hale[223] and Lord Bingham in *Gillan*.[224] Quite why the House seems to have rejected its own well-chosen words expressed on two separate occasions not long before is not made at all clear.

Secondly, on closer inspection several of the cases—*X v FRG*,[225] *Guenat v Switzerland*,[226] *Nielsen v Denmark*,[227] *HM v Switzerland*[228]—cited as authority for the assertion that motive and purpose should play a role in determining whether a deprivation of liberty had taken place do not offer unmitigated support. In Lord Walker's view, it was clear from *Saadi v UK*[229] that 'the state of mind of the person responsible for the alleged detention can be a relevant factor in deciding whether Article 5 has been infringed'.[230] There the Grand Chamber held that short-term detention pending fast-track asylum/immigration assessment was not unlawful under Article 5(1)(f). However, closer reading of the relevant

---

Human Rights—The Protection of Liberty and Security of the Person Human Rights Files No 12 (revised) (Strasbourg, Council of Europe Publishing, 2002). In none of these is there any discussion of the Court at Strasbourg taking an approach premised on 'balance' either to 'deprivation of liberty' or to the various permitted restrictions under Art 5(1)(a)–(f). The closest that we come is the assertion by Clayton and Tomlinson (at 10.93) that the application of the prohibition on arbitrariness in Art 5(1)—see for an example *Loukanov v Bulgaria* (1997) 24 EHRR 12 at [41]— is similar to assessing whether the limitations on Articles 8–11 are necessary in a democratic society. This in turn is taken from J Murdoch, 'Safeguarding the liberty of the person: recent Strasbourg jurisprudence' (1993) 42 *International Comparative Law Quarterly* 494, 499. Closer inspection of this and of the case-law reveals that arbitrariness—presumed in the word 'lawful' in each of Art 5(1)(a)–(f)—means that the law should not be misused for improper purposes, or be driven by bad faith or be an abuse of power outside the purposes of Art 5: *Bozano v France* (1987) 9 EHRR 297.

[218] *Witold Litwa v Poland* (2001) 33 EHRR 1267 at [78]. van Dijk and van Hoof, above n 217, 470 indicate that in their view Art 5(1)(b) does include a balance between the importance in a democratic society of securing immediate fulfilment of an obligation and the importance of the right to liberty.

[219] *R (JJ) v Secretary of State for the Home Department (SSHD)* [2007] UKHL 45; *R (MB) v SSHD* [2007] UKHL 46; and *R (EE) v SSHD* [2007] UKHL 47.

[220] *Gillan* [2006] UKHL 12 at [21]–[26] (Lord Bingham), at [38] (Lord Hope), at [58] (Lord Scott), at [70] (Lord Walker) and at [71] (Lord Brown).

[221] The relevant passages in *JJ* are [35]–[37], referred to by Lord Hope in *Austin* [2009] UKHL 5 at [16], [20] and [29] and by Lord Neuberger at [5] and [52].

[222] *JJ*, above n 219, at [42]. His dissent, like Lord Carswell's, was premised on rejecting the approach of the majority, favouring as it did a comparison with the detainee's normal life and an assessment of the measures in question on someone in the position of the particular detainee.

[223] *JJ*, above n 219, at [57].

[224] *Gillan*, above n 220, at [25].

[225] *X v Federal Republic of Germany* (1981) 24 DR 158.

[226] *Guenat v Switzerland* (App 24722/94) EComHR admissibility decision 10 April 1995.

[227] *Nielsen v Denmark* (1998) 11 EHRR 175.

[228] (2002) 38 EHRR 314.

[229] *Saadi v United Kingdom* (2008) 48 EHRR 17 (Grand Chamber).

[230] *Austin* [2009] UKHL 5 at [54] referring to *Saadi*, above n 229, at [69]: detention even if complying with national law could be contrary to Article 5 if there had been 'an element of bad faith or deception'.

passage shows that this does not go to whether or not Article 5 is engaged at all—the issue in *Austin*—but to whether the deprivation was lawful; that is, whether it was arbitrary.

Last, the decision is even more questionable in that it seems to disregard the principle established in *Gough v CC Derbyshire*: that restrictions on rights must only be imposed after giving *individual* consideration to each person affected, and thus tailored to their threat.[231] Blanket decisions—here, where there was no specific danger or worry—are susceptible to challenge. Of course, *Gough* arose in the context of a public law proportionality challenge in judicial review—under a qualified right—not, as *Austin* was, a challenge founded on tort and private law, albeit tinged with publicness in the shape of Article 5. It is somewhat of an irony that a judgment which rests on the novel transmutation of proportionality into a determining factor in the ambit of Article 5 seems to ignore this key element in the notion of what it means to balance rights and interests.

2. Conceptual coherence? At a conceptual level, the comparisons with football crowds and motorway crashes seem to support the conclusion reached: our initial thought is probably that being kept behind after a game—for one's own and others' safety—and being held up on a motorway by the police after an accident would not fall into the same category. But if we unpack it a little we can see a different truth. If only one person were held in those same conditions for seven hours, are we really saying that would not be a deprivation of liberty? Austin could only move in a small, cramped space. She could not hope to break out without being arrested for obstruction or to prevent a breach of the peace. In lay terms, as Jim Murdoch put it, she 'lost control over [her] liberty'.[232] If Article 5(1) has as its underlying purpose the protection of citizens from 'arbitrary or unjustified deprivations of liberty'[233] by the state, what better example of it in action? Why should it make any difference that it is done en masse? If anything that makes it worse.

Justifying detentions and arrests by reference to Article 5(1)(a)–(f) and the effects generally on individuals will be defined out by earlier considerations of state of mind; what I have referred to as 'ill-defined public welfare benevolence'.[234] We are edging towards a concept of 'illegal gathering', dealing with protesters en masse based on suspicion about a handful. The police are able to call upon collective guilt by association: they need not assess the specific threat posed by individuals provided the group contains possible troublemakers whom they cannot isolate and deal with separately.[235]

---

[231] *Gough v Chief Constable of Derbyshire Police* [2002] EWCA Civ 351 at [68].

[232] Murdoch, above n 217, 499.

[233] *McKay v UK* (2006) 44 EHRR 827 at [30]. This it must be said does not answer whether Art 5(1) is engaged—the Court was referring to Art 5 as a whole.

[234] Mead, above n 193, 393.

[235] This point was developed by the JCHR in its G20 policing follow-up report to *Demonstrating respect for rights*, paras 17–30 (22nd report of session 2008–09) available at: www.publications.parliament.uk/pa/jt200809/jtselect/jtrights/141/14102.htm, accessed 17 August 2009. At para 28, it set out its view: 'containment can be a useful and lawful tactic in some circumstances but it must be used in a proportionate manner with due regard to the human rights of the people contained. This requires the police's careful consideration in advance and during the protest of whether the tactic overall remains necessary and proportionate. It also requires individual officers policing the perimeter of the contained area to consider whether, in an individual case, it is appropriate to maintain that cordon for that individual, given his or her particular circumstances. It is this second aspect of containment—respecting the rights of individuals being contained—which we consider that the Metropolitan Police did not give sufficient weight to during the G20 protests. In our view, it would be a disproportionate and unlawful response to cordon a group of people and operate a blanket ban on individuals leaving the contained area, as this fails to consider whether individual circumstances require a different response'.

(f) *Austin*—the aftermath

Lois Austin lodged an application at Strasbourg in July 2009.[236] Her case will probably be heard sometime in 2010 or 2011 by the European Court. Interim, it seems inevitable that further challenges will be taken before the domestic courts if for no other reason than to clarify some crucial aspects of the Lords' judgment.[237] *Austin* seems to have been taken or perceived by the police to sanction a much wider use of the controversial tactic of kettling, almost a use per se, at the G20 protests in the City of London in April 2009.

The first question is thus 'the extent to which the police were correct to view *Austin* as authorising 'kettling' as a legitimate pre-meditated tactic [at the G20 protests] rather than a spontaneous response'.[238] The second question is linked. What exactly is the ratio of *Austin*, and specifically how fact-specific is it? Lord Hope was clear: kettling as a crowd-control measure can only be (but presumably is not always) lawful if it is not arbitrary. It must be resorted to in good faith, must be proportionate and must be enforced for no longer than is reasonably necessary.[239] However, his speech does not provide the only criteria by which lawfulness can be measured. Lord Neuberger was very clear about the fact-sensitive nature of the claim.[240] There are question marks over the decisive quality of the eight factors listed by him and the extent to which they were adopted by the remainder of the court as part of the ratio. Much of the evidence and discussion by the Joint Committee on Human Rights (JCHR) in its follow-up report seems to revolve around the criteria iterated by Lord Neuberger, rather than Lord Hope's more general ones—although there is a good deal of overlap. Lord Neuberger was prepared to hold the imposition of the cordon lawful, that is outside Article 5, and thus not even a deprivation of liberty where, as was the case,

(i) It was imposed purely for crowd control purposes, to protect people and property from injury;
(ii) It was necessary as many of the demonstrators were bent on violence and impeding the police, and its imposition was in no way attributable to policing failures;
(iii) The purpose and reason for imposing it were at all times plain to those constrained within it;
(iv) It lasted for as short a time as possible; during its imposition, the police attempted to raise it on a number of occasions, but decided that it was impractical;
(v) The inclusion of the appellant and the demonstrators constrained with her within it was unavoidable;
(vi) Those who were not demonstrators, or were seriously affected by being confined, were promptly permitted to leave;
(vii) Although the appellant suffered some discomfort, it was limited, and the police could not have alleviated it; further, she could move around within the cordon; and
(viii) The appellant knew in advance that many of the demonstrators intended to cause violence, and that the police were concerned about this.

---

[236] 'Metropolitan police's 'kettling' tactic challenged in European Court', *The Guardian*, 20 July 2009. A second protester caught up in the 2001 cordon as he made his way to a bookshop is also bringing a challenge.
[237] The same piece reported that a challenge from those caught up in Bishopsgate at the G20 protests is being lodged.
[238] Mead, above n 193, 394.
[239] *Austin* [2009] UKHL 5 at [37].
[240] ibid at [57].

356 *Preventive Action by the Police*

Clearly, *Austin* does not give the police carte blanche to kettle and to cordon at the slightest sign of trouble during or even before a protest, but where the police do, will it only be lawful if all of his eight factors are complied with?[241] Underlying many of the speeches is the more nebulous concept of 'crowd control'. Is this an independent criterion or umbrella? Is it even a test or criteria at all or merely shorthand?

F. Binding Over to Prevent Breaches of the Peace

The fourth and last aspect of breach of the peace we shall consider is the power to bind someone over to keep the peace—a power often linked with a power to bind over to be of good behaviour. We shall look at both together.[242]

(i) The Origins and Source of the Power

Magistrates have powers to bind over under section 115 of the Magistrates' Courts Act 1980, under common law and under the Justices of the Peace Act 1361.[243] A binding over order requires the person bound over to enter into what is called a recognizance. This is an undertaking, secured by a sum of money fixed by the court, to keep the peace or be of good behaviour for a specified period of time. If the protester refuses to consent to the order the court may commit him or her to prison, for up to six months in the case of an order made under the 1980 Act or for an unlimited period in respect of orders made under the 1361 Act or common law. If an order is made but breached within the specified time period, the person bound over forfeits the sum of the recognizance.

The difference between the power in the 1980 Act on one hand, and on the other those at common law and under the 1361 Act, lies mainly in by whom and how the process is initiated. At common law and under the Act of 1361, magistrates have the power, at any stage in proceedings before them, to bind over any participant in the proceedings (for example, a witness, an acquitted defendant or a defendant who has not yet been acquitted or convicted), if they consider that the conduct of the person concerned is such that there might be a breach of the peace or that his or her behaviour has been *contra bonos mores*.[244]

Under section 115 of the 1980 Act the process is usually begun by a police officer laying a formal complaint. Before the magistrates can make an order, they must be satisfied, on the basis of admissible evidence, that first the defendant's conduct caused a breach of the peace

---

[241] The Metropolitan Police for example do not accept that Lord Neuberger's eight criteria are the measure by which the legality of any future kettling can be judged. Stressing the fact that at [56] Lord Neuberger himself indicated that determining whether or not a deprivation of liberty had occurred 'a fact sensitive question', AC Chris Allison wrote to the chair of the JCHR during the course of its follow-up inquiry into protest as follows. 'The MPS legal position is that we do not accept that this is what paragraph 57 of the judgment says. It does not provide any sort of measure against which future public order containments can be tested . . . Far from being put forward by Lord Neuberger as comprising any sort of objective test for judging the legality of a police containment, he was setting them out as being a summary of the most significant considerations *in Ms Austin's case*': see *Demonstrating respect for rights: follow-up* (22nd report of session 2008/9, 28 July 2009), at: www.publications.parliament.uk/pa/jt200809/jtselect/jtrights/141/141.pdf Ev 50 (accessed 13 August 2009).

[242] Much of what follows by way of legal background is taken from the ECtHR decision in *Steel v UK* (1998) 28 EHRR 603 at [31]–[37]. See generally K Kerrigan, 'Breach of the Peace and Binding Over—Continuing Confusion' (1997) 2 J Civ Lib 30.

[243] For details of procedure, readers should refer to Law Commission Report No 222, *Binding Over* (February 1994).

[244] This is defined as 'conduct which has the property of being wrong rather than right in the judgment of the vast majority of contemporary fellow citizens' *Hughes v Holley* (1988) 86 Cr App R 130 (Glidewell LJ).

or was likely to cause one[245] and secondly unless the order is made, there is a real risk that the defendant will cause a further breach of the peace in the future. Although a binding over order is not a criminal conviction,[246] these proceedings have been described as analogous to criminal proceedings. In the past it was unclear whether the court should apply the criminal or the civil standard of proof when deciding whether facts exist which warrant a binding over. In *Nicol v DPP*, Simon Brown LJ stated that it was 'common ground that, although no criminal conviction results from finding such a complaint proved, the criminal standard of proof applies to the procedure'.[247] A fairly standard sequence of events is for a protest to be taking place, for those using or threatening violence or damage (or provoking others to do so) to be arrested if the threat to the peace is (now after *Laporte*) thought to be imminent, and for the police formally to bring them before the magistrates by laying a section 115 complaint for them then to be bound over.

(ii) Steel v UK

Some clarification of the domestic position was provided by Strasbourg in *Steel v UK*.[248]

(a) Background

The proceedings involved three different sets of protesters. The first applicant was arrested for breach of the peace after she attempted to obstruct a grouse-shoot by walking in front of one member of the shoot as he lifted his gun. She was detained for 44 hours before being released on conditional bail. She was charged with breach of the peace and using threatening words or behaviour, contrary to section 5 of the POA 1986. She was convicted of the section 5 offence and for breaching the peace. On appeal, the Crown Court upheld the convictions and ordered her to be bound over for 12 months in the sum of £100. She refused to be bound over and was committed to prison for 28 days. The second applicant took part in a protest against the building of an extension of a motorway. The protesters repeatedly broke into the construction site. The second applicant was arrested whilst standing under a digger, for conduct likely to provoke a disturbance of the peace. She was detained for approximately 17 hours. Magistrates found the allegation of conduct likely to cause a breach of the peace to have been made out. She was ordered to be bound over for a year to keep the peace in the sum of £100. She refused and was imprisoned for seven days.

The third, fourth and fifth applicants attended a 'Fighter Helicopter II' conference in order to protest with three others against the sale of fighter helicopters. They handed out leaflets and held up banners saying 'Work for peace not war'. The three were arrested, taken to a police station and detained for acting in breach of the peace. After seven hours they were taken before the magistrates, who adjourned through lack of time. The applicants were released and when proceedings were resumed a month later the prosecution called no evidence and the magistrates dismissed the case. All five brought various challenges before the Strasbourg Court, largely based on Article 5(1), Article 6 and Articles 10–11.[249] The first

---

[245] *R v Morpeth Ward Justices Ex parte Ward* (1992) 95 Cr App R 215.
[246] *R v London Quarter Sessions Ex parte Metropolitan Police Commissioner* [1940] 1 KB 670.
[247] *Nicol v DPP* (1996) 160 JP 155. As the EComHR pointed out in *Steel* above n 242 at [70], Article 6(2) of the Convention does not, however, lay down any specific rights in relation to the standard or burden of proof: *Salabiaku v France* (1991) 13 EHRR 379 at [26]–[30].
[248] *Steel v UK*, above n 242. The case is discussed by K Kerrigan (1999) 4 J Civ Lib 129.
[249] Some—such as Arts 5(3), 6(2) and 6(3)(b) and (c)—were raised before the Commission but were never pursued before the Court.

two applicants complained under Article 5(1) in respect of both their initial arrest and detention—as did the 3rd to 5th applicants—and their subsequent detention for refusing to be bound over.

(b) The European Court's Findings

Though it may not be considered a criminal offence in domestic law, for the purposes of the ECHR 'breach of the peace' is.[250] As the Court explained,

> the duty to keep the peace is in the nature of a public duty; the police have powers to arrest any person who has breached the peace or whom they reasonably fear will breach the peace; and the magistrates may commit to prison any person who refuses to be bound over not to breach the peace where there is evidence beyond reasonable doubt that his or her conduct caused or was likely to cause a breach of the peace and that he or she would otherwise cause a breach of the peace in the future.[251]

Those arrested for actual or threatened breaches are therefore entitled to the presumption of innocence in Article 6(2) as well as the additional procedural rights in Article 6(3).[252] It also means that those arrested for breach of the peace so as to be bound over under section 115 are deprived of their liberty but that their arrest potentially falls within Article 5(1)(c).[253] Whether or not it does so will depend on the arrest being 'lawful'. This—as the Court decided in *Steel* itself—evokes the same lack of arbitrariness found in the 'prescribed by law' test under Articles 8(2)–11(2). As we saw at the start of this chapter, the Court decided the offence in English law was—or had been—sufficiently clearly defined as to provide the requisite degree of certainty. The Court held that the initial arrests of the first two applicants were lawful under Article 5(1): there was no reason to consider their arrests and detentions as arbitrary or to doubt the reasonableness of the police view that if allowed to continue, their behaviour might provoke others to violence. However, in the absence of any national court ruling for the 3rd to 5th applicants, the three anti-war protesters (since the cases against all three were dismissed), the ECtHR felt able to exert a more stringent review. Here the Court concluded there was a violation of Article 5(1):

> Having itself considered the evidence available to it relating to the arrests of these three applicants, the Court sees no reason to regard their protest as other than entirely peaceful. It does not find any indication that they significantly obstructed or attempted to obstruct those attending the conference, or took any other action likely to provoke these others to violence. Indeed it would not appear that there was anything in their behaviour which could have justified the police in fearing that a breach of the peace was likely to be caused. For this reason, in the absence of any national decision on the question, the Court is not satisfied that their arrests and subsequent detention for seven

---

[250] *Steel* (1998) 28 EHRR 603 at [49] and [86].
[251] ibid, at [48].
[252] ibid, at [84]–[87]. The Art 6(2) point was not taken before the Court but discussion of it can be found in the Commission Opinion at [63]–[72].
[253] ibid, at [50]. If protesters are arrested for breach of the peace when there is no intention of bringing them before magistrates to be bound over or prosecuted for a more specific public order offence, but purely to remove them from a site of conflict, Art 5(1)(c) will not be satisfied. As Reid and Nicolson mention, above n 51, 771, there was considerable criticism during the 1984 miners' strike that the police used arrests followed by a binding over to have (or even merely to seek) stringent bail restrictions imposed on picketing. Though they do not mention it, the case is *R v Mansfield JJ ex parte Sharkey* [1985] 1 All ER 193 (DC). There is credible evidence that in recent protests too the police have been imposing very restrictive conditions that interfere with the right of peaceful protest—as part of police bail rather than as part of a binding over process: 'Lawyers to fight bail conditions that 'stifle' climate protests': *The Guardian*, 3 May 2009. Conditions imposed on four protesters who glued themselves to a statue inside the House of Commons included being prevented from going within 1km of Parliament.

hours complied with English law so as to be 'lawful' within the meaning of Article 5(1). It follows that there has been a violation of Article 5(1) in respect of the third, fourth and fifth applicants.[254]

The detentions of the two who refused to be bound over fell to be decided under Article 5(1)(b), non-compliance with an order of the court.[255] As to the lawfulness, in Convention terms, the applicants had argued that it was unclear, first, what conduct could trigger an order to be bound over to keep the peace and be of good behaviour and, secondly, what conduct would amount to a breach of such an order; the expression *contra bonos mores* in particular was very vague. In addition, there was no limit to the possible duration of an order, the amount of the recognizance or, under the common law, the length of detention following refusal to enter into an order.[256] Here the Court was satisfied that the binding over orders applied to the applicants were specific enough properly to be described as a 'lawful order of a court'. Although the orders were expressed in rather vague and general terms and the expression 'to be of good behaviour' was particularly imprecise and offered little guidance as to the type of conduct which would amount to a breach of the order, in each case the binding over order was imposed after a finding that she had committed a breach of the peace. Having considered all the circumstances, the Court was satisfied that, given the context, it was sufficiently clear that the applicants were being requested to agree to refrain from causing further, similar, breaches of the peace during the ensuing 12 months.[257]

The last issue the Court had to assess was whether or not there had been a violation of the right to peaceful protest under Articles 10–11.[258] As we saw in chapter three, in respect of the first two applicants, the Court rejected the Government's argument that Article 10 was not engaged by the form their protests took: physical impedance could still constitute expressions of opinion within Article 10. The earlier finding that the arrest of the 3rd to 5th applicants was not 'lawful' under Article 5(1), as not being prescribed by law, meant that there was a violation in their three cases. The measures were also, in the Court's view, disproportionate for the same reasons as it considered the arrests were not lawful.[259] For the first two applicants, the Court considered that the initial arrests and detention—and subsequent detentions—were capable of achieving the legitimate aims of preventing disorder, protecting the rights of others and upholding the authority of the judiciary. The first two applicants sought to argue that all the measures were disproportionate: in the context of non-violent protest activity, arrest was too extreme a measure since it totally extinguished the possibility further to participate in the demonstration and since the threat of arrest had a 'chilling' effect on the exercise of Article 10 rights. Secondly, they pointed out that they had each been detained for a long period of time when other less restrictive measures could have been used. Last, their freedom to protest would have been unreasonably restricted had they agreed to the vague and general terms of the binding over orders, and they had been imprisoned for long periods of time as a result of their refusal to accept these restrictions.

The Court, as is usual, did not engage a great deal with nor become overly troubled by the question of proportionality other than largely to rehearse the facts and conclude. In

---

[254] *Steel*, above n 250, at [64]–[65].
[255] ibid, at [70].
[256] ibid, at [72]
[257] ibid, at [75]–[76].
[258] No separate issues were raised under Art 11 (*ibid*, at [113]). There was on the facts no violation of Art 5(5) or of Art 6(3)(a): (at [82]–[83] and [87]).
[259] ibid, at [110] referring to its reasoning at [64], set out in the text to n 254 above.

respect of the first applicant's initial arrest and detention it merely noted the dangers inherent in the applicant's particular form of protest activity; the risk of disorder arising from the persistent obstruction by the demonstrators of the members of the grouse-shoot as they attempted to carry out their lawful pastime; and the risk of an early resumption by her, if released, of her protest against field sports, and the possible consequences of this eventuality. All of these latter issues the police were best placed to assess.[260] 28 days' detention for refusing to be bound over was also proportionate, given her earlier activities and the importance in a democratic society of maintaining the rule of law and the authority of the judiciary.[261] The second applicant troubled the Court even less in terms of reasoning.[262]

(c) Assessment

What does the case tell us? First, that Strasbourg is prepared to take a more flexible approach to, and to provide a more inclusive definition of, protest than purely marches, demonstrations and vigils. It was quite a leap to extend protection for the right of peaceful protest to encompass direct action protest of an obstructive type perpetrated by the 1st and 2nd applicants. Secondly, affirmation that the binding over process was criminal proceedings under the autonomous interpretation of 'offence' means too that important procedural protections should in future be offered to those before English courts, not the least of which ought to be a right to bail, as Kerrigan points out.[263]

Next, it is clear that 'breach of the peace' at common law should not cause problems under the HRA purely because of its perceived lack of clarity and precision. The ECtHR did not, it must be pointed out, accurately distill the *Howell* test. The Court in *Steel* was of the view that breach of the peace at common law was where 'an individual causes harm, or appears likely to cause harm, to persons or property or acts in a manner the natural consequence of which would be to provoke others to violence'. In *Howell*, as we can recall, the Court of Appeal held that it occurred when 'harm is actually done or likely to be done to a person or, in his presence, his property or he is put in fear of being harmed through an assault, affray, riot, unlawful assembly or other disturbance'.[264] As Collins J explained in *Percy v DPP* it was implicit that 'harm' connotes violence or a threat of violence as a constituent element.[265] The *Steel* test does not limit harm to property as occurring only where this is done in someone's presence. This was a necessary qualification, as was explained in *Percy*, since only then is violence a likely result. Nor does it limit 'harm' to violent harm or damage. Thus, despite Lord Bingham's thoughts in *Laporte*, there is in fact a lack of symmetry between the common law and the ECHR albeit at the peripheries.[266] Since the ECtHR was merely trying to summarise, so as to establish the English position, we must assume that the binding interpretation under section 2 of the HRA will remain that of the English courts at common law. This infelicity also explains the misleading simplification in *Steel* of the power to take action to prevent a breach of peace: 'a person may be arrested for causing a breach of the peace or where it is reasonably apprehended that he or she is likely

---

[260] ibid, at [102]–[105]
[261] ibid, at [107]. There was a 5:4 split on both aspects with the minority clearly holding that a 44-hour detention and 28-day imprisonment for what was not an especially violent or troubling protest by the 1st applicant was excessive.
[262] ibid, at [109] totalling six lines.
[263] Kerrigan, above n 248, 135–7.
[264] *R v Howell* [1981] 3 All ER 383 (CA) Watkins LJ.
[265] *Percy v DPP*, above n 107, 1393–4 (DC).
[266] *Laporte*, above n 44, at [28] (Lord Bingham).

to cause a breach of the peace', an interpretation omitting any notion of immediacy or imminence. Not surprisingly, this was latched onto by counsel for the police in *Laporte*. It was ultimately rejected unanimously by the House, as we have seen.

Lastly, for Convention jurisprudence generally it was important for the Court to read 'lawful' in Article 5(1) as implying the 'prescribed by law' test of Articles 10–11. The Court remains reluctant to second guess national courts; it was largely only because the 3rd to 5th applicants had been released without being tried that the Strasbourg Court felt able to hold their initial arrests and detention were unlawful and thus were breaches of both Article 5 and Article 10. Neither the arrests nor the detentions were in accordance with domestic law: as the group was entirely peaceful all along, the *Howell* test was not made out. In the latter case, by the same reasoning the arrests and detentions were also viewed as disproportionate. As Kevin Kerrigan comments, the Court 'clearly found that the reason for the violation [in respect of the 3rd–5th applicants] was a failure to abide by domestic law; not a defect in the law itself'.[267] As he notes, this was all the more surprising in light of the Law Commission's 1994 recommendation that the power to bind over be abolished.[268]

As we saw in chapter three, binding over to be of good behaviour *has* been held to be a violation of the right to peaceful protest on the ground that the *contra bonos mores* test lacks clarity and foreseeability.[269] Who can predict how right-thinking people will view the (protesting) behaviour of others? What, then, about binding over to keep the peace? The imputation of the prescribed by law test into Article 5 was intended to serve the goals of predictability and clarity, for protesters as to their future behaviour. Does this hold? There is, it must be said, a fine line between the following two scenarios: on the one hand, the situation where it is obviously impossible for me to predict what I can lawfully do afterwards given the lack of objectivity to the common law test, and on the other, a situation where I should well be able to predict that I would be arrested (and/or bound over) to prevent the peace in a *Nicol*- or a *Pretty*-type protest, with violence stemming from a third party reacting reasonably to my own protest by threatening violence. That situation does not, on any reading of *Steel*, appear to trouble the ECtHR and did not later when *Nicol* itself reached Strasbourg.[270] The case was declared inadmissible. The initial arrest and detention served the twin aims of preventing disorder and protecting the rights of others; there was a serious risk the protesters would return. The committal served those aims as well as maintaining the impartiality of the judiciary. None was disproportionate, given the risk of provoking disorder or violence from others.

---

[267] Kerrigan, above n 248, 135.
[268] It reported that it was 'satisfied that there are substantial objections of principle to the retention of binding over to keep the peace or to be of good behaviour. These objections are, in summary, that the conduct which can be the ground for a binding over order is too vaguely defined; that binding over orders when made are in terms which are too vague and are therefore potentially oppressive; that the power to imprison someone if he or she refuses to consent to be bound over is anomalous; that orders which restrain a subject's freedom can be made without the discharge of the criminal, or indeed any clearly defined, burden of proof; and that witnesses, complainants or even acquitted defendants can be bound over without adequate prior information of any charge or complaint against them'. Law Commission Report, above n 243, at para 6.27.
[269] *Hashman and Harrup v United Kingdom* (1999) 30 EHRR 241
[270] *Nicol and Selvanayagam v UK* (App 32213/96) ECtHR inadmissibility decision 11 January 2001.

IV. Anti-Social Behaviour Orders

The Crime and Disorder Act 1998 introduced the concept we now know by the convenient shorthand, the ASBO—the anti-social behaviour order.[271] The scheme in the 1998 Act was designed primarily as a measure that would enable action to be taken against the rowdier, ill-disciplined elements on housing estates where everyone lives in close proximity to one another. As we can see, there is nothing in the wording of the scheme that would so restrict it.

A. The Statutory Scheme

Section 1 of the 1998 Act entitles the Chief Constable (or the local council amongst other bodies, all public) to apply to a magistrate for an ASBO provided the person

> has acted ... in an anti-social manner, that is to say, in a manner that caused or was likely to cause harassment, alarm or distress to one or more persons not of the same household as himself; and that such an order is necessary to protect those in the local government area in which harassment, alarm or distress was caused or was likely to be caused from further anti-social acts by him.[272]

The first point to note is that the absence of any mens rea. If the conditions are proved, the court may make an ASBO prohibiting the defendant from 'doing anything' prescribed in the order, this power being limited only by the necessity that the purpose of any prohibitions is to protect persons in the same or adjoining local government area from further anti-social acts by the defendant. There is no list; the prohibitions could be unimaginably wide. They have ranged from applications being sought—and granted—against children with Tourette's syndrome to ban them from swearing or to ban those with Asperger's Syndrome from staring over a neighbour's fence,[273] to an actual ban on a Scottish woman answering the door in her underwear.[274] The minimum period for an ASBO is two-years, though a defendant can apply for a variation or discharge; in the latter case this requires consent of both parties at any time within the two-year period: section 1(7)–(9).

B. Commentary

Most of the concern surrounding ASBOs has focused on four matters. First, the sheer number being granted prompted Alvaro Gil-Robles, the Council of Europe's Human Rights Commissioner, in June 2005 to talk of the UK being in grip of 'Asbo-mania'.[275] Second is the disproportionate impact on disaffected teenagers: almost exactly the same number have been imposed on those in the age bracket 10–17 as on those aged 18–87.[276] Thirdly, the data

---

[271] See eg, P Squires (ed), *Asbo Nation* (Bristol, Policy Press, 2008) and R Mathews et al (eds), *Assessing the Use of ASBOs* (Bristol, Policy Press, 2007).
[272] Linked to this is s 50 of the Police Reform Act 2002. Under this when a uniformed officer has reason to believe that a person has been acting, or is acting, in an anti-social manner, it will be an offence to fail to tell that officer your name and address or to provide a false or inaccurate name or address if asked to do so.
[273] BBC news on-line, 15 August 2005, at: news.bbc.co.uk/1/hi/health/4144840.stm, accessed 2 May 2008.
[274] 'Welcome to ASBO nation', *The Observer*, 12 June 2005.
[275] Quoted, *ibid*.
[276] Liberty reported the Home Office's own statistics as showing that until June 2004, the respective figures were 1425 and 1479: Liberty paper, 'Anti-social behaviour orders and human rights' (2004) p7, at: www.liberty-human-rights.org.uk/issues/pdfs/asbos-and-human-rights.PDF, accessed 2 May 2008.

very much supports the view that those against whom ASBOs are sought are presumed not to be innocent: of 3,111 ASBOs applied for in England and Wales between 1999 and June 2004, only 42 were not granted.[277] Lastly, although applying for an ASBO is a civil procedure, such that hearsay evidence alone can lead to an order being imposed,[278] with an ostensibly civil sanction—albeit one where the criminal standard of proof obtains as to whether someone has acted in an anti-social fashion—breach can lead to quite severe criminal consequences. Breaching an ASBO without reasonable excuse is itself a criminal offence triable either way—with a six-month penalty on summary conviction and up to five years on indictment: section 1(10). We met similar concerns before when we considered breaches of Protection From Harassment Act (PFHA) injunctions in chapter six. This fusion of criminal and civil law, with the former dependent on establishing only a breach of the latter, is becoming common. Control orders to deal with the threat of terrorism would be another. All that needs to be proved is that there was an ASBO and that Joe Bloggs is in breach of its terms. There will be no assessment of the original order at any future criminal trial for its breach,[279] so all the usual criminal protections that do then apply—and those under Article 6—are largely misplaced.

C. Peaceful Protest Concerns

Those concerns are not misplaced but lengthy discussion would be out of place in this book. Instead, we shall look briefly at their use to contain peaceful protest. In 2005 *The Observer* reported that an animal rights activist, Heather Nicholson, had been given a five-year ASBO banning her from many of the UK's animal research laboratories, after taking part in what she described as a normal demonstration.[280] In the same year, an application to have an ASBO imposed on veteran peace campaigner Lindis Percy—following complaints by the MoD about her behaviour at protests at the US listening post at Menwith Hill in Yorkshire—was rejected by a judge in Harrogate.[281] The newspaper report indicated the judge's trenchant view that the law clearly intended the orders to be used against 'oafish and intimidating' behaviour: here, in none of the incidents was there aggressive behaviour, abusive language or threats of violence. It was, he said, an attempt to 'use a club to beat down the expression of legitimate comment and the expression of views on matters of public concern'.[282] However, the judge did warn that the right to protest did not override the right of others to use the highway, or of police officers to carry out their duties and he said that 'there could be circumstances where anti-social behaviour orders may be used against those engaging in political or other protests, if they indulged in intimidating behaviour'. In the event, he ordered that Ms Percy be tagged and subjected to an eight-week nighttime curfew, after being found guilty of various offences, such as aggravated trespass and obstructing the highway.

---

[277] Liberty paper, above n 276, p 4.
[278] *R (McCann) v Crown Court at Manchester* [2002] UKHL 39 but since the need to impose an ASBO is an evaluative task, this involves no standard of proof, criminal or civil.
[279] See similarly in the context of the PFHA, *Moseley v Director of Public Prosecutions*, unreported High Court decision, 9 June 1999, *The Times*, 23 June 1999, that we considered in the last chapter.
[280] *The Observer*, above n 274.
[281] 'Anti-war protester escapes ASBO', *The Guardian*, 18 May 2005.
[282] Contrast the views expressed in Bailey, Harris and Jones, *Civil liberties*, above n 45, 516 that it is unlikely that Art 11 challenges would succeed, provided the ASBO were drafted clearly, since they serve the interests of preventing crime and disorder.

As with harassment injunctions under the PFHA, it is clear the Act is being used—or is capable of being misused—to provide restrictions on peaceful protest that were not in the minds of its drafters. Protesters should, like Lindis Percy, have properly been dealt with under normal criminal law powers—which, as we have seen, are vast—rather than by using the hybrid 'civimal' procedure. If someone has, for example, obstructed the highway or disrupted a motorway project, they should be tried—and then acquitted or freed—for specific crimes. By applying for an ASBO, the police and prosecutors can fill any evidential gaps with untested hearsay and can deprive protesters of the additional protection in Articles 6(2) and 6(3). It is a point well made by Alex Gask, Legal Officer at Liberty.[283] An ASBO 'can serve as a shortcut to obtaining a criminal conviction without the need actually to prove the original crime' and furthermore a conviction that might mean a five-year sentence. This is quite possibly more than would be passed down for the free-standing offence. It is true that section 1(5) creates a reasonableness defence in that acts which are shown by the defendant to be reasonable in the circumstances are to be disregarded in the assessment of whether she has acted in an anti-social manner. It is not so much a defence as a potential reversal of the actus reus.[284] Whether the same cases under section 5 of the POA 1986, that we looked at in chapter five, would 'clearly also apply' as Fenwick asserts—cases such as *DPP v Clarke*,[285] holding that reasonableness must be judged objectively—must be moot. Irrespective of that point, as with the PFHA as we saw with *DPP v Moseley*, a court may well take the view that anti-social behaviour cannot be reasonable, so effectively depriving a defendant of an opportunity to set up the reasonableness of any subsequent breach as a defence.[286] *Moseley* was declared inadmissible by Strasbourg on that point.[287]

V. Dispersal Orders

Linked to the topic of ASBOs is the power that the police now have under section 30 of the Anti Social Behaviour Act 2003 to issue dispersal orders.[288] Its potential for use in the context of even peaceful protest is apparent.

A. The Statutory Scheme

Section 30 allows senior police officers to give written authorisation[289] for officers on the ground to issue dispersal orders. These can last up to six months. The senior officer needs reasonable grounds for believing both that

---

[283] Liberty paper, above n 276, p 5.
[284] Fenwick, *Civil Liberties*, above n 36 796.
[285] *Director of Public Prosecutions v Clarke* [1992] Crim LR 60.
[286] Above chapter six, p 273.
[287] *Selvanayagam and Moseley v United Kingdom* (App 57981/00) ECtHR inadmissibility decision 12 December 2002.
[288] See generally A Crawford and S Lister, *The Use and Impact of Dispersal Orders: Sticking Plasters and Wake-Up Calls* (Bristol, Policy Press, 2007).
[289] The full procedural requirements for a valid authorisation are set out in s 31. Reading s 31(1)(c), the Divisional Court in *Sierny v DPP* [2006] EWHC 716 (Admin) held that an authorisation must specify, if only in summary form, the grounds upon which it is made so as to "inform the reader, albeit in broad terms, of the nature of the problem and the mischief at which the authorisation is aimed' (Hallett J at [23]). Such an approach would

(a) any members of the public have been intimidated, harassed, alarmed or distressed as a result of the presence of behaviour of groups of two or more person; and
(b) anti-social behaviour (that is behaviour which causes or is likely to cause harassment, alarm or distress to one or more people[290]) is a significant and persistent problem in the area.

If an authorisation is given (which must then be publicised[291]), uniformed officers with reasonable grounds for believing that the presence or behaviour of a group of two or more persons in any public place in the relevant locality has resulted, or is likely to result, in any members of the public being intimidated, harassed, alarmed or distressed may give one or more of the following directions:

(a) a direction requiring the persons in the group to disperse (either immediately or by such time as he may specify and in such way as he may specify);
(b) a direction requiring any of those persons whose place of residence is not within the relevant locality to leave the relevant locality or any part of the relevant locality (either immediately or by such time as he may specify and in such way as he may specify); and
(c) a direction prohibiting any of those persons whose place of residence is not within the relevant locality from returning to the relevant locality or any part of the relevant locality for such period (not exceeding 24 hours) from the giving of the direction as he may specify.[292]

It is an offence knowingly to contravene a dispersal order. Officers may not give a direction—dispersal order—to anyone engaged in lawful industrial action (lawful that is under section 220 of the Trade Union and Labour Relations (Consolidation) Act 1992) or who is taking part in a public procession where the correct notice under section 11 of the POA 1986 has been given (or is not required).[293] There is no exemption in the 2003 Act for assemblies to which no conditions have been attached either because the police have chosen not to or because the trigger conditions are not met.

An officer needs to have some objectively reasonable basis—relating to the group that is ordered to disperse—for her belief that the public might be intimated, harassed or distressed. In *Bucknell v DPP*, the Divisional Court decided—on appeal by way of case stated—that unless there were exceptional circumstances a real belief for the purposes of section 30 of the Act had normally to depend in part at least on some behaviour—rather than mere presence—by the group that indicated harassment, alarm, intimidation or distress.[294] If that were not so, it would amount to an illegitimate interference in the rights of people to go where they pleased in public. In the case, the only evidence was of two large groups of teenage boys loitering after school in Wimbledon. In those circumstances, it had not been a proportionate response for the officer to act as he had because the apparent characterisation of those groups alone was not capable objectively of giving rise to the necessary reasonable

ensure there was a proper thought-out basis for making the authorisation and expressing that basis in written form, which can later be examined and challenged, and which explains to the police, who may later be required to give dispersal directions, information as to the nature of the problem which gave rise to the authorisation and hence in what circumstances the need for directions may arise' (Nelson J at [28]).

[290] Section 36.
[291] Section 31.
[292] Section 30(2)–(4). For the power to be renewed, that is for it to cover a second 24-hour period, the trigger conditions will need satisfying de novo.
[293] Section 30(5).
[294] *Bucknell v Director of Public Prosecutions* [2006] EWHC 1888 (Admin) at [8] (May LJ).

belief. It would appear that, assuming a group of protesters is in a designated dispersal area, there would need to be more than just previous experience of trouble and previous experience of trouble by them. That was why after all, in *Bucknell*, the authorisation had been given: there had been an increasing trend of inter-school fighting in the streets, and of the area being used to congregate and to frighten the public.

B. *R (Singh) v Chief Constable of West Midlands*

The omission of public assemblies from those exempted from the reach of the power in section 30 was the main issue at the heart of *R (Singh) v Chief Constable of West Midlands*.[295] There the Court of Appeal held, first, that the section 30 power can be called upon to disperse an assembly or gathering that is protesting, and secondly that this is so even though the authorisation was originally granted out of fear of other acts of harassment and alarm.

(i) Background and Arguments

Worried about anti-social seasonal revelry in the build-up to Christmas 2004, the Chief Superintendent granted a six-week section 30 authorisation covering Birmingham city centre. During that period, a controversial play, staged at the local repertory theatre, provoked immense outrage and offence among the local Sikh community.[296] The applicant was one of about 30 who protested inside and outside the theatre about the play. The group had started to become threatening. Some minor acts of violence had been committed by a few and the group as a whole was attempting, or large numbers were attempting, to have the play closed. The group refused to leave when asked and became increasingly hostile, agitated and abusive, towards the police at least. There were signs, according to the police, of impending violence.[297] An order under section 30(4)(a) was given requiring immediate dispersal of the group, but Mr Singh refused to move. He was cautioned under section 32 for knowingly contravening a direction. He challenged the legality of the direction by judicial review on three grounds. First, section 30 did not apply to protesters exercising their rights under Article 10 (the interpretation point). Secondly, a direction under section 30(4) could not lawfully be made to the protesters pursuant to an authorisation which was specifically limited to dealing with the problem of seasonal revellers (the authorisation point). Lastly, in any event the decision to order dispersal was one that was a disproportionate interference with the right of peaceful protest. The Queen's Bench Divisional Court dismissed the claim.[298] The Court of Appeal (Wall, Wilson and Hallett LJJ) affirmed the lower court's decision on all grounds and held for the Chief Constable.

On the interpretation point, though there was some dispute here about the peaceful nature of the protest, counsel for the claimant based her case around two linked arguments. First, Parliament should not be taken to have intended by general and ambiguous words to interfere with the fundamental right to protest lawfully, the principle of legality.[299] Secondly, even if Parliament had intended such a result, it would be incompatible with the

---

[295] *R (Singh) v Chief Constable of West Midlands* [2006] EWCA Civ 1118.
[296] The play *Behzti* (meaning dishonour) was set in a Sikh temple and depicted, inter alia, a Sikh priest committing sexual acts in the temple.
[297] *Singh*, above n 295, at [2]–[14] provides the factual background and build-up.
[298] *R (Singh) v Chief Constable of West Midlands* [2005] EWHC 2840 (Admin) Maurice Kay LJ and Penry-Davey J.
[299] *R v Secretary of State for the Home Department (SSHD) ex parte Simms and O'Brien* [2000] 2 AC 115 (HL) 131 (Lord Hoffman) and *R v SSHD ex parte Pierson* [1998] AC 539 (Lord Steyn).

Dispersal Orders 367

European Convention on Human Rights. She invited the Court to utilise section 3 of the HRA to read down section 30 in such a way that it did not apply to lawful protests.

On the authorisation point, counsel asserted that

> it could not have been Parliament's intention that whether one type of activity should be the subject of [a dispersal order] should depend upon the adventitious statutory identification (following consultation and publicity) of a totally different type of problematic activity.[300]

Section 31(9) says:

> The giving or withdrawal of an authorisation does not prevent the giving of a further authorisation in respect of a locality which includes the whole or any part of the relevant locality to which the earlier authorisation relates.

This meant Parliament clearly envisaged there being more than one, and overlapping, authorisations for the same locality, as indeed was the case at the time in Birmingham itself, with the second directed at skateboarders in the city centre. Counsel also relied on dicta in *Sierny* by Nelson J that a written, thought out authorisation 'explains to the police information as to the nature of the problem which gave rise to the authorisation and hence in what circumstances the need for directions may arise'.[301] This was taken as authority for the proposition that an authorisation could only be used for the purposes of dispersing groups engaged in the kind of anti-social behaviour specified in it.

On the last point, the dispersal order was disproportionate in two ways: the threat of violence was not serious enough to warrant dispersal of what was essentially a peaceful protest—or certainly was on the applicant's part—and there were, in any event, less restrictive measures (targeted arrests of those responsible for trouble; continued monitoring; or imposing conditions) available and the police had failed to show why—for some—these were not considered, and for others, considered and then rejected.

(ii) Reasoning: The Interpretation Point

Hallett LJ rejected the argument that section 30 was ambiguous. She did not consider it necessary to have recourse to the parliamentary debates under *Pepper v Hart* as she was satisfied, by the express language as a whole and in context, that Parliament intended section 30 to cover protests.[302] She did not accept that section 30 needed to be read down so as to be compatible with a protester's fundamental human rights. A dispersal order to cover protests of this kind was necessary in a democratic society to meet several legitimate aims, namely the prevention of crime and disorder, the protection of public safety and the protection of the rights and freedoms of others.[303]

She stressed several points. The exclusion of two sorts of protest (industrial disputes and properly notified processions) necessarily implied that Parliament intended to include static assemblies: 'Parliament has clearly decided to distinguish static protests of the kind we have here from processions over which the police would have some control and the impact of which on a local community would be transitory'.[304] Secondly, it was problem-

---

[300] Skeleton argument set out in *Singh*, above n 295, at [60].
[301] *Sierny*, above n 289.
[302] *Singh*, above n 295, at [79].
[303] ibid, at [97].
[304] ibid, at [82]. Her Ladyship drew on Lord Hobhouse in *R (Morgan Grenfell & Co Ltd) v Special Commissioner of Income Tax* [2003] 1 AC 563 at [45]. See too Wall LJ at [120]–[128] drawing on *R (W) v Commissioner of Police for the Metropolis* [2006] EWCA Civ 458: it was 'convincingly clear' that Parliament had in mind rights such as

atic to seek an exemption for 'protesters' when the only definition offered was someone exercising their right to freedom of expression. This was far from satisfactory. It could cover a multitude of situations and produce an absurd and unworkable result: it could encompass drunken revellers, refused entry to a nightclub, who decide to protest vociferously on the streets about their right to be admitted.[305] This problem largely disappears if the definition of 'demonstration' offered earlier in chapter three is adopted and accepted.[306] The third point concerned the discrepancy between the dispersal power (effectively to break up a protest) with its lower threshold—requiring only harm or distress—and the power to impose conditions on assemblies in section 14 of the POA 1986, ostensibly a less restrictive measure but with a higher threshold such as serious public disorder. This argument did not impress Hallett LJ. The powers under the two Acts complemented each other and were not inconsistent. Section 14 contained a lower risk test but with a higher conduct test. Under it, the police have powers to impose conditions where nothing has yet happened, but they may only do so where there are reasonable grounds for believing something serious may occur. By contrast, section 30 allows officers to disperse protesters but only where they have reasonable grounds for believing that any members of the public *have* been intimidated, harassed, alarmed or distressed or *are likely* to be. These latter situations are ones of an urgent kind not dealt with in section 14.[307] That said, both authorisations and dispersal orders—since they could be based on causing on alarm to just two people—had to be 'properly justified on an objective basis. If used improperly or disproportionately they may be challenged'.[308] In general terms, the dispersal power is

> limited both temporally and geographically. This is not a case of the authorities being empowered to prevent static protest generally or for any significant length of time. The authorisation may last a maximum of six months and the dispersal directions just 24 hours and then only if the circumstances fall with section 30(4)(c). Both may be withdrawn. The provisions apply to a narrowly defined locality ... [T]here is no sweeping power to force individuals to stop protesting and move on. Significant anti-social behaviour must have already become a persistent problem in the locality or there would be no authorisation in place. And, it is only when the behaviour of a group of people moves beyond legitimate protest and into the realms of behaviour that causes actual or likely intimidation, harassment, alarm and distress that an officer can use an authorisation to direct them to disperse. The peaceful member of the group who behaves in this fashion may have his rights infringed, but it is only for a relatively short time and it is for the greater good namely the protection of the rights of others.[309]

Three quick points might be made here. The first is that it conflates, not for the first time as we have seen, 'legitimate protest' with the absence of intimidation, harassment, alarm or distress. If we assume that 'legitimate protest' equates to the right to peaceful protest recognised in Articles 10–11, it is doubtful that this is a correct summation of the law.[310] Secondly, a right infringed for a short time is still a right infringed; even more, this takes no account of the chilling effect on potential protesters of the effective removal, albeit short-

those contained in Arts 10 and 11 when it passed s 30 and thus that it had by implication authorised something in breach of fundamental rights.

[305] *ibid*, at [84] or indeed those protesting about the 2003 Act itself (or even a dispersal order) in the anti-social way envisaged in the authorisation.
[306] See above pp 58.
[307] *Singh*, above n 295, at [86]–[87].
[308] *ibid*, at [90].
[309] *ibid*, at [91]–[92].
[310] See generally chapter three.

term. Thirdly, that something is—or might be—for the greater good does not mean it is also necessary or proportionate.

On the facts, it was clear that any restriction on the right to protest peacefully was made out, given that in the balance were not just the applicant's rights but also the competing rights and interests of those wishing to see the play.[311]

> [T]he protesters were able to protest before, during and after 16 December outside the theatre whilst the play was running. As long as the protest did not impinge upon the rights of others they would have been allowed to continue protesting. Even after they were directed to disperse, the protesters could have continued their protest elsewhere in the city just a few hundred yards away. They could have returned and did return to the theatre the very next day or the day after. That day Inspector Phillips was prepared to allow other protesters to gather in a cordoned off area and continue the protest in an organised and peaceful manner.

This does seem the better and safer analysis.

(iii) Reasoning: The Authorisation Point

Both Hallett and Wall LJJ found the authorisation point more troubling. They decided that a validly made authorisation could lawfully be used by officers to disperse a group of people acting in an anti-social manner of a kind not contemplated at the time the authorisation was made. *Sierny*, which had been relied on to assert the reverse, was construed as a case where the issue was the legality of the authorisation, not its application to a different situation. Nelson J there was at best speaking obiter.[312] Her Ladyship provided positive support for her conclusion.[313]

(i) Had Parliament intended to limit the use of dispersal directions to anti-social behaviour of the kind specified in the authorisation, it could and no doubt would have said so.
(ii) On a strict reading of the section, the power to direct a dispersal did not relate back to the kind of behaviour referred to in the authorisation or to the kind of groups addressed when the authorisation was made. If an authorisation is in place for one locality it may be used for any anti-social behaviour in that locality which meets the statutory criteria.
(iii) Logically, that argument led to the position that if an authorisation were given to cover anti-social behaviour by teenagers drinking alcohol and behaving badly on a particular street corner, the police would have to seek another authorisation to deal with a group of middle-aged men doing the same with the same effect.[314] That would be unworkable and absurd.
(iv) It was irrelevant that another partially overlapping authorisation was in place for the same locality.

Wall LJ was perturbed by the fortuitous and adventitious possibility that a second group could be ordered to disperse using an authorisation previously granted for unrelated

---
[311] *Singh*, above n 295, at [75]–[76].
[312] *ibid*, at [101].
[313] *ibid*, at [102]–[106].
[314] Hallett LJ admitted that in the present situation the anti-social behaviour was qualitatively different but that was 'beside the point': 'I cannot accept that police officers, faced with a volatile and threatening situation as, they say, was the case on 16 December 2004, would have been entitled to disperse drunken revellers who behaved in an anti-social fashion but not this particular group of protesters who were behaving in a potentially more alarming anti-social fashion' (at [105]).

behaviour but where a new authorisation could not be granted since section 30(1) requires intimidation, harassment, alarm or distress to have occurred) to prevent anticipated future anti-social behaviour. The problem was resolved by taking the view that sufficient safeguards surrounded the exercise of the power to remove any elements of arbitrariness. The power also had to be exercised proportionately: any improper exercise was open to challenge on public law grounds.[315]

(iv) Reasoning: Proportionality

On the third limb, the dispersal order was justified and proportionate given the intelligence the police had received and the events over the two days. Wall LJ drew on the words of Tugendhat J in the Divisional Court in *Austin* that 'the court should accord a high degree of respect for the police officers' appreciation of the risks of what the members of the crowd might have done if not contained'.[316] The operational decision here was made in good faith to prevent violence. It was the least restrictive, least intrusive and least inflammatory way of dealing with what, by any description, was no longer a peaceful protest. The police faced what to them seemed an intractable problem between two entrenched groups, one exercising their right to freedom of expression and the other, having failed to achieve their objectives by peaceful protest, deciding to distress and alarm if not also to intimidate. Other measures (arrest for breach of the peace or under section 5 of the POA 1986 or imposing conditions under section 14 of the POA 1986) were considered and rejected for good reason; doing nothing was clearly not sensible or appropriate. Furthermore, the direction to disperse constituted less of an interference with the claimant's rights than did immediate arrest under the POA 1986. The dispersal direction applied to a narrow geographical location and for a limited period of time. There was nothing to prevent the protesters from continuing their protest outside the area covered by the notice or returning the following day.[317]

(v) Analysis

Let us now consider the case critically. It is difficult to argue with the view taken by the Court of Appeal about Parliament's intention and about necessary implication. *Inclusio unus, altio exclusus* has considerable appeal here: by specifically exempting lawful pickets and properly notified processions, all other forms of protest fell within the scope of section 30. Yet the application of section 30 to an event such as the one here prompts a feeling of unease. But why? One reason is the realisation that the police are far from powerless. To apply section 30 to protests suggests that the balance has been tipped too far. They could have imposed conditions under section 14, arrested individual troublemakers under (say) section 5 of the POA 1986 (though it was argued that dispersal is a less restrictive and thus more proportionate measure) or called on their common law powers to preserve the peace. These existing powers taken together (it was submitted) reflect a careful compromise between freedom and the risk of serious disorder. There are various other ways in which the Court's reasoning and analysis is open to criticism.

---

[315] ibid, at [129]–[134].
[316] ibid, at [136] referring to the High Court decision in *Austin* [2005] EWHC 480 at [166].
[317] ibid, at [108]–[114] and Wall LJ at [135]–[137].

(a) Indiscriminate Nature of the Power

The power to order a dispersal is fairly indiscriminate in its target. Once an authorisation has been given (based on actual distress caused), ordering a dispersal is an all-or-nothing approach. Even if officers wished only to single out those 'troublemakers' actually or even likely to be causing harassment alarm or distress, on the natural meaning of section 30(3)–(4) that would not be possible: uniformed officers who have the requisite reasonable belief that members of the public have been or are likely to be intimidated, harassed, alarmed or distressed may give a direction 'requiring the persons in the group to disperse'. There need only be a reasonably believed threat from a group of two or more—possibly even part of a larger group—for the whole group to be obliged to disperse, on pain of arrest. If we assume that the purpose of section 30 is not to outlaw large groups but to outlaw large groups that threaten trouble, one solution would be this. Officers would be required to act only against those threatening or actually causing distress (for example) so as not to act outside the statutory purpose; only if they took action solely against troublemakers would those purposes be achieved—or not frustrated.[318]

Another solution would be to consider how the section in bare terms holds up to the gaze of Articles 10 and 11. Strasbourg case law such as *Bukta* is fairly clear: a measure of inconvenience and disturbance (query alarm and distress?) is the price to be paid for the exercise of the right of assembly with its functional, public value.[319] It would not be beyond imagination for a court to hold that, utilising section 3 of the HRA, section 30 should be read as permitting—requiring?—officers to disperse only those who they reasonably believe are likely to intimidate, harass, alarm or cause distress. This could be done simply by reading the section as saying 'requiring the persons in the group *who are likely to intimidate, harass, alarm or cause distress* to disperse'. That approach is dependent on (a) the actual wording being incompatible with the right to peaceful protest and (b) the proposed new wording being both compatible and a possible reading.

What about protests that become violent? We could perhaps more easily accept section 30 covering protests if we could limit its application not just to those who are, or are likely to be, causing harassment alarm or distress or intimidating others but to those who are violent or who are threatening violence, rather than covering the group as a whole. Again, we might argue that such a reading is required of courts under section 3. It is here that the Court of Appeal appears to have misread or misapplied one of the leading Strasbourg cases, *Ezelin v France*. It is clear from that case (at least) that a protester's right of peaceful protest is not lost merely because a *group* becomes violent. The behaviour of the individual is the key. As we have seen on several occasions, Article 11 does not avail a disruptive, obstructive or intimidating protester of protection,[320] but there is no reason why a protester should lose the benefit of their Convention rights merely because others are causing distress or engaging in obstructive direct action and a section 30 dispersal order has been made.

Hallett LJ, in *Singh*, sought to distinguish and marginalise *Ezelin* in several ways. In each all she did was to justify the order by attributing liability to the group en masse, a criticism we might recall of the collective round-up approach sanctioned by the House of Lords in

---

[318] See on this Lord Bingham in *Gillan* [2006] UKHL 12.
[319] *Bukta v Hungary* (App 25691/04) ECtHR judgment 17 July 2007, at [37]; and also *Galstyan v Armenia* (App 26986/03) ECtHR judgment 15 November 2007, at [116].
[320] See chapter three generally.

Austin.[321] It is unlikely that Strasbourg would treat the matter the same way: far too much weight was given to the domestic configuration.

> First ... if the police officers are correct on the facts of this case in their assessment of the situation, this protest was no longer peaceful. Acting as a group, these protesters forced their way into the theatre, refused to leave, they had to be forcibly ejected, they allegedly issued threats to those at the scene and refused to resume a peaceful protest outside the theatre. Members of the theatre staff were frightened and distressed. Other members of the public including hundreds of children were potentially affected. In my view, those are very different circumstances from the situation in the *Ezelin* case ... Secondly, the European court was not concerned, as here, with the interpretation of a law which specifically governs the behaviour of groups of people. The exercise of the powers under section 30 depends on the effect of conduct on members of the public by a group acting as a group. It does not depend on proving that any individual has behaved reprehensibly. In the *Ezelin* case no such provision was in play and Mr Ezelin, having himself done nothing wrong, was disciplined as an individual for failing to dissociate himself from the actions of his fellow protesters.[322]

The Court of Appeal has confirmed that the dispersal power can lawfully be used—and was intended by Parliament to be used—to order a protesting group, not just individual members, to disperse based only on a low threshold of alarm or distress. As counsel put it, perhaps only one or two people might react unreasonably to (an otherwise) legitimate protest and for whose reaction perhaps only one or two members of the group may have been responsible. Protesters' conduct which is merely offensive and irritating might become subject to these powers simply because one or two people are distressed by them. This cannot amount to a 'pressing social need' sufficient to justify interfering with the right to freedom of expression. At a public protest, people are likely to communicate their ideas vocally and in strong terms, and by its very nature a protest is reasonably likely to be 'intimidating'—even perhaps just by dint of size or location or other circumstance[323]—at any rate, to some. Yet this alone could not sensibly justify terminating such protests.

(b) Disproportionality

Similar concerns apply to *Singh* as they do to *Austin* in that both attribute to individuals the unlawful or threatening qualities of all, or of a sizeable number. Ordering an entire assembly to disperse simply because of the behaviour of one or two seems not to be a proportionate response. It would certainly seem at first blush to be out of line with, the reverse in fact of, what the ECtHR held in *Ezelin*. There, as we saw, the Court emphasised reprehensible behaviour. As Andrew Ashworth noted in his comment on *Singh*,[324] the court's approach was to consider the general situation as it was, rather than proportionality in relation to any particular individual, and on this point the House of Lords decision in *Laporte* may be relevant.[325]

---

[321] See above pp 354.
[322] *Singh*, above n 295, at [93]–[94]. It is true that her third reason (at [95]) holds good: in *Ezelin* there was not the clash of rights as there was on the facts in *Singh*. Also relevant were the rights of the play's author and producers to freedom of expression, of members of the public to see the play and to go about their lawful business in the square without being intimidated, harassed, alarmed or distressed.
[323] We noted a similar concern in the context of s 14 of the POA 1986, chapter five above p 186.
[324] A Ashworth [2007] *Crim LR* 243, 246.
[325] *Laporte* [2006] UKHL 55 at [84].

(c) Misplaced Comparison with Section 14

Hallett LJ countered the analogy with section 14—that the latter has stricter triggers for a less restrictive measure—by arguing that the stricter triggers (serious disorder for example) were tempered by a lower risk: nothing untoward needs actually to have happened. This does not hold true. Section 30 permits dispersal of what is in effect a section 14 public assembly on lesser conduct (mere alarm or distress) but without the same lesser risk. It can be triggered by a reasonable belief (ie need not actually be shown to be true) that members of the public *are likely* to be harassed, alarmed distressed or intimidated, in other words the same predictive risk as section 14. Indeed, Hallett LJ seemed herself to recognise this: if members of a group behave in such a way that members of the public

> are or are likely to be intimidated, harassed, alarmed or distressed, I fail to see why the police should necessarily be forced to wait for them to be actually harmed or for serious disorder to erupt before they can step in and direct the group to disperse.[326]

This must leave a big question mark over the continued use of section 14 to regulate protesting groups in future.

(d) Unworkability

Singh has produced an absurd result. The express exclusion of notified public processions means that the police will be acting unlawfully if they purport to disperse a procession—a moving protest—but not if they disperse a static protest. There is no basis for thinking that static protests are less important, or involve a lesser engagement with human rights, than moving protests. In fact, as we saw in chapter five, in 1986 the government accepted the greater value of assemblies over protests as being behind the differential treatment in what was then sections 11–14 of the POA 1986.[327] As counsel argued, if anything the reverse is true: almost all moving processions come to a halt at some point before disbanding. It is often at the very point that the procession stops moving, and becomes an assembly—perhaps when speeches start—that the interest in freedom of expression becomes most intense. It cannot be that by its nature a procession is on the move and so cannot become the static threat that is at the heart of the section 30 power: in other words, in some shape or form it is 'dispersing' anyway. Such a proposition, if put, clearly does not hold. The procession could be moving slowly and in circular fashion, with no intention of leaving the Town Square.

VI. Strasbourg Case Law

We have looked at a few Strasbourg cases in this chapter. Domestic cases are now, of course, argued along Strasbourg lines. We saw this most noticeably in *Laporte*, *Austin* and *Singh*, three of the cases we have looked at in some detail.

---

[326] *Singh*, above n 295, at [89].
[327] See above pp 169 and 184.

Aside from the handful of breach of the peace cases,[328] there is little by way of precedent within the Court's case law that is on all fours with (or even similar to) the sorts of policing decisions we have considered. Much of its time is taken up with bans on marches and processions, or the arrests of those who participate in those more formal protests without permission. Even still there is much by way of general principle in several cases that is pertinent to the sorts of situations we have looked at. We have seen in previous chapters that whenever protest threatens to become or does actually become obstructive, there is almost no chance of any sympathy being shown to the protesters' rights. This is certainly so when it disrupts the activity complained about[329] and historically it has often been so when there is only incidental disruption to, say, traffic or everyday business.[330] Recently, that latter position has been in a state of flux. For example, in *Galstyan v Armenia*, one ground submitted for justifying a conviction relating to a demonstration was that G had made a loud noise. The Court offered its view, finding it 'hard to imagine a huge political demonstration at which people express their opinion not generating a certain amount of noise'.[331] An earlier Commission decision, holding an application against Austria to be inadmissible, would have pointed to a different conclusion.[332]

Several factors would need to be borne in mind by officers when exercising preventive powers in advance. The first is the obvious one: all measures and decisions must properly balance the right of peaceful protest against competing social interests. It is not just a question of finding a balance; there is a presumption in favour of free speech and peaceful protest, since these are rights. If there is doubt, they should trump other interests. In other words, there needs to be a clear, rationally connected case—'convincing and compelling reasons'[333]—that this preventive measure is needed, and needed in respect of this protester, and needed now: other means are unavailable or they have been tried, tested and found wanting. It is this last aspect of the proportionality formula that does seem, from the domestic cases, to be overlooked. Such an approach would involve officers, and then courts on review or challenge, asking themselves why measures against entire groups are needed on the basis of possible wrongdoing by only some of its members. Thus in *Ezelin*, the Court placed such stock on the right that it should not be restricted 'so long as the person concerned does not himself commit any reprehensible act'.[334] If there were doubt about what 'reprehensible' means, and we considered this in chapter three, clarity has been provided more recently. In *Oya Ataman*, as just one example, the Court ruled where 'demonstrators do not engage in acts of violence, it is important for public authorities to show a certain

---

[328] We looked at *Steel*, *Hashman and Harrup* and *Nicol and Selvanyagam* in some detail. Other breach of the peace cases would be *Donnan v United Kingdom* (App 3811/04) ECtHR inadmissibility decision 8 November 2005 (failure to exhaust local remedies, viz the HRA), *Lucas v United Kingdom* (App 39013/02) ECtHR inadmissibility decision 18 March 2003 (arrest and conviction for breach of the peace after a road block sit-in outside Faslane naval base as justified in the interests of public safety and preventing disorder) and *McBride v United Kingdom* (App 27786/95) ECtHR inadmissibility decision 5 July 2001 (not disproportionate to arrest M who refused to discontinue walking towards an arms fair and remove her from the scene where there was a domestic finding of a high risk of violence given the need to prevent disorder and protect the rights of others).
[329] See as an example *Driemann v Norway* (App 33678/96) ECtHR inadmissibility decision 4 May 2000.
[330] See as an example *GS v Austria* (App 14923/89) EComHR inadmissibility decision 30 November 1992.
[331] *Galstyan v Armenia* (App 26986/03) ECtHR judgment 15 November 2007, at [116].
[332] *S v Austria* (App 13812/88) EComHR inadmissibility decision 3 December 1990. This makes the police tactics at the Kingsnorth climate camp in August 2008 even more ironic: 'Protesters fought the law but the law fought back ... very very loudly', *The Guardian*, 12 March 2009.
[333] *Makhmaduv v Russia* (App 35082/04) ECtHR judgment 26 July 2007.
[334] *Ezelin v France* (1991) 14 EHRR at [53].

degree of tolerance towards peaceful gatherings'.[335] The Joint Committee in its 2009 report on the policing of protest must be right to conclude that this means 'the police should be exceptionally slow to prevent or interfere with a peaceful demonstration simply because of the violent actions of a minority'.[336] This clearly has application to both *Austin* and *Singh*, amongst other cases. It is of 'particular importance for persons holding unpopular views or belonging to minorities' said the Court in *Baczowski v Poland*.[337]

The second factor is this. The police and other states parties might come under positive duties to facilitate protest, not merely to abstain from restricting it, so as to secure its 'effective enjoyment'.[338] We saw in chapter three how a state might breach this by applying an unreasonable indirect restriction. The example given was an excessive charge for a permit to use council land.[339] More obviously, it will require states to maintain an appropriate level of policing so as to allow protests to proceed;[340] arresting demonstrators—as the easier option—or taking other pre-emptive action simply because enough officers were not assigned on the day to keep the peace or opposing factions apart is not likely to withstand scrutiny. This was very clearly one of the factors at play in *Öllinger*[341] and was behind, as we saw earlier in this chapter, some of the thoughts expressed by the House in *Laporte*. However, as it involves the imposition of a positive duty, the obligation is not an absolute one.[342]

VII. Conclusions

Revisions to this chapter were first made in the week during which the police tactics at the G20 summit, as they tried to keep order, came under intense scrutiny. It was the week in which clear evidence of the assault on Ian Tomlinson—hit around the back of the legs with a baton and pushed in the back so he fell to the ground—became public and, thanks to the modern 'democratised' media, became globally known within hours. Just a few moments later he died. There is an investigation into Tomlinson's death being carried out by the Independent Police Complaints Commission but there are calls already for a public inquiry into his death and events generally on the day as well as the police response immediately afterwards. The police initially denied any involvement with Tomlinson at all and then claimed they were unable to treat him as they were being bombarded by missiles thrown by the protesters. Sadly, this 47-year-old newsagent, on his way home from work and in the wrong place at the wrong time, is destined to be remembered in much the same way as Blair Peach who died in similar fashion in 1979. It also seems likely that the Metropolitan Police is going to face a multitude of civil claims for injuries sustained. *The Guardian* contains

---

[335] *Oya Ataman v Turkey* (App 74552/01) ECtHR judgment 5 December, at [41]–[42].
[336] JCHR 7th report of session 2008–09, *Demonstrating respect for rights? A human rights approach to policing protest*, 3 March 2009 at: www.publications.parliament.uk/pa/jt200809/jtselect/jtrights/47/4702.htm, accessed 13 August 2009.
[337] *Baczowski v Poland* (App 1543/06) ECtHR judgment 3 May 2007.
[338] See *Djavit An v Turkey* (App 20652/92) ECtHR judgment 20 February 2003, at [57] and *Balçik v Turkey* (App 25/02) ECtHR judgment 29 November 2007, at [46]–[47].
[339] Above pp 71.
[340] *Plattform Ärzte fur das Leben v Austria* (1991) 13 EHRR 204.
[341] *Öllinger* (2008) 46 EHRR 38.
[342] *Plattform Ärzte* above n 340.

reports of several protesters: a press photographer with a broken elbow, a student whose wrist was broken, a young environmental consultant who was thrown up and back in to the cordon and a 71-year-old man bruised after being rugby tackled.[343]

No sensible person would deny that the police are between a rock and a hard place when it comes to maintaining order, or trying to, at events and occasions such as the G20 summit. It has become clear that there are within and among the vast majority of (near) peaceful anti-globalisation protesters a hard-core intent on violence and damage. The tension between the various conflicting imperatives—maintaining order, allowing bystanders to shop or to work while also positively permitting and guaranteeing the right to dissent and to make known one's feelings about global capitalism—is thrown into very sharp relief at such times. Nonetheless, it is not helpful and in fact likely to be positively provocative publicly to insist that all were 'up for it and up to it', as senior officers were reported to have done.[344]

The same time period also saw adverse press coverage of another controversial tactic in relation to protests: surveillance of those taking part in demonstrations and protests.[345] What these reports make clear, for the first time, is that the police not only take photos of both activists and occasional protesters, but they have compiled a database of photos, video footage and other personal details, if known, on thousands of protesters and campaigners, all of it being stored for up to seven years. This information is open to inter-force exchange to facilitate the better policing of protests nationwide. They are, obviously, serious human rights concerns regarding such a system under Article 8, used indiscriminately without the need for guilt or even (reasonable) suspicion. It could similarly have a chilling effect on the right to protest and, as the reports indicate the press has been targeted too, on journalists' free speech under Article 10.

It was widely known that the police regularly photographed those participating in peaceful protests. That was the issue before the courts in *Wood v Commissioner of Police for the Metropolis*.[346] In the Administrative Court, McCombe J held that where a protester, the media co-ordinator of the Campaign Against the Arms Trade, a high-profile NGO, was photographed leaving the AGM of a company that organised arms fairs, he had no reasonable expectation of privacy, his photo being taken on a public street.[347] There had been no interference with Article 8's guarantee of respect for private life. This was overturned by a majority in the Court of Appeal. Although in general taking of photos on public streets does not engage Article 8, in certain situations—and this was one—it would or could do. It was wrong, Laws LJ thought, to compartmentalise the taking of photos and their retention. Here, if the position was looked at in the round—taking, retention (and by whom), purposes, effects on the subject—there were 'aggravating circumstances'. Although the most

---

[343] 'G20 officers may face multiple claims over brutality allegations' 'The G20 protesters' stories: allegations over police treatment on the frontline', *The Guardian*, 11 April 2009.

[344] 'Police tactics queried as Met says G20 protests will be "very violent"' *The Guardian*, 28 March 2009.

[345] 'Revealed: police databank on thousands of protesters' and 'Caught on film and stored on a database: how the police keep tabs on activists', *The Guardian*, 7 March 2009. In contrast, there is a widespread view gaining currency that taking photos of officers has been criminalised by s 76 of the Counter-Terrorism Act 2008. This makes it an offence to elicit or attempt to elicit information about an individual who is or has been a constable 'which is of a kind likely to be useful to a person committing or preparing an act of terrorism.' Though this seems unlikely on its face and in light of the Explanatory Notes, the JCHR accepted that it might have created a chilling effect on journalists: JCHR *Demonstrating respect for rights*, above n 336, para 95.

[346] *Wood v Commissioner of Police for the Metropolis* [2009] EWCA Civ 414 (Laws and Dyson LJJ and Lord Collins).

[347] *Wood* [2008] EWHC 1105 (Admin).

Conclusions 377

common instance was the violent and aggressive paparazzi scrum, not the case here, in the circumstances the court, unanimously, held that Article 8 was engaged. It was not as if the applicant was either suspected of a crime or even actually involved in a protest at the time. In the mind of Laws LJ, it was important

> to recognise that State action may confront and challenge the individual as it were out of the blue. It may have no patent or obvious contextual explanation, and in that case it is not more apparently rational than arbitrary, nor more apparently justified than unjustified. In this case it consists in the taking and retaining of photographs, though it might consist in other acts. The Metropolitan Police, visibly and with no obvious cause, chose to take and keep photographs of an individual going about his lawful business in the streets of London. This action is a good deal more than the snapping of the shutter. The police are a State authority. And as I have said, the appellant could not and did not know why they were doing it and what use they might make of the pictures.[348]

The Court was split only on the issue of whether the interference with Mr Wood's privacy was proportionate. Dyson LJ and Lord Collins considered it was not. In the words of Dyson LJ,

> the only justification advanced by the police for retaining the photographs for more than a few days after the meeting was the possibility that the appellant might attend and commit an offence at [a subsequent event] several months later. But in my judgment, even if due allowance is made for the margin of operational discretion, that justification does not bear scrutiny. First, [that event] was not the principal focus of the evidence-gathering operation. The principal concern of the police was what might happen at the AGM and/or in the vicinity of the hotel. But for that concern, the evidence would suggest that the operation would not have taken place in the first place. Secondly, the sole reason why the photographs were taken was to obtain evidence in case an offence had been committed at the AGM. Thirdly, once it had become clear that . . . the appellant had not committed any offence at the AGM, there was no reasonable basis for fearing that, even if he went to the [subsequent event], he might commit an offence there. His behaviour on 27 April was beyond reproach, even though he was subjected to what he considered to be an intimidating experience. There was no more likelihood that the appellant would commit an offence if he went to the fair than that any other citizen of good character who happened to go to the fair would commit an offence there.

A few points are worth making, albeit in brief. First, the Court of Appeal has recognised, to some extent, that there is quite a conceptual difference between (a) my being seen by others in a public street, (b) my being photographed by the press in a public street, and (c) my being photographed by the police in a public street.[349] For McCombe J in the Administrative Court to conflate all three without realising this or justifying it is an analytical flaw. Secondly, the Court did not go so far as to say that retaining photos is not permitted nor that taking and retaining photographs of those actually present at protests is not permitted; neither was that a question before it on the facts. Just to be photographed—without having done anything wrong—while on a march can constitute a chilling effect; clearly the photos will almost certainly be retained—unless taking photos is being used as some form of free-standing intimidation!—and so the same, in-the-round approach as was favoured by the Court of Appeal would be appropriate on any future challenge. Last, there is still a world of difference between taking photos and retaining them. In fact events since the Administrative Court's decision have shown that there is not limited use and restricted

---

[348] *Wood* [2009] EWCA Civ 414 at [45].
[349] See generally N Moreham, 'Privacy in public places' (2006) 65 *CLJ* 606.

circulation by the police but much more general disclosure and general dossiers being compiled. The police have accepted it is probably unlawful to film journalists and to subject them to surveillance.[350] But the only reason that can sensibly be offered must be the chilling effect. If so, why does this not apply equally to protesters? After all, if no one turns up to a demo, for fear of being captured on film, what have the press got to report? There is a symbiosis between the two and just as we all lose out by restrictions on the press, so the wider public interest is not served by measures that restrict participation in protest.

Nonetheless, the Court of Appeal decision in *Wood* is, from a protesting perspective, a far more welcome decision, though inevitably one that will make the task of policing, regulating and controlling protests and protesters a harder one. How hard seems to be a matter of conjecture. It largely depends on which side of the fence a protagonist sits. Essentially this goes to the root of the problem and tension in the whole area. Reliable data on the impact of legal changes on operational decision-making, in terms of effective policing, is to all intents and purposes unknown. That there will be *some* difference resulting from an effective ban on the police retaining photographs (or, we must assume, any personal data) for more than a few days is obvious. Will it mean the police cannot take photos at all? As we have seen, the judgment does not go that far. Clearly, some retention is permitted and foreseen but it is only lawful and proportionate so far as it relates to possible disorder or crimes at the venue itself. What limits are now placed, following *Wood*, on the police's ability to build up, maintain and develop an intelligence database of possible 'troublemaker' protesters? The Court has clarified one aspect but laid down little by way of guidance for the future. It seems inevitable that further challenges will be brought. It must be beyond dispute that some forms of protest and some protesters are either intent on or disposed towards violence, disorder and bare criminality. Some forms of persuasion, advocacy and 'protest', loosely described, will and should remain beyond the pale, even if—as will be suggested in our conclusion—the legal framework needs realignment. How can and should the police protect target companies from having bricks thrown through windows, and prosecute those who send death threats to individuals without being able to keep watch? These are standard, basic policing techniques. The problem is where—and by whom—should the dividing line be drawn? It must at least be triggered only when the police have some evidence, any suspicion that the person in question has committed any wrongdoing. If all someone is doing is engaging in peaceful, communicative, persuasive protest, they should not be watched, they should not be photographed and their details should certainly not be recorded and entered onto a general database. They should quite properly assume they will no more be watched by the police, or a database on them be built up, than would any citizen on daily business.

In this chapter, we have analysed a selection of preventive powers that the police have at their disposal to prevent peaceful protests. We did not dwell on some powers we considered elsewhere, notably the giving of directions where failure to obey means a protester has committed a separate offence. In chapter six we looked at directions in relation to trespassory assembly under section 69 of the CJPOA 1994 and in chapter four, directions to leave land under section 61 of the CJPOA 1994. Neither did we re-visit any substantive crimes which of course give rise to a power of arrest in the hands of the police, but after the event. We have assessed the preventive powers in doctrinal terms and we have also seen how they measure up in terms of Convention compatibility and Convention compliance. Suggestions have been offered as to how, and where, they might be found wanting but these

---

[350] '"We were wrong to film journalists covering protest", say Kent police', *The Guardian*, 10 March 2009.

are, at best, tentative. With the exception of breach of the peace, Strasbourg has yet to rule on most of the scenarios imagined or which have taken place—whether against the UK or other states—and where it has done so, has largely found in favour of the police on grounds of preventing disorder or protecting the rights of others. The exceptions have been where the protest has been entirely peaceful—as it was for the three anti-arms protesters in *Steel v UK*. Even there, much of the finding in their favour was predicated on there being no domestic decision.

In *Gillan* the House of Lords did very little to rein in the incredibly wide stop and search power contained in section 44 of the Terrorism Act. We touched on some examples of the misapplication of counter-terrorism powers in the conclusion to our last chapter, on direct action. As the JCHR noted, although there could be credible evidence that a protest or demonstration was being used to mask a terrorist attack, it had heard of no examples arising in practice. It was a matter of considerable concern.[351] In 2008, at the time of Plane Stupid's direct action against airport expansionism, John Wilding, a pensioner was on his way to Heathrow to a rally about the third runway. He was stopped on the basis that Heathrow bye-laws permitted access only to air passengers or those meeting them. 'Oddly only members of the party wearing ['Stop Airport Expansion'] t-shirts appeared to be in breach of those bye-laws', he wrote.[352] The new ACPO guidance in 2008 does clearly assert in bold font that 'Terrorism Act 2000 powers must only be used to stop and search people in relation to terrorism'.[353]

We saw how in *Austin*, albeit with no Strasbourg case law on the point, the House fashioned a new power, that of mass round up and corral on suspicion of the activities of a small group. If those concerns were not enough, the policing tactics at the G20 summit were founded on a vastly expanded reading of the judgment. In their view it entitled them not only to deal with a group that had already formed but also to herd protesters in the first place.[354] It has become a pro-active tool, rather than being used responsively, ie reacting to a group that has already formed where there is potential for it to get out of hand. In turn, and the evidence at the G20 bears this out, it created and then fuelled an inflammatory situation rather than quelling and containing it. The crowd's natural reaction to being contained was to lash out, provoking a cycle of escalating violence. Last, in *Singh* we saw how the courts have sanctioned the use of a power, conferred for a purpose unconnected with protest, to be used to quell and dampen a demonstration, despite other perhaps more appropriate powers being available but not called on. That last brings us back to a major concern in relation to policing of protest: the differential use of different public order powers. We looked at some data in the introduction that shows both significant disparities across the UK and significant concentrations in one Force on one single power.[355] For example, the vast majority of aggravated trespass cases proceeded with before the magistrates across England and Wales occurred in Suffolk. It recorded 19 out of 54 and 12 out of 74 in 2003. In that light, calls to increase the number and range of offences or to give the

---

[351] JCHR, *Demonstrating respect for rights*, above n 336, para 93.
[352] Letter to *The Guardian*, 3 June 2007.
[353] National Policing Improvement Agency, *Practice Advice on Stop and Search in Relation to Terrorism* 2008 p10, at: www.npia.police.uk/en/docs/Stop_and_Search_in_Relation_to_Terrorism_-_2008.pdf, accessed 11 April 2009.
[354] See for example a letter to *The Guardian*, 3 April 2009, written by Izzy Koksal and Luke Sheldon: 'We arrived to protest against the government's failure to tackle climate change, to be told by a policeman that "once you go in, you can't get back out . . . it could be an hour or it could be tomorrow morning"'.
[355] See above p 19.

police greater power to 'deal' with protest *might* assist in reducing the 'problem' of protest, but it will for certain vastly increase the range and scope of police discretion, at both macro- and micro-levels on the street. This in turn raises the usual concerns.

Those concerns do not appear in the context of the subject-matter of our last chapter, the regulation and restriction of protest by private law means, perhaps by the target companies. That does not mean that where, say, private target companies take action against protesters that is unproblematic.

Before we address the issue of public right of peaceful protest being regulated by private means and actors, we might usefully note three developments in the policing of protest from the first months of 2010.[356] Most important is the judgment of the European Court of Human Rights in *Gillan*.[357] This is the appeal from the House of Lords decision that we considered above.[358] There are really three aspects to the decision. First, Strasbourg has given a clear steer that a stop in general terms (that is stops under PACE as well as those stops not requiring "reasonable suspicion" under section 44 of the Terrorism Act 2000) could engage Article 5.[359] In the domestic proceedings, the House of Lords was very clear that a stop and search would not constitute a deprivation of liberty. Secondly, the House was not even entirely certain that such a stop and search would engage Article 8. The ECtHR was clear that it does.[360] Last, matters such as the breadth of discretion and the limited efficacy of safeguards meant that the stop and search scheme under section 44 was arbitrary and so not "prescribed by law".[361] A violation was found on that ground without the need to consider the proportionality of the measures, either in general or as specifically utilised for the two applicants. The next development relates to stop and search as well. We considered earlier the judicial review challenge to the policing operation at the Kingsnorth climate camp in the summer of 2008.[362] On the same day as the *Gillan* decision it was reported that Kent police had conceded the unlawful nature of those blanket stops and search purportedly carried out under PACE.[363] The last development is one that we have adverted to throughout this book, as well as earlier in this chapter: the increasing conflation of direct action with terrorism, or at least certain forms of direct action. We took a step nearer a full merger a little later on in January when the Ministry of Justice, in its instructions to probation officers, seemed to equate eco-environmental protesters with Al Qaeda and Irish republicans. In contrast to the first two developments, this last is not something to be welcomed.[364] Let us now turn to the topic of our final chapter and address the concerns that surround the use of private law remedies to control protest.

---

[356] Furthermore, in early August 2009, a few days after the manuscript was completed, the Independent Police Complaints Commission concluded its various investigations into the policing of the G20 that we considered a few pages ago, including the death of Ian Tomlinson and various allegations of brutality: see "Update on G20 investigations" at http://www.ipcc.gov.uk/news/pr04082009_g20update.htm (accessed 1st February 2010).
[357] *Gillan and Quinton v UK* (App 4158/05) ECtHR judgment 12 January 2010.
[358] Above p 316.
[359] *Gillan and Quinton* above n 357 at [57].
[360] Ibid at [61]–[65] and see above n 34.
[361] Ibid at [79]–[87].
[362] Above n 9.
[363] "Police admit stops and searches on 11-year olds at Kingsnorth protests" *The Guardian* 12 January 2010
[364] See further "Ministry of Justice lists eco-activists alongside terrorists" *The Guardian* 26 January 2010.

8

Private Law Remedies and Proceedings

Previous chapters have explored the various ways in which the police can, in advance, utilise the law to prevent or to control a protest. This might be by imposing conditions or bans under the Public Order Act (POA) 1986—administrative regulation—that we looked at in chapter five, or by giving directions backed up by the threat of arrest. This might be at common law, to prevent a breach of the peace, or under section 69 of the Criminal Justice and Public Order Act (CJPOA) 1994, in relation to aggravated trespass. We looked at this in chapters seven and six respectively. All of these operate in the public sphere. This chapter will consider the rights and remedies in private law that those directly affected by a protest have.

The law that regulates protest is multi-layered and multi-faceted. Increasingly the public and private spheres overlap or are interdependent. We have seen how several criminal offences depend on the fact that protesters are trespassing, that is exceeding their private law rights to use land. Aggravated trespass under section 68 of the CJPOA 1994 is one such. We also saw in chapter six, for animal rights activists at least, that exactly the same protest might constitute one of the economic torts—that is, in the private sphere of the common law—as well as founding criminal liability under sections 145–146 of the Serious Organised Crime and Police Act (SOCPA) 2005. This chapter, the last substantive one in the book, explores how the same event—say, a static demonstration outside an animal research lab—might give rise not just to overlapping criminal liability (obstruction, breach of the peace, trespassory assembly) so as to trigger different police powers of arrest or prevention but to a range of civil remedies in the hands of the corporate or individual targets. In most cases, these obtain irrespective of whether the protest is peaceful or direct action. We have looked at one in detail: civil injunctions under section 2 of the Protection From Harassment Act (PFHA) 1997. We shall not traverse this ground again but will focus instead on several other remedies that might be pursued. We touched upon some of the wider issues and concerns that surround the privatisation of protest regulation in our introductory chapter. We shall touch upon some more in this one and in our concluding chapter, which follows.[1]

---

[1] One other is the whole area of private investigation into protesters and protest groups by or on behalf of private target companies, described by Stephanie Harrison of counsel as privatising criminal justice: joint Liberty/Norton Rose seminar: 'The right to protest', 5 May 2009. This is aside from any concerns about agents provocateurs and the reliability of the information gleaned, where those doing the surveillance are likely to have an interest in maintaining an output. In the public arena, this topic came to the fore in early 2009 when it was revealed that the police had tried to recruit a Plane Stupid activist as a spy: 'Police caught on tape trying to recruit Plane Stupid protester as spy', *The Guardian*, 24 April 2009. The furore surrounding this seemed to indicate surprise that it was going on, surprising in itself.

I. Introduction

Simply put, protesters and their commercial targets are in a private relationship: neither is a public authority in the sense that term is used in section 6 of the Human Rights Act (HRA).[2] This means that neither owes the other any *direct* duties to protect or to guarantee their Convention rights. Thus, *AnimalExperimenters plc* or *CoalPolluters R Us* are under no obligation to ensure that a protest against them goes ahead as planned or goes ahead unrestricted: they may seek whatever remedies are available in domestic law and, unlike the police, not be obliged to act only where it is proportionate to do so.[3] Matters are rarely so simple and clear-cut. This is no different. Whatever claims the target company or its directors seek to employ will nowadays still be mediated, as would criminal proceedings brought by the state, by the requirements of the HRA and the right to peaceful protest ... but how?

A. Indirect Horizontal Effect

Whatever powers a company seems to have, they will be tempered in one of two ways: through the new interpretative canon of section 3 or through the development of the common law by virtue of the indirect horizontal effect of the HRA.

The majority of private law remedies, with the exception of PFHA injunctions, lie at common law.[4] Thus there can be no question of protesters seeking to avail themselves of section 3 of the HRA against the company's claim, arguing for a Convention-compatible meaning, since that course of action depends on the restriction being in *statutory* form. It means that cases will come before the courts and be argued in a very different way to, say, *Connolly v DPP*.[5] There, as we saw in chapter six, Connolly succeeded in persuading Dyson LJ that the offence of sending an indecent or grossly offensive message through the post should be subject to a form of implied free speech defence.

Protesters instead will need to frame their arguments around the status of the court as a public authority, bound by section 6 of the HRA to reach Convention-compliant decisions as between litigating parties. We looked at this when we considered the operation of the HRA in chapter two. It has been seen most commonly where the media intrudes into private life,[6] though there is no reason that such 'pen-poised'[7] judicial activism should not infiltrate the law of protest. It would be fair to say that arguments along the lines that judges should

---

[2] We considered in some detail the scope of s 6 in chapter two p 44. We identified some institutions that may fall under the functional test or definition. Likely targets of protest that may also fall into this hybrid category were posited as universities and hospitals. They would only be liable under s 6 where the act they perform, which allegedly restricts the right to protest, is one that is public in nature: see s 6(5). This, we saw, possibly raises more questions than it answers—what are the qualities or criteria by which we may judge 'publicness'?

[3] This is not a one-way street. If corporate targets decide to respond to a protest by themselves publishing statements about the group or individual members or, as has taken place, making public names and addresses and other details on a 'Hall of Shame' website, then they leave themselves exposed to actions in defamation or for breach of confidence, following cases such as *McKennit v Ash* [2006] EWCA Civ 1714. As with the reverse scenario, courts would be asked to balance the competing rights of free speech and privacy. This second tactic is more usually called on by counter-pressure groups in the field of abortion rights.

[4] It is possible but unlikely for a company to initiate a private prosecution under say s 5 of the POA 1986 ... in which case s 3 would then bite on that criminal relationship between protester and private company.

[5] *Connolly v Director of Public Prosecutions* [2007] EWHC 237 (Admin).

[6] See as an example *McKennit*, above n 3.

[7] Lord Irvine LC, House of Lords Committee, Hansard HL Deb 24 November 1997, col 784.

develop or re-align the common law rules of nuisance or trespass in tort so as better to protect the right of peaceful protest have featured far less in protest cases than section 3/*Connolly*-type arguments. It was, in effect, what took place in *DPP v Jones*, where the House of Lords was concerned with criminal charges for trespassory assembly under section 14B of the POA 1986.[8] As we saw in chapter five, a majority of the House considered that a person's private law right at common law to use the highway should not have remained in stasis from the Victorian era; instead it should now include a limited 'right' of peaceful non-obstructive protest. Therefore, if all a group did was to protest peacefully without obstruction, it was not trespassing on the highway. An argument along similar lines was mounted—unsuccessfully—before the ECtHR in *Appleby*: there should be a limited right to assemble and demonstrate in a shopping centre irrespective of the owner's permission.[9]

B. The Court's Balancing Act in the Private Sphere

To comply with their section 6 duty judges cannot simply—and one-sidedly—protect the rights of protesters under Article 10 and Article 11 in isolation. Those who are targeted by or are victims of either peaceful protest or direct action may well also have Convention rights that will require protecting. This task is not the same as where a judge is considering the balance between the right of peaceful protest and any countervailing Article 10(2) and 11(2) social interests in, say, preventing crime and disorder and maintaining public safety. What we are talking about here is a clash before the court of two *rights* that both require resolution as part of the horizontal duty under section 6.

First, all protests must occur somewhere.[10] That will engage Article 1 of the First Protocol—the right peacefully to enjoy possessions.[11] That right covers not just interests in and over land but has been defined at Strasbourg as wide enough to comprise economic and commercial rights relating business as well. In other words, protests aimed at damaging trade or disrupting an enterprise have the potential to engage the right in exactly the same way as if the group squatted on the company's land.[12] That said, the Article is concerned with preventing 'deprivations' not just interference with possessions. The possessor's legal rights or her entitlement to use those possessions needs to be extinguished or to disappear altogether, not just become less (economically) valuable or less easy to use or to exploit.[13] That might counter an excessive reliance on using the First Protocol to defeat the right of peaceful protest. It is clear that if a group of direct action protesters ripped up GM crops in a field, any attempt by them to found a defence based on Article 11 could be met with the farmer's right not to have his GM crop 'possessions' destroyed. This would in fact apply

---

[8] *Director of Public Prosecutions v Jones* [1999] 2 AC 240 (HL).
[9] *Appleby v UK* (2003) 37 EHRR 38.
[10] In chapter four we considered the various issues surrounding the interplay between ownership of land and the right to protest especially in light of the changing nature of land holding.
[11] This is usually but incorrectly referred to as a right to 'property': the French text refers to 'biens'.
[12] The term includes company shares—*Bramelid v Sweden* (App 8588-9/79) (1982) 29 DR 64—and economic goodwill *van Marle v Belgium* (1986) 8 EHRR 483. In *Tre Traktörer AB v Sweden* (1989) 13 EHRR 309 the revocation of a restaurant's licence to sell alcohol had adverse effects on the value and goodwill of the restaurant and so was held to be a possession because an economic interest connected with running the restaurant. For more on Art 1 of the First Protocol, readers should consult the relevant chapter in a specialist work such as D Harris, M O'Boyle and C Warbrick, *The Law of the European Convention on Human Rights*, 2nd edn (Oxford, Oxford University Press, 2009).
[13] *Sporrong and Lonnröth v Sweden* (1983) 5 EHRR 35.

384 *Private Law Remedies and Proceedings*

equally if criminal charges (for offences contained in a statute) were brought as it would to common law claims by the farmer, the subject of this chapter. If members of a different group decided to chain themselves to diggers to prevent a new motorway being built, the position is clearly very different. It is hard to see how anything of economic value belonging to the construction company has been extinguished.

Secondly, those subjected to protest in or around their homes (such as harassment of an arms company director) or places of work[14] (such as a doctor at an abortion clinic) could claim it was infringing their rights under Article 8. This protects the right to respect for the home, for private and family life too. Article 8 has been given potentially quite wide scope at Strasbourg level—in cases such as *Pretty v UK*[15]—so as to encompass aspects of individual autonomy. It might have been thought that conferring a quasi-right to live as I choose would open up the opportunities to counter the right to protest. Domestically, the chances of someone targeted by a protest successfully claiming that it had infringed her 'life choice' to go fishing or to grow GM crops or to watch a controversial play or to bank with Barclays have been cut drastically as a result of the House of Lords decision in *R (Countryside Alliance) v Attorney-General*.[16] There, Parliament's decision to ban fox-hunting was argued as having infringed the group's rights under Article 8. It had adversely affected the private life, cultural lifestyle and the use of the homes of its members as well as resulting in loss of livelihood. The House provided a significant narrowing of the potential width of *Pretty*. In Lord Bingham's words, the scope of Article 8 was concerned with protecting 'the individual against intrusion by agents of the state, unless for good reason, into the private sphere within which individuals expect to be left alone to conduct their personal affairs and live their personal lives as they choose'.[17] In Lord Rodger's view Article 8 protected 'those features of a person's life which are integral to his identity'[18]—giving it potentially a much wider scope—but held against the applicants because they hunted in full knowledge that it was a public, rather than private, spectacle.[19]

II. Possible Claims by Private Parties

We shall focus on claims arising in tort, specifically trespass, nuisance and harassment. We considered some of the land law issues by implication in chapter four. Situations where a protest might have an impact on contractual relations are hard to imagine, though the same arguments about section 6 and horizontal development and re-moulding would apply. Perhaps P made an on-line order for a football from *SportsGoodsRUs.com* but between the order and delivery, she discovered they were made in South Asia in breach of International Labour Organisation rules. In protest P sought to rescind the contract.[20] In fact, a not entirely dissimilar situation occurred early in 2009. Cai Mingchao bid £13m for two bronze

---

[14] *Niemitz v Germany* (1992) 16 EHRR 97.
[15] *Pretty v United Kingdom* (2002) 35 EHRR 1.
[16] *R (Countryside Alliance) v Attorney-General* [2007] UKHL 52.
[17] *ibid*, at [10], Lord Hope at [54]–[55] and Baroness Hale at [116]. At [15] Lord Bingham explained why in his view none of the varied aspects of the applicants' Article 8 claims was made out on the facts.
[18] *ibid*, at [101] and similarly widely—as an aspiration rather than as a holding—Lord Brown at [139]–[140].
[19] *ibid*, at [108].
[20] Of course, one immediate problem with this scenario is that it might well not meet the definition of protest we established in chapter three.

artworks looted by the British or French from the Chinese Imperial Palace in 1860. They were being auctioned by Christie's as part of the estate of the designer Yves St Laurent. Cai Mingchao won but immediately announced he would not pay, calling his decision to bid a 'patriotic' act.[21] To what extent, if at all, if he were sued by Christie's for the full sum in British courts could Cai Mingchao defend his actions by claiming that when he bid, and entered into a binding contract, he was exercising his right to peaceful protest?[22] Much more likely than our imagined scenario would be where P induces a third party, say The Football Association, to breach its contract with *SportsGoodsRUs*, raising issues about the economic torts. We touch on these below.

A. Defamation[23]

Cyber protests might lead to claims in defamation by those companies or individuals targeted, just as they might by more traditional pamphletting or banners or slogans on a march.[24] These protests might take the form of a spoof website or a campaigning website making assertions about (say) the 'real' destination of tanks and rocket launchers or 'the truth' about company X employing under-age workers in the developing world. They run the risk of being held liable in damages for libel (if in permanent form) and otherwise slander.[25] Although there might be practical reasons (impecunious protesters) or Public Relations-related reasons that might militate against any claim actually being brought, if they were to be sued, English libel law means all a claimant needs to establish is that a protester has published a prima facie defamatory statement. Then, the onus shifts to the protester, as the defendant, to assert one of various defences. So, if a protester does publish something that 'tend[s] to lower the [claimant] in the estimation of right-thinking members of society generally'[26]—the test for whether a publication is prima facie defamatory—they must show on the balance of probabilities that it was justified (ie true), or is 'fair comment' on a matter of public interest, or is protected by absolute privilege (such as a report of Parliamentary or court proceedings) or by qualified privilege.

It is that last defence where there has been considerable development. Once material is deemed to attract qualified privilege, the *defence* can only be defeated if the claimant (this time) proves actual malice: Was the statement published either knowing it was false or recklessly, not caring as to its truth? The defence (broadly) resembles the *New York Times v Sullivan* public interest defence in the USA.[27] It is in fact wider, since it is not concerned only with political figures. If established, it shifts the onus back to the claimant and so is able to protect protesters who publish material which they cannot show to be true, something

---

[21] 'China 'patriot' sabotages auction', at: news.bbc.co.uk/1/hi/world/asia-pacific/7918128.stm, accessed 12 April 2009.

[22] This would of course be calling on Art 11 as a shield, under s 7(1)(b), using it collaterally to a claim brought against him: this is the fourth type we identified in chapter two, p 51 above.

[23] I am grateful to my UEA colleague Alastair Mullis for some assistance with this section.

[24] It should not be forgotten, for example, that in *Hubbard v Pitt* [1976] QB 142, alongside injunctions to prevent nuisance and disturbance of their estate agency business, the three claimants were also seeking libel damages for what was written on the placards. A more recent example were the toxic waste dumping signs at issue in *Culla Park v Richards* [2007] EWHC 1850. These were put up by the protesting defendants on their own property and held during a demonstration.

[25] The recognised specialist work is *Gatley on Libel and Slander*, 11th edn (London, Sweet and Maxwell, 2008) edited by Patrick Milmo QC and others.

[26] *Sim v Stretch* (1936) 62 TLR 669 (HL) 671 (Lord Atkin).

[27] *New York Times v Sullivan* 376 US 254 (1964).

that might in fact be difficult to show to the satisfaction of a court. Whether or not defendants fall four-square within the defence is a matter of crucial importance. Much recent case law on the topic generally (that is, outside the confines of protesters being sued) has surrounded the extent and scope of this possible defence. In very broad, loose terms a story will attract qualified privilege where there is both an interest in reading the story and a duty to publish it and it is published meeting the requirements of what is called the 'responsible journalist' test.[28]

Although we do not have clear domestic authority, it seems very likely that this rule would apply to publications in non-traditional media and by campaigning groups more generally. In 2008, the Privy Council ruled in *Seaga v Harper*, a Jamaican case, that in principle the *Reynolds* defence was of wider ambit than being available only to the press and broadcasting media.[29] The Privy Council could see no valid reason why the liberalising intention of *Reynolds* should not extend to publications made by any person who published material of public interest in any medium, so long as the conditions framed by Lord Nicholls in that case as being applicable to 'responsible journalism' were satisfied. Whether this will mean uniform or fragmented standards, dependent on the type of publisher, of what is connoted by 'responsible journalism' will need pinning down over time. The Privy Council was unable to accept that confining the defence to media publications, as had been done in *Kearns v General Council of the Bar*, was correct in principle.[30] A few years before, in the McLibel trial, the Court of Appeal had accepted that the duty to publish was not confined to the mainstream media but could also apply to members of campaign groups, such as London Greenpeace. However, to satisfy the test, the duty to publish had to override the requirement to verify the facts.[31]

We should not underestimate the McLibel case.[32] McDonalds brought proceedings against two environmental campaigners (and members of London Greenpeace) responsible for distributing a British or even European pamphlet 'What's Wrong With McDonalds?' The pair defended themselves before the UK courts—in the longest running civil case in history (313 days in the High Court covering two and a half years). They lost on almost all the issues. UK and US McDonalds combined was awarded damages of £60,000, reduced on appeal to £40,000. No steps were ever taken to enforce the award. The pair pursued a claim under the ECHR, *Steel and Morris v UK*,[33] arguing that the denial of legal aid and the

---

[28] *Reynolds v Times Newspapers* [2001] 2 AC 127; *Jameel v Wall Street Journal* [2006] UKHL 44; *Galloway v Telegraph Group* [2006] EWCA Civ 17; and *Charman v Orion Publishing* [2007] EWCA Civ 927.

[29] *Seaga v Harper* [2008] UKPC 9 at [11]. Lord Carswell based his view in part on the speeches in *Jameel* above by Lord Hoffmann at [54], Lord Scott at [118] and Baroness Hale at [146].

[30] *Kearns v General Council of the Bar* [2003] 1 WLR 1357. The Privy Council in *Seaga* concluded that such a finding was not necessary in any event to dispose of the appeal in that case.

[31] Details of the Court of Appeal decision (31 March 1999) are taken from the ECtHR judgment in *Steel and Morris v United Kingdom* (2005) 41 EHRR 22 at [30]–[32]. Privilege was more likely to be extended to a publication that was balanced, properly researched, in measured tones and based on reputable sources. In the instant case, the leaflet 'did not demonstrate that care in preparation and research, or reference to sources of high authority or status, as would entitle its publishers to the protection of qualified privilege'. Campaign groups could perform a valuable role in public life, but they should be able to moderate their publications so as to attract a defence of fair comment without detracting from any stimulus to public discussion which the publication might give. The relaxation of the law contended for would open the way for 'partisan publication of unrestrained and highly damaging untruths', and there was a pressing social need 'to protect particular corporate business reputations, upon which the well-being of numerous individuals may depend, from such publications'.

[32] MNCs resorting to libel against those who question their business practices is not just a problem in Britain or Europe: 'Writers criticise Tesco for 'chilling' Thai libel actions', *The Guardian*, 30 April 2008.

[33] *Steel and Morris*, above n 31, noted by E O'Dell (2005) 121 *Law Quarterly Review* 395.

possibility of excessive damages being awarded constituted breaches of their rights to a fair trial under Article 6 and unwarranted and unnecessary violations of Article 10.

The Court found for them on both counts: the lack of procedural fairness and the lack of legal aid contributed to a disproportionate interference, as did the size of the award relative to their income and resources. The lack of legal aid also rendered the trial unfair as it led to an inequality of arms.[34] It is clear too that the Strasbourg Court took a stricter line on the balance between litigants as to the burden of proving the truth of the allegations and on the tolerance permitted to value judgements. Although the Court upheld the presumption of falsity, the massive imbalance between the parties made the additional burden that it imposed one that pushed the case over the limits of proportionality. This was all the more so given the greater latitude of acceptable criticisms—made by both 'small and informal campaign groups . . . outside the mainstream' as well as by traditional journalists—of large corporations and multi-national corporations (MNCs) given the importance of free speech and the role and influence of such companies in modern society.[35] It is worth recalling that in the domestic proceedings, the Court of Appeal (Pill and May LJJ and Keene J) rejected an argument that in English law MNCs such as McDonalds should have no right at common law to sue in defamation—the unsuccessful argument effectively being put that *Derbyshire v Sunday Times*[36] should be extended. The Court also rejected an argument that *Reynolds*-type qualified privilege should extend to discussion of issues of public importance relating to public corporations.[37]

B. Causing Economic Harm

Protesters are perfectly free to lobby or urge customers to boycott certain companies on grounds, say, of their human rights or environmental record. Nestlé in the 1990s and Barclays throughout the 1970s and 1980s spring to mind as good examples, even if the drive there was not necessarily either of those two reasons. This is nothing more than the exercise of free speech—though of course protesters would need to be aware of the risks of defamation, as we saw in our last section.[38]

There is though a fine line between P urging X to boycott company Y—lawful—and P inducing X to break an existing contract with company Y, which is not. Where protesters do cause financial harm to companies or to individuals they might leave themselves

---

[34] Most libel cases are now funded by conditional fee agreements (CFAs)—under which claimants pay no legal costs if they lose but if successful their costs are paid by the media publisher. There is debate about whether CFAs with, say, 100% costs 'uplift' make it too much of a risk for the press to defend libel writs, thus constituting a chilling effect on free speech: see as an example *Campbell v MGN (No 2) (Costs)* [2005] UKHL 61, which is in fact a privacy case. I am grateful to Alastair Mullis for these points.

[35] *Steel and Morris*, above n 31, at [89]–[96].

[36] *Derbyshire v Sunday Times* [1993] AC 534.

[37] On the first point, the Court decided that commercial corporations had a clear right under English law to sue for defamation, and that there was no principled basis upon which a line might be drawn between strong corporations which should, according to the applicants, be deprived of this right, and weaker corporations which might require protection from unjustified criticism.

[38] Where say a local council seeks to exert pressure in that way in their terms of business or refusing to deal with certain companies, a whole host of public law concerns—competitive tendering, government contracts—arise as well as more mainstream public law judicial review principles: see as examples *R v Lewisham London Borough Council ex parte Shell UK Ltd* [1988] 1 All ER 938 and *R v Ealing London Borough Council ex parte Times Newspapers Ltd* (1986) 85 LGR 316.

exposed to being sued for one of the economic torts:[39] conspiracy, procuring or inducing a breach of contract, or the new tort of causing loss by unlawful means established by the House of Lords in *Mainstream Properties*.[40] We considered these briefly when we looked at the new offence contained in sections 145–146 of SOCPA 2005: interfering with contractual relationships so as to cause harm to an animal research organisation.

When a group of Greenpeace activists occupied a Range Rover factory in Solihull in the west Midlands, in protest at the car's CO_2 emissions and environmental impact, there were newspaper reports that the company obtained an injunction and had served a writ claiming £12m damages. This was said to represent the loss in production, £1m for each hour of the 12-hour occupation.[41] My own research has not tracked down any evidence that a writ was served, though it is understood that there is an extant injunction. Similarly, there were media reports that Ryanair, the airline that suffered most from the Plane Stupid disruption at Stansted in 2008, had not ruled out making a claim against all those protesters convicted, as well as against BAA itself, to cover its estimated £2.2m loss.[42] The reports about both are sketchy but we must rule out a contractual basis for the claims—neither group of protesters had any conceivable such relationship with either Range Rover or Ryanair—so the only realistic legal avenue would be under one of the economic torts. If either case does still proceed, the defendants might try to impress on the court the need to mould private law so as better to accommodate and reflect the right to peaceful protest. Much play would be made of the clear chilling effect created by even the institution of claims such as these for damages. They might have argued for the establishment of a 'golden formula' to protect protest, or certain forms of it at least, similar to that which exists for trade disputes[43] or that damages for those torts should not be awarded so high as effectively to silence opposition.

The problem, though, they would inevitably face is this. These protests were 'peaceful' in the non-violent, *Ezelin* sense and thus capable at least of engaging Article 10 or 11. But, as both were fairly obstructive and disruptive forms of direct action sit-in, any restrictions—in the form of either ex post facto awards of damages or preventive injunctions—would

---

[39] In *Department of Transport v Williams*, The Times, 7 December 1993, a group was protesting against the M3 motorway extension at Twyford Down and damaged vehicles and tore down fences. The Court of Appeal held that the criminal offence under s 303 of the Highways Act 1980 (wilfully obstructing any person carrying out his lawful duties under that Act) despite it only leading to a fine was also capable of constituting the tort of wrongful interference with business and thus could be restrained by injunction. However, a common purpose or intention to commit trespass did not equate to a common intention to commit violence or to interfere with business.

[40] *Mainstream Properties v Young; OBG v Allan; Douglas v Hello!* [2007] UKHL 21 as interpreted in *Total Network SL v Revenue and Customs Commissioners* [2008] UKHL 19. In *Mainstream Properties*, the House rejected the unified theory—a super-tort of 'unlawful interference with contractual relations' (comprising both procuring breach of contract and unlawful interference)—in favour of two separate torts, procuring breach of contract alongside the wider tort of 'causing loss by unlawful means'. This latter encompassed unlawful interference and subsumed within it intimidation as well. Procuring breach of contract is dependent on a third party's primary wrongdoing—breaching its contract with X—whereas causing loss by unlawful means is primary rather than accessory liability. These two torts though separate could overlap and in the right circumstances the same activity could give rise to concurrent liability. See generally H Carty, 'The economic torts in the 21st century' (2008) 124 LQR 641.

[41] *The Guardian* (G2 section) 19 May 2005. Fiona Donson reports how the Department of Transport threatened and did institute proceedings for damages totalling £1.9m against 76 Twyford Down protesters representing the costs of delay and damage, though there was little evidence it proceeded. In fact, she notes the Department was willing to settle for £1000: F Donson, *The Road to Conflict—Case Studies in the Effectiveness of Public Law as a Mechanism of Participation in Environmentally-Sensitive Decision Making* (Unpublished PhD thesis, Kings' College London, 1997) 218.

[42] 'Plane Stupid protesters face £2m claim from Ryanair', *The Evening Standard*, 8 January 2009.

[43] Section 219 of the Trade Union and Labour Relations (Consolidation) Act 1992 sets out (in terms) that 'acts done in furtherance or contemplation of a trade dispute' shall not be actionable as one of the economic torts.

likely be seen by Strasbourg, and thus under the HRA, as proportionate. Such protests as we have seen tend to be declared inadmissible or, if not, given no protection; the first two applicants in *Steel v UK* would be a good example in point.[44] There is little chance of the domestic position being held as out of line. Whatever protection the common law gives—none—for such activities, and thus whatever restrictions on protest it imposes—absolute—means there is simply no need for judges to develop the common law relating to the economic torts, pursuant to section 6 of the HRA. In all likelihood, a court would hold that the common law already balances the various competing interests and rights.

C. Corporate Remedies

Corporate targets have several distinct rights and remedies derived from commercial or company law.[45] We have already seen that companies can protect information about their directors.[46] Individual—or even groups of—shareholders who own fewer than 51 per cent of the shares and who have, say, concerns about the change in direction that a company is taking—in conflict with their own beliefs—have little option but to cave in. In *Re Waste Management plc*, a minority shareholder was unsuccessful in his attempt to prevent a scheme of arrangement and takeover of a publicly listed recycling company by a private company whose narrower commercial interests, it was argued, might collide with wider environmental objectives.[47] It was reported that Burberry, the famous exclusive clothing manufacturer, banned the vice-president of PETA (People for the Ethical Treatment of Animals) from its AGM despite his having a valid voucher and proxy card.[48] Either it had the power—in which case a review of this area of company law seems timely—or it did not but carried on regardless, in which case we see again the disjuncture between law and practice. Whichever is the case, they both clearly have deleterious consequences for participation and for the right to protest. If institutional shareholders tried to use their votes to alter a company's articles of association to prevent socially-minded, environmentally-friendly (individual) shareholders from putting forward their own company resolutions, or to try to take the company in a different direction, or just allow them to attend the AGM to ask questions of the directors and maintain pressure, how would and should company law respond?[49] If those small, individual critical shareholders challenged the proposed measure, would a Chancery judge hold that they would not be denied the right to protest and free speech, they would merely be denied one forum for exercising it or would she hold that it was an abuse of majority power to seek to restrict that participatory right in such a way for such a reason?

---

[44] *Steel v United Kingdom* (1998) 28 EHRR 603.
[45] We considered on-line protests and misuse of company logos in chapter five.
[46] Chapter six, above p 298.
[47] *Re Waste Management plc* [2003] EWHC 2065 (Ch). Does this chime with moves to a more stakeholder-based corporate agenda?
[48] *Eastern Daily Press*, 18 July 2008.
[49] See 'Exxon investors propose ban on green activism', *The Guardian*, 27 May 2008 and P Gadd, 'Being heard at the AGM' (1996) 1 *Commercial Law* 6. This article looks at shareholder protests against British Aerospace plans to change the articles of association governing conduct of business at general meetings in order to avoid disruption by protestors.

D. Trespass to Land

Protesters who enter or remain on someone else's land without permission or who exceed what limited permission they have to be or to remain there will be trespassing. They run the risk that the owners of the land—technically the person entitled to possession[50]—might try one of two approaches. They might take eviction proceedings to repossess the land (under RSC Ord 113, now CPR 50) or where the protest is temporary rather than a long-term squat they might seek an injunction to bring the trespass to an end and prevent it from reoccurring.[51] Both generally require a court order, although the remedy of self-help remains available to dispossessed occupiers and owners in certain situations.

Possession proceedings have tended to crystallise around two separate topics. The first is the quintessentially procedural one of standing: who may bring possession proceedings in private law? *Manchester Airport v Dutton* established that a licensee (that is, not the owner, occupier or even someone in de facto possession at the time of the trespassory occupation) could still seek eviction of protesters on a third party's land.[52] The second issue is that of collateral public law defences to the private law action, specifically alleged non-compliance with domestic or EC planning and environmental law. In each of *Secretary of State for Transport v Haughian*[53] and *Secretary of State for Transport v Fillingham*[54] the courts found against the protesters. In *Haughian*, it was argued that the alleged unlawfulness of a compulsory purchase order underpinning the Newbury bypass (through failing to carry out an environmental impact assessment, in breach of EC law) was a defence to possession proceedings. *Fillingham* also concerned the Newbury bypass, the habitat of a rare snail protected under various EC Directives. The protesters argued this justified their occupation as one that was necessary to preserve an endangered species, so as to defeat any claim to possession. The Court was not open to such an argument: whatever environmental obligations

---

[50] Even where a local public social amenity is built and owned privately under the Private Finance Initiative (PFI) the site will be occupied by the local hospital or school, pursuant to some form of lease. The person with the right to possession, and thus to sue any trespassing protesters, will be the NHS Trust or Board of Governors of the school not the PFI company owners.

[51] In such cases, the names of likely protesters do not have to be known or even made clear on the writ provided the description used is sufficiently certain that the terms of the order identify both those who are included and those who are not: *Hampshire Waste Services Ltd v Intending Trespassers in Chineham Incinerating Site* [2004] EWHC 1738 (Ch) at [8]–[9] Sir Andrew Morrit V-C, granting a so-called 'Harry Potter' order (*Bloomsbury Publishing Group plc v News Group Newspapers Ltd (Continuation of Injunction)* [2003] EWHC 1205). The order should be directed to 'persons entering or remaining without the consent of the claimants'.

[52] *Manchester Airport v Dutton* [2000] QB 133 (CA), Kennedy, Chadwick and Laws LJJ. Protesters opposed to a second runway at the airport set up camp (with tree houses and tunnels) in trees on land owned by the National Trust. The trees were to be removed or lopped by the airport authorities so as to clear a flight path. The protesters had no permission to be there and so were trespassers as against the Trust. Soon after, the airport authorities were given a licence to enter and to remove the trees. The Court by a majority (Chadwick LJ dissenting) nonetheless concluded that a licensee with a right to occupy land (as BAA was), whether or not he was in actual occupation, was entitled to bring an action for possession against a trespasser in order to give effect to, so as to enjoy, the rights under the licence. An estate in or a right to exclusive possession of the land was not required before an order under the summary procedure could be obtained. See too *Monsanto v Tilly*, Court of Appeal decision, 25 November 1999 (Stuart-Smith, Mummery and Pill LJJ), noted in full [2000] *Environmental Law Review* 313 and *Bromley London Borough Council v Susannah* (1999) *Journal of Planning and Environment Law* 361, Court of Appeal, noted (1998) 7 *Environmental Law and Management* 11. The issue in the latter was whether the local authority had title—so as to be able to seek possession proceedings in order then to sell the land for redeveloping Crystal Palace—where the land had originally been common land. An application to register land as common land is unlikely to provide a defence to possession proceedings, even if the protest concerns the ultimate development use of that land: *Epsom Borough Council v Nicholls* (1999) 78 P & CR 348 (QBD).

[53] *Secretary of State for Transport v Haughian* [1997] 2 CMLR 497 (CA), Hutchison, Pill and Rose LJJ.

[54] *Secretary of State for Transport v Fillingham*, unreported High Court decision, 26 March 1996 (Sedley LJ), noted [1997] Env LR 73.

there were (on the facts there were held to be none, there being no breach of EC law), these were not a defence to possession proceedings where land was occupied without consent or authority. The court would not balance whatever public law duties the Crown was said to owe against its private law rights to possess land in such circumstances.

Injunction proceedings too have tended to focus on procedural matters such as the representative status of defendants and the scope of relief—as we saw in the previous chapter under the PFHA 1997—as well as matters of substance. For example in *NIREX v Barton* Henry J held that an injunction to prevent protesters obstructing the lawful activity of developing land for disposing of nuclear waste, or obstructing entry onto that land (effectively supporting the tort of interference with business) could only be maintained against those actually involved.[55] Injunctions were therefore discharged against those whose only connection with the protest was that they held office in one of the two unincorporated protest associations involved at the site when the torts of obstruction or trespass were committed.[56] Though it has arisen mostly in connection with injunctive relief under the PFHA 1997, courts have grappled with the question whether or not injunctions bind those who are not actually parties to proceedings but who have notice of its terms and who act in concert with those who are named and bound, or those who are in any event given written notice of the injunction. The courts have favoured width.[57] The rationale—and which lends support to its use in trespass cases—is that the

> convenient administration of justice demanded that the courts should be able to afford effective protection to the victims of threatened illegal action by members of associations whose declared aims were in line with or calculated to promote such illegal action. It was a proper exercise of the judge's discretion to grant injunctions.[58]

By contrast, *Monsanto Plc v Tilly* featured an attempt to raise the substantive defence of necessity to the company's claim for an injunction.[59] Monsanto was licensed to carry out GM crop trials across the UK. Tilly was a member of an environmental interest group known as GenetiX Snowball. During its campaign, Tilly and others entered one of Monsanto's trial sites and uprooted a number of GM crops as a symbolic gesture. Monsanto applied for summary judgment for a permanent injunction to prevent any repeat trespass to land or goods, arguing that there was no defence to the claim. At first instance Tilly succeeded and was given leave to defend the action on the ground that the trespass to land or goods was in the public

---

[55] *NIREX v Barton*, unreported High Court decision, *The Times*, 14 December 1986.
[56] Unincorporated associations are unable to sue or be sued in their own names. In order to sue a protesting group in its entirety—including all its members—a representative action must be embarked on, suing perhaps one member or an identifiable select core such as the central organising committee. The effect is that each and every member of the association in question is bound by any orders made, injunctions granted or judgment given. It is for the court to decide if such a course of action is proper. It will only be so (absent an express or implied statutory provision) where all members share the same interest, even as to methods: *M Michaels (Furriers) Ltd v Askew*, unreported Court of Appeal decision, 23 June 1983 and *News Group v SOGAT '82* [1986] IRLR 337. There Stuart-Smith J refused to make representative orders against individual branches of a union where there was or might be a difference of opinion as to the achievement of the common goal by commission of torts. On the facts in *NIREX* Henry J discharged the representative orders. By contrast, the central tenets of the protest group GenetiXSnowball in *Monsanto v Tilly* [2000] Env LR 313 were said to be direct action such that joining up as a member meant implicit endorsement of unlawful activity.
[57] See *Huntingdon Life Sciences v Curtin*, unreported High Court decision, *The Times*, 11 December 1997, discussed K Kerrigan (1998) 3 *Journal of Civil Liberties* 37; *DPP v Moseley*, unreported High Court decision, *The Times*, 23 June 1999; and *Silverton v Gravett*, unreported High Court decision, 19 October 2001, Bentley QC sitting as a judge.
[58] Purchas LJ in *M Michaels (Furriers)*, above n 56.
[59] *Monsanto Plc v Tilly* [2000] Env LR 313 (CA).

interest and/or was necessary to protect third parties and their property. The protesters asserted that they were protecting two separate groups. First, those in the vicinity of the crops, such as organic farmers whose crops might be cross-pollinated (thereby losing their organic status) and organic bee-keepers who would be similarly affected if their bees harvested pollen from the GM crops. Second, the wider public, convinced as the protesters were that the crops presented a danger to mankind in general and farmers in the Third World in particular. The Court of Appeal allowed Monsanto's appeal: Tilly could not rely on either defence. Having reviewed the cases, public interest was not a defence known to law separate from the defence of necessity. That latter was available only in very limited circumstances: in cases of emergency where it was necessary for private citizens to act in the face of immediate, obvious and serious danger to life or property, where a reasonable person would conclude there was no alternative but to trespass and where the citizen acted reasonably in all the circumstances. Even accepting there was such a danger, on the facts the defence could not be made out, since the protesters had deliberately chosen to uproot some but not all the crop.[60] The real aim of the campaign had clearly been to attract publicity, further advanced by a public court hearing. Stuart-Smith LJ put that last point thus:

> The defendants are frustrated that they have been unable to change government policy by the strengths of their arguments. It is the breaking of the law, with its potential for martyrdom which affords far better publicity than any other. Indeed I think this is the real answer to the question which the court posed ... why do the defendants need to break the law to obtain publicity? It seems to be implicit in [the GenetiX Snowball] method of operating that they cannot attract sufficient attention to their cause without breaking the law. It would in my judgement be an astonishing proposition if the law were to recognise this as justification for law breaking.[61]

Further, even in circumstances of emergency—that is, immediate and serious danger to life or property—trespass was not justified where a public authority—here the Department for the Environment—was responsible for the protection of public interests. The Court was concerned that the protesters were challenging the wrong person in the wrong court by the wrong means. The essence of their complaint, on which they wanted a conclusive judicial determination, was the decision to grant the licence, an issue that was not justiciable in the common law courts on a private law action for trespass. As Mummery LJ put it,

> [t]hese are not public law proceedings challenging the legality of the decision by the Department of the Environment to grant licences to Monsanto ... These are adversarial private law proceedings to which no public authority is a party; in which the issues before the court are defined by the parties; in which the court will be confined at trial to consideration of the documentary and oral evidence of fact and expert opinion which the parties choose to call; and in which the court will only hear the arguments which the parties and their advisers wish to advance. In these rather unpropitious circumstances the court will be invited by the defendants to make a seemingly authoritative final 'judgment' on ... political choices and controversial policies the lawfulness of which are unchallenged in this action. Decisions on broad policy questions concerning the potential risks and rewards of GM crops clearly require input and back-up from sources of information, advice and specialist scientific and technical guidance to which the court does not have access. By running this line of defence the defendants are directly inviting the court to trespass beyond the proper limits of the judicial function, away from the world of triable issues of hard fact and law and deep into the territory of state policy and political judgement involving matters which have no bearing on Monsanto's claim for trespass. The court must resist the invitation to assume juris-

[60] We might just pause to note that it is a strange defence that exculpates worse and more damaging behaviour.
[61] Above n 59 at 323.

diction to resolve an issue of a kind which it is not its constitutional function to decide and which it is not competent and equipped to decide. Civil proceedings for trespass are not an appropriate vehicle for a determination on whether the growing of GM crops is in the public interest. The defendants and their supporters can continue to argue freely and to campaign strenuously elsewhere that the growing of GM crops is not in the best interests of the public.[62]

It is clear from this last extract that the Court did not—and courts will not—look kindly on being used as a facility for agit-prop activity. Neither will they allow protesters deliberately to infringe the property rights of others so as to attract publicity or persuade the government to legislate.

> [W]here the object of the respondent's campaign is to change government policy . . . [i]n a democratic society that must be effected by lawful and not unlawful means. Those who suffer infringement of their lawful rights are entitled to the protection of the law; if others deliberately infringe those rights in order to attract publicity to their cause, however sincerely they believe in its correctness, they must bear the consequences of their lawbreaking. This is fundamental to the rule of law in a civilised and democratic society.[63]

This presumption in favour of property and property rights reflects the historic preference of the common law. That is not surprising. What is surprising is that the case is fought against a backdrop devoid of any discussion, reference or even passing mention and then rejection of the right to protest. This is not to say that the appellants would have succeeded. Pulling up crops is some way past peacefully handing out anti-war leaflets, so any restrictions are likely to be proportionate, but a full year after the HRA was passed and some months after the re-invigoration of the common law of trespass on the highway in *DPP v Jones*, the right of protest is the dog that didn't bark. The right to peaceful enjoyment of possessions on the other hand simpers quietly, noises off, implicit in the judgment of Mummery LJ. Any argument would no doubt have been given short shrift and rejected after just a few lines' analysis—as we have seen repeatedly, Strasbourg case law is not supportive of anything approaching obstructive or disruptive protest—but the activity taking place here was a protest. The fact that the target of the protesters' ire was properly the government and its policy—though not solely—does not mean this is any the less a public protest, albeit one that was ultimately destructive. As the *Environmental Law Review* commentator put it, 'the court's final decision centred around a strict legalistic interpretation of the relevant provisions. Accordingly, there was either an explicit or implicit judicial rejection of the values or arguments which the protest groups were putting forward'.[64] Though Mummery LJ is almost certainly correct to say that the civil law procedures for the grant of injunctions do not lend themselves to more policy-oriented disputes,[65] he is not correct to hold that courts should 'resist the invitation to assume jurisdiction to resolve an issue of a kind which it is not its constitutional function to decide'. In a rights-based democracy, with powers conferred under section 6 of the HRA specifically by Parliament in 1998, that is no longer an answer.[66] Deciding normative questions and balancing competing rights claims or tension

---

[62] *Monsanto v Tilly* [2000] Env LR 313, 341–2. This bears a striking resemblance to the approach adopted by the courts, in several of the Iraq war cases, to the issue of the prerogative to declare war and deploy troops: see as examples *R v Margaret Jones* [2006] UKHL 16 (more in the lower courts) and *R (Gentle) v Prime Minister* [2008] UKHL 20.
[63] *Monsanto*, above n 59, 329 (Stuart-Smith LJ).
[64] *Monsanto*, above n 59, 341.
[65] Another way to look at this would be to conclude that the informed resolution of questions properly allocated to the judiciary should be facilitated not hindered by procedural rules.
[66] See on this J Jowell, 'Judicial Deference: servility, civility or institutional capacity?' [2003] *Public Law* 592, 597.

between rights and social interests is now—rightly or wrongly—quintessentially the judicial task and their constitutional function (or one of them), just as it was in the Belmarsh case, where Lord Bingham addressed that same issue.[67]

E. Nuisance and Harassment at Common Law

Nuisance comes in two flavours, public and private, and both also exist as either crimes or torts.[68] Private nuisance is the misuse of land to the detriment of a third party in connection with their ownership or use of it. Where A does something (perhaps even a state of affairs on A's land that A allows to continue[69])—whether lawfully or not—that interferes with B's enjoyment or use of her land or of a right connected to her land, private nuisance is committed. As the tort is dependent on an interference with B's rights in relation to land, in order to claim B must own or lease the land or be a licensee with an exclusive right to possession.[70]

On the other hand, public nuisance has no obvious and immediate connections to land. We encountered the crime in chapter six when we looked at the House of Lords decision in *Rimmington* in the context of direct action protests.[71] In short, knowingly inflicting damage, injury or inconvenience on everyone or all members of a class constitutes the crime, although—and this is the effect of *Rimmington*—prosecutors should only charge where there is no possible statutory alternative. Anyone who suffers special damage over and above that suffered by everyone (or everyone within the class) has a tortious claim in public nuisance. As no possessory or proprietary interest in the land is needed,[72] a claim in public nuisance could be instituted by anyone who suffers greater loss than any other through misuse of, say, the pavement.

Incidents potentially covered by the umbrella of tortious nuisance could include: loud and noisy protest marches along the roads, setting up a vigil outside the home of a director of an arms company, assembling in large numbers on the highway with the express purpose of obstructing free passage,[73] perhaps even using one's own home as a base for protests—festooned with posters and placards—affecting the value of surrounding houses. Of course in each, the claimants would need to prove special damage for public nuisance and in private nuisance some interest in or over land: without the former, as Scott J commented in *Thomas v NUM* we would arrive at the 'startling proposition that the plaintiffs can, without special damage, sue in tort for obstruction to the highway'.[74]

Perhaps the most well-known nuisance case in the context of protest is *Hubbard v Pitt*.[75] A group of local people in Islington, North London campaigned against a particular local

---

[67] *A v Secretary of State for the Home Department* [2004] UKHL 56 at [42].

[68] See generally A Dugdale and M Jones (eds), *Clerk and Lindsell on Torts*, 19th revised edn (London, Sweet and Maxwell, 2007).

[69] In fact, if a council allows a group of protesters to remain on its land and the group uses it as a base for causing unlawful disturbance to neighbours, the council may be liable in nuisance itself where a third party's enjoyment of the use of their land is affected. Once the council fails 'to exercise its power to turn out the travellers once their habitual misbehaviour became apparent' it effectively adopts the protesters' nuisance as its own: *Lippiatt v South Gloucestershire County Council* [2000] QB 51, 65, Sir Christopher Staughton.

[70] *Hunter v Canary Wharf Ltd* [1997] AC 655.

[71] *R v Rimmington* [2005] UKHL 63.

[72] *Tate & Lyle Industries Ltd v GLC* [1983] 2 AC 509.

[73] *Broome v DPP* [1974] AC 587 (HL) 597 (Lord Reid).

[74] *Thomas v National Union of Mineworkers* [1986] Ch 20, 63.

[75] *Hubbard v Pitt* [1976] QB 142, discussed by P Wallington, 'Injunction and the right to demonstrate' (1976) 35 Cambridge Law Journal 82.

estate agency, which was said to be instrumental in the 'gentrification' of the area by turning a blind eye to the dubious practices of landlords seeking repossession so as to sell on and develop. A picket was organised outside their offices for a couple of hours every Saturday for several weeks. The claimant partners in the estate agency sought damages for libel, nuisance and conspiracy at common law, as well as injunctions to prevent the campaigners besetting their premises, molesting their employees and committing nuisance. That last was the issue before the Court of Appeal. Forbes J at first instance had granted an interim injunction restraining the protesters from besetting the premises. He held that using the highway for a picket is not lawful unless it is done in contemplation or furtherance of a trade dispute.[76]

> Stationing of pickets on the public highway is not a legal exercise of the right of passage and, if it renders the highway less commodious, amounts to a public nuisance ... It may ... be an unreasonable user of the highway and therefore a common law nuisance. This will always be a question of fact, and what is or is not a reasonable user of the highway will be determined by reference to the purposes for which the highway was dedicated. As picketing is a use of the highway wholly unconnected with the purposes of dedication and is, in fact, designed to interfere with the rights of an adjoining owner to have unimpeded access from the highway, it is likely to be found to be an unreasonable user unless it is so fleeting and so insubstantial that it can be ignored under the de minimis rule.[77]

The protesters appealed, arguing that they were doing nothing unlawful save exercising their right peacefully to protest, to communicate and to make others aware of their points of concern. The Court of Appeal by a majority (Stamp and Orr LJJ; Lord Denning MR dissenting) still found for the claimants but on a different basis to the lower court. Before the Court of Appeal, the issue had become commission of private nuisance (affecting the estate agency's use of its office) rather than public nuisance which had been argued before Forbes J. In the interim, the House of Lords had handed down judgment in *American Cyanamid* and so for the Court of Appeal, the issue was now about granting interim relief using the new balance of convenience test.[78] This was, in the view of the majority, overwhelmingly in favour of maintaining the status quo: damages would not adequately compensate the possibly serious damage to the value of estate agents' business. There was also evidence of a serious issue to be tried, so it could not be said that the claimants would not succeed in their claim for a permanent injunction. Lord Denning did not think the *American Cyanamid* test should necessarily apply—given that it was a case on patents—but if it did, the balance of convenience did not necessarily favour the claimants.[79] It was a case where a court should assess the relative strength of each party's case before deciding whether to grant an injunction. Here, the 'uncompensatable disadvantages' were so evenly balanced: it was also the case that an interlocutory injunction would virtually decide the whole action in favour of the plaintiffs, as the protesters would be restrained from picketing until trial (perhaps for two years, or more) by which time the campaign would be over.[80]

---

[76] In this Forbes J favoured *J Lyons & Sons v Wilkins* [1899] 1 Ch 255 over *Ward, Lock and Co Ltd v Operative Printers' Assistants' Society* (1906) 22 TLR 327. We considered both of these cases in chapter six, pp 290 above.

[77] *Hubbard*, above n 75, decision of Forbes J cited at 157–9. Much of what he says concerning the illegality of using the highway for picketing—as it is a use that is not responsive to the purposes for which the highway was dedicated and thus is a trespass—is no longer good law, following *DPP v Jones* [1999] 2 AC 240.

[78] *American Cyanamid Co v Ethicon Ltd* [1975] AC 396 (HL).

[79] *Hubbard*, above n 75, 178.

[80] In his view the facts did not even give rise to nuisance: the claimants' annoyance could only stem from the content of the placards, in effect libel, something considered as not subject to restraint pending trial since *Bonnard v Perryman* [1891] 2 Ch 269.

All three judges were critical of the approach Forbes J took to the issue of the picket. The majority thought his conclusion was predicated on the scope of the right to use the highway rather than the scope of the tort of nuisance at common law. Stamp LJ considered that the conclusions drawn by Forbes J on the application of the law to the facts were not satisfactory.[81] Lord Denning went further, clearly demonstrating a preference for *Ward Lock* over *J Lyons*. The case that the group was committing private nuisance had not been made out. Using the highway for a picket unless it was in connection with or furthering a trade dispute was not per se unlawful. There was no such tort as 'watching or besetting' and picketing someone's premises, even if done with a view to compel or persuade, is only wrongful if it is combined with other conduct (for example, obstruction or violence) such that the whole conduct amounts to a nuisance at common law.

> Picketing is not a nuisance in itself. Nor is it a nuisance for a group of people to attend at or near the plaintiffs' premises in order to obtain or to communicate information or in order peacefully to persuade. It does not become a nuisance unless it is associated with obstruction, violence intimidation, molestation, or threats. [Here] there was no obstruction, no violence, no intimidation, no molestation, no noise, no smells, nothing except a group of six or seven people standing about with placards and leaflets outside the plaintiffs' premises, all quite orderly and well-behaved. That cannot be said to be a nuisance at common law. This question can be tested by supposing that the placards and leaflets contained nothing derogatory of the plaintiffs, but commended them and their services. No one could suggest that there was a nuisance at common law. This shows that the real grievance of the plaintiffs is that the words on the placards and leaflets were defamatory of them. Their real cause of action, if it exists, is for libel and not for nuisance.

The courts

> should not interfere by interlocutory injunction with the right to demonstrate and to protest any more than they interfere with the right of free speech; provided that everything is done peaceably and in good order [which was] the case here.[82]

There is clearly considerable doubt over the extent to which picketing, or even communicative peaceful protests more widely, can and should constitute either form of nuisance. Forbes J was not strictly overruled by the majority in the Court of Appeal.[83] Neither was there satisfactory resolution of the seeming inconsistency between *Ward Lock* and *JS Lyons*. Whether courts would now or should now permit landowners inconvenienced or disrupted by protests (assuming they suffer special damage, for public nuisance) to sue in nuisance must be arguable. There are two limbs to this. First, Lord Denning though was clear:

> Picketing is lawful so long as it is done merely to obtain or communicate information, or peacefully to persuade; and is not such as to submit any other person to any kind of constraint or restriction of his personal freedom.[84]

This is in sharp contrast given by Forbes J to the doctrinal pre-eminence to the right of property within nuisance at common law. He maintained it was

> quite wrong to argue ... that political conduct of a particular kind ... becomes clothed with a legality which it would not possess in a non-political context ... A man's right to enjoy his property

---

[81] *Hubbard*, above n 75, 180 and 189.
[82] ibid, 179.
[83] Indeed, it was assumed by Scott J in *Thomas v NUM* [1986] Ch 20, 64 still to hold true: regular picketing of a working miner's home, irrespective of the numbers and peaceful nature, would constitute nuisance at common law.
[84] *Hubbard*, above n 75, 177–8.

which abuts on the highway and to have access to that property both for himself and his invitees is a right which is fully entitled to the support of the courts if and when the courts are asked to support it.[85]

As we have seen on several occasions throughout this book, it is a problem of conceptualisation. Lord Denning's view is certainly more closely in line with the domestication of the right of peaceful protest, enshrined by the HRA. The common law must now be read as subject to that statutory imprimatur. Should there be any doubt, section 6 of the HRA would entitle (require?) courts to develop and confirm the law along those lines. As Beatson J acknowledged in *The Church of Jesus Christ of the Latter Day Saints v Price*,[86]

> [p]art of the claim involved nuisance and we can see in the case, albeit not expressly acknowledged, the role of the court as a public authority under s.6 being asked to mould and to develop the common law so as to accommodate Convention rights, albeit that the defendant was defeated on the facts—that is, so that they are not disproportionately restricted as a result of common law doctrine.

Secondly, the majority's holding was in turn based largely on the application of the *American Cyanamid* test. Under the HRA, there have been developments here such that it would not today provide the same rock-solid basis for disposing of the case. Section 12 of the HRA contains a presumption in favour of the Convention right of freedom of expression, something we must assume would include some peaceful protest cases where free speech rather than assembly predominates. Section 12 has meant some tinkering with the balance of convenience test in favour of protesters and free speech when applied to Article 10 cases. Following *Cream Holdings v Bannerjee*, the party seeking an injunction must show not just an arguable case but that it will more likely than not succeed at trial.[87]

As well as existing in statutory form since 1997 in the PFHA, unreasonable harassment of people wanting to exercise their own right to use the highway is said to exist as a separate tort, a species of private nuisance at common law.[88] In *Thomas v NUM*, Scott J declared (in a case arising out of the 1984–85 miners' strike):

> All citizens have the right to use the public highway. Suppose an individual were persistently to follow another on a public highway, making rude gestures or remarks in order to annoy or vex. If continuance of such conduct were threatened no one can doubt but that a civil court would, at the suit of the victim, restrain by an injunction the continuance of the conduct. The tort might be described as a species of private nuisance, namely unreasonable interference with the victim's rights to use the highway ... They are, in my judgment entitled under the general law to exercise that right without unreasonable harassment by others. Unreasonable harassment of them in their exercise of that right would, in my judgment, be tortious.[89]

The existence of—and need for—this new tort was doubted by Stuart-Smith J in another mass picket strike case, *News Group v SOGAT '82*, because it was one where liability was founded on unreasonable interference with the general rights of others, without proof of any damage.[90] For the same reasons as for nuisance, its continued existence in the HRA-era as a means by which private parties might control protesters must be open to question.

---

[85] *Hubbard*, above n 75, decision of Forbes J cited at 158.
[86] *The Church of Jesus Christ of the Latter Day Saints v Price* [2004] EWHC 3245 (QB) at [173].
[87] *Cream Holdings v Bannerjee* [2004] UKHL 44. This would be one reason to argue a case under Art 10 not Art 11 before the domestic courts: s 12 makes clear reference to 'the Convention right to freedom of expression', that is to Art 10, and not free speech more generally.
[88] *Thomas*, above n 74, 64.
[89] ibid.
[90] Above n 56.

III. Conclusions

An important consequence flowing from the privatised regulation of protest relates to the cost of enforcement. The financial burden shifts onto those who are directly affected by the protest rather than being borne directly by the state, as is the case where the police arrest under, say, section 5 of the POA 1986 or for watching and besetting. In reverse, the criminalisation of trespass, through the creation of the offence of aggravated trespass, has brought not only speedier resolution—immediate arrest rather than county court proceedings—but a resolution to incidents of protest where the costs are defrayed through being borne indirectly by us all, through taxation, including of course being borne by those actually doing the protesting. There are also concerns that relate to accountability of the private entities involved, as contrasted with the police (and local councils where bans on processions and assemblies are being considered), and about transparency and consistency of approach.

Another concern in any analysis of the incidental privatisation of protest (relying on and adapting historic common law remedies) as contrasted with deliberate privatisation—where the state creates bespoke private law remedies such as under the PFHA—is the suitability of the common law or chancery courts. There is, it must be conceded, some strength to the justiciability point made by Mummery LJ in *Monsanto v Tilly*.[91] The problem is that if protest points are raised in essentially private law cases, the conceptualisation of the case may well be different. In both the eviction and injunction cases, founded on trespass, the cases tend to be fought in a private law sea of technicality without a causeway to wider public law issues such as the specifics of the protest at hand or free speech more generally. We can see in these cases a clear rejection of any argument based on rights (to protest) or about the wider political/public context within which the protest and debate—and ultimately claim for repossession—was taking place. For Hutchison LJ (in *Haughian*) the simple question was this. Did the applicants have an arguable defence to claims for possession?

> They cannot, in my judgement, by asserting or admitting that the motive for their presence is to protest as against the implementation of the scheme, convert their status as mere trespassers into something conferring rights or entitling them to maintain their right to remain against the claim by the Secretary of State whose title is undoubtedly, in my view, sufficient to maintain these claims against them.[92]

There is, as we have seen, a wider public interest and functional value to protest. Should it really be left to private actors to determine its scope and extent consequential on private litigation?[93] We shall address this and several other wider issues as we bring this book to a close with some concluding words, in our next—and last—chapter.

---

[91] Above n 59.
[92] *Haughian*, above n 53, at [31].
[93] In some respects, the words of Lord Bingham in *R (Laporte) v Chief Constable of Gloucestershire* [2006] UKHL 55 at [52] are as valid here as when discussing the development of breach of the peace at common law: 'if (on which I express no opinion) the public interest requires that the power of the police to control demonstrations of this kind should be extended, any such extension should in my opinion be effected by legislative enactment and not judicial decision ... Any prior restraint ... must be scrutinised with particular care ... Assessment of whether a new restriction meets the exacting Convention test of necessity calls in the first instance for the wide consultation and inquiry and democratic consideration which should characterise the legislative process, not the more narrowly focused process of judicial decision. This is not a field in which judicial development of the law is at all appropriate'.

9

Conclusion

> Rights worth having are unruly things. Demonstrations and protests are liable to be a nuisance. They are liable to be inconvenient and tiresome, or at least perceived as such by others who are out of sympathy with them.[1]

2009 was a year of some moment and frenetic activity for those interested in peaceful protest. London has seen three major demonstrations: the protest against the Israeli actions in Gaza in January, the long-term protest outside Parliament by Tamil supporters and the G20 summit in April. There has been considerable public disquiet surrounding the policing of each, especially the last. As well as generating thousands of column inches—both hard-copy and virtual—there have been two parliamentary inquiries dedicated to the policing of the G20 protests. The first was conducted by the Home Affairs Select Committee and the second by the Joint Committee on Human Rights (JCHR), as well as its more general report into the policing of protest in March 2009.[2] Her Majesty's Inspectorate of Constabulary published the results of its investigation in July.[3] The death of Ian Tomlinson, on his way home from his job as a news vendor, is itself the subject of a separate Independent Police Complaints Commission (IPCC) inquiry (ongoing at the time of writing). That tragedy apart—thanks in most part to the speed and ease of modern technology—during the first few days of April we were also witness to Nicola Fisher being slapped across the face by burly male officer from the Territorial Support Group. This was at an event to mark the death of Mr Tomlinson the day before. A little later in the year, that same technology and user-generated media content spreading virally brought us—on the international stage—the brutal death of Neda Agha-Soltan, protesting at the outcome of Iran's election results. From a more strictly legal perspective, there were two crucial decisions in 2009 assessing the extent of policing tactics and strategy. In January, the House of Lords handed down judgment in *Austin* and in May in *Wood* the Court of Appeal issued its verdict on police surveillance tactics.[4] As we saw in chapter seven, the result was a one-all draw.

---

[1] Laws LJ in *Tabernacle v Secretary of State for Defence* [2009] EWCA Civ 23 at [43].

[2] JCHR 7th report of session 2008–09 (23 March 2009) *Demonstrating respect for rights: a human rights approach to policing protest* at: www.publications.parliament.uk/pa/jt200809/jtselect/jtrights/47/4702.htm, accessed 9 July 2009 and follow up report (22nd report of session 2008–09 (28 July 2009) at: www.publications.parliament.uk/pa/jt200809/jtselect/jtrights/141/14102.htm, accessed 16 August 2009. Home Affairs Select Committee 8th report of session 2008–09, *The policing of the G20 protests* (23 June 2009) available at: www.publications.parliament.uk/pa/cm200809/cmselect/cmhaff/418/41802.htm, accessed 10 July 2009.

[3] HMIC, *Adapting to protest*, 7 July 2009 at: inspectorates.homeoffice.gov.uk/hmic/docs/ap/, accessed 7 July 2009.

[4] *Austin v Commissioner of Police for the Metropolis* [2009] UKHL 5; *Wood v Commissioner of Police for the Metropolis* [2009] EWCA Civ 414.

I. A Strasbourg Snapshot: The Right of Peaceful Protest Under the ECHR in 2010

What picture has been painted of the state of play of protest law today? At European level (chapter three) two things are clear. First, intentionally obstructive and deliberately disruptive direct action protest, although it is not outwith the protection of Article 11 per se, has almost no chance of being protected. Restrictions—whether by way of arrests, or by administrative regulation, or by measures taken in advance—are without exception so far seen as proportionate, given the need to prevent disorder and protect the rights of others, howsoever nebulous those 'rights' might be. Secondly, the general trend of cases over the past five years has been one that advocates much greater acceptance of incidentally disruptive protests. Older cases where there was disruption—of traffic, passers-by, of business and every-day activities—would quite possibly be decided rather differently today. These would be cases like *G and E v Norway* (the four-day Lapplander protest outside Parliament),[5] *GS v Austria* (demonstration banned because of a fear of excessive noise)[6] and *Chorherr v Austria* (the arrest of two peace protesters at the air force fly-past).[7]

This new view is underpinned by an acceptance of the wider socio-political function served by the ability to protest freely. Though it has never really been made explicit, behind the Court's approach in more recent cases has been the idea of protest as something of benefit to us all in the longer term. Even if we cannot see protest as being of any immediate value and even if, in fact, its exercise is an immediate burden, relatively minor delays and disturbances to our daily lives are something that Strasbourg now enjoins us to endure for the greater public good. The prevailing view in the ECtHR has started to disjoin disruption from disorder in its reasoning: 'any demonstration in a public place may cause a certain level of disruption to ordinary life and may encounter hostility'. Since that case, *Aldemir v Turkey*, involved forcible dispersal with tear gas and truncheons, that must have made the Court's task and conclusions easier, we can safely assume.[8] In *Aya Otaman v Turkey* the Court asserted that 'where demonstrators do not engage in acts of violence, it is important for public authorities to show a certain degree of tolerance towards peaceful gatherings if [Article 11] is not to be deprived of all substance'.[9] It has repeated this mantra in many cases since, keen to emphasise that an individual's right to peaceful protest is not lost just because a protest becomes violent. As it asserted as long ago as *Ezelin v France* in 1991, what is crucial is whether the individual commits 'reprehensible' acts.[10] This is something we should keep to the forefront of our minds when we start to consider domestic developments. *Öllinger*, as we considered in chapter three and again in chapter five, cannot be seen as anything but a rejection of the straightjacket created by *Chorherr*.[11] The possibly disruptive reaction of third parties at the scene—perhaps we might even go so far as to say the effect

---

[5] *G and E v Norway* (Apps 9278/81 and 9415/81) EComHR inadmissibility decision 3 October 1983.
[6] *GS v Austria* (App 4923/89) EComHR inadmissibility decision 30 November 1992.
[7] *Chorherr v Austria* (1994) 17 EHRR 358.
[8] *Aldemir v Turkey* (App 32124/02) ECtHR judgment 18 Dec 2007 at [42]. A violent or forceful police reaction is not always frowned on: see *Çiloglu v Turkey* (App 73333/01) ECtHR judgment 6 March 2007, decision by five votes to two.
[9] *Aya Otaman v Turkey* (App 74552/01) ECtHR judgment 5 December 2005 at [41]–[42].
[10] *Ezelin v France* (1991) 14 EHRR 362 at [53]).
[11] *Öllinger v Austria* (2008) 46 EHRR 38.

of the protest on others at the time and at the scene—will become, at best, one factor for the authorities to bear in mind, not one that can largely determine the policing response.

The extent to which that applies to large-scale protests and demonstrations is unclear. At first glance, a case like *Patyi* might seem to herald a more relaxed approach. We might recall that the Court there took the view that a protest on the pavement outside the Prime Minister's residence was not one that called for an absolute ban, given that there was no danger to public order and no likelihood of violence.[12] That might seem to call for a revision of a case such as *Rai v UK*.[13] An outright ban on any demonstrations in Trafalgar Square was upheld (the application being declared inadmissible) irrespective of any possible disorder or disruption. In *Patyi* though, there were at most only 20 proposed protesters. Strasbourg in more modern times has yet to confront the same sort of situation as occurred in *Rai*: both *Kandzhov v Bulgaria* and *Kuznetsov v Russia* involved at most a handful of protesters.[14] In fact, *Molnar v Hungary* comes closest and there was held to be a violation, although a mass demonstration, which brought traffic to a standstill, was allowed to continue for several hours before being dispersed.[15] The dispersal was proportionate to the need to protect the rights of others, free movement and traffic. This was not an advance ban; the Court in its more tolerant guise has still not had the opportunity to revisit and revise *Rai*.

II. A Domestic Snapshot: The Right of Peaceful Protest in England and Wales in 2010

On the domestic front, it is not as easy to summarise the extent of the right. Any form of direct action, that is intentional and deliberate obstruction, disruption or intimidation, aimed at a commercial target or at an activity to ensure it stops, is rejected as a legitimate campaigning tool, just as it is at Strasbourg. Over time, peaceful, persuasive protest, seeking to communicate an idea or to change viewpoints has become looked on more favourably, though not consistently so.

However, there is a real risk that in seeking to outlaw and to limit direct action, the response of the law has been to cast too wide a net and in doing so, whether by design or by oversight, has captured far more political activity than is appropriate and balanced. We have encountered many examples throughout this book. One should make the point. In chapter six we saw how harassing someone in the vicinity of their home has been regulated. Originally, under section 42 of the Criminal Justice and Police Act 2001 (CJPA), the power was limited to directing someone to leave. It kicked in if a protester was present outside someone's home and two triggers were met: (i) they intended to persuade their victim not to do something they were entitled to do (or to do something they were not obliged to do); and (ii) their presence was likely to cause alarm or distress towards that victim or to harass them. That power was extended in two ways in 2005 in the Serious Organised Crime and

---

[12] *Patyi v Hungary* (App 5529/05) ECtHR judgment 7 October 2008.
[13] *Rai v United Kingdom* (App 25522/94) EComHR inadmissibility decision 6 April 1995.
[14] *Kandzhov v Bulgaria* (App 68294/01) ECtHR judgment 6 November 2008 and *Kuznetsov v Russia* (App 10877/04) ECtHR judgment 23 October 2008.
[15] *Molnar v Hungary* (App 10346/05) ECtHR judgment 7 October 2008.

Police Act (SOCPA). First, section 42A created the free-standing offence of harassing someone in the vicinity of their home. That is not our concern. Secondly, under section 42 as amended, protesters can now also be directed to leave and not to return within three months. This is the problem. Having been ordered to leave, they will commit a further offence if they return within three months with the purpose of persuading their victim not to do something they are permitted to do (or to do something they were not obliged to do). There is no further requirement, as there is with the original power of directing someone to leave, that they return and harass, alarm or distress someone as part of their persuasive tactics. It is enough if protesters, having been warned not to return, do so within three months merely to engage in peaceful communicative persuasive protest including, it would seem, persuasion directed at a wholly new activity of the householder. As we saw in chapter six, an anti-abortion protester could not return within three months to persuade a doctor to sell his shares in an arms manufacturer or to vote for a different political party—even, perhaps, to persuade him to tidy up an unsightly garden. The drafting of the new section must create an unnecessary restriction on the right of peaceful protest by being overly broad. Whether it could be 'saved' by section 3 of the Human Rights Act—limiting the new offence to situations where the returning protester does cause harassment, alarm or distress—is moot.

This potentially excessive width is not limited solely to instances where Parliament has chosen to intervene; judges have done so as well either at common law or as an aspect of interpretation. We saw—again in chapter six—how the Divisional Court decision in *Winder v DPP* has widened the scope of aggravated trespass under section 68 of the Criminal Justice and Public Order Act (CJPOA) 1994.[16] The fox-hunt protesters were guilty because (i) they were trespassing on land; (ii) someone else was engaged in (what was then) a lawful activity; and (iii) they had the intention of disrupting that lawful activity as and when they reached it from the adjacent field and had done an act—carrying citronella—that was more than merely preparatory to that end. The judgment criminalises those who are remote in time and place from actually causing any harm, as well as those whose objectives might be impossible to achieve. The protesters were guilty from the moment they entered the adjacent field even if—unbeknown to them—the hunt been cancelled earlier that day. We have to ask what social ill is here being outlawed and whether or not the law has struck the correct balance between the rights, freedoms and interests of all concerned.

We might well think of the outcome in *Haw* in the same light.[17] Indeed, that case might be viewed as worse, given that the judges there were faced with seemingly clear-cut legislative instructions limiting the impact on protest. Though it might not have been Parliament's intention to exclude his lengthy protest outside Westminster from the operative provisions of SOCPA 2005—indeed many would say that Brian Haw was the presumed target—sections 132–133 made clear that seven days' advance notice was needed only for 'demonstrations starting on or after 1st August 2005'. For the commencement order then to try to explain this as meaning 'starting or continuing on or after 1st August 2005' and for the Court of Appeal to accept this was judicial conjuring of the highest order. To reiterate the points made in chapter four, if the commencement date was clear on the face of the statute, why was there a need to clarify it in the Order? If it was not, the principle of doubtful penalty should have kicked in. How could and why should someone on 1 August have

---

[16] *Winder v Director of Public Prosecutions* (1996) 160 JP 713 (DC), discussed in chapter six above pp 260.
[17] *Director of Public Prosecutions v Haw* [2006] EWCA Civ 532.

complied with the seven-day requirement when, at a point seven days in advance (24 July), there was no need to have given any notice at all?

Chapters four to eight portray a picture of protest that is very mixed. It is impossible to sum up succinctly or even confidently to set out its direction and trends. For every *Evans and Blum*[18] there is a *Laporte*;[19] for every *Singh*,[20] there is a *Tilly*.[21] This really is the problem. There is little by way of an overarching scheme or an underpinning theory. Though they deal with very different factual matrices, the two main cases in 2009 portray a very confused message. How can it be lawful in January to hold protesters in a cordon for seven hours, without any suspicion that individuals have either done anything wrong or are even threatening trouble, yet by May be unlawful for the police to take and retain photos (for any length of time over a day or so) without any suspicion that individuals have either done anything wrong or are even threatening trouble?[22]

If we were to attempt mathematically to depict 'protest in 2010', the case law trend would be, at best, no change and would probably evince a subtle regressive shift. Cases over the past decade or so on the credit side would be:

- *Kay*, especially its potentially wider holding that the Critical Mass cycle rides are not only ones that are 'customarily and commonly held' but are possibly not even processions that require notice at all under section 11 of the POA 1986.[23]
- *Laporte* establishing the requirement that for the police even to take action short of arrest, a breach of the peace must be imminent.[24]
- *Tilly* holding that aggravated trespass cannot be committed unless there is someone present on the land capable of being disrupted or obstructed or intimidated.[25]
- *Redmond-Bate*, which placed relatively onerous constraints in the way of officers who seek to rein in free speech on grounds that others might react violently or unsympathetically, the so-called heckler's veto.[26]
- *Connolly v DPP* where Dyson J was prepared to hold that the words 'grossly offensive' or 'indecent' in section 1 of the Malicious Communications Act should be given a heightened meaning to reflect the importance of political communication (on the facts, sending a photo of an aborted foetus) or to read in its disapplication where not doing so would disproportionately restrict free speech.[27]
- *Wood*, as we discussed above.
- *Huntingdon Life Science*, or at least the dicta of Eady J that in his view the PFHA was clearly not intended by parliament 'to be used to clamp down on discussion of matters of public interest or upon the rights of political protest and public demonstration which was so much part of our democratic tradition'.[28] Sadly, those words in 1997 have been overtaken and sidelined by several cases since, as we saw in chapter six.

---

[18] *Evans and Blum v Director of Public Prosecutions* [2006] EWHC 3209 (Admin).
[19] *Laporte v Chief Constable of Gloucestershire* [2006] UKHL 55.
[20] *R (Singh) v Chief Constable of West Midlands* [2006] EWCA Civ 1118.
[21] *Director of Public Prosecutions v Tilly* [2001] EWHC Admin 821.
[22] Contrast *Austin* and *Wood*, both above n 4.
[23] *Kay v Commissioner of Police for the Metropolis* [2008] UKHL 69.
[24] *Laporte*, above n 19.
[25] *Tilly*, above n 21.
[26] *Redmond-Bate* (1999) 7 BHRC 375. However, the status of cases that display less empathy with protesters, such as *ex parte Ward*, *Nicol* and *Duncan v Jones* from the 1930s is unclear. The first two can be distinguished as being forms of peaceful but direct action and easily disposed of on that basis. *Duncan* is clearly different.
[27] *Connolly v Director of Public Prosecutions* [2007] EWHC 237 (Admin).
[28] *Huntingdon Life Science v Curtin*, unreported High Court decision, *The Times*, 11 December 1997.

404 *Conclusion*

On the other hand, cases on the debit side would be

- *Haw*, as we discussed above.
- *Winder*, as we discussed above.
- *Austin*, as we discussed above.
- *Singh*, in which the Court of Appeal confirmed that as a matter of law, a dispersal authorisation under section 30 of the Anti-Social Behaviour Act 2003 that was granted to control pre-Christmas revelry, was capable of being used to order the dispersal of a protesting group, unforeseen at the time of the initial authorisation.
- *Thomas v Sawkins*, still with us from the 1930s, empowering the police to enter even private meeting halls on suspicion only of potential (but now imminent?) breaches of the peace.[29]
- *Hammond v DPP* is a decision that many would probably put on the other side of the equation, but it is one in which viewpoint might cloud our judgement about the bigger picture.[30] Though many more would probably support the outcome in *Norwood*, the BNP organiser who was prosecuted under section 5 of the POA 1986 for his 'Islam out of Britain' poster, the conviction of Mr Hammond under the same section (for his 'stop immorality—stop homosexuality—stop lesbianism' signs) creates a certain unease. Is peaceful protest to be regulated such that the expression of honestly-held controversial views—where the audience reacts violently—is out of bounds?
- *Broughton* and *Smash EDO* as two cases among many that cumulatively extend the reach of the PFHA into the sphere of protest.[31] The holding by Treacy J in *Broughton* (the Oxford animal research lab) that 'interaction, even by a limited number of people, is likely to have the effect of amounting to intimidation and harassment' effectively removed at a stroke even peaceful persuasive proselytising protest from the arena.[32] It was a much wider injunction than was needed to restrain those who deliberately engage in intentionally hostile protest towards identifiable employees, which creates feelings of fear, worry and alarm. Similarly in the *EDO* case, the claimant arms manufacturer was able to obtain an interim ex parte injunction restraining the protesters from, inter alia, (a) assaulting, molesting, harassing, threatening, or otherwise interfering with them by doing acts which cause harassment, intimidation or harm to them by any means whatsoever including . . . using any instruments whatsoever (whether or not designed for the purpose) in order to make artificial or musical noise and (b) knowingly picketing, demonstrating or loitering within 100 yards of any houses belonging to them.[33] The first was overturned on an inter partes hearing before Gross J but the second was upheld. In his mind, there was 'no legitimate reason for wishing to picket, demonstrate or loiter within 100 yards of [their] homes . . . That would be capable of amounting to harassment, on any view'.[34] Peaceful protest has effectively been ruled out as a legitimate tactic by anyone if certain members of a group had previously engaged in harassing behaviour.

Of course, such statistical plotting does not inform us of anything worth knowing. The data portray a crude mathematical equation, a profit and loss account which takes no heed

---

[29] *Thomas v Sawkins* [1935] 2 KB 249.
[30] *Hammond v Director of Public Prosecutions* [2004] EWHC 69 (Admin).
[31] *University of Oxford v Broughton* [2008] EWHC 75 (QB); *EDO Technology Ltd v Campaign to Smash EDO* [2005] EWHC 837 (QB) Gross J.
[32] *Broughton*, ibid at [23].
[33] *EDO*, above n 31, at [12].
[34] ibid, at [80] and [83].

of the relative quality and impact of the constraints or of the toleration. Are more people able to protest as a result of *Laporte* than are likely to have been prevented by *Singh*? Clearly, this question is meaningless both to pose and to answer from raw legal judgments, yet resolving it is integral to knowing how healthy the reality of the right to peaceful protest is in the UK today.

With the exception of the Human Rights Act itself, what is abundantly clear is that any gains made by protesters in their ability to protest—what we might call the de-regulation of protest—have not come from Parliament. Legislative intervention has been singly one-way traffic. Examples in the last decade would include the requirement of authorisation to demonstrate near Parliament in sections 132–138 of SOCPA 2005 (chapter four); the outlawing of harassing someone in the vicinity of their home as part of a protest contained in section 42 of the CJPA 2001 and its extension in 2005 (chapter six); and the continuation of the ban on political advertising contained in section 321 of the Communications Act 2003 (chapter five). Despite the well-meaning aim of that piece of legislation—to produce a level playing-field—it in fact results in the opportunities for well-funded but politically marginal protest and campaigning groups being restricted. Furthermore, legislative intervention has not all been directed at direct action protests—the reduction in 2003 from 20 to two as the minimum number needed before the police can impose conditions on assemblies under section 14 of the POA 1986 would be a good example—but much more effort has gone in that direction. The discrete and targeted criminalisation of those who interfere with contractual relationships so as to harm an animal research organisation and intimidate those connected with animal rights organisations, under sections 145–146 of SOCPA 2005 (chapter six) springs to mind. Likewise, to fill the gaps (perceived or actual) in an already wide prohibition, harassment under the Protection From Harassment Act 1997 was extended in 2005 to encompass secondary and group harassment (chapter six). Since 2003, it has been possible to commit aggravated trespass indoors (chapter six). The legal position for protesters has been altered even when Parliament was not deliberately trying to do so. The new definition of 'terrorism' under section 1 of the Terrorism Act 2000 is capable, as we saw in chapter six, of bringing certain sorts of direct action protest—most likely GM protesters—within its realm. There is some change afoot. At the instigation of Government, Parliament is in the process of repealing sections 132–138 of SOCPA 2005 in relation to Westminster, as we noted in chapter four. Similarly, it is consulting more widely—given the implications for policing low-level disorder on the street—on the removal of 'insulting' (words or behaviour) as one of the triggers in section 5 of the POA 1986. This was recommended by the JCHR in March 2009.[35]

Of course, to say 'except the HRA' does not really capture the full flavour of possible or likely change. The HRA is just one Act but its principles pervade, or are capable of pervading, all others and indeed the common law too. Though it does not 'incorporate' the ECHR, its scheme allows for all legislation to be interpreted in its light, so far as is possible to do so, and all public authorities are bound to act, that is reach decisions, that not only accommodate the right to peaceful protest but in some cases positively guarantee it. Victims—those directly affected—may challenge decisions they perceive to be in breach of the right, either by bringing judicial review proceedings or waiting until they are charged and then relying on the right collaterally. Even the common law and private law—tort, contract and the rules

---

[35] JCHR report, 'Demonstrating respect for rights', above n 2, para 85 and Government reply at: www.official-documents.gov.uk/document/cm76/7633/7633.pdf p5, accessed 9 July 2009.

relating to land ownership—are not for that reason immune. As we have often seen, courts are under duties too to develop or mould common law rules as an aspect of their public authority status—what we know as indirect horizontal effect. Similarly, apparently clear criminal provisions have been read under section 3 of the HRA as being subject to the right of peaceful protest. *Connolly v DPP* would be a good case in point.[36] We saw the right of peaceful protest acting as a sword in *Brehony*: the provisions allowing the police to impose conditions on assemblies were challenged and read as being subject to the requirement of proportionality, a term not even appearing on the face of section 14 of the POA 1986.[37] Of course, and this is the rub, the extent to which both statutes must be re-read and the police subjected to duties of proportionality is a function of Strasbourg case law: the duty in section 3 and sections 6–7 only requires that the UK's position be rendered compatible or compliant. If whatever activity is being engaged in is one that is not protected by Strasbourg as legitimate peaceful protest, or if restrictions on it are deemed to be proportionate, then domestic courts are fully justified in maintaining the pre-HRA position. In general, as we have seen throughout this book, protest was heavily restricted at common law and under statute. The extent of Strasbourg case law—and its strong approval of some activities and its heavy disapprobation of other types of protests—was the subject of chapter three.

Thus, in several cases and situations that we identified, the 'problem' was not one of domestic law—its interpretation or development—but of Strasbourg law, which largely prescribes the result. At least that is the view of the British courts. *Evans and Blum v DPP* is probably the best example.[38] There the High Court effectively decided in accordance with the earlier admissibility decision in *Ziliberberg v Moldova*.[39] This held that requiring someone to seek authorisation in advance for a demonstration was normally compliant with Article 11, as was taking action against those who did not do so. As we saw in chapter four there are normative and policy-based arguments for not adhering so rigidly to that near-absolutist position but it seems the High Court did not feel able, under section 2 of the HRA, to depart. It could surely have done so, though, if it had compared the possible sanctions: in *Ziliberberg*, it was about €3 whereas under SOCPA it can include imprisonment for up to 51 weeks or a fine of up to £2500. That, very clearly, could be argued as being a disproportionate penalty.[40] In other cases, it is not the law itself or its meaning that is the stumbling block but how it is applied by the courts as they seek to reflect Strasbourg law and principle within the UK. Again, we might think of *Brehony*, the protest outside the central Manchester branch of Marks and Spencer. The positive side of the case was to hold that although section 14 of the POA 1986 did not impose a requirement of proportionality on the police when they set conditions on public assemblies, the effect of the HRA is that such a gauge is 'read in' as a control on all such decisions. That approach was not only consistent with the approach under the ECHR but undeniably compelled by it. The problem, again, is Strasbourg law. As we discovered in chapter three, largely—certainly historically—European law has permitted restrictions being imposed on protesters on rather flimsy

---

[36] Above n 27.
[37] *R (Brehony) v Chief Constable of Greater Manchester* [2005] EWHC 640 (Admin).
[38] Above n 18.
[39] *Ziliberberg v Moldova* (App 61821/00) ECtHR inadmissibility decision 4 May 2004.
[40] In any event, as and when the matter comes before the domestic courts again, they would have to take account not only of *Bukta v Hungary* (App 25691/04) ECtHR judgment 17 July 2007 (a system of authorisation that admits of no exception for immediate response is very likely to breach Art 11) but also *Kuznetsov v Russia* (App 10877/04) ECtHR judgment 23 October 2008. There, giving notice of a few days less than was required where that does not cause difficulties for policing was not a sufficient and relevant reason for subsequent prosecution.

evidence of fairly nebulous social goals. We need only think of *S v Austria* (upholding of a ban applied to a demonstration on the ground of possible excessive noise) and *GS v Austria* (convicted of demonstrating without permission after he erected two trestles to drum up support, on the grounds it hindered the safe flow of traffic[41]). We can see how *Brehony* is doing no more than following Strasbourg. Any complaints we have—that this gives undue preponderance to ill-defined social interests and concerns while underplaying the right and its attendant public and political utility—should be directed there. To some extent, Strasbourg has not been deaf to this. As we identified in chapter three and at the start of this conclusion, there is a new wind blowing through the ECtHR.

Another set of cases is deceptively favourable. A casual first glance would view them as certainly approving of peaceful protest (if not effusive about it) but in fact, on closer inspection and familiarity, they are wearing the emperor's new clothes. *Jones and Lloyd* would be one.[42] It does not contain, despite appearances to the contrary, a ringing endorsement of the *right* of protest. As we saw in chapter four, although the speeches of the majority can be seen to favour the two protesters, it is a decision largely predicated on private law. The right of passage is still predominant and the determining factor is whether there has been unreasonable and obstructive interference with it.[43] Another case would be *Hirst and Agu*, which asserted that protests that are minimally obstructive but otherwise lawful were not in themselves unlawful obstructions of the highway.[44] Much is left to subsequent development and interpretation and is very fact dependent. We saw its limitations in chapter four in the later case of *Birch*.[45] Similarly, *Percy* (the 'No to Star Wars' protester outside the US Air Force airbase) *seems* to constitute a strong defence of the right of free speech. In reality it falls some way short, as we saw in chapter five. The magistrate's decision was overturned but not because the conviction under section 5 of the POA 1986 *was* a disproportionate restriction. Instead, it was because the magistrate had not taken account of the full range of factors that the Divisional Court considered he should have done. Some of these were circular, some were otiose and some were misdirected in Article 10 terms.[46] It is impossible to tell from the decision if Ms Percy's protest was in fact reasonable or whether instead the conviction would have been upheld if the correct factors had been borne in mind. Lastly the harassment case *Smash EDO* established that the prevention of crime defence in section 1(3)(a) of the PFHA 1997 was to be interpreted subjectively rather than objectively: it would be enough for the defendant to establish that they thought their direct action protest was aimed at preventing crime. However, the crime in question had to be specific, with an identifiable victim and threat, and one that was immediate or imminent.[47] This obviously and necessarily lessens the utility of this as a potential argument for the defence.

---

[41] *GS v Austria* (App 14923/89) EComHR inadmissibility decision 30 November 1992.
[42] *Director of Public Prosecutions v Jones and Lloyd* [1999] 2 AC 240.
[43] It is furthermore a decision solely about the use of the highway to protest, not about any other public land such as council recreation areas or Town Hall foyers.
[44] *Hirst and Agu v Chief Constable of West Yorkshire* (1986) 85 Cr App Rep 143.
[45] *Birch* [2000] *Criminal Law Review* 301.
[46] Above pp 225.
[47] *EDO Technology Ltd v Campaign to Smash EDO (preliminary issues)* [2005] EWHC 2490 (QB) Walker J.

III. The Wider Picture: A Recap of Some Key Themes

The foregoing few pages have concentrated on the legal rules and legal position that surround the right of peaceful protest in the UK today. As the introduction made clear, the focus of this book has been doctrinal: it has offered a critical perspective on the cases and the legislation. Important as that is for our study, any appreciation of the right must acknowledge that the law does not just exist; it is operated by human actors, usually police officers within a legal system (of permitting and forbidding) that is itself a social construct. We have touched on both these themes throughout this book. It is that wider and bigger picture, as much as the specific rules for example contained in sections 12–14A of the POA 1986 that determines whether the right can be exercised at all, as well as settling whether or not it is effective. Any sensible debate about the nature and extent of that right, about the policing and control of it and about its future direction and trajectory can only take place if it is structured within and acknowledges those other constraints, underpinnings and wider socio-legal concerns. We shall bring this book to a close by, first, harking back to some of those in order, secondly, to suggest a way forward.

The scope of the right to protest is only partly a function of rules that are tailored specifically to curb certain forms or certain effects of protest. As we saw at the outset, forming the canvas on which that right is painted are common law rules of general application relating to land ownership and control. We saw in chapter four how, unless a private landowner agrees to a protest being held, no one can force their hand. This is the result of *Appleby* at Strasbourg giving effect to the domestic pre-eminence of the private law.[48] Much of that chapter on the locus of protest was dedicated to that aspect. We noted, for example, how the socio-political demographic skew of landholding means that certain types of messages and protests may be favoured and others sidelined entirely. We saw a similar undermining of the public law right of peaceful protest by private law rules in *Jones and Lloyd*, as well as throughout our study of private law remedies and proceedings in chapter eight. We also saw how public law regulation is parasitic on private law concepts, particularly trespass. Thus, the expansion and the erosion of the right to peaceful protest meanders with judicial developments in the Chancery Division and the Queen's Bench, as much as with those at the Old Bailey and the Divisional Court.

This entwining of the two is a matter of some concern. It merits much greater study for three reasons. First are the cost implications: if there is a public interest in protest, as there undoubtedly is, it must also be right that the 'tab' is picked up by the public purse. This would allow it to be shared between us all, either as targets or as beneficiaries (should it succeed). We all have an interest—extant or putative at any one time—in a properly balanced, properly regulated framework for protest, not one that is—or can be—in the hands of large-scale commercial operators who will, naturally, have vested interests that are different to ours as citizens. Secondly, there is a real risk that wider free speech concerns might be lost in what was described in chapter eight as 'a private law sea of technicality'. This does not mean solely private law procedural issues, though those are clearly important and can influence an outcome.[49] The whole topic of protest needs to be reviewed and considered in the

---

[48] *Appleby v UK* (2003) 37 EHRR 38.
[49] Although we have yet to see it in the area of protest, the effects of cross-fertilisation and inter-dependence can be seen in another public law arena. Whether the police can enter and search residential property with

round. Any gains made by removing 'insulting' as a trigger under section 5 of the POA 1986—so as to lessen the insulation offered to company directors criticised by their shareholders in vituperative terms—will be offset if those companies can alter their Articles of Association at will to remove the right of shareholding protesters to propose motions at the AGM condemning its environmental pollution record.[50] Thirdly, the increasing utility and adaptability of the private law as a means to control peaceful protest, in the hands of course of those who can afford to go to court, has meant an expansion of the private law and sidelining of public law remedies. These latter tend to be more transparent—not without notice injunctions behind closed doors—and for the exercise of which, bodies such as the Crown Prosecution Service (CPS) and police are better accountable to us all as citizens rather than only to some of us as shareholders.[51] It is troubling if the police decide not to bring charges under, say, section 5 of the POA 1986 or to impose conditions under section 14 but a target company itself decides to seek an injunction under the PFHA 1997, outwith Parliament's carefully crafted democratic balancing of the competing tensions and rights.[52] In *Laporte* Lord Bingham was very clear. One of the factors that underlay his decision not to broaden the scope of the power to keep the peace at common law was that the POA 1986 already struck the proper balance, specifically with public order and protest in mind. This

> conferred carefully defined powers and imposed carefully defined duties ... Parliament plainly appreciated the need for appropriate police powers to control disorderly demonstrations but was also sensitive to the democratic values inherent in recognition of a right to demonstrate. It would, I think, be surprising if, alongside these closely defined powers and duties, there existed a common law power and duty, exercisable and imposed not only by and on any constable but by and on every member of the public, bounded only by an uncertain and undefined condition of reasonableness ... Any extension [of the power of the police to control demonstrations of this kind] should in my opinion be effected by legislative enactment and not judicial decision ... Assessment of whether a new restriction meets the exacting Convention test of necessity calls in the first instance for the wide consultation and inquiry and democratic consideration which should characterise the legislative process, not the more narrowly focused process of judicial decision. This is not a field in which judicial development of the law is at all appropriate.[53]

That said, he was of course discussing the balance between judicial development at common law and legislative development by Parliament. We cannot necessarily transpose this onto our discussion of public vs. private law.

As we saw in chapter six, the result of using the civil injunction route under the PFHA makes it much easier to criminalise a protester in the future for a single repeat occurrence. An anti-harassment injunction can be obtained on the lower civil standard of proof with hearsay evidence much more the norm. It may of course have been granted against 'persons unknown' who will be bound provided they are given notice of its terms (perhaps only by posting on a relevant fence) and will almost certainly have been granted without protesters being given notice of the hearing. Cumulatively these all raise serious concerns for the fairness of the proceedings that determine a protester's civil obligations under Article 6 of the

---

consent is dictated by common law rules relating to trespass, and the grant and withdrawal of limited licences. Nothing in the few cases that exist is dedicated to the conceptualisation of the situation as a public law, state/citizen interchange.

[50] See above p 389.
[51] That last was a point made by Stephanie Harrison of counsel at a joint Liberty/Norton Rose seminar, 'The right to protest' on 5 May 2009.
[52] *ibid.*
[53] *Laporte*, above n 19, at [46] and [52].

ECHR.[54] These are exacerbated where those civil proceedings are used as the foundations of a criminal charge: once obtained, breach of a section 2 injunction without reasonable excuse itself constitutes a crime under section 2(6). The existence of this 'civimal' procedure offers the hard pressed, cash-strapped police the opportunity to privatise criminal investigations and enforcement of protest in part at least. In those circumstances, is it any wonder that Sussex police, in the *EDO* case,[55] did not try to use section 5 of the POA 1986? Instead, assuming (knowing?) the company was going to use some if its hard-earned but finite resources, officers could sit back and reap the fruits of EDO's labour, should they choose to do so. Too cynical a view perhaps, but one tinged with realism and certainly not one that is too fantastical.

None of this is to gainsay the clear and obvious relationship between policing and protest, between the police and protesters. Instead, it is to highlight the fact that we should not underestimate the influence of private law—its actors, institutions and principles—on the public sphere of protest. There is much to explore in the arena. As will be offered shortly, where a new framework for regulating peaceful protest is to be drawn up, we ignore private law and private remedies at our peril. There is considerable potential for the private sphere to restrict that which we might seek to place beyond the capabilities of the public sphere.

Before we move on to consider that new framework, we should reflect a little on the socio-legal aspect. How do protests pan out in practice? What do we know and what can we say about the everyday reality of protesting, for both protesters and police? Again, little work has been conducted in this area. Much is anecdotal. Even if, for much of what follows, there is a considerable amount of supporting evidence, little if anything is empirically proven. The actions of the police have been in the spotlight for most of the year. It is self-evident that the law does not always—cannot always—make for an adequate constraint on behaviour.

It is clear that officers on duty at protests should never hide their shoulder numbers and identification, so that they might remain publicly accountable and not be (seen to be) hiding anything.[56] The view of both the Independent Police Complaints Commission and the Metropolitan Police Commissioner, expressed to the Home Affairs Select Committee, established that very clearly. According to Nick Hardwick, it was an 'absolute obligation' on the part of the police. Sir Paul Stephenson called it a 'statement of the blindingly obvious. Uniformed officers should always be identifiable'.[57] Yet it is clear too that not all officers do so when policing protests and maintaining order. For example, *The Guardian* reported how two protesters at the Climate Camp demonstration in Kent in the summer of 2008 asked

---

[54] Another is the cost of defending an action like this in the High Court, impossible for someone of average means: see evidence presented by Dr Peter Harbour (of Save Radley Lakes) to the JCHR during its policing and protest enquiry, 7th report of session 2008–09 (*Demonstrating respect for rights*, above n 2) Ev 140.

[55] Above n 31.

[56] Although the legal basis for this requirement is hazy, to say the least: nothing in any of the recent reports into policing establishes its source. There is no legislative basis. It is a matter for individual Chief Constables, force guidance and dress codes. Breach of force guidance would be a disciplinary issue: HMIC report, above n 3, p 57, quoting Home Office Minister for Security and Counter-Terrorism, speaking in the House of Lords, 29 April 2009.

[57] Home Affairs Select Committee report, above n 2, para 21. There are of course good reasons for some not to be doing so but there is dispute between the various protagonists over its extent. Liberty's written evidence to the JCHR inquiry into the policing of the G20 summit, para 12, at: www.liberty-human-rights.org.uk/pdfs/policy-09/liberty-s-written-evidence-to-the-jchr-re-policing-and-protest.pdf (accessed 10 July 2009) cites a Police Review survey where 45% of officers said they did not always wear their badges. Contrast this with the evidence given by the Metropolitan Police Commissioner and Gold Commander to the Home Affairs Select Committee (19 May 2009) Ev 361, *ibid.*

for identification, it not being on show, and were themselves immediately arrested, restrained and held for four days on charges of assault and obstruction.[58] According to the report, at least four members of West Yorkshire Police were not showing badge numbers. One of the pair repeatedly asked the officer, who refused to divulge any details. They took a photograph of him so as to lodge a complaint; moments later they were wrestled to the ground. A formal complaint has been made to the IPCC. The JCHR in its July 2009 follow-up report on policing the G20 recommended that it be a legal duty on all officers to wear identification numbers or to identify themselves when asked.[59]

We saw in chapter five how the courts, in cases such as *Percy v DPP*, have placed limits on the use of section 5 as a means to control peaceful persuasive protest. Yet we also read how it had been used by the police to warn a teenager holding a sign declaring that scientology was not a religion but a dangerous cult. The CPS later advised this was a misuse. How the law *does* play out may be very different to how the law *should* play out. That same incident also raises the spectre of what I have called, in a different policing context, 'uninformed acquiescence':[60] unless citizens are very much up to speed on the law, they tend to assume orders by an officer in uniform are given lawfully and that they must obey.[61]

Another area where there is a fairly clear divergence between law and practice is in the area of stop and search, especially under section 44 of the Terrorism Act 2000, and similar investigative powers. We touched on this in chapter seven. There is now a wealth of evidence that the power is used by the police at demonstrations to such excess as to constitute a clear misuse and, it has been suggested, as a tactic of intimidation. This is despite Lord Bingham in *Gillan* making it clear, or so he must be presumed to have thought, that the power should not be used on those who were not 'obviously terrorist suspects'.[62] Following the judgment, as we saw in our chapter on preventive police powers, the Association of Chief Police Officers drew up new guidance. This made clear the link to thwarting terrorism.[63] Despite all that, Liberty recorded how

> the police frequently use stop and search powers [under s 44 and s 50 of the Police Reform Act 2002] to obtain the identity details of individuals. In some cases identity details have been demanded before protesters are allowed to leave areas of containment and we have heard numerous reports of protesters being told that a failure to provide identity details will lead to arrest.[64]

More worrying are the reports of excessive, broad blanket searches conducted under section 1 of PACE. For these searches to be lawful (unlike section 44), reasonable suspicion relating to that individual is required. *The Guardian* reported how over the summer of 2008, at Climate Camp, about 10,000 protesters were 'corralled into airport-style "checkpoints" used for blanket stop and searches'. Those stopped and searched in this way

---

[58] 'Caught on film: campaigner who asked for police identification' and 'Police footage reveals treatment of pair who asked for badge number', *The Guardian*, 22 June 2009.

[59] Above n 2, paras 37–39.

[60] D Mead, 'Informed consent to police searches in England and Wales—a critical (re-) appraisal in the light of the Human Rights Act?' [2002] *Crim LR* 791.

[61] Closely related to Robert Reiner's 'Ways and Means Act': R Reiner, 'Policing and the police' in M Maguire, R Morgan and R Reiner, *The Oxford Handbook of Criminology*, 2nd edn (Oxford, Oxford University Press, 1997) 1002.

[62] *R (Gillan) v Commissioner of Police for the Metropolis* [2006] UKHL 12 at [35].

[63] National Policing Improvement Agency, *Practice Advice on Stop and Search in Relation to Terrorism* 2008 p 14 at: www.npia.police.uk/en/docs/Stop_and_Search_in_Relation_to_Terrorism_-_2008.pdf, accessed 11 April 2009.

[64] Liberty evidence, above n 57, p6.

included two children aged 11. They launched judicial review proceedings against Kent police. In May 2009, Keene LJ gave leave to proceed to a full hearing on the merits.[65]

It has to be said that the law does not always pan out in practice to the detriment of protesters. It is clear, as we saw in chapter five, that there is very limited opportunity for direct action protesters to argue prevention of crime, lawful excuse, protection of property or a similar defence if charged with one of a range of offences. This is the cumulative effect of decisions such as *Jones*, holding that the 'crime' that is being prevented must be one recognised in domestic law,[66] *Blake* on the remoteness of the crime being prevented,[67] *Bayer* that the act that is to be prevented must itself be unlawful,[68] and *EDO* on the specificity and identifiability of the crime and victim (albeit under section 3 of the PFHA 1997).[69] Nonetheless, despite the paucity of defences, direct action protesters are not always convicted. In September 2008, eight Greenpeace activists were acquitted of causing £30,000 worth of criminal damage after they climbed a 200 metre coal power station chimney at Kingsnorth in Kent.[70] They admitted trying to shut down the station by occupying the smokestack and painting the word 'Gordon' down the chimney, but argued they were legally justified because they were trying to prevent climate change causing greater damage to property around the world. It is believed to be the first case in which preventing property damage caused by climate change had been used as part of a 'lawful excuse' defence in court. Despite the seemingly clear test set out in *Bayer*, in 2000 a jury in Norwich found various members of Greenpeace not guilty of causing criminal damage to a field of GM crops. How juries react to this sort of protest merits greater and more rigorous investigation—details are hazy and partial. For example, what led to two protesters, charged with conspiracy to commit criminal damage (to B-52s), being acquitted by a Bristol jury—their argument being that it was reasonable to prevent war crimes and property damage in Iraq—but another two protesters to be found guilty six weeks later also in Bristol after they used boltcutters and hammers to disable fuel tankers, again for the same reason?[71] Was it only because one pair actually committed damage whereas the first pair was arrested before they could do anything?[72]

IV. An Agenda for Change

Sadly, the policing of the G20 summit in April 2009—both what actually took place and what was widely circulated as having taken place—has led to the spotlight being shone on

---

[65] 'Court says police can be challenged on 'stop and search' powers', *The Guardian*, 6 May 2009.
[66] *R v Jones and Others; Ayliffe v DPP* [2006] UKHL 16, discussed above p 249.
[67] *Blake v Director of Public Prosecutions* [1993] Crim LR 586 (DC), discussed above p 247.
[68] *Bayer v Director of Public Prosecutions* [2003] EWHC 2567 (Admin), discussed above p 251.
[69] *EDO (preliminary issues)*, above n 47.
[70] 'Not guilty: the Greenpeace activists who used climate change as a legal defence', *The Guardian*, 11 September 2008.
[71] 'Fairford two strike blow for anti-war protesters after jury decide they were acting to prevent crime', *The Guardian*, 26 May 2007; and 'Protesters at RAF base guilty of damaging US vehicles', *The Guardian*, 7 July 2007. The four involved were those who had taken the preliminary issue to the House of Lords in *Jones* above n 66: Phil Pritchard, Toby Olditch, Margaret Jones and Paul Milling.
[72] War crimes, rather than crimes of aggression, we might recall from *Jones*, above n 66, at [22] were floated by Lord Bingham in obiter as being a domestic as well as internal law crime—such that the prevention of crime defence under s 3 of the Criminal Law Act 1967 could be run.

An Agenda for Change 413

the subject of protest in the UK today: whether and how it takes place, how and why it is managed and controlled. The various official reports and institutional responses[73] to the policing of disorder on this scale are something that has not been seen for over a quarter of a century, since the first Scarman Inquiry in the mid-1970s.[74] They have all focused on one particular type of protest from one particular angle: how have the police handled mass demonstrations with the potential (either because of their size or subject-matter) to become inflamed or violent? None considered localised, one-off protests of short duration or small-scale, long-term protests as being within their terms of reference. Although purely peaceful and clearly communicative protests tend to be more easily containable and manageable that does not mean they take place without incident or without restriction. A criticism of the recent round of inquiries and the heightened media attention has been the skew towards large-scale protests with clear potential for flash-points while overlooking the more mundane. This book has related the issues and problems that surround the policing of these everyday sorts of protests, issues and problems that too often pass under the radar of formal recognition. We might recall the arrest of the teenager with the anti-scientology placard or the arrests of the two grandmothers from Yorkshire who trespassed 15 feet onto a designated site, the listening base at Menwith Hill.[75]

A third example would be the incidents relayed to the JCHR by Jim Brann, long-term anti-war protester. These merit a fuller recounting, since they portray very vividly two themes of this book: first, the capability and potential that overly broad discretion has for misuse and secondly, the understanding of legal rules displayed by officers on the street.

> I was leafleting outside my local tube station. Two British Transport Police officers came up to me. They asked whether I had 'permission' to leaflet. I pointed out that I was on the public highway, that I was not obstructing it, that I had a right to be there and that there was no such thing as 'permission' for me to be there. They remained there for 20 minutes or more, blocking my access to the public. I repeatedly pointed out that the incident was being captured on CCTV and that they had no right to be there. After about 20 minutes they threatened to arrest me and confiscate my leaflets. I said that would be illegal. They then called the Metropolitan Police, apparently thinking that the 'problem' was that, as Transport Police, they did not have 'jurisdiction'. The Metropolitan Police sergeant who came realised there was no 'problem' to deal with and took no action . . . I took part in a demonstration of about 20 people in Bloomsbury in central London. There was no tension or disorder. A police constable got agitated, said it was an 'unauthorised demonstration' and began ordering people around. I pointed out that there was no such thing as an 'unauthorised demonstration'. He cited the Serious Organised Crime and Police Act 2005 ('SOCPA') which includes the 'Parliament Square ban'. I pointed out that we were well outside the designated zone around Parliament . . .
>
> Around 2005 my local London Borough attempted to ban political leafleting and stalls in the area around the tube station and to limit such activity on the main road to two 'designated places' subject to permission and/or a 'licence'. Provisions of the London Local Authorities Acts 1990 and

---

[73] See above n 2–3.
[74] Sir Leslie Scarman, *Report on the Red Lion Square Disorders of 15 June 1974* (Cmnd 5919, 1974) (London, HMSO, 1975) There was never any official response to the policing of the Miners' Strike in the 1980s and Lord Scarman's second inquiry had as its focus disorder simpliciter, not protesting, demonstrations and marches. That was the inquiry into the urban disorder in the summer of 1981: Lord Scarman, *The Brixton Disorders 10–12 April 1981* (Cmnd 8427, 1981) (London, HMSO, 1981). There has been a Law Commission Report No 123, *Criminal Law: offences relating to public order* (London HMSO, 1983) alongside the Home Affairs Select Committee Fifth Report of 1979–80, *The law relating to public order* HC 756 and Government Green Paper in response, *Review of the Public Order Act 1936* (Cmnd 7891, 1980) (London, HMSO, 1980).
[75] 'Helen and Sylvia, the new face of terrorism', *The Independent*, 6 April 2006.

1994 regarding 'Distribution of Free Literature' and 'Street Trading' were cited as justification. I was warned in a letter that 'market staff and the police have been very patient with you so far' and that I faced prosecution if I continued to 'defy' the ban. I wrote to the relevant manager saying that I thought the 'ban' contravened sections 10 and 11 of the Human Rights Act. I copied my letter to the Borough Solicitor. Whilst the manager wrote back strongly defending the ban, a Senior Prosecutions Officer wrote to me saying that I was right. However, the council continued to 'uphold' the ban for the next two years.[76]

The limitations of the current round of inquiries and reports, when set against the criticisms, uncertainties and limitations identified in this book, mean the time has come for a comprehensive inquiry into all aspects of the law and practice of protest. We shall conclude this book by outlining some terms of reference for this suggested Royal Commission.[77] It would need to be wide-ranging so as to cover both the single campaigner standing outside the high street supermarket (dedicated to publicising the fact that it buys up land solely to prevent competitors doing so) and the sorts of mass protests we witnessed in 2009.

A. Public Debate

Its first task would be to involve the public more widely in a debate about what it means to have the right to protest; to engage in what Andrew Geddis has called (in the context of section 5 of the POA 1986) a 'transformative' rather than 'pro-civility' discourse.[78] Without this debate and thus approval for any subsequent meta-framework and micro-level rules, and consideration of underlying values and priorities, how can the state seek to coerce people into tolerating the conflicting views and objectionable behaviour of others?[79]

There is little doubt in the minds of most people about the role and value of free speech, perceived as it is in the public psyche as a key aspect of British liberalism, even if this would not be expressed by many in consequentialist tones. Certainly, its penumbra—where doubts creep in about its value, its role and whether we really should allow people to voice views on topic X—seems to be much smaller. The same cannot really be said about protest, affected as it is by what could be termed protest 'nimby-ism' where toleration is dictated either by the location or by the topic. The idea that we defend to the death people's right to demonstrate and to protest in places that inconvenience us or about matters we disagree with seems a long way from reality. Some public opinion research was conducted as part of the HMIC inquiry into the policing of the G20. One aspect was to ask respondents to consider the extent to which disruption should be a factor in controlling protests. 44 per cent answered that protesters should not be allowed to protest on roads that are used by public transport; 54 per cent thought business and workers should not be disrupted by protesters.[80] Clearly, some public relations work is needed—and fuller discussion engaged in—to challenge the dominant discourse, a discourse that we might call the counter-right to peace-

---

[76] JCHR follow up report, above n 2, Ev 52.
[77] We will not here look at specific criticisms of legislation or common law—these have been sprinkled liberally throughout the book—but at structural or institutional or conceptual changes and problems: the 'bigger picture' in other words.
[78] A Geddis, 'Free speech martyrs or unreasonable threats to social peace?—'insulting' expression and section 5 of the Public Order Act 1986' [2004] PL 853, 869–70.
[79] D Feldman, 'Protest and tolerance: legal values and the control of public-order policing' in R Cohen-Almagor (ed), Liberal democracy and the limits of tolerance—essays in honor and memory of Yitzhak Rabin (Ann Arbor M, University of Michigan Press, 2000) 60.
[80] HMIC report, above n 3, at 86.

ful shopping. It is not necessarily selfish to view protest and protesters in that way but it is rather blinkered and short-term viewed: today's disrupted local shopper is someone who tomorrow will want to protest against an out-of-town retail development. Some comfort in this regard must be taken from moves at Strasbourg to distinguish disruption from disorder: only the latter features as a legitimate claw-back in Article 11(2). Some disruption is inevitable for a successful protest.

B. Underpinning Principles

Its second task would be to establish some linch-pins that would inform and configure the debate and against which we could measure future developments. Historically, domestic law relating to protest has been determined by a mindset of order maintenance and the political imperative to respond, and be seen to respond, to individual events and perceived social ills, rather than as a considered, structured and balanced framework with rights to the fore. Even in the era of the HRA, recent history shows a pattern of restriction and limitation against only a backdrop of rights protection.

Though ultimately a matter for the Royal Commission, the following six criteria seem a sensible place to start. There should be:

- serious consideration given to a single Protest Act.
- a protest-impact statement for all future legislation.
- a statutory guarantee of an individual's right of peaceful protest.
- a statutory definition of 'peaceful protest' that properly distinguishes the politically legitimate and politically illegitimate.
- sensitivity to different sorts of protests.
- a commitment to clarity and certainty in drafting.

(i) A Protest Act?

If not a codification then there should be at least a consolidation. In our new rights-based age it is symbolically important that we acknowledge the founding value of protest rather than continuing to recognise the continuation of the founding value of order maintenance, implicit as that must be in something called the Public Order Act. It would signify a new marker, a new start and a new—and welcome—orientation. Implicit in this call for a Royal Commission is demonstrable need, now more than ever, for a thorough overhaul and review of the various discrete pieces of legislation to reduce overlap and minimise misuse. Many of these have been identified throughout this book. Further, so far as is possible, the common law as it relates to protest should be put onto a statutory footing, with the democratic imprimatur that brings. A Protest Act could make a firm commitment too, based on the public's acceptance of its wider public utility and value, something to which they would have been converted as a result of the public debate we foreshadowed above. We would see that it is not just a right vested in individuals but vested in individuals to exercise on behalf of the polity. Lastly, although it is implicit in section 6 of the HRA, the adoption of an explicit statutory duty on the police (at least) and councils positively to facilitate peaceful protest would greatly enhance the chances of the right balance being struck between competing tensions, interests and rights. This magnetic north would clearly orientate all future operational, tactical and strategic decisions by the police in relation to protest. While this would not be to the exclusion of other rights, it would highlight the need to ensure not just that lawful protests (see below) are not hindered but that peaceful protests are positively supported and guaranteed under the usual proportionality basis.

(ii) Protest-impact Statements?

Whenever new legislation is proposed, it should be made clear what aim it is serving.[81] The statement would explain the gap in the existing law and how large that gap is, as well as setting out how it is envisaged it will be filled. It would set out why this power is needed—and why no lesser or other powers will suffice. We have seen throughout this book that the right to protest is regulated by a matrix of overlapping powers, several of which can be brought to bear on any one single protest 'activity'. Why is it that none of these laws is adequate? Some, like the common law power to keep the peace, are very broad. Is the problem, as we discussed in our introduction, one of insufficient law or are the difficulties ones of enforcement and application? The latter calls for a different response, not one that merely increases the amount of law. Are we passing laws to deal with solitary incidents? We saw in chapter six how one-third (19 from 54) of all cases brought before magistrates in 2002 under section 68 of the CJPOA 1994 (aggravated trespass) were brought by Suffolk Police—and (but?) under one-sixth (12 from 74) in 2003. Likewise, of the 63 defendants proceeded against under section 241 of Trade Unions and Labour Relations (Consolidation) Act (TULRCA) 1992 in 2003 (watching and besetting), 49 occurred in one county, Surrey. Of course not all these may have been protesters. Clearly there must be a reason why one county calls on these two arrest powers—in contrast both to its own use of other powers and to the use made by other counties of the same power. This necessarily leads to much greater institutional support for socio-legal research on protest and its regulation, much more than has taken place before. One last point. There should also be an institutional reflective review after a short period to assess whether the law does what it set out to do, or whether it has been relegated to the cupboards to be dragged out and contorted at an inopportune moment?[82]

(iii) A Statutory Guarantee of an Individual's Right of Peaceful Protest?

At first sight, it appears to be surplusage, given the clear terms of Article 11 but it would serve two linked goals. The guarantee would ensure first a concentration on the activities of individuals, not assemblies or groups and secondly, that the determining factor in interfering or restricting that right is that protest's peaceful quality, in the Strasbourg sense.

The first, as we shall see, will lead us into the operative mindset of the police and the authorities. It is on this idea that blanket, indiscriminate approaches to policing protest, such as 'kettling', are predicated. It is also behind recent moves towards greater pre-emptive action. It is out of keeping with Strasbourg case law, the vast majority of which, from *Ezelin* onwards to *Galstyan* in 2007,[83] seeks to distinguish peaceful prot*esters* not

---

[81] A similar position could be adopted for changes to force or ACPO guidance on public order management as well as it being required of all strategy and tactics in advance of a protest.

[82] This recommendation applies equally to all legislation and has been made inter alia by the House of Lords Select Committee on the Constitution (14th report of session 2003–04, 29 October 2004) *Parliament and the legislative process* ch 5 at: www.publications.parliament.uk/pa/ld200304/ldselect/ldconst/173/17302.htm, accessed 18 August 2009.

[83] *Ezelinv France* (1992) 14 EHRR 362; *Galstyan v Armenia* (App 26986/03) ECtHR judgment 15 November 2007.

peaceful protests. Action can only be taken—which in any event must be proportionate—on evidence relating to individual behaviour, not a 'gut feeling' that protesting crowds tend to violence or disorder.

The second would be to bring an end to the nonsensical—but politically convenient—epithet of 'lawful' protest. We can see a good example in the Government's response to the JCHR report *Demonstrating respect for rights?* in 2009: that the PFHA 1997 is not intended to 'criminalise people who campaign lawfully against particular activities'.[84] Facilitating 'lawful protest' was also the leading objective in the Gold Strategy document at the heart of policing the G20 summit in April 2009.[85] It is circular—or at least self-fulfilling—but serves the purpose of tending to label, with disapprobation, certain types of protesters: lawfulness is good, unlawfulness a bad thing. It can thus serve, misleadingly, to validate in the public mind the justifications and explanations of the policing response after the event as well as, mistakenly, to structure the policing response on the day.

Many, many protests are unlawful under domestic law, as we have seen, and thus very many could be broken up.[86] The real test is not the lawfulness—of a protester of course, not her group—but whether her protest is 'non-peaceful', 'politically illegitimate' perhaps even 'disproportionately disruptive, intimidating and obstructive'. We will consider these below. For example, march organisers act unlawfully if they fail to give notice under section 11 of the POA 1986. That infraction, though, should not determine the policing response (though clearly it may be a factor in determining that response). We have seen at Strasbourg on this point that it may still be a disproportionate restriction on the right of peaceful protest to punish protesters for 'merely formal breaches' of the notification rules.[87] Similarly, a charge of obstruction of the highway—despite *Hirst and Agu*[88]—is still very much a possibility for some static, long-term protests as are charges under section 5 of the POA 1986. These would be 'unlawful' (as presumably would be protests committing tortious wrongs?) but Strasbourg would not necessarily sanction as proportionate their disruption by the police.

(iv) A New, Clear Statutory Definition of 'Peaceful Protest'?

This should properly, and in a workable fashion, distinguish the politically legitimate and politically illegitimate. Domestic law takes little or no proper account of the functional importance (to a pathologically healthy democracy) of people expressing views, one side-effect of which might be temporary disturbance or suspension of 'normal' life.

As this book has shown, for too long and too consistently the line has been drawn in the wrong place, though there are signs of a reconfiguration at Strasbourg level. On one side are all protesters who cause no or perhaps de minimis disruption, and on the other are violent direct action protesters alongside whom are those whose protest necessarily disrupts every-day activities—though not the targeted activity, which is crucial—but no more than could be expected where large numbers congregate together. Do we ban the Selfridges sale for the disruption it causes when people queue for several nights? Do we ban football matches because of the snaking processions of fans at five o'clock making their way to railway stations and car parks? Neither of these—certainly not the first—comes anywhere near the

---

[84] The Government response can be found alongside the JCHR report itself, above n 2. The reference is on p 6.
[85] As set out in the HMIC report, above n 3, p 38.
[86] Unless we mean by this, lawful in HRA terms, which would tend to confuse yet more.
[87] *Kuznetsov v Russia* (App 10877/04) ECtHR judgment 23 October 2008 at [43].
[88] Above n 44.

social utility of incidentally and non-intentionally disruptive peaceful protest. This links to the Royal Commission's first task. Unless the disruption is disproportionately great—as a result of duration, location or numbers—and bearing in mind the social importance (accepting this subjectively laden term) of the subject-matter, this should be just one of those things that we all accept we must put up with as part and parcel of living in a healthy democracy. Though this is implicit in the Article 11 proportionality test, the onus must always be on the state and its agents—police and councils—to make a convincing case on evidence to displace the presumption that protests of that sort should go ahead.

There does also need to be clear legal water between two different types of direct action, both of which are aimed at the activity itself. On one hand there is acceptable civil disobedience—ie to highlight a legitimate concern (developed below) where the cessation or disruption is minimal in time and effect—and on the other civil disruption. This is where activists attempt to bring an end to the activity itself, if not for good, then for a period of time as to make resumption excessively costly (accepting this is not especially well-defined as a term of art) or impossible to perform on that day. In short, the law and its responses—perhaps at the level only of punishment (as informally occurs now)?—should cater differently to (for example) a few protesters laying in the road outside an air base as a convoy leaves, knowing they will be hauled away, or hijacking a goods train en route for a power station solely to take one polluting bag of coal 'hostage' than to (for example) a group who dismantle an entire fighter plane (in contrast to those who remove a few bolts and inform the crew of that fact) or who pile up railway sleepers on the track to topple the train over. There seems to be the world of difference between these two sets—and of course steps in between that make hard cases—though many (most?), not least the targets, would disagree. But, without a debate, this position will remain through stasis and inertia rather than one that has been positively endorsed.

A necessary aspect of this overhaul and review—and one that is much wider—would be to look at the place of protest, and of direct action *sui generis*, within our existing democratic structures. It is impossible to set out a new normative framework for protest without looking at what facilitates and hinders political engagement and public participation. If that is absent, any framework will be short-lived for being on shaky foundations. Disengagement and disenfranchisement is a widely known and well-accepted phenomenon, not just in the UK today. Whether those millions are justified in feeling so is not really the point so much as their perception that they are so disenfranchised, say, on climate change or abortion that they feel they have no alternative—no effective and efficient alternative?—than to resort to less peaceful, less persuasive means of protest and political engagement. There is a clear-cut distinction, in terms of legitimacy, between direct action on a topic that is high on the political agenda—only the majority consensus reached differs from that of the protesters—and a topic that is marginalised and outside mainstream political discourse. Whether, conceptually, both or only the former should be treated as having engaged in illegitimate protest—reasonable alternatives being available—as trying to impose minority will on the majority is something our Royal Commission would need to grapple with. It might here draw something from the mismatch of votes and seats under our current first-past-the-post electoral system for general elections.[89]

---

[89] This disregards any questions over lobbying and collusion—that seem to favour organised interests, largely commercial ones. We touched upon this in our introduction but it raises concerns that are much wider than this book can cater for.

(v) Sensitivity to Different Sorts of Protests

This takes us back to something we touched on a little earlier. There is a real danger—because of media attention and the sheer size—that the new framework of the law regulating protest will be driven by large-scale demonstrations that have clear potential for disruption and disorder. The framework needs to cater as well to the teenaged anti-Scientologist protester as it does to a march of thousands or a chanting mob, lest the former be overlooked and captured unnecessarily by laws targeted at other types. A linked point would be to consider the need for bespoke laws for protests or formal caveats for protest carved out of existing laws. There is something inherently problematic about seeking to control vituperative protesters and foul-mouthed drunks at pub closing time, both using section 5 of the POA 1986, or a protest outside an embassy and those attending an open-air concert in a park by means of section 14 and section 14A of the same Act.

(vi) Certainty

We have seen throughout this book that several measures have been drafted without adequate attention being given to making clear—for potential protesters—any limits and scope. The potential chilling effect is obvious. Examples would include disruption to the 'life of the community' in section 14 of the POA 1986, the meaning of 'demonstration' in section 132 of SOCPA or the uncertain scope of the economic torts such that the new offence in section 145 of SOCPA 2005—interfering with a contractual relationship—is also unclear. A legislative deficiency is never so bad that it cannot be compounded by judicial pronouncement. As we saw in chapter six in *Garman*, the Climate Change camp around Heathrow, Swift J opined that

> harassment cannot . . . be confined to conduct which would place the victim in fear of violence. Neither in my view can it be right that harassment is confined just to conduct that will cause alarm and distress. Quite where the line is to be drawn and whether a particular type of conduct can properly be considered to amount to harassment will depend on the particular facts and circumstances of the incident in question. It is not a matter that can—save in a clear case—be predicted in advance. All I am able to say at this stage is that the fact that the actions of protestors will or may cause annoyance and inconvenience to the travelling public (whether by a blockade or any other form of action) does not necessarily mean that their conduct will amount to harassment. It may do. It may not.[90]

C. Public and Private Law Regulation

The various inquiries did not look at what are thought of as peripheral issues—landholding and access to space as well as private law regulation and remedies—but which in many cases, as this book has shown, are central or at least have the potential to play a more leading role. Thirdly, the Commission would have to look holistically at the legal system that regulates and guarantees protest. Any overhaul and consolidation would need to take account of how the lawfulness of protest is now a function of a host of legal interactions much more complex than can be resolved simply by asking 'is it an offence to . . .?' To that end, recent inquiries have all been skewed towards the public arena of policing, legislative measures, executive decision-making and the like. Though these are clearly important

---

[90] *Heathrow Airport v Garman* [2007] EWHC 1957 (QB) at [99].

matters that need to be explored, the shape and face of protest—both on the ground and legally—have changed quite dramatically over the past 10 years or so. In essence the regulation (and so the restriction) of protest is now increasingly (if not yet) as much a function of private law rules as it is of criminalisation and other public regulation.

We have touched in several places on the entanglement of land ownership and protest. So that the state accords with its positive duty to facilitate protest, it would be open to our Royal Commission to conclude that owners of quasi-public land should be under a limited, balanced duty (of a type we sketched in chapter four) to allow protests to take place. That would involve recommendations being reached on definitions: land that was once in public hands?[91] Land that is used (generally) for public social purposes such as recreation in all its various guises? The increase in land that is privately held means fewer places where protest can take place.[92] Alternatively, this increase might buttress claims that there is a positive duty on councils under Article 11 (using an *Airey*-type argument based on effectiveness[93]) to provide protest space like permanent communal Speaker's Corners (as instituted in Nottingham)[94] or at least that they should not unduly restrict access to council land for protesters. The demographic skew of landholding in the UK—farmers' fields bedecked in 'Ban Hunting' posters—only serves to exacerbate this problem. The liberal assumption is that political equality will be bestowed merely by granting a right equally, whereas people who own land are unlikely to permit 'The Land is Ours' protest group onto it. Private law principles of absolute title bring important ramifications for participation in the public sphere.

Equally, regard would need to be had to the increasing extent and potential for the private law more generally to encumber or to 'chill' protests by threats. As we have seen, the regulation of protest and protesters is as much, and in some ways more, a function of civil injunctions and claims as it is one of public criminal proceedings and administrative rules. Can it be right that the PFHA can be used by Mohammed Al-Fayed to bar anti-fur protesters shouting outside Harrods and from walking along the Brompton Road or that EDO in Brighton were able to seek a harassment exclusion zone that included the home of one of the protesters?[95] We might obtain a valuable insight into the extent of this power if we consider one option that was open in the City of London on 1 April 2009 at the G20. It was fairly clear that banks were going to be targeted: the directors of RBS could, given past case law, have very easily obtained an injunction under section 3 of the PFHA against 'persons unknown' preventing them harassing any employees who did (against advice) decide to come to work that day. Although harassment requires a course of conduct (ie a repeat), an injunction can be granted if there is an apprehended breach—that is an apprehension that harassment will be repeated—which over the course of a day-long protest there would be. That injunction having been granted, likely as not without notice and without those who

---

[91] A precursor would have to be to conduct a survey of the extent of hiving off of once publicly-owned or publicly-held land. As we saw in chapter four, accurate data on this is extremely hard to obtain.

[92] As was outlined in chapter four, access to state/public land for the purposes of protest is regulated by standard public law/judicial review considerations—with of course the s 6 HRA duty on councils not to take decisions in relation to land that disproportionately restrict the right of peaceful protest. Strasbourg case law will provide here at best only marginal protection, given the scope of Art 11 to provide pubic protest space (no case so far) and only limited incursions into a state's ability to regulate access.

[93] *Airey v Ireland* (1979–80) 2 EHRR 305.

[94] This would not be in the sense of American 'free speech' zones, which tend to be corralled protest pens at some distance.

[95] Examples related by Stephanie Harrison of counsel at the Liberty seminar, above n 51: no case details provided or traced.

would eventually be bound (under CPR Ord 19.6) being represented, it would be a criminal offence, under section 3(6) to breach its terms without reasonable excuse. All that would have been needed would be for the terms of the order to be publicised on the day, at which point any actions covered by it would have allowed the police immediately to step in, absent any other free-standing criminal behaviour.

It was suggested in chapter eight that one response might be to consider the development of something akin to the golden formula in trade disputes. If that route were pursued, it would need to cater for and respond to the nuances on the spectrum of protest; legitimate protest (certainly including incidental disruption) that caused loss would be protected, whereas deliberate destruction of a firm's goods would not—unless some pressing social interest suggested otherwise, making it proportionate to protect even that. It is hard to think of a situation that would satisfy that test. A re-ordering of the private law along those—or similar—lines would also ensure that the state, through its courts, accords with the positive duty in Article 11 not just to protect but to guarantee, to facilitate protest. Should companies be able to exclude from an AGM a known protester?[96] If Burberry did have the power to ban the vice-president of PETA (the animal rights group) despite his having a voucher and proxy card, a revisit seems needed. If it did not, such activities create a chilling effect, which in turn requires a state response to assuage.

In short, solutions to the 'problems' of protest that consider only criminal or policing responses would be partial and possibly short-lived.

D. The Role of the Police

That said, a clear imperative for the Commission would be to look at the control of protest in the public sphere by the police. Relevant issues here would include the working assumptions of the police—such as the mindset of collective unlawfulness—and associated matters of training and leadership, as well as issues of accountability and the role played by the Home Office and central government generally.[97] Some of this has been highlighted in the reports produced in 2009. Linked to this is a real concern: loss of public support for the police. This is something that needs addressing and might require, for mainland UK, radical solutions.

No one could sensibly doubt the invidious position many officers have found themselves in during large-scale protests and demonstrations over the past 10 years or so. It is hard to accept that not one person present at events such as the G20 and on May Day 2001 (perhaps even the Countryside Alliance demonstration in 2004), if they were not there with the underlying purpose of provoking, causing or committing violence, disruption, disorder and disturbance, was disposed to join in once it started. The likely size of this group is not our concern, assuming it is more than a handful out of thousands. The real issue is the police response to those who get caught up in the violence and trouble or—worse—where no violence or trouble eventuates, the police attitude in advance towards them. Increasingly, media reports of protests over the past few years (the Kinsgnorth camp in the summer of 2008 as well as the G20 being good examples) across a broad spectrum indicate concerns about an initial mindset: reports that the police were 'up to it and up for it' set an incendiary tone for

---

[96] *Eastern Daily Press*, 18 July 2008.
[97] These last two were noted by the JCHR in its follow-up report (22nd of session 2008–09), above n 2, at paras 58 and 60.

the policing at the G20.[98] A perfectly reasonable conclusion to draw from the police response at these events is that a working assumption of likely trouble, rather than a presumption of innocence, is becoming increasingly prevalent. Worries that a peaceful group will be infiltrated or used as subterfuge for violence (perhaps even terrorism?) seem to shape and determine how the police deal with protesters. Whether this is at the level of operational tactics or 'on the ground', reactive decisions is hard to know.[99] What is true, of the G20 protests, is that of 11 Gold strategy objectives, only one referred positively to protest: the rest concerned strategies of preventing disruption, security and protection.[100] That single one, as we noted above, was to 'facilitate lawful protest'. This set the tone. It implicitly means—and this is explored in the HMIC report—that protests that showed even minor levels of obstruction and disruption would be unlawful and so would be stopped or regulated. This does not accord with the Strasbourg view that a degree of tolerance towards disruptive protests is needed, absent any violence, if the right is not to be deprived of its value and substance.[101] We might think of similar concerns arising over the role of the National Extremism Tactical Coordination Unit (NETCU) and its portrayal of even peaceful protesters as 'eco-terrorists', something we touched on in our introduction.[102]

The viewpoint that sees protesters—or the vast majority of them—as likely law-breakers seems to have taken hold. It has several worrying side-effects. The first is an indiscriminate policing response. This is at the heart of the reliance on 'kettling', not as a measure of last resort but as a standard tactic. As Jeremy Paxman wryly commented during a 'round-table' on BBC's *Newsnight* just after the G20 summit, the problem with kettles is that they come to the boil.[103] It was also used at the Gaza protest in January 2009 when a group was herded into the Hyde Park underpass. The Gaza protest captures one of the best examples of indiscriminate policing, one that would be humorous were it not so worrying. A lone protester stands in the road as a phalanx of 15 to 20 officers, en route urgently to some other part of the demonstration, jog straight through/over him. Some of the officers do try to avoid him; others do not appear even to be bothered that he is in the way.[104] Similarly, there must be serious concerns about the increasingly catch-all nature of surveillance that protesters are subject to. This comes out not only in *Wood* but also in the media reports of the recording, long-term storage, and database creation and sharing by FIT (forward intelligence

---

[98] 'Police tactics queried as Met says G20 protests will be "very violent"', *The Guardian*, 28 March 2009. Having reviewed the media briefings, it seemed to the JCHR that the 'main responsibility for talking up the prospect of violence and severe disruption rests with the media' taking perhaps ill-chosen words out of context (JCHR follow-up report, *ibid*, para 33). Media reporting of protest and disorder—and the policing of it—continues to remain a topic worthy of separate and lengthy examination.

[99] Officers on the ground and in positions of semi-seniority will be influenced by the wider picture and political discourse. Is it a coincidence that all this occurred against a back-drop of political support for the dilution of innocence? We need only think of the coverage given to the twelve terrorism arrests in early April 2009. All were released without charge but not before the Prime Minister had described MI5 as having uncovered a 'very big plot' and the links being made to student visas and calls for a crackdown: 'All 12 men arrested during anti-terror raids released without charge', *The Guardian*, 22 April 2009.

[100] The Gold Strategy (HMIC report, above n 3, p 38)

[101] *Balçik v Turkey* (App 0025/02) ECtHR judgment 29 November 2007 at [51]–[52] among many.

[102] Above pages 21 and see the piece by G Monbiot, 'Otter-spotting and birdwatching; the dark heart of the eco-terrorist peril', *The Guardian* 'Comment Is Free', 23 December 2008, at: www.guardian.co.uk/commentisfree/2008/dec/23/activists-conservation-police, accessed 16 June 2009.

[103] My own personal recollection, mid-late April 2009.

[104] 'Riot police knock down peaceful protestor on Gaza demo', at: www.youtube.com/watch?v=NPB5q8gvCWo access 6 July 2009.

teams).[105] Those practices must raise serious concerns under both Article 8 and Articles 10–11.

The second worry is pre-emptive policing. Two examples here will illustrate the point. In *Laporte* the police were held to have intervened at too early a stage and thus to have done so unlawfully.[106] More recently, in April 2009 over 100 environmental protesters were arrested in Nottingham on suspicion of conspiracy to commit aggravated trespass and criminal damage at an Eon power station. All were released without charge but bailed.[107] It is hard to dispel the suspicion that it was a pre-emptive strike to undertake a mass trawl for evidence and impose bail conditions relating to power stations, as was reported to be commonplace in the miners' strike.[108] The third concern is the more than occasional disproportionality of the police response. Undoubtedly there has been an escalation of violence and the indications are of a significant shift in policing practice. Whether this is one or a few bad apples or a rotten barrel is the million-dollar question. As we saw in chapter seven, it is now well documented that the use of stop and search at Kingsnorth in the summer of 2008 was excessive. Reference has already been made to a report written by members of the Liberal Democrats in March 2009.[109] This indicated that among the 2,000 items seized at the Climate Camp were board games, a clown outfit and soap 'because protesters might use it to make themselves slippery and evade the grip of the police'. We also considered the police search of the bedroom belonging to Bertie Russell, arrested after taking over a coal train bound for Drax power station in June 2008. The search was for 'evidence of a political nature'. This included removing copies of *The New Statesman* but strangely did not include letters from his MP, clearly political. His father filmed this all and it was made available by *The Guardian* newspaper.[110]

All of these create in the minds of protesters a climate of fear, or have the potential to do so. Some, maybe many, will be dissuaded from ever engaging in protest, even ones that are avowedly peaceful and remain so. Liberty has raised concerns about the alleged abuse of section 50 of the Police Reform Act 2006.[111] This makes it a criminal offence to fail to give a name and address when asked by a police constable who has reason to believe that someone has been acting, or is acting, in an anti-social manner. In the light of what we have read about anti-social behaviour and its sibling harassment, it is no surprise that Liberty's concern was its use by the police to request names and addresses of peaceful protesters as a deliberate tactic of intimidation. They received reports of section 50 demands being made in the City of London as a condition of being able to leave a police cordon. That must simply be beyond the power contained in the section. The desire to leave a protest cannot trigger a belief about possible anti-social behaviour. The mentality of the police towards protest is captured well in the apology by Assistant Chief Constable Allyn Thomas of Kent Police towards journalists subjected to surveillance at the Kingsnorth climate camp over the

---

[105] *Wood*, above n 4. See for example 'Revealed: police databank on thousands of protesters', *The Guardian*, 7 March 2009 and 'Caught on film: campaigner who asked for police identification', *The Guardian*, 22 June 2009.
[106] *Laporte v Chief Constable of Gloucestershire* [2006] UKHL 55.
[107] 'Power station protest plot suspects released on bail', *The Guardian*, 14 April 2009.
[108] See *R v Mansfield Justices ex parte Sharkey* [1985] 1 All ER 193 (DC).
[109] Above chapter seven p 314.
[110] www.guardian.co.uk/environment/video/2009/apr/19/police-activism, accessed 20 June 2009.
[111] Liberty submission to JCHR inquiry into policing and protest after the G20, available at: www.liberty-human-rights.org.uk/pdfs/policy-09/liberty-s-written-evidence-to-the-jchr-re-policing-and-protest.pdf, accessed 14 July 2009. As they also comment, there is no justification for a criminal offence of failing to give a name and address when stopped on mere suspicion of committing a non criminal act, when it is not a criminal offence to fail to give a name and address in respect of suspicion of criminal offences.

summer of 2008.[112] There was no realisation that the same measure had created a potentially vast chilling effect on protesters, by which we would all lose out ... and what would the press report then? The long-term, deleterious effects cannot be overstated.

The challenge facing our Royal Commission is to plot a way forward to deal with the dramatic loss of public confidence evoked by this telling comment from the father of Bertie Russell, the Drax protester. After the search his father is reported as saying:

> We are a completely clean, middle-class family from west London and I was the sort of person who would ask a policeman for the time, but now I would steer clear. I no longer have any trust in the police and, especially after seeing the vast violence by police against the G20 protesters, I worry about the safety of anyone near them.

That standpoint is likely to have been fortified by the coverage of the G20 protests and the tragedy that befell Ian Tomlinson and the slapping of Nicola Fisher. To that end, a Royal Commission may well adopt—and adapt—several of the recommendations made throughout 2009:

- putting human rights at the forefront of all policing, not least the policing of protest. This would include access to 'on the spot' legal advice;[113]
- greater and regular human rights training and public order training, based in de-briefings as well as being informed by those who have participated in protest;[114]
- improved dialogue and greater negotiations with protesters in advance and on the day, what has been called 'no surprises' policing;[115]
- a system for the speedy resolution of disputes about police operations and decisions, that would be trusted—an ACAS for protests; and
- a form of standing council at national and local levels with membership drawn from all stakeholders and interested groups, where identifiable.

The difficulty facing moves towards greater communication is the reality—perceived or actual—that confronts many protesters today: herded into cordons faced by officers from a special task force and presumed to be likely trouble-makers. What will be key to the future of policing of protests will be rebuilding confidence in police impartiality and consistency. The police will have to be seen by their actions to acknowledge the value of protest and publicly to recognise that the key term is 'peaceful' not 'lawful' protest and that it is protesters not protests that are peaceful or not. This may require not only tolerance on their part but, at the outset, for them to err on the side of caution and to be seen to be doing so.

---

[112] 'We were wrong to film journalists covering protest', *The Guardian*, 10 March 2009.

[113] This is largely based on the practice in Northern Ireland and the PSNI: see JCHR report, above n 2, at paras 163–9. See also 'New ACPO chief wants human rights to be put at the core of policing', *The Guardian*, 21 June 2009, referring to an interview with Sir Hugh Orde, then Chief Constable of the PSNI.

[114] The ACPO manual, *Keeping the peace* contains very little on human rights principles, save for a handful of very general mentions of proportionality and necessity. It provides no examples as it does for many other issues and the police reader would see them as afterthoughts or tag-ons: www.acpo.police.uk/asp/policies/Data/keeping_the_peace.pdf, accessed 14 July 2009.

[115] JCHR report, above n 2, at para 174. Dialogue requires a named contact: do all groups have such 'leaders'. Even if they do, or collectively realise the benefit, which individual would be willing to go forward knowing that if it all goes horribly wrong, the police have at least have one person they can turn to and bring charges against! Some form of statutory amnesty for these dedicated communicators might prove advantageous. Though that might explain why no protester comes forward as spokesperson, that does not explain why the police themselves offered up no nominated point of contact either in advance or on the day, for the purposes of open dialogue: JCHR follow up report, above n 2, at para 14.

What is likely to be of greatest significance would be the positive endorsement of human rights at the heart of all policing interactions. As the Home Officer Minister with responsibility for policing, Vernon Coker, told the JCHR: 'You do not have to choose between strong and effective policing or the human rights approach. You can marry the two'.[116] We seem to be a long way away, even after 10 years of the HRA, from such a state of wedded bliss. The regulation of the right of peaceful protest in the Human Rights Act era might best be described as bickering courtship. The next two to three years will see if this becomes a fully-fledged betrothal, remains a love-hate relationship or is cuckolded by increasing reliance on private law remedies and interactions.

---

[116] JCHR report, above n 2, Q51.

Appendix I

European Convention for the Protection of Human Rights and Fundamental Freedoms 1950

The governments signatory hereto, being members of the Council of Europe,

Considering the Universal Declaration of Human Rights proclaimed by the General Assembly of the United Nations on 10th December 1948;

Considering that this Declaration aims at securing the universal and effective recognition and observance of the Rights therein declared;

Considering that the aim of the Council of Europe is the achievement of greater unity between its members and that one of the methods by which that aim is to be pursued is the maintenance and further realisation of human rights and fundamental freedoms;

Reaffirming their profound belief in those fundamental freedoms which are the foundation of justice and peace in the world and are best maintained on the one hand by an effective political democracy and on the other by a common understanding and observance of the human rights upon which they depend;

Being resolved, as the governments of European countries which are like-minded and have a common heritage of political traditions, ideals, freedom and the rule of law, to take the first steps for the collective enforcement of certain of the rights stated in the Universal Declaration,

Have agreed as follows:

Article 1—Obligation to respect human rights

The High Contracting Parties shall secure to everyone within their jurisdiction the rights and freedoms defined in Section I of this Convention.

Section I—Rights and freedoms

Article 2—Right to life

1 Everyone's right to life shall be protected by law. No one shall be deprived of his life intentionally save in the execution of a sentence of a court following his conviction of a crime for which this penalty is provided by law.
2 Deprivation of life shall not be regarded as inflicted in contravention of this article when it results from the use of force which is no more than absolutely necessary:
   a in defence of any person from unlawful violence;
   b in order to effect a lawful arrest or to prevent the escape of a person lawfully detained;
   c in action lawfully taken for the purpose of quelling a riot or insurrection.

Article 3—Prohibition of torture

No one shall be subjected to torture or to inhuman or degrading treatment or punishment.

Article 4—Prohibition of slavery and forced labour

1. No one shall be held in slavery or servitude.
2. No one shall be required to perform forced or compulsory labour.
3. For the purpose of this article the term "forced or compulsory labour" shall not include:
   a. any work required to be done in the ordinary course of detention imposed according to the provisions of Article 5 of this Convention or during conditional release from such detention;
   b. any service of a military character or, in case of conscientious objectors in countries where they are recognised, service exacted instead of compulsory military service;
   c. any service exacted in case of an emergency or calamity threatening the life or well-being of the community;
   d. any work or service which forms part of normal civic obligations.

Article 5—Right to liberty and security

1. Everyone has the right to liberty and security of person. No one shall be deprived of his liberty save in the following cases and in accordance with a procedure prescribed by law:
   a. the lawful detention of a person after conviction by a competent court;
   b. the lawful arrest or detention of a person for non- compliance with the lawful order of a court or in order to secure the fulfilment of any obligation prescribed by law;
   c. the lawful arrest or detention of a person effected for the purpose of bringing him before the competent legal authority on reasonable suspicion of having committed an offence or when it is reasonably considered necessary to prevent his committing an offence or fleeing after having done so;
   d. the detention of a minor by lawful order for the purpose of educational supervision or his lawful detention for the purpose of bringing him before the competent legal authority;
   e. the lawful detention of persons for the prevention of the spreading of infectious diseases, of persons of unsound mind, alcoholics or drug addicts or vagrants;
   f. the lawful arrest or detention of a person to prevent his effecting an unauthorised entry into the country or of a person against whom action is being taken with a view to deportation or extradition.
2. Everyone who is arrested shall be informed promptly, in a language which he understands, of the reasons for his arrest and of any charge against him.
3. Everyone arrested or detained in accordance with the provisions of paragraph 1.c of this article shall be brought promptly before a judge or other officer authorised by law to exercise judicial power and shall be entitled to trial within a reasonable time or to release pending trial. Release may be conditioned by guarantees to appear for trial.
4. Everyone who is deprived of his liberty by arrest or detention shall be entitled to take proceedings by which the lawfulness of his detention shall be decided speedily by a court and his release ordered if the detention is not lawful.
5. Everyone who has been the victim of arrest or detention in contravention of the provisions of this article shall have an enforceable right to compensation.

Article 6—Right to a fair trial

1. In the determination of his civil rights and obligations or of any criminal charge against him, everyone is entitled to a fair and public hearing within a reasonable time by an independent and impartial tribunal established by law. Judgment shall be pronounced publicly but the press and public may be excluded from all or part of the trial in the interests of morals, public order or national security in a democratic society, where the interests of juveniles or the protection of the private life of the parties so require, or to the extent strictly necessary in the opinion of the court in special circumstances where publicity would prejudice the interests of justice.

2 Everyone charged with a criminal offence shall be presumed innocent until proved guilty according to law.
3 Everyone charged with a criminal offence has the following minimum rights:

   a to be informed promptly, in a language which he understands and in detail, of the nature and cause of the accusation against him;
   b to have adequate time and facilities for the preparation of his defence;
   c to defend himself in person or through legal assistance of his own choosing or, if he has not sufficient means to pay for legal assistance, to be given it free when the interests of justice so require;
   d to examine or have examined witnesses against him and to obtain the attendance and examination of witnesses on his behalf under the same conditions as witnesses against him;
   e to have the free assistance of an interpreter if he cannot understand or speak the language used in court.

Article 7—No punishment without law

1 No one shall be held guilty of any criminal offence on account of any act or omission which did not constitute a criminal offence under national or international law at the time when it was committed. Nor shall a heavier penalty be imposed than the one that was applicable at the time the criminal offence was committed.
2 This article shall not prejudice the trial and punishment of any person for any act or omission which, at the time when it was committed, was criminal according to the general principles of law recognised by civilised nations.

Article 8—Right to respect for private and family life

1 Everyone has the right to respect for his private and family life, his home and his correspondence.
2 There shall be no interference by a public authority with the exercise of this right except such as is in accordance with the law and is necessary in a democratic society in the interests of national security, public safety or the economic well-being of the country, for the prevention of disorder or crime, for the protection of health or morals, or for the protection of the rights and freedoms of others.

Article 9—Freedom of thought, conscience and religion

1 Everyone has the right to freedom of thought, conscience and religion; this right includes freedom to change his religion or belief and freedom, either alone or in community with others and in public or private, to manifest his religion or belief, in worship, teaching, practice and observance.
2 Freedom to manifest one's religion or beliefs shall be subject only to such limitations as are prescribed by law and are necessary in a democratic society in the interests of public safety, for the protection of public order, health or morals, or for the protection of the rights and freedoms of others.

Article 10—Freedom of expression

1 Everyone has the right to freedom of expression. This right shall include freedom to hold opinions and to receive and impart information and ideas without interference by public authority and regardless of frontiers. This article shall not prevent States from requiring the licensing of broadcasting, television or cinema enterprises.
2 The exercise of these freedoms, since it carries with it duties and responsibilities, may be subject to such formalities, conditions, restrictions or penalties as are prescribed by law and are necessary in a democratic society, in the interests of national security, territorial integrity or public safety, for the prevention of disorder or crime, for the protection of health or morals, for the protection of the reputation or rights of others, for preventing the disclosure of information received in confidence, or for maintaining the authority and impartiality of the judiciary.

Article 11—Freedom of assembly and association

1 Everyone has the right to freedom of peaceful assembly and to freedom of association with others, including the right to form and to join trade unions for the protection of his interests.
2 No restrictions shall be placed on the exercise of these rights other than such as are prescribed by law and are necessary in a democratic society in the interests of national security or public safety, for the prevention of disorder or crime, for the protection of health or morals or for the protection of the rights and freedoms of others. This article shall not prevent the imposition of lawful restrictions on the exercise of these rights by members of the armed forces, of the police or of the administration of the State.

Article 12—Right to marry

Men and women of marriageable age have the right to marry and to found a family, according to the national laws governing the exercise of this right.

Article 13—Right to an effective remedy

Everyone whose rights and freedoms as set forth in this Convention are violated shall have an effective remedy before a national authority notwithstanding that the violation has been committed by persons acting in an official capacity.

Article 14—Prohibition of discrimination

The enjoyment of the rights and freedoms set forth in this Convention shall be secured without discrimination on any ground such as sex, race, colour, language, religion, political or other opinion, national or social origin, association with a national minority, property, birth or other status.

Article 15—Derogation in time of emergency

1 In time of war or other public emergency threatening the life of the nation any High Contracting Party may take measures derogating from its obligations under this Convention to the extent strictly required by the exigencies of the situation, provided that such measures are not inconsistent with its other obligations under international law.
2 No derogation from Article 2, except in respect of deaths resulting from lawful acts of war, or from Articles 3, 4 (paragraph 1) and 7 shall be made under this provision.
3 Any High Contracting Party availing itself of this right of derogation shall keep the Secretary General of the Council of Europe fully informed of the measures which it has taken and the reasons therefor. It shall also inform the Secretary General of the Council of Europe when such measures have ceased to operate and the provisions of the Convention are again being fully executed.

Article 16—Restrictions on political activity of aliens

Nothing in Articles 10, 11 and 14 shall be regarded as preventing the High Contracting Parties from imposing restrictions on the political activity of aliens.

Article 17—Prohibition of abuse of rights

Nothing in this Convention may be interpreted as implying for any State, group or person any right to engage in any activity or perform any act aimed at the destruction of any of the rights and freedoms set forth herein or at their limitation to a greater extent than is provided for in the Convention.

Article 18—Limitation on use of restrictions on rights

The restrictions permitted under this Convention to the said rights and freedoms shall not be applied for any purpose other than those for which they have been prescribed.

* * *

1st Protocol to the Convention for the Protection of Human Rights and Fundamental Freedoms (1952)

Article 1—Protection of property

Every natural or legal person is entitled to the peaceful enjoyment of his possessions. No one shall be deprived of his possessions except in the public interest and subject to the conditions provided for by law and by the general principles of international law.

The preceding provisions shall not, however, in any way impair the right of a State to enforce such laws as it deems necessary to control the use of property in accordance with the general interest or to secure the payment of taxes or other contributions or penalties.

Article 2—Right to education

No person shall be denied the right to education. In the exercise of any functions which it assumes in relation to education and to teaching, the State shall respect the right of parents to ensure such education and teaching in conformity with their own religious and philosophical convictions.

Article 3—Right to free elections

The High Contracting Parties undertake to hold free elections at reasonable intervals by secret ballot, under conditions which will ensure the free expression of the opinion of the people in the choice of the legislature.

* * *

Protocol No. 4 to the Convention for the Protection of Human Rights and Fundamental Freedoms (1963)

Article 2—Freedom of movement

1 Everyone lawfully within the territory of a State shall, within that territory, have the right to liberty of movement and freedom to choose his residence.
2 Everyone shall be free to leave any country, including his own.
3 No restrictions shall be placed on the exercise of these rights other than such as are in accordance with law and are necessary in a democratic society in the interests of national security or public safety, for the maintenance of *ordre public*, for the prevention of crime, for the protection of health or morals, or for the protection of the rights and freedoms of others.
4 The rights set forth in paragraph 1 may also be subject, in particular areas, to restrictions imposed in accordance with law and justified by the public interest in a democratic society.

Appendix II

Bringing an Individual Case to Strasbourg: An Overview

The introduction of the HRA was intended by the Government to reduce the need for those dissatisfied by the English courts to make the journey to Strasbourg. Nonetheless, cases will still wend their way to the European Court. Some appreciation, as well as providing context for the discussion of Article 11 case law that follows, is therefore needed of the procedure.

The original mechanism envisaged by the drafters, as is the usual enforcement mechanism in many treaties and not just those dealing with human rights, is for inter-state petitions under Article 33. "Any High Contracting Party may refer to the Court any alleged breach of the provisions of the Convention and the protocols thereto by another High Contracting Party." Very few of these Article 33 cases have been brought and the vast majority of cases are now brought under Article 34 by means of individual petition.

—Any person, non-governmental organisation or group of individuals claiming to be the victim of a violation by a Member State has the right of individual petition to the Court under Article 34.
—Applications might be ruled inadmissible on various criteria, contained in Articles 34—35. Of most immediate and likely concern will be the requirements that

- Applicants must first exhaust domestic remedies, those that are capable and sufficient to afford redress. In other words, applicants must—in the UK—appeal up to the Supreme Court, though applicants will not be so required where binding authority means there is no reasonable prospect of success; counsel's opinion will be adequate to show this.
- Applicants must be a "victim" of the violation; that is they must be someone directly affected. This has generally been narrowly interpreted and broadly this removes the right for NGOs to bring cases on behalf of others save where they themselves have suffered a direct violation—their own march banned, the group disbanded or their advertisements censored. Not all successful applicants have been required to show that a restriction has actually been applied to them if they can show the mere existence of legislation or an administrative rule has created a "chilling effect": those potentially affected and covered by the rule may well have had to modify their behaviour as a result—see e.g. *Klass v FRG* (1994) 18 EHRR 305 or Norris v Ireland (1991) 13 EHRR 186. In Article 2, right to life cases, surviving relatives may bring actions on behalf of others, not surprisingly: *McCann v UK* (1996) 21 EHRR 97. As before domestic courts, there is a growing trend on the part of the Court to allow the participation of NGOs, not as victims *per se* but as intervenors making written submissions: see *Murray v UK* (1996) 22 EHRR 29 (Liberty, Amnesty and Justice, among others)
- Applicants must not be anonymous
- Claims must be brought within six months
- Claims must not be substantially the same as a matter already examined by the ECtHR or already submitted to another procedure of international investigation or settlement—such as the UN Human Rights Committee—and contains no relevant new information.
- Claims cannot be manifestly ill-founded or an abuse of process
- Claims must not be incompatible *rationae materiae, rationae loci* or *rationae temporis*

—Once lodged, all applications will be assigned, to one of the five sections—Chambers—of the Court. Each is aimed at achieving among the judges a geographical and gender balance and mix of different legal systems represented. Unless a three-judge committee unanimously decides the application can be declared inadmissible or struck out without further examination, it will be referred onto a seven-judge chamber. This will

- decide all other admissibility issues
- investigate facts, attempt any friendly settlement, hear the case argued—first with written submissions and then at a public hearing—and reach a decision on the merits and give reasoned judgment

The former system was overhauled in 1998 under the 11th Protocol. It introduced a full time, permanent Court with a compulsory right of individual petition in place of the former voluntary system (that is, states were not required to permit their citizens to petition directly). Formerly, the Commission decided admissibility, investigated the facts, tried to reach a friendly settlement and gave an opinion, not judgment (as it was not formally comprised of judges). Applicants and states effectively had a right of appeal to the Court for a re-hearing and reasoned judgment. The change means there is a reduced chance of two-tier decisions with possible conflicts between Commission and Court, with the latter taking precedence, and to considerable duplication. The Commission has disappeared and its roles subsumed into that of the now single Court. There is also now a more limited supervisory role for the political body of the Council of Europe, the Committee of Ministers.

The 17-judge Grand Chamber comes into play in two situations in the context of individual applications:

- under Article 30, a seven-judge Chamber may relinquish original jurisdiction where the application raises a "serious question affecting the interpretation of the Convention" or where resolution of a question before it might have a result inconsistent with a judgment previously delivered by the Court.
- under Article 43, either party—i.e. member state or applicant—may (within three months of judgment) ask that the decision of a seven-judge Chamber be referred. A five-judge panel of the Grand Chamber shall accept the request if the case raises a serious question affecting the interpretation or application of the Convention or the protocols thereto, or a serious issue of general importance.

—If the application succeeds, the remedy is limited to "just satisfaction". This will be pecuniary only; the ECtHR has no power to order that a member state changes its law or administrative practice, or that the individual violator be punished or that the applicant be released or retried. Historically, awards have not been especially generous; in many cases the Court has considered that its finding of a violation to be just satisfaction without more. A finding against a state imposes a legal obligation to end the breach and to make reparation for its consequences in such a way as to restore the *status quo ante* (see *Papamichalopoulos v Greece* (1996) 21 EHRR 439 at [34]). In keeping with the subsidiary and supervisory nature of the ECHR, deciding how to respond to a Strasbourg finding that there has been a violation is left to the member state concerned. If they fail to do so properly, the original applicant is left having to bring a second claim. The judgment only covers the respondent state—no other state is formally required to alter its rules/practices even if they are the same as those held to be a violation.

Further details can be found in the Court's own

- *Basic Information on Procedures* available at http://www.echr.coe.int/ECHR/EN/Header/The+Court/How+the+Court+works/Procedure+before+the+Court/ access 12th January 2010
- Case processing flow chart at http://www.echr.coe.int/NR/rdonlyres/BA3F06A3-133C-4699-A25D-35E3C6A3D6F5/0/PROGRESS_OF_A_CASE.pdf access 10th January 2010.

Appendix III

A Summary of Strasbourg Case Law on the Right to Peaceful Protest

Applicant	State	App no	Type of protest	Facts and basis of claim	Article	Admissible?	Commission/ Court finding	Reasoning on the issue of peaceful protest
ADALI	TURKEY	38187/97	C	Refusal of permission to cross green line from TNRC to attend a public meeting organised by a radio station and attended by journalists (as well as claims relating to disappearances, deaths and failures to investigate)	2, 3, 6, 8, 10–11 and 13–14	Yes: 31 Jan 2002	Court—violation of Arts 2 (no separate issue under Art 10), 11 and 13: 31 March 2003	The refusal to allow her to cross was not prescribed by law, following *Djavit An v Turkey* (App 20652/92) ECtHR judgment 20 February 2003.
AHMET	TURKEY	18877/91	C (E)	Candidate for minority party (totalling 1 MP) convicted and sentenced to 18 months imprisonment for disturbing public peace, sowing discord and inciting violence between Greek Muslims and Greek Christians after distributing critical leaflets during successful re-election campaign.	5, 6, 9–11, 14 and Art 3, 1st Protocol	Partially: Arts 9–11 and 14 admissible—8 July 1994.	Commission—violation of Art 10. Court: no violation: 25 October 1996.	Comm'n—In the circumstances, it was not necessary to restrict freedom of speech in order to prevent disorder especially as it took place during an election campaign. Court—reopened the question of exhaustion of local remedies and decided in favour of the state.
ALDEMIR AND OTHERS	TURKEY	32124/02	A, C	Violent dispersal of a TU organised demonstration (and march) on the basis that it allegedly took place in breach of Turkish law as it was not in a permitted place; charged with breaches of domestic law but acquitted.	3, 6, 7 10–11 and 13	Partially: Arts 10–11 admissible; Arts 3, 6 and 13 inadmissible for failing to exhaust domestic remedies; Art 7 manifestly ill-founded: 18 December 2007	Court—violation of Art 11 by 5:2 majority: 18 December 2007.	Forceful intervention was not necessary to prevent disorder or to protect public safety: no evidence of serious danger to public order yet authorities acted swiftly with considerable force.
ANDERSSON	SWEDEN	12781/87	A	Requirement of a permit and fee of 60 Swedish Krona to hold a demonstration (c £5.16 in 1983)	6, 8, 10–11, 13 and 14	Inadmissible: 13 December 1987		Even assuming that requiring a permit on payment was an interference with the right in Art 11, it was justified on grounds of public safety and preventing disorder and crime. Any restriction

A Summary of Strasbourg Case Law on the Right to Peaceful Protest 435

APPLEBY	UK	44306/98	C	Refusal by owners of private shopping centre to permit a small protest group to set up stalls and seek signatures for a petition.	10, 11 and 13	Yes—12 November 2002 or on Art 13: 6 May 2003	Court—no violation of Arts 10–11 (six votes to one)	was one that was necessary to regulate traffic and otherwise maintain order in public places. The low amount also militated in favour of it being proportionate. In the circumstances, the state had not failed in its positive duty to protect freedom of expression, given alternative locations existed.
ARROW-SMITH	UK	7050/75	C	Pacifist convicted under the Incitement to Disaffection Act 1934 after distributing leaflets to serving troops urging them to desert or to refuse to obey orders if posted to Northern Ireland.	5, 9, 10 and 14	Yes—16 May 1977	Commission—no violation of any Article	Art 10: the 1934 Act served the legitimate aims of protecting national security and preventing disorder in the army. By 11 votes to 1, in view of the applicant's manifest intention to continue her action unless stopped by prohibitive measures, neither her prosecution nor her conviction were disproportionate. The fact that others were not prosecuted was explained by the fact that they had stopped when requested. Art 9: distributing the leaflet was not a manifestation of pacifist views.
ASHUGHYAN	ARMENIA	33268/03	A (B)	A was arrested for 'violent public disorder'—making a loud noise and obstructing the traffic—after she participated in a political demonstration, part of a series of political rallies organised by opposition parties after the presidential election. She was	5–6 and 10–11	Partially: only the application under Art 5 was manifestly ill-founded: 17 July 2008.	Court—violation of Arts 6 and 11 (no separate issue under Art 10): 17 July 2008.	The first arrest was not necessary to protect the rights of others and to prevent disorder; there was no reason to depart from the decision in *Galstyan* (arising from the same protest)—it was clear she was arrested for the mere fact of being present and proactive

Applicant	State	App no	Type of protest	Facts and basis of claim	Article	Admissible?	Commission/ Court finding	Reasoning on the issue of peaceful protest
ASHUGHYAN (*cont.*)				detained, searched and questioned. A second demonstration and march at which she was present was dispersed violently, and then she was arrested. The application related only to the arrest, not the dispersal.				at the demonstration (one that had not been banned, was intended to remain peaceful and where no attempt was made at the time to disperse it) rather than for committing anything illegal, violent or obscene in the course of it. There was also a violation in relation to her second arrest: the reasons adduced by the domestic court were not sufficient to justify the interference especially in the form of such a harsh penalty as five days of detention.
ASPROFTAS	TURKEY	16079/90	A	Arrest at and treatment following participation in 19 July 1989 demonstration in TRNC.	3, 5, 6, 7, 11 and 13	Yes— 26 September 2002	Unknown	
OYA ATAMAN	TURKEY	74552/01	A, B and C	An unauthorised public demonstration (with 40–50 holding placards), march and press conference was dispersed violently by the police using tear gas and pepper spray. Those who refused to obey the order to disperse were arrested. The application challenged the dismissal by the Turkish authorities of the protesters' claims.	3 and 11	Partially: Arts 3 and 11 admissible— 8 March 2005.	Court— violation of Art 11 but no violation of Art 3: 5 December 2006.	Art 11: the restriction pursued the legitimate aims of preventing disorder and preserving the rights of others to move freely in public without restriction. Nonetheless, the forceful intervention by the police had not been necessary to prevent disorder. The fact that the demonstration was unlawful did not justify infringing the right of assembly. There was no evidence to suggest the group had represented any danger to public order, apart from possibly disrupting traffic. There had been at most 50 people who had wished to draw public attention to

A Summary of Strasbourg Case Law on the Right to Peaceful Protest

						a topical issue. The Court was particularly struck by the authorities' impatience in seeking to end the demonstration, which it did within half an hour. Where demonstrators did not engage in acts of violence it was important for the public authorities to show a certain degree of tolerance towards peaceful gatherings if the freedom of assembly guaranteed by the Convention was not to be deprived of all substance. Art 3—no medical evidence had been submitted to substantiate the claims of inhuman treatment.
AYLIFFE	UK	33294/06	D	Greenpeace activists were acquitted of various offences relating to boarding a cargo ship but were not awarded their costs	6 and 10	Struck out—no longer wished to proceed: 10 February 2009.
BACZKOW-SKI	POLAND	1543/06	A, B	A group planned to hold a march and several assemblies in Warsaw. In the case of the first, the traffic department refused permission—though it did take place anyway—as a 'traffic organisation plan' had not been submitted as allegedly required. The assemblies were banned by the mayor but overturned on appeal. The protests concerned the treatment of and discrimination towards minorities, especially gays and lesbians.	11, 13 and 14	Yes: 3 May 2007	Court—violation of Arts 11, 13 and 14: 3 May 2007.	The march was held and the decisions in respect of both the assemblies and the march were eventually overturned; the applicants did constitute victims as they were held without the presumption of legality, since the decisions were eventually overturned as being contrary to the constitutional guarantee of freedom of assembly, the restrictions were not prescribed by law.

438 Appendix III

Applicant	State	App no of protest	Type	Facts and basis of claim	Article	Admissible?	Commission/Court finding	Reasoning on the issue of peaceful protest
BALÇIK	TURKEY	0025/02	A (D)	Violent dispersal of a public assembly and making of a press announcement (having also planned to obstruct a tram line) in protest at F-type prisons. A police request to disperse, based on the absence of any prior notice and thus its unlawful nature, was refused. Arrested and charged and it took five years to be acquitted of taking taking part in an unlawful assembly and failing to disperse.	3, 10–11, 7, 17–18	Yes: 29 November 2007	Court—violation of Art 3 and Art 11. No separate ruling on Arts 7, 17–18 needed: 29 November 2007.	The nature of the police intervention was disproportionate to the aim of preventing disorder.
BARIKAN	TURKEY	29674/02	A	Dispersal of demonstration by security forces on grounds of public order—and subsequent initiating of criminal charges.	6 and 10	Struck out for delay: 12 February 2008		
BUKTA	HUNGARY	25691/04	A	Police disbanded (after a small detonation noise was heard) a rally—of about 150 people—protesting that the Hungarian PM should refrain from attending a state function hosted by the Rumanian PM during a state visit.	10 and 11	Yes: 17 July 2007	Court—violation of Art 11: 17th July 2007.	Not necessary in order to prevent disorder and protect the rights of others. Despite the fact that the police had had no prior notice of the assembly, in the special circumstances, when an immediate response to a political event might be justified, a decision to disband where there was no illegal conduct by the demonstrators solely because of no prior notice would be disproportionate.
C S	GERMANY	13858/88	D	Arrested and convicted of 'unlawful coercion' after sit-in on road in front of US barracks.	7, 11 and 14	No—6 March 1989		Necessary for preventing disorder and crime: applicant was not punished for participating in any demonstration as

						such, but for particular behaviour, namely the blocking of a public road, thereby causing more obstruction than would normally arise from the exercise of the right of peaceful assembly.
ÇETİNKAYA	TURKEY	75569/01	C	Arrested and convicted of participating in an illegal assembly after being present at a press conference where statement condemning government action was read out.	6, 10–11	Yes	Ct—violation of Art 11; no separate issue under Art 10. No violation of Art 6: 27th June 2006	Turkey made a general claim based on Art 11(2) by implication covering preventing crime and disorder, national security, rights and freedoms of others. The conviction was akin to a general ban on the content of assemblies and meetings save where permitted by the state and as such defeated the democratic principles underpinning Art 11.
CHORHERR	AUSTRIA	13308/87	C	Arrested and fined for the administrative offence of being 'likely to cause annoyance' after distributing anti-arms leaflets at ceremony to mark 40 years of peace.	5 and 10	Yes—1 March 1991	Commission—violation of Art 10 (by 7 votes to 7 with President's casting vote) but no violation of Art 5 (by 12:2): 21st May 1992. Court—no violation of Art 10 (6 votes to three) and unanimous finding of no violation of Art 5 25th August 1993.	No violation of Art 10—the measures were prescribed by law to prevent disorder and within the margin of appreciation as not to be disproportionate. No violation of Art 5 because of Austria's reservation.

Appendix III

Applicant	State	App no	Type of protest	Facts and basis of claim	Article	Admissible?	Commission/Court finding	Reasoning on the issue of peaceful protest
CHRISTIAN DEMO-CRATIC PEOPLE'S PARTY	MOLDOVA	28793/02	A	Temporary ban imposed on the party's activities for organising an allegedly unauthorised demonstration.	10 and 11	Yes—22 March 2005	Court—violation of Art 11 (by 6 votes to 1). No separate issue under Art 10: 14th February 2006.	None of the reasons provided was relevant or sufficient to ban, even temporarily, an opposition minority party. No submissions were made by Moldova on the issue of the legitimate aim and it was arguable that the restrictions were not prescribed by law: this last was the basis for Judge Pavlovschi's partly concurring opinion.
CHRISTIANS AGAINST RACISM & FASCISM (CARAF)	UK	8440/78	B	A general ban on all marches, so as to prohibit one by the National Front, incidentally caught a proposed march by CARAF.	5, 10, 11 and 14	No—16 July 1980		Comm'n accepted UK's claim that the ban was necessary in the interests of public safety, preventing disorder or crime, and protecting the rights and freedoms of others. It emphasised the need to prevent disorder. In all the circumstances, CARAF could reasonably be expected to sustain the effects of the ban which were not disproportionate.
CHRISTO-DOULIDOU	TURKEY	16085/90	A	Arrest at and treatment following participation in 19 July 1989 demonstration in TRNC.	3 and 11	Yes—7 Dec 1999	UNKNOWN	
CIESIELCZYK	POLAND	12575/02	A	Town mayor decided to ban a demonstration planned by 100 or so after hearing representations only from local inhabitants in the area affected.	11	Struck out of the list (Friendly settlement): 5 September 2006		

A Summary of Strasbourg Case Law on the Right to Peaceful Protest 441

ÇILOĞLU	TURKEY	73333/01	A	Tear gas dispersal of sit-in protest of about 60 or so, held regularly in Istanbul in support of prisoners' protest at the building a new type of prison.	3 and 11	Yes: 6 March 2007	Court—no violation of Art 11 (by 5 votes to 2): 6 March 2007	The demonstration had been unlawful and the participants informed; it had had a clearly disruptive effect on traffic as well as breaching the peace. It had been held for about three years in a public place every Saturday such that the protesters had had adequate opportunity to attain their objective, drawing attention to a matter of public concern. The state's reaction was within the margin of appreciation as a proportionate measure to meet the legitimate aim of maintaining order and protecting the rights of others.
ÇIRAKLAR	TURKEY	19601/92	A	Arrest and conviction by national security court for taking part in an unauthorised demonstration protesting about Turkish repression of the Kurds.	Arts 3, 5(1)(c), 5(3)–(4), 6(1)–(3), 8, 9–11.	Partially; only claim in relation to Art 6(1). Claim relating to participation in demonstration (Arts 9–11) declared inadmissible—19 January 1995.	Court—violation of Art 6 (by seven votes to two): 28 October 1998.	
CISSÉ	FRANCE	51346/99	D	Forcible evacuation of protesters using a church for a sit-in protest about French immigration law.	11	Yes—16 Jan 2001	Court—no violation of Art 11: 9 April 2002.	The protest had been peaceful and taken place with consent of the religious authorities and had not entailed any disturbance of public order. Despite that, given the deterioration in the protesters' health and sanitary conditions, it was not a disproportionate measure, given the state's wide margin of appreciation, to prevent disorder.

Applicant	State	App no	Type of protest	Facts and basis of claim	Article	Admissible?	Commission/Court finding	Reasoning on the issue of peaceful protest
DANIS	TURKEY	24564/94	A (C)	Arrest and prosecution for participating in a political demonstration and disseminating 'separatist propaganda'.	6, 10 and 11	No—Out of time		
DAVYTAN	ARMENIA	22382/05	A	Arrested for disobeying a police order when they came to question him ostensibly about a neighbour dispute but real reason suspected to be participation in a demonstration the previous day.	11	Struck out: 19 Oct. 2006		
DENMARK AND OTHERS ('THE GREEK CASE')	GREECE	3321-4/67 3344/67	A, C	Near total prohibition on political meetings except with permission from military authorities.	11 (inter alia)	Yes—24 January and 31 May 1968	Commission: violation of Art 11— 4 October 1969.	No evidence was produced to show the prohibition and restrictions were necessary to prevent disorder and crime.
DİREKÇİ	TURKEY	47826/99	A	Arrest and trial following participating in a TU demonstration (along with subsequent denial of medical treatment and death).	2, 3, 6 and 11	No as to Arts 2 and 3: 31 March 2005. No as to Arts 6 and 11 incompatible rationae personae (on ground that parents of the deceased protester could not be 'victims' under Art 34): 3 October 2006		

A Summary of Strasbourg Case Law on the Right to Peaceful Protest 443

DONNAN	UK	3811/04	A	Arrested for breach of the peace at a protest about the treatment of soldiers with PTSD.	7, 10	No—8 Nov 2005. Applicant didn't exhaust domestic remedies—he hadn't utilised HRA to challenge decision by judicial review.	
DRIEMAN	NORWAY	33678/96	D	Arrest detention and conviction for obstruction following Greenpeace anti-whaling protest at sea.	10 and 11	No—4 May 2000	The measure was within Norway's margin of appreciation and so was necessary either to prevent disorder or crime or to protect the rights and freedoms of others. The Court attached weight to the coercive/direct action nature of protest and to the fact that alternative measures were open.
DÜZGÖREN	TURKEY	56827/00	C	A military court convicted a journalist of inciting others to evade military service. He had distributed (outside the state security court) a leaflet consisting largely of a press release (issued a few years previously by a conscientious objector who had himself been convicted on the basis of its contents) and had organised a petition that the public prosecutor himself should be charged for a crime after bringing the prosecution.	6, 10 and 13	Yes as to Arts 6 and 10; claim under Art 13 manifestly unfounded—28 September 2004	Violation of Art 6 (tribunal could not be considered impartial) and 10: 9 November 2006. The Court considered that the restriction was prescribed by law and was intended to prevent disorder but it was not proportionate/'necessary in a democratic society': (a) although the words used in the impugned article connoted hostility to military service, they did not encourage violence, armed resistance or insurrection and did not constitute hate speech; (b) *Arrowsmith* distinguished in terms of potential impact—here the offending leaflet was distributed in a public place. It did not seek, either in its form or in its content, to precipitate immediate desertion.

Appendix III

Applicant	State	App no	Type of protest	Facts and basis of claim	Article	Admissible?	Commission/Court finding	Reasoning on the issue of peaceful protest
EZELIN	FRANCE	11800/85	A	Disciplinary sanction was imposed by a Guadeloupe court on a barrister for participating in a demonstration and holding a placard.	10 and 11	Yes—13 March 1989	Comm'n—violation of Art 11 and no separate issue under Art 10 (by 15 votes to 6). Court—violation of Art 11 (by 6 votes to 3): 26 April 1991	Even the minor penalty of a reprimand was a disproportionate impairment of the right to peaceful assembly and so was not necessary in the prevention of disorder.
FAIRFIELD	UK	24790/04	C	Arrested and convicted for an offence under s 5 Public Order Act 1986 after preaching in public about the sin of homosexuality.	9 and 10	No—8 March 2005. Application was brought by the relatives of the now deceased protester; they were not victims.		
FRIEDL	AUSTRIA	15225/89	D	Applicant was asked to leave an unauthorised sit-in demonstration in an underground pedestrian passage and was then photographed.	8, 11 and 13	Partially. Arts 8 and 13 only admissible: 30 November 1992	Friendly settlement on Art 8, relating to the photos	Art 11: manifestly inadmissible. Not a disproportionate measure given the need to balance the applicant's rights and the public interest in preventing disorder.
G	GERMANY	13079/87	D	Arrested and convicted of using unlawful coercion after refusing an order to leave a sit-in/road block demonstration outside US military barracks.	7, 11 and 14	No—6 March 1989		The conviction was not disproportionate to prevent disorder and crime: see *CS v Germany* above.

A Summary of Strasbourg Case Law on the Right to Peaceful Protest

G AND E	NORWAY	9278/81 9415/81	D	Environmental and ethnic protest by Lapplanders in the form of setting up a tent outside Parliament in excess of authorisation.	10, 13, 14 and Art 1, 1st Protocol	No: inadmissible for all applications—3rd October 1983	Permission to protest for four hours on one day but in fact lasted four days and nights: interference therefore reasonably necessary to protect public order
G S	AUSTRIA	14923/89	D	Convicted on two occasions for holding a demonstration (erecting two small tables so as to provide information) on a public road without authorisation, contrary to Austrian road traffic legislation.	10 and 11	No—30 November 1992	Neither conviction was unnecessary given the proportionate need to prevent disorder, in the form of unhindered and safe traffic.
GALSTYAN	ARMENIA	26986/03	A	Arrested near a demonstration; G. was an authorised election attendant for a minority party MP, ordered by police not to attend but arrested after observing a large rally.	6 and 10–11 (and Protocol 7, Art 2)	Yes: 15 November 2007	Violation of Art 6(1) and 6(3)(b) and Art 11 and 7th protocol; no violation of Art6(3)(c) by 5:2 —15 November 2007 The measure was not necessary to prevent disorder or to protect the rights of others.
GEFFEN AND OTHERS	UK	26049/94 26056/94	D	Arrested and detained without charge after protesting about the M11 motorway extension or against the policies of the World Bank.	5, 6, 10, 11 and 13	Struck out following withdrawal	
GREECE	UK	176/56	A, B, C	Banning of public processions, meetings and assemblies of five or more save for those that were peaceful and for the purpose of performing religious duties, social intercourse or business/profession.	11 (inter alia)	Yes	Comm'n: no violation of Art 11 The decision was justified for reasons of national security and public safety.

Applicant	State	App no	Type of protest	Facts and basis of claim	Article	Admissible?	Commission/ Court finding	Reasoning on the issue of peaceful protest
GÜL	TURKEY	4870/02	A, C	Convicted of facilitating the operation of an illegal Marxist-Leninist group, partly on the basis of participation at workers' day demonstrations at which Marxist-Leninist slogans were shouted and posters held, near which G was standing	6, 10–11	Partially: adjourned for Government response on Arts 10–11: 11 December 2007	AWAITED	
GULIYEV AND RAMAZANOV	AZER-BAIJAN	34553/02	A (E)	Interference with internal organisation and activities of opposition party; disruption of party meeting; refusal of permission to hold a protest; arrest and detention of those at meeting.	3, 5, 6, 8, 10–11 and 14	No—9 September 2004 and 14 February 2006. Inadmissible as to fair trial, violation of free speech and assembly and discrimination on ground of political opinion for failure to exhaust local remedies and incompatibility rationae temporis.		
GUNERI AND OTHERS	TURKEY	42853/98 43609/98 44291/98	A	The case involved two challenges. The first was a ban on national party officials of the Democracy and Peace Party (DBP) from entering certain towns in south-east Turkey as part of a plan to meet the local population	11, 13 and 14	Yes—8 July 2003	Violation of Arts 11 and 13: 12 July 2005	As to Art 11, the Court accepted that the restrictions could at least serve the aims of public safety and territorial integrity (sic)—whereas Turkey had argued they could also serve to protect national security and to prevent crime.

A Summary of Strasbourg Case Law on the Right to Peaceful Protest

			and civil organisations. Second was a ban imposed by the regional governor on a proposed outdoor meeting in one of those towns on the ground that the situation was tense and that, because of its size, the meeting was likely to lead to unruly incidents with placards, rallying cries and slogans being used to stir up the people and criticise governmental measures.		The measure though was not proportionate. Although account could be taken of the tense political/terrorist situation, advance notice of the contents of the speeches etc had been given to the governor. States could require permission to be sought but here there was nothing to suggest that the planned visits were liable to serve as a platform to advocate violence and the rejection of democracy or to have any potentially harmful consequences that would justify their prohibition.
H	UK	10888/84 C	Special Branch attempted to gain entry to property by subversion, following publication of letters written by H to a local newspaper indicating opposition to nuclear weapons. Her letters were interpreted as 'indicating that she might be prepared to support or become involved in public protests of a nature which could become disorderly or even violent'.	10 and 13	No— 3 December 1986. She was no longer a victim at the time of her application. Her complaint had been dealt with by the Chief Constable (after representations through her MP). This included issuing an apology, censuring the officers and taking measures to prevent re-occurrence.

Applicant	State	App no	Type of protest	Facts and basis of claim	Article	Admissible?	Commission/ Court finding	Reasoning on the issue of peaceful protest
HASHMAN AND HARRUP	UK	25594/94	D	Fox-hunt protesters bound over to be of good behaviour.	5, 10 and 11	Yes—26 June 1996	Commission— violation of Art 10 (by 25 votes to 4): 6 July 1998. Court—violation of Art 10, the only remaining challenge before it (by 16 votes to 1): 25 November 1999.	The restriction (ie the binding over order) was not prescribed by law: it was not apparent what they were not meant to do (but on this, see the dissent of Judge Baka).
HEIKKILÄ AND OTHERS	FINLAND	25472/94	A	A group of anti-motor race demonstrators was arrested, detained and convicted of acting 'in a refractory manner' and obstructing the police after they refused to obey an instruction to move to the other side of the street, in the vicinity of the town hall where a reception for the race drivers was being held.	5, 6, 10–11, 14 and Art 2, 4th Protocol	No—15 May 1996		Under Art 10, the group was not and had not been prevented from participating in the earlier demonstration. The order to cross the street was prescribed by law and necessary in the interest of public safety and to prevent disorder.
HYDE PARK	MOLDOVA	18491/07	A	Dispersal of demonstration in Chisinau; local council approved only one day of protest. That declaration was quashed by the court of appeal who ordered a three-day protest could be held. Council refused to comply as it did not consider the order was final. The protest was broken up as being	3, 5, 6, 8, 11 and 13	Partially: Arts 3, 8 and 13 treatment of (the protesters) inadmissible. Art 11 and 5 admissible (no	Court—violation of Art 11: 7 April 2009	The restrictions on protest were not prescribed by law

A Summary of Strasbourg Case Law on the Right to Peaceful Protest 449

INCAL	TURKEY 22678/93	C (E)	Member of the Executive Committee of the People's Labour Party (HEP) was convicted of propagating separatist propaganda and inciting racial hatred after distributing hostile and vituperative leaflet criticising certain measures taken by the authorities in Izmir: 'We call upon all Kurdish and Turkish patriots to assume their responsibilities and oppose this special war being waged against the proletarian people'.	6(1), 6(3)(b), 9–10 and 14	Yes—16 October 1995	Commission—violation of Art 10 (together with breaches of Art 6). Court—violation of Art 10 and no separate issue under Art 9. Violation of Art 6 (12 votes to 8): 9 June 1998	Given the especial importance of free speech for political parties and their members, the measures were disproportionate and so not necessary to prevent disorder. There was nothing to suggest the applicant was responsible for the terrorist problems in Turkey and Izmir.
IOAKIM	TURKEY 16076/90	A	Arrest at and treatment following participation in 19 July 1989 demonstration in TRNC.	3, 5, 7, 9–11, 13 and Art 1, 1st Protocol	Struck off list—9 March 1998		
IVANOV	BULGARIA 46336/99	A	Ban on two UMO Ilinden-Pirin rallies (together with improper refusal to hear appeal against ban).	11, 13 and 14	Yes—9 September 2004	Court—violation of Art 11 (by 5 votes to 2) and violation of Art 13 unanimously. No need to decide about Art 14: 24 November 2005	As to Art 11: relevant and sufficient reasons had not been given to justify the ban on grounds of public order.

Applicant	State	App no	Type of protest	Facts and basis of claim	Article	Admissible?	Commission/ Court finding	Reasoning on the issue of peaceful protest
JK	NETHER-LANDS	15928/89	C	Removed from platform of Amsterdam railway station after unfurling a 'No Olympics' banner to protest at Amsterdam's candidature for the 1992 Olympics.	9 and 10	No—13 May 1992		No violation of Art 10—prior permission was regarded as necessary to prevent disorder; furthermore, the applicant was not prosecuted nor prevented from protesting elsewhere. No violation of Art 9: this was not a manifestation of belief.
KANDZHOV	BULGARIA	68294/01	C	Prosecuted after setting up a stall to drum up support for a petition calling for the resignation of the Minister of Justice and local politican as well as for displaying posters referring to him a 'a top idiot'. The protest was planned for 9:00 am–5:00 pm over three days. K gave notice but permission was refused on grounds of public order and safety. When he continued he was arrested, detained and charged. His conviction was later overturned.	5 and 10	Yes: 6 Nov 2008	Court—violation of Art 10 (and Art 5): 6 Nov 2008	(i) The arrest and detention were not lawful under Art 5 and so were not prescribed by law. There was no power to detain for the privately-prosecutable offence of insult and the constituent elements of the offence of hooliganism were not made out. (ii) The measures were not necessary to prevent disorder and protect the rights of others; this was a political debate which was critical but not violent. In a democracy, acts and omissions of government and its members must be subject to close scrutiny. Furthermore, their dominant position requires them to show restraint in resorting to criminal proceedings especially where other means are available to reply to criticisms and attacks.
KARAKAYA AND PIROGLU	TURKEY	37581/02 36370/02	C	Prosecutions of five members of the Izmir Human Rights Association for issuing collective press statement	6, 10 and 11	Yes—2 May 2006	Court—violation of Arts 6, 10–11: 18 March	The conviction and sentence for being part of an illegal organisation where what was done was to highlight a

KESK	TURKEY	27794/02	A	about US military involvement in Afghanistan, thereby constituting an illegal organisation, and for the failure to dismiss members of the association with criminal convictions.			matter of social concern was not prescribed by law under Art 10(2)
				Violent dispersal of TU protest meeting.	3, 6, 7, 10–11 and 13	Art 11 adjourned (no separate issue under Art 10): 15 November 2005. Remainder declared inadmissible rationae materiae, rationae personae & manifestly ill-founded. Struck out of list: presumed applicant no longer wishes to pursue –21 November 2006.	2008
KUZNETSOV	RUSSIA	10877/04	A, C	Picket in front of the regional court daily over four days for about two hours per day in order to attract public attention to alleged violations of the human right of access to a court. K distributed information about the President of the Court (allegedly corrupt) and collected signatures	11 (and 10)	Yes: 23 Oct 2008	Court— violation: 23 October 2008.	The reasons given were not relevant or sufficient to the legitimate aim of preventing disorder and protecting the rights of others; the relatively small fine did not detract from this. The fact that K should have given 10 days' notice (but gave only 8) did not impair the authorities' ability to make

Applicant	State	App no of protest	Type	Facts and basis of claim	Article	Admissible?	Commission/ Court finding	Reasoning on the issue of peaceful protest
KUZNETSOV (*cont.*)				calling for his dismissal. There was no dispersal of the picket but in administrative proceedings brought after the event, K was found guilty of giving insufficient notice, breach of public order for the obstruction and conducting the protest at variance with notified aims.				necessary preparations. Any demonstration in a public place inevitably causes a certain level of disruption to ordinary life, including disruption of traffic. It is important for the public authorities to show a certain degree of tolerance towards peaceful gatherings, thus the alleged obstruction of passage was not a relevant and sufficient reason for the interference. The materials distibuted, though they might have been insulting, were not defamatory, inciting or reject democracy.
LUCAS	UK	39013/02	D	Arrest and conviction for committing a breach of the peace (contrary to Scottish law) at a road block sit-in outside Faslane navy base.	5 and 10–11	No— 18 March 2003		Both claims were manifestly ill-founded. As to Arts 10–11, the measures were justified in the interests of public safety and/or preventing disorder. As to Art 5, the law was sufficiently certain and complied with.
MAKHMA-DUV	RUSSIA	35082/04	A	Organiser fined after permission for an assembly complaining about local government and planning regime was withdrawn the day before	3, 5, 11 and 14	Partially— Arts 5 and 11 admissible: 26 July 2007	Violation of Art 11: 26 July 2007	Failure to produce any evidence substantiating the claim of a terrorist threat combined with the fact that M's meeting was the only one cancelled and the only one directed at Moscow's policies—whereas public festivities organised by Moscow were not banned despite the supposed threat—meant the ban on grounds of preventing disorder and crime and protecting the rights of others was arbitrary and not justified.

A Summary of Strasbourg Case Law on the Right to Peaceful Protest

McBRIDE	UK	27786/95	A	The applicant refused to discontinue walking along the public highway in the direction of an arms fair about 15 minutes distant (and away from a static demonstration where she had been previously). She was arrested and detained (then released without charge) for 90 minutes in order to prevent a breach of the peace.	5 and 10–11	No: 5 July 2001	Both claims were manifestly ill-founded. As to Art 5, the initial purpose of detention was to bring her before court even if there was a subsequent decision not to charge. As to Arts 10–11 it was not disproportionate to arrest and remove her from the scene of a protest, where there was a domestic finding of a very high risk of violence, so as to prevent disorder or to protect the rights of others.
METAXA	TURKEY	16077/90	A	Arrest at and treatment following participation in 19th July 1989 demonstration in TRNC.	3, 5, 7, 9–11, 13 and 1st Protocol	Struck off list: 9 March 1998	
MKRTCHYAN	ARMENIA	6562/03	B	Convicted of organising an unlawful procession, after an authorised demonstration.	11 and 13	Partially. Art 11 admissible and Art 13 inadmissible—20 October 2005	Violation of Art 11: 11 January 2007. The rules prescribing penalties for organising street rallies and processions were not formulated with sufficient precision to be 'prescribed by law'.
MOLNAR	HUNGARY	10346/05	A, C	The police dispersed a demonstration (numbers estimated at 300 to several thousand) without force for failing to comply with the three day prior notification rule. The protesters were demanding a general election recount on suspicion of vote-rigging. The demonstration blocked a central road bridge in Budapest with their cars, bringing traffic to a standstill.	11	Yes: 7 October 2008	Court—no violation: 7 October 2008. The dispersal was proportionate to the need to protect the rights of others (freedom of movement and traffic flow), which also comprised part of the state's positive duty. The protest was allowed to continue for several hours uninterrupted and in any event the facts did not disclose special circumstances to which the only adequate response was an immediate demonstration. The procedure was

Applicant	State	App no	Type of protest	Facts and basis of claim	Article	Admissible?	Commission/ Court finding	Reasoning on the issue of peaceful protest
MOLNAR (cont.)								notification not authorisation. Nearly two months had passed since the results of the elections had been made public. The Court was not persuaded that this matter would have become obsolete had the demonstrators respected the notification rule.
MOOSMAN	AUSTRIA	14093/88	C	Removal of crosses (symbolising death of nature) from private property adjoining road construction, on the instructions of member of regional government.	10	Yes— 15 October 1991. Friendly settlement reached— 9 July 1992		
NICOL AND SELVANA- YAGAM	UK	32213/96	D	After disturbing a fishing competition, the applicants were arrested (and detained for two days pending a hearing) to prevent breach of the peace then committed to prison for 21 days for refusing to be bound over.	5 (1), 5(5), 10, 11 and 13	No— 11th January 2001		As to Arts 10–11, the initial arrest and detention served the twin aims of preventing disorder and protecting the rights of others. There was a serious risk they would return. The committal served those aims and maintaining the authority of the judiciary. None was disproportionate given the risk of provoking disorder or violence from others.
ÖLLINGER	AUSTRIA	76900/01	A	Prohibition of public meeting on All Saints' Day that would coincide with popular commemoration ceremony by surviving SS members on ground that it would endanger public order and security and to protect the rights under Art 9 of other cemetery-goers.	11	Yes— 24 March 2005	Court—violation by 6 votes to 1: 29 June 2006	The ban struck the wrong balance. In all the circumstances, the domestic authorities attached too much weight to the Art 9 rights of other cemetery goers and too little to the rights of the applicant and so the ban was not necessary either to prevent disorder or to protect the rights of others.

A Summary of Strasbourg Case Law on the Right to Peaceful Protest 455

OLYMBIOU	TURKEY	16091/90	A	Arrest at and treatment following participation in 19 July 1989 demonstration in TRNC.	1, 3, 5–6, 7, 8–11, 13, 14 and 1st Protocol	Partially. Arts 3, 5–6, 7, 8, 11, 13, 14 and Art 1, 1st Protocol admissible—26 September 2002.	UNKNOWN
ÖNER AND 18 OTHERS	TURKEY	68684/01	C (E)	Complaint about the treatment of a group (including regional administrators of People's Democratic Party) on hunger strike protest together with a subsequent conviction for aiding an illegal terrorist organisation.	6, 8, 11 and 14	No as to Arts 8, 11 and 13 and adjourned as to Art 6—1 June 2004	The application under Art 11 was rejected because they were not taken into custody as a result of the hunger strike but because of suspicions about their criminal activity. Rejected both the claim that detention and search of party offices interfered with hunger strike and that the conviction wrongfully interpreted the hunger strike as showing support for PKK. Both were manifestly ill-founded.
OSMANI	MAC'-DONIA	50841/99	C (E): the sole example of inflammatory speech which may warrant a category of its own	The Mayor of Gostivar was convicted of stirring up national and racial hatred for his role in organising and speaking at a public meeting, defending the Albanian flag and using inflammatory language such as 'we're going to reply to a slap with a slap'.	10 and 11	No—11 October 2001	The claim was manifestly ill-founded; the prison sentence was not disproportionate in light of his encouragement to armed resistance and riots. Several aims were put forward and accepted: preventing crime and disorder, national security, public safety, and protecting the rights and freedoms of others.

Appendix III

Applicant	State	App no	Type of protest	Facts and basis of claim	Article	Admissible?	Commission/ Court finding	Reasoning on the issue of peaceful protest
PANAYI	TURKEY	16097/90	A	Arrest at and treatment following participation in 19th July 1989 demonstration in TRNC.	3, 5, 7, 9–11, 13 and Art 1, 1st Protocol	Struck off list—2 March 1998		
PAPI (ANDREOU)	TURKEY	16094/90	A	Arrest at and treatment following participation in 19th July 1989 demonstration in TRNC.	1, 3, 5–6, 7, 8–11, 13, 14 and Art 1, 1st Protocol	Partially. Arts 3, 5–6, 7, 8, 11, 13, 14 and Art 1, 1st Protocol admissible—26 Sept 2002.	UNKNOWN	
PATYI	HUNGARY	5529/05	A	Prohibition on holding a demonstration in front of the PM's house; planned to be about 20 in number, standing silently in line on a 5m wide pavement	11 (and 10); 6, 9, 13 and 14	Partially: only the claims in relation to Arts 11–10 were admissible: 7 Oct 2008	Court—violation of Art 11: 7 October 2008.	Reasons were neither relevant nor sufficient to meet a pressing social need: there was no evidence of violence and no likely danger to public order; there was not likely to be a significant impeding of traffic or of passers-by on foot, given the width of the pavement. The ban was therefore not necessary to protect the rights of others.
PETRAKIDOU	TURKEY	16081/90	A	Arrest at and treatment following participation in 19 July 1989 demonstration in TRNC.	1, 3, 5–6, 7, 8–11, 13, 14 and Art 1, 1st Protocol	Partially. Arts 3, 5–6, 7, 8, 11, 13, 14 and Art 1, 1st admissible—26 Sept 2002.	UNKNOWN	

A Summary of Strasbourg Case Law on the Right to Peaceful Protest 457

PETROPAV-LOVSKIS	LATVIA	44230/06	A, C	Refused naturalisation on grounds of previous political activities including protesting against the removal/reduction in rights of Russian-speaking minorities in education	10–11 and 13	Yes: 3 June 2008, despite the state's arguments that there was no interference with his right to protest and express views and was in fact a disguised attempt to claim a right (naturalisation) not protected in the ECHR	AWAITED
PIERMONT	FRANCE	15773/89 15774/89	A, B and C	Exclusion and expulsion of a German MEP from French Polynesia following participation in public meeting and march organised by the independence and anti-nuclear movement, along with her subsequent exclusion from New Caledonia.	10, 14 and Art 2, 4th Protocol	Yes— 3 December 1992	Commission—violation of Art 10 only (eight votes to six) resulting from the exclusion and expulsion in French Polynesia. Court—violation of Art 10 in both the exclusion and expulsion and the exclusion by New Caledonia. No need to decide the issue under	Art 10: the Court rejected France's defence based on both Art 63 ('local requirements' did not encompass a tense, sensitive political situation) and on Art 16 ('aliens' did not extend to nationals of other EU members especially those who were MEPs in which members of France's OTs also voted). As to Art 10(2), the Court accepted the government's claim that the restriction sought both to prevent disorder and to preserve territorial integrity but decided the measures did not strike a fair balance: despite the tense political atmosphere, the utterances were made in the course of a peaceful authorised demonstration.

Applicant	State	App no	Type of protest	Facts and basis of claim	Article	Admissible?	Commission/ Court finding	Reasoning on the issue of peaceful protest
							Art 14. No breach of Art 2, 4th Protocol: 27 April 1995.	At no time was there a call for violence or disorder and much of what was said reflected the demands made by several local parties. Her speech was therefore a contribution to a democratic debate. Moreover, the demonstration was not followed by any disorder and the Government did not show that the stances taken up by the applicant caused any unrest.
PLATTFORM 'ÄRZTE FÜR DAS LEBEN'	AUSTRIA	10126/82	A, B (C)	Group claimed that its authorised pro-life march and meeting were disrupted by counter-demonstrators due to inadequate police protection.	9–11 and 13	Partially: Art 13 application admissible—17 October 1985. Arts 9–11 manifestly ill-founded on the facts, though Comm'n accepted that Art 11 does comprise a positive duty to protect against counter-demonstrators.	Court—no violation of Art 13: 21 June 1988.	Art 13 only applies to 'arguable' claims that there have been violations of rights in the remainder of Convention. Though Art 11 does impose an element of positive obligation on states to allow protest and demonstrations to take place, on the facts Austria did not fail to take reasonable and though appropriate measures.

A Summary of Strasbourg Case Law on the Right to Peaceful Protest 459

PROTOPAPA	TURKEY	16084/90	A	Arrest at and treatment following participation in 19th July 1989 demonstration in TRNC.	1, 3, 5–6, 7, 8–11, 13, 14 and Art 1, 1st Protocol	Partially; admissible as to Arts 3, 5–6, 7, 11, 13, 14–26 September 2002.	Court—no violations of any article: 24 February 2009.	No violation of Art 11 because of the wide margin of appreciation. The demonstration engaged in acts of violence and so the response was proportionate to the need to protect national security, public safety and preventing disorder.
RAI, ALLMOND AND NEGO-TIATE NOW!	UK	25522/94	A	Challenge to the general policy of refusing permission to hold rallies about Northern Ireland in Trafalgar Square unless they were 'entirely uncontroversial'.	9–11, 13, 14 and 18	No— 6 April 1995		Arts 10–11: the application was manifestly ill-founded. Despite the discretion to control assemblies in Trafalgar Square being broad and vague, the interference was prescribed by law. The policy was not disproportionate to the aim of preventing disorder or protecting the rights and freedoms of others, given the UK's margin of appreciation. No arguable claim therefore no violation of Art 13. The group was treated no differently from any other seeking to protest at the same location, so no difference in treatment and no violation of Art 14.
RASSEMBLE-MENT JURAS-SIEN ET UNITÉ JURASSIENNE	SWITZ-ERLAND	8191/78	A,C	Ban on all political meetings imposed by executive council of Canton Berne meant that the two pro-Jura separatist organisations could not demonstrate or meet.	10–11 and 14	No— 10 October 1979		In all the circumstances of tension and possible violence, this was not a disproportionate measure to prevent disorder and protect public safety, given the state's margin of appreciation.
S	AUSTRIA	13812/88	A	Prohibition of a demonstration protesting about 'repression in Austria'.	11 and 14	No— 3 December 1990		Given the history and the organisers' intention to create 'excessive noise', the ban was proportionate to preventing disorder and protecting the rights of others.

460 Appendix III

Applicant	State	App no	Type of protest	Facts and basis of claim	Article	Admissible?	Commission/Court finding	Reasoning on the issue of peaceful protest
SALDZUZ	TURKEY	36391/02	A, C	Convicted of aiding and abetting PKK after participating in an illegal demonstration in support of imprisoned leader and hanging an illegal placard on a bridge.	5, 6, 7 and 10–11	Partially; Arts 10–11 inadmissible— 28 March 2006.		The claim under Arts. 10–11 was manifestly ill-founded. S was not convicted for expressing an opinion or for membership of a party but for aiding and abetting an illegal organisation
SAYA	TURKEY	4327/02	B (A)	Violent dispersal of group en route to May Day celebrations without any prior warning; arrested but released without charge the following day	3, 5–6 and 11	Partially; Arts 5–6 manifestly ill-founded: 7 October 2008	Court—violation of Arts 3 and 11: 7th Oct 2008.	Violent dispersal where there was no danger to public order and where the body was not engaging in acts of violence was disproportionate to prevent disorder.
SCHIEFER	GERMANY	13389/89	D	Arrested after refusing order to leave a sit-in/road block demonstration outside US military barracks. Convicted for using unlawful coercion.	7 and 11	No—6 March 1989 Inadmissible		Conviction was not disproportionate to prevent disorder and crime: see CS v Germany above.
SELVA-NAYAGAM	UK	57981/00	D	An animal rights protester was subject to a restraining order preventing her from 'harassing' a mink farmer. She was also found guilty of the crime of harassment. As a matter of domestic law, breaching an ex parte interim anti-harassment injunction (as she had done) meant she was deprived of the chance to argue the statutory defence of 'reasonable conduct'.	6(1), 6(2), 6(3)(d) and 10–11	No— 12 December 2002		(a) The interference with Arts 10–11 by way of restraining order was necessary to protect the rights of others and/or prevention disorder or crime and (b) the interference with Arts 10–11 by way of conviction based on breach of ex parte injunction was also necessary; the applicant acted in full knowledge of it and had taken no steps to have it varied or discharged.
SOLOMOU	TURKEY	36832/97	D	Shot dead while trying to remove the Turkish flag from a pole in Cyprus.	1, 2, 3, 8, 10, 14	Yes— 18 May 1999	Violation of Art 2: 24 June 2008	No need for a separate assessment under Art 10

STANKOV AND UMO ILINDEN	BULGARIA	29221/95 & 29225/95	A	Prohibition of meetings over the period 1990–97, arranged by a group (denied authorisation on grounds of unconstitutionality) to commemorate events of historic importance to Macedonians living in Bulgaria.	11	Yes—29 June 1998	Court—violation of Art 11 (by 6 votes to 1): 2 October 2001.	The ban exceeded the state's margin of appreciation and was therefore disproportionate as a means to protect national security and territorial integrity, to protect the rights and freedoms of others, to guarantee public order or to prevent disorder and crime, either because the reasons were not supported by evidence or could not in the circumstances justify a blanket ban.
STEEL AND MORRIS	UK	68416/01	C	McDonalds brought defamation proceedings against the couple responsible for distributing the pamphlet 'What's Wrong with McDonalds?'. They argued that being denied legal aid and the excessive damages award constituted an interference with free speech.	6 and 10	Yes—22 October 2002	Court—violation of both Arts 6 and 10: 15 February 2005.	As to Art 10, the lack of procedural fairness and lack of legal aid contributed to disproportionate interference as did the size of the award relative to defendants' income and resources. Lack of legal aid also rendered the trial unfair because of the inequality of arms.
STEEL AND OTHERS	UK	24838/94	C (for the 3rd–5th applicants) D (for the 1st & 2nd applicants)	The first two applicants engaged in obstructive direct action (in relation to a grouse shoot and a motorway extension respectively) The 3rd to 5th applicants distributed leaflets and held up banners outside an arms conference. All were arrested and temporarily detained initially for a limited time to prevent a breach of the peace. The first two applicants were committed to prison for 28 days and 7days respectively after they refused to be bound over to keep the peace.	All five claimed a breach of Art 5(1)(c), Art 5(5) and Arts 10–11 for the initial arrest and detention. The 1st and 2nd applicants claimed	Yes—26 June 1996, save for a 6th applicant who had not exhausted local remedies	Commission—only violation was in respect of the 3rd–5th applicants' Art 10 claim: 9 April 1997. Court—violation of Art5(1)(c) only for arrest of 3rd–5th applicants; no violation of Art5(1)(b) for	'Breach of the peace': sufficiently clearly defined as to be both 'lawful' within Art 5 and 'prescribed by law' within Art 10. As to the 1st and 2nd applicants, good reason to fear a breach of the peace. The 3rd–5th applicants were entirely peaceful and in the absence of a domestic decision, the Court was not satisfied that the police did fear a breach. The binding over orders were sufficiently clear for Art 5(1)(b). All arrests and all detentions served legitimate aims but the initial detention of 3rd–5th

Applicant	State	App no	Type of protest	Facts and basis of claim	Article	Admissible?	Commission/ Court finding	Reasoning on the issue of peaceful protest
STEEL AND OTHERS (*cont.*)					separate breaches of Art 5(1)(b) and Art 6(3)when they were charged and then committed.		first two applicants when committed; no violation of Art 5(5) for any of the five; no violation of Art 6(3)(a) for the first two applicants; violation of Art 10 in respect of 3rd–5th applicants; no separate issue under Art 11: 23rd September 1998.	applicants was a disproportionate response to the need to prevent disorder and protect rights of others.
STEFANEC	CZECH REPUBLIC	75615/01	B	Fined as organiser of a banned march (to highlight the negative impact of road traffic on the environment and health) during which S announced that the march had been arbitrarily banned, as well as relaying the authority's messages to avoid violence.	6 and 10	Yes— 25 August 2005.	Court–violation of both: 18 July 2006.	As to Art 10, it was essentially because of the content of his remarks, not because he had "organised or managed" the march, that the applicant had been held to be its organiser and fined. In the Court's view, the way the administrative authorities had interpreted Czech law constituted an extension of its scope which it had been impossible, within reason, to foresee. As to Art 6, his appeal to the Constitutional Court was not sufficiently independent and review was not of sufficient scope.

A Summary of Strasbourg Case Law on the Right to Peaceful Protest   463

STRATI	TURKEY	16082/90	A	Arrest at and treatment following participation in 19 July 1989 demonstration in TRNC.	1, 3, 5–6, 7, 8–11, 13, 14 and Art 1 1st Protocol	Partially. Arts 3, 5–6, 7, 8, 11, 13, 14 and Art 1, 1st Protocol admissible—26 September 2002.	UNKNOWN
TV VEST	NORWAY	21132/05	C (E)	TV company fined by state media authority for transmitting party political broadcast by minority Pensioner's Party (1.3% vote nationally) in the days before local and regional elections.	10	Yes: 29 November 2007	Court—violation of Art 10: 29 November 2007.	There was no reasonable relationship of proportionality between the legitimate aim (the right of free elections on a level playing field) and the restriction. Here it was akin to a blanket ban yet one which in effect disadvantaged the very type of group it sought to protect; in reverse, the party was not conceivably the real target which were parties with relative financial strength who could take advantage. Paid TV advertising was the only way to get its message across.
UMO ILINDEN AND IVANOV	BULGARIA	44079/98	A	Prohibition of meetings, over the period 1998–2003, arranged by a group (denied authorisation on grounds of unconstitutionality) to commemorate events of historic importance to Macedonians living in Bulgaria.	11	Yes— 9 September 2004	Court— violation of Art 11: 20 October 2005	No material difference to situation declared unlawful in Stankov; the measure was therefore still unnecessary in order to protect national security, and territorial integrity, to protect the rights and freedoms of others, to guarantee public order or to prevent disorder and crime.

Applicant	State	App no	Type of protest	Facts and basis of claim	Article	Admissible?	Commission/ Court finding	Reasoning on the issue of peaceful protest
VAJNAI	HUNGARY	33629/06	C	Convicted of wearing a banned totalitarian symbol in public, the red star of the international workers' movement, at a public demonstration	10	Yes: 8 July 2008	Court—violation of Art 10: 8 July 2008.	(i) The application was not inadmissible on Art 17 grounds: the display was not intending to justify or propagate totalitarian oppression; it was merely the symbol of a lawful left-wing movement. (ii) The ban was too broad. The red star has multiple meanings, some of which could encompass activities protected by Art 10. There was no satisfactory way to sever its different meanings and indeed, Hungarian law did not attempt to do so. Even if such distinctions had existed, uncertainties might have arisen entailing a chilling effect on freedom of expression and self-censorship. The containment of a mere speculative danger, as a preventive measure for the protection of democracy, cannot be seen as a 'pressing social need'. Furthermore, Hungary has a number of offences which aim to suppress public disturbances if they were to be provoked by the use of the red star. The potential propagation of an offensive underlying ideology cannot be the sole reason to limit the display by way of a criminal sanction. Despite the fact that displaying a symbol which was ubiquitous

VEREIN GEGEN TIERFABRI- KEN (VGT)	SWITZER- LAND	24699/94	C	Prohibition on the association from transmitting a TV commercial with clear political character, about the meat industry.	10, 13 and 14	Yes— 6 April 2000	Violation of Art 10 but no violation of Arts 13 or 14: 28 June 2001.	Not a proportionate measure, in terms of protecting the rights of others, given the narrowness of the margin of appreciation which was relevant here as the effect of the refusal was to limit an individual's ability to participate in a debate on matters of public concern.
VRAHIMI	TURKEY	16078/90	A	Arrest at and treatment following participation in 19 July 1989 demon- stration in TRNC.	1, 3, 5–6, 7, 8–11, 13,14 and Art 1, 1st Protocol	Partially. Arts 3, 5–6, 7, 8, 11, 13, 14 and Art 1, 1st Protocol admissible— 26 September 2002.	UNKNOWN	
W G	AUSTRIA	15509/89	C	Anti-nuclear campaigner challenged his conviction for unlawfully using a public road without authorisation for an assembly and to impart information after setting up a table and distributing environmental protest leaflets.	10 and 11	No— 30 November 1992		Requirement of prior authorisation was justified, on facts and in circumstances, to ensure the security and free flow of traffic, ie to prevent disorder.
W M AND H O	GERMANY	13235/87	D	Arrested after refusing order to leave a sit-in/road block demonstration outside US military barracks. Convicted for using unlawful coercion.	7 and 11	No— 6 March 1989		Conviction was not disproportionate to prevent disorder and crime; see CS v Germany above.

during the systematic regime of terror under Communism might create unease and be seen as disrespectful, such sentiments cannot alone set the limits of freedom of expression (cf *Rekvenyi v Hungary* (2000) 30 EHRR 519).

Applicant	State	App no	Type of protest	Facts and basis of claim	Article	Admissible?	Commission/ Court finding	Reasoning on the issue of peaceful protest
ZILIBERBERG	MOLDOVA	61821/00	A	Arrested and convicted of being an active participant in an unauthorised demonstration (against abolition of urban transport privileges for students).	6(1), 11 and 13	Partially. Art 11 inadmissible; Art 6(1) admissible: 4 May 2004.		The claim under Art 11 was manifestly ill-founded. Art 11 allows states to require authorisations for such protests, so as to prevent disorder, and so must allow for the imposition of sanctions on those who do not comply. The sanction here was at the lower end of the penalty scale, equivalent to c €3.

Appendix IV

Human Rights Act 1998
Chapter 42

An Act to give further effect to rights and freedoms guaranteed under the European Convention on Human Rights; to make provision with respect to holders of certain judicial offices who become judges of the European Court of Human Rights; and for connected purposes.

[9th November 1998]

Be it enacted by the Queen's most Excellent Majesty, by and with the advice and consent of the Lords Spiritual and Temporal, and Commons, in this present Parliament assembled, and by the authority of the same, as follows:—

Introduction

1 The Convention Rights

(1) In this Act "the Convention rights" means the rights and fundamental freedoms set out in—

   (a) Articles 2 to 12 and 14 of the Convention,
   (b) Articles 1 to 3 of the First Protocol, and
   (c) Articles 1 and 2 of the Sixth Protocol,

   as read with Articles 16 to 18 of the Convention.

(2) Those Articles are to have effect for the purposes of this Act subject to any designated derogation or reservation (as to which see sections 14 and 15).

(3) The Articles are set out in Schedule 1.

(4) The Secretary of State may by order make such amendments to this Act as he considers appropriate to reflect the effect, in relation to the United Kingdom, of a protocol.

(5) In subsection (4) "protocol" means a protocol to the Convention—

   (a) which the United Kingdom has ratified; or
   (b) which the United Kingdom has signed with a view to ratification.

(6) No amendment may be made by an order under subsection (4) so as to come into force before the protocol concerned is in force in relation to the United Kingdom.

2 Interpretation of Convention rights

(1) A court or tribunal determining a question which has arisen in connection with a Convention right must take into account any—

   (a) judgment, decision, declaration or advisory opinion of the European Court of Human Rights,
   (b) opinion of the Commission given in a report adopted under Article 31 of the Convention,
   (c) decision of the Commission in connection with Article 26 or 27(2) of the Convention, or
   (d) decision of the Committee of Ministers taken under Article 46 of the Convention,

   whenever made or given, so far as, in the opinion of the court or tribunal, it is relevant to the proceedings in which that question has arisen.

(2) Evidence of any judgment, decision, declaration or opinion of which account may have to be taken under this section is to be given in proceedings before any court or tribunal in such manner as may be provided by rules.

...

Legislation

3 Interpretation of legislation

(1) So far as it is possible to do so, primary legislation and subordinate legislation must be read and given effect in a way which is compatible with the Convention rights.
(2) This section—

  (a) applies to primary legislation and subordinate legislation whenever enacted;
  (b) does not affect the validity, continuing operation or enforcement of any incompatible primary legislation; and
  (c) does not affect the validity, continuing operation or enforcement of any incompatible subordinate legislation if (disregarding any possibility of revocation) primary legislation prevents removal of the incompatibility.

4 Declaration of incompatibility

(1) Subsection (2) applies in any proceedings in which a court determines whether a provision of primary legislation is compatible with a Convention right.
(2) If the court is satisfied that the provision is incompatible with a Convention right, it may make a declaration of that incompatibility.
(3) Subsection (4) applies in any proceedings in which a court determines whether a provision of subordinate legislation, made in the exercise of a power conferred by primary legislation, is compatible with a Convention right.
(4) If the court is satisfied—

  (a) that the provision is incompatible with a Convention right, and
  (b) that (disregarding any possibility of revocation) the primary legislation concerned prevents removal of the incompatibility,

  it may make a declaration of that incompatibility.
(5) In this section "court" means—

  (a) the House of Lords;
  (b) the Judicial Committee of the Privy Council;
  (c) the Courts-Martial Appeal Court;
  (d) in Scotland, the High Court of Justiciary sitting otherwise than as a trial court or the Court of Session;
  (e) in England and Wales or Northern Ireland, the High Court or the Court of Appeal.

(6) A declaration under this section ("a declaration of incompatibility")—

  (a) does not affect the validity, continuing operation or enforcement of the provision in respect of which it is given; and
  (b) is not binding on the parties to the proceedings in which it is made.

5 Right of Crown to intervene

(1) Where a court is considering whether to make a declaration of incompatibility, the Crown is entitled to notice in accordance with rules of court.

...

Public authorities

6 Acts of public authorities

(1) It is unlawful for a public authority to act in a way which is incompatible with a Convention right.
(2) Subsection (1) does not apply to an act if—

  (a) as the result of one or more provisions of primary legislation, the authority could not have acted differently; or
  (b) in the case of one or more provisions of, or made under, primary legislation which cannot be read or given effect in a way which is compatible with the Convention rights, the authority was acting so as to give effect to or enforce those provisions.

(3) In this section "public authority" includes—

  (a) a court or tribunal, and
  (b) any person certain of whose functions are functions of a public nature,

  but does not include either House of Parliament or a person exercising functions in connection with proceedings in Parliament.
(4) In subsection (3) "Parliament" does not include the House of Lords in its judicial capacity.
(5) In relation to a particular act, a person is not a public authority by virtue only of subsection (3)(b) if the nature of the act is private.
(6) "An act" includes a failure to act but does not include a failure to—

  (a) introduce in, or lay before, Parliament a proposal for legislation; or
  (b) make any primary legislation or remedial order.

7 Proceedings

(1) A person who claims that a public authority has acted (or proposes to act) in a way which is made unlawful by section 6(1) may—

  (a) bring proceedings against the authority under this Act in the appropriate court or tribunal, or
  (b) rely on the Convention right or rights concerned in any legal proceedings,

  but only if he is (or would be) a victim of the unlawful act.
(2) In subsection (1)(a) "appropriate court or tribunal" means such court or tribunal as may be determined in accordance with rules; and proceedings against an authority include a counter-claim or similar proceeding.
(3) If the proceedings are brought on an application for judicial review, the applicant is to be taken to have a sufficient interest in relation to the unlawful act only if he is, or would be, a victim of that act.
(4) If the proceedings are made by way of a petition for judicial review in Scotland, the applicant shall be taken to have title and interest to sue in relation to the unlawful act only if he is, or would be, a victim of that act.
(5) Proceedings under subsection (1)(a) must be brought before the end of—

  (a) the period of one year beginning with the date on which the act complained of took place; or
  (b) such longer period as the court or tribunal considers equitable having regard to all the circumstances,

  but that is subject to any rule imposing a stricter time limit in relation to the procedure in question.
(6) In subsection (1)(b) "legal proceedings" includes—

  (a) proceedings brought by or at the instigation of a public authority; and
  (b) an appeal against the decision of a court or tribunal.

(7) For the purposes of this section, a person is a victim of an unlawful act only if he would be a victim for the purposes of Article 34 of the Convention if proceedings were brought in the European Court of Human Rights in respect of that act.
(8) Nothing in this Act creates a criminal offence.

...

8 Judicial remedies

(1) In relation to any act (or proposed act) of a public authority which the court finds is (or would be) unlawful, it may grant such relief or remedy, or make such order, within its powers as it considers just and appropriate.
(2) But damages may be awarded only by a court which has power to award damages, or to order the payment of compensation, in civil proceedings.
(3) No award of damages is to be made unless, taking account of all the circumstances of the case, including—

   (a) any other relief or remedy granted, or order made, in relation to the act in question (by that or any other court), and
   (b) the consequences of any decision (of that or any other court) in respect of that act,

   the court is satisfied that the award is necessary to afford just satisfaction to the person in whose favour it is made.
(4) In determining—

   (a) whether to award damages, or
   (b) the amount of an award,

   the court must take into account the principles applied by the European Court of Human Rights in relation to the award of compensation under Article 41 of the Convention.
(5) A public authority against which damages are awarded is to be treated—

   (a) in Scotland, for the purposes of section 3 of the Law Reform (Miscellaneous Provisions) (Scotland) Act 1940 as if the award were made in an action of damages in which the authority has been found liable in respect of loss or damage to the person to whom the award is made;
   (b) for the purposes of the Civil Liability (Contribution) Act 1978 as liable in respect of damage suffered by the person to whom the award is made.
(6) In this section—

   "court" includes a tribunal;
   "damages" means damages for an unlawful act of a public authority; and
   "unlawful" means unlawful under section 6(1).

9 Judicial acts

(1) Proceedings under section 7(1)(a) in respect of a judicial act may be brought only—

   (a) by exercising a right of appeal;
   (b) on an application (in Scotland a petition) for judicial review; or
   (c) in such other forum as may be prescribed by rules.
(2) That does not affect any rule of law which prevents a court from being the subject of judicial review.
(3) In proceedings under this Act in respect of a judicial act done in good faith, damages may not be awarded otherwise than to compensate a person to the extent required by Article 5(5) of the Convention.
(4) An award of damages permitted by subsection (3) is to be made against the Crown; but no award may be made unless the appropriate person, if not a party to the proceedings, is joined.

(5) In this section—

"appropriate person" means the Minister responsible for the court concerned, or a person or government department nominated by him;
"court" includes a tribunal;
"judge" includes a member of a tribunal, a justice of the peace and a clerk or other officer entitled to exercise the jurisdiction of a court;
"judicial act" means a judicial act of a court and includes an act done on the instructions, or on behalf, of a judge; and
"rules" has the same meaning as in section 7(9).

Remedial action

10 Power to take remedial action

(1) This section applies if—

   (a) a provision of legislation has been declared under section 4 to be incompatible with a Convention right and, if an appeal lies—

   (i) all persons who may appeal have stated in writing that they do not intend to do so;
   (ii) the time for bringing an appeal has expired and no appeal has been brought within that time; or
   (iii) an appeal brought within that time has been determined or abandoned; or

   (b) it appears to a Minister of the Crown or Her Majesty in Council that, having regard to a finding of the European Court of Human Rights made after the coming into force of this section in proceedings against the United Kingdom, a provision of legislation is incompatible with an obligation of the United Kingdom arising from the Convention.

(2) If a Minister of the Crown considers that there are compelling reasons for proceeding under this section, he may by order make such amendments to the legislation as he considers necessary to remove the incompatibility.

(3) If, in the case of subordinate legislation, a Minister of the Crown considers—

   (a) that it is necessary to amend the primary legislation under which the subordinate legislation in question was made, in order to enable the incompatibility to be removed, and
   (b) that there are compelling reasons for proceeding under this section,

   he may by order make such amendments to the primary legislation as he considers necessary.

(4) This section also applies where the provision in question is in subordinate legislation and has been quashed, or declared invalid, by reason of incompatibility with a Convention right and the Minister proposes to proceed under paragraph 2(b) of Schedule 2.

(5) If the legislation is an Order in Council, the power conferred by subsection (2) or (3) is exercisable by Her Majesty in Council.

(6) In this section "legislation" does not include a Measure of the Church Assembly or of the General Synod of the Church of England.

(7) Schedule 2 makes further provision about remedial orders.

Other rights and proceedings

11 Safeguard for existing human rights

A person's reliance on a Convention right does not restrict—

   (a) any other right or freedom conferred on him by or under any law having effect in any part of the United Kingdom; or

(b) his right to make any claim or bring any proceedings which he could make or bring apart from sections 7 to 9.

12 Freedom of expression

(1) This section applies if a court is considering whether to grant any relief which, if granted, might affect the exercise of the Convention right to freedom of expression.
(2) If the person against whom the application for relief is made ("the respondent") is neither present nor represented, no such relief is to be granted unless the court is satisfied—

(a) that the applicant has taken all practicable steps to notify the respondent; or
(b) that there are compelling reasons why the respondent should not be notified.

(3) No such relief is to be granted so as to restrain publication before trial unless the court is satisfied that the applicant is likely to establish that publication should not be allowed.
(4) The court must have particular regard to the importance of the Convention right to freedom of expression and, where the proceedings relate to material which the respondent claims, or which appears to the court, to be journalistic, literary or artistic material (or to conduct connected with such material), to—

(a) the extent to which—

(i) the material has, or is about to, become available to the public; or
(ii) it is, or would be, in the public interest for the material to be published;

(b) any relevant privacy code.

(5) In this section—
"court" includes a tribunal; and
"relief" includes any remedy or order (other than in criminal proceedings).

13 Freedom of thought, conscience and religion

(1) If a court's determination of any question arising under this Act might affect the exercise by a religious organisation (itself or its members collectively) of the Convention right to freedom of thought, conscience and religion, it must have particular regard to the importance of that right.
(2) In this section "court" includes a tribunal.

Derogations and reservations

14 Derogations

...

15 Reservations

...

16 Period for which designated derogations have effect

...

17 Periodic review of designated reservations

...

Judges of the European Court of Human Rights

18 Appointment to European Court of Human Rights

. . .

Parliamentary procedure

19 Statements of compatibility

(1) A Minister of the Crown in charge of a Bill in either House of Parliament must, before Second Reading of the Bill—

   (a) make a statement to the effect that in his view the provisions of the Bill are compatible with the Convention rights ("a statement of compatibility"); or
   (b) make a statement to the effect that although he is unable to make a statement of compatibility the government nevertheless wishes the House to proceed with the Bill.

(2) The statement must be in writing and be published in such manner as the Minister making it considers appropriate.

Supplemental

20 Orders etc. under this Act

. . .

21 Interpretation, etc

(1) In this Act—

"amend" includes repeal and apply (with or without modifications);
"the appropriate Minister" means the Minister of the Crown having charge of the appropriate authorised government department (within the meaning of the Crown Proceedings Act 1947);
"the Commission" means the European Commission of Human Rights;
"the Convention" means the Convention for the Protection of Human Rights and Fundamental Freedoms, agreed by the Council of Europe at Rome on 4th November 1950 as it has effect for the time being in relation to the United Kingdom;
"declaration of incompatibility" means a declaration under section 4;
"Minister of the Crown" has the same meaning as in the Ministers of the Crown Act 1975;
"Northern Ireland Minister" includes the First Minister and the deputy First Minister in Northern Ireland;
"primary legislation" means any—

   (a) public general Act;
   (b) local and personal Act;
   (c) private Act;
   (d) Measure of the Church Assembly;
   (e) Measure of the General Synod of the Church of England;
   (f) Order in Council—
      (i) made in exercise of Her Majesty's Royal Prerogative;
      (ii) made under section 38(1)(a) of the Northern Ireland Constitution Act 1973 or the corresponding provision of the Northern Ireland Act 1998; or
      (iii) amending an Act of a kind mentioned in paragraph (a), (b) or (c);

and includes an order or other instrument made under primary legislation (otherwise than by the National Assembly for Wales, a member of the Scottish Executive, a Northern Ireland Minister or a Northern Ireland department) to the extent to which it operates to bring one or more provisions of that legislation into force or amends any primary legislation;

"the First Protocol" means the protocol to the Convention agreed at Paris on 20th March 1952;

"the Sixth Protocol" means the protocol to the Convention agreed at Strasbourg on 28th April 1983;

"the Eleventh Protocol" means the protocol to the Convention (restructuring the control machinery established by the Convention) agreed at Strasbourg on 11th May 1994;

"remedial order" means an order under section 10;

"subordinate legislation" means any—

(a) Order in Council other than one—
   (i) made in exercise of Her Majesty's Royal Prerogative;
   (ii) made under section 38(1)(a) of the Northern Ireland Constitution Act 1973 or the corresponding provision of the Northern Ireland Act 1998; or amending an Act of a kind mentioned in the definition of primary legislation;
(b) Act of the Scottish Parliament;
(c) Act of the Parliament of Northern Ireland;
(d) Measure of the Assembly established under section 1 of the Northern Ireland Assembly Act 1973;
(e) Act of the Northern Ireland Assembly;
(f) order, rules, regulations, scheme, warrant, byelaw or other instrument made under primary legislation (except to the extent to which it operates to bring one or more provisions of that legislation into force or amends any primary legislation);
(g) order, rules, regulations, scheme, warrant, byelaw or other instrument made under legislation mentioned in paragraph (b), (c), (d) or (e) or made under an Order in Council applying only to Northern Ireland;
(h) order, rules, regulations, scheme, warrant, byelaw or other instrument made by a member of the Scottish Executive, a Northern Ireland Minister or a Northern Ireland department in exercise of prerogative or other executive functions of Her Majesty which are exercisable by such a person on behalf of Her Majesty;

"transferred matters" has the same meaning as in the Northern Ireland Act 1998; and

"tribunal" means any tribunal in which legal proceedings may be brought.

(2) The references in paragraphs (b) and (c) of section 2(1) to Articles are to Articles of the Convention as they had effect immediately before the coming into force of the Eleventh Protocol.

(3) The reference in paragraph (d) of section 2(1) to Article 46 includes a reference to Articles 32 and 54 of the Convention as they had effect immediately before the coming into force of the Eleventh Protocol.

(4) The references in section 2(1) to a report or decision of the Commission or a decision of the Committee of Ministers include references to a report or decision made as provided by paragraphs 3, 4 and 6 of Article 5 of the Eleventh Protocol (transitional provisions).

(5) Any liability under the Army Act 1955, the Air Force Act 1955 or the Naval Discipline Act 1957 to suffer death for an offence is replaced by a liability to imprisonment for life or any less punishment authorised by those Acts; and those Acts shall accordingly have effect with the necessary modifications.

22 Short title, commencement, application and extent

(1) This Act may be cited as the Human Rights Act 1998.
(2) Sections 18, 20 and 21(5) and this section come into force on the passing of this Act.

(3) The other provisions of this Act come into force on such day as the Secretary of State may by order appoint; and different days may be appointed for different purposes.

(4) Paragraph (b) of subsection (1) of section 7 applies to proceedings brought by or at the instigation of a public authority whenever the act in question took place; but otherwise that subsection does not apply to an act taking place before the coming into force of that section.

(5) This Act binds the Crown.

(6) This Act extends to Northern Ireland.

(7) Section 21(5), so far as it relates to any provision contained in the Army Act 1955, the Air Force Act 1955 or the Naval Discipline Act 1957, extends to any place to which that provision extends.

SCHEDULE 1

THE ARTICLES

...

SCHEDULE 2

REMEDIAL ORDERS

...

SCHEDULE 3

DEROGATION AND RESERVATION

...

BIBLIOGRAPHY

TRS Allen 'Parliamentary Sovereignty: Law Politics and Revolution' (1997) 113 *LQR* 443
Archbold Criminal Pleading Evidence and Practice (London, Sweet and Maxwell, 2006)
Dame Mary Arden 'Human rights in the age of terrorism' (2005) 121 *LQR* 604
A Ashworth 'Commentary on R (Singh) v Chief Constable of the West Midlands' [2007] *Crim LR* 243
A Ashworth 'Public order: police powers to control demonstration' [2007] *Crim LR* 576
S Bailey 'Wilfully obstructing the freedom to protest?' [1987] *PL* 495
S Bailey and N Taylor *Bailey Harris and Jones Civil Liberties cases, materials and commentary* 6th edn (London, Butterworths, 2009)
S Bailey, D Harris and S Jones *Civil Liberties cases and materials* 5th edn (London, Butterworths, 2001)
D Baker 'From Batons to Negotiated Management: The Transformation of Policing Industrial Disputes in Australia' (2007) 1 *Policing* 390
E Barendt 'Freedom of assembly' in J Beatson and Y Cripps (eds) *Freedom of Expression and Freedom of Information* (Oxford, OUP, 2000)
E Barendt *Freedom of Speech* 2nd edn (Oxford, OUP, 2007)
C Barnard and I Hare 'The right to protest and the right to export: police discretion and free movement of goods' (1997) 60 *MLR* 394
S Barnes and M Kaase (eds) *Political Action: Mass Participation in Five Western Democracies* (Beverley Hills CA, Sage, 1979)
DG Barnum 'Freedom of Assembly and the Hostile Audience in Anglo-American Law' 29 *Am J Comp Law* 59 (1981)
H Becker *Outsiders* (New York, Free Press, 1963)
D Beetham 'Political Participation Mass Protest and Representative Democracy' (2003) 56 *Parl Aff* 597
V Bettinson 'Section 4A Public Order Act 1986: accommodating freedom of expression, Dehal v Crown Prosecution Service [2005] EWHC 2154' [2006] 5 *Web JCLI*
W Birtles 'The Common Law Power of the Police to Control Public Meetings' (1973) 36 *MLR* 587
E Bittner 'Florence Nightingale in search of Willie Sutton: a theory of the police' in H Jacob (ed) *The potential for reform of criminal justice* (Beverley Hills CA, Sage, 1974)
D Bonner and R Stone 'The Public Order Act 1986: steps in the wrong direction?' [1987] *PL* 202
J Brewer et al *The Police, Public Order and the State* 2nd edn (London, Macmillan, 1996)
D Brown and T Ellis *Policing low-level disorder: police use of section 5 of the Public Order Act 1986* (HORS 135, 1994)
T Bucke and Z James *Trespass and Protest: Policing under the Criminal Justice and Public Order Act 1994* HORS 190 (London, Home Office, 1998)
M Button 'Private security and the policing of quasi-public space' (2003) 31 *Int J Soc of Law* 227
M Button, T John and N Brearley 'New challenges in public order policing: the professionalisation of environmental protest and the emergence of the militant environmental activist' (2002) 30 *Int J Soc Law* 17
K Cahill *Who Owns Britain* (Edinburgh, Canongate Press, 2001)
R Card *Public Order Law* (Bristol, Jordans, 2000)
H Carty 'The economic torts in the 21st century' (2008) 124 *LQR* 641
C Clarkson 'Necessary action—a new defence' [2004] *Crim LR* 81
G Clayton 'Reclaiming public ground: the right to peaceful assembly' (2000) 63 *MLR* 252
R Clayton and H Tomlinson *The Law of Human Rights* 2nd edn (Oxford, OUP, 2009)

S Cohen *Folk Devils and Moral Panics* (St Albans, Paladin, 1973)
J Collins 'The Theft Act and it commentators' [1968] *Crim LR* 638
K Connolly 'Case comment—Redmond-Bate v DPP' [1999] *J Civ Lib* 382
Lord Cooke 'Shoreham-by-sea' in J Beatson and Y Cripps *Freedom of Expression and Freedom of Information: Essays in Honour of Sir David Willliams* (Oxford, OUP, 2000)
P Craig *Administrative Law* 7th edn (London, Sweet and Maxwell 2008)
A Crawford and S Lister *The Use and Impact of Dispersal Orders: Sticking Plasters and Wake-Up Calls* (Bristol, Policy Press, 2007)
C Critcher and D Waddington (eds) *Policing public order: theoretical and practical issues* (Aldershot, Ashgate, 1996)
C Critcher *Critical readings: Moral Panics in the Media* (Berkshire, Open University Press, 2006)
T Crocker 'Displacing Dissent: The Role of 'Place' in First Amendment Jurisprudence' 75 *Fordham Law Review* 2587 (2007)
T Daintith 'Disobeying a policeman—a fresh look at Duncan v Jones' [1966] *PL* 248
W de Lint 'Public order policing—a tough act to follow?' (2005) 33 *Int J Soc Law* 179
D della Porta & H Reiter (eds) *Policing Protest: The Control of Mass Demonstrations in Western Democracies* (Minneapolis, University of Minnesota Press, 1998)
D della Porta & M Diani *Social Movements* (Oxford, Blackwell, 1999)
D della Porta *The Policing of Protest in Contemporary Democracies* (San Domenico Italy, European University Institute, Robert Schuman Centre, 1997)
D della Porta, M Andretta, L Mosea and H Reiter *Globalization from below: transnational activists and protest networks* (Minneapolis, University of Minnesota Press, 2006)
AV Dicey *An Introduction to the Study of the Law of the Constitution* 10th edn (London, MacMillan, 1959)
B Doherty, A Plows and D Wall ' "The preferred way of doing things": the British direct action movement' (2003) 56 *Parl Aff* 669
D Donnelly 'Anti-roads protests, the community and the police' (1996) *Police Journal* 207
F Donson *The Road to Conflict—Case Studies in the Effectiveness of Public Law as a Mechanism of Participation in Environmentally-Sensitive Decision Making* (Unpublished PhD thesis Kings' College London, 1997)
J Driscoll 'Protest and Public Order: The Public Order Act' [1987] *J Soc Wel L* 280
R Dworkin *Taking Rights Seriously* (Cambridge Mass, Harvard UP, 1977)
T A El-Haj 'The neglected right of assembly' 56 *UCLA Law Rev* 543 (2009)
A Etzioni *Demonstration Democracy* (New York, Gordon and Breach, 1977)
K Ewing and C Gearty *The Struggle for Civil Liberties: Political Freedom and the Rule of Law in Britain 1914–1945* (Oxford, OUP, 2000)
M Falcón y Tella 'Civil disobedience and test cases' (2004) 17 *Ratio Juris* 315
D Feldman 'The King's Peace, the Royal Prerogative and Public Order: the roots and early history of binding over powers' (1988) 47 *CLJ* 101
D Feldman 'Containment, deprivation of liberty and breach of the peace' (2009) 68 *CLJ* 243
D Feldman 'Property and Public Protest' in F Meisel and P Cook (eds) *Property and Protection* (Oxford, Hart Publishing, 2000)
D Feldman 'Protest and tolerance: legal values and the control of public-order policing' in R Cohen-Almagor (ed) *Liberal democracy and the limits of tolerance—essays in honor and memory of Yitzhak Rabin* (Mich, University of Michigan Press Ann Arbor, 2000)
D Feldman *Civil Liberties and Human Rights in England and Wales* 2nd edn (Oxford, OUP, 2002)
H Fenwick and G Phillipson 'Direct Action, Convention Values and the Human Rights Act' (2001) 21 *LS* 535
H Fenwick and G Phillipson *Media Freedom and the Human Rights Act* (Oxford, OUP, 2006)
H Fenwick *Civil liberties and human rights* 4th edn (Abingdon, Routledge-Cavendish, 2007)
E Finch 'Legitimate protest or campaign of harassment—protestors, harassment and reasonableness' [1999] *Web JCLI* 5

B Fitzpatrick and N Taylor 'A Case of Highway Robbery' (1997) 147 *NLJ* 338
P Gadd 'Being heard at the AGM' (1996) 1 *Comm Law* 6
D Galligan 'Preserving public protest: the legal approach' in L Gostin (ed) *Civil Liberties in Conflict* (London, Routledge, 1998)
S Gardner 'Direct action and necessity' [2005] *Crim LR* 371
J Garman 'Today's protesters, tomorrow's saviours' *The Guardian* 'Comment is Free' 8th December 2008
G Gaskell and R Benewick *The Crowd in Contemporary Britain* (London, Sage, 1987)
C Gearty and K Ewing *Freedom Under Thatcher Civil Liberties in Modern Britain* (Oxford, OUP, 1990)
R Geary *Policing industrial disputes 1893–1985* (Cambridge, CUP, 1985)
A Geddis 'Brooker v Police' (2008) 8 *OUCLJ* 117
A Geddis 'Free speech martyrs or unreasonable threats to social peace?—'insulting' expression and section 5 of the Public Order Act 1986' [2004] *PL* 853
A Geddis 'You Can't Say 'God' on the Radio: Freedom of Expression, Religious Advertising and the Broadcast Media After Murphy v Ireland' [2004] *EHRLR* 181
AL Goodhart '*Thomas v Sawkins*: A Constitutional Innovation' (1936) 6 *CLJ* 22
W Grant 'Pressure politics: the changing world of pressure groups' (2004) 57 *Parl Aff* 408
K Gray 'Equitable Property' (1994) 47(2) *Current Legal Problems* 157
K Gray and S Gray 'Civil Rights, Civil Wrongs and Quasi-Public Space' [1999] *EHRLR* 46
K Greenwalt 'Free speech justifications' 89 *Col LR* 119 (1989)
S Greer *The margin of appreciation: interpretation and discretion under the European convention on Human Rights* (Strasbourg, Human Rights files No 17, Council of Europe Publishing, 2000)
T Hadden 'The draft Theft Bill' [1967] *Crim LR* 669
S Hall et al *Policing the Crisis: Mugging, the State and Law and Order* (London, MacMillan, 1978)
M Hamilton 'Freedom of assembly, consequential harms and the rule of law: liberty-limiting principles in the context of transition' (2007) 27 *OJLS* 75
I Harden *The Contracting State* (Buckingham, Open University Press, 1992)
I Hare and C Barnard 'Police discretion and the rule of law: Economic Community rights versus civil rights' (2000) 63 *MLR* 681
I Hare and C Barnard 'The right to protest and the right to export: police discretion and the free movement of goods' (1997) 60 *MLR* 394
D Harris, M O'Boyle, E Bates and C Buckley *The Law of the European Convention on Human Rights* 2nd edn (Oxford, OUP, 2009)
J Harris *Property and Justice* (Oxford, OUP, 1996)
M Hornsey et al 'Why Do People Engage in Collective Action? Revisiting the Role of Perceived Effectiveness' (2006) 36 *J App Soc Psych* 1701
M Humphreys 'Free Movement and roadblocks: the right to protest in the Single Market' (2004) 6 *Env L Rev* 190
M Hutchinson 'The margin of appreciation doctrine in the European Court of Human Rights' (1999) *ICLQ* 638
Lord Irvine 'The Human Rights Act Two Years On: An Analysis' [2003] *PL* 308
G Jordan and W Moloney 'Protest businesses and democratic activity' in G Jordan & W Moloney *The Protest Business—Mobilizing Campaign Groups* (Manchester University Press Manchester, 1997)
S Joseph, J Schultz, and M Castan *The International Covenant on Civil and Political Rights Cases, Materials, and Commentary* 2nd edn (Oxford, OUP, 2003)
J Jowell 'Judicial Deference: servility, civility or institutional capacity?' [2003] *PL* 592
JUSTICE *Legislating for Human Rights—the parliamentary debates on the Human Rights Bill* (Oxford, Hart Publishing, 2000)
J Keane *The Life and Death of Democracy* (London, Simon and Schuster, 2009)
K Kerrigan 'Case comment—Steel v UK' (1999) 4 *J Civ Lib* 129
K Kerrigan 'Breach of the Peace and Binding Over—Continuing Confusion' (1997) 2 *J Civ Lib* 30

K Kerrigan 'Case comment—DPP v Moseley' (1999) 4 *J Civ Lib* 390
K Kerrigan 'Case comment—Huntingdon Life Sciences v Curtin' (1998) 3 *J Civ Lib* 37
M King and N Brearley *Public Order Policing—contemporary perspectives on strategies and tactics* (Basingstoke, Palgrave MacMillan, 1995)
J Klear 'Comparison of the Federal Courts' and the New Jersey Supreme Court's treatments of free speech on private property: where won't we have the freedom to speak next?' 33 *Rutgers Law Journal* 589 (2002)
C Knight 'Monkeying around with free speech' (2008) 124 *LQR* 557
H Kriesi et al *New Social Movements in Western Europe: A Comparative Analysis* (Minnesota, University of Minnesota Press, 1995)
H Kriesi, D Della Porta & D Rucht (eds) *Social Movements in a Globalizing World* (London, Macmillan, 1998)
J Landau 'Functional Public Authorities after *YL*' [2007] *PL* 630
Sir John Laws 'Is the High Court the guardian of fundamental constitutional rights?' [1993] *PL* 59
G LeBon *The crowd—a study of the popular mind* (New Brunswick NJ, Viking Press, 1895)
I Leigh and L Lustgarten *In from the cold: national security and parliamentary democracy* (Oxford, OUP, 1994)
Lord Lester 'The art of the possible—interpreting statutes under the Human Rights Act' [1998] *EHRLR* 665
Liberty *Anti-social behaviour orders and human rights* (2004)
Liberty *Casualty of War: Eight Weeks of Counter-Terrorism in Rural England* (July 2003)
Liberty *Criminalising Diversity Criminalising Dissent: a Report on the Use of the Public Order Provisions of the Criminal Justice and Public Order Act 1994* (1995)
Liberty 'Response to the JCHR *Demonstrating Respect for Rights? A Human Rights Approach to Policing Protest*' (May 2009)
Liberty *Liberty* magazine Summer 2008
Liberty 'Supplementary evidence to the JCHR inquiry into policing and protest: private property' (June 2008)
Liberty 'Evidence to JCHR inquiry into policing and protest' (June 2008)
I Loveland 'Public Protest in Parliament Square' [2007] *EHRLR* 252
S Lukes *Power—a radical view* (London, MacMillan, 1974)
D MacAusland 'Policing parades and protest in Northern Ireland' [2007] *EHRLR* 211
N MacEwan 'The Computer Misuse Act 1990: lessons from its past and predictions for its future' [2008] *Crim LR* 955
A Marsh 'Explorations in Unorthodox Political Behaviour: A Scale to Measure Protest Potential' (1974) 2 *European Journal of Political Research* 107
A Marsh *Protest and Political Consciousness* (Beverley Hills CA, Sage, 1977)
G Marshall 'Two kinds of compatibility: more about section 3 of the Human Rights Act 1998' [1999] *PL* 377
J Marston and P Tain *Public Order: The Criminal Law* (London, Callow Publishing, 2001)
R Masterman 'Section 2(1) of the Human Rights Act 1998: Binding Domestic Courts to Strasbourg?' [2004] *PL* 725
R Mathews et al (eds) *Assessing the Use of ASBOs* (Bristol, Policy Press, 2007)
D McBarnet 'The Police and the State' in G Littlejohn et al *Power and the State* (London, Croom-Helm, 1978)
D McBarnet *Conviction* (London, MacMillan, 1981)
S McCabe and P Wallington (eds) *The police, public order, and civil liberties: legacies of the miners' strike* (London, Routledge, 1988)
C McPhail et al 'Policing Protest in the United States: 1960–1995' in D della Porta & H Reiter (eds) *Policing Protest: The Control of Mass Demonstrations in Western Democracies* (Minneapolis, University of Minnesota Press, 1998)

C McPhail *The Myth of the Madding Crowd* (New York, Aldine de Gruyter, 1991)

D Mead 'Informed consent to police searches in England and Wales—a critical (re-) appraisal in the light of the Human Rights Act?' [2002] *Crim LR* 791

D Mead 'It's a funny old game—privacy, football and the public interest' [2006] *EHRLR* 541

D Mead 'Judicial mis-behavin' : a defence of process-based review of public authority decisions under the Human Rights Act' Norwich Law School Working Papers 08/02

D Mead 'Of kettles, cordons and crowd control—Austin v Commissioner of Police for the Metropolis and the meaning of deprivation of liberty' [2009] *EHRLR* 376

D Mead 'Rights, relationships and retrospectivity: the impact of Convention rights on pre-existing private law relationships following *Wilson* and *Ghaidan*' [2005] *PL* 459

D Mead 'Strasbourg discovers the right to counter-demonstrate: a case-note on Öllinger v Austria' [2007] *EHRLR* 133

D Mead 'Strasbourg succumbs to the temptation 'To Make a God of the Right of Property': peaceful protest on private land and the ramifications of Appleby v UK' [2004] *J Civ Lib* 98

D Mead 'The Human Rights Act—A Panacea for Peaceful Protest' part I (1998) 3 *J Civ Lib* 206 and part II (1999) 4 *J Civ Lib* 7

D Mead 'The likely effect of the Human Rights Act on everyday policing decisions in England and Wales' (2000) 5 *J Civ Lib* 5

D Mead 'The right to peaceful protest under the European Convention on Human Rights—a content study of Strasbourg case law' [2007] *EHRLR* 345

D Mead 'Will peaceful protesters be foxed by the Divisional Court decision in Capon v DPP?' [1998] *Crim LR* 870

A Meiklejohn 'The First Amendment is an absolute' *Sup Ct Rev* 245 (1961)

K Milne *Manufacturing Dissent: Single-Issue Protest, the Public and the Press* (London, Demos Publishing, 2005)

D Moeckli 'Stop and Search under the Terrorism Act 2000: A Comment on R (Gillan) v Commissioner of Police for the Metropolis' (2007) 70 *MLR* 659

G Monbiot 'Attack of the baby eaters' *The Guardian* 18th August 2007

G Monbiot 'Otter-spotting and birdwatching; the dark heart of the eco-terrorist peril' *The Guardian* 'Comment Is Free' 23rd December 2008

N Moreham 'Privacy in public places' (2006) 65 *CLJ* 606

G Morse et al *Palmer's Company Law Annotated guide to the Companies Act 2006* (London, Sweet and Maxwell 2007)

A Mowbray *The Development of Positive Obligations under the European Convention on Human Rights by the European Court of Human Rights* (Oxford, Hart Publishing, 2004)

J Murdoch 'Safeguarding the liberty of the person: recent Strasbourg jurisprudence' (1993) 42 *ICLQ* 494

J Murdoch *Article 5 of the European Convention on Human Rights—The Protection of Liberty and Security of the Person* Human Rights Files No 12 (revised) (Strasbourg, Council of Europe Publishing, 2002)

T Murphy 'Freedom of assembly' in D Harris and S Joseph *The International Covenant on Civil and Political Rights and UK Law* (Oxford, Clarendon, 1995)

S Neff 'Idealism in action: International Law and nuclear weapons in Greenock Sherriff Court' (2002) 4 *Edin LR* 74

E O'Dell 'Case note—Steel and Morris v UK' (2005) 121 *LQR* 395

D Ormerod 'Commentary on DPP v Tilly' [2002] *Crim LR* 128

D Ormerod and D Tausz 'Commentary on DPP v Avery' [2002] *Crim LR* 142

C Ovey and R White *Jacobs and White: The European Convention on Human Rights* 4th edn (Oxford, OUP, 2006)

S Palmer 'Public private and the Human Rights Act 1998—an ideological divide' (2007) 66 *CLJ* 559

D Pannick 'Principles of interpretation of Convention rights under the Human Rights Act and the discretionary area of judgment' [1999] *PL* 545

J Penner *The Idea of Property in Law* (Oxford, Clarendon Press, 1997)

G Phillipson 'Judicial reasoning in breach of confidence cases under the Human Rights Act: not taking privacy seriously?' [2003] *EHRLR Supp* (special issue privacy) 54

G Phillipson and H Fenwick 'Public protest, the Human Rights Act and judicial responses to political expression' [2000] *PL* 627

J Rawls *Political Liberalism* (New York, Columbia UP, 1993)

S Reicher et al 'Knowledge-based public order policing: principles and practice' (2007) 1 *Policing* 403

K Reid and D Nicolson 'Arrest for Breach of the Peace and the European Convention on Human Rights' [1996] *Crim LR* 764

R Reiner 'Policing the police' in M Maguire R Morgan and R Reiner *The Oxford Handbook of Criminology* 2nd edn (Oxford, OUP 1997) 4th edn (Oxford, OUP, 2007)

F Ridley and G Jordan *Protest politics: causes groups and campaigns* (Oxford, OUP, 1998)

J Roach and J Thomaneck (eds) *Police and Public Order in Europe* (Beckenham, Croom Helm, 1985)

N Robinson 'Fuel protests: governing the ungovernable' (2003) 56 *Parl Aff* 423

J Rowbottom 'Property and Participation: A Right of Access for Expressive Activities' [2005] *EHRLR* 186

G Rudé *The Crowd in History: A Study of Popular Disturbances in France and England, 1730–1848* (London, Wiley, 1964)

D Sanders, H Clarke, M Stewart and P Whiteley 'The dynamics of protest in Britain 2000–2002' (2003) 56 *Parl Aff* 687

M Sanderson 'Free speech in public places: the privatisation of human rights in *Appleby v UK*' (2004) 15 *KCLJ* 159

F Schauer *Free speech: a philosophical enquiry* (Cambridge, CUP, 1982)

SchNEWS issue 637 (27th June 2008)

SchNEWS issue 684 'Call off the hounds' (17th July 2009)

B Seel and A Plows 'Coming Live and Direct—strategies of Earth First!' in B Seel (ed) *Direct Action in British Environmentalism* (Abingdon, Routledge, 2000)

J Seymour 'Injunctions enjoining non-parties: distinction without a difference?' (2007) 66 *CLJ* 605

J Seymour 'Who can be harassed? Claims against animal rights protestors under section 3 of the Protection from Harassment Act 1997' (2005) 64 *CLJ* 57

A Sherr *Freedom of Protest, Public Order and the Law* (Oxford, Blackwell, 1989)

ATH Smith 'Public order law 1974–1983: development and proposals' [1984] *Crim LR* 643

ATH Smith 'The Public Order Act 1986 Part 1: the new offences' [1987] *Crim LR* 156

ATH Smith 'The Criminal Justice and Public Order Act 1994—the public order elements' [1995] *Crim LR* 19

ATH Smith 'Protecting protest—a constitutional shift' (2007) 66 *CLJ* 253

ATH Smith *Offences against public order* (London, Sweet and Maxwell,1987)

JC Smith 'Burglary under the Theft Bill' [1968] *Crim LR* 295

JC Smith 'Commentary on R v Morpeth Ward Justices ex p Ward' [1992] *Crim LR* 497

S Sottiaux 'Anti-democratic associations: content and consequences in Article 11 adjudication' (2004) 22 *NQHR* 585

J Spencer 'Commentary on Percy v DPP' [1995] *Crim LR* 714

J Spencer 'Commentary on Todd v DPP' [1996] *Crim LR* 344

P Squires (ed) *Asbo Nation* (Policy Press Bristol, 2008)

R Stone 'Breach of the Peace: the case for abolition' [2001] 2 *Web JCLI*

R Stone *Textbook on Civil Liberties* 7th edn (Oxford, OUP, 2008)

C Sunstein 'Social and Economic Rights? Lessons from South Africa' John M Olin Law & Economics Working paper No 124 (2D series) The Law School, University of Chicago, May 2001

M Supperstone and J Coppel 'Judicial review after the Human Rights Act' [1999] *EHRLR* 301

M Supperstone *Brownlie's Law of public order and national security* 2nd edn (London, Butterworths, 1981)

A Sydenham *Public Rights of Way and Access to Land* 3rd edn (Bristol, Jordans 2007)

N Taylor and B Fitzpatrick 'Freedom of assembly' (1999) 4 *J Civ Lib* 253

N Taylor and B Fitzpatrick 'Trespassers might be prosecuted: the European Convention and restrictions on the right to assemble' [1999] *EHRLR* 292

C Townshend *Making the peace: public order and public security in modern Britain* (OUP Oxford 1993)

R Turner and L Killian *Collective Behavior* (Englewood Cliffs N J, Prentice-Hall, 1957, 4th edn 1993)

P Van Dijk, F von Hoof, A van Rijn and L Zwaak (eds) *The Theory and Practice of the European Convention on Human Rights* 4th edn (Antwerp, Intersentia, 2006)

D Vick and K Campbell 'Public protests, private lawsuits and the market: the investor response to the McLibel trial' (2001) 28 *J Law Soc* 204

A von Hirsch and C Shearing 'Exclusion from public spaces' in A von Hirsch, D Garland & A Wakefield *Ethical and social perspectives on situational crime prevention* (Oxford, Hart Publishing, 2000)

D Waddington 'Seattle and its aftershock: some implications for theory and practice' (2007) 1 *Policing* 380

D Waddington *Contemporary issues in public disorder: a comparative and historical approach* (London, Routledge, 1992)

D Waddington, K Jones and C Critcher *Flashpoints—studies in public disorder* (London, Routledge, 1989)

PAJ Waddington (editorial) 'Policing of public order' (2007) 1 *Policing* 375

PAJ Waddington 'Both arms of the law: institutionalised protest and the policing of public order' British Society of Criminology conference 1995

PAJ Waddington 'Dying in a ditch: the use of police powers in public order' (1993) 21 *Int J Soc Law* 335

PAJ Waddington 'Policing public order and political contention' in T Newburn (ed) *Handbook of Policing* (Cullumpton, Willan, 2003)

PAJ Waddington *Liberty and order: public order policing in a capital city* (London, UCL press, 1994)

PAJ Waddington *The strong arm of the law: armed and public order policing* (Oxford, OUP, 1991)

W Wade and C Forsyth *Administrative Law* 10th edn (Oxford, OUP, 2009)

C Walker 'Commentary on R (Gillan) v Commissioner of Police for the Metropolis' [2006] *Crim LR* 751

C Walker *Blackstone's Guide to the Anti-Terrorism Legislation* 2nd edn (Oxford, OUP, 2009)

C Walker 'Commentary on R v Margaret Jones' [2007] *Crim LR* 66

P Wallington 'Injunctions and the right to demonstrate' (1976) 35 *CLJ* 82

P Wallington 'Policing the miners' strike' (1985) 14 *ILJ* 145

W Waluchow (ed) *Free expression: essays in law and philosophy* (Oxford, Clarendon 1994)

P Whiteley 'The state of participation in Britain' (2003) 56 *Parl Aff* 610

A Williams 'YL v Birmingham City Council: contracting out and "functions of a public nature"' [2007] *EHRLR* 524

DGT Williams 'Processions, assemblies and the freedom of the individual' [1987] *Crim LR* 167

DGT Williams *Keeping the peace: the police and public order* (London, Hutchinson, 1967)

DGT Williams 'The principle of Beatty v Gillbanks—a reappraisal' in A Doob and E Greenspan (eds) *Perspectives in Criminal Law: Essays in Honour of John L. J. Edwards* (Aurora, Ont Canada Law Book, 1985)

G Williams 'Dealing with Breaches of the Peace' (1982) 146 *JPN* 199 and 217

Lord Woolf 'Human Rights: Have the Public Benefitted?' British Academy Lecture October 2002

Lord Woolf 'Droit Public –English style' [1995] *PL* 57

R Youngs 'G8 protests: controlling the right to demonstrate' (2008) 14 *EPL* 69

H Yourow *The Margin of Appreciation Doctrine in the Dynamics of European Human Rights Jurisprudence* (The Hague/Boston/London, Kluwer, 1996)

INDEX

abortion protests:
  aggravated trespass, 255
  classification of offences, 137
  excessive powers against, 402
  forms of protest, 63
  harassment outside homes, 15
  intimidation, 238
  malicious communications, 224, 296–8
  offensive language, 221–2
  professional protesters, 20
  Strasbourg jurisprudence, 71–2, 73, 128
  watching and besetting, 292
abuse *see* language
access to land:
  equality, 120
  issues, 118–21
  place-specific restrictions on protest
    highway obstruction, 138–41
    national security sites, 141–5
    overview, 138–61
    Trafalgar Square *see* Trafalgar Square
    Westminster *see* Westminster
  police powers, 162–7
    CJPOA 1994 (s61), 162–3
    criminalisation of trespass, 162–5
    Fuller case, 165–7
    travellers, 162–3
  private land
    absolute title, 129–30
    Appleby v UK, 74–5, 129, 132–6, 163, 200, 201, 408
    categories of ownership, 130–1
    overview, 129–38
    quasi-public land, 131–2, 133, 420
    rights of way, 136–8
    shopping centres, 64, 74, 129, 132–6
  protesters' rights, 5, 121–38
    private land, 129–38
    public land, 122–9
    public v private land, 22, 24, 121–2, 162
  public land
    bans from council land, 127–8
    failing to provide venue, 128–9
    general historic position, 122–6
    HRA 1998 impact, 126–9
    illegal refusal, 124–6
    irrational refusal, 123–4
    non-discrimination, 127–8
    overview, 122–9
  title, see land ownership
  trespass *see* trespass
ACPO, 21, 317, 379, 411, 424
actual bodily harm, 246

advertising, 233–4
Aegis Defence Services, 24
affray, 242, 243, 245, 323
agenda for change:
  certainty, 419
  definition of peaceful protest, 417–18
  human rights, 424–5
  overview, 412–25
  Protest Act, call for, 415–16
  protest-impact statements, 416
  public and private regulation, 419–21
  public debate, 414–15
  role of police, 421–5
  sensitivity to diversity of protest, 419
  statutory guarantee of right to peaceful protest, 416–17
  underpinning principles, 415–19
aggression, 249–50, 412n72
Agha-Soltan, Neda, 399
aiding and abetting, 246, 277
airbases, 141, 142, 143, 146, 249, 332, 407
Al-Fayed, Mohammed, 420
alarm, language causing, 218–19
Aldermaston, 143
Aldermaston Women's Peace Camp, 51
angling competitions, 89–90, 223, 330–2
animal research organisations, intimidating those connected with, 304–6
animal rights protests:
  aggravated trespass, 255
  anti-fur protesters, 420
  arson attacks, 247n54
  ASBOs, 363
  broadcasting rights, 234
  confidentiality orders and, 299
  damage to property, 247
  economic torts, 381
  enforcement of legislation and, 15
  extreme groups, 14
  harassment, 282, 404
  impact of direct action, 299–306
  interfering with contractual relationships, 23, 300–4, 405
  intimidating those connected with animal research, 304–6
  intimidation, 238
  malicious communications, 294n257, 294n259
  new legislation and, 16–17, 310
  port authorities and, 312
  professional protesters, 20
  s42A CJPA 2001 directions and, 289
  watching and besetting, 291

anti-Muslim protests, 227–9
anti-social behaviour orders see ASBOs
anti-social manner, 423
Arden, Mary Dame, 318
Armenia, protest cases in Strasbourg, 60, 66, 69, 105, 108, 111
arms trade, 15, 20, 63, 75, 105, 110–11, 225, 231–2, 270–1, 316, 357, 376
arrest powers, breach of the peace:
    Beatty v Gillbanks, 328–9
    Duncan v Jones, 327–8
    heckler's veto, 327–8
    Nicol v DPP, 330–2, 357
    Percy v DPP, 332, 411
    preventive powers, 325–34
    Redmond-Bate v DPP, 332–4, 346, 403
    scope of power, 326–7
    Ward, 328–9
arsenals, 141
arson, 247n54
ASBOs:
    "ASBO-mania", 362
    assessment, 362–3
    breach, criminal penalties, 363
    hearsay evidence, 363, 364
    hybrid procedure, 364
    mens rea and, 362
    objectives, 363
    peaceful protest and, 363–4
    presumption of innocence and, 363
    preventive action, 362–4
    standard of proof, 121n11, 363
    statutory scheme, 362
    time limit, 362
    width of prohibitions, 362
Ashworth, Andrew, 347, 372
assault and battery, 245–6, 323
assemblies see public assemblies
attempts, criminal, 246, 248, 249
Austria:
    abortion protests, 71–2, 97–8, 113, 128
    All Saints' Day, 67
    Brenner Pass blocking, 235
    competing rights, 73
    counter-demonstrations (Öllinger), 104, 114, 128, 231
    effect of protest on third parties, 110–15, 231
    energy policy, 81
    freedom of thought and religion, 89
    margin of appreciation, 96
    meaning of assembly, 65–6
    military policy, 110
    noise of protests, 75–6, 407
    nuclear protests, 81, 238
    positive obligations, 97–8, 128
    proportionality of restrictions, 104
    protest cases in Strasbourg, 60
    traffic obstruction, 90, 106, 407
    use of roads, 81n114, 238
Azerbaijan, 60

BAA, 247, 282, 388
Bailey, Stephen, 259, 326
Barclays, 387
Batt, Jonathan, 183n82
Bedau, Hugo Adam, 58
Belgium, 60
besetting, 19, 284, 290–2, 395, 396, 398, 416
binding over:
    abolition of power, 361
    breach of the peace
        cases, 321, 323, 328–32
        prevention, 356–61
    contra bonos mores test, 86–7, 308, 356–7, 361
    criminal proceedings, 357, 360
    legal basis, 356–7
    meaning, 356
    origins, 356
    standard of proof, 357
    Strasbourg jurisprudence, 75n86, 86–7, 308
        Steel v UK, 61, 88–9, 105, 357–61
    vague law, 61, 308, 360–1
biotech industry, 24
Bittner, Egon, 15
blackmail, 17n54, 246
Blackshirts, 214
Blair, Tony, 9, 146, 151, 241
blogging, 20
Bonner, David, 182, 186, 189, 234–5
boycotts, 205, 304, 306, 387–8
Brann, Jim, 413–14
breach of confidence, 298
breach of the peace
    see also binding over
    aggravated trespass or, 19
    arrest powers
        Beatty v Gillbanks, 328–9
        Duncan v Jones, 327–8
        heckler's veto, 327–8
        Nicol v DPP, 330–2, 357
        Percy v DPP, 332, 411
        preventive powers, 325–34
        Redmond-Bate v DPP, 332–4, 346, 403
        scope of power, 326–7
        Ward, 328–9
    caused by police, 221
    entry powers
        human rights and, 324–5
        preventive powers, 322–5
        property rights, 324
        proportionality, 324–5
        Thomas v Sawkins, 322–3, 404
    meaning, 320–1, 324
    overlap with POA 1986, 170
    prevention, 319–61
        arrest powers, 325–34
        Austin v MPC, 335, 349–56, 379
        binding over, 356–61
        common law powers, 162, 170, 319, 321
        disruption from third parties, 345–8
        entry powers, 322–5
        heckler's veto, 321, 345–8
        imminence test, 336, 337–43
        innocent third parties, 343–5
        kettling, 51n148, 349–56
        Laporte, 334–48, 403, 409, 423

Moss v McLachlan, 341–3
O'Kelly v Harvey, 344–5
reasonable other powers, 334–56
protest and, 24
sanctions, 104
Strasbourg jurisprudence, 104, 231–2, 325
vague law, 88–9, 320, 360–1
British Aerospace, 389n49
British National Party (BNP), 8, 227
British Transport Police, 413
Brown, Gordon, 10n32, 152n173, 422n99
Buckingham Palace, 143–4
Bulgaria, protest cases in Strasbourg, 60, 66–7, 90n156, 96, 98–9, 102, 107–9
Burberry, 389
Burke, Edmund, 10
Bursey, Brett, 119n4
Bush, George W, 119n4, 241
bylaws, 309
bypasses, 13, 21, 282, 390–1

Campaign Against the Arms Trade, 376
Campaign for Nuclear Disarmament (CND), 170, 204
Canada, Bill of Rights, 41
Card, Richard, 243, 246, 290n241, 291
censorship, meaning, 7
certainty of law, 33–5, 85, 86–8 164, 203, 263, 267, 358, 419
Chakrabarti, Shami, 146
charities, HRA 1998 and, 47–8
Chequers, 143, 145
choice, 7, 8, 31
Christie's, 385
citizen journalism, 20
civil disobedience, 12, 69, 307
  civil disruption, contrasted with, 418
class actions, 50
Climate Change Camps, 269, 282, 309, 314, 410–11, 411–12, 419, 423
clothing:
  communication through, 213–17
  concealing identity, 216–17
  proscribed organisations, 217
  Strasbourg jurisprudence, 215
Cohen, Stan, 17–18
Coker, Vernon, 425
collective action, 12–14
communication of dissent:
  advertising, 233–4
  assemblies *see* public assemblies
  clothing, 213–17
  direct action *see* direct action
  forms, 168–9
  information technology, 168, 174, 233
  language and placards, 217–30
  legal responses, 169
  marches *see* public processions
  overview, 213–32
  restrictions on, generally, 168–236
  Strasbourg jurisprudence, 230–2
  targets, 168–9
  uniforms, 213–16

community:
  disruption, 150, 152, 154–7, 182, 184, 185–7, 190–1, 212–13, 234–5
  meaning, 153
companies:
  boycotting, 205, 304, 306, 387–8
  company law remedies, 389, 409, 421
  confidentiality orders, 298–9
  defamation, 51, 386–7
  harassment
    companies cannot be harassed, 273–4
    injunctions taken by, 264
  misusing personal information on, 298–9
  property rights, 311
computer misuse, 298
confidence, breach of, 298
confidentiality orders, 298–9
conscience *see* free thought, conscience and religion
conspiracy, 17n54, 246, 248–9, 388, 412
constitutionalism, 4, 40
contra bonos mores, binding over, 86–7, 308, 356–7, 361
contract:
  inducing breach of contract, 388
  interfering with contractual relationships, 300–4
control orders, terrorism, 240–1, 286n226, 363
copyright, 233
Council of Europe, 29, 60
counter-demonstrations, 68, 104, 114, 128, 208, 231
Countryside Alliance, 120, 421
Countryside March (2002), 120
courts, public authorities, 45, 47–8, 334
  duty to develop the common law, 47, 202, 382–4, 388
crime prevention defence:
  direct action, 412
  ECHR Art 11, 89, 90
  harassment, 270–1, 407
  violence, 249–50
criminal damage, 246–8, 412
Critical Mass, 176–82
customary international law, 249–50
cyber-protests, 233, 385
Cyprus, 70–1, 85
Czech Republic, protest cases in Strasbourg, 60, 86

damage to property, 246–8, 412
defamation:
  chilling effect, 22–3
  free speech and, 33, 75, 233, 385–7
  multinational corporations, 51
  qualified privilege, 385–7
deforestation, 63
Deloitte & Touche, 300
democracy:
  anti-democratic speech, 7, 8
  characteristics, 99, 107
  deliberative democracy, 119
  demonstration democracy, 9
  direct action and, 9
  ECHR and, 32, 36–8
  effectiveness of elections, 1
  forms of protest, 174

488 Index

democracy (*cont.*):
  free speech and, 4, 7–8
  participatory democracy, 9, 146
  pluralism, 16, 32
  right to protest and, 4–5, 6, 9–10
  Strasbourg jurisprudence and, 57–8, 62, 94–6, 94–114, 116
  UK defective democracy, 9
demonstrations:
  assemblies *see* public assemblies
  definition, 59, 152–3, 368, 419
  marches *see* public processions
Denmark, 60, 84
designated sites, 142–4, 241
deviance, construction of,16–18
Dicey, Albert Venn, 4, 26, 200, 328
dignity, right to protest and, 8
direct action:
  aggravated trespass *see* trespass
  animal rights, 299–306
  civil liability, 292
  climate change and, 10
  computer misuse, 298
  confidentiality orders, 298–9
  democracy and, 9–10
  forms, 9–10, 237
  harassment *see* harassment
  incidental v inevitable disruption, 11
  increase, 306–7
  increased regulation, 310
  interfering with contractual relationships, 300–4
  intimidating those connected with animal research, 304–6
  intimidation strategy, 238
  legitimacy, 418
  malicious communications, 294–8
  meaning, 9
  misusing company information, 298–9
  ordinary criminal law, 241–2
  overview, 238
  protest and, 11–12
  protesters as terrorists, 14, 239–41, 379, 411
  public nuisance, 293–4
  public policy, 401
  reasonable excuse defence, 262–4
  restrictions on, generally, 237–310
  Strasbourg jurisprudence, 61, 62, 63, 75–6, 89–90, 238
    monochromatic approach, 308
    unfavourable treatment, 244, 281–2, 312
  symbolic disruption, 11, 75
  threats, 11
  trespass *see* trespass
  violence
    crime prevention defence, 249–50, 412
    defences, 249–52
    harm, 11, 241–6
    inchoate offences, 246, 248–9, 412
    lawful excuse defence, 247–8, 412
    necessity defence, 251–2
    property damage, 246–8, 412
    self-defence, 250–1

discretionary powers:
  access to public land, 124–6
  breach of the peace
    arrest powers, 326–34
    reasonable powers, 334–56
  police control of protest, 18–19
    breadth, 15–16, 413
    Strasbourg jurisprudence, 87–8
    vagueness, 189–90
  stop and search powers, 380
dispersal orders:
  assembly conditions or, 370, 373
  authorisation points, 369–70
  exclusions, 365, 367, 370
  indiscriminate power, 371–2
  preventive action, 364–73
  proportionality, 365–6, 367, 370, 372
  Singh, 366–73, 379, 404
  statutory scheme, 364–6
  time limit, 364, 368
  unworkability, 373
disruption:
  aggravated trespass, 252, 253, 254
  community, 150, 152, 154–7, 182, 185–7, 190–1, 212–13, 234–5
  electronic systems, 239, 240
  from third parties, 345–8
  inevitable and incidental, contrasted with direct and deliberate, 11–12, 415
  peaceful protest and, 417–9
  symbolically disruptive action, 11, 75
distress, language causing, 218–19
dockyards, 141, 143
Doherty, Brian, 306n317, 307
Donson, Fiona, 388n41
Downing Street, 143
Drax power station, 282, 283, 423, 424
Driscoll, Jim, 183, 186
Druids, 100, 194n133
Dworkin, Ronald, 195

economic torts, *see* torts
education:
  ECHR right to education, 430
  public education, 236
elections:
  access to public land, 123
  ECHR right, 430
  effectiveness, 1
  proportional representation, 9
electronic systems, disruption, 239, 240
embassies, 154, 173, 186, 419
entry powers, breach of the peace:
  human rights and, 324–5
  preventive powers, 322–5
  property rights, 324
  proportionality, 324–5
  Thomas v Sawkins, 322–3, 404
environmental protests, 31–2, 63, 291, 389, 390–4, 423
Eon power station, 11, 423
Equality and Human Rights Commission, 39
Esso, 233

Etzioni, Amitai, 9
European Convention on Human Rights
  see also specific rights and freedoms
  absolute and relative rights, 33–8
  balance of rights, 33–8, 374–5
  claim procedure, 431–2
  common law standards and, 27
  derogations, 33–4, 429
  DPP v Jones and Lloyd and, 200–3
  Drittwirkung 33
  ECtHR case law *see* Strasbourg jurisprudence
  enforcement of rights, 31
  HRA 1998 and, 39–40
  living instrument, 31, 40n90
  membership, 29–30
  objectives, 29
  origins, 29
  peaceful protest and, 58
  positive obligations, 31–2
    access to land, 128–9, 133
  prohibition of abuse of rights (Art 17), 8, 429
  purposive interpretation, 31
  restrictions on rights
    legitimacy, 36
    margins of appreciation, 37–8, 54, 96–9
    necessary in democratic society, 36–8, 62, 94–114
    prescribed by law, 34–5, 62, 84–9, 267–8, 308, 360–1
    proportionality, 33, 36–8, 62, 200–3
    public interest, 36
  scope, 30–3
  state liability, 33
  text, 426–30
  UK dualism and, 27–8
  UK ratification, 29
European Court of Human Rights *see* Strasbourg jurisprudence
European Union:
  compatibility of domestic legislation, 42
  direct effect of law, 40
  environmental protection, 250
  free movement, 235
Ewing, Keith, 27n8, 186, 223, 327n90

Fagan, Michael, 144
fair trial/hearing:
  balance of arms, 387
  burden of proof, 188, 229
  ECHR (Art 6), 30, 427–8
  harassment injunctions, 409–10
  legal aid, 32, 386–7
  presumption of innocence, 358, 363
  Strasbourg jurisprudence, 386–7
Fairford airbase, 143, 335, 339, 346, 412n71
fall guys, 16
false imprisonment, 349–56
Fascism, 324
Faslane naval base, 104
Fathers4Justice, 146
Feldman, David, 154n177, 186
Fenwick, Helen:
  aggravated trespass, 263
  on ASBOs, 364
  bans on all marches, 206
  bans on assemblies, 187
  breach of the peace, 320
  direct action, 237n3
    on *DPP v Jones and Lloyd,* 195, 198
    on *Gillan,* 318
  harassment, burden of proof, 273, 278
  intimidation at marches, 186
  intimidation strategy, 238
    on *Laporte,* 347–8
  legitimate protest, 12
  mechanistic statutory interpretation, 254
  POA s14A, 190, 212
  Strasbourg jurisprudence, 207–8
  symbolically disruptive direct action, 11
Finland, protest cases in Strasbourg, 60, 70
Fisher, Nicola, 399, 424
fishing competitions, 89–90, 223, 330–2
folk devils, 17, 239
football banning orders, 54, 286n226
forward intelligence teams, 422–3
fox-hunting protests, 9, 16, 35, 86–7, 252, 259, 260, 262, 307, 308, 326, 420
fox-hunting supporters, 120, 146
France:
  Cissé v France, 61, 65, 70, 81, 93, 97
  colonial territories, 230
  Ezelin v France, 68–9, 77, 105, 115
  free expression and intellectual property rights, 233
  immigration rules, 70, 93, 97
  Lindon v France, 98
  protest cases in Strasbourg, 60
freedom of assembly:
  access to land *see* access to land
  balance of rights, 34, 283
  ECHR (Art 11), 31
    balance of rights, 34
    DPP v Jones and Lloyd and, 200–3, 383
    list of defences, 89
    text, 57, 429
  entry powers and, 324–5
  historical development, 4–6
  HRA impact, 55–6
    access to land, 127
  police conditions and, 52
  right to peaceful protest and, 58, 169
    free speech or, 63–7
    positive obligations, 32, 70–5
    Strasbourg jurisprudence, 63–76
  shopping centres, 64, 74, 129, 132–6
  Strasbourg jurisprudence
    content study, 59–63
    democracy and, 57–8, 94–6, 116
    direct action, 75–6
    free speech or, 63–7
    legal nature of restrictions, 84–9
    legitimacy of restrictive policies, 89–94
    marches and assemblies, 206–13
    meaning of assembly, 65–7
    necessary restrictions, 62, 94–114
    peaceful assembly, 67–70
    positive obligations, 70–5
    private land, 64, 74–5

freedom of assembly (*cont.*):
  Strasbourg jurisprudence (*cont.*):
    proportionality, 62, 94–114
    public order defence, 64, 90–4
    restrictions, overview, 76–114
    types of interferences, 77–84
    UK cases, 66, 68, 71, 74–5, 93, 101–2, 103
  violence and, 239–40, 242, 243–4
  Westminster area, 27
Freedom of expression
  see also language
  balance of rights, 283
  choices and, 7
  common law right, 28
  defamation and, 33, 75, 233, 385–7
  ECHR (Art 10), 31
    list of defences, 89
    text, 428
  entry powers and, 324–5
  free speech zones, 119n4, 420n94
  function, 6–8
  harassment and, 52
  historical development, 4–6, 27
  HRA and
    abusive language, 223–4
    impact, 55–6
    presumption in favour of, 397
    proportionality, 234
  intellectual property rights and, 233
  malicious communications and, 224, 296
  market place of ideas, 7–8
  political discourse, 8
  racist speech, 8, 169
  right to peaceful protest and, 58, 169
    free assembly or, 63–7
  state liability, 33
  Strasbourg jurisprudence
    access to land, 133–4
    choice of clothing, 215
    defamation laws and, 33, 75
    overview, 230–2
    positive obligations, 74–5
    proportionality of restrictions, 96, 99, 102, 105
    public order defence, 90, 91
    restrictions, classification, 84
  uniform wearing and, 215
  venues, 118
  Westminster restrictions and, 160
free movement:
  EC law, 235
  ECHR Protocol 4, 73, 430
Freedom of thought, conscience and religion:
  ECHR (Art 9), 31, 428
  malicious communications and, 296
  Strasbourg jurisprudence, 89, 111
    UK case, 100
funerals, 214

G20 protests:
  anti-bank protests, 420
  camera phones and, 20
  costs of policing, 23
  Gold Strategy, 417, 422
  impact, 412–13
  inquiries, 399, 414
  JCHR report, 354n235
  kettling, 349, 354n235, 355, 422
  legitimacy, 6
  media role, 421–2
  police conduct, 314–15, 375–6, 379, 424
  pre-emptive police coercion, 11
  Tomlinson death, 20, 375, 399, 424
  unidentified police, 411
Gask, Alex, 364
Gaza protest (2009), 399, 422
Gearty, Conor, 27n8, 186, 223, 327n90
Geddis, Andrew, 224, 226, 227, 235, 236, 414
Germany:
  anti-military protests, 65, 308
  Klass v Germany, 78
  road obstruction, 91–2
  sit-in cases, 65, 66, 86, 106, 139
  surveillance, 79n103
Gil-Robles, Alvaro, 362
GlaxoSmithKline, 299
GM crops, 9, 239, 240, 244, 250, 251, 254, 257, 293, 303, 391–3, 412
Goldman, Emma, 1
Goodhart, Arthur L, 323
Google, 168
graffiti, 247
Greece, 73n73, 79n102, 84
Greenham Common, 65, 164–5
Greenpeace, 10, 100, 233, 240n13, 386, 388, 412
Gulf War (1991), 247–8
gypsies *see* travellers

habeas corpus, 26
harassment:
  civil and criminal wrong, 23, 264, 265
  dispersal orders, 365
  in homes, s42A CJPA 2001 directions, 288–9
  injunctions, 22–3, 56
    apprehended harassment, 266
    balance of rights, 279–84
    identifiable targets, 274–6
    increase, 264
    Strasbourg jurisprudence, 75n86
  judicial hardening, 268–9
  language, 52, 218–19, 221, 228, 289
  meaning, 24, 267–9
  outside homes
    CJPA 2001 (s42), 284–8
    enforcement of previous legislation, 15
    excessive powers, 15, 401–2, 420
    forms, 63
    proportionality, 288
    statutory directions, 285–6
    three-month return rule, 286–7
  PFHA 1997, 264–84
    balance of rights, 279–84
    burden of proof, 273, 278
    certainty and, 419
    companies cannot be harassed, 273–4
    course of conduct, 265–7
    crime prevention defence, 270–1, 412

Index 491

group harassment, 265, 266, 405
identifiable targets, 274–6
impact on protesters, 273–84, 409–10
inchoate offences, 277–8
malicious communications, 295
political attitudes, 417
procedural safeguards, 278–9, 363
protest exclusion orders, 279–84
questionable regulation, 15, 16
questionable use of regulation, 21
reasonableness defence, 272–3, 309, 407
secondary harassment, 265–6, 269, 309, 405
standard of proof, 265, 409
statutory defences, 270–3
statutory offence, 264–5
unnamed protesters, 276–8, 391, 420
putting in fear of violence, 244–5
watching and besetting, 290–2
Fidler v DPP, 291–2
statutory offence, 290–1
Hardwick, Nick, 410
Harris, David, 259, 326, 420
Harrods, 283
hate speech, 8, 169
Haw, Brian, 59, 148, 152, 155–7, 164–5, 402
hearsay evidence, 265, 278, 363, 364, 409
Heathrow, 10, 276, 282, 309, 379
heckler's veto, 220, 235–6, 321, 327–8, 345–8
Hertfordshire Police, 19
highway *see* public highway
Hill Grove Farm, 23
Her Majesty's Inspectorate of Constabulary (HMIC)
 report *Adapting to Protest* (July 2009), 399, 410, 414, 417, 422
Hohfeld, Wesley Newcomb, 4, 90, 119, 333
Home Affairs Select Committee, 399, 410
homes:
 harassment in, 288–9
 harassment outside, 284–9, 420
homosexuality, 28–9, 127–8, 223, 226
Horsmonden Horse Fair, 90
hospitals, 48–9, 131–2
HUDOC database, 60
human rights
 see also specific rights and freedoms
 agenda for change, 424–5
 balance of rights, 33–8, 313, 374–5
 common law protection, 25, 26–9
 ECHR *see* European Convention on Human Rights
 HRA *see* Human Rights Act (1998)
 positive obligations
  access to land, 128–9, 133
  ECHR, 32–3
  v negative obligations, 122
 stop and search powers and, 316
Human Rights Act (1998):
 access to public land and, 126–9
 assessment of compliance, 52–4
 Convention Rights, 39n85
 declarations of incompatibility, 42, 43, 234
 duties of private bodies, 47–8
 duties of public bodies, 44–54
 ECHR and, 39–40
 enforcement, 50–2
 impact on peaceful protest, 46–7, 55–6, 405–6
 indirect horizontal effect, 47, 49, 51, 334, 382–3
 institutions, 39
 legislative compatibility, 40–4, 55–6, 137, 205–6, 244, 256, 296–7
 necessary restrictions, 53–4
 origins, 38–9
 overview, 38–54
 parliamentary sovereignty and, 39, 40, 41
 proportionality of restrictions, 52–4, 203–5, 223–4
 remedies, 40n89
 restrictions prescribed by law, 52, 360
 statutory interpretation, 40–4
 taking account of Strasbourg case law, 63, 406–7
 text, 467–75
 UK Bill of Rights, 39–40
 victims, 50
Hungary:
 authorisation as interference, 80, 81–3
 ban on wearing red star, 99, 102, 105, 109, 215, 236
 Bukta v Hungary, 73, 81–3, 108, 111, 115, 173, 212–13, 308
 Freedom of assembly, 67
 Patyi v Hungary, 67, 103
 positive obligations, 73
 protest cases in Strasbourg, 60
 public order defence, 108
 traffic obstruction, 91
 Vajnai v Hungary, 99, 111
Huntingdon Life Sciences, 300, 403

Identification
 duty on individuals under s.60A CJPOA 1994, 216–17
 duty on police officers, 410–11, 423
inchoate offences, 246, 248–9, 261, 277–8, 412
incitement, 248
inclusio unus, altio exclusus, 370
Independent Police Complaints Commission, 375, 399, 410
industrial disputes, 186, 290, 365, 367, 388, 395, 397, 421
information technology, 168, 174, 298, 399
injunctions:
 balance of convenience, 395
 harassment, 22–3, 56
  apprehended harassment, 266
  balance of rights, 279–84
  criminalisation of protesters, 409
  identifiable targets, 274–6
  increase, 264
  Strasbourg jurisprudence, 75n86
  unnamed protesters, 276–8, 391, 420
 nuisance, 47, 56, 394–7
 trespass, 47, 391–3
Innovation Fund, 122
insults *see* language
intellectual property rights, 233
interfering with business, 391
interfering with contractual relationships:
 criminalisation of economic torts, 304, 405, 419
 intentions, 302

interfering with contractual relationships (*cont.*):
  legislative duplication, 303
  peaceful protest issues, 303–4
  proportionality, 304
  relevant acts, 301
  scope, 302–3
  statutory offence, 300
  triggers, 301–2
internet, 168, 174, 233, 385
intimidation:
  definition, 240, 291
  strategy, 238
IRA, 214
Iran, 399
Iraq War, 9–10, 16, 59, 119n4, 148, 160, 241, 259–60, 307, 318, 334–5, 412
Irvine of Lairg, Lord, 39–40
Italy, 60

Joint Committee on Human Rights (JCHR):
  Brann testimony, 413–14
  Coker submission, 425
  G20 protests, 354n235, 399, 411
  harassment in homes, 289
  harassment outside homes, 287
  inconsistent law enforcement, 152
  interference with contractual relationships, 304
  Liberty submission to, 314n13, 423
  political responses to, 417
  protesters and terrorism, 379
  secondary harassment, 309
  on Westminster demonstration, 151
  work and function, 39
Jones, Barry, 259, 326
judicial review:
  access to land, 123–6
  common law principles, 123–6, 311–12
  HRA 1998 and, 44
    v common law, 53–4
  standing, 50
  Wednesbury test of unreasonableness, 28, 53

Kent, Bruce, 170
Kerrigan, Kevin, 360, 361
kettling, 51n148, 349–56, 422
key themes, 408–12
Kingsnorth power station, 309, 314, 412, 421, 423–4
knee-jerkism, 15

Lakenheath airbase, 143
land:
  access to *see* access to land
  definition, 256, 257
  ownership *see* land ownership
  trespass *see* trespass
Land League, 345
land ownership:
  absolute title, 129–30
  categories, 130–1
  privatisations, 74, 118
  quasi-public land, 131–2, 133, 420
  right to protest and, 74–5, 120–1, 408
  rights, 121–2
  stakeholder society, 120
  underpinnings, 119
  unegalitarianism, 121
landlord and tenant, 121, 127–8
language: *see also* freedom of expression
  freedom of expression, 223–4
    HRA and proportionality, 223–4, 229
  offensiveness, 221–2
  pro-civility discourse, 236
  threatening, abusive or insulting, 24, 52
    audience veto, 220, 235–6
    defences, 219
    English case law, 219–30
    Hammond v DPP, 226–7, 404
    harassment, alarm or distress, 218–21, 289
    judicial preferences, 220, 227
    meaning, 221–3
    Norwood v DPP, 227–9
    Percy v DPP, 224–6
    POA 1986 (ss4–5), 218–19
    reasonable conduct defence, 223–30
    violence and, 218
Latvia, 77
Law Commission, 242, 243, 361
Le Pen, Jean-Marie, 98
legal aid, 32, 386–7
legal certainty, 33–5, 85, 86–8, 164, 203, 263, 267, 358, 419
legal representation, 28
legislation
  see also regulation of protest
  compatibility with HRA 1998, 40–4, 55–6, 137, 205–6
    aggravated trespass, 256
    declarations of incompatibility, 42, 43, 234
    direct actions and violence, 244
    malicious communications and, 296–7
  duplication, 303, 319, 339, 347–8, 432
  protest-impact statements, 416
  restrictions on human rights
    certainty, 33–5
    ECHR, 34–5
    Strasbourg jurisprudence, 84–9
  restrictions on right to protest
    certainty, 85– 88, 164, 203, 263, 267, 358, 360–1, 419
    improper application, 88–9
    no legal regime, 85
    Strasbourg jurisprudence, 62, 84–9
    unforeseeable application, 86, 88
  unforeseeable application, 86, 88, 167
Leigh, Ian, 313
Lester, Lord, 42
Liberty, 314–15, 318–19, 364, 423
liberty and security:
  Austin, 349–56, 379
  ECHR (Art 5), 30, 427
  kettling, 349–56
  Steel v UK, 357–61
  stop and search and, 316, 380
  Strasbourg jurisprudence, 352–3, 357–61
Linslade bypass, 282

locus see access to land
Lustgarten, Laurence, 313

McBarnet, Doreen, 16
Macedonia, 69–70
McLibel Two, 33, 51, 75, 386
Make Poverty History, 13
malice, 385–5
malicious communications:
    Connolly v DPP, 137, 296–8, 382, 403, 406
    definition, 294–5
    direct actions, 294–8
    free expression and, 224
Mandela problem, 69
marches *see* public processions
Marston, John, 184n85, 190n121, 192
May Day disturbances (2001), 51n148, 349–56
media:
    24-hour rolling news, 20
    citizen journalism, 20
    communication of protest, 168, 307
    democratisation, 20
    large protests and, 421–2
    ownership, 120
    protesters' use of, 20n74
meetings *see* public assemblies
Menwith Hill airbase, 143, 145, 146, 241, 363
Mildenhall airbase, 143
Milne, AA, 331
miners' strike, 186, 342, 343, 397, 423
Mingchao, Cai, 384–5
Moldova:
    Christian Democratic People's Party v Moldova, 86n136, 90n152, 98
    protest cases in Strasbourg, 60
    Ziliberberg v Moldova, 69, 79–81, 87, 91, 104, 105, 115, 157–8, 160, 161, 174, 181
Monbiot, George, 21
moral panic, 17–18, 239
Mosley, Oswald, 214
motorways, 20–1, 75, 222, 237, 291, 354, 357, 364, 384

National Extremism Tactical Coordination Unit (NETCU), 21, 422
National Front, 5, 77–8, 92, 170, 208
national security:
    critique, 144–5
    ECHR Art 11 defence, 89
    exclusions from specific sites, 141–5, 318–19
    Official Secrets Act 1911–1989, 141–2
    trespass on designated sites, 142–4, 241
necessity
    see also proportionality
    defence, 251–2
    false imprisonment, 350–6
Nestlé, 387
Netherlands:
    Greek dictatorship and, 84
    Olympics protest, 115, 232
    protest cases in Strasbourg, 60
new social movements, 9
New Zealand, Bill of Rights, 41
Newbury bypass, 21, 390–1

NGOs:
    HRA 1998 and, 47–8, 50
    Strasbourg jurisprudence and, 99
Nicholson, Heather, 363
Nicolson, Donald, 326, 342, 358n253
noise, 75–6, 374, 394, 400, 407
non-discrimination:
    access to land, 120, 127–8
    ECHR (Art 14), 31, 429
    equal worth, 135
    sexual orientation, 227
Northern Ireland law, 3
Norway:
    anti-whaling protests, 97, 100, 308
    direct actions, 75
    Greek dictatorship and, 84
    Lapp protest, 91, 106, 165, 400
    protest cases in Strasbourg, 60
Not in My Name, 13
Nottingham Speaker's Corner, 420
nuclear protests, 81, 91–2, 238, 307, 312
nuisance:
    direct actions, 293–4
    Hubbard v Pitt, 394–7
    injunctions, 47, 56, 394–7
    public and private nuisance, 394

Öcalan, Abdullah, 83
offensive weapons, 314
Orange Order parades, 180
organisers, public processions, 173–5, 181
Ovey, Clare, 36

parliamentary sovereignty, 26–7, 39, 40, 41
Paxman, Jeremy, 422
Peach, Blair, 375
Percy, Lindis, 363, 364
PETA, 389
Peterloo Massacre (1819), 5
petitions, 168
pharmaceutical industry, 24
Phillipson, Gavin, 11, 12, 237n3, 238, 254, 263
picketing, 394–7
placards, 217–30
places of protest *see* access to land
Plane Stupid, 10, 20n74, 269, 276, 307, 379, 388
Plows, Alexandra, 306n317, 307
Poland:
    bans on assemblies, 35, 78, 89n147
    minority views, 71
police:
    causing breach of the peace, 221
    costs of protest policing, 23, 398
    entry *see* entry powers
    general duties, 311–13
    identification tags, 410–11
    indiscriminate policing, 422–3
    politics of protest policing, 19–20
    powers *see* police powers
    pre-emptive policing, 423–4
    proportionality of actions, 309–10
    public authority status, 311
    rigid approaches, Strasbourg jurisprudence, 102–4

police (*cont.*):
  role and behaviour, 18–20, 421–5
  surveillance of protesters, 79n102, 376–8, 399, 422–3, 423–4
  targets of protest, 313
police powers:
  access to land
    CJPOA 1994 s61, 162–3
    criminalisation of trespass, 162–5
    Fuller case, 165–7
    overview, 162–7
    travellers, 162–3
  arrest *see* arrest powers
  assemblies *see* public assemblies
  common law powers, 170
  discretionary powers, 18–19
    breach of the peace *see* breach of the peace
    breadth, 15–16, 413
    Strasbourg jurisprudence, 87–8
    vagueness, 189–90
  marches *see* public processions
  reforming, 421–5
  stop and search *see* stop and search powers
political parties, 13, 174
politics:
  meaning of political, 20
  peaceful protest and, 58
  policing of protest, 19–20
  political advertising, 233–4
  role of free speech, 8
presumption of innocence, 358, 363
preventive action:
  aggravated trespass, 261–4
  ASBOs, 362–4
  breach of the peace *see* breach of the peace
  dispersal orders, 364–73
  general duties of police, 311–13
  pre-emptive policing, 11, 423–4
  stop and search powers, 313–19
  Strasbourg jurisprudence and, 373–5
prisoners, freedom of expression, 4
private and family life:
  common law rights, 26
  ECHR (Art 8), 30–1, 428
  fox-hunting rights, 384
  non-absolute right, 135
  police action and, 311
  reasonable expectation of privacy, 298
  stop and search and, 316
  Strasbourg jurisprudence, 384
  surveillance of protesters, 376–8
  uniform wearing and, 215
private finance initiative (PFI), 132
private law remedies:
  balance of rights, 383–4
  causing economic harm, 387–8
  company law remedies, 389, 409, 421
  defamation, 385–7
  indirect horizontal effect, 47, 49, 334, 382–3
  nuisance, 394–7
  possible remedies, overview, 384–97
  privatisation of protest regulation, 22–3, 381, 398, 402, 408–10
  costs of, 22, 398, 408
  property rights *see* property rights
  public v private law
    access to land, 22, 24, 118–21, 162
    agenda for change, 419–21
    economic torts, 304
    interdependence, 22
    Strasbourg jurisprudence, 73–4
    trespass to land, 390–4
Pro-Test, 310
professional protesters, 20–1
property rights:
  balance of rights, 383–4
  companies, 311
  defence of property, 249, 251
  demographic skew, effect on protest, 120
  ECHR Protocol, Art 1, 31, 430
  entry powers and, 324
  inequality, 121
  land *see* land ownership
  presumption in favour of, 393
  protest rights and, 324
  trespass *see* trespass
proportional representation, 9
proportionality:
  dispersal orders, 365–6, 367, 370, 372
  entry powers, breach of the peace, 324–5
  harassment, s42 CJPA 2001 directions, 288
  HRA restrictions, 52–4, 223–4, 229
    free expression, 234
    Public Order Act 1986, 203–5
  interfering with contractual relationships, 304
  police action, 309–10
  protest exclusion orders, 279–84
  public processions, conditions, 182
  regulation of protest, 417, 418
  restrictions on ECHR rights, 33, 36–8
    DPP v Jones and Lloyd and, 200–3
  restrictions on human rights
    ECHR, 36–8, 200–3
    HRA 1998, 53–4, 203–5
  stop and search, 314
  Strasbourg jurisprudence
    blanket bans, 101–2
    counter-demonstrations, 114, 208, 231
    democracy, 94–6, 99, 116
    factors, 99–114, 193–4
    margin of appreciation, 96–9
    restrictions on protest rights, 62, 76, 80, 81, 82, 94–114, 359–60
    rigid police approaches, 102–4
    sanctions, 104–5, 158–59, 161
    third party effect, 109–14
    time, manner and place, 100–1
    types of protest, 106–9
  UK preventive action and, 374–5
proscribed organisations, 217
protest:
  changing face, 20–4
  civil disobedience, 12
  collective action, 12–14
  definition, 58–9
  democracy and, 9–10

direct action *see* direct action
ECtHR *see* Strasbourg jurisprudence
forms, 168–9, 419
function, 6–8
land ownership, relationship between, 2, 22, 118–121, 167, 200–1, 256, 408, 420
litigation as a form of protest, 307
locus *see* access to land
professional protesters, 20–1
public inconvenience, 6
regulation *see* regulation of protest
right *see* right to peaceful protest
support *see* communication of dissent
targets, 168–9
technology and, 20–1, 294, 298, 375–6, 385, 399, 422
violent *see* violence
Protest Act, call for 415–16
protest exclusion orders, 279–84
protest-impact statements, 416
psychological harm, 246
public assemblies:
  bans (s14A POA 1986), 184–5
    conditions compared, 187–92
    DPP v Jones and Lloyd, 194–203, 257–8, 383, 408
    extent of power, 192–203
    offences (ss14B/C POA 1986), 185
    Trafalgar Square, 87–8, 93–4, 101, 127, 202, 203, 208, 401
    trespassory assemblies, 184–5
  breach of the peace powers, 170
  conditions (s14 POA 1986), 184, 368, 406
    Broadwith v DPP, 190–2
    comparison with bans, 187–92
    dispersal orders or, 370, 373
    failure to comply, 190–2
    minimum numbers, 184, 190
    triggers, 185–7, 204
  definition, 183–4
  dispersal orders, 366–73
  offences, 185
  Public Order Act 1986, 169
    comparison with processions, 187–92
    effect of HRA 1998, 203–6
    overview, 170–1
  Strasbourg jurisprudence, 206–13
    Cetinkaya v Turkey, 211
    Güneri v Turkey, 211–12
    Makhmaduv v Russia, 212
    Öllinger, 210–11
    Patyi v Hungary, 212
  unlawful assembly, 242
public authorities:
  courts, 334, 382–3
  functional public authorities, 45, 46, 48–9
  HRA compliance
    assessment, 52–4
    enforcement rights, 50–2
    overview, 44–54
    right to protest and, 46–7
  judicial deference, 54
  meaning, 45–9, 135

police, 311
public debate, 414–15
public education, 236
public health, 89
public highway:
  aggravated trespass and, 257–8
  definition, 194n134, 257
  leafleting, 413
  obstruction, 24, 138–41
    Birch v DPP, 140–1
    direct action, 241
    Hirst and Agu, 140
    offence, 138–9
    picketing, 395–7
    Strasbourg jurisprudence, 139
  right to protest on, 5–6, 130–1
  trespassory assemblies, 194–203
public housing, privatisation, 118n2
public interest, right to protest, 4, 5, 58, 408
public libraries, 125
public morals, 89
public places, meaning, 171
public processions
  see also public assemblies
  advance notice
    ad hoc marches, 173
    Kay, 176–82
    customarily held events, 173, 177–9, 181, 403
    defences, 173
    exemptions, 173
    intentions, 175–82
    meaning of public places, 171
    non-compliance, 417
    organisers' liability, 173–5, 181
    POA 1986 (s11), 171–82
    routes, 172, 173, 179–80
    specifications, 172–3
    spontaneous events, 176–82
    time limits, 172, 173, 177
    written notice, 172
  bans (s13 POA 1986), 183
    comparison with conditions, 187–92
    failing to comply, 183
    police powers, 170, 172
  conditions (s12 POA 1986), 52, 182
    comparison with assembly regime, 187–92
    comparison with bans, 187–92
    failing to comply, 183
    police powers, 52, 170, 172, 182–3
    triggers, 182, 185–7, 204
  demonstration, definition, 59, 152–3
  lawfulness, 182
  meaning, 171–2
  POA 1986 (ss 12–14C)
    assembly/procession comparison, 187–92
    breach of the peace and, 347
    effect of HRA 1998, 203–6
    intimidation trigger, 182, 184, 186–7
    overview, 171–82, 182–213
    public assemblies, 183–5
    public processions, 182–3
    serious disruption trigger, 182, 184, 185–6
    triggers for conditions, 182, 184, 185–7

public processions (*cont.*):
  Strasbourg jurisprudence, 206–13
  UK cases, 77–8, 92
public safety defence, 89

quarries, 13
quasi-military organisations, 14
quasi-public land, 131–2, 133, 420

racist speech, 8, 169, 293
Radley Lakes, 21
Range Rover, 388
Rawls, John, 135
RBS, 420
Reclaim the Streets, 237
recognizance, 356, 359
regulation, meaning, 2
regulation of protest:
  access to land *see* access to land
  certainty *see* legal certainty
  conditions, 8
  discretionary powers *see* discretionary powers
  distortion of powers, 15
  increased regulation, 310, 401–5
  indiscriminate regulation, 416
    dispersal orders, 371–2
    Westminster protests, 153–5
  knee-jerkism, 15
  marches *see* public processions
  misdirection, 16
  multi-agency, 24
  private law concepts, 22
  privatisation, 22–3, 381, 398, 402, 408–10
  proportionality, 417, 418
  questionable necessity, 15, 16–18
  reactive regulation, 15
  socio-legal aspects, 14–18, 239, 408–12
Reid, Kiron, 326, 342, 358n253
religion *see* freedom of thought, conscience and religion
remedy, right to effective remedy, 71–2, 429
Remembrance Day parades, 180
residing, meaning, 164
right to life:
  common law right, 28
  ECHR Art 2, text, 426
  positive obligations, 32
right to peaceful protest:
  agenda for change, 412–25
  amalgam of free speech and free assembly, 58, 169
  definition of peaceful protest, 11–12, 417–18
  definition of protest, 58–9
  demonstrations *see* public assemblies; public processions
  ECtHR *see* Strasbourg jurisprudence
  England and Wales 2010 snapshot, 401–7
  European constitutions, 62
  historical development, 4–6
  HRA 1998 and
    likely influence, 55–6
    meaning of public authority, 46–7
  key themes, 408–12
  legitimacy, 11–12, 368

marches *see* public processions
public debate, 414–15
public sphere and, 58
statutory guarantee, 416–17
Strasbourg 2010 snapshot, 400–1
unreasonable protest, 6
venues *see* access to land
rights of way, 136–8
riot, 242, 243
Rosyth Dockyard, 143
rout, 242
Rowbottom, Jacob, 135, 136, 167
Royal Commission, 415, 418, 419, 420, 424
rule of law:
  Dicey, 26n3
  ECHR and, 33, 62
    restrictions on right to protest, 84–9
  free speech and, 4
  HRA restrictions and, 52
  UK constitution, 40
Russell, Bertie, 20, 423, 424
Russia, protest cases in Strasbourg, 76, 82–3, 116
RWE Npower, 21
Ryanair, 388

St-Laurent, Yves, 385
Salford Council, 71n67
Scarman Inquiry (1974), 413
schools, 13, 48
Scottish law, 3, 257
secondary legislation, *ultra vires*, 28
sedition, 233, 324
self-defence, 249, 250–1
self-immolation, 59
self-incrimination, privilege against, 27
separation of powers, 40
sexual orientation, 28–9, 127–8, 223, 226
Seymour, Jillaine, 274
Sharon, Ariel, 241
Shell, 154
Sherr, Avrom 220
shopping centres, 64, 74, 129, 132–6
silence, right to, 27
socio-legal perspectives, 14–18, 239, 408–12
Spain, 60
Speakers' Corners, 420
Speakers' Corners Trust, 122–3
Spencer, John, 291
stakeholder society, 120
stalking, 16, 264, 273, 281
standing:
  enforcement of HRA 1998, 50–2
  private law remedies, 390
Stansted, 9, 307, 388
state liability, ECHR and, 33
statutory interpretation:
  HRA 1998 and, 40–4, 137
  mechanistic, 254
  Pepper v Hart, 367
  purposive approach, 155
Stephenson, Paul, 410
Stone, Richard, 182, 186, 189, 234–5, 347
Stonehenge, 5, 100, 194

Index 497

stop and search powers:
  anticipation of violence, 315
  blanket searches, 314, 380, 411–12
  clothing and, 216–17
  excessive use, 314
  human rights and, 316
  no reasonable suspicion, 315–19
  overview, 313–19
  proportionality, 314
  reasonable suspicion, 313–15
  Strasbourg jurisprudence, 380
  terrorism, 241, 315–19
    Gillan, 316–18, 353, 379, 380
Stop Huntingdon Animal Cruelty, 274, 300
Strasbourg jurisprudence:
  binding over, 75n86, 308
    Steel v UK, 61, 88–9, 105, 357–61
  breach of the peace, 231–2, 325
  class actions, 50
  communication of dissent, 230–2
    audience sensitivity, 236
  democracy and free assembly, 57–8
  direct action *see* direct action
  fair trial, 386–7
  HRA duty to take account of (s2), 63, 406–7
  HUDOC database, 60
  indirect horizontal effect, 47, 49, 51, 334, 382–3
  intimidation, 255
  legal nature of restrictions
    discretionary powers, 87–8
    improper application of laws, 88–9
    no legal regime, 85
    overview, 84–9
    unforeseeable application, 86, 88
    vague laws, 35, 86–8, 360–1
  legitimacy of restrictions on right to protest
    list of defences, 89
    overview, 89–94
    range of disorder, 64, 90–4
  liberty and security, 352–3
  marches and assemblies
    Cetinkaya v Turkey, 211
    Güneri v Turkey, 211–12
    limited protection, 207–10
    Makhmaduv v Russia, 212
    new expansionism, 210–13, 308–9
    Öllinger, 210–11
    overview, 206–13
    Patyi v Hungary, 212
  peaceful protest and, 55–6
  positive obligations, 32–3
  preventive action in UK and, 373–5
  private and family life, 384
  procedure, 431–2
  proportionality, restrictions on right to protest
    binding over, 359–60
    blanket bans, 101–2
    Chorherr v Austria, 110–11, 114, 116, 231, 232, 347
    counter-demonstrations, 114, 208, 231
    democracy, 94–6, 99, 116
    factors, 99–114, 193–4
    margin of appreciation, 96–9
    Öllinger v Austria, 111–14, 116, 210–11, 231, 344
    overview, 62, 94–114
    rigid police approaches, 102–4
    sanctions, 104–5, 158–9, 161
    third party effect, 109–114, 231
    time, manner and place, 100–1
    types of protest, 106–9
    UK preventive action and, 374–5
  proportionality, restrictions on rights, 33, 36–8
    margin of appreciation, 37–8, 54, 96–9
  protest cases
    content study, 59–63
    defending countries, 60–1
    outcomes, 62–3
  purposive interpretation, 31
  restrictions on right to protest
    access to land, 129, 132–6
    advance bans, 77–9, 101–2
    authorisation requirements, 79–83, 157–61, 193–4
    balance of rights, 33–8, 374–5
    Bukta v Hungary, 73, 81–3, 108, 111, 115, 173, 212–13, 308
    highway obstruction, 139
    indiscriminate practices, 416–17
    legitimate aims, 89–94
    nature of interference, 77–84
    necessity, 62, 94–114
    noise reason, 75–6, 374, 400
    overview, 76–114
    prescribed by law, 84–9, 267–8, 308, 360–1
    proportionality, 62, 76, 80, 81, 82, 94–114
    public order, 64, 89, 90–4
    punishment, 77, 104–5
    state definition of interferences, 83–4
    surveillance, 79n102
    Ziliberberg v Moldova, 69, 79–81, 82, 87, 91, 104, 105, 115, 157–8, 160, 161, 174, 181
  right to peaceful protest
    2010 snapshot, 400–1
    assessment, 114–17
    free speech or free assembly, 63–7
    lawful restrictions, 76–114
    marches and assemblies, 206–13
    meaning of assembly, 65–7
    peaceful assembly, 67–70, 127, 232
    positive obligations, 70–5
    regulation of private sphere, 73–4
    scope of right, 63–76
    summary of cases, 434–66
    stop and search powers, 380
  UK cases, 60
Straw, Jack (Foreign Secretary), 241
Suffolk Police, 19, 379, 416
suffragettes, 12
Sunstein, Cass, 119
Surrey Police, 19, 416
surveillance, 79n102, 376–8, 399, 422–3, 423–4
Swampy, 307
Sweden, 60, 79n102, 84
Switzerland:
  meat industry protests, 231
  protest cases in Strasbourg, 60

Switzerland (cont.):
　separatist tension, 92–3, 97, 109
　time-limited ban, 100

Tain, Paul, 184n85, 190n121, 192
Tamil Protest (2009), 23, 399
Tate Modern, 59
Territorial Support Group, 399
terrorism:
　control orders, 240–1, 286n226, 363
　definition, 14, 217, 239–41
　police role, 422n99
　proscribed groups, 14
　protesters as terrorists, 239–41, 379, 411
　stop and search powers, 241, 315–19
　　Gillan, 316–18, 353, 379, 380
　use of legislation for ordinary protest, 241, 309, 318–19
Thatcher, Margaret, 9
third parties:
　breach of the peace and, 349–56
　　disruption from third parties, 345–8
　　innocent third parties, 343–5
　effect of protest on, Strasbourg jurisprudence, 89, 109–14, 231
　harassment and, 278
　heckler's veto, 220, 235–6, 321, 327–8, 345–8
threats
　see also language
　criminal offence, 303
　interfering with contractual relationships, 300
　malicious communications, 294
Tomas, Allyn, 423–4
Tomlinson, Ian, 20, 375, 399, 424
torts
　see also specific torts
　direct actions, 292
　economic torts, 381, 388, 405
　　criminalisation, 304, 381, 419
　peaceful protest and, 384–97
torture, inhuman or degrading treatment:
　absolute right, 33
　ECHR Art 3, text, 426
　state liability, 33
trade unions, 2, 31, 57, 107, 159, 174, 186, 429
Trafalgar Square, 87–8, 93–4, 101, 127, 202, 203, 208, 401
transformative approach, 236, 414
travellers, 90, 92, 100, 103, 162–3
trespass
　see also entry powers
　aggravated trespass
　　breach of the peace or, 19
　　CJPOA 1994 (s68), 252
　　criminalisation of trespass, 252, 402
　　defences, 251
　　elements, 253–61
　　increase, 379–80
　　lawfulness of activity, 258–60
　　misdirected regulation, 16
　　more than simple trespass, 253–4
　　objectives, 252
　　overview, 252–64

　　penalties, 137
　　permission to enter, 256–7
　　police prevention, 261–4
　　pre-emptive action, 423
　　preparing for, 260–1
　　presence of others, 254–6
　　privatisation of regulation, 381, 402
　　protesters' property rights, 256–8
　　public land, 257–8
　　reasonable excuse defence, 262–4
　　time factor, 260–1
　criminalisation, 162–5, 247
　　CJPOA 1994 s68, 252
　　Fuller case, 165–7
　designated sites, 142–4, 241
　litigation, 11n34
　police and, 322, 323
　privacy and, 26
　private law remedy, 390–4
　　injunctions, 47, 391–3
　　public law defences, 390–3
　　standing, 390
　public and private sphere, 22, 24, 162
　right to protest and, 120–1
　Scottish law, 257
　travellers, 162
　trespassory assemblies, 190
　　bans, 184–5
　　DPP v Jones and Lloyd, 194–203, 257–8, 383, 408
　　extent of banning power, 192–203
Turkey:
　coercive dispersal, 78, 80, 103, 107, 400
　Cyprus and, 70–1, 79, 85
　Democratic and Peace Party, 230
　free association, 86, 116–17
　illegal assembly, 65, 68
　illegal restrictions, 85
　notification of demonstrations, 106
　PKK demonstrations, 83
　proportionality, 61
　protest cases in Strasbourg, 60
　trade unions, 107
twitter, 20
Twyford Down, 21, 388n39, 388n41

Ulster Volunteer Force (UVF), 217
uniforms, 213–16
unincorporated associations, 391
United States:
　abusive language, 217
　constitutional review, 41
　costs of policing protests, 23
　free speech zones, 119n4, 420n94
　1st Amendment, 23, 100
　UK airbases, 142, 143
　wearing Nazi uniforms, 216
universities, public authorities, 48–9

vague laws *see* legal certainty
victim status, 50
victims, HRA 1998, 50–2
Vietnam War, 147

violence:
    anticipation of violence, stop and search powers, 315
    common law crimes, 242
    communication of dissent and, 232
    direct action and, 11, 241–52
    peaceful assembly and, 67–70
    putting in fear of violence, 244–5
    sporadic violence, 55, 69, 242
    terrorism, 239–40
    threatening, abusive or insulting language, 218
    unlawful violence, 242, 243
    violent disorder, 242, 243

Waddington, Jim, 19, 183n82
Walker, Clive, 318
Wall, Derek, 306n317, 307
Wallinger, Mark, 59, 152
Wapping, 186
war crimes, 250, 259–60, 260, 270–1, 412n72
watching and besetting, 19, 284, 290–2, 396, 398, 416
Welford airbase, 318
Westminster, protest around:
    2005 changes, 16, 27, 148–57
        commencement, 155–6, 403–4
    critique, 151–5
    definition of demonstrations, 59, 152–3
    Evans and Blum v DPP, 160–1
    Haw's case, 59, 148, 155–7, 402
    indiscriminate regulation, 153–5
    statutory scheme, 149–51
    Strasbourg jurisprudence and, 157–60
    abolishing provisions, 405
    experiences, 413
    history, 146–8
    media coverage, 20n74
    overview, 146–61
    Tamil protest (2009), 23
whaling, 97, 100, 308
White, Robin, 36
Wilding, John, 309, 379
Williams, David, 218n257, 242n27, 319n41, 322n61, 323–4
Williams of Mostyn, Lord, 38
Windsor Castle, 143
Wolfgang, Walter, 241, 309, 318
Wombles, 335
Woolf, Lord, 53

YouTube, 20